ALL NEW!

GREAT AMERICAN

FAVORITE BRAND NAME

COOKBOOK

Collector's Edition

PUBLICATIONS INTERNATIONAL, LTD.

Front cover photography: Peter Dean Ross Photographs, Chicago

Pictured on the front cover (*clockwise from top left*): Pineberry Smoothie *(page 10)*, Peach-Melon Cooler *(page 10)*, Ginger Shrimp Salad *(page 94)*, Steak Nachos *(page 48)*, Chicken with Walnuts *(page 162)*, Fruit Pizza *(page 538)*, Triple Chocolate Brownies *(page 480)*, Chocolate Surprise Cookies *(page 464)*, Garden Vegetable Pasta Salad with Bacon *(page 118)* and Stuffed Chicken with Apple Glaze *(page 158)*.

Pictured on the back cover (*clockwise from top left*): Mexican Lasagna *(page 212)*, The Best Cherry Pie *(page 498)* and Frank's™ Southwest Steak *(page 236)*.

ISBN: 0-7853-2471-2

Library of Congress Catalog Card Number: 97-66765

Manufactured in U.S.A.

8 7 6 5 4 3 2 1

Microwave Cooking: Microwave ovens vary in wattage. Use the cooking times as guidelines and check for doneness before adding more time.

Contents

CONTENTS

· · · · · · · · · · ·

· · · · · · · · · · ·

Introduction

The *All New Great American Favorite Brand Name Cookbook* is jam-packed with an exceptional assortment of recipes that will delight beginners as well as seasoned cooks. This all-new collection features the finest kitchen-tested recipes—many from America's favorite brand name companies. Undoubtedly, it will quickly become the cookbook you turn to first for that perfect dish for any occasion. And with more than 900 mouthwatering recipes, this book will continue to provide you with great ideas to choose from for years to come.

As you turn the pages, you'll encounter a wide variety of flavors. If you're planning a quick meal one night and a showstopping dinner the next, you'll have plenty of choices, from popular dishes to time-tested classics. And all the recipes have easy-to-follow instructions that make it a cinch to create delicious homemade meals and treats. Each chapter has a colorful identifier at the top of each page and there is a simple to follow index to help you quickly locate exactly what you want. All this to make cooking effortless and enjoyable for you!

At your fingertips are 18 chapters designed to take you on a delicious journey from appetizers to desserts with many fabulous stops in between. You'll find quick party snacks, elegant hors d'oeuvres, creamy dips and thirst-quenching beverages in "Appetizers & Drinks." To escape winter's chill, look to "Soups & Chili" to warm you on a cold, snowy night. Or, if a light, refreshing dish is appealing, the fresh flavors of "Salads" and "Sandwiches & Pizzas" will revitalize your tastebuds. Satisfying, home-cooked dinners start with a savory main dish and you'll find endless choices in the meat, poultry, seafood, pasta and casserole chapters. Complement your carefully selected entrée with a variety of tasty side dishes. And for the finishing touch to every good meal, the indulgent dessert section is sure to leave you blissfully satisfied.

On top of all that, special chapters not found in other cookbooks were created to meet all your culinary needs. In "Barbecue," you'll be delighted to discover plenty of recipes to keep you grilling all summer long. Planning a leisurely brunch for a special occasion? Turn to "Breakfast & Brunch" to dazzle your closest friends with simple-to-fix dishes that get you out of the kitchen fast. Don't call for takeout, but flip to "International Fare" to fulfill your exotic craving. And for the unrivaled aroma of freshly baked bread, see "Breads & Muffins" for many sweet and savory treats.

The *All New Great American Favorite Brand Name Cookbook* offers you hundreds of imaginative ideas. Leaf through this comprehensive collection and you'll see the unlimited number of scrumptious dishes at your fingertips. Happy cooking from our kitchen to yours!

Appetizers & Drinks

FEATURING:

Dips & Spreads

Party Fare

Blender Drinks

Chili Chip Party Platter (page 42)

Bloody Marys RedHot™ Style

- 1 quart tomato juice
- ½ cup vodka
- 2 tablespoons FRANK'S® Original REDHOT® Cayenne Pepper Sauce
- 2 tablespoons FRENCH'S® Worcestershire Sauce
- 2 tablespoons prepared horseradish
- 1 tablespoon lemon juice
- 1 teaspoon celery salt

Combine all ingredients in large pitcher; refrigerate. Serve over ice.   *Makes 4 servings*

Prep Time: 5 minutes
Chill Time: 30 minutes

Sangrita

- 3 cups DEL MONTE® Tomato Juice
- 1½ cups orange juice
- ½ cup DEL MONTE® Traditional Salsa
- Juice of 1 medium lime

1. Mix all ingredients in large pitcher; chill. Serve over ice with fruit garnishes, if desired.
   Makes 6 (6-ounce) servings

Prep Time: 3 minutes

Bronze Nectarine Margaritas

- 10 Frozen California Nectarine Cubes (recipe follows)
- ¾ cup orange juice
- 2 tablespoons lime juice
- 2 tablespoons sugar
- 10 ice cubes, cracked

Combine all ingredients in blender or food processor; blend until smooth. Pour into stemmed glasses.
Makes 2 servings

FROZEN CALIFORNIA NECTARINE CUBES: Slice 4 fresh nectarines. Combine in blender or food processor with ¼ cup lime juice; blend until smooth. Pour into ice cube trays; freeze.
Makes 20 cubes

*FAVORITE RECIPE FROM **CALIFORNIA TREE FRUIT AGREEMENT***

Bahama Slush

- 1 cup DEL MONTE® Tomato Juice, chilled
- 1 cup DEL MONTE® Pineapple Juice, chilled
- 1 tablespoon lime juice
- Crushed ice

1. Combine juices; serve over crushed ice.
   Makes 2 (8-ounce) servings

Prep Time: 2 minutes

Real Old-Fashioned Lemonade

- Juice of 6 SUNKIST® Lemons (1 cup)
- ¾ cup sugar (or to taste)
- 4 cups cold water
- 1 SUNKIST® Lemon, sliced crosswise
- Ice cubes

In large pitcher, combine lemon juice and sugar; stir until sugar dissolves. Add remaining ingredients and blend well. Serve immediately.
Makes 6 (8-ounce) servings

Pink Lemonade: *Add a few drops red food coloring or grenadine syrup.*

Honeyed Lemonade: *Add honey to taste in place of sugar.*

Bloody Marys RedHot™ Style

Fuzzy Banana Navel

**2 medium ripe DOLE®
Bananas, quartered
1 pint DOLE® Orange
Sorbet or 2 cups
orange sherbet,
slightly softened
1 cup DOLE® Mandarin
Tangerine Juice**

• **Combine** bananas, sorbet
and juice in blender or food
processor container. Blend until
thick and smooth. Garnish with
orange slices and curls, if
desired. Serve immediately.
Makes 4 servings

Prep Time: 5 minutes

*Fuzzy Peach Navel: Substitute
DOLE® Orchard Peach Juice for
Mandarin Tangerine Juice.*

Pineberry Smoothie

**1 medium ripe DOLE®
Banana, quartered
1 cup DOLE® Pineapple
Juice
½ cup vanilla or plain
nonfat yogurt
½ cup fresh or frozen
strawberries,
raspberries or
blueberries**

• **Combine** banana, juice,
yogurt and strawberries in
blender or food processor
container. Blend until thick and
smooth. Garnish with additional
strawberries, if desired. Serve
immediately.
Makes 2 servings

Prep Time: 5 minutes

Peach-Melon Cooler

**3 cups cubed DOLE®
Cantaloupe
5 cups DOLE® Orchard
Peach Juice or
Pineapple Orange
Juice, divided**

• **Place** melon and 1 cup juice
in blender or food processor
container. Blend until smooth.

• **Combine** melon mixture and
remaining juice in large pitcher.
Chill 1 hour before serving. Stir
before serving. Garnish with
skewered fresh fruit, if desired.
Makes 7 servings

Prep Time: 10 minutes
Chill Time: 1 hour

Dole® Juice Spritzer

**½ cup DOLE® Country
Raspberry Juice or
other DOLE® Juice
½ cup mineral or sparkling
water**

• **Pour** juice and mineral water
over ice cubes in large glass.
Garnish with lime wedge and
citrus curl, if desired.
Makes 1 serving

Prep Time: 5 minutes

Strawberry-Banana Yogurt Energy Drink

**1 box (10 ounces) BIRDS
EYE® frozen
Strawberries, partially
thawed
2 medium bananas
¾ cup plain yogurt**

• Place all ingredients in blender
or food processor; blend until
smooth.   *Makes 2½ cups*

Prep Time: 5 minutes

*SERVING SUGGESTION: ADD
2 TEASPOONS WHEAT GERM OR
¼ CUP FRUIT JUICE.*

California Shake

**¾ cup DOLE® Pitted Dates,
halved
1 medium ripe DOLE®
Banana, quartered
1 cup fat-free or low-fat
frozen vanilla yogurt,
slightly softened
½ cup low-fat or nonfat
milk**

• **Combine** dates and banana
in blender or food processor
container. Blend until dates are
finely chopped.

• **Add** yogurt and milk; blend
until thick and smooth. Serve
immediately. Garnish with
banana slices, if desired.
Makes 2 servings

Prep Time: 5 minutes

*Clockwise from top: California Shake,
Pineberry Smoothie and
Fuzzy Banana Navel*

Mulled Apple Cider

2 quarts bottled apple cider or juice (not unfiltered)
¼ cup packed brown sugar
1 square (8 inches) double-thickness cheesecloth
8 allspice berries
4 cinnamon sticks, broken into halves
12 whole cloves
1 large orange
Additional cinnamon sticks (optional)

Slow Cooker Directions:
COMBINE apple juice and brown sugar in slow cooker. Rinse cheesecloth; squeeze out water. Wrap allspice berries and cinnamon stick halves in cheesecloth; tie securely with cotton string or strip of cheesecloth. Stick cloves randomly into orange; cut orange into quarters. Place spice bag and orange quarters in juice mixture. Cover and cook on HIGH 2½ to 3 hours. Once cooked, cider may be turned to LOW and kept warm up to 3 additional hours. Discard spice bag and orange; ladle cider into mugs. Garnish with additional cinnamon sticks, if desired.

Makes 10 servings

Tip: *To insert cloves into orange, first pierce orange skin with point of wooden skewer. Remove skewer and insert clove.*

New Mexican Hot Chocolate

¼ cup unsweetened cocoa
¼ cup sugar
½ teaspoon ground cinnamon
¼ teaspoon ground nutmeg
Dash of salt
⅔ cup water
3⅓ cups milk
1 teaspoon vanilla extract
4 cinnamon sticks *or* dash ground nutmeg

Combine cocoa, sugar, ground cinnamon, ¼ teaspoon nutmeg, salt and water in medium saucepan. Cook, stirring occasionally, over medium heat until cocoa and sugar are dissolved. Add milk and vanilla. Heat to simmering. Whip mixture with rotary beater or portable electric mixer until frothy. Pour into 4 mugs. Place 1 cinnamon stick in each mug or sprinkle each serving lightly with nutmeg.

Makes 4 servings

Kahlúa® Brave Bull

1½ ounces KAHLÚA® Liqueur
1½ ounces sanza tequila
Lemon twist for garnish

Pour Kahlúa® and tequila over ice in glass. Stir. Garnish with lemon twist.

Makes 1 serving

Pineapple Margarita

⅔ cup DOLE® Pineapple Juice
1½ ounces tequila
1 ounce Triple Sec
Juice of 1 lemon
Crushed ice

• **Combine** pineapple juice, tequila, Triple Sec and lemon juice in blender. Add ice; blend until slushy. Serve in frosted glasses. *Do not put salt on rim.*

Makes 2 servings

Peach Fizz

3 fresh California peaches, peeled, halved, pitted and sliced
1 can (6 ounces) pineapple juice
¼ cup frozen limeade or lemonade concentrate
¼ teaspoon almond extract
Finely crushed ice
3 cups club soda, chilled

Add peaches to food processor or blender. Process until smooth to measure 2 cups purée. Stir in pineapple juice, limeade and almond extract. Fill six 12-ounce glasses ⅔ full with crushed ice. Add ⅓ cup peach base to each. Top with club soda. Stir gently. Serve immediately.

Makes 6 servings

FAVORITE RECIPE FROM **CALIFORNIA TREE FRUIT AGREEMENT**

Mulled Apple Cider

Herbed Blue Cheese Spread with Garlic Toasts

1 1/3 cups 1% low-fat cottage cheese
1 1/4 cups (5 ounces) crumbled blue, feta or goat cheese
1 large clove garlic
2 teaspoons lemon juice
2 green onions with tops, sliced (about 1/4 cup)
1/4 cup chopped fresh basil or oregano or
1 teaspoon dried basil or oregano leaves
2 tablespoons toasted slivered almonds
Garlic Toasts (recipe follows)

1. Combine cottage cheese, blue cheese, garlic and lemon juice in food processor; process until smooth. Add green onions, basil and almonds; pulse until well blended but still chunky.

2. Spoon cheese spread into small serving bowl; cover. Refrigerate until ready to serve.

3. When ready to serve, prepare Garlic Toasts. Spread 1 tablespoon cheese spread onto each toast slice. Garnish, if desired.   *Makes 16 servings*

GARLIC TOASTS
32 (1/2-inch-thick) French bread slices
1/4 teaspoon garlic powder
1/8 teaspoon salt

1. Place bread slices on nonstick baking sheet. Lightly coat both sides of bread slices with nonstick cooking spray. Combine garlic powder and salt in small bowl; sprinkle evenly onto bread slices. Broil 6 to 8 inches from heat, 30 to 45 seconds on each side or until bread slices are lightly toasted on both sides.
Makes 32 pieces

Tip: To toast almonds, place almonds in shallow baking pan. Bake at 350°F about 10 minutes or until lightly toasted, stirring occasionally. (Watch almonds carefully—they burn easily.)

Speedy Spam™ Dip

1 (12-ounce) can SPAM® Luncheon Meat
1 onion
2 jalapeño peppers, seeded
4 tablespoons mayonnaise or salad dressing
Chips and/or crackers

In food processor fitted with metal blade, process Spam®, onion and jalapeño peppers until smooth. Stir in mayonnaise. Cover and refrigerate 1 hour. Serve with chips and crackers.
Makes 2 cups dip

Five-Layered Mexican Dip

1/2 cup low-fat sour cream
1/2 cup GUILTLESS GOURMET® Salsa (mild, medium or hot)
1 jar (12.5 ounces) GUILTLESS GOURMET® Bean Dip (Black or Pinto, mild or spicy)
2 cups shredded lettuce
1/2 cup chopped tomato
1/4 cup (1 ounce) shredded sharp Cheddar cheese
Chopped fresh cilantro and cilantro sprigs (optional)
1 large bag (7 ounces) GUILTLESS GOURMET® Baked Tortilla Chips (yellow, white or blue corn)

Combine sour cream and salsa in small bowl. Spread bean dip in shallow glass bowl. Top with sour cream-salsa mixture, spreading to cover bean dip.* Just before serving, top with lettuce, tomato and cheese. Garnish with cilantro, if desired. Serve with tortilla chips.   *Makes 8 servings*

*Dip may be prepared to this point, then covered and refrigerated up to 24 hours.

Herbed Blue Cheese Spread with Garlic Toasts

French Onion Dip

1 container (16 ounces) sour cream
½ cup HELLMANN'S® or BEST FOODS® Real or Light Mayonnaise or Low Fat Mayonnaise Dressing
1 package (1.9 ounces) KNORR® French Onion Soup and Recipe Mix

1. In medium bowl, combine sour cream, mayonnaise and soup mix.

2. Cover; chill to blend flavors.

3. Stir dip before serving. Accompany with fresh vegetables or potato chips. Garnish as desired.

Makes about 2½ cups

Celebration Brie

1 (12- to 16-ounce) round Brie cheese, room temperature
1 teaspoon coarsely ground black pepper
½ cup SMUCKER'S® Strawberry Preserves
1 tablespoon balsamic vinegar
½ cup chopped BLUE RIBBON® Calimyrna or Mission Figs
Assorted crackers

Sprinkle top of Brie with pepper; press gently into cheese. Mix preserves with vinegar. Stir in figs. Spoon mixture over cheese. Serve with assorted crackers.

Makes 12 servings

Cucumber Dill Dip

1 package (8 ounces) light cream cheese, softened
1 cup HELLMANN'S® or BEST FOODS® Real or Light Mayonnaise or Low Fat Mayonnaise Dressing
2 medium cucumbers, peeled, seeded and chopped
2 tablespoons sliced green onions
1 tablespoon lemon juice
2 teaspoons snipped fresh dill *or* ½ teaspoon dried dill weed
½ teaspoon hot pepper sauce

1. In medium bowl, beat cream cheese until smooth. Stir in mayonnaise, cucumbers, green onions, lemon juice, dill and pepper sauce.

2. Cover; chill to blend flavors.

3. Serve with fresh vegetables, crackers or chips. Garnish as desired.

Makes about 2½ cups

Spinach Dip

1 package (10 ounces) frozen chopped spinach, thawed and drained
1½ cups sour cream
1 cup HELLMANN'S® or BEST FOODS® Real or Light Mayonnaise or Low Fat Mayonnaise Dressing
1 package (1.4 ounces) KNORR® Vegetable Soup and Recipe Mix
1 can (8 ounces) water chestnuts, drained and chopped (optional)
3 green onions, chopped

1. In medium bowl, combine spinach, sour cream, mayonnaise, soup mix, water chestnuts and green onions.

2. Cover; chill to blend flavors.

3. Stir dip before serving. Accompany with fresh vegetables, crackers or chips. Garnish as desired.

Makes about 3 cups

Left to right: Spinach Dip, Cucumber Dill Dip and French Onion Dip

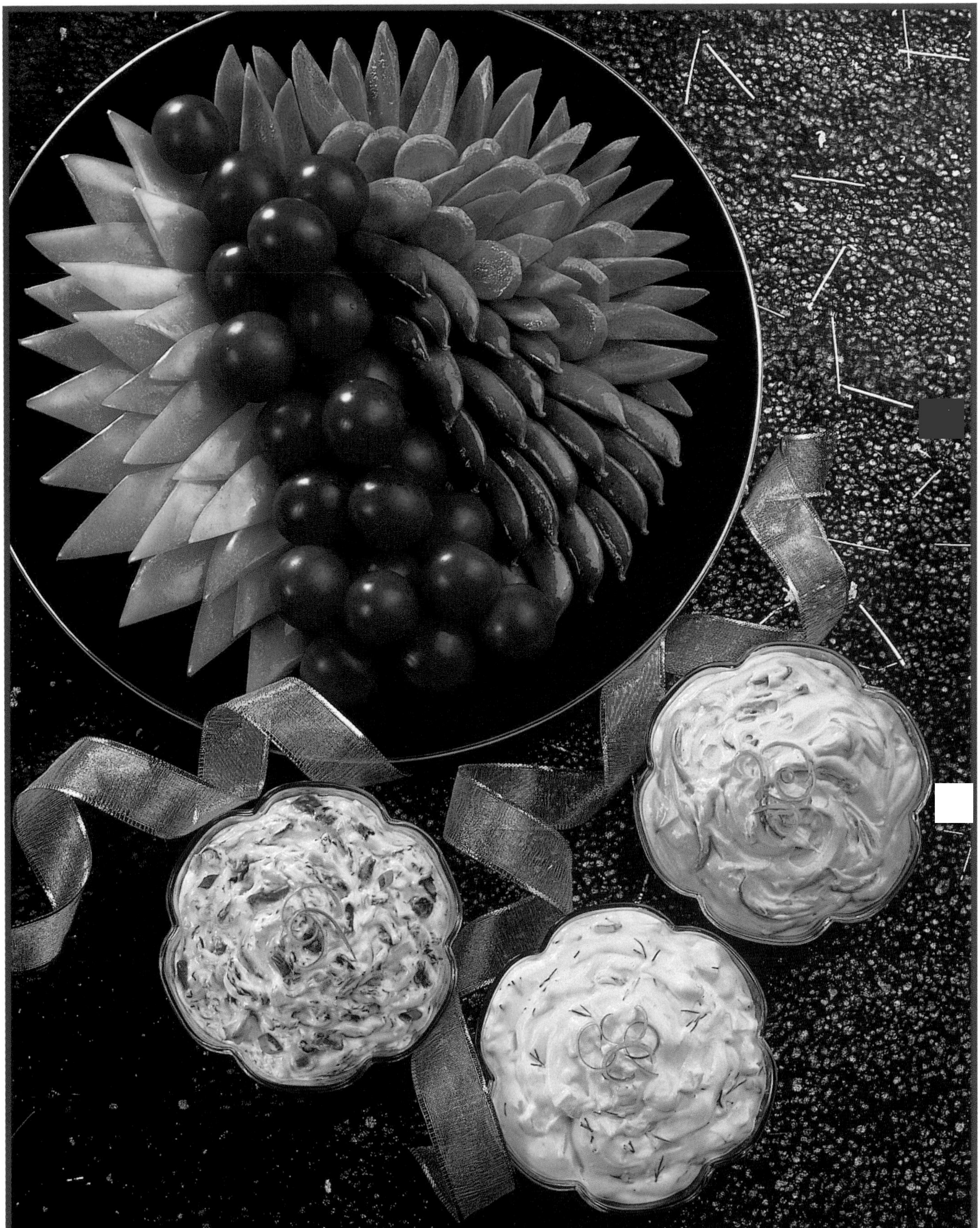

Spectacular Shrimp Spread

½ pound rock shrimp, cooked, peeled and deveined
1 can (13 ounces) artichoke hearts, drained
1 cup mayonnaise*
½ cup shredded Parmesan cheese
¼ teaspoon ground lemon pepper
⅛ teaspoon salt
   Dash cayenne pepper

May substitute ½ cup mayonnaise and ½ cup plain yogurt for mayonnaise.

Preheat oven to 400°F. Finely chop rock shrimp and artichoke hearts; place in medium bowl. Add mayonnaise, cheese, lemon pepper, salt and cayenne pepper; mix well. Spoon shrimp mixture into 9-inch pie pan or 1-quart shallow baking dish. Bake 10 minutes or until hot and bubbly. Serve hot with crackers, if desired.

Makes about 3¾ cups

FAVORITE RECIPE FROM **FLORIDA DEPARTMENT OF AGRICULTURE AND CONSUMER SERVICES, BUREAU OF SEAFOOD AND AQUACULTURE**

Roasted Pepper Dip

1 jar (7 ounces) roasted red peppers, drained
1 clove garlic, chopped
¼ cup reduced-fat mayonnaise
2 tablespoons FRENCH'S® Dijon Mustard
2 tablespoons FRANK'S® Original REDHOT® Cayenne Pepper Sauce
¼ teaspoon salt
   Crackers
   Vegetable dippers

1. Place roasted peppers and garlic in food processor or blender. Cover; process on high until very smooth.

2. Add mayonnaise, mustard, RedHot® sauce and salt. Process until well blended. Cover; refrigerate 30 minutes.

3. Serve with crackers and vegetable dippers.

Makes 1 cup dip

Prep Time: 10 minutes
Chill Time: 30 minutes

Santa Fe Pineapple Salsa

1 DOLE® Fresh Pineapple
1 can (8¼ ounces) whole kernel corn
1 can (8 ounces) red pinto or kidney beans, drained and rinsed
1 cup chopped DOLE® Red or Green Bell Pepper
½ cup finely chopped DOLE® Red Onion
2 tablespoons chopped fresh cilantro
1 to 2 teaspoons chopped seeded fresh jalapeño pepper
½ teaspoon grated lime peel
2 tablespoons lime juice

• **Twist** off crown from pineapple. Cut pineapple in half lengthwise. Refrigerate one half for later use. Cut remaining piece in half. Core and skin fruit; finely chop fruit.

• **Combine** pineapple, corn, beans, bell pepper, onion, cilantro, jalapeño, lime peel and juice in large serving bowl. Cover and chill at least 30 minutes to allow flavors to blend.   *Makes 10 servings*

Prep Time: 20 minutes
Chill Time: 30 minutes

Spectacular Shrimp Spread

Pesto Brie

- 2 tablespoons GREY POUPON® Dijon Mustard
- 2 tablespoons prepared pesto sauce
- 1 (8-ounce) wheel Brie cheese
- 2 tablespoons PLANTERS® Walnuts, finely chopped
  Chopped tomatoes and fresh basil leaves for garnish
  Assorted crackers or breadsticks

In small bowl, blend mustard and pesto; set aside. Cut cheese in half horizontally. Place bottom half on greased baking sheet, cut side up; spread with half the pesto mixture. Replace top of Brie, cut side down; spread with remaining pesto mixture and sprinkle with nuts.

Bake at 350°F for 3 to 4 minutes or until cheese is slightly softened. *Do not overbake.* Transfer to serving dish. Garnish with chopped tomatoes and basil leaves. Serve with assorted crackers or breadsticks.

Makes 6 to 8 servings

Nutty Broccoli Spread

- 1 box (10 ounces) BIRDS EYE® frozen Chopped Broccoli
- 4 ounces cream cheese
- ¼ cup grated Parmesan cheese
- 1 teaspoon dried basil leaves
- ¼ cup walnuts
- 1 loaf frozen garlic bread

• Cook broccoli according to package directions; drain well.

• Preheat oven to 400°F. Place broccoli, cream cheese, Parmesan cheese and basil in food processor or blender; process until ingredients are mixed. *Do not overmix.* Add walnuts; process 3 to 5 seconds.

• Split garlic bread lengthwise. Spread broccoli mixture evenly over bread.

• Bake 10 to 15 minutes or until bread is toasted and broccoli mixture is heated through.

• Cut bread into bite-size pieces; serve hot.

Makes about 2 cups spread

Prep Time: 10 minutes
Cook Time: 10 to 15 minutes

Baked Artichoke and Chile Dip

- 2 cups (14-ounce can) artichokes, drained and chopped
- 1 cup (7-ounce can) ORTEGA® Diced Green Chiles
- 1 cup (4 ounces) shredded Cheddar cheese, divided
- ½ cup (2 ounces) grated Parmesan cheese
- ½ cup sour cream
- 4 tablespoons (about 3) sliced green onions, divided

COMBINE artichokes, chiles, *¾ cup* Cheddar cheese, Parmesan cheese, sour cream and *2 tablespoons* green onions in medium bowl.

SPREAD onto bottom of 8-inch square baking pan. Sprinkle with *remaining ¼ cup* Cheddar cheese and *remaining 2 tablespoons* green onions.

BAKE, uncovered, in preheated 350°F. oven 15 to 20 minutes or until heated through. Serve with chips or crackers.

Makes 6 to 8 servings

Pesto Brie

Smoky Eggplant Dip

- 1 large eggplant (about 1 pound)
- ¼ cup olive oil
- 3 tablespoons FRANK'S® Original REDHOT® Cayenne Pepper Sauce
- 2 tablespoons peanut butter or tahini paste
- 1 tablespoon lemon juice
- 2 cloves garlic, minced
- ¾ teaspoon salt
- ½ teaspoon ground cumin
  Spicy Pita Chips (recipe follows)

1. Prepare grill. Place eggplant on oiled grid. Grill, over hot coals, 15 minutes or until soft and skin is charred, turning often. Remove from grill; cool until easy enough to handle.

2. Peel skin from eggplant with paring knife; discard. Coarsely chop eggplant. Place in strainer or kitchen towel. Press out excess liquid.

3. Place eggplant in food processor; add oil, RedHot® sauce, peanut butter, lemon juice, garlic, salt and cumin. Cover; process until mixture is very smooth. Spread eggplant mixture on serving platter. Cover; refrigerate until chilled. Serve with Spicy Pita Chips.

Makes 1½ cups dip

SPICY PITA CHIPS: Split 4 pita bread rounds in half lengthwise. Combine *½ cup* olive oil, *¼ cup* FRANK'S® Original REDHOT® Cayenne Pepper Sauce and *1 tablespoon* minced garlic in small bowl. Brush mixture on both sides of pitas. Place pitas on grid. Grill, over medium coals, about 5 minutes or until crispy, turning once. Cut pitas into triangles.

Prep Time: 30 minutes
Cook Time: 20 minutes
Chill Time: 30 minutes

Hot Artichoke Spread

- 1 cup MIRACLE WHIP® Salad Dressing
- 1 cup (4 ounces) KRAFT® 100% Grated Parmesan Cheese
- 1 (14-ounce) can artichoke hearts, drained and chopped
- 1 (4-ounce) can chopped green chilies, drained
- 1 clove garlic, minced
- 2 tablespoons green onion slices
- 2 tablespoons chopped tomato

- Preheat oven to 350°F.

- Mix all ingredients except onion and tomato until well blended.

- Spoon into shallow ovenproof dish or 9-inch pie plate.

- Bake 20 to 25 minutes or until lightly browned. Sprinkle with onion and tomato. Serve with toasted bread cutouts.

Makes 2 cups

Prep Time: 10 minutes
Cook Time: 25 minutes

Savory Seafood Spread

- 2 packages (8 ounces each) light cream cheese, softened
- 1 package (8 ounces) imitation crabmeat, flaked
- 2 tablespoons minced green onion
- 1 tablespoon prepared horseradish
- 1 tablespoon FRANK'S® Original REDHOT® Cayenne Pepper Sauce
- 1 teaspoon FRENCH'S® Worcestershire Sauce
- ½ cup sliced almonds
  Paprika
  Crackers
  Vegetable dippers

1. Preheat oven to 375°F. Beat or process cream cheese in electric mixer or food processor until smooth and creamy. Add crabmeat, onion, horseradish, RedHot® sauce and Worcestershire; beat or process until well blended.

2. Spread cream cheese mixture onto 9-inch pie plate. Top with almonds and sprinkle with paprika. Bake 20 minutes or until mixture is heated through and almonds are golden.

3. Serve with crackers and vegetable dippers.

Makes 3 cups spread

Prep Time: 10 minutes
Cook Time: 20 minutes

Smoky Eggplant Dip

Tomato-Pesto Stuffed Brie

1 cup boiling water
1 package (3 ounces) unsalted sun-dried tomatoes (about 2 cups)
4 tablespoons FRANK'S® Original REDHOT® Cayenne Pepper Sauce
2 green onions, chopped
2 (5-inch) whole Brie rounds (about 13 ounces each), well chilled
1 jar (1¾ ounces) pine nuts, toasted
3 tablespoons butter, softened
¾ cup chopped parsley

1. Pour boiling water over tomatoes in medium bowl. Let stand 4 minutes or until just softened; drain well and pat dry with paper towels. Place tomatoes, RedHot® sauce and onions in food processor; process until smooth paste forms.

2. Using large sharp knife, split each Brie round in half horizontally. Spread tomato mixture over cut sides of bottom halves. Sprinkle evenly with pine nuts. Cover bottom halves with top halves, cut side down. Press gently. Spread butter on edges of rounds; roll in chopped parsley. Refrigerate about 1 hour. Cut into wedges; serve with crackers or French bread.   *Makes 12 servings*

Note: *Filled Brie may be served warm. (Do not coat with butter and parsley.) Place in baking dish; bake at 325°F 5 to 10 minutes or until slightly softened.*

Potted Cheese Paté

2 cups (8 ounces) shredded ALPINE LACE® Reduced Sodium Muenster Cheese
⅓ cup fat free mayonnaise
⅓ cup finely chopped red bell pepper
3 tablespoons minced white onion
2 tablespoons fresh snipped dill *or* 2 teaspoons dried dill weed
1 tablespoon fresh lemon juice

1. In a medium-size bowl, with an electric mixer set on high, beat the cheese and mayonnaise just until blended. Stir in the remaining ingredients. Spoon into a small serving "pot" or dish and cover with plastic wrap. Refrigerate for at least 1 hour or until thoroughly chilled. Garnish as desired. Serve with melba toast rounds.
Makes 2 cups

Layered Sombrero Dip

1¾ cups (1-pound can) ORTEGA® Refried Beans
1 cup (7-ounce can) ORTEGA® Diced Green Chiles, divided
2 medium very ripe avocados, pitted, peeled and mashed
1¾ cups (16-ounce jar) ORTEGA® Thick & Chunky Salsa, medium or mild, divided
¼ cup sour cream
1 cup (4 ounces) shredded Cheddar cheese
½ cup (2¼-ounce can) sliced ripe olives, drained
Sliced green onions (optional)
Diced tomatoes (optional)
Tortilla chips

COMBINE beans and ½ cup chiles in small bowl. Spread onto bottom of 8-inch square baking pan.

COMBINE avocados, ¼ cup salsa and sour cream in small bowl; blend well.

SPREAD avocado mixture over bean mixture. Top with *remaining 1½ cups* salsa, cheese, *remaining ½ cup* chiles, olives, green onions and tomatoes. Serve with chips.
Makes 10 to 12 servings

Cheesy Crab Mousse

2 cups fresh shelled crabmeat *or* 2 cans (6 ounces each) canned crabmeat
1½ cups (6 ounces) shredded ALPINE LACE® Reduced Fat Colby Cheese
½ cup finely chopped celery
½ cup finely chopped green onions
½ cup finely chopped red bell pepper
1 cup sour half-and-half
½ cup reduced fat mayonnaise
¼ cup bottled chili sauce
2 tablespoons fresh lemon juice
3 tablespoons cold water
1 tablespoon unflavored gelatin

1. Lightly oil a 1-quart fish-shaped or other shaped mold.

2. Rinse the crabmeat, drain well and pick through for shells. Place in a large bowl. Toss with the cheese, celery, green onions and bell pepper.

3. In a small bowl, blend together the half-and-half, mayonnaise, chili sauce and lemon juice. Into a small saucepan, pour the cold water and stir in the gelatin. Heat over low heat, stirring constantly, until thoroughly dissolved. Stir quickly into the half-and-half mixture.

4. Fold half-and-half mixture into the crab mixture and spoon into the mold. Cover with plastic wrap and refrigerate for 3 hours or until set. Unmold onto a serving platter. Garnish with the cucumber slices and sprigs of dill, if you wish.

Makes 32 appetizer servings

Mexican Fiesta Dip

1 package (8 ounces) cream cheese, softened
1 cup plain yogurt
1 package (1¼ ounces) ORTEGA® Taco Seasoning Mix
1 cup shredded iceberg lettuce
½ cup (4-ounce can) ORTEGA® Diced Green Chiles
¼ cup chopped red onion
¼ cup chopped cucumber
¼ cup sliced ripe olives
½ cup (2 ounces) shredded Monterey Jack cheese
ORTEGA® Thick & Chunky Salsa, hot, medium or mild
Tortilla chips

COMBINE cream cheese, yogurt and taco seasoning mix in medium bowl. Spread onto bottom of 10-inch plate.

TOP with lettuce, chiles, onion, cucumber, olives, Monterey Jack cheese and salsa. Chill at least 1 hour. Serve with chips.

Makes 8 to 10 servings

Easy Cheddar Mustard Beer Dip

12 ounces pasteurized processed Cheddar cheese spread, cubed
4 ounces cream cheese, cubed
⅔ cup beer
½ cup GREY POUPON® Dijon Mustard
⅓ cup chopped green onions
Chopped red bell pepper for garnish
Pretzel chips, breadsticks or bagel chips for dipping

In medium saucepan, over low heat, heat cheese spread and cream cheese until melted and smooth. Slowly blend in beer and mustard. Stir in green onions. Pour into serving bowl; garnish with chopped bell pepper. Serve with pretzel chips, breadsticks or bagel chips.

Makes 2½ cups

Angelic Deviled Eggs

6 eggs
¼ cup 1% low-fat cottage cheese
3 tablespoons prepared fat-free Ranch dressing
2 teaspoons Dijon mustard
2 tablespoons minced fresh chives or dill
1 tablespoon diced well-drained pimiento or roasted red pepper

1. Place eggs in medium saucepan; add enough water to cover. Bring to a boil over medium heat, stirring gently and frequently. Remove from heat; cover. Let stand 20 minutes. Drain. Add cold water to eggs in saucepan; let stand until eggs are cool. Drain. Remove shells; discard.

2. Cut eggs lengthwise in half. Remove yolks, reserving 3 yolk halves. Discard remaining yolks. Place egg whites, cut sides up, on serving plate; cover with plastic wrap. Refrigerate while preparing filling.

3. Combine cottage cheese, Ranch dressing, mustard and reserved yolk halves in mini food processor; process until smooth. (Or, place in small bowl and mash with fork until well blended.) Transfer cheese mixture to small bowl; stir in chives and pimiento. Spoon into egg whites; cover with plastic wrap. Refrigerate until chilled, at least 1 hour.

Makes 12 servings

Neufty Cups

2 (18×14-inch) sheets phyllo dough, thawed according to package directions
2 tablespoons butter
1 package (6 ounces) FLEUR DE LAIT® Neufchâtel® cheese, Garden Vegetables variety

Preheat oven to 350°F. Cover phyllo with damp cloth.

Melt butter; brush a small amount onto sides and bottoms of 12 miniature muffin pan cups.

Cut phyllo into 36 (3¼-inch) squares. Place 1 phyllo square into each muffin pan cup with corners pointing upward. Lightly brush phyllo with butter. Top each with another phyllo square, alternating corners; brush with butter. Repeat once more, alternating corners, so that there are 3 phyllo squares arranged in each cup.

Brush all edges of phyllo lightly with melted butter. Bake 8 to 10 minutes or until golden. Remove shells to wire racks; cool completely. Fill with Fleur de Lait®; garnish as desired.

Makes 12 appetizers

Hummus-Stuffed Vegetables

1 can (15 ounces) chick-peas, rinsed and drained
1 medium clove garlic
1 tablespoon lemon juice
1 tablespoon olive oil
½ teaspoon ground cumin
¼ teaspoon salt
¼ teaspoon black pepper
1 cup snow peas (about 24)
¾ pound medium fresh mushrooms (about 24)

1. Combine chick-peas, garlic, lemon juice, oil, cumin, salt and pepper in food processor. Process until mixture is smooth. Transfer to piping bag fitted with fluted tip.

2. Remove string portions of snow peas by pinching stem end of each snow pea and pulling back on string. (Some snow peas will not have a stringy portion.) Carefully split snow peas with tip of paring knife. Remove stems from mushrooms; discard.

3. Pipe bean mixture into snow peas and into cavities of inverted mushrooms. Store loosely covered in refrigerator until ready to serve. Garnish just before serving, if desired.

Makes 12 servings

Variation: *Substitute cucumber slices or red or green bell peppers, cut into 1½-inch triangles, for snow peas and mushrooms.*

Angelic Deviled Eggs

Herbed Croutons with Savory Bruschetta

½ cup regular or reduced-fat mayonnaise
¼ cup FRENCH'S® Dijon Mustard
1 tablespoon finely chopped green onion
1 clove garlic, minced
¾ teaspoon dried oregano leaves
1 long thin loaf (18 inches) French bread, cut crosswise into ½-inch-thick slices
Savory Bruschetta (recipe follows)

Combine mayonnaise, mustard, onion, garlic and oregano in small bowl; mix well. Spread herbed mixture on one side of each slice of bread.

Place bread, spread sides up, on grid. Grill over medium-low coals 1 minute or until lightly toasted. Spoon Savory Bruschetta onto herbed croutons. Serve warm.

Makes 6 appetizer servings

Tip: Leftover croutons may be served with dips or cut up and served in salads.

Prep Time: 10 minutes
Cook Time: 1 minute

SAVORY BRUSCHETTA

1 pound ripe plum tomatoes, cored, seeded and chopped
1 cup finely chopped fennel bulb or celery
¼ cup chopped fresh basil leaves
3 tablespoons FRENCH'S® Dijon Mustard
3 tablespoons olive oil
3 tablespoons balsamic vinegar
2 cloves garlic, minced
½ teaspoon salt

Combine ingredients in medium bowl; toss well to coat evenly.

Makes 3 cups

Prep Time: 15 minutes

Baked Brie

½ pound Brie cheese, rind removed
¼ cup chopped pecans
¼ cup KARO® Dark Corn Syrup

1. Preheat oven to 350°F.

2. Place cheese in shallow oven-safe serving dish. Top with pecans and corn syrup.

3. Bake 8 to 10 minutes or until cheese is almost melted. Serve warm with plain crackers or melba toast.

Makes about 8 servings

Prep Time: 5 minutes
Bake Time: 8 minutes

Sausage Pinwheels

2 cups biscuit mix
½ cup milk
¼ cup butter or margarine, melted
1 pound BOB EVANS FARMS® Original Recipe Roll Sausage

Combine biscuit mix, milk and butter in large bowl until blended. Refrigerate 30 minutes. Divide dough into two portions. Roll out one portion on floured surface to ⅛-inch-thick rectangle, about 10×7 inches. Spread with half the sausage. Roll lengthwise into long roll. Repeat with remaining dough and sausage. Place rolls in freezer until hard enough to cut easily. Preheat oven to 400°F. Cut rolls into thin slices. Place on baking sheets. Bake 15 minutes or until golden brown. Serve hot. Refrigerate leftovers. *Makes 48 appetizers*

SERVING SUGGESTION: THIS RECIPE MAY BE DOUBLED. REFREEZE EXTRA PINWHEELS AFTER SLICING. WHEN READY TO SERVE, THAW SLICES IN REFRIGERATOR AND BAKE.

Herbed Croutons with Savory Bruschetta

Chicken Saté

Chicken Kabobs (recipe follows)
1 teaspoon MAZOLA® Corn Oil
1 teaspoon dark sesame oil
¼ cup finely chopped onion
1 clove garlic, minced
½ teaspoon grated fresh ginger
¼ teaspoon crushed red pepper (optional)
½ cup SKIPPY® Creamy Peanut Butter
¼ cup KARO® Light or Dark Corn Syrup
1 tablespoon soy sauce
1 tablespoon cider vinegar
⅔ cup milk

1. Begin preparing Chicken Kabobs.

2. Meanwhile, in small saucepan, heat oils over medium heat; add onion, garlic, ginger and crushed red pepper. Stirring constantly, cook 3 to 4 minutes or until onion is translucent.

3. Stir in peanut butter, corn syrup, soy sauce and vinegar until smooth. Gradually stir in milk. Stirring constantly, bring to a boil. Remove from heat. Cool slightly.

4. Serve as dipping sauce for Chicken Kabobs.

Makes 1⅓ cups sauce or about 3 dozen appetizers

CHICKEN KABOBS: Soak about 36 wooden skewers in water at least 20 minutes. In medium bowl, combine 2 tablespoons MAZOLA® Corn Oil and 2 tablespoons light teriyaki sauce. Cut 1 pound boneless skinless chicken breasts into 1-inch pieces; stir into teriyaki mixture. Cover and let stand at room temperature no longer than 30 minutes or refrigerate several hours or overnight.

Thread chicken onto skewers. Place on foil-lined baking sheet. Broil about 6 inches from heat, 6 to 8 minutes or until lightly browned.

Prep Time: 25 minutes, plus marinating
Broil Time: 6 minutes

Mustard-Glazed Shrimp

MAZOLA NO STICK® Corn Oil Cooking Spray
2 tablespoons hot water
1 tablespoon dry mustard
¼ cup KARO® Light or Dark Corn Syrup
¼ cup prepared duck or plum sauce
2 tablespoons rice wine or sake
1 tablespoon soy sauce
1 tablespoon dark sesame oil
1 pound large shrimp, shelled and deveined, or sea scallops
¾ pound sliced bacon, cut crosswise in half
Bamboo skewers, soaked in cold water 20 minutes

1. Line broiler pan rack with foil; spray with cooking spray.

2. In small bowl, stir water and mustard until smooth. Stir in corn syrup, duck sauce, rice wine, soy sauce and sesame oil.

3. In large bowl, toss shrimp with about ¼ cup of the mustard glaze. Wrap half slice bacon around each shrimp and thread about 1 inch apart onto skewers.

4. Broil 6 inches from heat 8 to 10 minutes or until shrimp are tender, turning and brushing occasionally with remaining mustard glaze.

Makes 6 to 8 appetizer servings

Prep Time: 20 minutes
Broil Time: 10 minutes

Savory Apricot Bites

4 ounces cream cheese, softened
12 fresh apricots, halved, pitted and brushed with lemon juice
½ cup pistachios, finely chopped

Stir cream cheese until smooth. Pipe or spoon cheese into pitted apricot halves. Top each half with 1 teaspoon pistachios.

Makes 2 dozen bites, 12 appetizer servings

*FAVORITE RECIPE FROM **CALIFORNIA APRICOT ADVISORY BOARD***

Top to bottom: Chicken Saté and Mustard-Glazed Shrimp

Sopes

¼ cup shortening or lard
2 cups masa harina flour
   (Mexican corn masa
   mix)
1¼ cups warm water
½ cup (4-ounce can)
   ORTEGA® Diced Green
   Chiles
3 teaspoons vegetable oil,
   divided
1¾ cups (1-pound can)
   ORTEGA® Refried
   Beans, warmed
1 cup (4 ounces) shredded
   Cheddar or Cotija
   cheese, crumbled
   ORTEGA® Thick &
   Chunky Salsa, mild
   Sour cream

CUT shortening into flour in
large bowl with pastry blender
or two knives until mixture
resembles coarse crumbs.
Gradually add water, kneading
until smooth. Add chiles; mix
well.

DIVIDE dough into 16 small
balls. Pat each ball into 3-inch
patty; place on waxed paper.

HEAT 1 teaspoon oil in large
skillet over medium-high heat
for 1 minute. Cook patties for
3 minutes on each side or until
golden brown, adding additional
oil as needed.

TOP with beans, cheese, salsa
and dollop of sour cream.
Makes 16 appetizers

*Tip: These crispy masa treats can
be topped with many ingredients:
grilled chicken or fish, chorizo,
crumbled cheeses such as Mexican
queso fresco, shredded lettuce or
sliced radishes.*

Bruschetta

1 can (14½ ounces) DEL
   MONTE® *FreshCut*™
   Diced Tomatoes,
   drained
2 tablespoons chopped
   fresh basil *or*
   ½ teaspoon dried basil
1 small clove garlic, finely
   minced
½ French bread baguette,
   cut into ⅜-inch-thick
   slices
2 tablespoons olive oil

1. Combine tomatoes, basil and
garlic in small bowl; cover and
refrigerate at least ½ hour.

2. Preheat broiler. Place bread
slices on baking sheet; lightly
brush both sides of bread with
oil. Broil until lightly toasted,
turning to toast both sides.
Cool on wire rack.

3. Bring tomato mixture to
room temperature. Spoon
tomato mixture over bread and
serve immediately. Sprinkle
with additional fresh basil
leaves, if desired.
Makes 8 appetizer servings

Prep Time: 15 minutes
Cook Time: 30 minutes

*Note: For a fat-free version, omit
olive oil. For a lower-fat variation,
spray bread with olive oil cooking
spray.*

Chile 'n' Cheese Spirals

4 ounces cream cheese,
   softened
1 cup (4 ounces) shredded
   Cheddar cheese
½ cup (4-ounce can)
   ORTEGA® Diced Green
   Chiles
½ cup (about 6) sliced
   green onions
½ cup chopped ripe olives
4 soft taco-size (8-inch)
   flour tortillas
   ORTEGA® Garden Style
   Salsa, medium or mild

COMBINE cream cheese,
Cheddar cheese, chiles, green
onions and olives in medium
bowl.

SPREAD ½ cup cheese mixture
on each tortilla. Roll up. Wrap
each roll in plastic wrap; chill
for 1 hour.

REMOVE plastic wrap; slice
each roll into six ¾-inch
pieces. Serve with salsa for
dipping.   *Makes 24 appetizers*

*Tip: Chili 'n' Cheese Spirals can be
made ahead and kept in the
refrigerator for 1 to 2 days. For
added variety, add diced red bell
pepper or use whole green chiles
instead of diced chiles.*

Sopes

East Meets West Cocktail Franks

1 cup prepared sweet and sour sauce
1 ½ tablespoons rice vinegar or cider vinegar
1 tablespoon grated fresh ginger *or* 1 teaspoon dried ginger
1 tablespoon dark sesame oil
½ teaspoon chili oil (optional)
1 package (12 ounces) HEBREW NATIONAL® Cocktail Beef Franks
2 tablespoons chopped cilantro or chives

Combine sweet and sour sauce, vinegar, ginger, sesame oil and chili oil, if desired, in medium saucepan. Bring to a boil over medium heat. Cook 5 minutes or until thickened. Add cocktail franks; cover and cook until heated through. Transfer to chafing dish; sprinkle with cilantro. Serve with frilled wooden picks.

Makes 12 appetizer servings
(2 cocktail franks per serving)

Mushrooms Stuffed with Walnuts & Feta Cheese

12 medium mushroom caps
1 tablespoon olive oil
1 tablespoon butter or margarine
½ cup finely chopped onion
2 tablespoons chopped walnuts
1 clove garlic, minced
5 ounces frozen chopped spinach, thawed and squeezed dry
1 ounce crumbled feta cheese
¼ cup (1 ounce) shredded Swiss cheese
2 tablespoons chopped fresh dill
Salt and black pepper to taste
Dry bread crumbs

Preheat oven to 400°F. Wipe mushroom caps with damp cloth; set aside. To prepare filling, heat oil and butter in large skillet over medium-high heat until hot; add onion. Cook, covered, until tender. Add walnuts and garlic. Cook and stir 1 minute. Stir in spinach, cheeses and dill. Remove from heat; blend well. Add salt and pepper. Stuff caps evenly with filling. Arrange caps, top side down, in 8×8-inch baking dish. Sprinkle with bread crumbs.

Bake 8 to 10 minutes or until browned. Serve warm. Refrigerate leftovers.

Makes 4 appetizer servings

FAVORITE RECIPE FROM **BOB EVANS FARMS®**

Cheesy Sun Crisps

2 cups (8 ounces) shredded Cheddar cheese
½ cup grated Parmesan cheese
½ cup sunflower oil margarine, softened
3 tablespoons water
1 cup all-purpose flour
¼ teaspoon salt (optional)
1 cup uncooked quick oats
⅔ cup roasted, salted sunflower seeds

Beat cheeses, margarine and water in bowl until blended. Mix in flour and salt. Stir in oats and sunflower seeds until combined. Shape into 12-inch-long roll; wrap securely. Refrigerate about 4 hours or up to 1 week.

Preheat oven to 400°F. Lightly grease cookie sheets. Cut roll into ⅛- to ¼-inch slices; flatten each slice slightly. Place on prepared cookie sheets. Bake 8 to 10 minutes or until edges are light golden brown. Remove immediately; cool on wire rack.

Makes 4 to 5 dozen crackers

FAVORITE RECIPE FROM **NATIONAL SUNFLOWER ASSOCIATION**

East Meets West Cocktail Franks

Spiral Reuben Dijon Bites

1 sheet puff pastry (½ package)
¼ cup GREY POUPON® Dijon Mustard
6 slices Swiss cheese (3 ounces)
6 slices deli corned beef (6 ounces)
1 egg, beaten
1 tablespoon caraway seeds
Additional GREY POUPON® Dijon Mustard

Thaw puff pastry sheet according to package directions. Roll puff pastry dough to 12×10-inch rectangle. Spread mustard evenly over dough; top with cheese and corned beef. Cut in half crosswise to form 2 (10×6-inch) rectangles. Roll up each rectangle from short end, jelly-roll fashion; pinch seams to seal.*

Cut each roll into 16 (¼-inch-thick) slices. Place slices, cut side up, on lightly greased baking sheets; brush with beaten egg and sprinkle with caraway seeds. Bake at 400°F for 10 to 12 minutes or until golden. Serve warm with additional mustard.

Makes 32 appetizers

*Rolls may be wrapped and frozen. To serve, thaw at room temperature for 30 minutes. Slice and bake as directed above.

Ham and Gouda Quesadilla Snacks

1½ cups shredded smoked Gouda cheese (6 ounces)
1 cup chopped ham (4 ounces)
½ cup pitted ripe olives, chopped
¼ cup minced red onion
½ cup GREY POUPON® COUNTRY DIJON® Mustard
8 (6- or 7-inch) flour tortillas
Sour cream, chopped peppers, sliced pitted ripe olives and cilantro for garnish

In small bowl, combine cheese, ham, olives and onion. Spread 1 tablespoon mustard on each tortilla; spread about ⅓ cup cheese mixture over half of each tortilla. Fold tortilla in half to cover filling.

In large nonstick skillet, over medium heat, heat filled tortillas for 4 minutes or until cheese melts, turning once. Cut each quesadilla into 3 wedges. Place on serving platter; garnish with sour cream, peppers, olives and cilantro.

Makes 24 appetizers

South-of-the-Border Quiche Squares

1 (8-ounce) package refrigerated crescent dinner roll dough
1½ cups shredded Monterey Jack and Colby cheese blend (6 ounces)
½ cup diced green chilies
½ cup chopped onion
4 eggs, beaten
1 cup milk
⅓ cup GREY POUPON® COUNTRY DIJON® Mustard
1 tablespoon chopped cilantro or parsley
½ teaspoon chili powder
Chopped tomato and yellow and green bell peppers for garnish

Unroll dough and press perforations together. Press dough on bottom and 1 inch up sides of greased 13×9×2-inch baking pan. Bake crust at 375°F for 5 to 8 minutes or until lightly golden. Remove from oven; sprinkle with half the cheese. Top with chilies, onion and remaining cheese.

In medium bowl, blend eggs, milk, mustard, cilantro and chili powder. Pour mixture evenly over cheese layer. Bake at 375°F for 25 to 30 minutes or until set. Cool 5 minutes. Garnish with tomato and bell peppers; cut into 2-inch squares. Serve hot.

Makes 24 appetizers

Spiral Reuben Dijon Bites

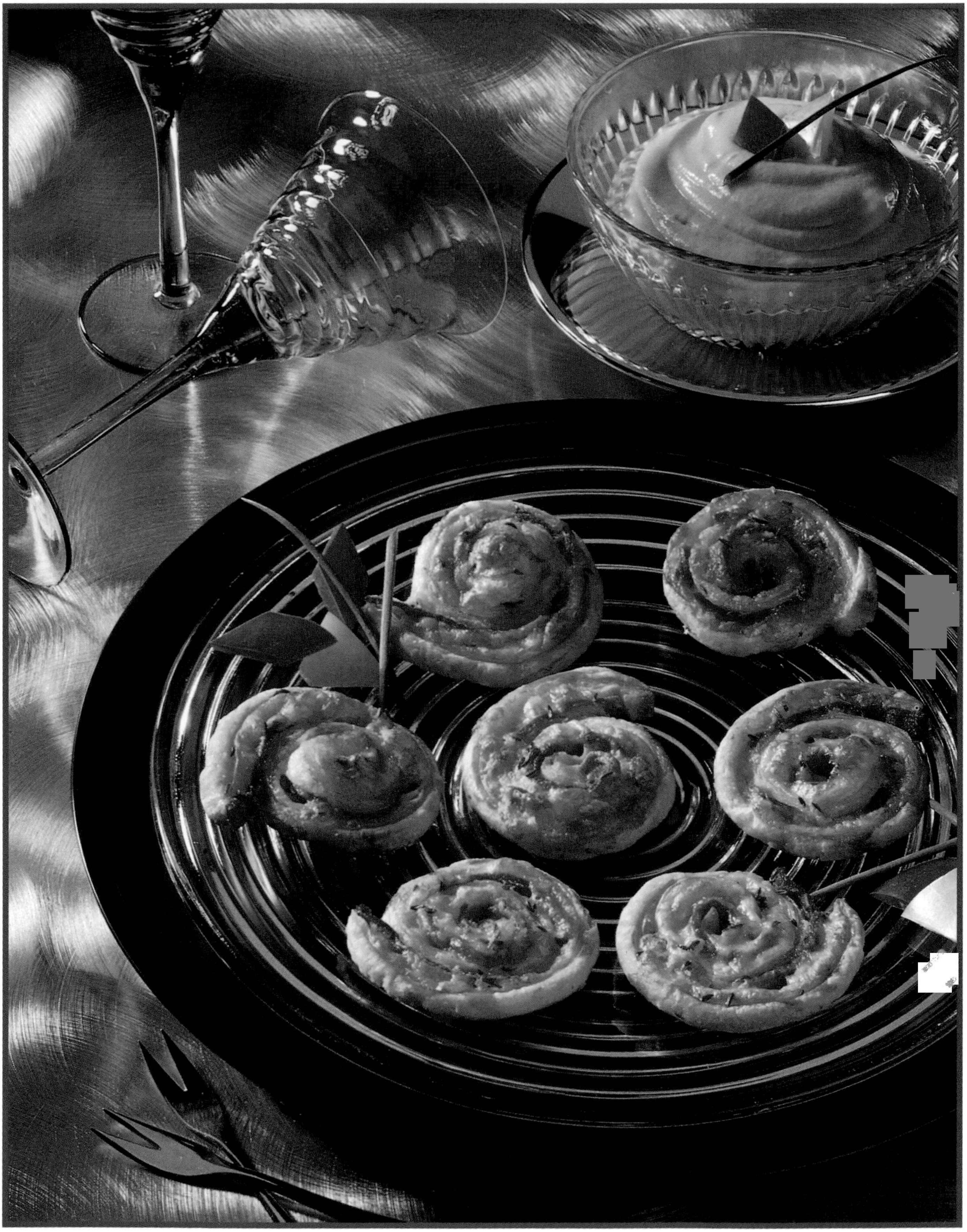

Tex-Mex Spring Rolls

- **2 tablespoons vegetable oil**
- **4 large green onions, finely chopped**
- **1 small red bell pepper, seeded and finely chopped**
- **5 cups shredded Romaine or iceberg lettuce**
- **½ cup drained and rinsed canned black beans**
- **½ cup frozen corn**
- **¼ cup chopped fresh cilantro**
- **3 tablespoons FRANK'S® Original REDHOT® Cayenne Pepper Sauce**
- **1 teaspoon ground cumin**
- **½ cup (2 ounces) shredded Monterey Jack cheese**
- **12 to 15 spring roll wrappers (6 inches), thawed if frozen***
- **Nonstick cooking spray**
- **Creamy Corn Salsa (recipe follows)**

Available from Asian markets or in the produce section of larger supermarkets.

1. Heat oil in large nonstick skillet over medium heat. Add green onions and bell pepper; cook and stir 2 minutes or until tender. Stir in lettuce, beans, corn, cilantro, RedHot® sauce and cumin. Cook 3 to 5 minutes or until liquid has evaporated, stirring occasionally. Cool 15 minutes. Stir in cheese.

2. Preheat oven to 400°F. Grease large baking sheet.

3. Place 1 wrapper on work surface like a diamond, with corner at bottom, keeping remaining wrappers covered with plastic wrap. Place about *2 tablespoons* filling across center. Brush edges of wrapper with cold water. Fold bottom corner of wrapper up over filling. Fold in and overlap the opposite right and left corners to form log. Continue rolling tightly up. Repeat with remaining wrappers and filling.

4. Place rolls on prepared baking sheet. Lightly spray rolls with cooking spray. Bake 15 minutes or until golden brown and crispy, turning halfway through baking time. Prepare Creamy Corn Salsa; serve warm with spring rolls.

Makes about 12 spring rolls

CREAMY CORN SALSA
- **1 cup frozen whole kernel corn, thawed and drained**
- **¼ cup milk**
- **2 tablespoons FRANK'S® Original REDHOT® Cayenne Pepper Sauce**
- **2 tablespoons chopped fresh cilantro**

Combine corn, milk and RedHot® sauce in blender or food processor. Cover; blend until puréed. Pour into small saucepan. Stir in cilantro. Cook over medium heat until heated through, stirring often.

Makes 1 cup salsa

Smoked Turkey Roll-Ups

- **2 packages (4 ounces each) herb-flavored soft spreadable cheese**
- **4 (8-inch) flour tortillas***
- **2 packages (6 ounces each) smoked turkey breast slices**
- **2 green onions, sliced lengthwise into quarters**
- **Whole pickled red cherry peppers (optional)**

To keep flour tortillas soft while preparing turkey roll-ups, cover with a slightly damp cloth.

1. Divide one package of cheese equally and spread over tortillas. Divide turkey slices equally and layer over cheese, overlapping turkey slices slightly to cover tortillas. Divide remaining package of cheese equally and spread over turkey slices.

2. At one edge of each tortilla, place 2 quarters of green onion. Roll up tortillas, jelly-roll style. Place turkey tortilla roll-ups, seam side down, in resealable plastic bag; refrigerate several hours or overnight.

3. To serve, cut each turkey tortilla roll-up crosswise into ½-inch slices to form pinwheels. If desired, arrange on serving plate and garnish with cherry peppers in center.

Makes 56 appetizer servings

FAVORITE RECIPE FROM NATIONAL TURKEY FEDERATION

Tex-Mex Spring Rolls

Cheesy Potato Skins with Black Beans & Salsa

6 medium potatoes (6 ounces each), baked
¾ cup GUILTLESS GOURMET® Black Bean Dip (mild or spicy)
¾ cup GUILTLESS GOURMET® Nacho Dip (mild or spicy)
¾ cup GUILTLESS GOURMET® Salsa (mild, medium or hot)
¾ cup low-fat sour cream
Fresh cilantro sprigs (optional)

Preheat oven to 400°F. Cut baked potatoes in half lengthwise and scoop out potato pulp, leaving ¼-inch pulp attached to skin (avoid breaking skin). (Save potato pulp for another use, such as mashed potatoes.) Place potato skins on large baking sheet, skin side down; bake 5 minutes.

Fill each potato skin with 1 tablespoon bean dip and 1 tablespoon nacho dip. Return to oven; bake 10 minutes. Remove from oven; let cool 5 minutes. Dollop 1 tablespoon salsa and 1 tablespoon sour cream onto each potato. Garnish with cilantro, if desired. Serve hot.

Makes 12 servings

Bell Pepper Nachos

1 green bell pepper
1 yellow or red bell pepper
2 Italian plum tomatoes, seeded and chopped
⅓ cup finely chopped onion
1 teaspoon chili powder
½ teaspoon ground cumin
1½ cups cooked white rice
½ cup (2 ounces) shredded reduced-fat Monterey Jack cheese
¼ cup chopped fresh cilantro
2 teaspoons jalapeño pepper sauce *or* ¼ teaspoon hot pepper sauce
½ cup (2 ounces) shredded reduced-fat sharp Cheddar cheese

1. Spray large nonstick baking sheets with nonstick cooking spray; set aside.

2. Cut bell peppers into 2×1½-inch strips; cut strips into bite-size triangles.

3. Spray large nonstick skillet with nonstick cooking spray. Add tomatoes, onion, chili powder and cumin. Cook over medium heat 3 minutes or until onion is tender, stirring occasionally. Remove from heat. Stir in rice, Monterey Jack cheese, cilantro and pepper sauce.

4. Top each pepper triangle with approximately 2 tablespoons rice mixture; sprinkle with Cheddar cheese. Place on prepared baking sheets.

5. Preheat broiler. Broil 6 to 8 inches from heat 3 to 4 minutes (or bake at 400°F 8 to 10 minutes) or until cheese is bubbly and rice is heated through. *Makes 8 servings*

Guiltless Quesadillas

¼ cup GUILTLESS GOURMET® Bean Dip (Black or Pinto, mild or spicy)
¼ cup GUILTLESS GOURMET® Nacho Dip (mild or spicy)
4 whole wheat tortillas
¼ cup low-fat sour cream
¼ cup GUILTLESS GOURMET® Salsa (mild, medium or hot)

Spread 1 tablespoon bean dip and 1 tablespoon nacho dip on each tortilla. Fold tortillas in half. Heat large nonstick skillet over medium-high heat until hot. Place 2 folded tortillas in skillet; cook until tortillas start to brown. Flip tortillas; cook until browned on other side. Slide tortillas onto warm serving plate; cut each quesadilla in half. Repeat with remaining 2 folded tortillas. Serve each quesadilla with 1 tablespoon sour cream and salsa. *Makes 4 servings*

Cheesy Potato Skins with Black Beans & Salsa

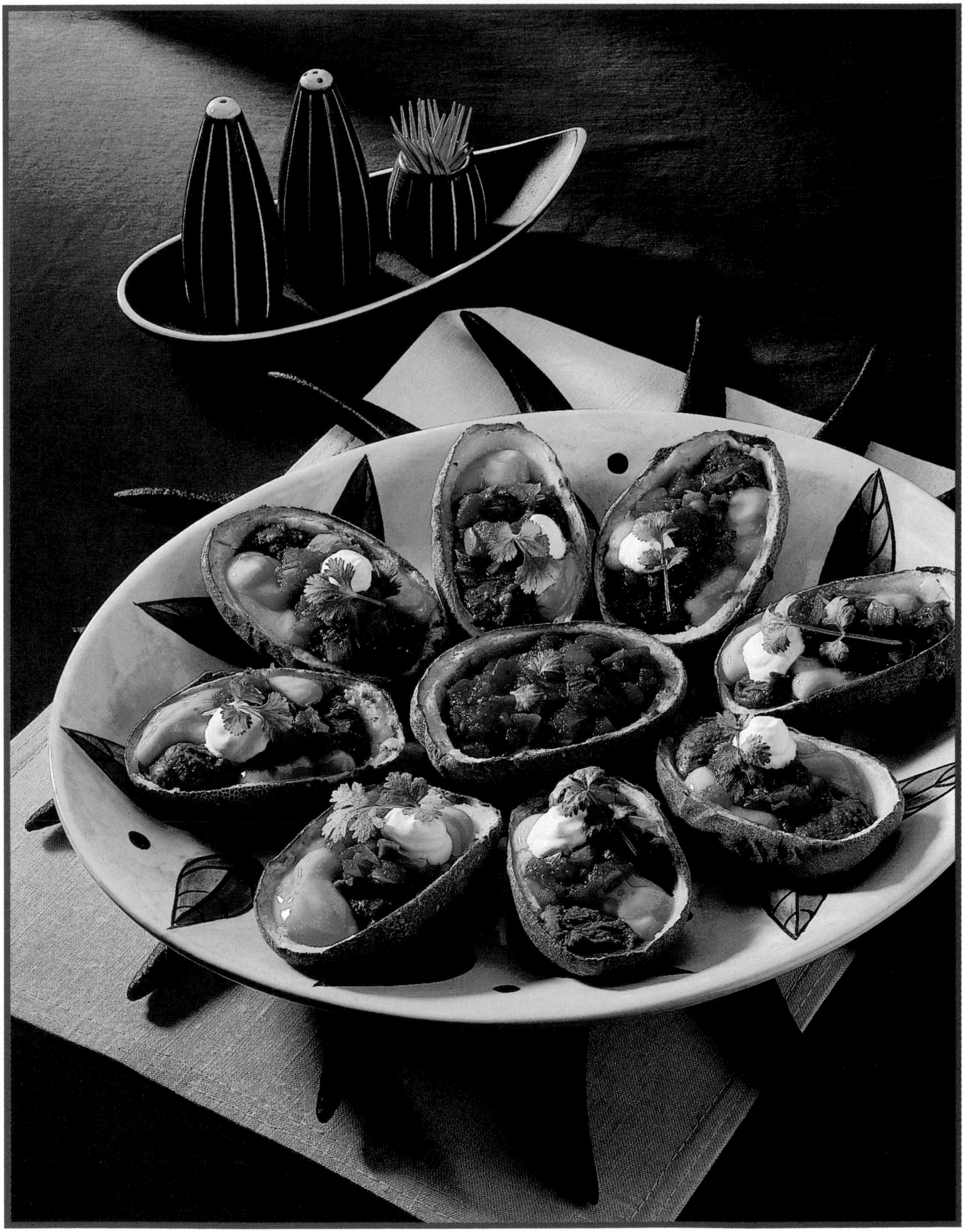

Chili Chip Party Platter

- **1 pound ground beef**
- **1 medium onion, chopped**
- **1 package (1.48 ounces) LAWRY'S® Spices & Seasonings for Chili**
- **1 can (6 ounces) tomato paste**
- **1 cup water**
- **1 bag (8 to 9 ounces) tortilla chips or corn chips**
- **1½ cups (6 ounces) shredded cheddar cheese**
- **1 can (2¼ ounces) sliced pitted ripe olives, drained**
- **½ cup sliced green onions**

In medium skillet, brown beef until crumbly; drain fat. Add onion, Spices & Seasonings for Chili, tomato paste and water; blend well. Bring to a boil. Reduce heat to low; simmer, uncovered, 15 minutes, stirring occasionally. Serve over tortilla chips. Top with cheese, olives and green onions.

Makes 4 servings

Presentation: *Serve with a cool beverage and sliced melon.*

Salmon Appetizers

- **1 package frozen puff pastry sheets**
- **4 ounces smoked salmon, flaked**
- **8 ounces cream cheese, softened**
- **2 tablespoons snipped chives**
- **1½ teaspoons lemon juice**

Preheat oven to 375°F. Cut 2-inch rounds of dough from pastry sheet; place in greased muffin cups. (Freeze remaining pastry sheet for later use.) Top dough rounds with salmon. Mix cream cheese, chives and lemon juice until creamy. Top salmon with about 1 tablespoon cream cheese mixture or pipe cream cheese over salmon, if desired. Bake 15 to 18 minutes. Serve warm. *Makes 12 appetizers*

Favorite recipe from **Wisconsin Milk Marketing Board**

Swiss Fondue-Wisconsin

- **2 cups dry white wine**
- **1 tablespoon lemon juice**
- **1 pound Wisconsin Gruyère cheese, shredded**
- **1 pound Wisconsin Fontina cheese, shredded**
- **1 tablespoon arrowroot**
- **2 ounces kirsch**
  Pinch ground nutmeg
  French bread cubes
  Pears, cut into wedges
  Apples, cut into wedges

Bring wine and lemon juice to a boil in fondue pot. Reduce heat to low. Toss cheeses with arrowroot. Gradually add to wine mixture, stirring constantly. When cheese is completely melted, stir in kirsch. Sprinkle with nutmeg and serve with French bread cubes, pears and apples.

Makes 6 servings

Favorite recipe from **Wisconsin Milk Marketing Board**

Elegant Antipasto

- **1 jar (16 ounces) mild cherry peppers**
- **1 package (9 ounces) frozen artichoke hearts, cooked and drained**
- **½ pound asparagus spears, cooked**
- **½ cup pitted ripe olives**
- **1 medium red onion, cut into wedges**
- **1 green bell pepper, cut into triangles**
- **1 red bell pepper, cut into triangles**
- **1 bottle (8 ounces) KRAFT® House Italian with Olive Oil Blend Dressing**
- **1 wedge (4 ounces) KRAFT® Natural Parmesan Cheese, shredded, divided**
- **1 package (8 ounces) OSCAR MAYER® Sliced Hard Salami**

• Arrange vegetables in rows in 13×9-inch glass baking dish.

• Pour dressing and ⅓ cup cheese over vegetables; cover. Refrigerate 1 to 2 hours.

• Drain vegetables, reserving marinade. Arrange vegetables and salami on serving platter. Drizzle with marinade; top with remaining cheese.

Makes 6 servings

Prep Time: *20 minutes plus refrigerating*

Variation: *Substitute mushrooms, green beans, cherry tomatoes or broccoli flowerets for any of the vegetables listed.*

Spicy Tomato, Onion and Cheese Tart

1 package (11 ounces) pie crust mix
⅓ cup cold water
2 tablespoons olive oil
3 cups thinly sliced red onions
3 tablespoons FRANK'S® Original REDHOT® Cayenne Pepper Sauce
¾ teaspoon dried tarragon leaves
1½ cups (6 ounces) shredded Monterey Jack cheese, divided
4 ripe plum tomatoes, thinly sliced, divided

1. Preheat oven to 450°F. Prepare pie crust mix according to package directions using water. Roll out dough to 14-inch circle on lightly floured board. Press dough into 12-inch pizza pan, folding edges under to fit inside pan. Prick dough with fork. Bake 15 minutes or until bottom of crust is golden brown. (Cover pan loosely with foil if crust browns too quickly.) Cool. Remove from oven. *Reduce oven temperature to 375°F.*

2. Heat oil in large nonstick skillet over medium heat. Add onions; cook and stir 5 minutes or until softened. Stir in RedHot® sauce and tarragon. Cook, covered, 5 minutes or until onions are very tender, stirring occasionally.

3. Sprinkle *¾ cup* cheese over crust. Top with *half* of the tomatoes and cover with onions. Layer remaining *¾ cup* cheese and tomatoes over onions. Bake 15 minutes or until cheese melts and tomatoes soften. Let stand 10 minutes. Cut into thin wedges to serve.
Makes 12 servings

Prep Time: 20 minutes
Cook Time: 40 minutes

Spam™ Quesadillas

1 (12-ounce) can SPAM® Luncheon Meat, chopped
4 cups (16 ounces) shredded Monterey Jack cheese with peppers
6 (8-inch) flour tortillas, divided
Guacamole and CHI-CHI'S® Salsa

In large bowl, combine Spam® and cheese. Spoon Spam™ mixture over each of 3 tortillas. Top with remaining 3 tortillas. On lightly greased griddle over medium-high heat, warm 1 quesadilla until soft and cheese is melted, turning once. Repeat with remaining 2 quesadillas. Cut each tortilla stack into 6 wedges. Serve with guacamole and salsa.
Makes 18 appetizer servings

Roasted Garlic & Spinach Spirals

1 whole head fresh garlic
3 cups fresh spinach leaves
1 can (15 ounces) white beans, rinsed and drained
1 teaspoon dried oregano leaves
¼ teaspoon ground black pepper
⅛ teaspoon cayenne pepper
7 (7-inch) flour tortillas

1. Preheat oven to 400°F. Trim top of garlic just enough to cut tips off center cloves; discard. Moisten head of garlic with water; wrap in foil. Bake 45 minutes or until garlic is soft and has a mellow garlicky aroma; cool. Remove garlic from skin by squeezing between fingers and thumb and place in food processor.

2. Rinse spinach leaves; pat dry with paper towels. Remove stems; discard. Finely shred leaves by stacking and cutting several leaves at a time. Place in medium bowl.

3. Add beans, oregano, black pepper and cayenne pepper to food processor; process until smooth. Add to spinach; mix well. Spread mixture evenly onto tortillas; roll up. Trim ½ inch off ends of rolls; discard. Cut rolls into 1-inch pieces. Transfer to serving plates; garnish, if desired.
Makes 10 servings

Tip: For best results, cover tortilla rolls and refrigerate 1 to 2 hours before slicing.

Crab Canapés

⅔ cup nonfat pasteurized
   process cream cheese
   product, softened
2 teaspoons lemon juice
1 teaspoon hot pepper
   sauce
1 package (8 ounces)
   imitation crabmeat or
   lobster, flaked
⅓ cup chopped red bell
   pepper
2 green onions with tops,
   sliced (about ¼ cup)
64 cucumber slices (about
   2½ cucumbers cut
   ⅜ inch thick) or melba
   toast rounds

1. Combine cream cheese,
lemon juice and hot pepper
sauce in medium bowl; mix
well. Stir in crabmeat, bell
pepper and green onions;
cover. Chill until ready to serve.

2. When ready to serve, spoon
1½ teaspoons crab mixture
onto each cucumber slice.
Place on serving plate; garnish
with parsley, if desired.

Makes 16 servings

Tip: *To allow flavors to blend, chill
crab mixture at least 1 hour before
spreading onto cucumbers or
melba toast rounds.*

Mariachi Drumsticks

1¼ cups crushed tortilla
   chips
1 package (1.0 ounce)
   LAWRY'S® Taco Spices
   & Seasonings
2 dozen chicken
   drumettes

In large resealable plastic bag,
combine chips and Taco Spices
& Seasonings. Dampen chicken
with water and shake off
excess. Place a few pieces at
a time in plastic bag; seal bag
and shake pieces thoroughly
to coat with chips. Arrange
chicken in greased shallow
baking pan; bake, uncovered,
in 350°F oven 30 to 45 minutes
or until crispy.

Makes 2 dozen appetizers

Presentation: *Serve with salsa
and dairy sour cream for dipping.*

MICROWAVE DIRECTIONS:
PREPARE AND COAT CHICKEN AS
DIRECTED. ARRANGE ON 10-INCH
GREASED GLASS PIE PLATE IN "SPOKE"
PATTERN WITH THICK ENDS OF CHICKEN
TOWARD OUTSIDE EDGE OF PLATE.
COVER WITH WAXED PAPER.
MICROWAVE AT **MEDIUM-HIGH**
(70% POWER) 10 MINUTES, TURNING
PLATE AFTER 5 MINUTES.

Hot & Spicy Buffalo Chicken Wings

1 can (15 ounces) DEL
   MONTE® Original
   Sloppy Joe Sauce
¼ cup DEL MONTE® Thick
   & Chunky Salsa,
   Medium
1 tablespoon red wine
   vinegar or cider
   vinegar
20 chicken wings (about
   4 pounds)

1. Preheat oven to 400°F.

2. Combine sloppy joe sauce,
salsa and vinegar in small
bowl. Remove ¼ cup sauce
mixture to serve with cooked
chicken wings; cover and
refrigerate. Set aside remaining
sauce mixture.

3. Arrange wings in single layer
in large, shallow baking pan;
brush wings with sauce mixture.

4. Bake chicken, uncovered, on
middle rack in oven 35 minutes
or until chicken is no longer
pink in center, turning and
brushing with remaining sauce
mixture after 15 minutes. Serve
with reserved ¼ cup sauce.
Garnish, if desired.

Makes 4 servings

Prep Time: 5 minutes
Cook Time: 35 minutes

Crab Canapés

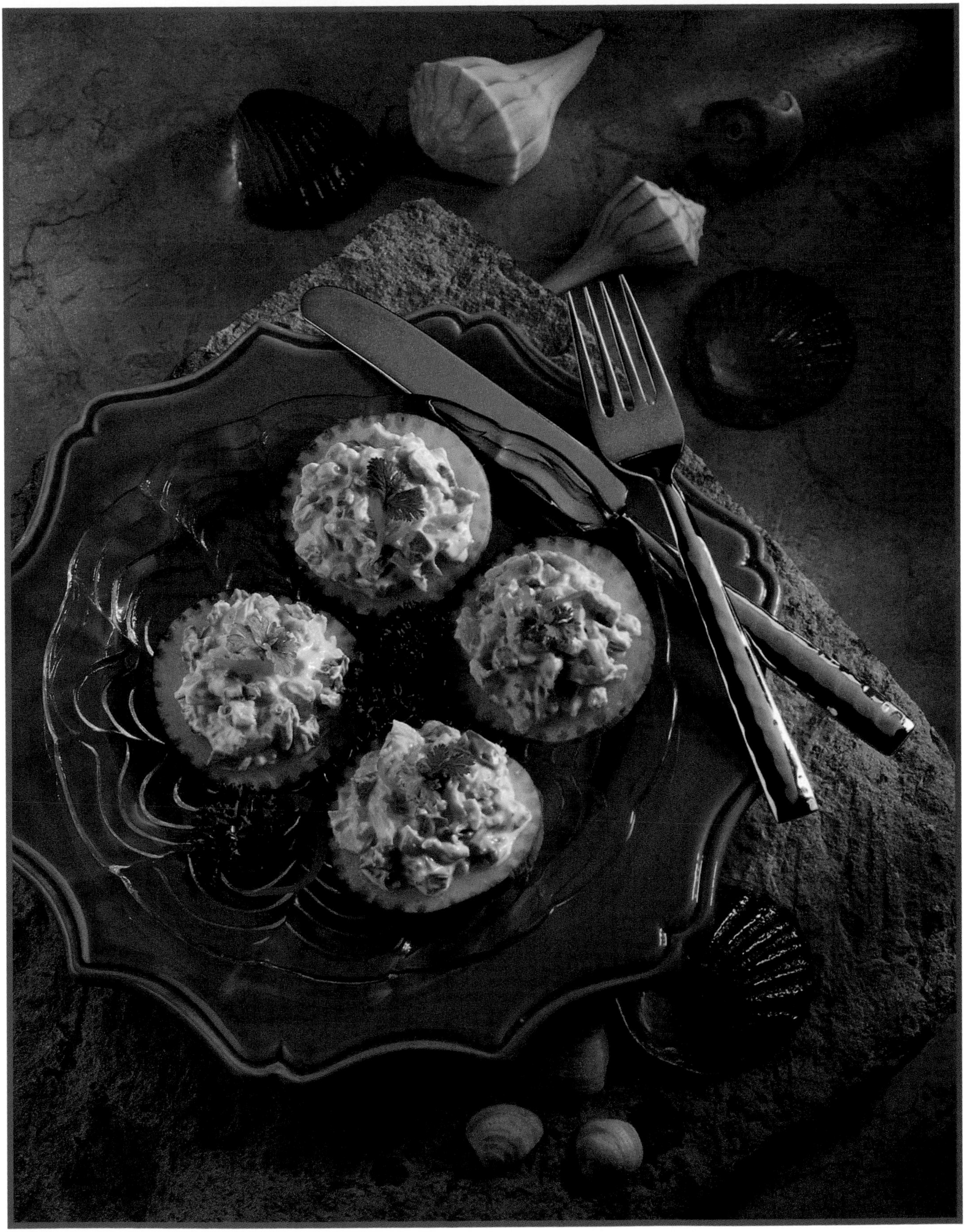

Smoked Chicken Bagel Snacks

⅓ cup nonfat pasteurized
   process cream cheese
   product, softened
2 teaspoons spicy brown
   mustard
¼ cup chopped roasted
   red peppers, drained
1 green onion with top,
   sliced
5 mini-bagels, split
3 ounces smoked chicken
   or turkey, cut into
   10 very thin slices
¼ medium cucumber, cut
   into 10 thin slices

1. Combine cream cheese and mustard in small bowl; mix well. Stir in peppers and green onion.

2. Spread cream cheese mixture evenly onto cut sides of bagels. Cover bottom halves of bagels with chicken, folding chicken to fit onto bagels; top with cucumber slices and tops of bagels.   *Makes 5 servings*

Mini Sausage Quiches

½ cup butter or margarine,
   softened
3 ounces cream cheese,
   softened
1 cup all-purpose flour
½ pound BOB EVANS
   FARMS® Italian Roll
   Sausage
1 cup (4 ounces) shredded
   Swiss cheese
1 tablespoon snipped
   fresh chives
2 eggs
1 cup half-and-half
¼ teaspoon salt
   Dash cayenne pepper

Beat butter and cream cheese in medium bowl until creamy. Blend in flour; refrigerate 1 hour. Roll into 24 (1-inch) balls; press each into ungreased mini-muffin cup to form pastry shell. Preheat oven to 375°F. To prepare filling, crumble sausage into small skillet. Cook over medium heat until browned, stirring occasionally. Drain off any drippings. Sprinkle evenly into pastry shells in muffin cups; sprinkle with Swiss cheese and chives. Whisk eggs, half-and-half, salt and cayenne until blended; pour into pastry shells. Bake 20 to 30 minutes or until set. Remove from pans. Serve hot. Refrigerate leftovers.
Makes 24 appetizers

SERVING SUGGESTION: POUR MIXTURE INTO 12 STANDARD 2½-INCH MUFFIN CUPS TO MAKE LARGER INDIVIDUAL QUICHES. SERVE FOR BREAKFAST.

Sweet & Sour Cocktail Meatballs

1 pound ground turkey
¾ cup plain dry bread
   crumbs
½ cup GREY POUPON®
   Dijon Mustard, divided
½ cup chopped green
   onions, divided
1 egg, beaten
½ teaspoon ground ginger
½ teaspoon ground black
   pepper
1 (8-ounce) can pineapple
   chunks, undrained
⅓ cup firmly packed light
   brown sugar
¼ cup apple cider vinegar
¼ cup diced red bell
   pepper
1 teaspoon cornstarch

In large bowl, combine turkey, bread crumbs, ¼ cup mustard, ¼ cup green onions, egg, ginger and black pepper. Shape into 32 (1-inch) balls. Place in greased 13×9×2-inch baking pan. Bake at 350°F for 20 minutes.

In medium saucepan, combine pineapple chunks with juice, sugar, vinegar, bell pepper, cornstarch and remaining ¼ cup mustard and green onions. Cook over medium heat until sauce thickens and begins to boil. Spoon pineapple sauce over meatballs. Bake 5 to 7 minutes or until meatballs are done. Spoon into serving dish and serve with toothpicks.
Makes 32 appetizers

Smoked Chicken Bagel Snacks

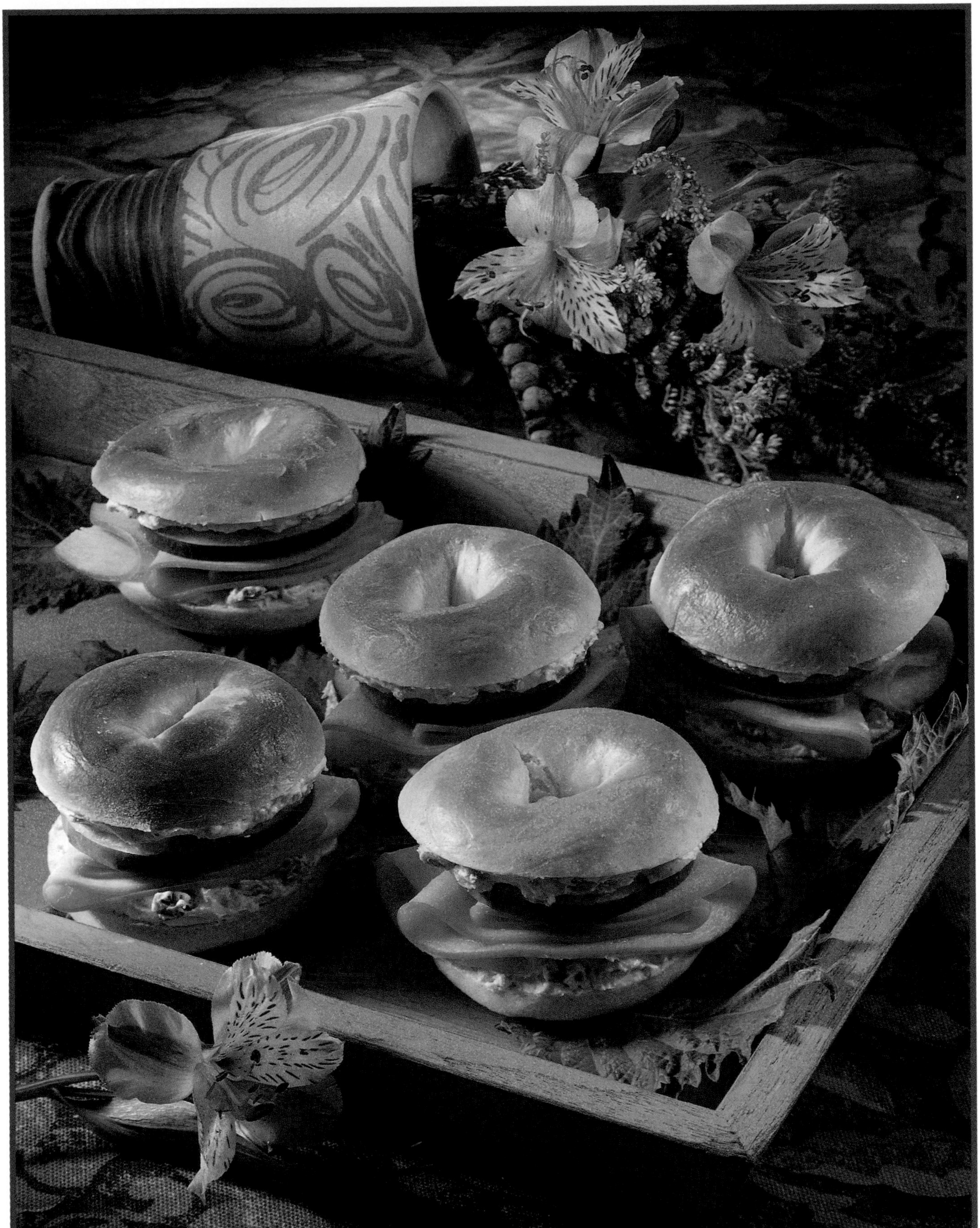

Buffalo Chicken Wings

24 chicken wings
1 teaspoon salt
¼ teaspoon ground black pepper
4 cups vegetable oil for frying
¼ cup butter or margarine
¼ cup hot pepper sauce
1 teaspoon white wine vinegar
Celery sticks
1 bottle (8 ounces) blue cheese dressing

Cut tips off wings at first joint; discard tips. Cut remaining wings into two parts at the joint; sprinkle with salt and black pepper. Heat oil in deep-fryer or heavy saucepan to 375°F. Add half the wings; fry about 10 minutes or until golden brown and crisp, stirring occasionally. Remove with slotted spoon; drain on paper towels. Repeat with remaining wings.

Melt butter in small saucepan over medium heat; stir in pepper sauce and vinegar. Cook until thoroughly heated. Place wings on large platter. Pour sauce over wings. Serve warm with celery and dressing for dipping.

Makes 24 appetizers

FAVORITE RECIPE FROM **NATIONAL BROILER COUNCIL**

Steak Nachos

1 (1-pound) beef top round steak, chopped
¼ cup chopped onion
1 tablespoon vegetable oil
½ cup A.1.® Original or A.1.® Bold & Spicy Steak Sauce
5 cups tortilla chips
2 cups (8 ounces) shredded Cheddar or Monterey Jack cheese
1 cup chopped fresh tomatoes
¼ cup diced green chilies or jalapeño pepper slices
¼ cup sliced pitted ripe olives
Dairy sour cream (optional)

In large skillet, over medium-high heat, sauté steak and onion in oil until steak is no longer pink; drain. Stir in steak sauce. Arrange tortilla chips on large heatproof platter or baking sheet. Spoon steak mixture over chips; sprinkle with cheese. Broil 6 inches from heat source 3 to 5 minutes or until cheese melts. Top with tomatoes, chilies and olives. Serve immediately with sour cream on the side, if desired.

Makes 6 appetizer servings

Deluxe Fajita Nachos

1 tablespoon vegetable oil
1 pound boneless skinless chicken breasts, thinly sliced
1 package (1.27 ounces) LAWRY'S® Spices & Seasonings for Fajitas
⅓ cup water
8 ounces tortilla chips
1¼ cups (5 ounces) grated cheddar cheese
1 cup (4 ounces) grated Monterey Jack cheese
1 large tomato, chopped
1 can (2¼ ounces) sliced ripe olives, drained
¼ cup sliced green onions
Salsa

In medium skillet, heat oil. Add chicken; sauté 5 to 8 minutes. Add Spices & Seasonings for Fajitas and water; blend well. Bring to a boil; reduce heat and simmer 7 minutes. In large shallow ovenproof platter, arrange chips. Top with chicken mixture and cheeses. Place under broiler to melt cheeses. Top with tomato, olives, green onions and desired amount of salsa. *Makes 4 appetizer or 2 main-dish servings*

Presentation: *Garnish with guacamole and dairy sour cream.*

Substitution: *1¼ pounds cooked ground beef can be used in place of shredded chicken.*

Hint: *For a spicier version, add sliced jalapeños.*

Buffalo Chicken Wings

Coconut-Orange Shrimp

2 ½ cups flaked coconut, divided
1 medium ripe banana
¼ cup FRANK'S® Original REDHOT® Cayenne Pepper Sauce
¼ cup orange juice
1 tablespoon olive oil
1 tablespoon grated orange peel
1 pound raw large shrimp, peeled and deveined

1. Combine ½ cup coconut, banana, RedHot® sauce, juice, oil and orange peel in blender or food processor; blend until puréed.

2. Pour into resealable plastic food storage bag. Add shrimp; toss to coat. Seal bag. Refrigerate 1 hour.

3. Preheat oven to 450°F. Line baking pan with foil; grease foil. Sprinkle remaining coconut onto sheet of waxed paper. Dip shrimp into coconut, pressing firmly to coat. (Do not shake off excess marinade from shrimp.) Place shrimp on prepared baking pan. Bake 6 to 8 minutes or until shrimp are opaque.   *Makes 6 servings*

Prep Time: 30 minutes
Marinate Time: 1 hour
Cook Time: 6 minutes

Blue Crab Stuffed Tomatoes

½ pound blue crabmeat
10 plum tomatoes
½ cup finely chopped celery
⅓ cup plain low-fat yogurt
2 tablespoons minced green onion
2 tablespoons finely chopped red bell pepper
½ teaspoon lemon juice
¼ teaspoon salt
⅛ teaspoon black pepper

Remove any shell or cartilage from crabmeat.

Cut tomatoes in half lengthwise. Carefully scoop out centers of tomatoes; discard pulp. Invert on paper towels.

Combine crabmeat, celery, yogurt, onion, bell pepper, lemon juice, salt and black pepper. Mix well.

Fill tomato halves with crab mixture. Refrigerate 2 hours.
Makes 20 appetizers

*FAVORITE RECIPE FROM **FLORIDA DEPARTMENT OF AGRICULTURE AND CONSUMER SERVICES, BUREAU OF SEAFOOD AND AQUACULTURE***

Clams Posilippo

2 dozen cherrystone clams, well scrubbed
½ cup finely chopped red or yellow bell pepper
½ cup finely chopped plum tomatoes
½ cup finely chopped green onions
¼ cup chopped Canadian bacon or boiled ham
¼ cup FRANK'S® Original REDHOT® Cayenne Pepper Sauce
2 tablespoons olive oil
2 tablespoons grated Parmesan cheese

1. Place clams in large nonstick skillet; add ¼ cup water. Cook, covered, over medium heat 6 to 8 minutes or until clams begin to open, removing them as they open. Rinse clams under water to remove excess sand, if necessary. Remove top shells; discard. With paring knife, loosen clam meat from bottom shell. Place clams in shallow ovenproof baking dish.

2. Preheat oven to 400°F. Combine bell pepper, tomatoes, onions, bacon, RedHot® sauce and oil in small bowl. Spoon about 1 tablespoon mixture over each clam. Sprinkle with cheese.

3. Bake clams 10 minutes or until heated through.
Makes 6 servings

Prep Time: 25 minutes
Cook Time: 10 minutes

Coconut-Orange Shrimp

Waldorf Appetizer Pizzas

½ package (5 ounces) washed fresh spinach or thawed frozen spinach
½ red apple, cored
1 tablespoon lemon juice
¼ cup (1 ounce) chopped walnuts
2 large cloves garlic, minced
2 tablespoons golden raisins
1 teaspoon olive oil
2 packages (8 ounces each) 6-inch Italian bread shells
¼ cup (1 ounce) crumbled Gorgonzola cheese or blue cheese
Cracked black pepper

1. Preheat oven to 450°F. Remove and discard stems from spinach; set aside. Thinly slice apple and then cut slices into ½-inch pieces. Place in small bowl with lemon juice and 1 tablespoon water; stir to completely coat apple pieces with juice. Drain; set aside.

2. Spray large skillet with nonstick cooking spray. Heat over medium-high heat until hot. Add walnuts; cook and stir 5 to 6 minutes or until nuts are light golden. Stir in apple, garlic and raisins. Add spinach and drizzle with olive oil. Cover and cook 1 minute or until spinach begins to wilt. Stir until spinach is just wilted and coated with oil.

3. Place bread shells on baking sheet. Divide spinach mixture evenly among shells, leaving ½-inch border. Crumble cheese over spinach. Sprinkle with pepper. Bake 6 minutes or until cheese is melted and shells are warm. Cut each shell into 4 wedges.   *Makes 8 servings (2 pieces each)*

California Quesadillas

1 small ripe avocado
2 packages (3 ounces each) cream cheese, softened
⅓ cup FRANK'S® Original REDHOT® Cayenne Pepper Sauce
¼ cup minced fresh cilantro leaves
16 (6-inch) flour tortillas (2 packages)
1 cup (4 ounces) shredded Cheddar or Monterey Jack cheese
½ cup finely chopped green onions
Sour cream (optional)

Halve avocado and remove pit. Scoop out flesh into food processor or bowl of electric mixer. Add cream cheese and RedHot® Sauce. Cover and process, or beat, until smooth. Add cilantro; process, or beat, until well blended. Spread rounded tablespoon avocado mixture onto each tortilla. Sprinkle half the tortillas with cheese and onions, dividing evenly. Top with remaining tortillas; press gently.

Place tortillas on oiled grid. Grill over medium coals 5 minutes or until cheese melts and tortillas are lightly browned, turning once. Cut into triangles. Serve with sour cream, if desired.   *Makes 8 servings*

Easy Caramel Popcorn

MAZOLA NO STICK® Corn Oil Cooking Spray
3 quarts popped popcorn
3 cups unsalted mixed nuts
1 cup packed brown sugar
½ cup KARO® Light or Dark Corn Syrup
½ cup (1 stick) MAZOLA® Margarine or butter
½ teaspoon salt
½ teaspoon vanilla
½ teaspoon baking soda

1. Spray large shallow roasting pan with cooking spray. Combine popcorn and nuts in pan; place in 250°F oven while preparing glaze.

2. In heavy medium saucepan, combine brown sugar, corn syrup, margarine and salt. Stirring constantly, bring to a boil over medium heat. Without stirring, boil 5 minutes. Remove from heat; stir in vanilla and baking soda. Pour syrup mixture over warm popcorn and nuts, stirring to coat.

3. Bake in 250°F oven 60 minutes, stirring occasionally. Cool; break apart. Store in tightly covered container.   *Makes about 4 quarts*

Easy Caramel Popcorn

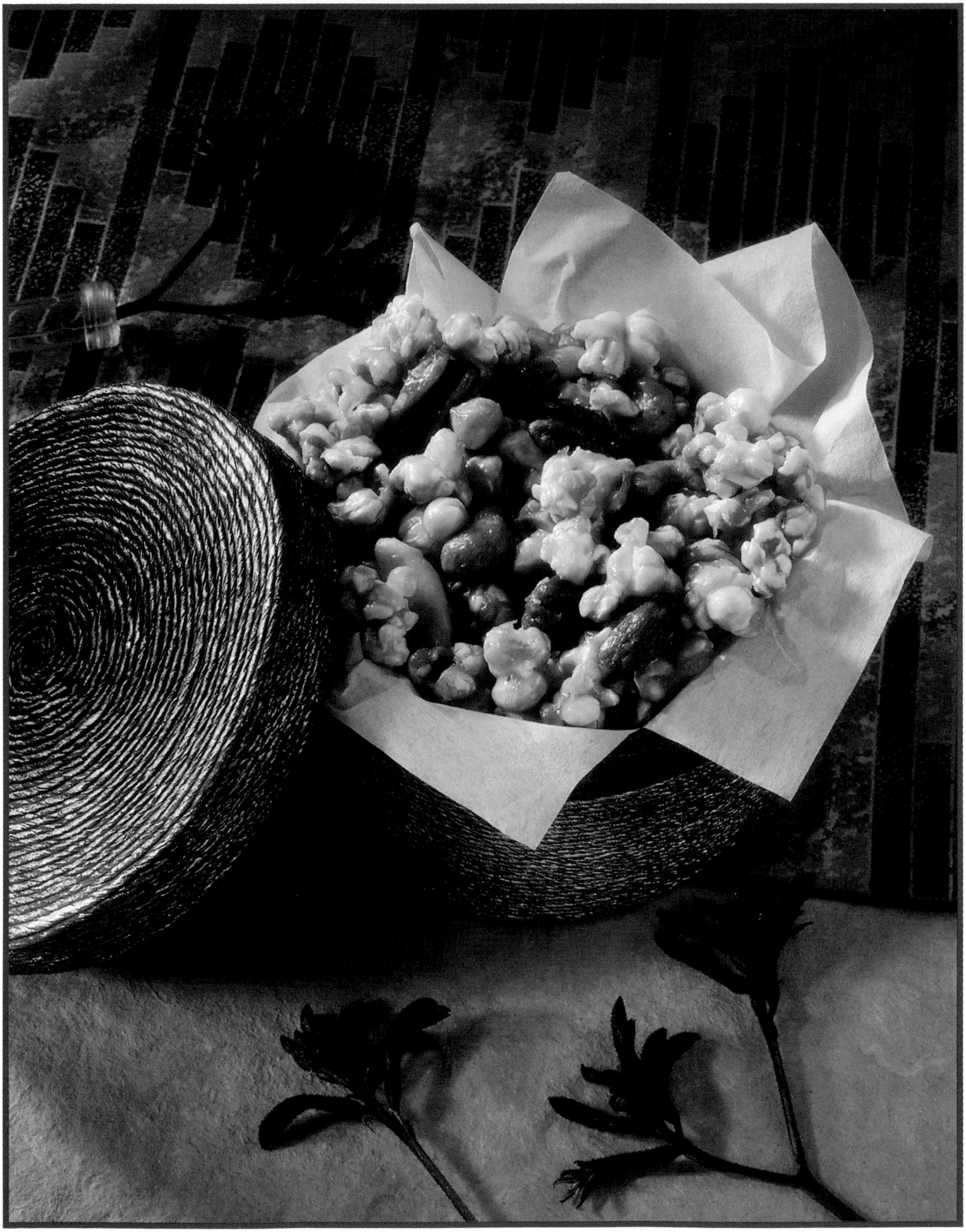

Honey Popcorn Clusters

6 cups air-popped popcorn
⅔ cup DOLE® Golden or Seedless Raisins
½ cup DOLE® Chopped Dates or Pitted Dates, chopped
⅓ cup DOLE® Slivered Almonds (optional)
⅓ cup packed brown sugar
¼ cup honey
2 tablespoons margarine
¼ teaspoon baking soda

• **Line** bottom and sides of 13×9-inch baking pan with large sheet of aluminum foil. Spray foil with vegetable cooking spray.

• **Stir** together popcorn, raisins, dates and almonds, if desired, in foil-lined pan.

• **Combine** brown sugar, honey and margarine in small saucepan. Bring to a boil over medium heat, stirring constantly; reduce heat to low. Cook 5 minutes. *Do not stir.* Remove from heat.

• **Stir** in baking soda. Pour evenly over popcorn mixture, stirring quickly to coat evenly.

• **Bake** at 300°F 12 to 15 minutes or until mixture is lightly browned, stirring once halfway through baking time.

• **Lift** foil from pan; place on cooling rack. Cool popcorn mixture completely; break into clusters. Popcorn can be stored in airtight container up to 1 week. *Makes 7 cups*

Prep Time: 20 minutes
Bake Time: 15 minutes

Chex® Brand Party Mix

¼ cup margarine or butter
5 teaspoons Worcestershire sauce
1¼ teaspoons seasoned salt
¼ teaspoon garlic powder
2⅔ cups CORN CHEX® brand cereal
2⅔ cups RICE CHEX® brand cereal
2⅔ cups WHEAT CHEX® brand cereal
1 cup mixed nuts
1 cup pretzels

1. Melt margarine in open roasting pan in preheated 250°F oven. Stir in seasonings.

2. Gradually add cereals, nuts and pretzels; stir to coat evenly.

3. Bake 1 hour, stirring every 15 minutes. Spread on absorbent paper to cool. Store in airtight container.

Makes 10 cups

MICROWAVE DIRECTIONS:
1. MELT MARGARINE IN LARGE MICROWAVE-SAFE BOWL AT **HIGH**. STIR IN SEASONINGS.

2. GRADUALLY ADD CEREALS, NUTS AND PRETZELS; STIR TO COAT EVENLY.

3. MICROWAVE AT **HIGH** 5 TO 6 MINUTES, STIRRING THOROUGHLY WITH RUBBER SPATULA EVERY 2 MINUTES. WHILE STIRRING, MAKE SURE TO SCRAPE SIDES AND BOTTOM OF BOWL. SPREAD ON ABSORBENT PAPER TO COOL. STORE IN AIRTIGHT CONTAINER.

Take-Along Snack Mix

1 tablespoon butter or margarine
2 tablespoons honey
1 cup toasted oat cereal, any flavor
½ cup coarsely broken pecans
½ cup thin pretzel sticks, broken in half
½ cup raisins
1 cup "M&M's"® Chocolate Mini Baking Bits

In large heavy skillet over low heat, melt butter; add honey until blended. Add cereal, nuts, pretzels and raisins, stirring until all pieces are evenly coated. Continue cooking over low heat about 10 minutes, stirring frequently. Remove from heat; immediately spread on waxed paper until cool. Add "M&M's"® Chocolate Mini Baking Bits. Store in tightly covered container.

Makes about 3½ cups

Cinnamon RedHot™ Popcorn

- 10 cups air-popped popcorn (½ cup unpopped)
- 1½ cups (7 ounces) coarsely chopped pecans
- ¾ cup granulated sugar
- ¾ cup packed light brown sugar
- ½ cup light corn syrup
- 3 tablespoons FRANK'S® Original REDHOT® Cayenne Pepper Sauce
- 2 tablespoons honey
- 6 tablespoons (¾ stick) unsalted butter, room temperature, cut into thin pats
- 1 tablespoon ground cinnamon

1. Preheat oven to 250°F. Place popcorn and pecans in large ovenproof bowl or Dutch oven. Bake 15 minutes.

2. Combine sugars, corn syrup, RedHot® sauce and honey in medium saucepan. Bring to a full boil over medium-high heat, stirring just until sugars dissolve. Boil about 6 to 8 minutes or until soft crack stage (290°F on candy thermometer). *Do not stir.* Remove from heat.

3. Gradually add butter and cinnamon to sugar mixture, stirring gently until well blended. Pour over popcorn, tossing to coat evenly.* Spread popcorn mixture on greased baking sheets, using two forks. Cool completely. Break into bite-size pieces. Store in airtight container up to 2 weeks. *Makes 18 cups*

*If popcorn mixture sets too quickly, return to oven to rewarm. Popcorn mixture may be shaped into 3-inch balls while warm, if desired.

Prep Time: 15 minutes
Cook Time: 8 to 10 minutes

Patchwork Pop Corn Party Mix

- 3 quarts popped JOLLY TIME® Pop Corn
- 2 cups rice or wheat cereal squares
- 1 cup coarsely chopped walnuts, toasted
- ½ cup dried cranberries or dried tart cherries
- 3 tablespoons butter or margarine
- ½ teaspoon maple extract

Place popped pop corn, cereal, walnuts and cranberries in large bowl. Melt butter in small pan. Stir in maple extract. Pour over pop corn mixture; toss well. *Makes about 3½ quarts*

Take-Along Snack Mix (page 54)

Soups & Chili

FEATURING:

Cream Soups

Vegetarian Chili

Seasonal Soups

Bounty Soup (page 64)

Zesty Noodle Soup

1 pound BOB EVANS FARMS® Zesty Hot Roll Sausage
1 (16-ounce) can whole tomatoes, undrained
½ pound fresh mushrooms, sliced
1 large onion, chopped
1 small green bell pepper, chopped
2½ cups tomato juice
2½ cups water
¼ cup chopped fresh parsley
1 teaspoon lemon juice
1 teaspoon Worcestershire sauce
1 teaspoon celery seeds
½ teaspoon salt
½ teaspoon dried thyme leaves
1 cup uncooked egg noodles

Crumble sausage into medium saucepan. Cook over medium-high heat until browned, stirring occasionally. Drain off any drippings. Add tomatoes with juice, mushrooms, onion and pepper; cook until vegetables are tender, stirring well to break up tomatoes. Stir in all remaining ingredients except noodles. Bring to a boil over high heat. Reduce heat to low; simmer, covered, 30 minutes. Add noodles; simmer just until noodles are tender, yet firm. Serve hot. Refrigerate leftovers.

Makes 6 servings

SERVING SUGGESTION: SERVE WITH CRUSTY FRENCH BREAD.

Hearty Chicken and Rice Soup

10 cups chicken broth
1 medium onion, chopped
1 cup sliced celery
1 cup sliced carrots
¼ cup chopped parsley
½ teaspoon cracked black pepper
½ teaspoon dried thyme leaves
1 bay leaf
1½ cups diced chicken (about ¾ pound)
2 cups cooked rice
2 tablespoons lime juice
Lime slices for garnish

Combine chicken broth, onion, celery, carrots, parsley, pepper, thyme and bay leaf in Dutch oven. Bring to a boil; stir once or twice. Reduce heat; simmer, uncovered, 10 to 15 minutes. Add chicken; simmer, uncovered, 5 to 10 minutes or until chicken is no longer pink in center. Remove and discard bay leaf. Stir in rice and lime juice just before serving. Garnish with lime slices.

Makes 8 servings

FAVORITE RECIPE FROM **USA RICE FEDERATION**

Tortilla Soup

1 tablespoon butter or margarine
½ cup chopped green bell pepper
½ cup chopped onion
½ teaspoon ground cumin
3½ cups (two 14½-ounce cans) chicken broth
1¾ cups (16-ounce jar) ORTEGA® Thick & Chunky Salsa, hot, medium or mild or Garden Style Salsa, medium or mild
1 cup whole kernel corn
1 tablespoon vegetable oil
6 corn tortillas, cut into ½-inch strips
¾ cup (3 ounces) shredded Monterey Jack cheese
Sour cream (optional)

MELT butter in medium saucepan over medium heat. Add bell pepper, onion and cumin; cook for 3 to 4 minutes or until tender. Stir in chicken broth, salsa and corn. Bring to a boil. Reduce heat to low; cook for 5 minutes.

HEAT oil in medium skillet over medium-high heat. Add tortilla strips; cook for 2 to 4 minutes or until light golden brown and crisp. Place on paper towels.

PLACE tortilla strips and cheese in 6 bowls; ladle soup into bowls. Top with dollop of sour cream and additional tortilla strips. *Makes 6 servings*

Tip: For a festive appearance, use yellow, blue and red corn tortilla chips in soup.

Zesty Noodle Soup

Minestrone

- 1 tablespoon extra virgin olive oil
- 1 cup chopped red onion
- 2 teaspoons minced garlic
- 5 cups low sodium chicken broth
- 1 cup water
- 1 can (16 ounces) low sodium whole tomatoes, chopped and juices reserved
- 1 bay leaf
- ½ teaspoon salt or to taste
- ¼ teaspoon freshly ground black pepper
- ¾ cup uncooked ditalini pasta (mini macaroni)
- 2 packages (10 ounces each) frozen Italian vegetables
- 1 can (16 ounces) cannellini beans, rinsed and drained
- ⅓ cup slivered fresh basil leaves
- 1 cup (4 ounces) shredded ALPINE LACE® Fat Free Pasteurized Process Skim Milk Cheese Product—For Parmesan Lovers

1. In an 8-quart Dutch oven, heat the oil over medium-high heat. Add the onion and garlic and sauté for 5 minutes or until the onion is soft.

2. Stir in the broth, water, tomatoes and their juices, the bay leaf, salt and pepper. Bring to a rolling boil, add the pasta and return to a rolling boil. Cook, uncovered, for 10 minutes or until the pasta is almost tender.

3. Stir in the vegetables and beans. Return to a boil. Reduce the heat to low and simmer 5 minutes longer or until the vegetables are tender. Remove the bay leaf and discard. Stir in the basil, sprinkle with the cheese and serve immediately.

Makes 10 first-course servings (1 cup each) or 5 main-dish servings (2 cups each)

Ravioli Soup

- 1 package (9 ounces) fresh or frozen cheese ravioli or tortellini
- ¾ pound hot Italian sausage, crumbled
- 1 can (14½ ounces) DEL MONTE® Italian Recipe Stewed Tomatoes
- 1 can (about 14 ounces) beef broth
- 1 can (14½ ounces) DEL MONTE® *FreshCut*™ Cut Green Italian Beans, drained
- 2 green onions, sliced

1. Cook pasta according to package directions; drain.

2. Meanwhile, cook sausage in large saucepan over medium-high heat until no longer pink; drain. Add tomatoes, broth and 1¾ cups water; bring to a boil.

3. Reduce heat to low; stir in pasta, green beans and green onions. Simmer until heated through. Season with pepper and sprinkle with grated Parmesan cheese, if desired.

Makes 4 servings

Prep & Cook Time: 15 minutes

Dijon Roasted Vegetable Soup

- 2 plum tomatoes, halved
- 1 medium zucchini, split lengthwise and halved
- 1 large onion, quartered
- 1 red bell pepper, sliced
- 1 cup sliced carrots
- 2 to 3 cloves garlic
- 5 cups COLLEGE INN® Chicken Broth or Lower Sodium Chicken Broth
- ¼ teaspoon ground cumin
- ¼ teaspoon red pepper flakes
- 2 cups diced cooked chicken (about 10 ounces)
- ½ cup GREY POUPON® Dijon Mustard
- ¼ cup chopped parsley

On large baking sheet, arrange tomatoes, zucchini, onion, bell pepper, carrots and garlic. Bake at 325°F for 30 to 45 minutes or until golden and tender. Remove from oven and cool. Chop vegetables.

In medium saucepan, over high heat, bring chicken broth, chopped vegetables, cumin and red pepper flakes to a boil; reduce heat. Simmer for 5 minutes. Stir in chicken and mustard; cook for 5 minutes more. Stir in parsley and serve warm. *Makes 8 servings*

Minestrone

Classic Matzoh Ball Soup

- 1 package GALIL® Cut-Up Whole Chicken (about 3½ pounds)
- 7 cups plus 2 tablespoons water, divided
- 3 carrots, cut into 1-inch pieces
- 3 ribs celery, cut into 1-inch pieces
- 1 medium onion, unpeeled, quartered
- 1 large parsnip, cut into 1-inch pieces (optional)
- 1 head garlic, separated into cloves, unpeeled
- 3 sprigs parsley
- 8 to 10 whole black peppercorns
- 4 eggs
- 1 cup matzoh meal
- ¼ cup parve margarine, melted, cooled
- 1 tablespoon grated onion
- ½ teaspoon salt
- ⅛ teaspoon ground white pepper *or* ¼ teaspoon freshly ground black pepper
- Chopped fresh parsley for garnish

Combine chicken and 7 cups water in Dutch oven. Bring to a boil over medium heat. Remove any foam from surface of water with large metal spoon; discard. Add carrots, celery, unpeeled onion, parsnip, garlic, parsley sprigs and whole peppercorns. Cover; simmer 3 hours or until chicken is no longer pink in center.

Remove from heat; cool 30 minutes. Strain broth; reserve chicken and broth separately. Discard vegetables, garlic, parsley and peppercorns. Remove skin and bones from chicken; discard.*

Beat eggs in large bowl on medium speed of electric mixer. Add matzoh meal, margarine, remaining 2 tablespoons water, grated onion, salt and ground pepper. Mix at low speed until well blended. Let stand 15 to 30 minutes. With wet hands, form matzoh mixture into 12 (2-inch) balls.

Bring 8 cups water to a boil in Dutch oven. Drop matzoh balls, one at a time, into boiling water. Reduce heat. Cover; simmer 35 to 40 minutes or until matzoh balls are cooked through. Drain well.

Add reserved broth to Dutch oven. Bring to a boil over high heat. Add salt to taste. Reduce heat; cover. Simmer 5 minutes or until matzoh balls are heated through.

Garnish with chopped parsley, if desired. *Makes 6 servings*

Chicken and broth may be covered and refrigerated up to 3 days or frozen up to 3 months.

Chicken Soup au Pistou

- ½ pound boneless skinless chicken breasts, cut into ½-inch pieces
- 1 large onion, diced
- 3 cans (about 14 ounces each) chicken broth
- 1 can (15 ounces) whole tomatoes, undrained
- 1 can (14 ounces) Great Northern beans, rinsed and drained
- 2 medium carrots, sliced
- 1 large potato, diced
- ¼ teaspoon salt
- ¼ teaspoon black pepper
- 1 cup frozen Italian green beans
- ¼ cup prepared pesto Grated Parmesan cheese (optional)

SPRAY large saucepan with nonstick cooking spray; heat over medium-high heat until hot. Add chicken; cook and stir about 5 minutes or until chicken is browned. Add onion; cook and stir 2 minutes.

ADD chicken broth, tomatoes with juice, Great Northern beans, carrots, potato, salt and pepper. Bring to a boil, stirring to break up tomatoes. Reduce heat to low. Cover and simmer 15 minutes, stirring occasionally. Add green beans; cook about 5 minutes or until tender.

LADLE soup into bowls. Top each with teaspoonful pesto and sprinkle with Parmesan cheese, if desired.

Makes 8 servings

Classic Matzoh Ball Soup

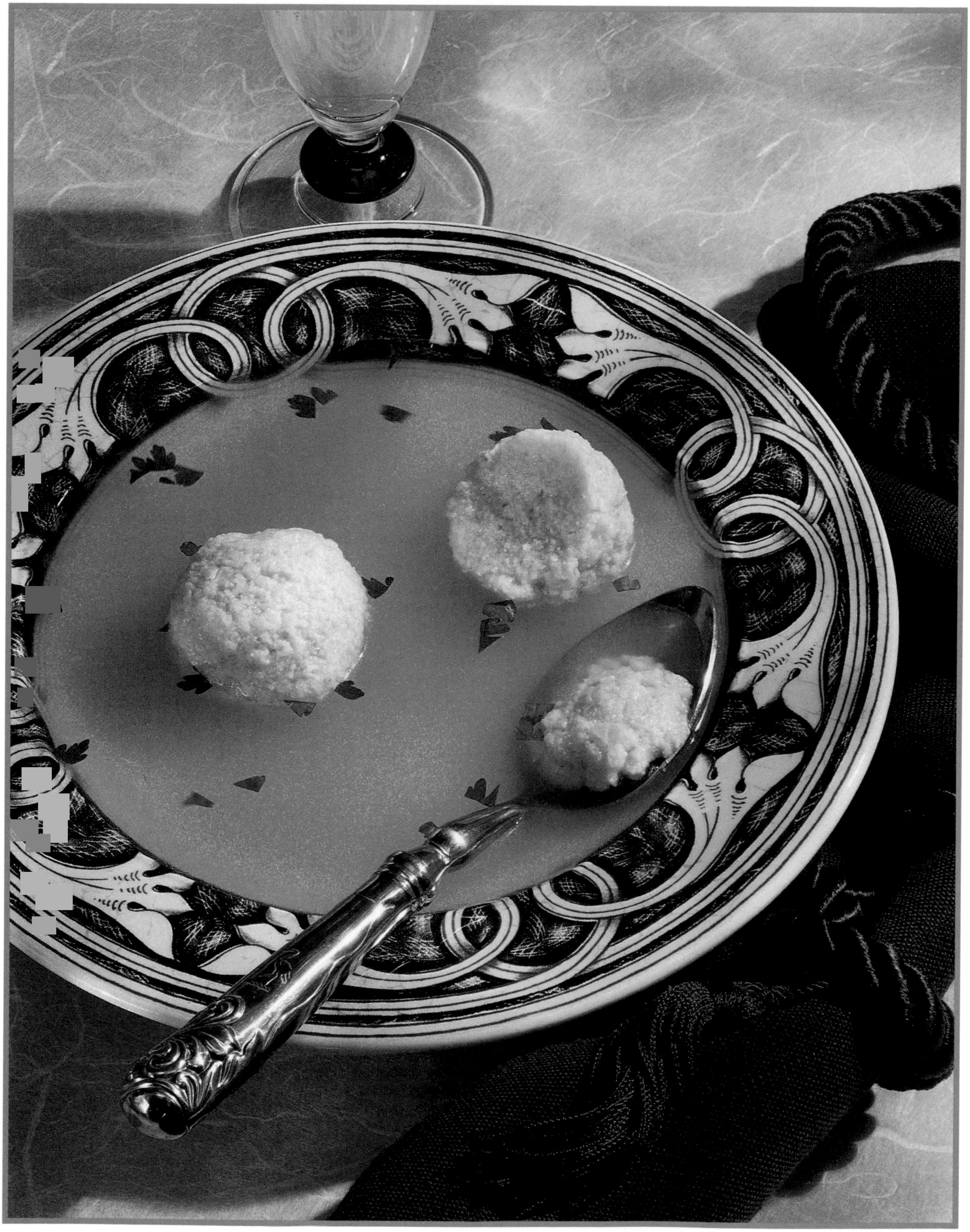

Fisherman's Soup

⅛ teaspoon dried thyme leaves
½ pound halibut or other firm white fish
2 tablespoons vegetable oil, divided
1 medium onion, chopped
1 clove garlic, crushed
3 tablespoons all-purpose flour
2 cans (about 14 ounces each) low-salt chicken broth
1 can (15¼ ounces) DEL MONTE® FreshCut™ Golden Sweet Whole Kernel Corn, No Salt Added, undrained
1 can (14½ ounces) DEL MONTE® FreshCut™ Whole New Potatoes, drained and chopped

1. Sprinkle thyme over both sides of fish. In large saucepan, cook fish in 1 tablespoon hot oil over medium-high heat until fish flakes easily when tested with fork. Remove fish from saucepan; set aside.

2. Heat remaining 1 tablespoon oil in same saucepan over medium heat. Add onion and garlic; cook until onion is tender. Stir in flour; cook 1 minute. Stir in chicken broth; cook until thickened, stirring occasionally. Stir in corn and potatoes.

3. Discard skin and bones from fish; cut fish into bite-size pieces.

4. Add fish to soup just before serving; heat through. Stir in chopped parsley or sliced green onions, if desired.

Makes 4 to 6 servings

Bounty Soup

½ pound yellow crookneck squash
2 cups frozen mixed vegetables
1 teaspoon dried parsley flakes
⅛ teaspoon dried rosemary
⅛ teaspoon dried thyme leaves
⅛ teaspoon salt
⅛ teaspoon ground black pepper
2 teaspoons vegetable oil
3 boneless skinless chicken breast halves (about ¾ pound), chopped
1 can (about 14 ounces) fat-free reduced-sodium chicken broth
1 can (14½ ounces) stewed tomatoes, undrained

1. Cut wide part of squash in half lengthwise; lay flat and cut crosswise into ¼-inch slices. Place squash, mixed vegetables, parsley, rosemary, thyme, salt and pepper in medium bowl.

2. Heat oil in large saucepan over medium-high heat. Add chicken; stir-fry 2 minutes. Stir in vegetables and seasonings. Add chicken broth and tomatoes with liquid, stirring to break up large tomatoes. Cover; bring to a boil. Reduce heat to low. Cover; cook 5 minutes or until vegetables are tender. *Makes 4 servings*

Prep & Cook Time: 30 minutes

Louisiana Shrimp and Chicken Gumbo

3 tablespoons vegetable oil
¼ cup all-purpose flour
2 medium onions, chopped
1 cup chopped celery
1 large green bell pepper, chopped
2 cloves garlic, minced
3 cups chicken broth
1 can (16 ounces) whole tomatoes in juice, undrained
1 package (10 ounces) frozen sliced okra
1 bay leaf
1 teaspoon TABASCO® pepper sauce
¾ pound shredded cooked chicken
½ pound raw shrimp, peeled and deveined
Hot cooked rice

Heat oil in large saucepan or Dutch oven. Add flour and cook over low heat until mixture turns dark brown and develops a nutty aroma, stirring frequently. Add onions, celery, bell pepper and garlic; cook 5 minutes or until vegetables are tender. Gradually add chicken broth. Stir in tomatoes with juice, okra, bay leaf and TABASCO® sauce; bring to a boil. Add chicken and shrimp; cook 3 to 5 minutes or until shrimp turn pink. Remove bay leaf. Serve with rice.

Makes 6 servings

Fisherman's Soup

Vegetable and Shrimp Chowder

1½ cups diced Spanish onions
½ cup sliced carrots
½ cup diced celery
2 tablespoons margarine or butter
2 cups peeled and diced baking potatoes
1 (10-ounce) package frozen corn
5 cups COLLEGE INN® Chicken Broth or Lower Sodium Chicken Broth
½ pound small shrimp, peeled and deveined
⅓ cup GREY POUPON® Dijon Mustard
¼ cup chopped parsley

In large saucepan, over medium heat, cook onions, carrots and celery in margarine 3 to 4 minutes or until tender. Add potatoes, corn and chicken broth; heat to a boil. Reduce heat; simmer 20 to 25 minutes or until potatoes are tender. Add shrimp, mustard and parsley; cook 5 minutes more or until shrimp are cooked. Garnish as desired. Serve warm. *Makes 8 servings*

Chicken Tortilla Soup

6 broiler-fryer chicken thighs, boned, skinned and cut into 1-inch pieces
2 tablespoons plus 2 teaspoons vegetable oil, divided
4 corn tortillas, halved and cut into ¼-inch strips
1 cup chopped onions
2 cloves garlic, minced
2 cans (about 14 ounces each) chicken broth
1 can (10 ounces) diced tomatoes with green chilies
½ cup water
1 cup frozen corn
¼ cup chopped cilantro
1 tablespoon lime juice
1 teaspoon ground cumin

In Dutch oven, place 2 tablespoons oil and heat to medium-high temperature. Add tortilla strips; cook 3 to 4 minutes or until crisp. Remove with slotted spoon; drain on paper towels. In same Dutch oven, add remaining 2 teaspoons oil and heat to medium-high temperature. Add chicken, onions and garlic; cook, stirring, 5 to 7 minutes or until chicken is lightly browned. Add chicken broth, tomatoes and water; heat to boiling. Reduce heat to medium-low; cover and cook 10 minutes. Add corn, cilantro, lime juice and cumin; cook 5 minutes. Spoon into bowls; top with tortillas. *Makes 4 servings*

Favorite recipe from **Delmarva Poultry Industry, Inc.**

Kaleidoscope Chowder

3 cups water
3 large potatoes, peeled and diced
1 (26-ounce) jar NEWMAN'S OWN® Diavolo Sauce
2 large carrots, peeled and thinly sliced
1½ to 2 pounds assorted seafood, such as fish fillets, bay scallops, shrimp or clams
½ cup dry white wine
2 cups shredded fresh spinach leaves
1 yellow bell pepper, seeded and diced
Freshly grated Parmesan cheese

In large stockpot, bring water to a boil. Add potatoes; cook 5 minutes. Stir in Diavolo Sauce and carrots. Bring to a boil; reduce heat and simmer 5 minutes.

Cut fish fillets into bite-size pieces. Peel and devein shrimp. Add seafood and wine to soup. Cook over medium-high heat, stirring often, until fish is opaque, 3 to 4 minutes. Add spinach and pepper; cover. Remove from heat and let stand until spinach and pepper are heated through, about 2 minutes. Serve with Parmesan cheese. *Makes 4 servings*

Note: *This chowder is also excellent with diced cooked chicken breast.*

Vegetable and Shrimp Chowder

Gazpacho

3 cups tomato juice
4 tomatoes, chopped
1 green bell pepper,
chopped
1 cucumber, chopped
1 cup chopped celery
1 cup chopped green
onions
3 tablespoons red wine
vinegar
2 tablespoons FILIPPO
BERIO® Olive Oil
1 tablespoon chopped
fresh parsley
1 to 2 teaspoons salt
1 clove garlic, finely
minced
Freshly ground black
pepper or hot pepper
sauce

In large bowl, combine tomato
juice, tomatoes, bell pepper,
cucumber, celery, green onions,
vinegar, olive oil, parsley, salt
and garlic. Cover; refrigerate
several hours or overnight
before serving. Season to taste
with black pepper or hot
pepper sauce. Serve cold.

Makes 10 to 12 servings

Kielbasa &
Chicken Gumbo

6 slices bacon
1 pound BOB EVANS
FARMS® Kielbasa
Sausage, cut into
1-inch pieces
½ pound boneless skinless
chicken breasts, cut
into 1-inch chunks
¼ cup all-purpose flour
1 can (12 ounces) tomato
juice
1 cup water
1 can (28 ounces) whole
tomatoes, undrained
2 cubes chicken bouillon
1 can (8 ounces) tomato
sauce
1½ cups sliced fresh okra *or*
1 package (10 ounces)
frozen cut okra,
thawed
1 medium onion, coarsely
chopped
1 medium green bell
pepper, coarsely
chopped
2 bay leaves
½ teaspoon salt
½ teaspoon ground red
pepper
⅛ teaspoon ground
allspice
1 pound uncooked
medium shrimp,
peeled and deveined
Hot cooked rice
(optional)

Cook bacon in large Dutch
oven over medium-high heat
until crisp. Remove bacon;
drain and crumble on paper
towel. Set aside. Cook and
stir kielbasa and chicken in
drippings over medium heat
until chicken is lightly browned.
Remove kielbasa and chicken;
set aside. Drain off all but
3 tablespoons drippings from
Dutch oven. Add flour to
drippings; cook over medium
heat 12 to 15 minutes or until
a reddish-brown roux forms,
stirring constantly. Gradually
stir in tomato juice and water
until smooth. Add tomatoes
with juice and bouillon, stirring
well to break up tomatoes.
Add reserved kielbasa, chicken,
tomato sauce, okra, onion, bell
pepper, bay leaves, salt, ground
red pepper and allspice; mix
well. Bring to a boil over high
heat. Reduce heat to low;
simmer, covered, 1 hour,
stirring occasionally. Add
shrimp and simmer, covered,
10 minutes more or until
shrimp turn pink and opaque.
Remove and discard bay
leaves. Stir in reserved bacon.
Serve hot over rice, if desired.
Refrigerate leftovers.

Makes 10 servings

*SERVING SUGGESTION: SERVE WITH
CORN BREAD.*

Sassy Sausage and Black Bean Soup

1 tablespoon vegetable oil
1 medium onion, chopped
2 cloves garlic, minced
1 can (16 ounces) black beans, rinsed and drained
1 can (14½ ounces) stewed tomatoes, undrained
1 can (10½ ounces) kosher condensed beef broth
½ cup prepared chunky salsa
½ cup water
1 package (12 ounces) HEBREW NATIONAL® Beef Hot Sausage
¼ cup chopped cilantro
Lime wedges for garnish

Heat oil in large saucepan over medium heat. Add onion and garlic; cook 8 minutes or until tender. Stir in beans, tomatoes with liquid, beef broth, salsa and water. Bring to a boil over high heat.

Cut sausage into ½-inch pieces; stir into soup. Reduce heat. Cover; simmer 15 minutes, stirring occasionally. Ladle into soup bowls; sprinkle with cilantro. Garnish with lime wedges, if desired.

Makes 4 to 5 servings

Tomato French Onion Soup

4 medium onions, chopped
2 tablespoons butter or margarine
1 can (14½ ounces) DEL MONTE® *FreshCut*™ Diced Tomatoes, undrained
1 can (10½ ounces) condensed beef consommé
¼ cup dry sherry
4 French bread slices, toasted
1½ cups (6 ounces) shredded Swiss cheese
¼ cup (1 ounce) grated Parmesan cheese

1. Cook onions in butter in large saucepan about 10 minutes. Add tomatoes, with liquid, 2 cups water, consommé and sherry to saucepan. Bring to a boil, skimming off foam.

2. Reduce heat to medium-low; simmer 10 minutes. Place soup in four broilerproof bowls; top with bread and cheeses. Broil until cheeses are melted and golden. *Makes 4 servings*

Prep & Cook Time: 35 minutes

Helpful Hint: If broilerproof bowls are not available, place soup in ovenproof bowls and bake at 350°F 10 minutes.

Gazpacho (page 68)

Creamy Corn Bisque with Spicy Red Pepper Cream

RED PEPPER CREAM
- **1 jar (7 ounces) roasted red peppers, drained and patted dry**
- **3 tablespoons sour cream**
- **2 tablespoons FRANK'S® Original REDHOT® Cayenne Pepper Sauce**

CORN BISQUE
- **1 tablespoon olive oil**
- **1 large leek (white portion only), well rinsed and chopped* (1½ cups)**
- **2 carrots, diced**
- **¾ teaspoon dried thyme leaves**
- **½ teaspoon dried basil leaves**
- **1 can (about 14 ounces) reduced-sodium chicken broth**
- **¾ pound potatoes, peeled and cut into ½-inch pieces (2 cups)**
- **1 can (10¾ ounces) condensed cream of corn soup**
- **1 cup half-and-half**
- **1 cup frozen corn**
- **¼ teaspoon salt**
- **1 tablespoon FRANK'S® Original REDHOT® Cayenne Pepper Sauce**

*You may substitute 6 small green onions (white portion only), chopped.

1. Combine roasted peppers, sour cream and *2 tablespoons* RedHot® sauce in blender or food processor. Cover; blend until puréed. Set aside.

2. Heat oil in large saucepan. Add leek and carrots; cook over medium heat 4 minutes or until just tender. Add thyme and basil; cook 1 minute. Stir in chicken broth and potatoes. Bring to a boil. Reduce heat to low; cook, covered, 5 minutes or until potatoes are just tender. Stir in corn soup, *1 cup water,* half-and-half, corn and salt. Bring just to a boil. Reduce heat to low; cook 3 minutes, stirring. Stir in *1 tablespoon* RedHot® sauce.

3. Ladle soup into bowls. Top with dollop of reserved red pepper cream; swirl into soup. Garnish with chives, if desired.

Makes 6 servings
(7 cups soup, 1 cup pepper cream)

Prep Time: 30 minutes
Cook Time: about 15 minutes

Hot 'n' Chilly Mango Melon Soup

- **1 medium cantaloupe, seeded and cut into 2-inch pieces (4 cups)**
- **2 mangoes, seeded and cut into 2-inch pieces (2 cups)**
- **1 cup plain yogurt**
- **¼ cup honey**
- **2 to 3 tablespoons FRANK'S® Original REDHOT® Cayenne Pepper Sauce**
- **1 tablespoon grated peeled fresh ginger**
- **1 can (12 ounces) cold ginger ale**

1. Combine cantaloupe and mangoes in blender or food processor. Cover; blend until very smooth. (Blend in batches if necessary.) Transfer to large bowl. Stir in yogurt, honey, RedHot® sauce and ginger. Cover; refrigerate at least 3 hours or overnight.

2. Stir in ginger ale just before serving. Garnish with mint, if desired. *Makes 6 cups*

Prep Time: 15 minutes
Chill Time: 3 hours

Creamy Corn Bisque with
Spicy Red Pepper Cream

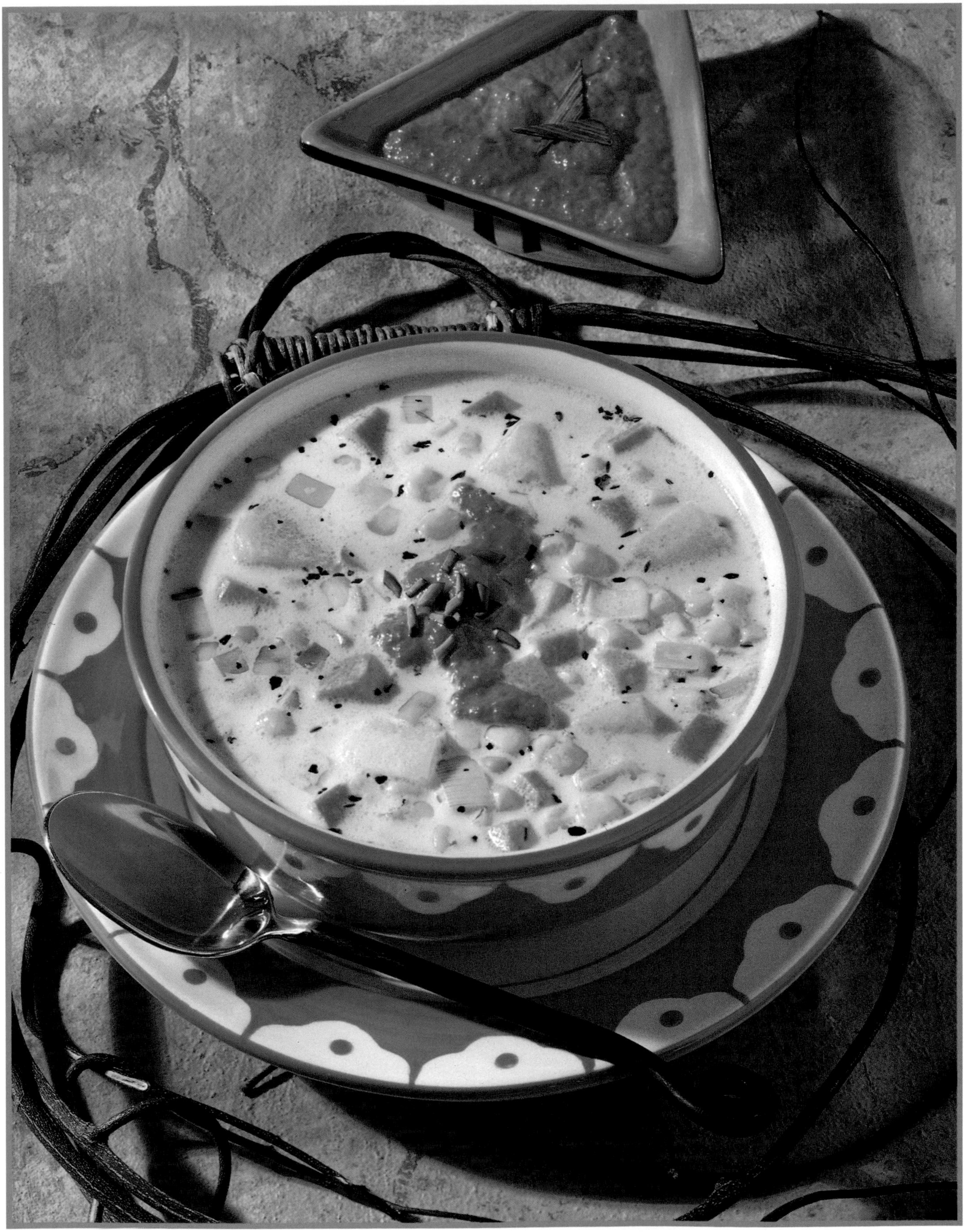

Savory Pea Soup with Sausage

8 ounces smoked sausage, cut lengthwise into halves, then cut into ½-inch pieces
1 package (16 ounces) dried split peas, rinsed
3 medium carrots, sliced
2 ribs celery, sliced
1 medium onion, chopped
¾ teaspoon dried marjoram leaves
1 bay leaf
2 cans (about 14 ounces each) reduced-sodium chicken broth

Slow Cooker Directions:
HEAT small skillet over medium heat. Add sausage; cook 5 to 8 minutes or until browned. Drain well. Combine sausage and remaining ingredients in slow cooker. Cover and cook on LOW 4 to 5 hours or until peas are tender. Turn off heat. Remove and discard bay leaf. Cover and let stand 15 minutes to thicken.   *Makes 6 servings*

Corn and Tomato Chowder

1 ½ cups diced peeled plum tomatoes
¾ teaspoon salt, divided
2 ears corn, husks removed
1 tablespoon margarine
½ cup finely chopped shallots
1 clove garlic, minced
1 can (12 ounces) evaporated skimmed milk
1 cup chicken broth
1 tablespoon finely chopped fresh sage *or* 1 teaspoon rubbed sage
¼ teaspoon black pepper
1 tablespoon cornstarch
2 tablespoons cold water

1. Place tomatoes in nonmetallic colander over bowl. Sprinkle ½ teaspoon salt on top; toss to mix well. Allow tomatoes to drain at least 1 hour.

2. Cut kernels off cobs into small bowl. Scrape cobs with dull side of knife to extract liquid into same bowl; set aside. Discard 1 cob; break remaining cob in half.

3. Heat margarine in heavy saucepan over medium-high heat until melted. Add shallots and garlic; reduce heat to low. Cover; cook about 5 minutes or until shallots are soft. Add milk, chicken broth, sage, pepper and reserved corn cob halves. Bring to a boil over high heat. Reduce heat to low; simmer, uncovered, 10 minutes. Remove and discard cob halves.

4. Add corn with liquid; return to a boil over medium-high heat. Reduce heat to low; simmer, uncovered, 15 minutes more. Dissolve cornstarch in water; add to chowder, mixing well. Stir until thickened. Remove from heat; stir in drained tomatoes and remaining ¼ teaspoon salt. Spoon into bowls. Garnish with additional fresh sage, if desired.
Makes 6 appetizer servings

Creamy Asparagus Potato Soup

1 can (14½ ounces) DEL MONTE® *FreshCut*™ Whole New Potatoes, drained
1 can (12 ounces) DEL MONTE® *FreshCut*™ Asparagus Spears, drained
½ teaspoon dried thyme
⅛ teaspoon garlic powder
1 can (about 14 ounces) chicken broth
1 cup milk or half-and-half

1. Place potatoes, asparagus, thyme and garlic powder in food processor or blender (in batches, if needed); process until smooth.

2. Pour into medium saucepan; add chicken broth. Bring to a boil. Stir in milk; heat through. *Do not boil.* Season with salt and pepper, if desired. Thin with additional milk or water, if desired.   *Makes 4 servings*

Savory Pea Soup with Sausage

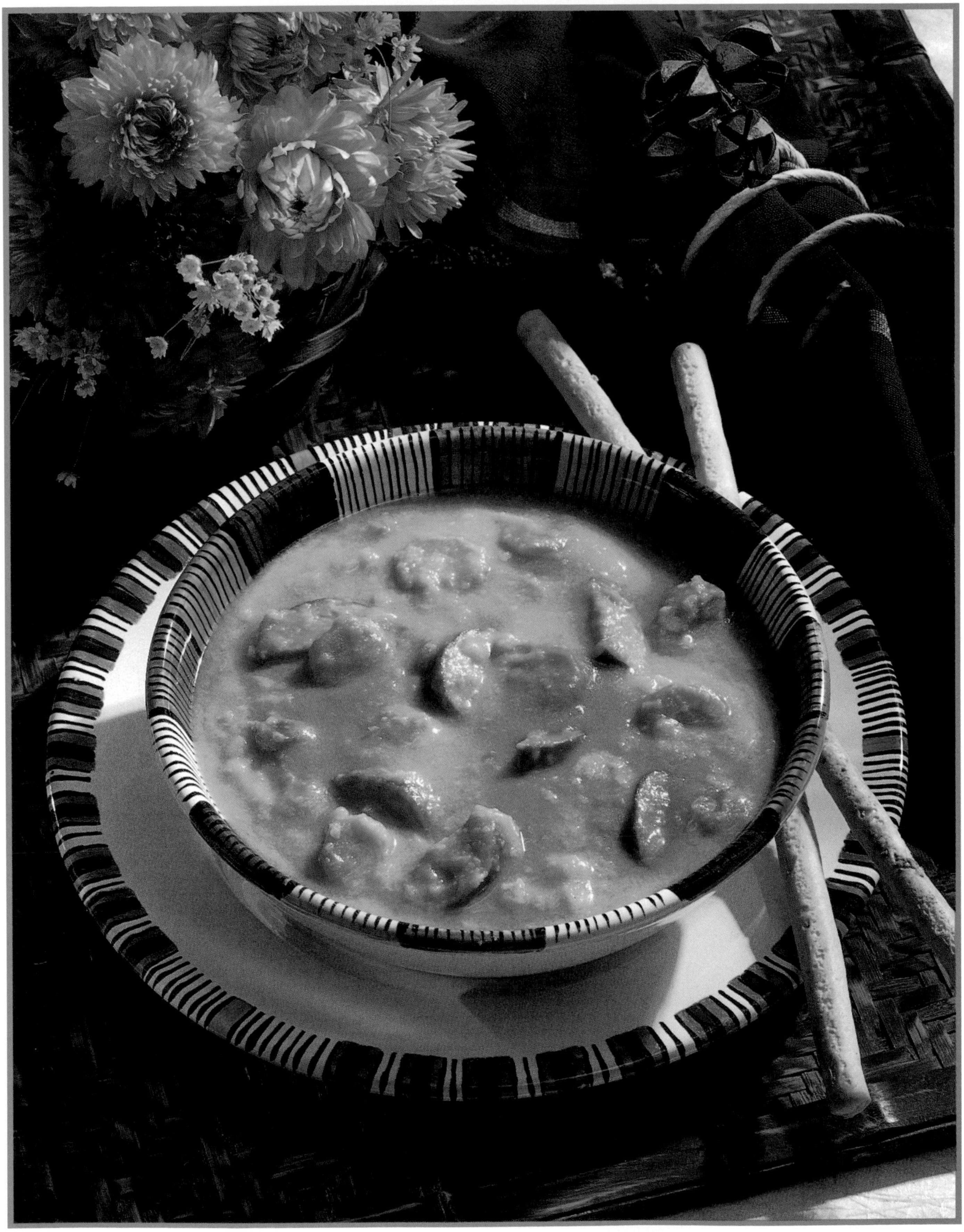

Ham and Cauliflower Chowder

1 bag (16 ounces) BIRDS EYE® frozen Cauliflower
2 cans (10¾ ounces each) cream of mushroom or cream of celery soup
2½ cups milk or water
½ pound ham, cubed
⅓ cup shredded colby cheese (optional)

• Cook cauliflower according to package directions.

• Combine cauliflower, soup, milk and ham in saucepan; mix well.

• Cook over medium heat 4 to 6 minutes, stirring occasionally. Top individual servings with cheese.

Makes 4 to 6 servings

Prep Time: 2 minutes
Cook Time: 10 to 12 minutes

Cream of Broccoli and Cheddar Soup

1 pound fresh broccoli
1 can (about 14 ounces) reduced-sodium or regular chicken broth
2 tablespoons butter or margarine
2 tablespoons all-purpose flour
2 cups milk
¼ teaspoon freshly ground black pepper
2 cups (8 ounces) SARGENTO® Classic Shredded Sharp or Mild Cheddar Cheese

Chop broccoli florets; thinly slice stems. Combine broccoli and chicken broth in medium saucepan; heat to a boil. Reduce heat; cover and simmer about 7 minutes or until broccoli is fork-tender.* Transfer (in thirds) to food processor or blender. Process until fairly smooth. Melt butter in same saucepan; add flour. Cook, stirring constantly, over medium heat until bubbly. Add milk and pepper; heat to a boil, stirring constantly. Reduce heat to medium; add broccoli purée. Stir in Cheddar cheese; heat just until cheese melts *(do not boil)*, stirring constantly. Ladle into soup bowls.

Makes 6 servings

For chunky soup, reserve 1 cup broccoli pieces; add to soup with purée.

Indonesian Curried Soup

1 can (14 ounces) coconut milk*
1 can (10¾ ounces) condensed tomato soup
¾ cup milk
3 tablespoons FRANK'S® Original REDHOT® Cayenne Pepper Sauce
1½ teaspoons curry powder

You may substitute 1 cup half-and-half for coconut milk BUT increase milk to 1½ cups.

1. Combine all ingredients in medium saucepan; stir until smooth.

2. Cook, over low heat, about 5 minutes or until heated through, stirring occasionally.

Makes 6 servings (4 cups)

Prep Time: 5 minutes
Cook Time: 5 minutes

Ham and Cauliflower Chowder

Hearty Vegetable Gumbo

½ cup chopped onion
½ cup chopped green bell pepper
¼ cup chopped celery
2 cloves garlic, minced
2 cans (about 14 ounces each) no-salt-added stewed tomatoes, undrained
2 cups no-salt-added tomato juice
1 can (15 ounces) red beans, drained and rinsed
1 tablespoon chopped fresh parsley
¼ teaspoon dried oregano leaves
¼ teaspoon hot pepper sauce
2 bay leaves
1½ cups uncooked quick-cooking brown rice
1 package (10 ounces) frozen chopped okra, thawed

1. Spray 4-quart Dutch oven with nonstick cooking spray; heat over medium heat until hot. Add onion, bell pepper, celery and garlic. Cook and stir 3 minutes or until crisp-tender.

2. Add stewed tomatoes, juice, beans, parsley, oregano, pepper sauce and bay leaves. Bring to a boil over high heat. Add rice. Reduce heat to medium-low. Simmer, covered, 15 minutes or until rice is tender.

3. Add okra; simmer, covered, 5 minutes more or until okra is tender. Remove bay leaves; discard. Garnish as desired.
Makes 4 (2-cup) servings

Summer Minestrone

2 carrots, sliced
1 cup halved green beans
½ cup sliced celery
½ cup thinly sliced leek
2 cloves garlic, minced
1 tablespoon fresh sage *or* ½ teaspoon dried sage leaves
1 tablespoon fresh oregano *or* ½ teaspoon dried oregano leaves
3 cans (about 14 ounces each) fat-free reduced-sodium chicken broth
1 zucchini, halved lengthwise and cut into ½-inch slices
1 cup quartered mushrooms
8 ounces cherry tomatoes, halved
¼ cup minced fresh parsley
3 ounces uncooked small rotini
8 teaspoons grated Parmesan cheese

1. Spray large saucepan with olive oil-flavored nonstick cooking spray. Heat over medium heat until hot. Add carrots, green beans, celery, leek, garlic, sage and oregano. Cook and stir 3 to 5 minutes. Add chicken broth; bring to a boil. Reduce heat and simmer about 5 minutes or until vegetables are crisp-tender.

2. Add zucchini, mushrooms, tomatoes and parsley to saucepan; bring to a boil. Stir in pasta. Reduce heat and simmer, uncovered, about 8 minutes or until pasta and vegetables are tender. Season to taste with salt and pepper, if desired. Ladle soup into bowls; sprinkle each serving with 1 teaspoon Parmesan cheese.
Makes 8 side-dish servings

Wild Rice Soup

½ cup lentils
3 cups water
1 package (6 ounces) long grain and wild rice blend
1 can (about 14 ounces) vegetable broth
1 package (10 ounces) frozen mixed vegetables
1 cup skim milk
½ cup (2 ounces) reduced-fat processed American cheese, cut into pieces

1. Rinse and sort lentils, discarding any debris or blemished lentils. Combine lentils and water in small saucepan. Bring to a boil; reduce heat to low. Simmer, covered, 5 minutes. Let stand, covered, 1 hour. Drain and rinse lentils.

2. Cook rice according to package directions in medium saucepan. Add lentils and remaining ingredients. Bring to a boil; reduce heat to low. Simmer, uncovered, 20 minutes. Garnish as desired.
Makes 6 servings

Hearty Vegetable Gumbo

Chile con Carne

- 2 tablespoons vegetable oil
- 2 pounds ground beef
- 2 cups (2 small) chopped onions
- 4 cloves garlic, finely chopped
- 3½ cups (two 15-ounce cans) kidney, pinto or black beans, drained
- 3½ cups (29-ounce can) CONTADINA® Crushed Tomatoes
- 1¾ cups (16-ounce jar) ORTEGA® Thick & Chunky Salsa, mild
- ½ cup dry white wine
- ½ cup (4-ounce can) ORTEGA® Diced Green Chiles
- 3 tablespoons chili powder
- 1 to 2 tablespoons ORTEGA® Diced Jalapeños
- 1 tablespoon ground cumin
- 1 tablespoon dried oregano leaves
- 2 teaspoons salt

HEAT oil in large saucepan over medium-high heat. Add beef, onions and garlic; cook for 4 to 5 minutes or until no longer pink; drain.

STIR in beans, crushed tomatoes, salsa, wine, chiles, chili powder, jalapeños, cumin, oregano and salt. Bring to a boil. Reduce heat to low; cover. Cook, stirring frequently, for 1 hour.

Makes 10 to 12 servings

Jalapeño Two-Bean Chili

- 1 tablespoon vegetable oil
- 1 medium onion, chopped
- 1 green bell pepper, seeded and chopped
- 2 cloves garlic, minced
- 1 can (16 ounces) pinto beans, rinsed and drained
- 1 can (16 ounces) black beans, rinsed and drained
- 1 can (14½ ounces) stewed tomatoes or Mexican-style stewed tomatoes, undrained
- 1 can (10½ ounces) kosher condensed beef or chicken broth
- ½ cup water
- 2 teaspoons chili powder
- 2 teaspoons ground cumin
- 1 to 2 teaspoons chopped bottled or fresh jalapeño peppers
- 1 package (12 ounces) HEBREW NATIONAL® Beef Hot Sausage or Lean Smoked Turkey Sausage
- Chopped cilantro (optional)
- Diced avocado (optional)

Heat oil in large saucepan over medium heat. Add onion, bell pepper and garlic; cook 8 minutes, stirring occasionally. Add pinto and black beans, tomatoes with liquid, beef broth, water, chili powder, cumin and jalapeño peppers; bring to a boil.

Cut sausage into ½-inch slices. Cut slices into quarters. Stir in sausage; reduce heat to medium-low. Simmer, uncovered, 15 minutes, stirring occasionally. Ladle into shallow bowls; top with cilantro and avocado, if desired.

Makes 6 servings

Chili con Carne Winchester

- 2 tablespoons vegetable oil
- ⅓ cup chopped onion
- ⅓ cup chopped green bell pepper
- 1 pound ground beef
- 1 clove garlic, minced
- 2 (15-ounce) cans kidney beans, drained
- 1 (1-pound) can stewed tomatoes
- 1 (15-ounce) can VEG-ALL® Mixed Vegetables, with liquid

1. Heat oil in medium stockpot over medium-high heat. Add onion and pepper; cook and stir until soft.

2. Add ground beef, garlic, kidney beans and stewed tomatoes. Bring to a boil; cover. Reduce heat and simmer 30 minutes.

3. Stir in Veg-All® vegetables and cook 10 minutes longer. Serve hot. *Makes 6 servings*

Chile con Carne

Scrumptious Spam™ Spring Chili

Nonstick cooking spray
4 cloves garlic, minced
2 green bell peppers, cut into strips
1 cup sliced green onions
3 (4¼-ounce) jars CHI-CHI'S® Diced Green Chilies
2 jalapeño peppers, seeded and minced
2 teaspoons dried oregano leaves
2 teaspoons ground cumin
2 (15-ounce) cans cannellini beans or kidney beans
2 (10¾-ounce) cans condensed chicken broth, undiluted
1 (12-ounce) can SPAM® Luncheon Meat, cubed

In large saucepan coated with cooking spray, sauté garlic over medium heat 1 minute. Add bell peppers, green onions, chilies, jalapeños, oregano and cumin; sauté 5 minutes. Stir in beans and chicken broth. Bring to a boil. Cover. Reduce heat and simmer 10 minutes. Stir in Spam®. Simmer 2 minutes.

Makes 4 to 6 servings

20-Minute White Bean Chili

1 cup chopped onions
1 clove garlic, minced
1 tablespoon vegetable oil
1 pound ground turkey
1 cup COLLEGE INN® Chicken Broth or Lower Sodium Chicken Broth
1 (14½-ounce) can stewed tomatoes
⅓ cup GREY POUPON® Dijon Mustard
1 tablespoon chili powder
⅛ to ¼ teaspoon ground red pepper
1 (15-ounce) can cannellini beans, drained and rinsed
1 (8-ounce) can corn, drained
Tortilla chips, shredded Cheddar cheese and cilantro (optional)

In medium saucepan, over medium-high heat, sauté onions and garlic in oil until tender. Add turkey; cook until done, stirring occasionally to break up meat. Drain. Stir in chicken broth, tomatoes, mustard, chili powder and pepper. Heat to a boil; reduce heat. Simmer for 10 minutes. Stir in beans and corn; cook for 5 minutes. Top with tortilla chips, shredded cheese and cilantro, if desired.

Makes 6 servings

Quick & Easy Chili

1 pound ground beef
1 cup (1 small) chopped onion
2 cloves garlic, finely chopped
3½ cups (two 15-ounce cans) kidney, pinto or black beans, drained
2½ cups (24-ounce jar) ORTEGA® Thick & Chunky Salsa, hot, medium or mild
½ cup (4-ounce can) ORTEGA® Diced Green Chiles
2 teaspoons chili powder
½ teaspoon dried oregano leaves
½ teaspoon ground cumin
Topping suggestions: ORTEGA® Thick & Chunky Salsa, shredded Cheddar cheese or Monterey Jack cheese, chopped tomatoes, sliced ripe olives, sliced green onions and sour cream

COOK beef, onion and garlic in large skillet over medium-high heat for 4 to 5 minutes or until beef is no longer pink; drain.

STIR in beans, salsa, chiles, chili powder, oregano and cumin. Bring to a boil. Reduce heat to low; cook, covered, for 20 to 25 minutes.

TOP as desired before serving.

Makes 6 servings

Scrumptious Spam™ Spring Chili

Spicy Tomato Chili with Red Beans

1 tablespoon olive oil
1 cup chopped onion
1 cup chopped green bell pepper
1 cup sliced celery
1 clove garlic, minced
1 can (15 ounces) diced tomatoes, undrained
1 can (15 ounces) red beans, drained and rinsed
1 can (10 ounces) diced tomatoes with green chilies
1 can (8 ounces) low-sodium tomato sauce
8 (6-inch) corn tortillas

1. Preheat oven to 400°F.

2. Heat oil in large saucepan over medium heat until hot. Add onion, bell pepper, celery and garlic. Cook and stir 5 minutes or until onion is translucent.

3. Add remaining ingredients except tortillas. Bring to a boil; reduce heat to low. Simmer, uncovered, 15 minutes.

4. Cut each tortilla into 8 wedges. Place on baking sheet; bake 8 minutes or until crisp. Crush about half of tortilla wedges; place in soup bowls. Spoon chili over tortillas. Serve with remaining tortilla wedges.

Makes 4 servings

California Turkey Chili

1¼ cups chopped onion
1 cup chopped green bell pepper
2 cloves garlic, minced
3 tablespoons vegetable oil
1 can (28 ounces) kidney beans, drained
1 can (28 ounces) stewed tomatoes, undrained
1 cup red wine or water
3 cups cubed cooked California-grown turkey
1 tablespoon chili powder
1 tablespoon chopped cilantro *or* 1 teaspoon dried coriander
1 teaspoon crushed red pepper
½ teaspoon salt
Shredded Cheddar cheese (optional)
Additional chopped onion (optional)
Chopped cilantro (optional)

Cook and stir onion, bell pepper, garlic and oil in large saucepan over high heat until tender. Add beans, tomatoes with liquid, wine, turkey, chili powder, cilantro, red pepper and salt. Cover; simmer 25 minutes or until heated through. Top with cheese, onion or cilantro, if desired.

Makes 6 servings

FAVORITE RECIPE FROM **CALIFORNIA POULTRY INDUSTRY FEDERATION**

Arizona Pork Chili

1 tablespoon vegetable oil
1½ pounds boneless pork, cut into ¼-inch cubes
Salt and black pepper (optional)
1 can (15 ounces) black, pinto or kidney beans, drained
1 can (14½ ounces) DEL MONTE® *FreshCut*™ Diced Tomatoes with Garlic & Onion, undrained
1 can (4 ounces) diced green chilies, drained
1 teaspoon ground cumin
Tortillas and sour cream (optional)

1. Heat oil in large skillet over medium-high heat. Add pork; cook until browned. Season with salt and pepper to taste, if desired.

2. Add beans, tomatoes, chilies and cumin. Simmer 10 minutes, stirring occasionally. Serve with tortillas and sour cream, if desired. *Makes 6 servings*

Prep Time: 10 minutes
Cook Time: 25 minutes

Spicy Tomato Chili with Red Beans

Texas RedHot® Chili

4 tablespoons vegetable oil, divided
2 large onions, chopped
3 large cloves garlic, minced
2 pounds boneless sirloin or round steak, cut into ½-inch cubes
1 pound ground beef
2 cans (16 ounces each) tomatoes in purée
1 can (15 to 19 ounces) red kidney beans, undrained
⅓ cup FRANK'S® Original REDHOT® Cayenne Pepper Sauce
¼ cup chili powder
2 tablespoons ground cumin
1 tablespoon dried oregano leaves
½ teaspoon ground black pepper

1. Heat *1 tablespoon* oil in large saucepan or Dutch oven. Add onions and garlic; cook 5 minutes or until tender. Transfer to small bowl; set aside.

2. Heat remaining *3 tablespoons* oil in saucepan. Add sirloin and ground beef in batches; cook about 15 minutes or until well browned. Drain off fat.

3. Stir in remaining ingredients. Bring to a boil over medium-high heat. Return onions and garlic to saucepan. Simmer, partially covered, 1 hour or until meat is tender. Garnish with shredded Cheddar cheese and chopped green onion, if desired.   *Makes 10 servings*

Prep Time: 15 minutes
Cook Time: 1 hour 20 minutes

Southern BBQ Chili

½ pound lean ground beef
1 medium onion, chopped
1 clove garlic, minced
1½ cups DEL MONTE® Traditional Salsa, Mild
1 can (15 ounces) barbecue-style beans
1 can (15 ounces) black beans, drained
1 can (8¾ ounces) *or* 1 cup kidney beans, drained

1. Brown meat with onion and garlic in large saucepan; drain.

2. Add salsa and beans. Cover and simmer 15 minutes or until heated through. Top with sour cream and sliced green onions, if desired.   *Makes 6 servings*

Prep Time: 5 minutes
Cook Time: 20 minutes

7-Spice Chili with Corn Bread Topping

1 pound ground turkey or lean beef
1 jar (16 ounces) Original or Spicy TABASCO® brand 7-Spice Chili Recipe
1 can (16 ounces) kidney beans, rinsed and drained
¾ cup water
1 package (12 ounces) corn muffin mix
1 can (7 ounces) whole kernel corn with sweet green and red peppers, drained
1 cup (4 ounces) shredded Cheddar cheese

In large skillet, brown turkey; drain. Stir in 7-Spice Chili Recipe, beans and water. Bring to a boil; reduce heat. Simmer 10 minutes.

Divide evenly among six 12-ounce individual ramekins.

Meanwhile, prepare corn muffin mix according to package directions. Stir in corn and cheese until well blended.

Pour about ½ cup muffin mixture over top of each ramekin. Bake at 400°F 15 minutes or until corn bread topping is golden brown.
Makes 6 servings

Texas RedHot® Chili

Turkey Chili with Black Beans

1 pound ground turkey breast
1 can (about 14 ounces) fat-free reduced-sodium chicken broth
1 large onion, finely chopped
1 green bell pepper, seeded and diced
2 teaspoons chili powder
½ teaspoon ground allspice
¼ teaspoon ground cinnamon
¼ teaspoon paprika
1 can (15 ounces) black beans, rinsed and drained
1 can (14 ounces) crushed tomatoes in tomato purée, undrained
2 teaspoons apple cider vinegar

1. Heat large nonstick skillet over high heat. Add turkey, chicken broth, onion and bell pepper. Cook and stir, breaking up turkey. Cook until turkey is no longer pink.

2. Add chili powder, allspice, cinnamon and paprika. Reduce heat to medium-low; simmer 10 minutes. Add black beans, tomatoes and vinegar; bring to a boil.

3. Reduce heat to low; simmer 20 to 25 minutes or until thickened to desired consistency. Garnish as desired.

Makes 4 servings

Chunky Vegetarian Chili

1 tablespoon vegetable oil
1 medium green bell pepper, chopped
1 medium onion, chopped
3 cloves garlic, minced
2 cans (14½ ounces each) Mexican-style tomatoes, undrained
1 can (15 ounces) kidney beans, rinsed and drained
1 can (15 ounces) pinto beans, rinsed and drained
1 can (11 ounces) whole kernel corn, drained
2½ cups water
1 cup uncooked rice
2 tablespoons chili powder
1½ teaspoons ground cumin
Sour cream (optional)

Heat oil in medium saucepan or Dutch oven over medium-high heat. Add bell pepper, onion and garlic; cook and stir 5 minutes or until tender. Add tomatoes, beans, corn, water, rice, chili powder and cumin; stir well. Bring to a boil. Reduce heat; cover. Simmer 30 minutes, stirring occasionally. To serve, top with sour cream, if desired.

Makes 6 servings

FAVORITE RECIPE FROM **USA RICE FEDERATION**

Cajun Chili

6 ounces spicy sausage links, sliced
4 boneless chicken thighs, skinned and cut into cubes
1 medium onion, chopped
⅛ teaspoon cayenne pepper
1 can (15 ounces) black-eyed peas or kidney beans, drained
1 can (14½ ounces) DEL MONTE® *FreshCut*™ Diced Tomatoes with Garlic & Onion
1 medium green bell pepper, chopped

1. Lightly brown sausage in large skillet over medium-high heat. Add chicken, onion and cayenne pepper; cook until browned. Drain.

2. Stir in remaining ingredients. Cook 5 minutes, stirring occasionally.

Makes 4 servings

Prep & Cook Time: 20 minutes

Head-'Em-Off-at-the-Pass White Chili

1 tablespoon olive oil
½ cup chopped onion
2 cans (15 ounces each) cannellini beans, undrained
1 jar (11 ounces) NEWMAN'S OWN® Bandito Salsa, divided
1½ cups chopped cooked chicken
½ cup chicken broth
1 teaspoon dried oregano leaves
½ teaspoon celery salt
1½ cups (6 ounces) shredded mozzarella cheese, divided

Heat oil in medium saucepan; add onion and cook and stir until tender. Stir in beans, ½ cup Bandito Salsa, chicken, chicken broth, oregano and celery salt. Cover; simmer over medium heat 10 minutes, stirring occasionally. Just before serving, stir in 1 cup mozzarella cheese. Divide chili evenly among serving bowls. Top each with a portion of remaining mozzarella and salsa.

Makes 4 servings

Championship Chili

1 pound lean ground beef
½ cup chopped onion
½ cup chopped green bell pepper
¼ cup chopped celery
1 package (1¼ ounces) chili seasoning mix
1 can (14½ ounces) stewed tomatoes, undrained
1 cup tomato juice
2 cans (15½ ounces each) light or dark red kidney beans, drained

Cook beef, onion, bell pepper and celery in large saucepan over medium-high heat until browned and vegetables are tender. Drain excess fat. Stir in seasoning mix, tomatoes, tomato juice and beans. Cover and simmer 30 minutes. Serve.

Makes 6 servings

FAVORITE RECIPE FROM **CANNED FOOD INFORMATION COUNCIL**

Turkey Chili with Black Beans (page 86)

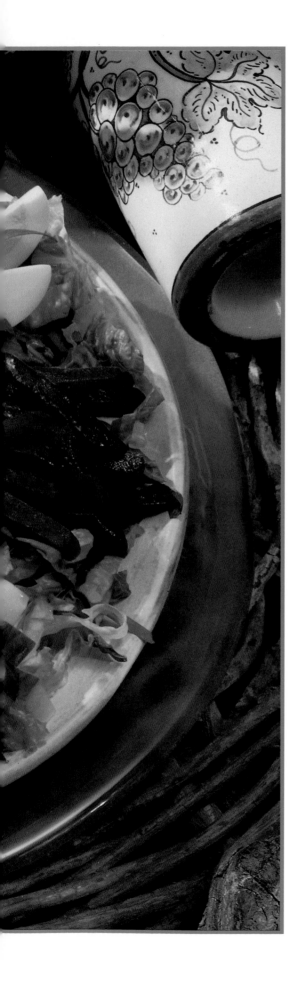

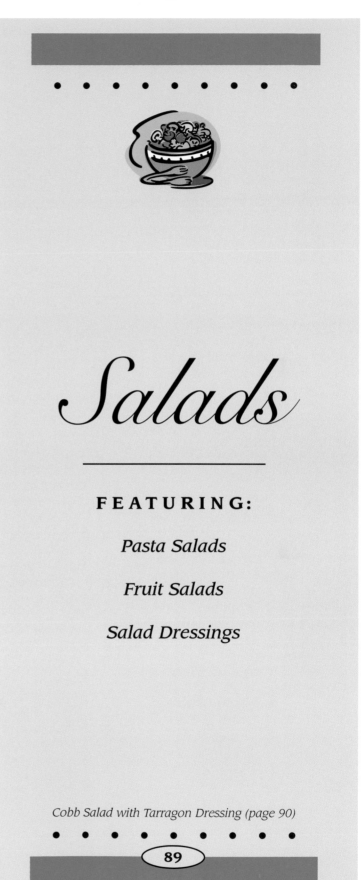

Salads

FEATURING:

Pasta Salads

Fruit Salads

Salad Dressings

Cobb Salad with Tarragon Dressing (page 90)

Mediterranean Greek Salad

½ **cup olive oil**
⅓ **cup red wine vinegar**
2 **teaspoons chopped fresh oregano** *or*
¾ **teaspoon dried oregano leaves**
1 **teaspoon LAWRY'S® Seasoned Salt**
1 **teaspoon LAWRY'S® Garlic Powder with Parsley**
3 **medium cucumbers, peeled and chopped**
3 to 4 **medium tomatoes, seeded and coarsely chopped**
1 **medium onion, thinly sliced and separated into rings**
1 **can (6 ounces) Greek or ripe olives, drained, pitted**
1 **cup (4 ounces) crumbled feta cheese**

In container with stopper or lid, combine oil, vinegar, oregano and seasonings. Cover; shake well. Set dressing aside. In medium bowl, combine cucumbers, tomatoes, onion, olives and cheese; mix lightly. Shake dressing. Add to salad; toss lightly to coat. Refrigerate 30 minutes.

Makes 8 servings

Cobb Salad with Tarragon Dressing

TARRAGON DRESSING
1 **cup plain yogurt**
½ **cup reduced-fat mayonnaise**
½ **cup chopped fresh parsley**
4 **tablespoons chopped fresh tarragon** *or*
1 **tablespoon dried tarragon leaves**
¼ **cup milk**
3 **tablespoons FRANK'S® Original REDHOT® Cayenne Pepper Sauce**
2 **tablespoons lime juice**
2 **teaspoons honey**

SALAD
8 **cups thinly sliced romaine lettuce**
2 **cups (10 ounces) chopped cooked chicken**
6 **slices crisply cooked bacon, crumbled**
3 **hard-cooked eggs, cut into wedges**
4 **plum tomatoes, diced**
1 **can (8¼ ounces) sliced beets, drained and cut into strips**
1 **small ripe avocado, diced**
1 **small red onion, diced**
1½ **cups diced seeded cucumber**
½ **cup (2 ounces) crumbled Gorgonzola cheese**

1. Combine dressing ingredients in medium bowl; mix until well blended.

2. Arrange lettuce on serving platter *or* in 8 individual salad bowls. Arrange chicken, bacon, eggs, tomatoes, beets, avocado, onion, cucumber and Gorgonzola in mounds or rows over lettuce. Serve with Tarragon Dressing.

Makes 8 servings
(2 cups dressing)

Prep Time: 45 minutes

Lime Vinaigrette

3 **tablespoons finely chopped fresh cilantro or parsley**
3 **tablespoons plain low-fat yogurt**
3 **tablespoons orange juice**
2 **tablespoons lime juice**
2 **tablespoons white wine vinegar**
2 **tablespoons water**
1 **tablespoon sugar**
1 **teaspoon chili powder**
½ **teaspoon onion powder**
½ **teaspoon ground cumin**

In small jar with tight-fitting lid, combine all ingredients. Shake well. Refrigerate until ready to use. Shake before serving. Serve with seafood or chicken salads.

Makes about ¾ cup

Mediterranean Greek Salad

Salad Niçoise

- 1 clove garlic, halved
- 1 small head iceberg lettuce, leaves separated
- 8 ounces fresh green beans, trimmed and steamed until crisp-tender
- 1 (6½-ounce) can tuna packed in water, drained and flaked
- 2 hard-cooked eggs, cut into wedges
- 3 tomatoes, cut into wedges
- 1 green bell pepper, seeded and cut into rings
- 1 small red onion, thinly sliced
- ¼ cucumber, sliced
- 1 (2-ounce) can anchovy fillets, drained
- 12 oil-cured black olives
- ¼ cup FILIPPO BERIO® Olive Oil
- 3 tablespoons white wine vinegar
- 1 to 2 tablespoons chopped fresh herbs (chives, parsley or marjoram)
- 1 teaspoon Dijon mustard
- ½ teaspoon sugar
  Salt and freshly ground black pepper

Rub inside of large bowl with cut garlic. Line bowl with lettuce leaves. Arrange green beans, tuna, eggs, tomatoes, bell pepper, onion, cucumber, anchovies and olives over lettuce, keeping each ingredient in a separate group.

In small screw-top jar, combine olive oil, vinegar, herbs, mustard and sugar. Shake vigorously until well blended. Drizzle over salad. Season to taste with salt and black pepper. *Makes 4 servings*

Blue Cheese Chicken Salad

- 1 can (14½ ounces) DEL MONTE® *FreshCut*™ Diced Tomatoes with Garlic & Onion, undrained
- ½ pound boneless chicken breasts, skinned and cut into strips
- ½ teaspoon dried tarragon leaves
- 6 cups torn assorted lettuces
- ½ medium red onion, thinly sliced
- ½ medium cucumber, thinly sliced
- ⅓ cup crumbled blue cheese
- ¼ cup Italian dressing

1. Drain tomatoes, reserving liquid. In large skillet, cook reserved liquid until thickened, about 5 minutes, stirring occasionally.

2. Add chicken and tarragon; cook until chicken is no longer pink, stirring frequently.

3. Cool. In large bowl, toss chicken and tomato liquid with remaining ingredients.
Makes 4 servings

Prep Time: 10 minutes
Cook Time: 10 minutes

Creamy Warm Bacon Dressing

- 4 slices OSCAR MAYER® Bacon, chopped
- 1 clove garlic, minced
- 1 cup MIRACLE WHIP® Salad Dressing
- ½ cup milk

• Cook bacon until crisp. Drain, reserving 1 tablespoon drippings.

• Heat reserved drippings, chopped bacon and garlic over low heat 1 minute.

• Stir in salad dressing and milk. Continue cooking, stirring occasionally, until thoroughly heated. Serve with spinach salad. *Makes 1½ cups*

Prep Time: 10 minutes
Cook Time: 10 minutes

Italian Herb Dressing

- ⅔ cup vegetable oil
- ⅓ cup HEINZ® Gourmet Wine Vinegar
- 1 clove garlic, split
- 1 teaspoon dry mustard
- ½ teaspoon salt
- ½ teaspoon dried basil leaves
- ½ teaspoon dried oregano leaves
- ¼ teaspoon crushed red pepper

In jar, combine all ingredients; cover and shake vigorously. Chill to blend flavors. Remove garlic; shake again before serving over tossed salad greens. *Makes 1 cup*

Salad Niçoise

Ginger Shrimp Salad

1 package (10 ounces) DOLE® French Blend Salad or Italian Blend Salad

6 ounces cooked peeled, deveined medium shrimp or cooked tiny shrimp

1 can (11 ounces) DOLE® Mandarin Oranges, drained

1 medium DOLE® Red, Yellow or Green Bell Pepper, cut into 2-inch strips

⅓ cup fat-free or reduced-fat mayonnaise

⅓ cup DOLE® Mandarin Tangerine Juice or Pineapple Juice

2 teaspoons finely chopped fresh ginger or ¼ teaspoon ground ginger

• **Toss** salad blend, shrimp, mandarin oranges and bell pepper in large serving bowl.

• **Stir** mayonnaise, juice and ginger in small bowl. Add to salad; toss to evenly coat.

Makes 3 servings

Prep Time: 20 minutes

Tarragon and Celery Seed Dressing

¼ small yellow onion

3 tablespoons tarragon vinegar or white wine vinegar

2 tablespoons sugar

½ teaspoon salt

½ teaspoon dry mustard

¼ cup extra-virgin olive oil

¼ cup vegetable oil

1 teaspoon celery seeds

Place onion and vinegar in food processor or blender. Process using on/off pulsing action until onion is finely chopped. Add sugar, salt and mustard. Process until blended.

With motor running, slowly pour olive and vegetable oils through feed tube. Process until smooth. Add celery seeds. Process using on/off pulsing action until mixture is blended. Serve with mixed green, seafood or chicken salads.

Makes about 1 cup

Yogurt Dressing

2 cups plain low-fat yogurt

4 teaspoons chopped fresh mint or ¼ teaspoon dried dill weed

⅛ teaspoon TABASCO® pepper sauce

In small bowl, combine yogurt, mint and TABASCO® sauce; mix well. Cover; refrigerate.

Makes 2 cups

Grilled Steak Caesar Salad

½ cup A.1.® Original or A.1.® Bold & Spicy Steak Sauce

3 tablespoons lemon juice

1 teaspoon minced anchovy fillets

1 teaspoon minced garlic

½ cup olive oil

1 (1-pound) beef top round steak, about 1 inch thick

4 (1-inch-thick) slices French bread

4 cups torn romaine lettuce leaves

2 ounces shaved Parmesan cheese

In small bowl, blend steak sauce, juice, anchovies and garlic; slowly whisk in oil until well blended. Place steak in nonmetallic dish; coat with ⅓ cup steak sauce mixture. Cover; refrigerate 1 hour, turning occasionally. Reserve remaining steak sauce mixture for dressing.

Remove steak from marinade; discard marinade. Grill steak over medium-high heat 6 minutes on each side or to desired doneness. Lightly brush cut sides of bread with some reserved dressing. Grill bread 2 to 3 minutes on each side or until golden.

In small saucepan, heat remaining reserved dressing until warm. Arrange lettuce on serving platter. Thinly slice steak; arrange on lettuce. Drizzle with warm dressing; top with cheese. Serve immediately with grilled bread.

Makes 4 servings

Colorful Crabmeat Salad

- **1 pound blue crab claw meat (fresh, frozen or pasteurized)**
- **6 cups cooked colorful pasta shells (beet, tomato, spinach or egg)**
- **1 cup cooked frozen green peas**
- **½ cup diced red bell pepper**
- **½ cup chopped red onion**
- **½ cup chopped parsley**
- **½ cup olive oil**
- **2 tablespoons lemon juice**
- **1 tablespoon dried basil leaves**
- **½ teaspoon salt**
- **½ teaspoon minced garlic**
- **¼ teaspoon white pepper**

Thaw crabmeat if frozen. Remove any pieces of shell or cartilage from crabmeat. Combine crabmeat, pasta, peas, bell peppers, onion and parsley in large salad bowl; toss. Cover; refrigerate 3 to 4 hours. Combine oil, lemon juice, basil, salt, garlic and white pepper in shaker or jar with tight-fitting lid; shake well. Pour dressing over salad immediately before serving.

Makes 6 servings

Favorite recipe from **Florida Department of Agriculture and Consumer Services, Bureau of Seafood and Aquaculture**

Mandarin Chicken Salad

- **1 can (15½ ounces) DEL MONTE® Pineapple Chunks in Heavy Syrup, undrained**
- **3 tablespoons vegetable oil**
- **3 tablespoons cider vinegar**
- **1 tablespoon soy sauce**
- **4 cups shredded cabbage or iceberg lettuce**
- **1 can (14½ ounces) DEL MONTE® FreshCut™ Diced Tomatoes, drained**
- **2 cups cubed cooked chicken**
- **⅓ cup packed cilantro, chopped, or ½ cup sliced green onions**

1. Drain pineapple, reserving ¼ cup syrup. In small bowl, combine reserved syrup, oil, vinegar and soy sauce; stir briskly with fork.

2. Toss cabbage with pineapple, tomatoes, chicken and cilantro in large bowl. Add dressing as desired; gently toss.

3. Sprinkle with crumbled dry noodles (from ramen noodle soup mix), toasted slivered almonds or toasted sesame seeds, if desired.

Makes 4 servings

Prep Time: 15 minutes

Mandarin Chicken Salad

Confetti Barley Salad

4 cups water
1 cup dried pearl barley
⅓ cup GREY POUPON® Dijon Mustard
⅓ cup olive oil
¼ cup REGINA® Red Wine Vinegar
2 tablespoons chopped parsley
2 teaspoons chopped fresh rosemary *or* ½ teaspoon dried rosemary
2 teaspoons grated orange peel
1 teaspoon sugar
1 ½ cups diced red, green or yellow bell peppers
½ cup sliced green onions
½ cup sliced pitted ripe olives
Fresh rosemary and orange and tomato slices for garnish

In medium saucepan, over medium-high heat, heat water and barley to a boil; reduce heat. Cover; simmer for 45 to 55 minutes or until tender. Drain and cool.

In small bowl, whisk mustard, oil, vinegar, parsley, rosemary, orange peel and sugar until blended; set aside.

In large bowl, combine barley, bell peppers, green onions and olives. Stir in mustard dressing, tossing to coat well. Chill several hours to blend flavors. To serve, spoon barley mixture onto serving platter; garnish with rosemary and orange and tomato slices.

Makes 6 to 8 servings

Albacore and White Bean Salad with Orange Dressing

2 cans (15 ounces each) Great Northern beans, rinsed and drained
3 hard-cooked eggs, chopped
⅓ cup chopped green onions, including tops
⅓ cup chopped red onion
¾ teaspoon salt
⅓ cup bottled Italian dressing
1 tablespoon frozen orange juice concentrate, thawed
2 teaspoons grated orange peel
½ to 1 teaspoon crushed red pepper
1 can (6 ounces) STARKIST® Solid White Tuna, drained and chunked
2 chopped plum tomatoes, drained
Quartered orange slices and chives for garnish

In large bowl, combine beans, eggs, onions and salt. In glass measuring cup, blend dressing, orange juice concentrate, orange peel and crushed red pepper. Add to salad in bowl. Chill several hours or overnight. Just before serving, gently toss in tuna and tomatoes. Garnish with orange slices and chives.

Makes 6 servings

Prep Time: 15 minutes

Zesty Wild Rice Salad

5 cups cooked wild rice
2 cups frozen cooked shrimp, thawed, or canned tuna, drained and flaked
½ cup chopped broccoli
½ cup chopped cauliflower
½ cup (2 ounces) cubed Cheddar cheese
¼ cup diced red bell pepper
¼ cup diced green bell pepper
¼ cup Italian dressing

Combine wild rice, shrimp, broccoli, cauliflower, cheese and peppers in large bowl. Cover; refrigerate. Just before serving, toss gently with dressing. Serve on lettuce leaves.

Makes about 4 servings

FAVORITE RECIPE FROM **MINNESOTA CULTIVATED WILD RICE COMMISSION**

Confetti Barley Salad

Sesame Green Beans and Red Pepper

- 1 tablespoon sesame seeds
- 3 tablespoons FRANK'S® Original REDHOT® Cayenne Pepper Sauce
- 1 tablespoon olive oil
- 1 tablespoon soy sauce
- 2 teaspoons grated peeled fresh ginger
- ¼ teaspoon dark sesame oil
- 1 clove garlic, minced
- 1 pound fresh green beans, washed, trimmed and cut in half crosswise
- ¼ teaspoon salt
- ½ red bell pepper, seeded and cut into very thin strips
  Lettuce (optional)

1. Heat large nonstick skillet over medium heat. Add sesame seeds. Cook 1 to 2 minutes or until golden, shaking skillet often. Transfer to small bowl. Whisk in RedHot® sauce, olive oil, soy sauce, ginger, sesame oil and garlic; set aside.

2. Bring *1 cup water* to a boil in large saucepan over high heat. Place green beans and salt in steamer basket; set into saucepan. *Do not let water touch beans.* Cover; steam 5 to 6 minutes or until beans are crisp-tender. Rinse with cold water; drain well.

3. Combine beans and bell pepper in large bowl. Pour sesame dressing over

vegetables; toss to coat evenly. Cover; refrigerate 1 hour. Toss just before serving. Serve on lettuce-lined plates, if desired.

Makes 6 servings

Mediterranean Couscous

- 1 (10-ounce) package couscous
- ⅓ cup GREY POUPON® COUNTRY DIJON® Mustard
- ¼ cup lemon juice
- ¼ cup chopped parsley
- 3 tablespoons chopped fresh mint
- 1 tablespoon grated lemon peel
- 1 clove garlic, minced
- ⅔ cup olive oil
- 4 ounces feta cheese, diced
- ½ cup chopped pitted ripe olives
- 1 (7-ounce) jar roasted red peppers, drained and chopped
  Sliced tomatoes and cucumbers for garnish

Prepare couscous according to package directions; cool.

In small bowl, whisk mustard, lemon juice, parsley, mint, lemon peel and garlic until blended. Whisk in oil.

In large bowl, combine couscous, cheese, olives and peppers; add mustard mixture, tossing to coat well. Chill at least 1 hour. To serve, arrange couscous mixture on serving plate; garnish with tomato and cucumber slices.

Makes 6 servings

Aztec Chili Salad

- 1 pound ground beef
- 1 package (1.48 ounces) LAWRY'S® Spices & Seasonings for Chili
- 1 can (15¼ ounces) kidney beans, undrained
- 1 can (14½ ounces) whole peeled tomatoes, cut up, undrained
- ½ cup water
- ½ cup sour cream
- 1 fresh medium tomato, diced
- ¼ cup chopped fresh cilantro
- 3 tablespoons mayonnaise
- ½ teaspoon LAWRY'S® Seasoned Pepper
- 1 head lettuce
- 1 red bell pepper, sliced
- ¼ cup sliced green onions
- 1½ cups (6 ounces) shredded Cheddar cheese
- ¼ cup sliced ripe olives

In large skillet, brown beef until crumbly; drain fat. Stir in Spices & Seasonings for Chili, beans, canned tomatoes and water; blend well. Bring to a boil; reduce heat and simmer, uncovered, 10 minutes. For dressing, in blender or food processor, blend sour cream, fresh tomato, cilantro, mayonnaise and Seasoned Pepper. Refrigerate until chilled. On 6 individual plates, layer lettuce, chili meat, bell pepper, onions, cheese and olives. Drizzle with chilled dressing. *Makes 6 servings*

Sesame Green Beans and Red Pepper

Roasted Red Pepper, Corn & Garbanzo Bean Salad

2 cans (15 ounces each) garbanzo beans
1 jar (11.5 ounces) GUILTLESS GOURMET® Roasted Red Pepper Salsa
1 cup frozen whole kernel corn, thawed and drained
½ cup GUILTLESS GOURMET® Green Tomatillo Salsa
2 green onions, thinly sliced
8 lettuce leaves
Fresh tomato wedges and sunflower sprouts (optional)

Rinse and drain beans well; place in 2-quart casserole. Add roasted red pepper salsa, corn, tomatillo salsa and onions; stir to combine. Cover and refrigerate 1 hour or up to 24 hours.

To serve, line serving platter with lettuce. Spoon bean mixture over top. Garnish with tomatoes and sprouts, if desired.   *Makes 8 servings*

Tabbouleh

¾ cup bulgur, rinsed and drained
Boiling water
2 cups chopped seeded cucumber
1 large tomato, seeded and chopped
1 cup snipped parsley
⅓ cup CRISCO® Oil or CRISCO® PURITAN® Canola Oil
⅓ cup chopped green onions
2 tablespoons lemon juice
1 teaspoon dried mint leaves
2 cloves garlic, minced
½ teaspoon salt
⅛ teaspoon white pepper
⅛ teaspoon ground red pepper

Place bulgur in medium bowl. Add enough boiling water to just cover bulgur. Let stand about 1 hour or until bulgur is rehydrated. Drain.

Combine bulgur, cucumber, tomato and parsley in large serving bowl; set aside. Blend remaining ingredients in small mixing bowl. Pour over bulgur mixture; toss to coat. Cover; refrigerate at least 3 hours. Stir before serving.
          Makes 10 to 12 servings

Black and White Bean Salad

½ cup MIRACLE WHIP® FREE® Nonfat Dressing
1 can (15 ounces) navy beans, drained and rinsed
1 can (15 ounces) black beans, drained and rinsed
½ cup green bell pepper strips
½ cup red onion slices
1 cucumber, chopped
3 tablespoons chopped fresh parsley
Dash black pepper

Mix together ingredients until well blended; refrigerate.
          Makes 4 cups

Prep Time: 10 minutes

Roasted Red Pepper, Corn & Garbanzo Bean Salad

Border Black Bean Chicken Salad

¼ cup olive oil, divided
1½ pounds boneless skinless chicken breasts, cut into 2-inch strips
1 clove garlic, minced
½ jalapeño pepper, seeded and finely chopped
1¼ teaspoons salt, divided
4 cups torn romaine lettuce
1 can (15 to 16 ounces) black beans, drained and rinsed
1 cup peeled and seeded cucumber cubes
1 cup red bell pepper strips
1 cup chopped tomato
½ cup chopped red onion
⅓ cup tomato vegetable juice
2 tablespoons fresh lime juice
½ teaspoon ground cumin
½ cup chopped pecans, toasted
Fresh parsley for garnish

Heat 2 tablespoons oil in large skillet over medium heat until hot. Add chicken; stir-fry 2 minutes or until no longer pink in center. Add garlic, jalapeño and ¾ teaspoon salt; stir-fry 30 seconds. Combine chicken mixture, lettuce, beans, cucumber, red pepper, tomato and onion in large salad bowl. Combine tomato juice, lime juice, remaining 2 tablespoons oil, cumin and remaining ½ teaspoon salt in small jar with lid; shake well. Add to skillet; heat over medium heat until slightly warm. Pour warm dressing over chicken mixture; toss to coat. Sprinkle with pecans. Garnish with parsley. Serve immediately.

Makes 4 servings

FAVORITE RECIPE FROM **NATIONAL BROILER COUNCIL**

Hot Mediterranean Chicken Salad

4 cups chicken broth
6 boneless skinless chicken breast halves
⅓ cup FILIPPO BERIO® Extra Virgin Olive Oil
1 medium onion, cut into thin strips
1 clove garlic, crushed
1 tablespoon chopped fresh oregano *or* 1½ teaspoons dried oregano leaves
1 cup cooked small green beans
1 cup quartered cherry tomatoes
¾ cup pitted ripe olives
2 teaspoons grated lemon peel
1 to 2 tablespoons white wine vinegar
Juice of 1 lemon
Salt and freshly ground black pepper
6 cups finely shredded lettuce
Additional lemon juice
Chopped fresh parsley

In large saucepan or Dutch oven, bring chicken broth to a boil over high heat. Add chicken. Cover; reduce heat to low and simmer about 20 minutes or until chicken is no longer pink in center. Drain; let cool slightly. Coarsely chop.

In large skillet, heat olive oil over medium heat until hot. Add onion and garlic; cook and stir 5 minutes. Sprinkle with oregano; cook and stir an additional 5 to 10 minutes or until onion is almost transparent. Add green beans, tomatoes, olives and lemon peel; cook and stir until heated through. Add chicken. Season to taste with vinegar, juice of 1 lemon, salt and pepper. Heat briefly.

In large bowl, toss lettuce with additional lemon juice. Season to taste with salt and pepper. Divide equally among 6 plates. Spoon hot chicken salad over lettuce; garnish with parsley.

Makes 6 servings

Border Black Bean Chicken Salad

Singapore Spam™ Salad

WARM SESAME DRESSING
  1 cup sugar
  ⅓ cup rice vinegar
  ¼ cup olive oil
  2 tablespoons sesame oil
  ¼ teaspoon garlic salt

SALAD
  ½ head iceberg lettuce, thinly sliced
  ½ head romaine lettuce, thinly sliced
  1 (12-ounce) can SPAM® Luncheon Meat, cubed
  3 carrots, grated
  1 cup chopped green onions
  1 cup chopped celery
  1 green bell pepper, chopped
  1 cup thinly sliced radishes
  1 (6½-ounce) package sliced almonds, toasted

In small saucepan over low heat, combine all dressing ingredients. Stir constantly until sugar dissolves. In large bowl, toss together all salad ingredients. Serve warm dressing with salad.

Makes 8 servings

Thai Beef Salad

DRESSING
  1 cup packed fresh mint or basil leaves, coarsely chopped
  1 cup olive oil vinaigrette dressing
  ⅓ cup FRANK'S® Original REDHOT® Cayenne Pepper Sauce
  3 tablespoons chopped peeled fresh ginger
  3 tablespoons sugar
  3 cloves garlic, chopped
  2 teaspoons FRENCH'S® Worcestershire Sauce

SALAD
  1 flank steak (about 1½ pounds)
  6 cups washed and torn mixed salad greens
  1 cup sliced peeled cucumber
  ⅓ cup chopped peanuts

1. Place dressing ingredients in blender or food processor. Cover; blend until smooth. Reserve *1 cup* dressing.

2. Place steak in large resealable plastic food storage bag. Pour remaining dressing over steak. Seal bag; refrigerate 30 minutes.

3. Prepare grill. Place steak on grid, reserving marinade. Grill, over hot coals, about 15 minutes for medium-rare, brushing frequently with marinade. Let stand 5 minutes. Slice steak diagonally; arrange over greens and cucumber.

4. Sprinkle with peanuts and drizzle with reserved *1 cup* dressing. Serve warm.

Makes 6 servings

Asian Cabbage & Carrot Slaw

  3 cups finely shredded napa (Chinese) cabbage or green cabbage
  1 cup finely shredded red cabbage
  1 cup finely shredded carrots
  1 can (8 ounces) sliced water chestnuts, rinsed and drained
  ¼ cup orange juice
  2 tablespoons olive oil
  2 tablespoons FRANK'S® Original REDHOT® Cayenne Pepper Sauce
  1 tablespoon soy sauce
  2 teaspoons grated peeled fresh ginger
  ½ teaspoon sugar
  ½ teaspoon dark sesame oil

1. Combine napa and red cabbages, carrots and water chestnuts in large bowl; set aside.

2. Whisk orange juice, olive oil, RedHot® sauce, soy sauce, ginger, sugar and sesame oil in small measuring cup. Pour over cabbage mixture; toss to coat evenly. Cover; refrigerate 1 hour.

Makes 6 servings
(5 cups salad, about
½ cup dressing)

Prep Time: 30 minutes
Chill Time: 1 hour

Singapore Spam™ Salad

Lamb Salad with Tomatoes and Feta

¾ **pound boneless lamb chops (1 inch thick)**
3 **tablespoons olive oil, divided**
1 **can (14½ ounces) DEL MONTE® FreshCut™ Diced Tomatoes with Garlic & Onion, undrained**
3 **tablespoons red wine vinegar**
2 **to 3 tablespoons minced fresh mint or**
½ **teaspoon dried mint**
½ **medium red onion, thinly sliced**
  Shredded lettuce
½ **cup crumbled feta cheese**

1. Season meat with salt and black pepper, if desired.

2. Heat 1 tablespoon oil over medium-high heat in large skillet. Add meat; cook about 4 minutes on each side or until desired doneness. Cut meat crosswise into thin slices.

3. Drain tomatoes, reserving ⅓ cup liquid. Combine reserved liquid with vinegar, mint and remaining 2 tablespoons oil.

4. Toss meat slices, tomatoes and onion with dressing. Arrange over lettuce; top with cheese. Garnish, if desired.
Makes 4 servings

Prep Time: 12 minutes
Cook Time: 8 minutes

Variation: *Grill lamb over hot coals instead of pan-frying.*

Colorado Potato & Prosciutto Salad

1¼ **pounds round red-skin Colorado potatoes, unpeeled (about 4 potatoes)**
½ **pound green beans, trimmed and sliced into 2½-inch lengths**
1 **red or green bell pepper, cored, seeded and cut into slivers**
1½ **cups cooked fresh or thawed frozen corn kernels**
6 **ounces mozzarella cheese, cut into ½-inch cubes**
3 **ounces thinly sliced prosciutto or ham, torn into strips**
3 **green onions, sliced**
⅓ **cup olive oil**
¼ **cup lemon juice**
2 **tablespoons water**
1 **or 2 cloves garlic, minced**
1 **tablespoon chopped fresh thyme or 1½ teaspoons dried thyme leaves**
  Salt and black pepper

Cook potatoes until tender. Cool; cut into ½-inch-thick slices, then cut into quarters. Cook green beans until tender; cool. In large serving bowl, combine potatoes, beans, bell pepper, corn, cheese, prosciutto and green onions. In small bowl, whisk together oil, lemon juice, water, garlic and thyme.

Season with salt and black pepper to taste. Pour dressing over potato mixture and toss to coat. Serve immediately or refrigerate.
Makes 6 to 8 servings

FAVORITE RECIPE FROM **COLORADO POTATO ADMINISTRATIVE COMMITTEE**

Rosemary Lemon Chicken Salad

2 **cups cubed cooked chicken**
1 **cup chopped onions**
1 **cup diced celery**
½ **cup chopped roasted red pepper**
⅓ **cup GREY POUPON® COUNTRY DIJON® Mustard**
¼ **cup olive oil**
2 **tablespoons lemon juice**
1½ **teaspoons dried rosemary leaves**
1 **teaspoon grated lemon peel**
½ **teaspoon coarsely ground black pepper**
¼ **teaspoon salt**

In large bowl, combine chicken, onions, celery and roasted red pepper. In small bowl, whisk mustard, oil, lemon juice, rosemary, lemon peel, black pepper and salt until blended. Pour over chicken mixture, tossing to coat well. Chill at least 1 hour. Serve as a salad or sandwich filling. Garnish as desired. *Makes 4 servings*

Lamb Salad with Tomatoes and Feta

Crab Salad with Chiles and Cilantro

1 cup sour cream
½ cup (4-ounce can) ORTEGA® Diced Green Chiles
½ cup finely chopped onion
¼ cup chopped fresh cilantro
2 tablespoons lime juice
½ teaspoon salt
1 pound fresh or chopped imitation crabmeat

COMBINE sour cream, chiles, onion, cilantro, lime juice and salt in medium bowl; add crabmeat. Toss to coat well; cover. Chill for at least 1 hour.

SERVE with crackers or tortilla chips or use as a topping for salads. *Makes 4 servings*

Tip: Serve this salad atop ORTEGA® Tostada Shells or inside ORTEGA® Taco Shells for an easy elegant seafood meal!

Dijon Asparagus Chicken Salad

1 cup HELLMANN'S® or BEST FOODS® Real or Light Mayonnaise or Low Fat Mayonnaise Dressing
¼ cup HELLMANN'S® or BEST FOODS® Dijonnaise Creamy Mustard Blend
2 tablespoons lemon juice
1 teaspoon salt
½ teaspoon black pepper
1 pound boneless skinless chicken breasts, cooked and cubed
1 package (10 ounces) frozen asparagus spears, thawed and cut into 2-inch pieces
6 ounces MUELLER'S® Twist Trio® (about 2½ cups), cooked, rinsed with cold water and drained
1 red bell pepper, cut into 1-inch squares

1. In large bowl, stir mayonnaise, creamy mustard blend, lemon juice, salt and black pepper.

2. Add chicken, asparagus, pasta and red bell pepper; toss to coat well. Cover; chill to blend flavors.

Makes 6 servings

Grilled Chicken Taco Salad

1 can (14½ ounces) DEL MONTE® *FreshCut*™ Diced Tomatoes with Garlic & Onion
⅓ cup DEL MONTE® Thick & Chunky Salsa, hot or medium
2 tablespoons vegetable oil
2 tablespoons red wine or cider vinegar
1 large head romaine lettuce, chopped (10 to 12 cups)
4 boneless chicken breast halves, grilled and cut into bite-size pieces*
1 can (8 ounces) kidney beans, drained (optional)
1 cup (4 ounces) shredded sharp Cheddar cheese
3 cups broken tortilla chips

Or, substitute 3 cups cubed cooked chicken.

1. Drain tomatoes, reserving 1 tablespoon liquid. Chop tomatoes; set aside.

2. Make dressing in small bowl by blending reserved tomato liquid, salsa, oil and vinegar.

3. Toss lettuce with tomatoes, chicken, beans and cheese in large bowl. Add dressing as desired. Add chips; toss. Season with salt and black pepper, if desired. Serve immediately. Garnish, if desired. *Makes 4 servings*

Crab Salad with Chiles and Cilantro

Market Salad

- **2 cups small cauliflower florets**
- **2 cups small broccoli florets**
- **2 cups (8 ounces) SARGENTO® Fancy Shredded Mozzarella Cheese**
- **2 medium carrots, cut into short, thin strips**
- **1 can (16 ounces) garbanzo beans, well drained**
- **¾ cup chopped red bell pepper**
- **⅓ cup white wine vinegar**
- **2 cloves garlic, minced**
- **1 teaspoon dried oregano leaves**
- **¼ teaspoon salt**
- **½ cup vegetable oil**
- **2 teaspoons capers (optional)**

In large bowl, combine cauliflower, broccoli, mozzarella cheese, carrots, beans and bell pepper; set aside. In small bowl, combine vinegar, garlic, oregano and salt. Slowly add oil, whisking until smooth and thickened. Stir in capers, if desired. Add to vegetable and cheese mixture. Toss gently. Cover; chill thoroughly, stirring several times. *Makes 8 servings*

Herbed Tomato Cucumber Salad

- **½ cup MIRACLE WHIP® FREE® Nonfat Dressing**
- **1 cucumber, peeled, seeded and chopped**
- **⅓ cup *each* finely chopped red onion and finely chopped fresh basil**
- **¼ teaspoon salt**
- **3 tomatoes, sliced**

MIX all ingredients except tomatoes until well blended; refrigerate. Spoon over tomatoes. *Makes 6 servings*

Prep Time: 10 minutes plus refrigerating

Classic Potato Salad

- **1 cup HELLMANN'S® or BEST FOODS® Real or Light Mayonnaise or Low Fat Mayonnaise Dressing**
- **2 tablespoons vinegar**
- **1½ teaspoons salt**
- **1 teaspoon sugar**
- **¼ teaspoon freshly ground black pepper**
- **5 to 6 medium potatoes, peeled, cubed and cooked**
- **1 cup sliced celery**
- **½ cup chopped onion**
- **2 hard-cooked eggs, diced**

1. In large bowl, combine mayonnaise, vinegar, salt, sugar and pepper.

2. Add potatoes, celery, onion and eggs; toss to coat well.

3. Cover; chill to blend flavors. *Makes about 8 servings*

Creamy Dijon Coleslaw

- **½ cup GREY POUPON® COUNTRY DIJON® Mustard**
- **½ cup prepared ranch, creamy Italian or blue cheese salad dressing**
- **2 tablespoons chopped parsley**
- **½ teaspoon celery seeds**
- **3 cups shredded green cabbage**
- **2 cups shredded red cabbage**
- **1 cup shredded carrots**
- **½ cup chopped onion**
- **⅓ cup chopped red bell pepper**

In small bowl, blend mustard, salad dressing, parsley and celery seeds; set aside.

In large bowl, combine green and red cabbages, carrots, onion and bell pepper. Add mustard mixture, tossing to coat well. Chill at least 1 hour before serving. *Makes about 5 cups*

Market Salad

Fruit Salad with Orange Poppy Seed Dressing

¼ cup orange juice
3 tablespoons cider vinegar
3 tablespoons FRENCH'S® Dijon Mustard
2 tablespoons honey
1 tablespoon FRENCH'S® Worcestershire Sauce
1 teaspoon grated orange peel
½ teaspoon salt
½ cup canola or corn oil
1 tablespoon poppy seeds
6 cups fruit: orange segments; cantaloupe, watermelon and/or honeydew melon balls; blueberries; blackberries; grapes; star fruit and/or strawberry slices; nectarine wedges
Lettuce leaves

To prepare dressing, place juice, vinegar, mustard, honey, Worcestershire, orange peel and salt in blender or food processor. Cover and blend until well blended. Gradually add oil in steady stream, blending until very smooth. Stir in poppy seeds.

Arrange fruit on lettuce leaves on large platter. Spoon dressing over fruit just before serving.
Makes 6 side-dish servings (about 1½ cups dressing)

Prep Time: 40 minutes

Orange-Berry Salad

½ cup prepared HIDDEN VALLEY RANCH® Original Ranch® salad dressing
2 tablespoons orange juice
1 teaspoon grated orange peel
½ cup heavy cream, whipped
1 can (11 ounces) mandarin orange segments, undrained
2 packages (3 ounces each) strawberry- or raspberry-flavored gelatin
1 can (16 ounces) whole-berry cranberry sauce
½ cup walnut pieces
Mint sprigs
Whole fresh strawberries and raspberries

In large bowl, whisk together salad dressing, orange juice and peel. Fold in whipped cream; cover and refrigerate. Drain oranges, reserving juice. Add water to juice to measure 3 cups; pour into large saucepan and bring to a boil. Stir in gelatin until dissolved. Cover and refrigerate until partially set. Fold orange segments, cranberry sauce and walnuts into gelatin. Pour into lightly oiled 6-cup ring mold. Cover and refrigerate until firm; unmold. Garnish with mint, strawberries and raspberries. Serve with chilled dressing.
Makes 8 servings

Confetti Apple Salad

1 Golden Delicious apple (about 6 ounces), cored and chopped
½ cup *each* flaked coconut, raisins and chopped carrot
½ cup lemon-flavored yogurt
⅓ cup coarsely chopped cashews or peanuts
Curly lettuce leaves

Combine all ingredients except nuts and lettuce; allow flavors to blend for 1 hour. Stir in nuts. Arrange salad on lettuce-lined plates.   *Makes 2 to 3 servings*

Note: Recipe can be multiplied.

FAVORITE RECIPE FROM WASHINGTON APPLE COMMISSION

Pistachio Pineapple Delight

1 package (4-serving size) JELL-O® Pistachio Flavor Instant Pudding and Pie Filling
1 can (20 ounces) crushed pineapple in syrup, undrained
1 cup miniature marshmallows
½ cup chopped nuts
1¾ cups thawed COOL WHIP® Whipped Topping

STIR pudding mix, pineapple, marshmallows and nuts in large bowl until well blended. Gently stir in whipped topping. Refrigerate until ready to serve. Garnish with additional whipped topping and fresh fruit, if desired.   *Makes 8 servings*

Prep Time: 15 minutes

Tuna Pilaf Salad

- 1 package (7.2 ounces) **RICE-A-RONI®** Rice Pilaf
- 1 package (10 ounces) frozen cut green beans
- 1 small red onion, thinly sliced, slices halved
- ¼ cup Italian dressing
- 2 cans (6 ounces each) white tuna in water, drained, flaked
- ½ cup ripe pitted olives (optional)
- 1 large tomato, cut into 12 wedges
- 1 tablespoon chopped parsley

Prepare Rice-A-Roni® Mix as package directs, reducing water to 1¾ cups and stirring in frozen green beans and onion during last 15 minutes of cooking. Remove from heat; stir in dressing.

Top rice mixture with tuna, olives, if desired, tomato and parsley. Serve warm or chilled with additional dressing, if desired.   *Makes 5 servings*

Garden Party Pasta Salad

- 1 package (16 ounces) multicolor rotini
- 1 package (8 ounces) refrigerated tricolor tortellini
- 2½ cups cauliflower florets or broccoli florets
- 1 cup diced carrots
- 1 cup diced green bell pepper
- 1 cup sliced ripe olives
- 1 cup frozen green peas
- ½ cup chopped green onions leaves
- 1 tablespoon dried oregano leaves
- 1 tablespoon dried basil leaves
- 1 jar (26 ounces) **NEWMAN'S OWN®** Diavolo Sauce
- ¾ cup **NEWMAN'S OWN®** Olive Oil & Vinegar Salad Dressing

Cook rotini and tortellini according to package directions; drain.

Mix together rotini, tortellini, cauliflower, carrots, bell pepper, olives, peas and green onions in large salad bowl.

Sprinkle oregano and basil over pasta mixture. Add Diavolo Sauce and Olive Oil & Vinegar Salad Dressing; toss and refrigerate at least 3 hours.
Makes 15 to 20 side-dish servings

Note: *May be made a day ahead.*

Centennial Apple Pasta Salad

- 2 cups dried pasta, cooked according to package directions
- 2 cups (about ¾ pound) cored and cubed Red Delicious apples
- 1 cup coarsely chopped walnuts
- ¼ cup chopped green onions
- ¼ cup *each* mayonnaise and plain yogurt
- 1 tablespoon Dijon mustard
  Salt and black pepper to taste

Combine all ingredients; toss to mix well. Refrigerate at least 1 hour.   *Makes 4 to 6 servings*

Prep Time: 15 minutes

FAVORITE RECIPE FROM **WASHINGTON APPLE COMMISSION**

Mozzarella & Tomato with Lemon Dijon Dressing

⅓ cup olive oil
¼ cup GREY POUPON®
    COUNTRY DIJON®
    Mustard*
2 tablespoons lemon juice
2 teaspoons finely
    chopped fresh basil
    leaves
½ teaspoon sugar
3 medium tomatoes,
    sliced
6 ounces mozzarella
    cheese, sliced
2 cups mixed salad greens
¼ cup coarsely chopped
    pitted ripe olives
    Chopped fresh basil
    leaves

*GREY POUPON® Peppercorn
Mustard may be substituted for
Country Dijon® Mustard.

In small bowl, whisk oil,
mustard, lemon juice, 2
teaspoons basil and sugar;
set aside.

Arrange tomato and cheese
slices over salad greens on
serving platter. Top with
chopped olives and basil
leaves; garnish as desired.
Drizzle with prepared dressing
before serving.

Makes 6 appetizer servings

Apple Pesto Potato Salad

    Pesto Sauce (recipe
        follows)
¾ cup cooked boiling
        potatoes
¼ cup sliced radishes
¼ cup sliced olives
1 green onion, diagonally
        sliced
1 tablespoon olive oil
1 tablespoon white wine
        vinegar
½ teaspoon sugar
½ teaspoon grated lemon
        peel
¼ teaspoon salt
¼ teaspoon ground black
        pepper
2 Golden Delicious apples,
        cored and thinly sliced

Prepare Pesto Sauce; set aside.
Peel potatoes, if desired; slice.
In large bowl, combine
potatoes, radishes, olives and
green onion. In small bowl,
blend 2 tablespoons Pesto
Sauce, olive oil, vinegar, sugar,
lemon peel, salt and pepper;
pour over potato mixture. Stir
gently to coat. Marinate 1 to
2 hours. Arrange salad on
serving plate with apple slices;
serve.   *Makes 4 servings*

PESTO SAUCE: In blender or
food processor, combine ½ cup
fresh basil leaves, ¼ cup grated
Parmesan cheese, 2 tablespoons
pine nuts, 1 tablespoon olive oil,
1 clove garlic and 1 teaspoon
lemon juice; purée until smooth.

FAVORITE RECIPE FROM **WASHINGTON
APPLE COMMISSION**

Mandarin Orange and Red Onion Salad

1 cup BLUE DIAMOND®
    Sliced Natural
    Almonds
1 tablespoon butter
2 tablespoons lemon juice
1 teaspoon Dijon mustard
½ teaspoon sugar
½ teaspoon salt
¼ teaspoon white pepper
½ cup vegetable oil
1 head romaine lettuce,
    torn into pieces
1 can (11 ounces)
    mandarin orange
    segments, drained
1 small red onion, thinly
    sliced, rings separated

Sauté almonds in butter until
golden; reserve. Combine
lemon juice, mustard, sugar,
salt and pepper in small bowl;
whisk in oil. Combine lettuce,
oranges, onion and almonds in
large bowl. Toss with dressing.
Makes 4 to 6 servings

*Mozzarella & Tomato with
Lemon Dijon Dressing*

Roasted Pepper and Avocado Salad

2 red bell peppers
2 orange bell peppers
2 yellow bell peppers
2 ripe avocados, halved, pitted and peeled
3 shallots, thinly sliced
¼ cup FILIPPO BERIO® Extra Virgin Olive Oil
1 clove garlic, crushed
Finely grated peel and juice of 1 lemon
Salt and freshly ground black pepper

Place bell peppers on baking sheet. Broil 4 to 5 inches from heat, 5 minutes on each side or until entire surface of each bell pepper is blistered and blackened slightly. Place bell peppers in paper bag. Close bag; cool 15 to 20 minutes. Cut around cores of bell peppers; twist and remove. Cut bell peppers lengthwise in half. Peel off skin with paring knife; rinse under cold water to remove seeds. Slice bell peppers into ½-inch-thick strips; place in shallow dish. Cut avocados into ¼-inch-thick slices; add to bell peppers. Sprinkle with shallots.

In small bowl, whisk together olive oil, garlic, lemon peel and juice. Pour over bell pepper mixture. Cover; refrigerate at least 1 hour before serving. Season to taste with salt and black pepper.

Makes 6 servings

Mediterranean Phyllo Twists with Grapes and Cheese

6 sheets phyllo dough
2 tablespoons olive oil, divided
5 to 6 ounces goat cheese
2 tablespoons chopped fresh basil
⅛ teaspoon medium-grind black pepper
2 cups California seedless grapes
3 quarts mixed greens
Mustard Vinaigrette (recipe follows)
12 small California grape clusters

Cut each sheet of phyllo dough into 4 equal (about 6½×8½-inch) pieces and keep under damp, clean towel to prevent drying. Working with 4 pieces at a time, brush each with oil and stack, alternating directions with each piece to enable the complete covering of filling. Portion one-sixth of cheese in center of dough. Combine basil and pepper; mix well. Top cheese with 1 teaspoon basil mixture and ⅓ cup grapes. Carefully gather dough to enclose filling, twisting dough at top to form small bundle. Brush lightly with oil to prevent drying. Place on greased baking sheet. Repeat with remaining ingredients. Bake at 400°F 10 minutes or until thoroughly heated. Toss mixed greens with Mustard Vinaigrette. Serve each phyllo packet on bed of mixed greens; garnish with grape clusters.

Makes 6 servings

MUSTARD VINAIGRETTE:
Combine 3 tablespoons balsamic vinegar, 1 tablespoon *each* olive oil and chopped parsley, 1 teaspoon Dijon mustard, ½ teaspoon *each* sugar and salt and ¼ teaspoon black pepper. *Makes ⅓ cup*

FAVORITE RECIPE FROM **CALIFORNIA TABLE GRAPE COMMISSION**

California Apricot Fruit Salad

2 cups sliced pitted fresh California apricots
1½ cups sliced fresh strawberries
1½ cups peeled and sliced kiwifruit
¼ cup California apricot nectar
¼ cup flaked coconut, lightly toasted
1 tablespoon finely chopped fresh mint

Combine all ingredients in medium bowl; refrigerate. Serve as salad or thread onto wooden skewers for fresh fruit kabobs. *Makes 5 servings*

FAVORITE RECIPE FROM **CALIFORNIA APRICOT ADVISORY BOARD**

Roasted Pepper and Avocado Salad

Garden Vegetable Pasta Salad with Bacon

12 ounces uncooked rotini or spiral pasta
½ pound bacon, thinly sliced
1 medium bunch broccoli, cut into florets
2 medium carrots, sliced diagonally
2 ribs celery, sliced diagonally
1 can (14½ ounces) pasta-ready tomatoes, drained
10 medium mushrooms, thinly sliced
½ medium red or yellow onion, thinly sliced
1 bottle (8 ounces) ranch salad dressing
½ cup (2 ounces) shredded Cheddar cheese
1 tablespoon dried parsley flakes
2 teaspoons dried basil leaves
¼ teaspoon black pepper

1. Cook pasta according to package directions. Drain and rinse well under cold water until pasta is cool.

2. Heat large skillet over medium-high heat. Add bacon; cook until browned. Remove bacon from skillet; drain on paper towels. Cool and crumble into small pieces.

3. Combine broccoli, carrots, celery, tomatoes, mushrooms and onion in large bowl. Add pasta and bacon; toss lightly. Add salad dressing, Cheddar cheese, parsley, basil and pepper; stir to combine.

Makes 6 servings

Pepperoni Pasta Salad

1 bag (16 ounces) BIRDS EYE® frozen Farm Fresh Mixtures Broccoli, Red Peppers, Onions and Mushrooms
2 cups cooked macaroni
1 package (3 ounces) thinly sliced pepperoni
¼ to ½ cup peppercorn or ranch salad dressing

• Cook vegetables according to package directions.

• Combine vegetables and macaroni in large bowl. Chill.

• Toss with pepperoni and dressing. Add salt and pepper to taste.

Makes 4 to 6 servings

Prep Time: 2 minutes, plus chilling time
Cook Time: 10 to 12 minutes

San Marcos Chili Pepper Penne Salad

1 (12-ounce) package PASTA LABELLA® Chili Pepper Penne Rigate
1 cup large diced avocado
¾ cup julienned red onion
1 cup sliced seeded Anaheim chilies
1 cup large diced tomato
¾ cup sliced seeded peeled cucumber
½ cup light soy sauce
½ cup fresh lime juice
⅓ cup extra-virgin olive oil
⅓ cup red wine vinegar
¼ cup chopped cilantro
¼ teaspoon garlic powder
¼ teaspoon onion powder
¼ teaspoon black pepper
¼ teaspoon salt

Cook pasta according to package directions. When pasta is al dente, rinse with cold water until cool to touch. Drain pasta well and put in large mixing bowl. Toss pasta with all vegetables and set aside. In small bowl, whisk together soy sauce, lime juice, oil and vinegar. Blend in cilantro and spices; mix well. Pour salad dressing over pasta and vegetables. Toss well and serve.

Makes 4 servings

Pepperoni Pasta Salad

Ragin' Cajun Spam™ Party Salad

SALAD

8 ounces uncooked
 wagon wheel-shaped
 pasta
1 (6-ounce) jar marinated
 artichoke hearts,
 undrained
1 (12-ounce) can SPAM®
 Luncheon Meat, cubed
1 cup diced green bell
 peppers
½ cup chopped red onion
½ cup sliced ripe olives
3 tablespoons finely
 chopped fresh basil

DRESSING

⅓ cup olive oil
¼ cup Creole seasoning
 mix
1 tablespoon lemon juice
1 tablespoon mayonnaise
 or salad dressing
1 tablespoon white wine
 vinegar
½ teaspoon dry mustard
½ teaspoon dried oregano
 leaves
½ teaspoon sugar
½ teaspoon dried thyme
 leaves
1 clove garlic, chopped

Cook pasta according to
package directions. Drain
artichokes, reserving marinade;
cut into quarters. In large bowl,
combine all salad ingredients.
In blender, combine reserved
artichoke marinade with
dressing ingredients; blend
until smooth. Add dressing to
salad, tossing well. Cover and
refrigerate several hours or
overnight.

Makes 8 to 10 servings

Warm Pasta Pepper Salad

1 package (9 ounces)
 refrigerated
 CONTADINA® Dalla
 Casa Buitoni Cheese
 & Basil Tortelloni,
 cooked, drained and
 rinsed
⅔ cup (7-ounce container)
 refrigerated
 CONTADINA® Pesto
 with Basil
½ cup chopped onion
3 cups (3 medium) thinly
 sliced red, orange,
 yellow or green bell
 peppers
⅓ cup apple cider vinegar
1 teaspoon dry mustard
¼ teaspoon salt
¼ teaspoon ground black
 pepper

SPOON oil from top of pesto
into large skillet; warm over
medium-high heat. Add onion;
cook 2 to 3 minutes or until
tender. Add bell peppers; cook
4 to 5 minutes or until peppers
are tender.

COMBINE pesto, vinegar,
mustard, salt and black pepper
in small bowl. Add pesto
mixture and tortelloni to bell
pepper mixture; cook 1 to 2
minutes or until heated
through.   *Makes 4 servings*

Santa Fe Chicken Pasta Salad

12 ounces uncooked spiral
 pasta
2 cups cooked chicken
 breast cubes
1 medium zucchini or
 yellow squash, cut in
 half lengthwise, then
 sliced crosswise
1 cup GUILTLESS
 GOURMET® Green
 Tomatillo Salsa
1 cup drained and
 coarsely chopped
 artichoke hearts
½ cup chopped green
 onions
½ cup sliced black olives
 Lettuce leaves
 Fresh dill sprigs
 (optional)

Cook pasta according to
package directions; drain.
Place pasta in large nonmetallic
bowl; add chicken, zucchini,
tomatillo salsa, artichoke
hearts, onions and olives. Toss
lightly. Refrigerate at least
6 hours before serving.

To serve, line serving platter
with lettuce leaves. Top with
pasta mixture. Garnish with
dill, if desired.

Makes 4 servings

Pasta, Chicken & Broccoli Pesto Toss

4 ounces (about 2 cups) uncooked vegetable spiral pasta
2 cups cubed cooked chicken or turkey breast meat
2 cups small broccoli florets, cooked crisp-tender, cooled
1½ cups (6 ounces) SARGENTO® Light Fancy Shredded Mozzarella Cheese
⅔ cup lightly packed fresh basil leaves
2 cloves garlic
1 cup mayonnaise
1 tablespoon lemon juice
½ teaspoon salt
½ cup (1½ ounces) SARGENTO® Fancy Shredded Parmesan Cheese
½ cup pine nuts or coarsely chopped walnuts, toasted

Cook pasta according to package directions until tender; drain and cool. Combine pasta, chicken, broccoli and mozzarella cheese in large bowl. Blend basil and garlic in covered blender or food processor until finely chopped. Add mayonnaise, lemon juice and salt. Blend to combine thoroughly. Stir in Parmesan cheese. Add to pasta mixture; toss to coat well. Stir in pine nuts. Serve immediately or cover and refrigerate. Remove from refrigerator and toss gently 30 minutes before serving. *Makes 8 servings*

Roast Beef and Pasta Salad

9 ounces uncooked radiatore pasta
6 ounces lean roast beef
1 can (15 ounces) kidney beans, rinsed
1 can (15 ounces) whole baby corn, rinsed
1 can (10 ounces) diced tomatoes and green chilies
1 cup cherry tomato halves
½ cup sliced ripe olives
2 tablespoons minced fresh parsley
1 tablespoon minced fresh oregano
¼ cup olive oil

1. Cook pasta according to package directions, omitting salt; drain. Rinse in cold water; drain.

2. Slice beef into thin strips. Combine pasta, beef and remaining ingredients in large bowl. Toss to coat. Garnish with fresh oregano, if desired.
Makes 6 servings

Roast Beef and Pasta Salad

Beef, Pork & Lamb

FEATURING:

Steaks & Chops

Roasts

Sausages & Ham

Stuffed Pork Tenderloin (page 144)

Beef & Broccoli Pepper Steak

- 1 tablespoon margarine or butter
- 1 pound well-trimmed top round steak, cut into thin strips
- 1 package (6.8 ounces) RICE-A-RONI® Beef Flavor
- 2 cups broccoli florets
- ½ cup red or green bell pepper strips
- 1 small onion, thinly sliced

1. In large skillet, melt margarine over medium heat. Add meat; sauté just until browned.

2. Remove from skillet; set aside. Keep warm.

3. In same skillet, prepare Rice-A-Roni® Mix as package directs; simmer 10 minutes. Add meat and remaining ingredients; simmer an additional 10 minutes or until most of liquid is absorbed and vegetables are crisp-tender.

Makes 4 servings

Marinated Flank Steak with Pineapple

- 1 can (15¼ ounces) DEL MONTE® Pineapple Slices In Its Own Juice, undrained
- ¼ cup teriyaki sauce
- 2 tablespoons honey
- 1 pound flank steak

1. Drain pineapple, reserving 2 tablespoons juice. Set aside pineapple for later use.

2. Combine reserved juice, teriyaki sauce and honey in shallow 2-quart dish; mix well. Add meat; turn to coat. Cover and refrigerate at least 30 minutes or overnight.

3. Remove meat from marinade, reserving marinade. Grill meat over hot coals (or broil), brushing occasionally with reserved marinade. Cook about 4 minutes on each side for rare; about 5 minutes on each side for medium; or about 6 minutes on each side for well done. During last 4 minutes of cooking, brush pineapple slices with marinade; grill until heated through.

4. Slice meat across grain; serve with pineapple. Garnish, if desired.   *Makes 4 servings*

Prep & Marinate Time: 35 minutes
Cook Time: 10 minutes

Note: Marinade that has come into contact with raw meat must be discarded or boiled for several minutes before serving with cooked food.

Gazpacho Steak Roll

- 1 (2-pound) beef flank steak, butterflied
- ⅔ cup A.1.® Steak Sauce, divided
- 1 cup (4 ounces) shredded Monterey Jack cheese
- ½ cup chopped tomato
- ⅓ cup chopped cucumber
- ¼ cup chopped green bell pepper
- 2 tablespoons sliced green onion

Open butterflied steak like a book on smooth surface and flatten slightly. Spread ⅓ cup steak sauce over surface. Layer remaining ingredients over sauce. Roll up steak from short edge; secure with toothpicks or tie with string if necessary.

Grill steak roll over medium heat 30 to 40 minutes or to desired doneness, turning and brushing often with remaining ⅓ cup steak sauce during last 10 minutes of cooking. Remove toothpicks; slice and serve garnished as desired.

Makes 8 servings

Beef & Broccoli Pepper Steak

Beef Kabobs with Apricot Glaze

1 can (15¼ ounces) DEL
  MONTE® Apricot
  Halves, undrained
1 tablespoon cornstarch
1 teaspoon Dijon mustard
½ teaspoon dried basil
  leaves
1 pound sirloin steak, cut
  into 1½-inch cubes
1 small green bell pepper,
  cut into ¾-inch pieces
4 medium mushrooms,
  cut in half
4 to 8 skewers

1. Drain apricot syrup into small saucepan. Blend in cornstarch until dissolved. Cook over medium heat, stirring constantly, until thickened. Stir in mustard and basil. Set aside.

2. Thread meat, apricots, bell pepper and mushrooms alternately onto skewers; brush with apricot syrup mixture. Grill kabobs over hot coals (or broil) about 5 minutes on each side or to desired doneness, brushing occasionally with additional syrup mixture. Garnish, if desired.

Makes 4 servings

Prep & Cook Time: 25 minutes

Tip: *To prevent burning of wooden skewers, soak skewers in water for 10 minutes before assembling kabobs.*

Beef Pot Roast

3 pounds beef eye of
  round roast
1 can (about 14 ounces)
  fat-free reduced-
  sodium beef broth
2 cloves garlic, peeled
1 teaspoon herbes de
  Provence *or*
  ¼ teaspoon *each* dried
    rosemary, thyme, sage
    and savory
4 small turnips, peeled
  and cut into wedges
10 ounces fresh brussels
  sprouts, trimmed
20 baby carrots
4 ounces pearl onions,
  outer skins removed
2 teaspoons cornstarch
  mixed with
  1 tablespoon water

1. Heat large nonstick skillet over medium-high heat. Place roast, fat side down, in skillet. Cook until evenly browned. Remove roast from skillet; place in Dutch oven.

2. Pour beef broth into Dutch oven; bring to a boil over high heat. Add garlic and herbes de Provence. Cover tightly. Reduce heat; cook 1½ hours.

3. Add turnips, brussels sprouts, carrots and onions to Dutch oven. Cover; cook 25 to 30 minutes or until vegetables are tender. Remove meat and vegetables from Dutch oven. Arrange on serving platter; cover with foil to keep warm.

4. Strain broth; return to Dutch oven. Stir cornstarch mixture into broth. Bring to a boil over medium-high heat; cook and stir 1 minute or until thick and bubbly. Serve immediately with pot roast and vegetables. Garnish as desired.

Makes 6 servings

The Original Baked Spam®

1 (12-ounce) can SPAM®
  Luncheon Meat
  Whole cloves
⅓ cup packed brown sugar
1 teaspoon water
1 teaspoon prepared
  mustard
½ teaspoon vinegar

Heat oven to 375°F. Place Spam® on rack in shallow baking pan. Score surface; stud with cloves. In small bowl, combine brown sugar, water, mustard and vinegar, stirring until smooth. Brush glaze over Spam®. Bake 20 minutes, basting often. Cut into slices to serve.

Makes 6 servings

Beef Kabobs with Apricot Glaze

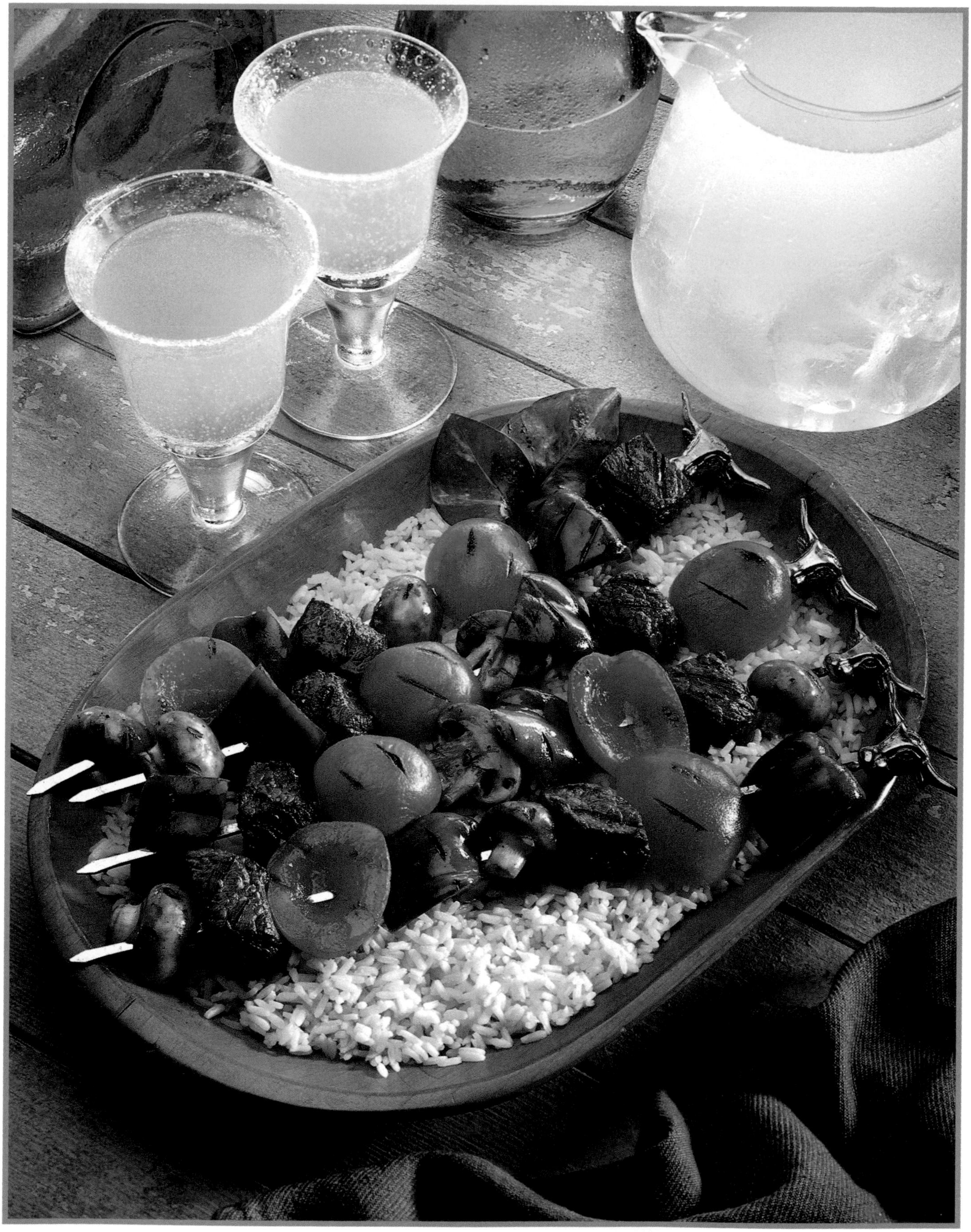

Blackened Steaks with Fresh Mango Salsa

1 mango, peeled, pitted and cut into ½-inch chunks (about 1½ cups)
½ cup chopped red onion
½ cup chopped fresh plum tomatoes
1 clove garlic, minced
1 tablespoon chopped fresh cilantro
⅓ cup A.1.® Thick & Hearty Steak Sauce
1 tablespoon paprika
1 teaspoon onion powder
1 teaspoon garlic powder
1 teaspoon ground red pepper
1 teaspoon ground black pepper
½ teaspoon dried thyme leaves
½ teaspoon dried oregano leaves
4 (4- to 6-ounce) beef top sirloin or strip steaks, about 1 inch thick

In medium bowl, combine mango, red onion, tomatoes, garlic and cilantro; stir in steak sauce. Cover; refrigerate at least 1 hour to blend flavors.

In small bowl, combine paprika, onion powder, garlic powder, peppers, thyme and oregano. Coat both sides of steaks with seasoning mixture, pressing firmly into steaks. In large skillet, over high heat, brown 2 steaks until underside looks blackened, about 2 to 3 minutes. Turn steaks and cook 2 to 3 minutes more or to desired doneness. Repeat with remaining steaks. Serve with chilled mango salsa. Garnish as desired. *Makes 4 servings*

Dijon Pesto Steak

½ cup finely chopped fresh basil or parsley
½ cup PLANTERS® Walnuts, finely chopped
⅓ cup GREY POUPON® Dijon Mustard
1 clove garlic, crushed
1 (2-pound) boneless sirloin or top round steak

In small bowl, combine basil, walnuts, mustard and garlic.

Broil steak 5 inches from heat source, about 10 minutes, turning once. Spread top of steak with basil mixture; broil 2 to 3 minutes more or until lightly browned and beef is cooked to desired doneness. Slice and serve.

Makes 6 to 8 servings

Rolled Teriyaki Steak

½ cup A.1.® Original or A.1.® Bold & Spicy Steak Sauce
⅓ cup teriyaki sauce
3 tablespoons GREY POUPON® Dijon Mustard
1 (1½-pound) beef flank steak, butterflied
½ cup coarsely chopped snow peas (about 2 ounces)
½ cup thinly sliced red bell pepper
4 green onions

In small bowl, combine steak sauce, teriyaki sauce and mustard. Open butterflied steak like a book on smooth surface and flatten slightly. Spread ¼ cup steak sauce mixture over surface. Arrange snow peas, pepper strips and green onions over sauce parallel to short edge of steak. Roll up steak from short edge; secure with wooden toothpicks or tie with string if necessary. Place, seam side down, in greased 13×9×2-inch baking pan. Top with remaining steak sauce mixture. Bake at 375°F 40 to 45 minutes or to desired doneness, basting every 15 minutes with sauce in pan. Remove toothpicks; let steak roll rest 10 minutes. Slice steak across grain. Serve immediately. Garnish as desired.

Makes 6 servings

Blackened Steak with Fresh Mango Salsa

Corned Beef with Horseradish Sauce

**1 HEBREW NATIONAL®
Pickled Corned Beef
(about 7 pounds)
1 pound fresh baby
carrots
5 to 6 new potatoes
1 pound fresh green
beans, trimmed
⅔ cup mayonnaise
3 tablespoons grated fresh
or prepared
horseradish
1 tablespoon fresh lemon
juice**

Preheat oven to 350°F. Place corned beef in large roasting pan; add water to cover. Cover; bake 2 hours.

Add carrots and potatoes to pan. Cover; bake 30 minutes. Add green beans to pan. Cover; bake 15 to 20 minutes or until corned beef and vegetables are fork-tender.

Combine mayonnaise, horseradish and lemon juice in small bowl. Cover; refrigerate until ready to serve.

Place corned beef on cutting board. Cut fat from corned beef; discard fat. Slice corned beef across the grain into ¼-inch-thick slices. Serve with vegetables and horseradish sauce for dipping.

Makes 8 servings

Feijoada Completa

**1½ pounds country-style
ribs or pork spareribs
1 corned beef
(1½ pounds)
½ pound smoked link
sausage, such as
Polish or andouille
½ pound fresh link
sausage, such as
bratwurst or breakfast
links
3 cups water
1 can (15½ ounces) black
beans, rinsed and
drained
1 cup chopped onion
4 cloves garlic, minced
1 jalapeño pepper,*
seeded and chopped
Chili-Lemon Sauce
(recipe follows)**

Slow Cooker Directions:
TRIM excess fat from ribs. Combine all ingredients except Chili-Lemon Sauce in slow cooker; stir to mix well. Cover and cook on LOW 7 to 8 hours or until meats are fork-tender. *Meanwhile,* prepare Chili-Lemon Sauce.

REMOVE meats to cutting board. Slice corned beef; place on large serving platter. Arrange remaining meats around corned beef. Cover and keep warm.

DRAIN liquid from beans, leaving just enough liquid so beans are moist. Transfer to serving bowl. Serve with Chili-Lemon Sauce.

Makes 10 to 12 servings

CHILI-LEMON SAUCE
**¾ cup lemon juice
1 small onion, coarsely
chopped
3 jalapeño peppers,*
seeded and chopped
3 cloves garlic, cut into
halves**

PLACE all ingredients in food processor or blender. Process until smooth. Serve at room temperature.

Makes about 1 cup

*Jalapeño peppers can sting and irritate the skin; wear rubber gloves when handling peppers and do not touch eyes.

Skillet Franks and Potatoes

- 3 **tablespoons vegetable oil, divided**
- 4 **HEBREW NATIONAL®️ Quarter Pound Dinner Beef Franks or Beef Knockwurst**
- 3 **cups chopped cooked red potatoes**
- 1 **cup chopped onion**
- 1 **cup chopped seeded green bell pepper or combination of green and red bell peppers**
- 3 **tablespoons chopped fresh parsley (optional)**
- 1 **teaspoon dried sage leaves**
- ½ **teaspoon salt**
- ¼ **teaspoon freshly ground black pepper**

Heat 1 tablespoon oil in large nonstick skillet over medium heat. Score franks; add to skillet. Cook franks until browned. Transfer to plate; set aside.

Add remaining 2 tablespoons oil to skillet. Add potatoes, onion and bell pepper; cook and stir 12 to 14 minutes or until potatoes are golden brown. Stir in parsley, if desired, sage, salt and black pepper.

Return franks to skillet; push down into potato mixture. Cook about 5 minutes or until heated through, turning once halfway through cooking time.

Makes 4 servings

Spicy Pot Roast

- 2 **tablespoons vegetable oil, divided**
- 4 **pounds chuck or beef rump roast**
- 2 **tablespoons all-purpose flour**
- 1 **tablespoon chili powder**
- 1½ **cups (two 8-ounce jars) ORTEGA®️ Thick & Smooth Taco Sauce, hot, medium or mild**
- ½ **cup beef broth**

HEAT 1 tablespoon oil in large saucepan over medium-high heat. Add roast; cook 4 to 5 minutes or until brown on all sides. Remove from saucepan; set aside.

HEAT remaining 1 tablespoon oil in same saucepan. Add flour and chili powder; cook 30 seconds. Add taco sauce and beef broth. Bring to a boil; reduce heat to low. Add roast to sauce. Cover; cook, stirring occasionally, 1½ to 2 hours or until roast is of desired doneness. Serve with sauce.

Makes 6 to 8 servings

Tip: Shred cooked roast with a fork and use as a meat filling for tacos, burritos or tamales.

Corned Beef with Horseradish Sauce (page 130)

Peppered Beef Tenderloin Roast

1 (3- to 4-pound) beef tenderloin, fat trimmed
5 cloves garlic, finely chopped
2 tablespoons finely chopped fresh rosemary
1 tablespoon green peppercorns in brine, drained and finely chopped
1 teaspoon salt
1 teaspoon freshly ground black pepper
2 tablespoons olive or vegetable oil
1¼ cups beef stock

Place beef on sheet of plastic wrap. Combine remaining ingredients except oil and beef stock; rub over roast. Wrap tightly and refrigerate at least 4 hours, but no longer than 48 hours. Return to room temperature before cooking. Preheat oven to 425°F. In large ovenproof skillet or roasting pan, heat oil over medium-high heat. Place roast in skillet; brown on all sides (about 4 minutes per side). Carefully lift roast with large carving fork and place roasting rack in skillet; place roast on rack. *Do not cover.* Insert meat thermometer into thickest part of roast. Roast until meat thermometer registers 155°F. (Roasts will usually increase about 5°F after removal from oven.) Remove to cutting board and let rest in warm place 15 minutes before carving.

Place skillet with pan drippings over high heat until hot. Stir in beef stock. Cook, stirring occasionally, until reduced to about ¾ cup. Strain and serve in sauce pitcher.

Makes 10 to 12 servings

FAVORITE RECIPE FROM **CALIFORNIA BEEF COUNCIL**

Herb-Crusted Roast Beef and Potatoes

1 (4½-pound) eye of round or sirloin tip beef roast
¾ cup plus 2 tablespoons FILIPPO BERIO® Olive Oil, divided
Salt and freshly ground black pepper
2 tablespoons paprika
2 pounds small red skin potatoes, cut into halves
1 cup dry bread crumbs
1 teaspoon dried thyme leaves
1 teaspoon dried rosemary
½ teaspoon salt
¼ teaspoon freshly ground black pepper

Preheat oven to 325°F. Brush roast with 2 tablespoons olive oil. Season to taste with salt and pepper. Place in large roasting pan; insert meat thermometer into center of thickest part of roast. Roast 45 minutes.

Meanwhile, in large bowl, combine ½ cup olive oil and paprika. Add potatoes; toss until lightly coated. In small bowl, combine bread crumbs, thyme, rosemary, ½ teaspoon salt, ¼ teaspoon pepper and remaining ¼ cup olive oil.

Carefully remove roast from oven. Place potatoes around roast. Press bread crumb mixture onto top of roast to form crust. Sprinkle any remaining bread crumb mixture over potatoes. Roast an additional 40 to 45 minutes or until meat thermometer registers 145°F for medium-rare or until desired doneness is reached. Transfer roast to carving board; tent with foil. Let stand 5 to 10 minutes before carving. Cut into ¼-inch-thick slices. Serve immediately with potatoes, spooning any remaining bread crumb mixture from roasting pan onto meat.

Makes 8 servings

Peppered Beef Tenderloin Roast

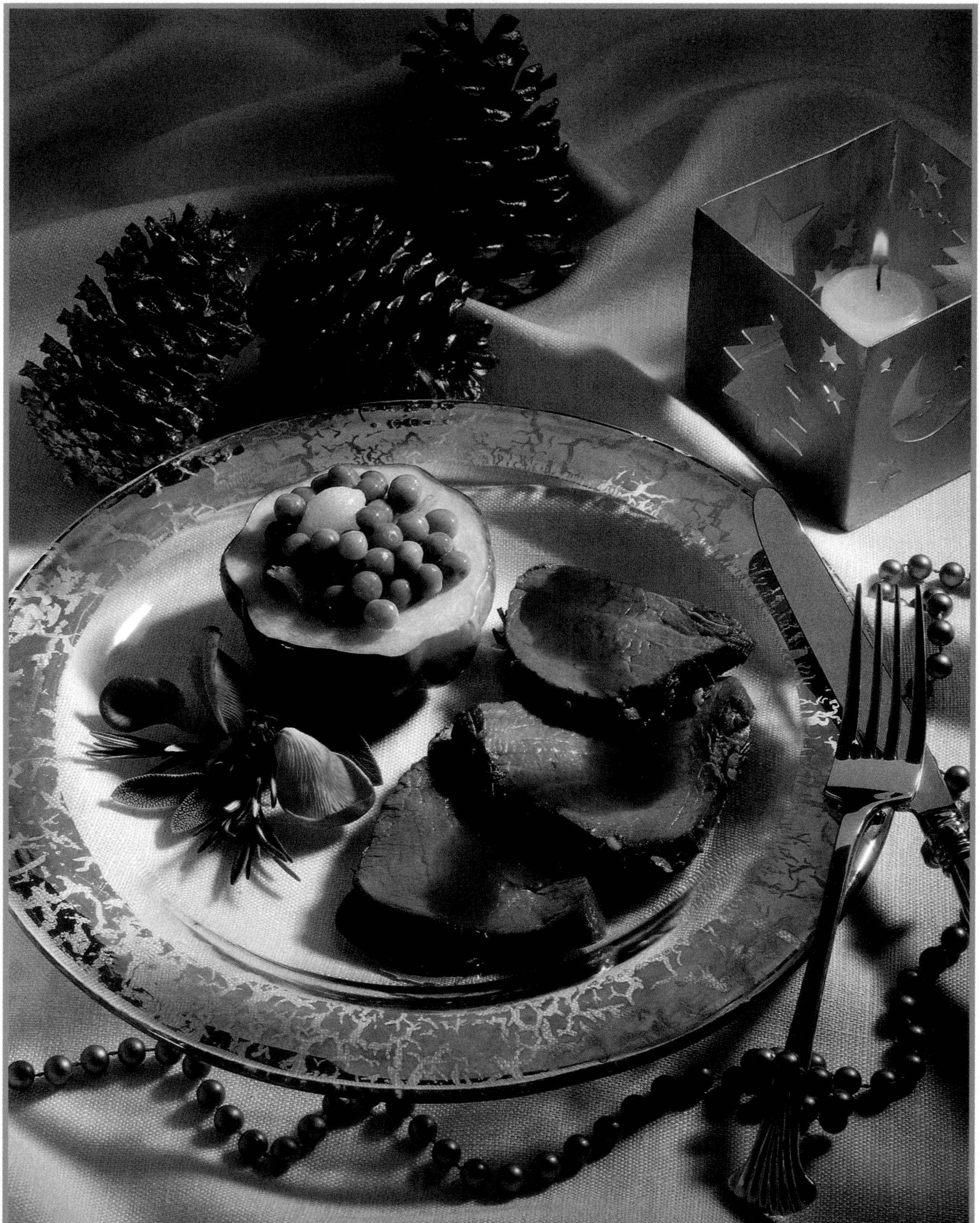

Ratatouille Smothered Steak

- 1 cup chopped eggplant
- 1 cup chopped yellow and/or green bell peppers
- 1 clove garlic, minced
- 2 tablespoons olive oil
- 1 cup chopped fresh tomatoes
- ½ cup A.1.® Thick & Hearty Steak Sauce
- ½ teaspoon dried basil leaves
- 1 (1-pound) beef top round steak, about ¾ inch thick
  Additional A.1.® Thick & Hearty Steak Sauce (optional)

In large skillet, over medium heat, sauté eggplant, peppers and garlic in oil until tender, about 5 minutes. Stir in tomatoes, ½ cup steak sauce and basil; heat to a boil. Reduce heat; simmer 5 minutes. Keep warm.

Grill steak over medium heat or broil 6 inches from heat source 6 minutes on each side or to desired doneness, basting with additional steak sauce, if desired. Slice steak; serve with warm sauce. Garnish as desired.   *Makes 4 servings*

Tournedos with Mushroom Wine Sauce Dijon

- ¼ cup chopped shallots
- 2 tablespoons margarine or butter
- 1 cup small mushrooms, cut into halves (about 4 ounces)
- ¼ cup GREY POUPON® Dijon Mustard, divided
- 2 tablespoons A.1.® Steak Sauce
- 2 tablespoons Burgundy wine
- 1 tablespoon chopped parsley
- 4 slices bacon
- 4 (4-ounce) beef tenderloin steaks (tournedos), about 1 inch thick
- ¼ teaspoon coarsely ground black pepper

In small saucepan, over medium heat, sauté shallots in margarine until tender. Add mushrooms; sauté 1 minute. Stir in 2 tablespoons mustard, steak sauce, wine and parsley; heat to a boil. Reduce heat and simmer 5 minutes; keep warm.

Wrap bacon slice around edge of each steak; secure with toothpicks. Coat steaks with remaining mustard; sprinkle with pepper. Grill steaks over medium heat 10 to 12 minutes or to desired doneness, turning occasionally. Remove toothpicks; serve steaks topped with warm mushroom sauce.
Makes 4 servings

Spinach Meatloaf Dijon

- 1½ pounds lean ground beef
- ¾ cup plain dry bread crumbs
- ½ cup GREY POUPON® Dijon Mustard, divided
- 2 eggs
- 1 (10-ounce) package frozen chopped spinach, thawed and well drained
- 1 cup shredded Swiss cheese (4 ounces)
- ½ cup minced onion
- 2 teaspoons chopped fresh dill
- 1 teaspoon coarsely ground black pepper
- 1 clove garlic, minced
- 2 tablespoons honey

In large bowl, combine ground beef, bread crumbs, 5 tablespoons mustard, eggs, spinach, cheese, onion, dill, pepper and garlic. Shape mixture into 9×5-inch loaf; place in greased 13×9×2-inch baking pan. Bake at 350°F for 60 to 70 minutes or until done. Blend remaining mustard and honey; brush on meatloaf during last 10 minutes of baking time. Remove from oven and let stand 10 minutes. Slice and serve.
Makes 6 to 8 servings

Ratatouille Smothered Steak

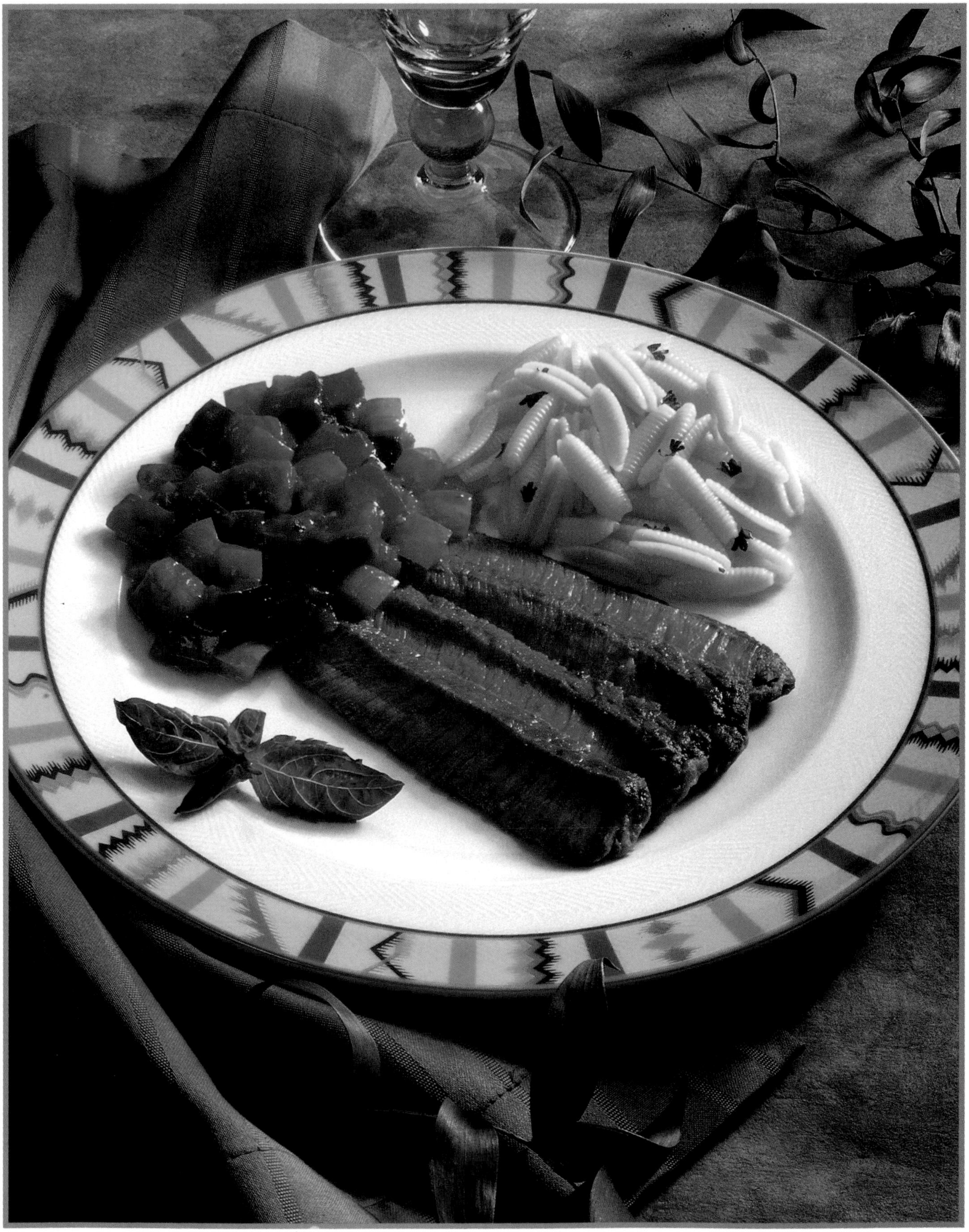

Saltimbocca

4 boneless thin veal slices
cut from the leg, or
thinly sliced veal
cutlets (about
1¼ pounds)
1 tablespoon FILIPPO
BERIO® Olive Oil
1 clove garlic, cut into
halves
4 slices prosciutto, cut
into halves
8 fresh sage leaves*
½ cup beef broth
5 tablespoons Marsala
wine or medium
sherry
¼ cup half-and-half
Freshly ground black
pepper

*Omit sage if fresh sage is
unavailable. Do not substitute
dried sage leaves.*

Pound veal between 2 pieces
waxed paper with flat side of
meat mallet or rolling pin until
very thin. Cut each piece in
half to make 8 small pieces. In
large skillet, heat olive oil and
garlic over medium heat until
hot. Add veal; cook until
brown, turning occasionally.
Top each piece with slice of
prosciutto and sage leaf. Add
beef broth and Marsala. Cover;
reduce heat to low and simmer
5 minutes or until veal is
cooked through and tender.
Transfer veal to warm serving
platter; keep warm. Add half-
and-half to mixture in skillet;
simmer 5 to 8 minutes, stirring

occasionally, until liquid is
reduced and thickened,
scraping bottom of skillet to
loosen browned bits. Remove
garlic. Spoon sauce over veal.
Season to taste with pepper.

Makes 4 servings

Veal Parmesan

¼ cup egg substitute *or*
1 large egg
1 large egg white
1 tablespoon water
¾ cup seasoned dry bread
crumbs
¼ cup (1 ounce) shredded
ALPINE LACE® Fat
Free Pasteurized
Process Skim Milk
Cheese Product—For
Parmesan Lovers
6 veal cutlets (3 ounces
each), pounded thin
2 tablespoons unsalted
butter substitute,
divided
½ cup chopped yellow
onion
2 teaspoons minced garlic
1 can (28 ounces) crushed
tomatoes, undrained
½ cup slivered fresh basil
leaves
½ teaspoon freshly ground
black pepper
2 cups (8 ounces)
shredded ALPINE
LACE® Reduced Fat
Low Moisture
Mozzarella Cheese
¼ cup finely chopped fresh
parsley

1. Preheat the oven to 425°F.
Spray a 13×9-inch baking dish
and a large nonstick skillet
with nonstick cooking spray.

2. In a pie plate, whisk the egg
substitute (or the whole egg)
with the egg white and water
until foamy. On a separate
plate, toss the bread crumbs
with the Parmesan. Dip the veal
into the egg mixture, letting
the excess drip off, then coat
with the bread crumb mixture.

3. In the skillet, melt 1
tablespoon of the butter over
medium-high heat. Sauté the
veal for 2 minutes on each side
or until golden brown, turning
once. Using a slotted spatula,
transfer to a plate.

4. In the same skillet, melt the
remaining tablespoon of butter;
add the onion and garlic and
sauté 5 minutes. Stir in the
tomatoes and their juices, the
basil and pepper. Lower the
heat; simmer, uncovered, for
5 minutes.

5. Spread half of the sauce in
the baking dish. Top with the
veal, then the remaining sauce
and the mozzarella. Bake,
uncovered, 10 minutes or until
bubbly. Sprinkle with the
parsley and serve hot.

Makes 6 servings

Saltimbocca

Lamb in Dill Sauce

2 large boiling potatoes, peeled and cut into 1-inch cubes
½ cup chopped onion
1½ teaspoons salt
½ teaspoon black pepper
½ teaspoon dried dill weed *or* 4 sprigs fresh dill
1 bay leaf
2 pounds lean lamb stew meat, cut into 1-inch cubes
1 cup plus 3 tablespoons water, divided
2 tablespoons all-purpose flour
1 teaspoon sugar
2 tablespoons lemon juice Fresh dill (optional)

Slow Cooker Directions:
LAYER ingredients in slow cooker in the following order: potatoes, onion, salt, pepper, dill, bay leaf, lamb and 1 cup water. Cover and cook on LOW 6 to 8 hours.

REMOVE lamb and potatoes with slotted spoon; cover and keep warm. Remove and discard bay leaf. Turn heat to HIGH. Stir flour and remaining 3 tablespoons water in small bowl until smooth. Add half of cooking juices from slow cooker and sugar. Mix well and return to slow cooker. Cover and cook 15 minutes. Stir in lemon juice. Return lamb and potatoes to slow cooker. Cover and cook 10 minutes or until heated through. Garnish with fresh dill, if desired.

Makes 6 servings

Lamb Chops with Parmesan-Herb Stuffing

LAMB CHOPS
8 loin lamb chops with bone (5 to 6 ounces each), cut 1 inch thick, well trimmed
½ cup dry red wine (with or without alcohol)

PARMESAN–HERB STUFFING
1 cup (4 ounces) grated ALPINE LACE® Fat Free Pasteurized Process Skim Milk Cheese Product—For Parmesan Lovers
½ cup fresh basil leaves, firmly packed
½ cup fresh mint leaves, firmly packed
½ cup fresh watercress leaves, firmly packed
2 tablespoons olive oil
1 tablespoon whole-grain Dijon mustard
2 large cloves garlic
1 tablespoon snipped fresh rosemary leaves *or* 1 teaspoon dried rosemary
½ teaspoon salt
½ teaspoon freshly ground black pepper

1. Preheat the grill or broiler and broiler pan. Lay each chop flat on a board; cut from the outer edge toward the bone, making a deep pocket.

2. To marinate the Lamb Chops: Place the chops in a single layer in a large shallow dish. Pour the wine over the chops; let stand at room temperature for 15 minutes, turning once. Drain the marinade into a small saucepan and bring to a boil over high heat. Meanwhile, prepare the Parmesan-Herb Stuffing: In a food processor or blender, place all ingredients for the stuffing. Process for 2 minutes or until blended.

3. Stuff the herb mixture into the pocket of each chop and close the opening with toothpicks. Grill or broil the chops 4 inches from the heat, basting frequently with the hot marinade, for about 4 minutes per side for medium doneness. Serve hot!   *Makes 8 servings*

Lamb in Dill Sauce

Mushroom Sausage Spinach Strudel

½ pound BOB EVANS FARMS® Original Recipe Roll Sausage
3 tablespoons olive oil
1 small onion, chopped
¼ pound fresh mushrooms, sliced
¼ cup chopped red bell pepper
1 clove garlic, minced
½ pound fresh spinach, washed, torn into small pieces and drained
¼ cup (1 ounce) shredded Swiss cheese
Salt and black pepper to taste
4 sheets phyllo dough, thawed according to package directions
¼ cup butter or margarine, melted
3 tablespoons dry bread crumbs
Fresh thyme sprig and red pepper strips (optional)

Crumble sausage into medium skillet. Cook over medium-high heat until browned, stirring occasionally. Drain off any drippings. Remove sausage to paper towels; set aside. Heat oil in same skillet until hot. Add onion, mushrooms, chopped bell pepper and garlic; cook and stir until vegetables are soft. Stir in sausage, spinach, cheese, salt and black pepper; cook until vegetables are tender. Set aside until cool.

Preheat oven to 375°F. Place 1 phyllo sheet on work surface. Brush entire sheet with some melted butter and sprinkle with ¼ of bread crumbs. (To keep remaining sheets from drying out, cover with damp kitchen towel.) Repeat layers three times. Spread sausage mixture over top; roll up, starting at one short side, until roll forms. Place on ungreased baking sheet. Brush with remaining butter; bake 15 minutes or until golden. Let stand 5 minutes. Cut into 1-inch slices. Garnish with thyme and red pepper strips, if desired. Serve hot. Refrigerate leftovers.

Makes 4 to 6 servings

Sausage-Chicken Creole

1 can (14½ ounces) whole tomatoes, undrained and cut up
½ cup uncooked rice
½ cup hot water
2 teaspoons FRANK'S® Original REDHOT® Cayenne Pepper Sauce
¼ teaspoon garlic powder
¼ teaspoon dried oregano
1 bag (16 ounces) frozen vegetable combination (broccoli, corn, red pepper), thawed and drained
1⅓ cups (2.8 ounce can) FRENCH'S® French Fried Onions, divided
4 chicken thighs, skinned
½ pound link Italian sausage, quartered and cooked*
1 can (8 ounces) tomato sauce

*To cook sausage, simmer in water to cover until done. Or, place in microwave-safe dish and cook, covered, at HIGH 3 minutes or until done.

Preheat oven to 375°F. In 12×8-inch baking dish, combine tomatoes, rice, hot water, RedHot® sauce and seasonings. Bake, covered, 10 minutes. Stir vegetables and ⅔ cup French Fried Onions into rice mixture; top with chicken and cooked sausage. Pour tomato sauce over chicken and sausage. Bake, covered, 40 minutes or until chicken is done. Top chicken with remaining ⅔ cup onions; bake, uncovered, 3 minutes or until onions are golden brown.

Makes 4 servings

Mushroom Sausage Spinach Strudel

Stuffed Green Peppers

**6 medium to large green
    bell peppers**
**1 pound BOB EVANS
    FARMS® Original
    Recipe Roll Sausage**
2 cups tomato sauce
2 cups water
1 small onion, chopped
**1 cup uncooked rice
    Sliced green onion
    (optional)**

Preheat oven to 350°F. Slice off
tops from peppers; scrape out
centers to remove seeds and
membranes. Combine all
remaining ingredients except
green onion in medium bowl;
mix well. Evenly stuff peppers
with sausage mixture. Place in
lightly greased deep 3-quart
casserole. Bake, covered,
20 minutes. Uncover; bake
5 to 10 minutes more or until
peppers are fork-tender and
filling is set. Garnish with green
onion, if desired. Serve hot.
Refrigerate leftovers.

Makes 6 servings

Tip: *For a pretty presentation,
slice 6 small peppers lengthwise
in half through stem; scrape out
centers to remove seeds and
membranes. Proceed as directed,
serving 2 halves to each guest.*

**SERVING SUGGESTION: SERVE WITH
MIXED SALAD OF CARROT, RADISH
AND CUCUMBER SLICES DRIZZLED
WITH A VINAIGRETTE.**

Ham Stroganoff

**12 ounces uncooked yolk-
    free egg noodles**
**1 teaspoon poppy seeds
    (optional)**
**2 tablespoons unsalted
    butter or margarine,
    divided**
**1 pound ALPINE LACE®
    Boneless Cooked
    Ham, cut into
    3×½×½-inch strips**
**8 ounces mushrooms,
    sliced ¼ inch thick
    (2½ cups)**
**½ cup finely chopped
    green onions**
**¾ cup low-sodium chicken
    broth**
**6 ounces (1 carton)
    ALPINE LACE® Fat
    Free Cream Cheese
    with Garlic & Herbs**
**¼ teaspoon freshly ground
    black pepper**
1 cup sour half-and-half
**1 tablespoon snipped
    fresh dill *or*
    1 teaspoon dill weed**

1. Cook the noodles according
to package directions. Toss
with the poppy seeds, if you
wish; keep hot.

2. Meanwhile, in a 12-inch
nonstick skillet, melt 1
tablespoon of the butter over
medium-high heat. Sauté the
ham for 7 minutes or until
brown. Transfer to a warm
platter. Melt the remaining
tablespoon butter in the same
skillet. Stir in the mushrooms
and onions and sauté 5 minutes
or until tender. Meanwhile, in a
small saucepan, bring the broth
to a boil over high heat. Add
the cheese and pepper and stir
until melted.

3. Stir the broth-cheese
mixture into the mushroom
mixture, stirring to scrape up
any browned bits. Bring to a
boil and simmer for 1 minute.
Reduce heat to medium.

4. Whisk in the sour half-and-
half until smooth. Stir in the
ham, any juices that have
collected on the platter and
dill. Heat 3 minutes or until
hot. (Do not let boil!) Serve
immediately over the hot
noodles.   *Makes 6 servings*

Honey Glazed Ham

**2 (8-ounce) fully cooked
    ham steaks**
¼ cup honey
3 tablespoons water
1½ teaspoons dry mustard
½ teaspoon ground ginger
¼ teaspoon ground cloves

Pan-fry or broil ham steaks
until lightly browned and
thoroughly heated. Remove
ham from skillet or broiler pan.
Combine honey, water and
spices; add to pan drippings
and bring to a boil. Simmer
1 to 2 minutes. Brush over
ham. Serve ham with remaining
sauce.   *Makes 4 servings*

*FAVORITE RECIPE FROM **NATIONAL
HONEY BOARD***

Stuffed Green Pepper

Pork Chops in Creamy Garlic Sauce

1 cup fat-free reduced-sodium chicken broth
¼ cup garlic cloves, peeled and crushed (about 12 to 15)
½ teaspoon olive oil
4 boneless pork loin chops, about ¼ inch thick
1 tablespoon minced fresh parsley
½ teaspoon dried tarragon leaves
¼ teaspoon salt
¼ teaspoon black pepper
1 tablespoon all-purpose flour
2 tablespoons water
1 tablespoon dry sherry
2 cups cooked white rice

1. Place chicken broth and garlic in small saucepan. Bring to a boil over high heat. Cover; reduce heat to low. Simmer 25 to 30 minutes or until garlic mashes easily with fork. Set aside to cool. Purée until smooth in blender or food processor.

2. Heat oil in large nonstick skillet over medium-high heat. Add pork; cook 1 to 1½ minutes on each side or until browned. Pour garlic purée into skillet. Sprinkle with parsley, tarragon, salt and pepper. Bring to a boil; cover. Reduce heat to low; simmer 10 to 15 minutes or until pork is juicy and barely pink in center. Remove pork from skillet; keep warm.

3. Combine flour and water in small cup. Slowly pour flour mixture into skillet; bring to a boil. Cook and stir until mixture thickens. Stir in sherry. Serve sauce over pork and rice. Garnish as desired.

Makes 4 servings

Stuffed Pork Tenderloin

2 teaspoons minced garlic
2 teaspoons snipped fresh rosemary leaves *or* ½ teaspoon dried rosemary
2 teaspoons snipped fresh thyme leaves *or* ½ teaspoon dried thyme
1 teaspoon salt
½ teaspoon freshly ground black pepper
1 boneless end-cut rolled pork loin with tenderloin attached (4 pounds), tied
1 tablespoon unsalted butter substitute
1 cup thin strips yellow onion
2 large tart apples, peeled, cored and thinly sliced (2 cups)
10 thin slices (½ ounce each) ALPINE LACE® Reduced Fat Swiss Cheese
1 cup apple cider or apple juice

1. Preheat the oven to 325°F. Fit a 13×9×3-inch baking pan with a rack. In a small bowl, combine the garlic, rosemary, thyme, salt and pepper. Untie and unroll the pork loin, laying it flat. Rub half of the spice mixture onto the pork.

2. In a medium-size skillet, melt the butter over medium-high heat. Add the onion and apples and sauté for 5 minutes or until soft. Spread this mixture evenly on the pork and cover with the cheese slices.

3. Starting from one of the widest ends, re-roll the pork, jelly-roll style. Tie the roast with cotton string at 1-inch intervals and rub the outside with the remaining spice mixture. Place the roast on the rack in the pan and pour the apple cider over it.

4. Roast, uncovered, basting frequently with the pan drippings, for 2 to 2½ hours or until an instant-read thermometer inserted in the thickest part registers 160°F. Let the roast stand for 15 minutes before slicing.

Makes 16 servings

Pork Chops in Creamy Garlic Sauce

Fruited Boneless Pork Loin

- 1 cup pitted prunes
- 1 cup dried apricots
- 1 (3-pound) boneless pork loin roast
- 1 clove garlic, cut into thin strips
- 3 tablespoons FILIPPO BERIO® Olive Oil, divided
  Salt and freshly ground black pepper
- 2 onions, each cut into 6 wedges
- 2 tart apples (such as Granny Smith), peeled, cored and each cut into 8 wedges
- 8 fresh sage leaves, chopped*
- 1 tablespoon lime or lemon juice
- 1 cup plus 2 tablespoons chicken broth, divided
- 3 tablespoons all-purpose flour
- 1/4 cup Madeira wine

Omit sage if fresh sage is unavailable. Do not substitute dried sage leaves.

Cover prunes and apricots with cold water; soak at least 2 hours or overnight. Drain, reserving liquid. Preheat oven to 400°F. With tip of sharp knife, cut slashes at 1-inch intervals in pork. Insert garlic into scored pork flesh. Place pork in large shallow roasting pan; insert meat thermometer into center of thickest part of pork. Drizzle pork with 2 tablespoons olive oil; season with salt and pepper. Roast 1 hour.

Add onions, apples and sage to fruit mixture. Drizzle with lime juice. Spoon around pork in roasting pan; baste pork with juices and remaining 1 tablespoon olive oil. Pour 2 tablespoons chicken broth over pork. Roast 30 to 40 minutes or until meat thermometer registers 160°F, turning and basting fruit mixture frequently with juices. Transfer pork to warm serving platter. Surround with fruit mixture; keep warm. Pour drippings from roasting pan into measuring cup; skim off fat. Return juices to roasting pan. In roasting pan over medium heat, gradually stir flour into juices until smooth. Cook and stir 1 minute. Add remaining 1 cup broth, 1/2 cup reserved prune-apricot liquid and Madeira. Bring to a boil, stirring frequently. Reduce heat to low; simmer 5 minutes. Season to taste with additional salt and pepper. Serve hot with pork and fruit mixture. Carve pork into thin slices.

Makes 4 to 6 servings

Herbed Tomato Pork Chops and Stuffing

- 1 tablespoon vegetable oil
- 4 pork chops, 1/2 inch thick
- 1 can (8 ounces) stewed tomatoes
- 1 can (8 ounces) tomato sauce
- 1 medium green bell pepper, chopped
- 1/2 teaspoon dried oregano leaves
- 1/4 teaspoon ground black pepper
- 2 cups STOVE TOP® Stuffing Mix for Chicken in the Canister
- 1 cup (4 ounces) shredded mozzarella cheese, divided

HEAT oil in large skillet over medium-high heat. Add chops; brown on both sides.

STIR in tomatoes, tomato sauce, bell pepper, oregano and black pepper. Bring to a boil. Reduce heat to low; cover and simmer 15 minutes or until chops are cooked through. Remove chops from skillet.

STIR stuffing mix and 1/2 cup cheese into skillet. Return chops to skillet. Sprinkle with remaining 1/2 cup cheese; cover. Remove from heat. Let stand 5 minutes.   *Makes 4 servings*

Prep Time: 5 minutes
Cook Time: 25 minutes

Fruited Boneless Pork Loin

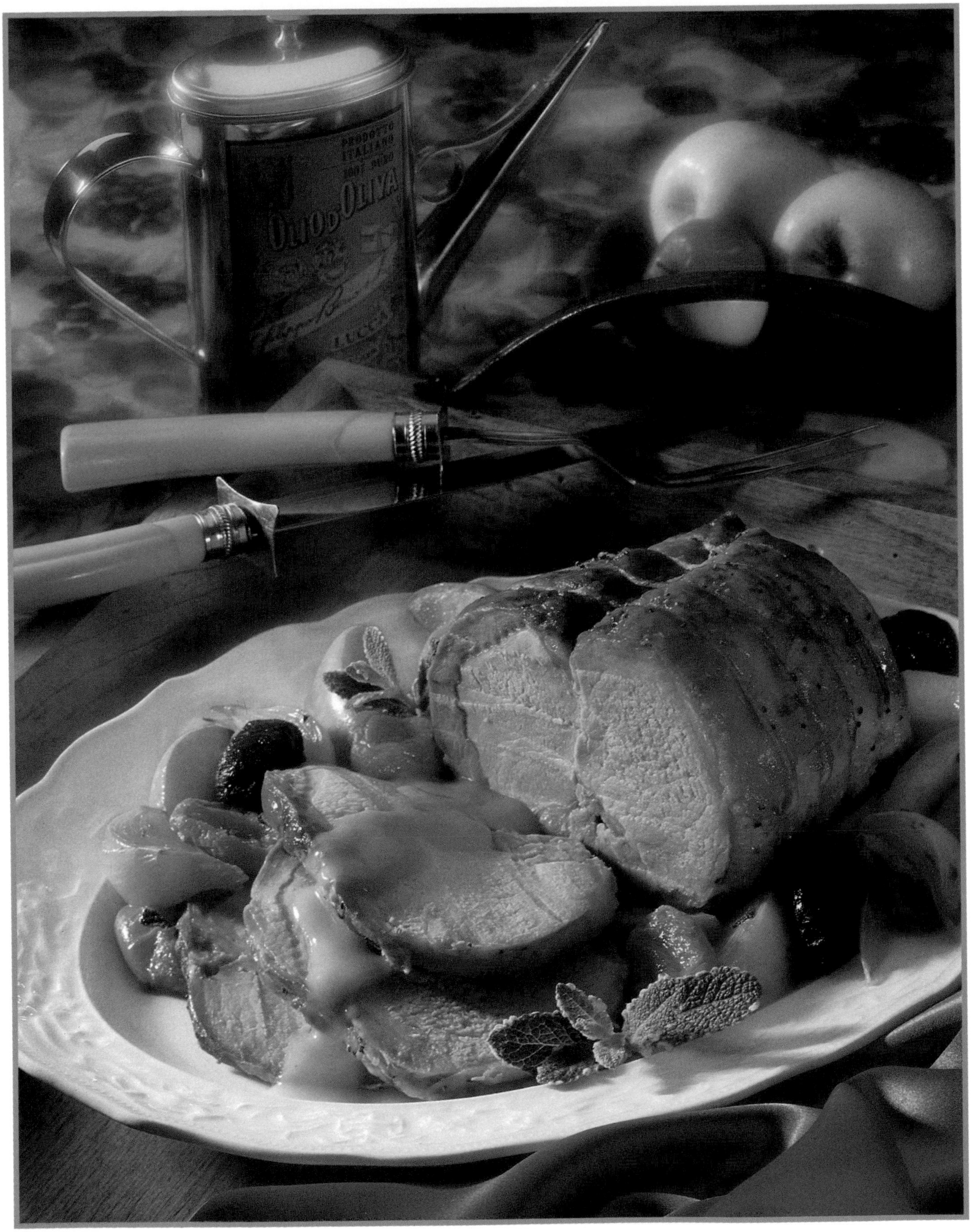
PRODOTTO
ITALIANO
OLIO D'OLIVA

Stuffed Pork Tenderloin with Cilantro-Lime Pesto

1 to 1½ pounds pork tenderloin
3 large cloves garlic, peeled
½ onion, cut into chunks
½ cup lightly packed fresh cilantro
2 tablespoons lime juice
1 teaspoon ORTEGA® Diced Jalapeños
2 tablespoons corn oil
½ cup (2 ounces) shredded Monterey Jack or crumbled Cotija cheese
ORTEGA® Green Chile Picante Sauce, mild

CUT tenderloin lengthwise almost in half. Open; lay flat between two pieces of waxed paper. Pound with meat mallet or rolling pin to ½-inch thickness.

PLACE garlic, onion, cilantro, lime juice and jalapeños in food processor or blender container; cover. Process until coarsely chopped. Process, while slowly adding oil, 10 to 15 seconds or until mixture is almost smooth. Spread half of cilantro mixture over tenderloin; top with cheese. Roll up; tie with cotton string. Spread remaining cilantro mixture over top. Place on rack in roasting pan.

BAKE in preheated 400°F oven 55 to 60 minutes or until internal temperature of 170°F is reached. Cool in pan on wire rack 5 minutes. Remove string; slice. Serve with picante sauce.
Makes 4 servings

Tip: Ladle ORTEGA® Thick & Chunky Salsa onto bottom of plate and top with tenderloin slices for a fantastic presentation!

Spareribs with Tex-Mex Barbecue Sauce

6 pounds pork spareribs, cut into 2-rib portions
½ cup HELLMANN'S® or BEST FOODS® Real or Light Mayonnaise
½ cup ketchup
¼ cup Worcestershire sauce
3 tablespoons chili powder
1 clove garlic, minced or pressed
⅛ teaspoon hot pepper sauce

1. In large shallow roasting pan, arrange ribs in single layer on rack. Roast in 325°F oven 1½ hours or until tender.

2. Meanwhile, prepare Tex-Mex Barbecue Sauce. Using wire whisk, combine mayonnaise, ketchup, Worcestershire sauce, chili powder, garlic and pepper sauce in small bowl until smooth.

3. Brush sauce on ribs, turning frequently, during last 20 minutes of roasting time.
Makes 6 servings

HOMESTYLE BARBECUE SAUCE: Follow recipe for Tex-Mex Barbecue Sauce, omitting chili powder and garlic and adding ¼ cup prepared mustard and ¼ cup KARO® Dark Corn Syrup or ¼ cup firmly packed brown sugar in step 2.

SWEET AND SOUR BARBECUE SAUCE: Follow recipe for Tex-Mex Barbecue Sauce, omitting Worcestershire, chili powder, garlic and pepper sauce and adding ¾ cup apricot preserves, ¼ cup soy sauce and 1 teaspoon ground ginger in step 2.

Welsh Pork Pasties

¼ cup margarine
½ pound ½-inch pork cubes
½ cup finely chopped onion
1 teaspoon dried thyme
½ teaspoon salt
¼ teaspoon black pepper
¼ cup all-purpose flour
1 can (about 14 ounces) chicken broth
1 (15-ounce) can VEG-ALL® Mixed Vegetables, drained
2 (9-inch) refrigerated pie crusts
1 egg beaten with 2 tablespoons milk

1. Heat margarine in large skillet over medium-high heat; add pork and onion. Cook and stir 15 minutes or until pork is barely pink in center.

2. Add thyme, salt and black pepper. Sprinkle flour over meat mixture; cook and stir until brown. Add chicken broth. Blend until thickened and well combined.

3. Add Veg-All® vegetables. Blend well. Remove from heat; refrigerate until chilled.

4. Preheat oven to 400°F. Cut pie crusts in half. Place ½ cup filling on each half circle. Fold in half and seal; crimp each pastie with decorative edge.

5. Brush with egg mixture and pierce tops with fork. Bake about 20 minutes or until golden. Serve immediately.

Makes 4 servings

Honey Sesame Tenderloin

1 pound whole pork tenderloin
½ cup soy sauce
2 cloves garlic, minced
1 tablespoon grated fresh ginger
1 tablespoon sesame oil
¼ cup honey
2 tablespoons packed brown sugar
4 tablespoons sesame seeds

Combine soy sauce, garlic, ginger and sesame oil. Place tenderloin in resealable plastic food storage bag; pour in soy sauce mixture. Marinate 2 hours or overnight in refrigerator. Preheat oven to 375°F. Remove pork from marinade; pat dry with paper towel. Mix honey and brown sugar on plate. Place sesame seeds on another plate. Roll pork in honey mixture, then in sesame seeds. Roast in shallow pan 20 to 30 minutes or until meat thermometer inserted into thickest part registers 160°F. Serve immediately.

Makes 4 servings

*FAVORITE RECIPE FROM **NATIONAL PORK PRODUCERS COUNCIL***

Stuffed Pork Tenderloin with Cilantro-Lime Pesto (page 148)

Poultry

FEATURING:

Whole & Cut-Up Chicken

Turkey Dishes

Cornish Hens & Capon

Roasted Chicken with Maple Glaze (page 160)

151

Chicken and Asparagus Hollandaise

1 package (1¼ ounces) hollandaise sauce mix
1 pound boneless chicken breasts, cut into strips
2 teaspoons lemon juice
1 box (10 ounces) BIRDS EYE® frozen Asparagus
Dash cayenne pepper

• Prepare hollandaise sauce according to package directions.

• Spray large skillet with nonstick cooking spray; cook chicken strips over medium-high heat 10 to 12 minutes or until browned, stirring occasionally.

• Add hollandaise sauce, lemon juice and asparagus.

• Cover and cook, stirring occasionally, 5 to 10 minutes or until asparagus is heated through. (Do not overcook.)

• Add cayenne pepper, salt and black pepper to taste.

Makes 4 to 6 servings

Prep Time: 10 minutes
Cook Time: 20 to 25 minutes

SERVING SUGGESTION: SERVE OVER RICE OR NOODLES.

Artichoke Chicken Pilaf

2 tablespoons butter or margarine
12 ounces boneless skinless chicken breasts, cut into strips
1 clove garlic, minced
1¾ cups water
1 package (6 ounces) FARMHOUSE® Rice Pilaf Mix
½ teaspoon dried basil leaves
1 jar (6 ounces) marinated artichokes, drained, rinsed and cut into halves
3 green onions, cut into ½-inch lengths
¼ cup toasted sliced almonds

Heat butter in large skillet over medium-high heat. Cook and stir chicken and garlic in butter 5 to 7 minutes or until browned. Add water, seasoning mix, rice and basil. Bring to a boil. Reduce heat to low. Cover and simmer 15 minutes. Stir in artichokes and green onions; cook 5 minutes more. Garnish with almonds.

Makes about 4 servings

Microwaved Garlic and Herb Chicken

8 broiler-fryer chicken thighs (about 2 pounds)
½ cup olive oil
1 large tomato, chopped
1 rib celery, thinly sliced
2 tablespoons dried parsley flakes
6 cloves garlic, chopped
1 teaspoon salt
½ teaspoon ground black pepper
½ teaspoon dried oregano leaves
¼ teaspoon dried basil leaves
⅛ teaspoon ground nutmeg

Microwave Directions:
In microwavable baking dish, mix together oil, tomato, celery, parsley, garlic, salt, pepper, oregano, basil and nutmeg. Microwave at HIGH 3 minutes; stir. Add chicken; mix well. Cover; refrigerate 3 hours or overnight. Cover baking dish with waxed paper; microwave at HIGH 10 minutes. Turn chicken over; cover again with waxed paper and microwave at HIGH 10 minutes or until chicken is no longer pink in center. Let stand 5 minutes. To serve, remove garlic; discard. Spoon sauce over chicken.

Makes 4 servings

FAVORITE RECIPE FROM **NATIONAL BROILER COUNCIL**

Chicken and Asparagus Hollandaise

Chicken Florentine with Lemon Mustard Sauce

2 whole boneless skinless chicken breasts, cut into halves (1 pound)
¼ cup EGG BEATERS® Healthy Egg Substitute
½ cup plain dry bread crumbs
1 teaspoon dried basil leaves
1 teaspoon garlic powder
2 tablespoons sweet unsalted margarine, divided
⅓ cup water
2 tablespoons GREY POUPON® Dijon Mustard
2 tablespoons lemon juice
1 tablespoon sugar
1 (10-ounce) package frozen chopped spinach, cooked, well drained and kept warm

Pound chicken breasts to ¼-inch thickness. Pour Egg Beaters® into shallow bowl. Combine bread crumbs, basil and garlic powder. Dip chicken breasts into Egg Beaters®, then coat with bread crumb mixture.

In large nonstick skillet, over medium-high heat, melt 1 tablespoon margarine. Add chicken; cook 5 to 7 minutes on each side or until browned and no longer pink in center.

Remove chicken from skillet; keep warm. In same skillet, melt remaining 1 tablespoon margarine; stir in water, mustard, lemon juice and sugar. Simmer 1 minute or until thickened. To serve, arrange chicken on serving platter. Top with spinach; drizzle with lemon-mustard sauce. Garnish as desired.

Makes 4 servings

Prep Time: 25 minutes
Cook Time: 15 minutes

Chicken with Artichokes and Mushrooms

4 whole broiler-fryer chicken breasts, cut into halves, boned and skinned
¾ teaspoon salt, divided
¼ cup butter or margarine, divided
½ pound fresh mushrooms, sliced
¼ cup chopped green onions
3 cloves garlic, minced
1 package (9 ounces) frozen artichoke hearts, thawed, drained and cut into halves
⅓ cup chicken broth
½ teaspoon dried thyme leaves
¼ teaspoon ground red pepper
⅓ cup dry white wine
2 teaspoons cornstarch
Fresh herbs for garnish

With meat mallet or similar flattening utensil, pound chicken to ¼-inch thickness. Sprinkle ½ teaspoon salt over chicken. In large skillet, melt 2 tablespoons butter over medium-high heat. Add chicken, 4 pieces at a time, and cook, turning, about 6 minutes or until browned on both sides. Remove chicken; set aside. To drippings in same skillet, add remaining 2 tablespoons butter and melt over medium heat. Add mushrooms, onions and garlic. Cook, stirring frequently, about 4 minutes or until vegetables are tender. Add artichoke hearts, chicken broth, remaining ¼ teaspoon salt, thyme and red pepper; stir to mix well. In small dish, mix wine and cornstarch. Stir into vegetable mixture and cook, stirring, until slightly thickened. Return chicken to pan, spooning sauce over chicken. Cover and cook about 3 minutes or until chicken is fork-tender and heated through. Garnish with fresh herbs.

Makes 8 servings

*FAVORITE RECIPE FROM **DELMARVA POULTRY INDUSTRY, INC.***

Chicken Florentine with Lemon Mustard Sauce

Chicken with Brandied Fruit Sauce

- 4 broiler-fryer chicken breast halves, boned and skinned
- ½ teaspoon salt
- ¼ teaspoon ground nutmeg
- 2 tablespoons butter or margarine
- 1 tablespoon cornstarch
- ¼ teaspoon ground red pepper
  Juice of 1 orange
  Juice of 1 lemon
  Juice of 1 lime
- ⅓ cup orange marmalade
- 2 tablespoons brandy
- 1 cup red seedless grapes

Pound chicken to ½-inch thickness on hard surface with meat mallet or rolling pin. Sprinkle salt and nutmeg over chicken. Heat butter in large skillet over medium-high heat. Add chicken and cook, turning, about 8 minutes or until chicken is brown and fork-tender. Mix cornstarch and red pepper in small bowl. Stir in orange juice, lemon juice and lime juice; set aside. Remove chicken to serving platter. Add marmalade to same skillet; heat until melted. Stir in juice mixture; cook and stir until mixture boils and thickens. Add brandy and grapes. Return chicken to pan; spoon sauce over chicken. Cook over low heat 5 minutes.

Makes 4 servings

FAVORITE RECIPE FROM **DELMARVA POULTRY INDUSTRY, INC.**

Chicken and Vegetable Couscous

- 3 boneless skinless chicken breasts (3 ounces each)
- 1 tablespoon vegetable oil
- ½ cup chopped green onions
- 3 cloves garlic, minced
- 1¼ cups tomato sauce
- 1¼ cups chopped carrots
- 1 cup canned small white beans, drained and rinsed
- 1 large potato, cut into cubes
- 1 yellow squash, chopped
- 1 medium tomato, chopped
- ¼ cup chopped seeded red bell pepper
- ¼ cup raisins
- 2 tablespoons brown sugar
- 2 teaspoons ground cumin
- ¾ teaspoon ground cinnamon
- 3 to 4 drops hot pepper sauce
- 1 cup dry couscous

Cut chicken into 3-inch cubes; set aside. Heat oil in skillet over medium heat. Add chicken and cook, turning to brown on all sides. Add green onions and garlic; cook and stir 1 minute. Stir in tomato sauce and ¼ cup water. Add remaining ingredients except couscous. Reduce heat to low. Cover and simmer 15 minutes. Meanwhile, bring 1½ cups water to a boil over high heat; add couscous.

Cover; remove from heat. Let stand 5 minutes. Serve chicken and vegetables over couscous.

Makes 6 servings

FAVORITE RECIPE FROM **THE SUGAR ASSOCIATION, INC.**

Almond Butter Chicken

- 4 boneless skinless chicken breast halves (about 1¼ pounds)
- 2 tablespoons all-purpose flour
- ½ teaspoon salt
- ½ teaspoon black pepper
- 1 egg, beaten
- 1 package (2¼ ounces) sliced almonds
- ¼ cup butter
  Orange Sauce (page 157)

Place each chicken breast half between 2 pieces of plastic wrap. Pound to ¼-inch thickness. Coat chicken with flour. Sprinkle with salt and pepper. Dip one side of each chicken breast into egg; press with almonds. Melt butter in large skillet over medium-high heat. Cook chicken, almond side down, 3 to 5 minutes or until almonds are toasted; turn chicken over. Reduce heat to medium-low; cook 10 to 12 minutes or until chicken is tender and juices run clear. Serve, almond side up, with Orange Sauce. Garnish as desired.

Makes 4 servings

ORANGE SAUCE
1 tablespoon brown sugar
2 teaspoons cornstarch
Juice of 1 orange (about ½ cup)
2 tablespoons butter
1 teaspoon grated orange peel

Combine brown sugar and cornstarch in saucepan. Add juice, butter and orange peel. Cook over medium heat, stirring constantly, until thickened. *Makes ⅔ cup*

FAVORITE RECIPE FROM **WISCONSIN MILK MARKETING BOARD**

Apple Raisin-Stuffed Chicken

1 package (6 ounces) STOVE TOP® Savory Herbs Stuffing Mix or STOVE TOP® Stuffing Mix for Chicken
1½ cups hot water
¼ cup (½ stick) margarine, cut into pieces
1 apple, cored and chopped
¼ cup raisins
¼ cup toasted chopped walnuts
6 boneless skinless chicken breast halves
Vegetable oil
Paprika

Heat oven to 375°F.

Mix contents of vegetable-seasoning packet, hot water and margarine in large bowl until margarine is melted. Stir in stuffing crumbs, apple, raisins and walnuts just to moisten. Let stand 5 minutes.

Pound chicken to ¼-inch thickness. Spoon ¼ cup of stuffing over each chicken breast half; roll up. Reserve remaining stuffing. Place chicken, seam side down, in 13×9-inch baking pan. Brush with oil; sprinkle with paprika.

Bake 20 minutes. Spoon reserved stuffing into center of pan. Bake 20 minutes or until chicken is no longer pink in center. *Makes 6 servings*

Sausage Stuffed Chicken Breast Olé

6 boneless skinless chicken breast halves
1 pound BOB EVANS FARMS® Original Recipe or Zesty Hot Roll Sausage
1 (8-ounce) block Monterey Jack cheese, divided
4 tablespoons butter or margarine, divided
1 large green bell pepper, sliced into rings
1 large onion, sliced into rings
2 cloves garlic, minced
2 (16-ounce) cans stewed tomatoes, undrained
1 (12-ounce) can large black olives, drained and sliced, divided
¼ cup chopped cilantro
3 tablespoons chopped jalapeño peppers (optional)
Sour cream (optional)
Fresh cilantro sprigs (optional)

Pound chicken into uniform thin rectangles with meat mallet or rolling pin. Divide uncooked sausage into 6 equal pieces. Cut 6 (½-inch-thick) sticks from cheese block. Shred remaining cheese; set aside. Wrap each sausage piece around each cheese stick to enclose cheese completely. Place each sausage bundle on each chicken piece at one narrow end; roll up and secure with toothpicks. Melt 2 tablespoons butter in large Dutch oven or skillet over medium heat until hot. Add chicken bundles; cook, covered, about 5 to 7 minutes on each side or until browned, turning occasionally. Remove chicken; set aside.

Melt remaining 2 tablespoons butter in same Dutch oven. Add bell pepper, onion and garlic; cook and stir until lightly browned. Stir in tomatoes with juice, ½ the olives, chopped cilantro and jalapeños, if desired. Cook and stir over medium-low heat about 10 minutes. Add reserved chicken bundles. Cook, covered, 30 to 40 minutes or until flavors blend. To serve, spoon tomato sauce mixture on top of chicken. Sprinkle with remaining cheese and olives. Garnish with dollop of sour cream and cilantro sprigs, if desired. Serve hot. Refrigerate leftovers. *Makes 6 servings*

Chicken Pot Pie

1½ **pounds chicken pieces, skinned**
1 **cup chicken broth**
½ **teaspoon salt**
¼ **teaspoon black pepper**
1 **to 1½ cups 2% milk**
3 **tablespoons margarine or butter**
1 **medium onion, chopped**
1 **cup sliced celery**
⅓ **cup all-purpose flour**
2 **cups frozen mixed vegetables (broccoli, carrots and cauliflower combination), thawed**
1 **tablespoon chopped fresh parsley** *or* **1 teaspoon dried parsley**
½ **teaspoon dried thyme leaves**
1 **(9-inch) refrigerated pastry crust**
1 **egg lightly beaten**

COMBINE chicken, chicken broth, salt and pepper in large saucepan over medium-high heat. Bring to a boil. Reduce heat to low. Cover; simmer 30 minutes or until chicken is no longer pink in center and juices run clear.

REMOVE chicken and let cool. Pour remaining chicken broth mixture into glass measure. Let stand; spoon off fat. Add enough milk to broth mixture to equal 2½ cups. Remove chicken from bones and cut into ½-inch pieces.

MELT margarine in same saucepan over medium heat. Add onion and celery. Cook and stir 3 minutes. Stir in flour until well blended. Gradually stir in broth mixture. Cook, stirring constantly, until sauce thickens and boils. Add chicken, vegetables, parsley and thyme. Pour into 1½-quart deep casserole.

PREHEAT oven to 400°F. Roll out pastry 1 inch larger than diameter of casserole on lightly floured surface. Cut slits in pastry for venting air. Place pastry on top of casserole. Roll edges and cut away extra pastry; flute edges. Reroll scraps to cut into decorative designs. Place on top of pastry. Brush pastry with beaten egg. Bake about 30 minutes or until crust is golden brown and filling is bubbling.

Makes 4 servings

Stuffed Chicken with Apple Glaze

1 **broiler-fryer chicken (3½ to 4 pounds)**
½ **teaspoon salt**
¼ **teaspoon black pepper**
2 **tablespoons vegetable oil**
1 **package (6 ounces) chicken-flavored stuffing mix plus ingredients to prepare mix**
1 **cup chopped apple**
¼ **cup chopped walnuts**
¼ **cup raisins**
¼ **cup thinly sliced celery**
½ **teaspoon grated lemon peel**
½ **cup apple jelly**
1 **tablespoon lemon juice**
½ **teaspoon ground cinnamon**

Preheat oven to 350°F. Sprinkle inside of chicken with salt and pepper; rub outside with oil. Prepare stuffing mix in large bowl according to package directions. Add apple, walnuts, raisins, celery and lemon peel; mix thoroughly. Stuff body cavity loosely with stuffing.* Place chicken in baking pan. Cover loosely with aluminum foil; roast 1 hour. Meanwhile, combine jelly, lemon juice and cinnamon in small saucepan. Simmer over low heat 3 minutes or until blended. Remove foil from chicken; brush with glaze. Roast chicken, uncovered, brushing frequently with glaze, 30 minutes or until meat thermometer inserted into thickest part of thigh registers 185°F and juices run clear. Let chicken stand 15 minutes before carving.

Makes 4 servings

Bake any leftover stuffing in covered casserole alongside chicken until heated through.

FAVORITE RECIPE FROM **DELMARVA POULTRY INDUSTRY, INC.**

Chicken Pot Pie

Chicken with Pineapple Salsa

1 can (20 ounces) DOLE®
Crushed Pineapple in
Juice, undrained
4 boneless skinless
chicken breast halves
1 large clove garlic,
pressed
1 teaspoon ground cumin
Salt and black pepper to
taste
1 tablespoon vegetable oil
½ cup minced DOLE® Red
Bell Pepper
¼ cup minced DOLE®
Green Bell Pepper
1 tablespoon minced
DOLE® Green Onion
2 teaspoons minced
cilantro
2 teaspoons minced fresh
or canned jalapeño
peppers
1 teaspoon grated lime
peel

• Drain ½ cup juice from
pineapple; reserve.

• Rub chicken with garlic;
sprinkle with cumin, salt and
black pepper.

• Brown chicken in hot oil. Add
reserved ½ cup pineapple juice
to chicken. Cover; simmer 7 to
10 minutes.

• For salsa, combine undrained
pineapple with remaining
ingredients.

• Cut each chicken breast into
slices. Serve with pineapple
salsa.   *Makes 4 servings*

Prep Time: 5 minutes
Cook Time: 15 minutes

Roasted Chicken with Maple Glaze

1 (3-pound) whole chicken
1 small orange, cut into
wedges
1 small onion, cut into
wedges
¾ cup apple cider
¼ cup maple syrup
¾ teaspoon cornstarch
¼ teaspoon pumpkin pie
spice

PREHEAT oven to 325°F.
Remove giblets and neck from
chicken; reserve for another
use. Rinse chicken under cold
water and pat dry with paper
towels.

PLACE orange and onion
wedges in cavity of chicken.
Tie legs together with wet
cotton string and place breast-
side up on rack in shallow
roasting pan coated with
nonstick cooking spray. Insert
meat thermometer into meaty
part of thigh, not touching bone.

COMBINE apple cider, maple
syrup, cornstarch and pumpkin
pie spice in small saucepan;
bring to a boil over medium
heat, stirring constantly. Cook
1 minute; brush apple cider
mixture over chicken.

BAKE chicken 1½ to 2 hours
or until meat thermometer
registers 180°F, basting
frequently with remaining
apple cider mixture.

REMOVE string, orange and
onion wedges; discard. Transfer
chicken to serving platter. Let
stand 10 minutes before
carving.   *Makes 12 servings*

Chicken Diane

6 ounces uncooked pasta
¾ cup unsalted butter,
divided
1 tablespoon plus
2 teaspoons CHEF
PAUL PRUDHOMME'S
Poultry Magic®
¾ pound boneless skinless
chicken breasts, cut
into strips
3 cups sliced mushrooms
(about 8 ounces)
¼ cup minced green onion
tops
3 tablespoons minced
fresh parsley
1 teaspoon minced garlic
1 cup skimmed chicken
stock or water

Cook pasta according to
package directions. Drain
immediately; rinse with hot
water, then with cold water.
Drain again.

Combine ¼ cup butter, Poultry
Magic® and chicken in medium
bowl. Heat large skillet over
high heat until hot, about 4
minutes. Add chicken pieces;
brown both sides. Add
mushrooms; cook 2 minutes.
Add green onion tops, parsley,
garlic and stock. Cook 2
minutes or until sauce boils
rapidly. Add remaining ½ cup
butter (cut into pats), stirring
constantly. Cook 3 minutes.
Add cooked pasta; mix well.
Serve immediately. Garnish as
desired.   *Makes 2 servings*

Chicken with Pineapple Salsa

Forty-Clove Chicken

1 frying chicken
  (3 pounds), cut into
  serving pieces
Salt and black pepper
1 to 2 tablespoons olive
  oil
¼ cup dry white wine
⅛ cup dry vermouth
2 tablespoons chopped
  fresh parsley *or*
  2 teaspoons dried
  parsley leaves
2 teaspoons dried basil
  leaves
1 teaspoon dried oregano
  leaves
Pinch red pepper flakes
40 cloves garlic (about
  2 heads), peeled
4 ribs celery, sliced
Juice and peel of
  1 lemon
Fresh herbs (optional)

Slow Cooker Directions:
REMOVE skin from chicken, if desired. Sprinkle with salt and black pepper. Heat oil in large skillet over medium heat. Add chicken; cook 10 minutes or until browned on all sides. Remove to platter.

COMBINE wine, vermouth, parsley, basil, oregano and red pepper flakes in large bowl. Add garlic and celery; coat well. Transfer garlic and celery to slow cooker with slotted spoon. Add chicken to remaining herb mixture; coat well. Place chicken on top of vegetables in slow cooker. Sprinkle lemon juice and peel in slow cooker; add remaining herb mixture. Cover and cook

on LOW 6 hours or until chicken is no longer pink in center. Garnish with fresh herbs, if desired.

Makes 4 to 6 servings

Coq au Vin

4 thin slices bacon, cut
  into ½-inch pieces
6 chicken thighs, skinned
¾ teaspoon dried thyme
  leaves
1 large onion, coarsely
  chopped
4 cloves garlic, minced
½ pound small red
  potatoes, cut into
  quarters
10 mushrooms, cut into
  quarters
1 can (14½ ounces) DEL
  MONTE® *FreshCut*™
  Diced Tomatoes with
  Garlic & Onion,
  undrained
1½ cups dry red wine

1. Cook bacon in large heavy saucepan until just starting to brown. Sprinkle chicken with thyme; season with salt and pepper, if desired.

2. Add chicken to saucepan; brown over medium-high heat. Add onion and garlic. Cook 2 minutes; drain.

3. Add potatoes, mushrooms, tomatoes and wine. Cook, uncovered, over medium-high heat about 25 minutes or until potatoes are tender and sauce thickens, stirring occasionally. Garnish with chopped parsley, if desired.

Makes 4 to 6 servings

Chicken with Walnuts

1 cup uncooked instant
  rice
½ cup chicken broth
¼ cup Chinese plum sauce
2 tablespoons soy sauce
2 teaspoons cornstarch
2 tablespoons vegetable
  oil, divided
3 cups frozen bell peppers
  and onions
1 pound boneless skinless
  chicken breasts, cut
  into ¼-inch slices
1 clove garlic, minced
1 cup walnut halves

1. Cook rice according to package directions. Set aside.

2. Combine chicken broth, plum sauce, soy sauce and cornstarch in small bowl; set aside.

3. Heat 1 tablespoon oil in wok or large skillet over medium-high heat until hot. Add frozen peppers and onions; stir-fry 3 minutes or until crisp-tender. Remove vegetables from wok. Drain; discard liquid.

4. Heat remaining 1 tablespoon oil in wok until hot. Add chicken and garlic; stir-fry 3 minutes or until chicken is no longer pink in center.

5. Stir broth mixture; add to wok. Cook and stir 1 minute or until sauce thickens. Stir in vegetables and walnuts; cook 1 minute more. Serve with rice.

Makes 4 servings

Prep & Cook Time: 19 minutes

Forty-Clove Chicken

Tomato, Basil & Broccoli Chicken

4 boneless skinless chicken breast halves
Salt and black pepper (optional)
2 tablespoons margarine or butter
1 package (6.9 ounces) RICE-A-RONI® Chicken Flavor
1 teaspoon dried basil
2 cups broccoli florets
1 medium tomato, seeded and chopped
1 cup (4 ounces) shredded mozzarella cheese

1. Sprinkle chicken with salt and pepper, if desired.

2. In large skillet, melt margarine over medium-high heat. Add chicken; cook 2 minutes on each side or until browned. Remove from skillet; set aside, reserving drippings. Keep warm.

3. In same skillet, sauté rice-vermicelli mix in reserved drippings over medium heat until vermicelli is golden brown. Stir in 2½ cups water, contents of seasoning packet and basil. Place chicken over rice mixture; bring to a boil over high heat.

4. Cover; reduce heat. Simmer 15 minutes. Top with broccoli and tomato.

5. Cover; continue to simmer 5 minutes or until liquid is absorbed and chicken is no longer pink in center. Sprinkle with cheese. Cover; let stand a few minutes before serving.

Makes 4 servings

Chicken with Pasta and Puttanesca Sauce

8 ounces uncooked ziti or other medium-sized pasta
1 package (1½ to 1¾ pounds) GALIL® Chicken Breast Cutlets, split
¼ teaspoon freshly ground black pepper
2 tablespoons olive oil
3 cloves garlic, minced
1 can (14½ ounces) diced tomatoes in juice, undrained
2 tablespoons tomato paste
1 tablespoon drained capers (optional)
1½ teaspoons dried basil leaves
¼ teaspoon red pepper flakes
10 kalamata olives, pitted
3 tablespoons chopped fresh Italian parsley (optional)

Cook pasta according to package directions. *Do not drain.* Set aside. Sprinkle chicken with black pepper. Heat oil in large deep nonstick skillet over medium-high heat. Add garlic and chicken. Cook chicken 2 minutes each side or until browned. Reduce heat to medium; add tomatoes with juice, tomato paste, capers, if desired, basil and crushed pepper. Simmer, uncovered, 12 to 15 minutes or until chicken is no longer pink in center. Coarsely chop olives; stir into sauce.

Transfer chicken to serving platter. Drain pasta; add to skillet. Toss well. Serve pasta with chicken. Garnish with fresh parsley, if desired.

Makes 4 servings

Cheesy Crispy Chicken

Vegetable cooking spray
1 bottle (8 ounces) blue cheese salad dressing
2 cups dry bread crumbs
½ teaspoon celery salt
½ teaspoon dried dill weed
¼ teaspoon black pepper
12 chicken drumsticks

Preheat oven to 350°F. Spray baking sheet with cooking spray; set aside. Pour dressing into medium bowl. Combine bread crumbs, celery salt, dill and pepper in shallow dish. Dip chicken in dressing; roll in bread crumb mixture. Place chicken in single layer on prepared baking sheet. Bake, uncovered, 50 minutes or until juices run clear, turning once. Serve hot or cold.

Makes 6 servings

FAVORITE RECIPE FROM **NATIONAL BROILER COUNCIL**

Tomato, Basil & Broccoli Chicken

Chicken Phyllo Wraps

Vegetable cooking spray
1 pound ground chicken
1 cup chopped fresh
   mushrooms
1 medium onion, chopped
3 cups cooked rice
   (cooked without salt
   and fat)
1 cup nonfat low-salt
   ricotta cheese
1 package (10 ounces)
   chopped spinach,
   thawed and well
   drained
1 can (2¼ ounces) sliced
   black olives, drained
¼ cup pine nuts, toasted*
2 cloves garlic, minced
1 teaspoon ground
   oregano
1 teaspoon lemon pepper
12 phyllo dough sheets

*To toast nuts, place on baking sheet. Bake at 350°F 5 to 7 minutes or until lightly browned.

Coat large skillet with cooking spray; heat over medium-high heat until hot. Add chicken, mushrooms and onion; cook and stir 2 to 4 minutes or until chicken is no longer pink and vegetables are tender. Reduce heat to medium. Add rice, ricotta cheese, spinach, olives, nuts, garlic, oregano and lemon pepper; cook and stir 3 to 4 minutes until well blended and thoroughly heated. Working with 1 phyllo sheet at a time, spray 1 sheet with cooking spray; fold sheet in half lengthwise. Place ¾ to 1 cup rice mixture on one end of phyllo strip. Fold left bottom corner over mixture, forming a triangle. Continue folding back and forth into triangle at end of strip. Repeat with remaining phyllo sheets and rice mixture. Place triangles, seam sides down, on baking sheets coated with cooking spray. Coat top of each triangle with cooking spray. Bake at 400°F 15 to 20 minutes or until golden brown. Serve immediately.

Makes 12 servings

FAVORITE RECIPE FROM **USA RICE FEDERATION**

Mexican Chicken Rolls

6 boneless skinless
   chicken breast halves
   (1½ pounds)
¼ cup plus 1½ tablespoons
   plain dry bread
   crumbs, divided
1 teaspoon chili powder
½ teaspoon ground cumin
¾ cup (3 ounces) shredded
   Monterey Jack cheese
2 tablespoons chopped
   pimientos, drained
1 green onion, chopped
3 tablespoons FRANK'S®
   Original REDHOT®
   Cayenne Pepper
   Sauce, divided
1½ tablespoons grated
   Parmesan cheese
½ teaspoon paprika
2 tablespoons butter,
   melted
   Salsa (optional)

1. Pound chicken breasts between 2 sheets of plastic wrap to ¼-inch thickness. Set aside. Combine ¼ cup bread crumbs, chili powder and cumin in medium bowl. Stir in Monterey Jack cheese, pimientos, onion and 2 tablespoons RedHot® sauce; mix well.

2. Preheat oven to 400°F. Spoon about 2 tablespoons filling down center of each chicken breast half, leaving 1-inch border along edges. Fold edges over filling; place, seam side down, in greased 2-quart baking dish.

3. Combine remaining 1½ tablespoons bread crumbs, Parmesan cheese and paprika in small bowl; set aside. Mix butter and remaining 1 tablespoon RedHot® sauce in another small bowl; brush over stuffed chicken breasts. Sprinkle bread crumb mixture over chicken breasts. Bake 30 minutes or until chicken is no longer pink. Serve with salsa, if desired.

Makes 6 servings

Prep Time: 20 minutes
Cook Time: 30 minutes

Lazy Gator Jambalaya

2 tablespoons vegetable
oil
8 chicken thighs
(2½ pounds)
8 hot Italian sausages
(1½ pounds), cut
crosswise into halves
1 large onion, chopped
1 green bell pepper,
chopped
3 ribs celery, chopped
3 large cloves garlic,
minced
1½ cups uncooked white
rice
1 can (10½ ounces)
condensed chicken
broth
1¼ cups water
½ cup dry white wine
½ cup barbecue sauce
¼ cup FRANK'S® Original
REDHOT® Cayenne
Pepper Sauce

1. Preheat oven to 350°F. Heat
oil in large saucepan or Dutch
oven. Cook chicken and
sausages in batches, about
10 minutes or until browned.
Transfer meat to plate; drain fat.

2. Add remaining ingredients
to saucepan; bring to a boil.
Return meat to saucepan;
cover.

3. Bake 45 minutes or until
rice is tender and chicken is
no longer pink near bone.

Makes 8 servings

Prep Time: 15 minutes
Cook Time: 1 hour

Chicken Fiesta

2½ to 3 pounds chicken
pieces
Salt
Black pepper
Paprika
2 tablespoons butter or
margarine
¼ pound pork sausage
¾ cup sliced celery
¾ cup sliced green onions
with tops
3 cups cooked rice
1 can (12 ounces) whole
kernel corn with
peppers, drained
2 teaspoons lemon juice

Preheat oven to 350°F. Season
chicken with salt, black pepper
and paprika. In large skillet,
melt butter. Add chicken to
skillet; brown well. Drain
chicken on paper towels; set
aside. Cook sausage, celery
and onions in same skillet
over medium-high heat, stirring
frequently until vegetables are
crisp-tender. Add rice, corn and
lemon juice; mix well. Pour
into greased shallow baking
dish. Arrange chicken on top of
rice mixture, pressing chicken
slightly into rice mixture. Cover
with foil. Bake 30 to 40 minutes
or until chicken is no longer
pink in center.

Makes 6 servings

FAVORITE RECIPE FROM **USA RICE
FEDERATION**

Chicken Phyllo Wrap (page 166)

New Year's Chicken

- **1 GALIL® Whole Chicken (about 3¾ pounds)**
- **½ teaspoon salt**
- **¼ teaspoon freshly ground black pepper**
- **1 orange, peeled and separated into segments**
- **1 medium onion, thinly sliced**
- **½ cup kosher dry white wine**
- **½ cup orange juice**
- **2 tablespoons grated fresh ginger**
- **2 tablespoons honey**

Preheat oven to 350°F. Sprinkle chicken with salt and pepper. Place half of orange slices in chicken cavity. Place onion slices in small shallow roasting pan or 8-inch square glass baking dish. Arrange remaining half of orange slices over onion slices in roasting pan. Pour wine over orange and onion slices. Place chicken, breast side down, over orange and onion mixture. Combine orange juice and ginger in glass measuring cup; pour over chicken. Bake, uncovered, 30 minutes.

Turn chicken, breast side up, and drizzle honey over surface. Bake 1 hour or until internal temperature of chicken reaches 180°F on meat thermometer inserted into thickest part of thigh. Baste with pan juices every 20 minutes. (If chicken is browning too quickly, tent with foil.) Transfer chicken to cutting board; tent with foil. Let stand 5 to 10 minutes.

Pour juices from roasting pan into small saucepan; discard orange and onion slices. Cook, stirring constantly, 2 to 3 minutes over medium-high heat or until slightly thickened. Serve with chicken.

Makes 6 servings

Spiced Orange Chicken with Lentils

- **3 tablespoons all-purpose flour**
- **1 teaspoon ground coriander**
- **1 teaspoon ground cumin**
- **½ teaspoon salt**
- **½ teaspoon dried mixed herbs (thyme, marjoram and rosemary)**
- **¼ teaspoon freshly ground black pepper**
- **8 chicken drumsticks**
- **2 tablespoons FILIPPO BERIO® Olive Oil, divided**
- **Finely grated peel and juice of 1 orange**
- **1 large onion, finely chopped**
- **2 cloves garlic, minced**
- **2½ cups chicken broth**
- **8 ounces dried lentils (about 1¼ cups), rinsed and drained**
- **Additional salt and freshly ground black pepper**
- **1 to 2 tablespoons honey**
- **Orange wedges and chopped fresh parsley (optional)**

In small brown paper bag or plastic food storage bag, combine flour, coriander, cumin, ½ teaspoon salt, dried herbs and ¼ teaspoon pepper; shake until well mixed. Place 1 chicken drumstick at a time into flour mixture; shake well to coat evenly. In large skillet, heat 1 tablespoon olive oil over medium-high heat until hot. Add drumsticks; cook 5 minutes or until brown, turning occasionally. Stir orange peel and juice into skillet. Cover; reduce heat to low and simmer 20 minutes or until chicken is no longer pink in center and juices run clear.

Meanwhile, in another large skillet, heat remaining 1 tablespoon olive oil over medium heat until hot. Add onion and garlic; cook and stir 5 minutes or until onion is softened. Add chicken broth and lentils; bring to a boil. Cover; reduce heat to low and simmer 20 minutes or until lentils are tender and broth is absorbed. Season to taste with additional salt and pepper. Arrange lentils on serving plate; place drumsticks on top. Stir honey into chicken juices remaining in skillet. Heat through, stirring occasionally. Spoon over chicken and lentils. Garnish with orange wedges and parsley, if desired.

Makes 4 servings

New Year's Chicken

Chicken and Black Bean Soft Tacos

- **1 package (10) ORTEGA® Soft Taco Dinner Kit (flour tortillas, taco seasoning mix and taco sauce)**
- **1 tablespoon vegetable oil**
- **1 pound (3 to 4) boneless skinless chicken breast halves, cut into 2-inch strips**
- **1 cup (1 small) chopped onion**
- **1¾ cups (15-ounce can) black beans, drained**
- **¾ cup whole kernel corn**
- **½ cup water**
- **2 tablespoons lime juice**

HEAT oil in large skillet over medium-high heat. Add chicken and onion; cook 4 to 5 minutes or until chicken is no longer pink in center. Stir in taco seasoning mix, beans, corn, water and lime juice. Bring to a boil. Reduce heat to low; cook, stirring occasionally, 5 to 6 minutes or until mixture is thickened.

REMOVE tortillas from outer plastic pouch. Microwave at HIGH 10 to 15 seconds or until warm. *Or* heat each tortilla, turning frequently, in small skillet over medium-high heat until warm.

FILL each tortilla with ½ cup chicken mixture and taco sauce. *Makes 10 tacos*

Chicken Fajitas Dijon

- **¼ cup GREY POUPON® Dijon Mustard**
- **2 tablespoons vegetable oil, divided**
- **2 tablespoons lime juice**
- **1 clove garlic, minced**
- **1 tablespoon chopped cilantro**
- **1 teaspoon chili powder**
- **½ teaspoon ground cumin**
- **¼ to ½ teaspoon red pepper flakes**
- **1 pound boneless skinless chicken breasts, cut into strips**
- **2 small onions, sliced**
- **1 medium red, yellow or green bell pepper, cut into strips**
- **8 (8-inch) flour tortillas, warmed**
- **Sour cream, chopped tomatoes and shredded Cheddar cheese (optional)**

In medium bowl, blend mustard, 1 tablespoon oil, lime juice, garlic, cilantro, chili powder, cumin and red pepper flakes. Add chicken, stirring to coat well. Refrigerate 1 hour.

In large skillet, over medium-high heat, sauté onions and bell pepper strips in remaining 1 tablespoon oil 2 to 3 minutes or until tender; remove from skillet. In same skillet, sauté chicken mixture 5 to 7 minutes or until done. Stir in onion mixture; heat through.

Serve chicken mixture in tortillas with sour cream, tomatoes and cheese, if desired. *Makes 4 servings*

Peanut Chicken

- **4 half boneless chicken breasts, skinned**
- **2 tablespoons vegetable oil**
- **1 can (14½ ounces) DEL MONTE® FreshCut™ Diced Tomatoes with Garlic & Onions**
- **2 cloves garlic, minced, or ¼ teaspoon garlic powder**
- **¼ teaspoon ground ginger or 1 teaspoon grated fresh ginger**
- **⅛ to ¼ teaspoon crushed red pepper flakes**
- **3 tablespoons chunky peanut butter**

1. Cook chicken in hot oil in large skillet over medium-high heat about 4 minutes on each side or until chicken is no longer pink in center. Remove chicken from skillet.

2. Add tomatoes, garlic, ginger and red pepper flakes to skillet; cook 2 minutes. Stir in peanut butter.

3. Return chicken to skillet; heat through. Sprinkle with chopped cilantro and peanuts for garnish, if desired. *Makes 4 servings*

Prep Time: 4 minutes
Cook Time: 12 minutes

Black Bean Garnachas

1 can (14½ ounces) DEL MONTE® FreshCut™ Diced Tomatoes with Garlic & Onion, undrained
1 can (15 ounces) black or pinto beans, drained
2 cloves garlic, minced
1 to 2 teaspoons minced jalapeño peppers (optional)
½ teaspoon ground cumin
1 cup cubed grilled chicken
4 flour tortillas
½ cup (2 ounces) shredded sharp Cheddar cheese

1. Combine undrained tomatoes, beans, garlic, jalapeño peppers, if desired and cumin in large skillet. Cook over medium-high heat 5 to 7 minutes or until thickened, stirring occasionally. Stir in chicken. Season with salt and black pepper, if desired.

2. Arrange tortillas in single layer on grill over medium coals. Spread about ¾ cup chicken mixture over each tortilla. Top with cheese.

3. Cook about 3 minutes or until bottoms of tortillas are browned and cheese is melted. Top with shredded lettuce, diced avocado and sliced jalapeño peppers, if desired.

Makes 4 servings

Prep Time: 5 minutes
Cook Time: 10 minutes

Variation: Prepare the chicken mixture as directed. Place a tortilla in a dry skillet over medium heat. Spread with about ¾ cup chicken mixture; top with 2 tablespoons cheese. Cover and cook about 3 minutes or until bottom of tortilla is browned and cheese is melted. Repeat with remaining tortillas.

Mexican Meatloaf

1½ pounds lean ground turkey or beef
1 cup GUILTLESS GOURMET® Salsa (mild, medium or hot), divided
1 cup (3½ ounces) crushed GUILTLESS GOURMET® Baked Tortilla Chips (yellow or white corn)
½ medium onion, chopped
3 egg whites, lightly beaten
½ teaspoon coarsely ground black pepper

Preheat oven to 350°F. Mix turkey, ½ cup salsa, crushed chips, onion, egg whites and pepper in large bowl until lightly blended. Shape into loaf and place in 9×5-inch loaf pan.

Bake 1 hour or until firm. Pour remaining ½ cup salsa over top; bake 10 minutes more. Let stand 10 minutes before slicing and serving.

Makes 4 servings

Camp Tacos

8 taco shells
1 pound ground turkey or lean ground beef
1 can (15 ounces) pinto beans, drained
½ (8-ounce) jar mild Mexican pasteurized process cheese spread*
½ cup chopped California ripe olives
Shredded lettuce
Chopped tomato
Additional chopped olives for topping

The cheese spread can be found on the grocery shelf, not in refrigerated section.

To warm taco shells, place shells on shell rack; cover with foil. Set over pot of boiling water that has been removed from heat (or warm shells in oven). Cook and stir turkey in large skillet over high heat until browned. Stir in beans, cheese spread and ½ cup chopped olives. Cook and stir until heated through. To serve, spoon turkey mixture into taco shells. Add lettuce, tomato and additional olives to shells.

Makes 4 servings

Prep Time: 14 minutes
Cook Time: 8 minutes

FAVORITE RECIPE FROM CALIFORNIA OLIVE INDUSTRY

Turkey Gyros

**1 turkey tenderloin
(8 ounces)**
**1½ teaspoons Greek
seasoning**
1 cucumber
⅔ cup plain nonfat yogurt
**¼ cup finely chopped
onion**
**2 teaspoons dried dill
weed**
**2 teaspoons fresh lemon
juice**
1 teaspoon olive oil
4 pita breads
**1½ cups washed and
shredded romaine
lettuce**
1 tomato, thinly sliced
**2 tablespoons crumbled
feta cheese**

1. Cut turkey tenderloin across grain into ¼-inch slices. Place turkey slices on plate; lightly sprinkle both sides with Greek seasoning. Let stand 5 minutes.

2. Cut two thirds of cucumber into thin slices. Finely chop remaining cucumber. Combine chopped cucumber, yogurt, onion, dill and lemon juice in small bowl.

3. Heat olive oil in large skillet over medium heat until hot. Add turkey. Cook 2 minutes on each side or until cooked through. Wrap 2 pita breads in paper towel. Microwave at HIGH 30 seconds or just until warmed. Repeat with remaining pita breads.

4. Divide lettuce, tomato, cucumber slices, turkey, cheese and yogurt-cucumber sauce evenly among pita breads. Fold edges over and secure with toothpicks.   *Makes 4 servings*

Tasty Turkey Pot Pie

**½ cup MIRACLE WHIP®
Salad Dressing**
2 tablespoons flour
**1 teaspoon instant
chicken bouillon**
⅛ teaspoon black pepper
¾ cup milk
**1½ cups chopped cooked
turkey or chicken**
**1 (10-ounce) package
frozen mixed
vegetables, thawed
and drained**
**1 (4-ounce) can
refrigerated crescent
rolls**

• Combine salad dressing, flour, bouillon and pepper in medium saucepan. Gradually add milk.

• Cook, stirring constantly, over low heat until thickened. Add turkey and vegetables; heat thoroughly, stirring occasionally.

• Spoon into 8-inch square baking dish. Unroll dough into two rectangles. Press perforations together to seal. Place rectangles side-by-side to form square; press edges together to form seam. Cover turkey mixture with dough.

• Bake at 375°F 15 to 20 minutes or until browned.
Makes 4 to 6 servings

Prep Time: 15 minutes
Bake Time: 20 minutes

Curried Turkey Dinner

**1 package (10 ounces)
frozen broccoli spears,
cooked and drained**
**2 cups cubed cooked
turkey**
**1 can (10½ ounces)
reduced-sodium cream
of mushroom soup**
**¼ cup reduced-calorie
mayonnaise**
1½ teaspoons lemon juice
1 teaspoon curry powder
1 cup seasoned croutons

1. Preheat oven to 350°F.

2. In 8-inch square baking dish, arrange broccoli; top with turkey.

3. In small bowl, combine soup, mayonnaise, lemon juice and curry powder. Pour over turkey and top with croutons.

4. Bake 20 to 25 minutes or until bubbly.
Makes 4 servings

FAVORITE RECIPE FROM **NATIONAL TURKEY FEDERATION**

Turkey Gyro

Turkey Breast Provençal with Vegetables

1 cup turkey or chicken bouillon
¼ cup white wine
¼ cup lemon juice
1 head garlic, cloves separated and unpeeled
1 bag (10 ounces) frozen onions
2 teaspoons dried rosemary
1 teaspoon dried thyme leaves
½ teaspoon salt
¼ teaspoon fennel seeds
¼ teaspoon black pepper
6 plum tomatoes, cut into quarters
1 package (9 ounces) frozen artichoke hearts, slightly thawed
1 package (10 ounces) frozen asparagus spears, slightly thawed
1 can (3¼ ounces) pitted ripe olives, drained
1 bone-in (4½-pound) turkey breast

1. Preheat oven to 325°F. In 13×9-inch baking pan, combine bouillon, wine, lemon juice, garlic, onions, rosemary, thyme, salt, fennel seeds and pepper. Cover pan with foil; bake 20 minutes.

2. Remove pan from oven. Add tomatoes, artichoke hearts, asparagus and olives. Place turkey breast on top of vegetables. Cover and bake 1 hour. Remove foil and bake 1 hour or until meat

thermometer inserted into thickest part of breast registers 170°F. Baste turkey and vegetables frequently with pan juices.

3. Remove turkey and vegetables to serving platter. Reserve 6 cloves garlic and pan juices.

4. Remove skin from reserved garlic. Combine garlic with pan juices in food processor; process 30 to 60 seconds or until mixture is smooth.

5. Serve sauce with turkey and vegetables.

Makes 12 servings

*FAVORITE RECIPE FROM **NATIONAL TURKEY FEDERATION***

Turkey Picadillo

1 tablespoon vegetable oil
1 large onion, chopped
2 cloves garlic, minced
1 pound ground turkey
1 can (14½ ounces) tomatoes, undrained and cut up
⅓ cup golden raisins
3 to 4 tablespoons FRANK'S® Original REDHOT® Cayenne Pepper Sauce
1 tablespoon balsamic vinegar
½ teaspoon dried oregano leaves
⅛ teaspoon ground cinnamon
⅓ cup blanched slivered almonds, chopped
¼ cup chopped fresh parsley
Shredded lettuce (optional)

1. Heat oil in large nonstick skillet over medium-high heat. Add onion and garlic; cook and stir until tender. Add turkey; cook and stir until no longer pink.

2. Add tomatoes with liquid, raisins, RedHot® sauce, vinegar, oregano and cinnamon to turkey mixture. Bring to a boil. Reduce heat to low; cook, uncovered, 15 minutes or until thickened and most of liquid is absorbed, stirring occasionally. Stir in almonds and parsley.

3. Spoon turkey mixture over bed of shredded lettuce, if desired. Serve with sour cream, Cheddar cheese, chopped green onions and red bell peppers, if desired.   *Makes 4 main-dish or 12 appetizer servings*

Prep Time: 20 minutes
Cook Time: 25 minutes

Turkey Breast Provençal with Vegetables

Roast Capon with Fruit and Nut Stuffing

4 tablespoons butter or
  margarine, divided
1 tart apple, diced
½ cup chopped golden
  raisins
¼ cup sliced green onions
¼ cup chopped celery
4 cups stale bread cubes
2 teaspoons poultry
  seasoning
1 teaspoon dried parsley
1 teaspoon salt
½ teaspoon black pepper
1½ cups reduced-sodium
  chicken broth
½ cup dry sherry
½ cup toasted slivered
  almonds
¼ cup honey
2 tablespoons mustard
½ teaspoon curry powder
1 capon (8 to 9 pounds)

PREHEAT oven to 325°F. *For stuffing,* **MELT** 2 tablespoons butter in skillet over medium-high heat. Add apple, raisins, onions and celery; cook and stir 3 minutes. Add bread cubes, poultry seasoning, parsley, salt and pepper; toss. Add chicken broth, sherry and almonds; toss. *For glaze,* **BRING** honey, remaining 2 tablespoons butter, mustard and curry powder to a boil in saucepan. Boil 1 minute; remove from heat.

REMOVE giblets and neck from capon; discard. Rinse capon under cold water and pat dry with paper towels. Stuff cavity loosely with stuffing (place remaining stuffing in baking dish). Tie legs together with wet cotton string and place, breast side up, on rack in shallow roasting pan coated with nonstick cooking spray. Insert meat thermometer into meaty part of thigh not touching bone. Bake 3 hours or until meat thermometer registers 170°F, brushing well with glaze every 30 minutes. Cover remaining stuffing; bake last 45 minutes of baking time.

TRANSFER capon to platter. Remove stuffing; add to remaining stuffing. Cover capon with foil; let stand 10 minutes.

SERVE capon with stuffing and pan juices.   *Makes 8 servings*

Glazed Cornish Hens

6 fresh or thawed frozen
  Rock Cornish game
  hens (1¼ to
  1½ pounds each)*
1 small onion, cut into
  6 wedges
1 lemon, cut into
  6 wedges
2 tablespoons butter,
  softened
  Salt (optional)
½ cup apricot preserves
1 tablespoon lemon juice
1 teaspoon shredded
  lemon peel

*A 1¼- to 1½-pound Rock Cornish game hen should take 1 to 2 days to thaw in the refrigerator. **Do not thaw at room temperature.**

Preheat oven to 350°F. Wash hens inside and out with cold running water; pat dry with paper towels. Place 1 onion wedge and 1 lemon wedge in cavity of each hen. Tuck wings under hens. Tie legs together with cotton string. Place hens on meat rack in shallow roasting pan. Spread butter evenly over hens; sprinkle with salt, if desired. Roast 45 minutes.

Meanwhile, combine apricot preserves, lemon juice and lemon peel. Brush half of mixture over hens; roast 15 minutes. Brush hens with remaining preserve mixture; roast 15 minutes more or until hens are glazed, juices run clear when hens are pierced with long-handled fork and internal temperature is 180°F.** Cut string with scissors; discard. Remove onion and lemon wedges from cavities; discard.   *Makes 6 servings*

**Since Rock Cornish game hens are so small, the most accurate way to measure the internal temperature is with an instant-read thermometer, which has a narrower stem than a standard meat thermometer. Insert thermometer into fleshy part of thigh. Do not leave the thermometer in the hen during roasting since the thermometer is not ovenproof.

Honey Dijon Cornish Hens

2 whole Cornish hens, split (about 2½ pounds total) *or* **1 (2½-pound) chicken, cut up**
⅔ cup GREY POUPON® Dijon Mustard
⅓ cup honey
¼ cup lemon juice
2 tablespoons minced onion
¾ teaspoon minced fresh rosemary
½ cup COLLEGE INN® Chicken Broth or Lower Sodium Chicken Broth
1 teaspoon cornstarch
6 lemon slices, cut into halves
Hot cooked long grain and wild rice

Place Cornish hens on rack in roasting pan. Bake at 350°F for 30 minutes.

Meanwhile, in small bowl, blend mustard, honey, lemon juice, onion and rosemary. Use ⅓ cup mustard mixture to brush over hens. Bake 30 to 40 minutes more or until done.

In small saucepan, blend remaining mustard mixture, chicken broth and cornstarch. Cook over medium heat until mixture thickens and begins to boil. Add lemon slices; cook 1 minute. Keep warm.

Serve hens with rice and heated mustard sauce. Garnish as desired. *Makes 4 servings*

Cajun Cornish Hens

4 ounces hot smoked sausage, chopped
½ cup long grain white rice
1 can (14½ ounces) DEL MONTE® *FreshCut*™ Diced Tomatoes with Garlic & Onion
½ cup sliced green onions
¼ cup chopped green bell pepper
1 clove garlic, minced
¼ teaspoon dried thyme leaves
4 Rock Cornish hens (20 ounces each)
1 tablespoon butter, melted

1. Brown sausage in saucepan. Stir in rice; cook 2 minutes.

2. Add tomatoes, onions, pepper, garlic and thyme. Bring to a boil. Cover; simmer 20 minutes (rice will be firm).

3. Rinse hens; drain well. Stuff with rice mixture. Place breast side up on rack in shallow pan. Brush with butter.

4. Bake at 375°F 1 hour or until done. *Makes 4 servings*

Roast Capon with Fruit and Nut Stuffing (page 176)

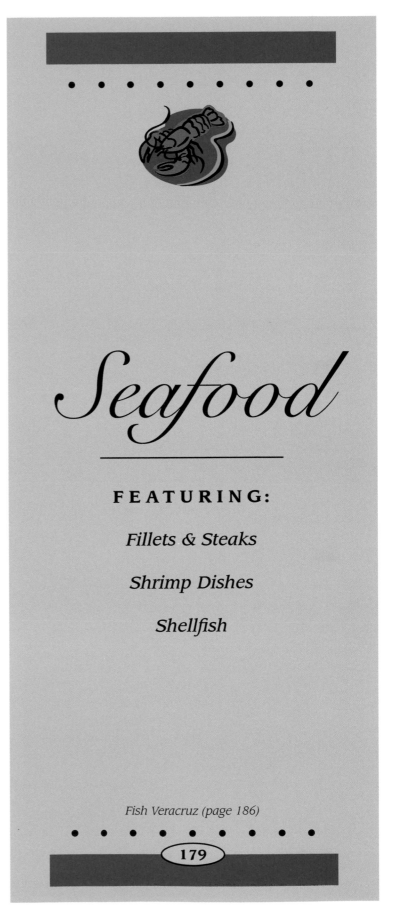

Seafood

FEATURING:

Fillets & Steaks

Shrimp Dishes

Shellfish

Fish Veracruz (page 186)

Baja Fish and Rice Bake

- **3 tablespoons vegetable oil**
- **¾ cup chopped onion**
- **½ cup chopped celery**
- **1 clove garlic, minced**
- **½ cup uncooked medium grain white rice**
- **3½ cups (two 14½-ounce cans) CONTADINA® Stewed Tomatoes, cut up, undrained**
- **1 teaspoon lemon pepper seasoning**
- **½ teaspoon salt**
- **⅛ teaspoon cayenne pepper**
- **1 pound fish fillets (any firm white fish)**
- **¼ cup finely chopped fresh parsley**
  Lemon slices (optional)

Heat oil in large skillet over medium heat; sauté onion, celery and garlic. Stir in rice; sauté about 5 minutes or until rice browns slightly. Add tomatoes and juice, lemon pepper, salt and cayenne pepper. Place fish fillets in bottom of 12×7½×2-inch baking dish. Spoon rice mixture over fish. Cover with foil; bake in preheated 400°F oven 45 to 50 minutes or until rice is tender. Allow to stand 5 minutes before serving. Sprinkle with parsley. Garnish with lemon slices, if desired.

Makes 6 servings

MICROWAVE DIRECTIONS: COMBINE ONION, CELERY AND GARLIC IN MICROWAVE-SAFE BOWL. MICROWAVE AT HIGH 3 MINUTES. STIR IN RICE, TOMATOES AND JUICE, LEMON PEPPER, SALT AND CAYENNE PEPPER. MICROWAVE AT HIGH AN ADDITIONAL 5 MINUTES. PLACE FISH FILLETS IN 12×7½×2-INCH MICROWAVE-SAFE BAKING DISH. SPOON TOMATO MIXTURE OVER FISH. COVER TIGHTLY WITH PLASTIC WRAP, TURNING UP CORNER TO VENT. MICROWAVE AT HIGH 20 TO 25 MINUTES OR UNTIL RICE IS TENDER. ALLOW TO STAND 5 MINUTES BEFORE SERVING. SERVE AS DIRECTED.

Dijon-Crusted Fish Fillets

- **¼ cup GREY POUPON® Dijon Mustard, divided**
- **2 tablespoons margarine or butter, melted**
- **½ cup plain dry bread crumbs**
- **2 tablespoons grated Parmesan cheese**
- **2 tablespoons chopped parsley**
- **4 (4- to 6-ounce) firm fish fillets (salmon, cod or catfish)**

In small bowl, blend 2 tablespoons mustard and margarine; stir in bread crumbs, cheese and parsley. Place fish fillets on baking sheet; spread fillets with remaining 2 tablespoons mustard and top with crumb mixture. Bake at 400°F for 10 to 12 minutes or until fish is golden and flakes easily when tested with fork.

Makes 4 servings

Salmon Steaks with Lemon Dill Sauce

- **½ cup finely chopped red onion**
- **2 teaspoons margarine**
- **2 tablespoons all-purpose flour**
- **1⅓ cups skim milk**
- **½ cup EGG BEATERS® Healthy Egg Substitute**
- **2 teaspoons grated lemon peel**
- **¼ cup lemon juice**
- **2 teaspoons dried dill weed**
- **8 (½-inch-thick) salmon steaks (2 pounds)**
  Fresh dill sprigs for garnish

In small saucepan, over low heat, sauté onion in margarine until tender-crisp. Stir in flour; cook 1 minute. Over medium heat, gradually stir in milk; cook, stirring until mixture thickens and boils. Boil, stirring constantly, 1 minute; remove from heat. Whisk in Egg Beaters®, lemon peel, lemon juice and dried dill; return to heat. Cook, stirring constantly, until thickened. *Do not boil.*

Meanwhile, grill or broil salmon steaks 3 to 5 minutes on each side or until fish flakes easily when tested with fork. Top with sauce. Garnish with dill sprigs. *Makes 8 servings*

Prep Time: 15 minutes
Cook Time: 15 minutes

Baja Fish and Rice Bake

Broiled Salmon Fillets with Lime Salsa

1½ pounds fresh salmon fillets, quartered
½ cup plus 2 tablespoons lime juice, divided
1 jar chunky green salsa or pico de gallo
⅓ cup finely chopped green onions, including tops
⅓ cup finely chopped fresh cilantro

1. Preheat broiler. Place fillets, skin sides up, in large casserole. Pour ½ cup lime juice over fillets; set aside. Lightly spray broiler pan with nonstick cooking spray; set aside.

2. Pour salsa into small bowl; mix in remaining 2 tablespoons lime juice, green onions and cilantro. Set aside.

3. Arrange fillets, skin sides up, on prepared broiler pan. Broil 6 inches from heat 4 to 5 minutes or until skin begins to brown and chars slightly. Remove pan; turn fillets over. Return to broiler 6 to 8 minutes or until fillets begin to brown and flake easily with fork. Serve immediately.

Makes 4 servings

Prep & Cook Time: 23 minutes

SERVING SUGGESTION: SERVE WITH ADDITIONAL SALSA, STEAMED WHITE RICE AND A FRESH GREEN SALAD.

Impossibly Easy Salmon Pie

1 can (7½ ounces) salmon packed in water, drained and deboned
½ cup grated Parmesan cheese
¼ cup sliced green onions
1 jar (2 ounces) chopped pimientos, drained
½ cup 1% low-fat cottage cheese
1 tablespoon lemon juice
1½ cups 1% low-fat milk
¾ cup reduced-fat baking and pancake mix
2 whole eggs
2 egg whites *or* ¼ cup cholesterol-free egg substitute
¼ teaspoon dried dill weed
¼ teaspoon salt
¼ teaspoon paprika (optional)

1. Preheat oven to 375°F. Spray 9-inch pie plate with nonstick cooking spray. Combine salmon, Parmesan cheese, onions and pimientos in prepared pie plate; set aside.

2. Combine cottage cheese and lemon juice in blender or food processor; purée until smooth. Add milk, baking mix, whole eggs, egg whites, dill and salt. Blend 15 seconds. Pour over salmon mixture. Sprinkle with paprika, if desired.

3. Bake 35 to 40 minutes or until lightly golden and knife inserted halfway between center and edge comes out clean. Cool 5 minutes before serving. Garnish as desired.

Makes 8 servings

Fish Françoise

1 can (14½ ounces) DEL MONTE® *FreshCut*™ Diced Tomatoes with Garlic & Onion, undrained
1 tablespoon lemon juice
2 cloves garlic, minced
½ teaspoon dried tarragon leaves
⅛ teaspoon black pepper
3 tablespoons whipping cream
Vegetable oil
1½ pounds firm white fish (such as halibut or cod)
Lemon wedges

1. Preheat broiler; position rack 4 inches from heat.

2. Combine tomatoes, lemon juice, garlic, tarragon and pepper in large saucepan. Cook over medium-high heat about 10 minutes or until liquid has evaporated.

3. Stir in cream. Reduce heat to low. Cook until tomato mixture is very thick; set aside.

4. Brush broiler pan with oil. Arrange fish in pan; season with salt and additional pepper, if desired. Broil 3 to 4 minutes on each side or until fish flakes easily when tested with fork.

5. Spread tomato mixture over top of fish. Broil 1 minute. Serve with lemon wedges.

Makes 4 servings

Prep Time: 5 minutes
Cook Time: 19 minutes

Broiled Salmon Fillet with Lime Salsa

Poached Salmon with Tarragon Cream Sauce

- 2 tablespoons butter or margarine
- 3 tablespoons minced shallots
- 1 clove garlic, minced
- 1 cup dry white wine, divided
- ½ cup clam juice
- ½ cup heavy cream
- 1 tablespoon chopped fresh parsley
- ½ teaspoon dried tarragon leaves
- 2 salmon steaks, 1 inch thick (about 8 ounces each)
- Fish Stock (recipe follows), clam juice or water
- Fresh tarragon for garnish (optional)

To make Tarragon Cream Sauce, melt butter in medium saucepan over medium heat. Add shallots and garlic; reduce heat to low and cook 5 minutes or until shallots are tender. Add ½ cup wine and clam juice. Bring to a simmer. Simmer 10 minutes or until sauce is reduced to ½ cup. Add cream and simmer 5 minutes or until sauce is reduced by half. (The sauce should heavily coat the back of a metal spoon.) Stir in parsley and dried tarragon; keep warm over very low heat.

Rinse salmon steaks and pat dry with paper towels. Place steaks in saucepan just large enough to hold them. Add remaining ½ cup wine and enough Fish Stock to barely cover fish. Bring liquid to a simmer over medium heat. *(Do not boil. This will cause fish to break apart.)* Adjust heat, if necessary, to keep liquid at a simmer. Simmer 10 minutes or until center is no longer red and fish flakes easily when tested with fork. Remove fish with slotted spatula; transfer to serving plates. Top fish with Tarragon Cream Sauce. Garnish, if desired. *Makes 2 servings*

FISH STOCK

- 1¾ pounds fish skeletons and heads from lean fish, such as red snapper, cod, halibut or flounder
- 2 medium onions, cut into wedges
- 3 ribs celery, cut into 2-inch pieces
- 10 cups cold water
- 2 slices lemon
- ¾ teaspoon dried thyme leaves
- 8 black peppercorns
- 3 fresh parsley sprigs
- 1 bay leaf
- 1 clove garlic

Rinse fish; cut out gills and discard. Combine fish skeletons and heads, onions and celery in stockpot or Dutch oven. Add remaining ingredients. Bring to a boil over high heat. Reduce heat to medium-low; simmer, uncovered, 30 minutes, skimming foam that rises to the surface. Remove stock from heat and cool slightly. Strain stock through large sieve or colander lined with several layers of dampened cheesecloth, removing all bones, vegetables and seasonings; discard. Use immediately or refrigerate in tightly covered container up to 2 days or freeze stock in freezer containers for several months.
Makes about 10 cups

Savory Salmon

- 6 small salmon steaks (about 6 ounces each)
- ¾ cup prepared HIDDEN VALLEY RANCH® Original Ranch® Salad Dressing
- 2 teaspoons chopped fresh dill *or* ¼ teaspoon dried dill weed
- 1 teaspoon chopped fresh parsley
- Lemon wedges
- Fresh dill sprigs (optional)

Preheat oven to 375°F. Arrange salmon in large buttered baking dish; spread 2 tablespoons salad dressing over each steak. Sprinkle with chopped dill and parsley. Bake until fish flakes easily when tested with fork, 10 to 15 minutes. Place under broiler 45 to 60 seconds to brown. Serve with lemon wedges; garnish with dill sprigs, if desired. *Makes 6 servings*

Savory Salmon

Fish Veracruz

FISH
1½ pounds red snapper or
   halibut fillets
½ cup lime juice
½ teaspoon salt

SAUCE
2 tablespoons vegetable
   oil
1 cup (1 small) sliced
   onion
1 cup (1 small) green bell
   pepper strips
3 cloves garlic, finely
   chopped
⅓ cup dry white wine
2½ cups (24-ounce jar)
   ORTEGA® Garden Style
   Salsa, mild
½ cup CONTADINA®
   Tomato Sauce
¼ cup ORTEGA® Sliced
   Jalapeños
¼ cup sliced ripe olives
1 tablespoon CROSSE &
   BLACKWELL® Capers
   Cilantro sprigs (optional)
   Lime wedges (optional)

FOR FISH: **ARRANGE** fish in
13×9-inch baking pan. Sprinkle
with lime juice and salt; cover.
Chill at least 20 minutes.

FOR SAUCE: **HEAT** oil in large
skillet over medium-high heat.
Add onion, bell pepper and
garlic; cook 1 to 2 minutes or
until vegetables are crisp-
tender. Add wine; cook 1
minute.

STIR in salsa, tomato sauce,
jalapeños, olives and capers.
Bring to a boil. Place fish in
sauce. Reduce heat to low.

COOK, covered, 8 to 10 minutes
or until fish flakes when tested
with fork. Serve with cilantro
and lime, if desired.

Makes 8 servings

Moroccan Swordfish

4 swordfish steaks
   (4 ounces each), about
   1 inch thick
1 tablespoon fresh lemon
   juice
1 tablespoon apple cider
   vinegar
2½ teaspoons garlic-
   flavored vegetable oil
1 teaspoon ground ginger
1 teaspoon paprika
½ teaspoon ground cumin
½ teaspoon hot chili oil
¼ teaspoon salt
¼ teaspoon ground
   coriander
⅛ teaspoon black pepper
2⅔ cups prepared couscous

1. Place swordfish in single
layer in medium shallow dish.
Combine lemon juice, vinegar,
vegetable oil, ginger, paprika,
cumin, chili oil, salt, coriander
and pepper in small bowl;
pour over swordfish, turning
to coat both sides. Cover and
refrigerate 40 minutes, turning
once.

2. Discard marinade; grill
swordfish on uncovered grill
over medium-hot coals 8 to
10 minutes or until swordfish is
opaque and flakes easily when
tested with fork, turning once.
Serve with couscous.

Makes 4 servings

Greek-Style Fish Fillets

2 tablespoons olive oil
1 cup (1 small) thinly
   sliced onion
3½ cups (two 14½-ounce
   cans) CONTADINA®
   Dalla Casa Buitoni
   Recipe Ready Diced
   Tomatoes, undrained
2 MAGGI® Vegetarian
   Vegetable Bouillon
   Cubes
1 pound firm fish fillets
1¾ cups (14-ounce can) cut
   green beans, drained
½ cup (2¼-ounce can)
   sliced ripe olives,
   drained
¾ cup (3 ounces) crumbled
   feta cheese
   Hot cooked couscous

HEAT oil in large skillet over
medium-high heat. Add onion;
cook 2 to 3 minutes or until
tender. Stir in tomatoes and
juice and bouillon; cook,
stirring occasionally, 2 to 3
minutes or until bouillon is
dissolved.

PLACE fish over sauce; spoon
some sauce over fish. Reduce
heat to low. Cook, covered,
15 to 20 minutes or until fish
flakes easily when tested with
fork.

DISTRIBUTE green beans,
olives and cheese over fish.
Cook, covered, 2 to 3 minutes
or until cheese is softened.
Serve with couscous.

Makes 4 servings

Trout Stuffed with Fresh Mint and Oranges

2 pan-dressed* trout (1 to 1¼ pounds each)
½ teaspoon coarse salt, such as Kosher salt
1 orange, sliced
1 cup fresh mint leaves
1 sweet onion, sliced

*A pan-dressed trout has been gutted and scaled with head and tail removed.

1. Rinse trout under cold running water; pat dry with paper towels.

2. Sprinkle cavities of trout with salt; fill each with orange slices and mint. Cover each fish with onion slices.

3. Spray 2 large sheets of foil with nonstick cooking spray. Place 1 fish on each sheet and seal using Drugstore Wrap technique.**

4. Place foil packets seam-side down directly on medium-hot coals; grill on covered grill 20 to 25 minutes or until trout flakes easily when tested with fork, turning once.

5. Carefully open foil packets; remove and discard orange-mint stuffing and trout skin. Serve immediately.

Makes 6 servings

**Drugstore Wrap: Place the food in the center of an oblong piece of heavy-duty foil, leaving at least a 2-inch border around the food. Bring the 2 long sides together above the food; fold down in a series of locked folds, allowing for heat circulation and expansion. Fold the short ends up and over again. Press folds firmly to seal the foil packet.

Trout with Apples and Toasted Hazelnuts

⅓ cup whole hazelnuts
5 tablespoons butter or margarine, divided
1 large Red Delicious apple, cored and cut into 16 wedges
2 butterflied rainbow trout fillets (about 8 ounces each)
Salt and black pepper
3 tablespoons all-purpose flour
1 tablespoon lemon juice
1 tablespoon snipped fresh chives
Lemon slices and fresh chives for garnish

Preheat oven to 350°F. To toast hazelnuts, spread in single layer on baking sheet. Bake 8 to 10 minutes or until skins split.

Wrap hazelnuts in kitchen towel; set aside 5 minutes to cool slightly. Rub hazelnuts in towel to remove as much of the papery skins as possible. Process hazelnuts in food processor until coarsely chopped; set aside.

Melt 3 tablespoons butter in medium skillet over medium-high heat. Add apple; cook 4 to 5 minutes or until crisp-tender. Remove from skillet with slotted spoon; set aside.

Rinse trout and pat dry with paper towels. Sprinkle fish with salt and pepper, then coat in flour. Place fish in skillet. Cook 4 minutes or until golden and fish flakes easily when tested with fork, turning halfway through cooking time. Return apple to skillet. Reduce heat to low and keep warm.

Melt remaining 2 tablespoons butter in small saucepan over low heat. Stir in lemon juice, chives and hazelnuts. Drizzle fish and apple with hazelnut mixture. Garnish, if desired.

Makes 2 servings

Mediterranean Cod

- 1 bag (16 ounces) BIRDS EYE® frozen Farm Fresh Mixtures Broccoli, Green Beans, Pearl Onions and Red Peppers
- 1 can (14½ ounces) stewed tomatoes, undrained
- ½ teaspoon dried basil leaves
- 1 pound cod fillets, cut into serving pieces
- ½ cup orange juice, divided
- 2 tablespoons all-purpose flour
- ¼ cup sliced black olives (optional)

• Combine vegetables, tomatoes and basil in large skillet. Bring to a boil over medium-high heat.

• Place cod on vegetables. Pour ¼ cup orange juice over fish. Cover and cook 5 to 7 minutes or until fish is tender and flakes with fork.

• Remove cod and keep warm. Blend flour with remaining ¼ cup orange juice; stir into skillet. Cook until liquid is thickened and vegetables are coated.

• Serve fish with vegetables; sprinkle with olives, if desired.

Makes about 4 servings

Prep Time: 5 minutes
Cook Time: 15 minutes

SERVING SUGGESTION: SERVE WITH RICE OR COUSCOUS.

Baked Stuffed Snapper

- 1 red snapper (1½ pounds)
- 2 cups hot cooked rice
- 1 can (4 ounces) sliced mushrooms, drained
- ½ cup diced water chestnuts
- ¼ cup thinly sliced green onions
- ¼ cup diced pimientos
- 2 tablespoons chopped parsley
- 1 tablespoon finely shredded lemon peel
- ½ teaspoon salt
- ⅛ teaspoon black pepper
- 1 tablespoon margarine, melted

Preheat oven to 400°F. Clean and butterfly fish. Combine rice, mushrooms, water chestnuts, onions, pimientos, parsley, lemon peel, salt and pepper; toss lightly. Fill cavity of fish with rice mixture; close with wooden toothpicks soaked in water. Place fish in 13×9-inch baking dish coated with nonstick cooking spray; brush fish with margarine. Bake 18 to 20 minutes or until fish flakes easily when tested with fork. Wrap any remaining rice in foil and bake in oven with fish.

Makes 4 servings

*FAVORITE RECIPE FROM **USA RICE FEDERATION***

Red Snapper Vera Cruz

- 4 red snapper fillets (1 pound)
- ¼ cup fresh lime juice
- 1 tablespoon fresh lemon juice
- 1 teaspoon chili powder
- 4 green onions with 4 inches of tops, sliced in ½-inch lengths
- 1 tomato, coarsely chopped
- ½ cup chopped Anaheim or green bell pepper
- ½ cup chopped red bell pepper

Microwave Directions:
1. Place red snapper in shallow microwavable baking dish. Combine lime juice, lemon juice and chili powder. Pour over snapper. Marinate 10 minutes, turning once or twice.

2. Sprinkle onions, tomato and peppers over snapper. Cover dish loosely with plastic wrap. Microwave at HIGH 6 minutes or just until snapper flakes in center, rotating dish every 2 minutes. Let stand, covered, 4 minutes before serving.

Makes 4 servings

Mediterranean Cod

Tuna with Peppercorns on a Bed of Greens

4 tuna steaks (about
   1½ pounds)
Salt
2 teaspoons coarsely
   ground black pepper
1 tablespoon butter or
   margarine
1 large onion, thinly sliced
¼ cup dry white wine
½ pound fresh kale or
   spinach, washed
1 tablespoon olive oil
½ teaspoon sugar
¼ teaspoon black pepper
12 julienne strips carrot
   Lemon slices and purple
   kale for garnish

Preheat oven to 325°F. Rinse tuna and pat dry with paper towels. Lightly sprinkle fish with salt, then press 2 teaspoons coarsely ground pepper into both sides of steaks; set aside.

Melt butter in large skillet over medium heat. Add onion; cook and stir 5 minutes or until crisp-tender. Add wine and remove from heat. Spread onion mixture on bottom of 13×9-inch glass baking dish. Top with fish. Bake 15 minutes. Spoon liquid over fish and bake 15 minutes more or until fish flakes easily when tested with fork.

Meanwhile, trim away tough stems from kale; cut leaves into 1-inch strips.

Heat oil in medium skillet over medium-high heat. Add kale, sugar and ¼ teaspoon pepper. Cook and stir 2 to 3 minutes or until tender. Place kale on plates. Top with fish and onion mixture. Top fish with carrot strips. Garnish, if desired. Serve immediately.

Makes 4 servings

Tuna-Stuffed Sole with Lime Sauce

½ cup carrots, cut into
   thin strips
½ cup zucchini or yellow
   squash, cut into thin
   strips
2 green onions, cut into
   thin strips
1 can (9 ounces)
   STARKIST® Tuna,
   drained and flaked
2 tablespoons lemon juice
1 teaspoon dried basil
   leaves
½ teaspoon dried dill weed
8 thin sole or other white
   fish fillets (about
   1½ pounds)
16 large fresh spinach
   leaves, washed

LIME SAUCE
   ½ cup chicken broth
   2 tablespoons butter or
      margarine
   2 tablespoons lime juice
   1 tablespoon cornstarch
   ¼ teaspoon black pepper
      Lemon or lime peel for
      garnish (optional)

Microwave Directions:
In 1-quart microwavable bowl, combine carrots, zucchini and onions. Cover with waxed paper; microwave at HIGH 2 to 3 minutes or until nearly tender, stirring once during cooking. Stir in tuna, lemon juice, basil and dill. Arrange one sole fillet on microwavable roasting rack or plate. Top with two spinach leaves, overlapping if necessary. Spoon equal portion of vegetable mixture over each fillet; roll up each fillet from short side, enclosing filling. Secure with wooden toothpicks; transfer to shallow microwavable dish, filling sides up. Repeat with remaining fillets and filling.

Cover dish with vented plastic wrap. Microwave at HIGH 8 to 11 minutes or until fish flakes easily, rotating dish once during cooking. Remove wooden toothpicks. Let stand while making Lime Sauce.

For Lime Sauce, in medium microwavable bowl, combine all sauce ingredients except garnish until well blended. Microwave, covered, at HIGH 1 to 3 minutes, or until thickened, stirring once. Serve fish with sauce. Garnish, if desired.   *Makes 4 servings*

Prep Time: 15 minutes

Soleful Roulettes

1 package (6 ounces) long-grain and wild rice mix
1 package (3 ounces) cream cheese, softened
2 tablespoons milk
32 medium fresh spinach leaves, washed
4 sole fillets (about 1 pound)
Salt and coarsely ground black pepper
¼ cup dry white wine

Cook rice mix according to package directions. Place 2 cups cooked rice in large bowl. (Refrigerate remaining rice for another use.) Combine cream cheese and milk in medium bowl. Stir into rice; set aside.

Place spinach in heatproof bowl. Pour very hot water (not boiling) over spinach to wilt leaves slightly. Rinse sole and pat dry with paper towels. Sprinkle both sides of each fillet with salt and pepper. Cover each fillet with spinach leaves. Divide rice mixture evenly and spread over top of each spinach-lined fillet. To roll fillets, begin with thin end of fillet, roll up and secure with toothpicks.

Combine wine and ½ cup water in large, heavy saucepan. Stand fillets upright on rolled edges in saucepan; cover. Simmer over low heat 10 minutes or until fish flakes easily when tested with fork. *(Do not boil. This will cause fish to break apart.)*
Makes 4 servings

Tuna Quesadilla Stack

4 (10-inch) flour tortillas
¼ cup plus 2 tablespoons pinto or black bean dip
1 can (9 ounces) tuna packed in water, drained and flaked
2 cups (8 ounces) shredded Cheddar cheese
1 can (14½ ounces) diced tomatoes, drained
½ cup thinly sliced green onions
1½ teaspoon butter or margarine, melted

1. Preheat oven to 400°F.

2. Place 1 tortilla on 12-inch pizza pan. Spread with 2 tablespoons bean dip, leaving ½-inch margin. Top with ⅓ each tuna, cheese, tomatoes and green onions. Repeat layers twice.

3. Top with remaining tortilla, pressing gently. Brush with melted butter.

4. Bake 15 minutes or until cheese melts and top is lightly browned. Cut into 8 wedges.
Makes 4 servings

Prep & Cook Time: 25 minutes

Tuna Quesadilla Stack

Tequila-Lime Prawns

- 1 pound medium shrimp, peeled and deveined
- 3 tablespoons butter or margarine
- 1 tablespoon olive oil
- 2 large cloves garlic, minced
- 2 tablespoons tequila
- 1 tablespoon lime juice
- ¼ teaspoon salt
- ¼ teaspoon red pepper flakes
- 3 tablespoons coarsely chopped cilantro
- Hot cooked rice (optional)

Pat shrimp dry with paper towels. Heat butter and oil in large skillet over medium heat. When butter is melted, add garlic; cook 30 seconds. Add shrimp; cook 2 minutes, stirring occasionally. Stir in tequila, lime juice, salt and red pepper flakes. Cook 2 minutes or until most of liquid evaporates and shrimp are pink and glazed. Add cilantro; cook 10 seconds. Serve over hot cooked rice, if desired. Garnish with lime wedges, if desired.

Makes 3 to 4 servings

Diavolo Seafood Loaves

- 1 to 1½ pounds shrimp*
- 1 bunch fresh cilantro
- 3 cloves garlic, divided
- 2 green onions
- 4 round loaves sourdough bread, each about 5 inches in diameter
- Olive oil or butter
- 1 cup white wine
- 1 small red bell pepper, diced
- 1 small yellow bell pepper, diced
- 1 small green bell pepper, diced
- 1 (26-ounce) jar NEWMAN'S OWN® Diavolo Sauce
- Softened butter
- Tomato and orange slices for garnish

Substitute 1½ pounds other fresh shellfish or red snapper if shrimp is unavailable.

1. Peel and devein shrimp. Chop cilantro to make about 1 cup, reserving a few sprigs for garnish. Chop 2 cloves garlic and green onions. Prepare bread by horizontally slicing top off of each loaf. Hollow out loaves to within 1 inch of sides and bottoms; reserve removed bread in separate bowl.

2. Heat 3 tablespoons oil in skillet. Add chopped garlic and green onions; cook and stir 3 to 5 minutes or until tender. Add wine; boil mixture until reduced to ½ cup. Add shrimp and peppers; cook and stir just until shrimp turn pink. *Do not overcook.* In large saucepan, heat Diavolo Sauce; add chopped cilantro.

3. Cut reserved bread into cubes; drizzle with small amount of olive oil. Chop remaining 1 clove garlic. Add half of chopped garlic to cubed bread mixture; stir well. Spread cubed bread mixture on ungreased baking sheet; bake 10 minutes in preheated 400°F oven or until golden brown.

4. Spread some softened butter on inside of each bread shell; sprinkle with remaining chopped garlic. Broil to brown lightly. Remove; set aside.

5. To serve, fill each bread shell with even amount of shrimp mixture; add heated Diavolo Sauce to within 1 inch of top of each filled bread shell. Garnish with bread cubes, reserved cilantro sprigs and tomato and orange slices.

Makes 4 servings

Tequila-Lime Prawns

Butterflied Shrimp Parmesan

1½ pounds large shrimp
1 cup (4 ounces) shredded ALPINE LACE® Fat Free Pasteurized Process Skim Milk Cheese Product—For Parmesan Lovers
¼ cup Italian seasoned dry bread crumbs
2 tablespoons unsalted butter substitute
¾ cup chopped red bell pepper
½ cup thinly sliced green onions
1 tablespoon minced garlic
⅛ teaspoon crushed red pepper flakes or to taste
⅓ cup minced fresh parsley
6 tablespoons 2% low fat milk

1. Peel the shrimp, leaving the tails on. Then butterfly each shrimp by cutting it along the outer curved edge almost all the way through. Open the shrimp up like a book and remove the dark vein. In a small bowl, toss the cheese with the bread crumbs and set aside.

2. In a large nonstick skillet, melt the butter over medium-high heat. Add the bell pepper, green onions, garlic and red pepper flakes and cook for 5 minutes or until soft. Add the shrimp and sauté for 5 minutes or just until the shrimp turn pink and opaque. Stir in the parsley.

3. In a small saucepan, bring the milk just to a boil, then stir into the shrimp mixture. Stir in the cheese mixture and cook until the cheese is melted. Serve immediately.

Makes 4 servings

Shrimp Miami

2 pounds shrimp, fresh or frozen
¼ cup olive or vegetable oil
2 teaspoons salt
½ teaspoon white pepper
¼ cup extra-dry vermouth
2 tablespoons lemon juice

Thaw frozen shrimp. Peel shrimp, leaving last section of shell on. Remove sand veins and wash. Preheat electric frying pan to 320°F. Add oil, salt, pepper and shrimp. Cook 8 to 10 minutes or until shrimp are pink and tender, stirring constantly. *Increase pan temperature to 420°F.* Add vermouth and lemon juice. Cook 1 minute longer, stirring constantly. Drain. Serve hot or cold as an appetizer or entrée.

Makes 6 servings

FAVORITE RECIPE FROM *FLORIDA DEPARTMENT OF AGRICULTURE AND CONSUMER SERVICES, BUREAU OF SEAFOOD AND AQUACULTURE*

Spicy Shrimp

2 tablespoons olive oil
1 large onion, finely chopped
1 large green bell pepper, finely chopped
3 cloves garlic, minced
1 can (8 ounces) tomato sauce
½ cup dry white wine
½ cup chopped parsley
1 jar (4 ounces) chopped pimientos, undrained
3 tablespoons FRANK'S® Original REDHOT® Cayenne Pepper Sauce or more to taste
¼ teaspoon salt
2 pounds raw large shrimp, peeled and deveined
Cooked white rice (optional)

1. Heat oil in large nonstick skillet over medium-high heat. Add onion, bell pepper and garlic; cook and stir until vegetables are tender. Add tomato sauce, wine, parsley, pimientos, RedHot® sauce and salt. Bring to a boil. Cover; cook over medium-low heat 10 minutes, stirring occasionally.

2. Stir in shrimp. Cover; cook over medium-low heat 5 to 8 minutes or until shrimp turn pink, stirring often. Serve over rice, if desired.

Makes 6 servings

Prep Time: 20 minutes
Cook Time: 23 minutes

Butterflied Shrimp Parmesan

Shrimp in Tomatillo Sauce over Rice

1 teaspoon olive oil
¼ cup chopped onion
1 cup GUILTLESS GOURMET® Green Tomatillo Salsa
¾ cup white wine
Juice of ½ lemon
12 ounces medium-size raw shrimp, peeled and deveined
4 cups hot cooked white rice
Lemon peel strip (optional)

Heat oil in large nonstick skillet over medium-high heat until hot. Add onion; cook and stir until onion is translucent. Add salsa, wine and juice, stirring just until mixture begins to boil. Reduce heat to medium-low; simmer 10 minutes. Add shrimp; cook about 2 minutes or until shrimp turn pink and opaque, stirring occasionally. To serve, place 1 cup rice in each of 4 individual serving bowls. Pour shrimp mixture evenly over rice. Garnish with lemon peel, if desired.

Makes 4 servings

Jazzy Jambalaya

1 package (6.8 ounces) RICE-A-RONI® Spanish Rice
1 cup chopped cooked chicken or ham
1 cup chopped onion
1 cup chopped green bell pepper
2 cloves garlic, minced
3 tablespoons vegetable oil
1 can (14½ ounces) tomatoes, undrained and chopped
Dash hot pepper sauce (optional)
½ pound raw shrimp, peeled and deveined *or* 8 ounces frozen cleaned precooked shrimp

1. In large skillet, combine rice-vermicelli mix, chicken, onion, bell pepper, garlic and oil. Sauté over medium heat, stirring frequently, until vermicelli is golden brown.

2. Stir in 2 cups water, tomatoes and juice, hot pepper sauce, if desired, and contents of seasoning packet; bring to a boil over high heat.

3. Cover; reduce heat. Simmer 10 minutes.

4. Stir in shrimp.

5. Cover; continue cooking 8 to 10 minutes or until liquid is absorbed, rice is tender and shrimp turn pink.

Makes 5 servings

Grilled Prawns with Salsa Vera Cruz

1½ cups DEL MONTE® Thick & Chunky Salsa, Mild
1 orange, peeled and chopped
¼ cup sliced green onions
¼ cup chopped cilantro or parsley
1 small clove garlic, crushed
1 pound medium shrimp, peeled and deveined

1. Combine salsa, orange, green onions, cilantro and garlic in medium bowl.

2. Thread shrimp onto skewers; season with salt and pepper, if desired.

3. Brush grill with oil. Cook shrimp over hot coals about 3 minutes on each side or until shrimp turn pink. Serve over rice and top with salsa. Garnish, if desired.

Makes 4 servings

Prep Time: 25 minutes
Cook Time: 6 minutes

Helpful Hint: Thoroughly rinse shrimp in cold water before cooking.

Shrimp in Tomatillo Sauce over Rice

Lemon-Garlic Shrimp

1 package (6.2 ounces) RICE-A-RONI® With ⅓ Less Salt Broccoli Au Gratin
1 tablespoon margarine or butter
1 pound raw medium shrimp, peeled and deveined *or* large scallops, cut into halves
1 medium red or green bell pepper, cut into short thin strips
2 cloves garlic, minced
½ teaspoon dried Italian seasoning
½ cup reduced-sodium or regular chicken broth
1 tablespoon lemon juice
1 tablespoon cornstarch
3 medium green onions, cut into ½-inch pieces
1 teaspoon grated lemon peel, divided

1. Prepare Rice-A-Roni® Mix as package directs.

2. While Rice-A-Roni® is simmering, heat margarine in second large skillet or wok over medium-high heat. Add shrimp, bell pepper, garlic and Italian seasoning. Stir-fry 3 to 4 minutes or until seafood is opaque.

3. Combine chicken broth, lemon juice and cornstarch, mixing until smooth. Add broth mixture and onions to skillet. Stir-fry 2 to 3 minutes or until sauce thickens.

4. Stir ½ teaspoon lemon peel into rice. Serve rice topped with shrimp mixture; sprinkle with remaining ½ teaspoon lemon peel.

Makes 4 servings

Shrimp Monterey

2 tablespoons butter or margarine
2 large cloves garlic, minced
2 pounds medium shrimp, peeled and deveined
¼ teaspoon ground red pepper
½ cup dry white wine
2 cups (8 ounces) SARGENTO® Fancy Shredded Monterey Jack Cheese
2 tablespoons chopped fresh parsley

In large skillet, melt butter; add garlic and cook over medium heat 1 minute. Add shrimp and red pepper; cook about 4 minutes, stirring often, until shrimp turn pink. Using slotted spoon, remove shrimp to 11×7-inch baking dish. Add wine to skillet; bring to a boil and cook about 5 minutes over high heat, stirring constantly, until liquid is reduced by half. Pour reduced liquid over shrimp in baking dish. Combine Monterey Jack cheese and parsley; spoon over shrimp. Bake in preheated 350°F oven about 10 minutes or until cheese is melted.

Makes 6 servings

Shrimp Classico

⅔ cup milk
2 tablespoons margarine or butter
1 package (4.8 ounces) PASTA RONI® Angel Hair Pasta with Herbs
1 clove garlic, minced
1 package (10 ounces) frozen chopped spinach, thawed and well drained
1 package (10 ounces) frozen precooked shrimp, thawed and well drained
1 jar (2 ounces) chopped pimientos, drained

Microwave Directions:
1. In 3-quart round microwavable glass casserole, combine 1⅔ cups water, milk and margarine. Microwave, uncovered, at HIGH 4 to 5 minutes or until boiling.

2. Gradually add pasta while stirring. Separate pasta with a fork, if needed. Stir in contents of seasoning packet and garlic.

3. Microwave, uncovered, at HIGH 4 minutes, stirring gently after 2 minutes. Separate pasta with a fork, if needed. Stir in spinach, shrimp and pimientos. Microwave at HIGH 1 to 2 minutes. Sauce will be very thin, but will thicken upon standing.

4. Let stand, uncovered, 2 minutes or until desired consistency. Stir before serving.

Makes 4 servings

Boiled Whole Lobster with Burned Butter Sauce

½ cup butter
2 tablespoons chopped
 fresh parsley
1 tablespoon cider vinegar
1 tablespoon capers
2 live lobsters*

Purchase live lobsters as close to time of cooking as possible. Store in refrigerator.

Fill 8-quart stockpot with enough water to cover lobsters. Cover stockpot; bring water to a boil over high heat. Meanwhile, to make Burned Butter Sauce, melt butter in medium saucepan over medium heat. Cook and stir butter until it turns dark chocolate brown. Remove from heat. Add parsley, vinegar and capers. Pour into 2 individual ramekins; set aside.

Holding each lobster by its back, submerge head first into boiling water. Cover and continue to heat. When water returns to a boil, cook lobsters from 10 to 18 minutes, according to size:

1 pound—10 minutes
1¼ pounds—12 minutes
1½ pounds—15 minutes
2 pounds—18 minutes

Transfer to 2 large serving platters. Remove bands restraining claws. Cut through underside of shells with kitchen shears and loosen meat from shells. Serve lobsters with Burned Butter Sauce.

Makes 2 servings

Mock "Étouffée"

¼ cup butter or margarine
1 green bell pepper,
 chopped
1 medium onion, chopped
2 ribs celery, chopped
3 cloves garlic, minced
1 can (14½ ounces) diced
 tomatoes, undrained*
1 can (10¾ ounces)
 condensed golden
 mushroom soup
2 tablespoons FRANK'S®
 Original REDHOT®
 Cayenne Pepper Sauce
1 pound raw large shrimp,
 peeled and deveined
½ cup chopped parsley
 Cooked white rice or
 pasta (optional)

You may substitute 1 can (14½ ounces) whole tomatoes, cut up, for diced tomatoes.

1. Melt butter in large nonstick skillet. Add bell pepper, onion, celery and garlic; cook and stir 3 minutes or until tender.

2. Stir in tomatoes with liquid, soup and RedHot® sauce. Bring to a boil. Simmer 5 minutes, stirring often. Add shrimp; simmer about 3 minutes or until shrimp turn pink, stirring occasionally.

3. Stir in parsley. Serve over rice or pasta, if desired.
Makes 4 servings

Boiled Whole Lobster with Burned Butter Sauce

Seafood Paella

- 1 tablespoon olive oil
- 4 cloves garlic, minced
- 4½ cups finely chopped onions
- 2 cups uncooked long-grain white rice
- 2 cups clam juice
- 2 cups dry white wine
- 3 tablespoons fresh lemon juice
- ½ teaspoon paprika
- ¼ cup boiling water
- ½ teaspoon saffron or ground turmeric
- 1½ cups diced peeled plum tomatoes
- ½ cup chopped fresh parsley
- 1 jar (8 ounces) roasted red peppers, drained and thinly sliced, divided
- 1 pound bay scallops
- 1½ cups frozen peas, thawed
- 10 clams, scrubbed
- 10 mussels, scrubbed
- 20 large shrimp (1 pound), peeled and deveined

Preheat oven to 375°F. Heat oil in large ovenproof skillet or paella pan over medium-low heat until hot. Add garlic and cook just until garlic sizzles. Add onions and rice; cook and stir 10 minutes or until onions are soft. Stir in clam juice, wine, lemon juice and paprika; mix well.

Combine boiling water and saffron in small bowl; stir until saffron is dissolved. Stir into onion mixture. Stir in tomatoes, parsley and half the red peppers. Bring to a boil over medium heat. Remove from heat; cover. Place on lowest shelf of oven. Bake 1 hour or until all of liquid is absorbed.

Remove from oven; stir in scallops and peas. *Turn oven off;* return paella to oven. Steam clams and mussels 4 to 6 minutes, removing each as shells open. (Discard any unopened clams or mussels.) Steam shrimp 2 to 3 minutes just until shrimp turn pink and opaque. Remove paella from oven and arrange clams, mussels and shrimp on top. Garnish with remaining red peppers. *Makes 10 servings*

Zesty Crab Cakes with Red Pepper Sauce

- ½ pound raw medium shrimp, peeled and deveined
- 1 egg white
- ⅔ cup heavy cream
- 3 tablespoons FRANK'S® Original REDHOT® Cayenne Pepper Sauce
- 1 tablespoon FRENCH'S® Worcestershire Sauce
- ¼ teaspoon seasoned salt
- 1 pound crabmeat or imitation crabmeat, flaked (4 cups)
- 1 red or yellow bell pepper, minced
- 2 green onions, minced
- ¼ cup minced parsley
- 1½ cups fresh bread crumbs
- ½ cup corn oil
  Red Pepper Sauce (recipe follows)

1. Place shrimp, egg white, cream, RedHot® sauce, Worcestershire and seasoned salt in food processor. Process until mixture is puréed. Transfer to large bowl.

2. Add crabmeat, bell pepper, onions and parsley. Mix with fork until well blended.

3. Shape crabmeat mixture into 12 (½-inch-thick) patties, using about ¼ cup mixture for each. Coat both sides in bread crumbs.

4. Heat oil in large nonstick skillet. Add crab cakes; cook until browned on both sides. Drain on paper towels. Serve with Red Pepper Sauce.
Makes about 1 dozen crab cakes

Prep Time: 30 minutes
Cook Time: 15 minutes

RED PEPPER SAUCE
- 1 jar (7 ounces) roasted red peppers, drained
- ¼ cup mayonnaise
- 3 tablespoons FRANK'S® Original REDHOT® Cayenne Pepper Sauce
- 2 tablespoons minced onion
- 1 tablespoon FRENCH'S® Deli Brown Mustard
- 1 tablespoon minced parsley
- 1 clove garlic

Place all ingredients in blender or food processor. Cover; blend until smooth.

Makes 1 cup sauce

Seafood Paella

Crab Cakes with Tomato Salsa

CRAB CAKES
- 1 pound crabmeat
- 1 tablespoon FILIPPO BERIO® Olive Oil
- 1 onion, finely chopped
- 1 cup fresh white bread crumbs, divided
- 2 eggs, beaten, divided
- 2 tablespoons drained capers, rinsed and chopped
- 2 tablespoons mayonnaise
- 1 tablespoon chopped parsley
- 1 tablespoon ketchup
  Finely grated peel of ½ lemon
- 1 tablespoon lemon juice
  Additional FILIPPO BERIO® Olive Oil for frying
  Salt and freshly ground black pepper

TOMATO SALSA
- 3 tablespoons FILIPPO BERIO® Olive Oil
- 4 large tomatoes, finely chopped
- 2 cloves garlic, crushed
- ¼ cup lemon juice
- 4½ teaspoons sweet or hot chili sauce
- 1 tablespoon sugar
  Salt and freshly ground black pepper

For Crab Cakes, pick out and discard any shell or cartilage from crabmeat. Place crabmeat in medium bowl; flake finely. In small skillet, heat 1 tablespoon olive oil over medium heat until hot. Add onion; cook and stir 3 to 5 minutes or until softened. Add to crabmeat. Gently mix in ½ cup bread crumbs, 1 egg, capers, mayonnaise, parsley, ketchup, lemon peel and 1 tablespoon lemon juice. Shape mixture into 8 round cakes; cover and refrigerate 30 minutes.

Meanwhile, for Tomato Salsa, in medium skillet, heat 3 tablespoons olive oil over medium heat until hot. Add tomatoes and garlic; cook and stir 5 minutes. Add ¼ cup lemon juice, chili sauce and sugar; mix well. Season to taste with salt and pepper.

Dip crab cakes into remaining beaten egg, then in remaining ½ cup bread crumbs. Press crumb coating firmly onto crab cakes.

In large nonstick skillet, pour in just enough olive oil to cover bottom. Heat over medium-high heat until hot. Add crab cakes; fry 5 to 8 minutes, turning frequently, until cooked through and golden brown. Drain on paper towels. Season to taste with salt and pepper. Serve hot with Tomato Salsa for dipping.

Makes 8 crab cakes

Maryland Crab Cakes

- 1 pound fresh backfin crabmeat, cartilage removed
- 10 low-salt crackers (2 inches each), crushed to equal ½ cup crumbs
- 1 rib celery, finely chopped
- 1 green onion, finely chopped
- ¼ cup cholesterol-free egg substitute
- 3 tablespoons nonfat tartar sauce
- 1 teaspoon seafood seasoning
- 2 teaspoons vegetable oil

1. Combine crabmeat, cracker crumbs, celery and onion in medium bowl; set aside.

2. Mix egg substitute, tartar sauce and seafood seasoning in small bowl; pour over crabmeat mixture. Gently mix so large lumps will not be broken. Shape into six ¾-inch-thick patties. Cover; refrigerate 30 minutes.

3. Spray skillet with nonstick cooking spray. Add oil; heat over medium-high heat. Place crab cakes in skillet; cook 3 to 4 minutes on each side or until cakes are lightly browned. Garnish with lemon wedges, if desired. *Makes 6 servings*

Crab Cakes with Tomato Salsa

Tarragon Scallops & Zucchini

1¼ pounds sea scallops
6 tablespoons butter or margarine
2 small zucchini, thinly sliced
¼ teaspoon onion powder
2 cups uncooked instant white rice
3 large green onions including tops, chopped
3 tablespoons chopped fresh tarragon *or*
¾ teaspoon dried tarragon leaves
¼ teaspoon salt
2 tablespoons lemon juice
2 teaspoons cornstarch

1. Rinse scallops; pat dry with paper towels. Cut large scallops in half.

2. Melt butter in large nonstick skillet over medium heat. Stir in scallops, zucchini and onion powder; cook and stir 2 minutes. Cover; reduce heat. Cook 7 minutes.

3. Meanwhile, prepare rice according to package directions. Combine green onions, tarragon and salt in small bowl. Blend lemon juice and cornstarch in another small bowl, stirring until cornstarch dissolves; set aside.

4. Stir green onion and cornstarch mixtures into skillet. Increase heat to medium; cook and stir 1 minute or until sauce thickens and scallops are opaque. Serve over rice.

Makes 4 servings

Fresh Shellfish Risotto

12 raw littleneck clams in the shell
12 raw mussels in the shell, or additional clams
1 tablespoon cornmeal
1½ pounds raw medium shrimp in the shell
8 ounces raw bay scallops
6½ cups low-sodium chicken broth, divided
1 cup dry white wine (with or without alcohol), divided
1 tablespoon olive oil
4 large shallots, minced
2 cups uncooked arborio rice
¼ teaspoon crushed saffron threads
1 cup (4 ounces) shredded ALPINE LACE® Reduced Sodium Muenster Cheese
1 cup coarsely chopped plum tomatoes
1 cup frozen peas, thawed
1 tablespoon snipped fresh dill *or* 1 teaspoon dried dill weed
¼ teaspoon black pepper

1. Using a stiff brush, scrub the clams and mussels under cold running water, discarding any shells that have opened. Remove any beards from the mussels. Half-fill a large bowl with cold water, stir in the cornmeal and add the clams and mussels. Let them stand for 15 minutes to disgorge their sand; rinse well. Peel and devein the shrimp, leaving the tails on. Rinse the scallops.

2. In a large saucepan, bring the chicken broth and ½ cup of the wine to a boil over high heat. Add the clams and mussels; reduce the heat. Cover and simmer 5 minutes or until the shells open. Using a slotted spoon, remove the clams and mussels, discarding any that do not open; keep warm. Keep the broth mixture at a simmer.

3. Meanwhile, in a large nonstick Dutch oven, heat the oil over medium-high heat and sauté the shallots for 5 minutes or until soft. Add the rice and saffron and sauté 3 minutes more. Slowly, add 1 cup of the hot broth mixture, stirring until it is absorbed. Continue adding 4 cups more of the broth, 1 cup at a time, stirring constantly.

4. Stir in the cheese, shrimp, scallops, tomatoes, peas, dill, pepper and the remaining 1½ cups of broth and ½ cup of wine; stir until creamy and most, but not all, of the liquid is absorbed. Transfer to a serving platter; arrange the clams and mussels on top of the risotto. Garnish with additional sprigs of dill, if you wish. Serve immediately.

Makes 6 main-dish or 9 side-dish servings

Surimi Seafood with Black Beans and Cilantro Sauce

Cilantro Sauce (recipe follows)
2 cups frozen corn
1 can (16 ounces) black beans, rinsed and drained well
¼ cup chopped red bell pepper
1 can (4 ounces) chopped green chilies, drained
¼ cup minced fresh cilantro
4 green onions with tops, minced
12 ounces lobster-flavored Surimi Seafood chunks, shredded or flake style
2 cloves garlic, minced
1 teaspoon ground cumin
¼ teaspoon freshly ground black pepper
2 tablespoons white wine vinegar
2 tablespoons water
2 teaspoons fresh lime juice
3 tablespoons olive oil
½ teaspoon minced jalapeño pepper (optional)

Prepare Cilantro Sauce; set aside. Place corn in fine mesh strainer; rinse with cold water to thaw. Drain well. In large bowl, combine corn, beans, bell pepper, chilies, cilantro, green onions and Surimi Seafood. On cutting board, with point of sharp knife, mash garlic, cumin and black pepper to form paste. Place paste in small bowl; whisk in vinegar, water and lime juice. Gradually whisk in oil. Drizzle vinaigrette over bean mixture and toss.

Serve salad at room temperature in individual bowls or lettuce cups. If chilling salad, taste and adjust seasonings before serving. Pass Cilantro Sauce separately. Garnish with jalapeño pepper, if desired.

Makes 4 servings

CILANTRO SAUCE

1 cup plain nonfat yogurt
¼ cup minced cilantro
½ teaspoon sugar
¼ teaspoon salt
⅛ to ¼ teaspoon ground red pepper

Combine ingredients in small bowl. *Makes 1½ cups*

FAVORITE RECIPE FROM **NATIONAL FISHERIES INSTITUTE**

Crab and Scallop Creole

1 tablespoon vegetable oil
1 large onion, chopped
1 large green bell pepper, chopped
2 cloves garlic, minced
1 can (15 ounces) crushed tomatoes, undrained
3 to 4 tablespoons FRANK'S® Original REDHOT® Cayenne Pepper Sauce, divided
½ teaspoon dried basil leaves
½ teaspoon dried thyme leaves
1 package (9 ounces) frozen corn
½ pound raw bay scallops
½ pound crabmeat or imitation crabmeat, flaked (2 cups)
Cooked white rice (optional)

1. Heat oil in large nonstick skillet over medium-high heat. Add onion, bell pepper and garlic; cook until tender. Add tomatoes with liquid, 2 to 3 tablespoons RedHot® sauce, basil and thyme. Cover; cook over medium-low heat 10 minutes, stirring occasionally.

2. Add corn and scallops. Bring to a boil. Reduce heat to low. Cover; cook 5 minutes or until scallops are translucent. Stir in crabmeat; heat through.

3. Stir in 1 to 2 tablespoons RedHot® sauce. Serve over rice, if desired. *Makes 4 servings*

Prep Time: 20 minutes
Cook Time: 20 minutes

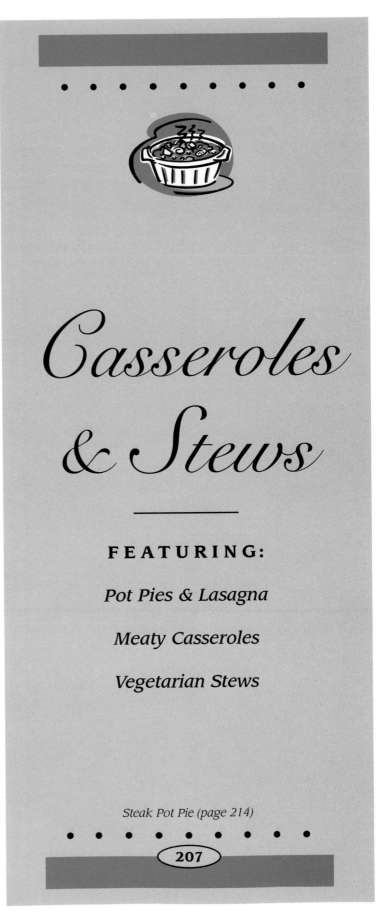

Casseroles & Stews

FEATURING:

Pot Pies & Lasagna

Meaty Casseroles

Vegetarian Stews

Steak Pot Pie (page 214)

French-Style Pork Stew

- 1 package (6.2 ounces) long-grain and wild rice
- 1 tablespoon vegetable oil
- 1 pork tenderloin (16 ounces), cut into ¾- to 1-inch cubes
- 1 medium onion, coarsely chopped
- 1 rib celery, sliced
- 2 tablespoons all-purpose flour
- 1½ cups chicken broth
- ½ package (16 ounces) frozen mixed vegetables (carrots, potatoes and peas)
- 1 jar (4½ ounces) sliced mushrooms, drained
- ½ teaspoon dried basil leaves
- ¼ teaspoon dried rosemary
- ¼ teaspoon dried oregano leaves
- 2 teaspoons lemon juice
- ⅛ teaspoon ground nutmeg

1. Prepare rice according to package directions, discarding spice packet, if desired.

2. While rice is cooking, heat oil in large saucepan over medium-high heat until hot. Add pork, onion and celery; cook 5 minutes or until pork is browned. Stir flour into chicken broth until dissolved; add to pork mixture. Cook over medium heat 1 minute, stirring constantly.

3. Stir in frozen vegetables, mushrooms, basil, rosemary and oregano; bring to a boil. Reduce heat to low; simmer, covered, 6 to 8 minutes or until pork is tender and barely pink in center. Stir in lemon juice, nutmeg and salt and pepper to taste. Serve stew over rice.

Makes 4 (1-cup) servings

Prep & Cook Time: 20 minutes

Maple Spam™ Stuffed Squash

- 3 small acorn squash (about 1 pound each), cut in half, seeds removed
- ½ cup chopped celery
- ¼ cup chopped onion
- 2 tablespoons butter or margarine
- 1 (12-ounce) can SPAM® Luncheon Meat, chopped
- 1½ cups frozen cubed hash brown potatoes, thawed
- ½ cup chopped apple
- ¼ cup pure maple syrup or maple-flavored syrup

Heat oven to 375°F. Place squash, cut side up, in 13×9-inch baking pan. In large skillet over medium-high heat, sauté celery and onion in butter until tender. Stir in Spam® and potatoes. Cook, stirring occasionally, until potatoes are lightly browned. Stir in apple and syrup. Spoon ½ cup Spam™ mixture into each squash half. Cover. Bake 40 to 50 minutes or until squash is tender.

Makes 6 servings

Salami Stuffed Peppers

- 4 large bell peppers (any color combination)
- 1½ cups (6 ounces) HEBREW NATIONAL® Beef Salami or Lean Beef Salami Chub, diced
- 2 tablespoons finely chopped onion
- 1 can (15 ounces) tomato sauce
- 2 teaspoons sugar
- 1½ cups cooked white or brown rice
- 1 cup frozen peas

Preheat oven to 350°F. Cut peppers lengthwise in half; remove seeds and membrane. Bring 5 cups water to a boil in large saucepan. Add peppers; cook 5 minutes. Rinse under cold running water; drain well.

Cook salami and onion in large nonstick skillet over medium heat 6 minutes, stirring occasionally. Combine tomato sauce and sugar in small bowl. Add ¾ cup tomato sauce mixture to skillet. Reserve remaining tomato sauce mixture. Add rice and peas to skillet; cook about 3 minutes or until heated through.

Arrange pepper halves, cut side up, in 13×9-inch baking pan. Fill pepper halves with salami mixture; top with reserved tomato sauce mixture. Bake, uncovered, 35 to 40 minutes or until heated through.

Makes 4 servings

French-Style Pork Stew

Kielbasa and Lentil Stew

- 1 pound kielbasa sausage or smoked Polish sausage
- 1 tablespoon olive oil
- 2 cups shredded cabbage
- 1 large onion, chopped
- 1 cup shredded carrots
- 2 cloves garlic, minced
- ½ pound dried lentils, rinsed and sorted
- 2 cans (about 14 ounces each) beef broth
- 1 can (14½ ounces) tomatoes, cut up, undrained
- 3 tablespoons FRANK'S® Original REDHOT® Cayenne Pepper Sauce Cooked white rice (optional)

1. Cut sausage lengthwise into halves. Cut halves into ¼-inch-thick slices. Heat oil in 5-quart saucepan or Dutch oven over medium-high heat. Add sausage; cook and stir 3 minutes or until lightly browned. Transfer to platter; set aside. Drain off all but *1 tablespoon* fat.

2. Add cabbage, onion, carrots and garlic to saucepan. Cook and stir 3 to 5 minutes or until tender. Return sausage to saucepan; add lentils, beef broth, tomatoes with liquid, *½ cup water* and RedHot® sauce. Bring to a boil. Reduce heat to low; cook, partially covered, 40 minutes or until lentils are tender.

3. Ladle into soup bowls. Serve over cooked rice, if desired.
Makes 6 servings (8 cups)

Knockwurst with White Beans and Tomatoes

- 1 tablespoon olive oil
- 1 small onion, chopped
- 2 cloves garlic, minced
- 1 can (14½ ounces) Italian-style stewed tomatoes, undrained
- 1 can (16 ounces) cannellini or Great Northern beans, drained
- 1 teaspoon dried basil leaves
- ½ teaspoon dried rosemary
- 1 package (12 ounces) HEBREW NATIONAL® Beef Knockwurst

Heat oil in large nonstick saucepan over medium-high heat. Add onion and garlic; cook 4 minutes, stirring occasionally. Add tomatoes with liquid, beans, basil and rosemary; bring to a boil. Cut knockwurst crosswise into ½-inch pieces; stir into saucepan. Cover; simmer 10 minutes. *Makes 4 servings*

Black Bean & Pork Stew

- 2 (15-ounce) cans cooked black beans, rinsed and drained
- 2 cups water
- 1 pound boneless ham, cut into ¾-inch cubes
- ¾ pound BOB EVANS FARMS® Italian Dinner Link Sausage, cut into 1-inch pieces
- ¾ pound BOB EVANS FARMS® Smoked Sausage, cut into 1-inch pieces
- 1 pint cherry tomatoes, stems removed
- 1 medium onion, chopped
- 1 teaspoon red pepper flakes
- 6 cloves garlic, minced
- ⅛ teaspoon grated orange peel
- Corn bread or rolls (optional)

Preheat oven to 350°F. Combine all ingredients except corn bread in large Dutch oven. Bring to a boil over high heat, skimming foam off top if necessary. Cover; transfer to oven. Bake 30 minutes; uncover and bake 30 minutes more, stirring occasionally. Serve hot with corn bread, if desired, or cool slightly, then cover and refrigerate overnight. Remove any fat from surface. Reheat over low heat. Refrigerate leftovers. *Makes 8 servings*

Knockwurst with White Beans and Tomatoes

Chicken & Tortilla Casserole

- ¼ cup low-sodium chicken broth, defatted, divided
- ½ cup finely chopped red bell pepper
- ½ cup finely chopped green bell pepper
- ½ cup finely chopped red onion
- 1 can (28 ounces) low-sodium tomatoes, undrained
- ¼ cup GUILTLESS GOURMET® Spicy Nacho Dip
- 3 ounces (about 60) GUILTLESS GOURMET® Unsalted Baked Tortilla Chips, divided
- 1 cup cooked and shredded boneless chicken breast
  Fresh herb sprig (optional)

NACHO SAUCE
- ¾ cup GUILTLESS GOURMET® Spicy Nacho Dip
- ¼ cup low-fat sour cream
- ¼ cup skim milk

Preheat oven to 350°F. Heat 2 tablespoons broth in medium nonstick skillet until hot. Add peppers and onion; cook about 5 minutes, stirring often. Add remaining 2 tablespoons broth and cook until peppers are soft. Remove from heat; set aside. Drain off about ¾ juice from tomatoes; discard. Coarsely chop tomatoes. To assemble casserole, spread ¼ cup nacho dip on bottom of 1½- to 2-quart casserole dish. Top with layer of tortilla chips (about 30). Cover with pepper mixture, followed by another layer of tortilla chips (about 30). Evenly spread chicken over chips; top with tomatoes and remaining juice. Combine Nacho Sauce ingredients in small saucepan; heat over medium heat 2 to 3 minutes or until warm. Drizzle half the mixture evenly over tomato layer.

Cover and bake about 25 to 35 minutes or until mixture bubbles. Drizzle casserole with remaining Nacho Sauce. Garnish with herb sprig, if desired.

Makes 4 servings

Mexican Lasagna

- ½ pound lean ground turkey
- ½ cup chopped onion
- ½ cup chopped bell pepper
- ½ teaspoon black pepper
- ½ teaspoon dried basil leaves, crushed
- 1 can (8 ounces) low-sodium tomato sauce
- 1 cup GUILTLESS GOURMET® Salsa (mild, medium or hot), divided
- 1 cup low-fat cottage cheese
- ½ cup GUILTLESS GOURMET® Nacho Dip (mild or spicy)
  Nonstick cooking spray
- 1 bag (7 ounces) GUILTLESS GOURMET® Unsalted Baked Tortilla Chips, crushed
  Carrot strip and fresh parsley sprig (optional)

Preheat oven to 350°F. Cook turkey, onion, bell pepper, black pepper and basil in nonstick skillet over medium heat until turkey is no longer pink, breaking up meat and stirring occasionally. Stir in tomato sauce and ½ cup salsa; remove from heat. Combine cottage cheese and nacho dip in small bowl. Coat 11×7-inch baking dish with cooking spray. Set aside.

To assemble lasagna, place ⅓ of crushed chips on bottom of prepared dish, spreading to cover. Top with half the turkey mixture. Spread half the cheese mixture over turkey mixture. Repeat layers once. Top with remaining crushed chips; pour remaining salsa evenly over chips.

Bake 30 minutes or until heated through. Let stand 10 minutes before serving. Garnish with carrot and parsley, if desired.

Makes 4 servings

Chicken & Tortilla Casserole

Zesty Zucchini Lasagna

1 pound ground beef
1 package (1.5 ounces) LAWRY'S® Original-Style Spaghetti Sauce Spices & Seasonings
1 can (6 ounces) tomato paste
1¾ cups water
2 tablespoons butter or margarine
½ teaspoon dried basil leaves
⅛ teaspoon dried thyme leaves
2 cups ricotta cheese
1 egg, slightly beaten
4 medium zucchini, thinly sliced lengthwise
1 cup shredded mozzarella cheese (about 4 ounces)

Preheat oven to 350°F. In medium saucepan, brown ground beef until no longer pink; drain. Stir in Spaghetti Sauce Spices & Seasonings, tomato paste, water, butter, basil and thyme. Bring to a boil, then simmer uncovered 10 minutes. In small bowl, combine ricotta cheese with egg; set aside. In medium saucepan, bring 1 quart water to a boil. Add zucchini and cook 2 minutes; remove and rinse under cold running water. In 12×8-inch casserole, layer half the zucchini, ricotta mixture and meat sauce. Repeat layers. Top with mozzarella cheese and bake, uncovered, 30 minutes or until cheese is melted.

Makes about 6 servings

Oven-Easy Beef & Potato Dinner

4 cups frozen hash brown potatoes, thawed
3 tablespoons vegetable oil
⅛ teaspoon black pepper
1 pound ground beef
1 cup water
1 package (about ¾ ounce) brown gravy mix
½ teaspoon garlic salt
1 package (10 ounces) frozen mixed vegetables, thawed and drained
1 cup (4 ounces) shredded Cheddar cheese, divided
1 can (2.8 ounces) FRENCH'S® French Fried Onions, divided

Preheat oven to 400°F. In 12×8-inch baking dish, combine potatoes, oil and pepper. Firmly press potato mixture evenly across bottom and up sides of dish to form a shell. Bake, uncovered, at 400°F for 15 minutes. Meanwhile, in large skillet, brown ground beef; drain. Stir in water, gravy mix and garlic salt; bring to a boil. Add mixed vegetables; reduce heat to medium and cook, uncovered, 5 minutes. Remove from heat and stir in ½ *cup* cheese and ½ *can* French Fried Onions; spoon into hot potato shell. *Reduce oven temperature to 350°F.* Bake, uncovered, at 350°F for 15 minutes or until heated through. Top with remaining cheese and onions; bake, uncovered, 5 minutes or until onions are golden brown.

Makes 4 to 6 servings

Steak Pot Pie

1 cup chopped onion
2 tablespoons margarine
3 tablespoons all-purpose flour
1½ cups COLLEGE INN® Beef Broth
½ cup A.1.® Original or A.1.® Bold & Spicy Steak Sauce
3 cups cubed cooked steak (about 1½ pounds)
1 (16-ounce) package frozen broccoli, cauliflower & carrot mixture
Prepared pastry for 1-crust pie
1 egg, beaten

In 2-quart saucepan, over medium-high heat, cook onion in margarine until tender. Blend in flour; cook 1 minute more. Add broth and steak sauce; cook and stir until mixture thickens and begins to boil. Stir in steak and vegetables. Spoon mixture into 8-inch square glass baking dish. Roll out and cut pastry crust to fit over dish. Seal crust to edge of dish; brush with egg. Slit top of crust to vent. Bake at 400°F 25 minutes or until crust is golden brown. Serve immediately. Garnish as desired.

Makes 4 servings

Cheese-Stuffed Beef Rolls

1 jar (15½ ounces) spaghetti sauce
1 egg, slightly beaten
¼ teaspoon dried oregano, crumbled
¼ teaspoon garlic powder
1 container (15 ounces) ricotta cheese
¼ cup (1 ounce) grated Parmesan cheese
1 cup (4 ounces) shredded mozzarella cheese
1 can (2.8 ounces) FRENCH'S® French Fried Onions
6 thin slices deli roast beef (about ½ pound)
2 medium zucchini, sliced (about 3 cups)

Preheat oven to 375°F. Spread ½ cup spaghetti sauce on bottom of 12×8-inch baking dish. In large bowl, thoroughly combine egg, seasonings, ricotta cheese, Parmesan cheese, ½ cup mozzarella cheese and ½ can French Fried Onions. Spoon equal amounts of cheese mixture on 1 end of each beef slice. Roll up beef slices jelly-roll style and arrange, seam side down, in baking dish. Place zucchini along both sides of dish. Pour remaining spaghetti sauce over beef rolls and zucchini. Bake, covered, at 375°F for 40 minutes or until heated through. Top beef rolls with remaining mozzarella cheese and onions. Bake, uncovered, 3 minutes or until onions are golden brown.

Makes 6 servings

French Beef Stew

1½ pounds stew beef, cut into 1-inch cubes
¼ cup all-purpose flour
2 tablespoons vegetable oil
2 cans (14½ ounces each) DEL MONTE® FreshCut™ Diced Tomatoes with Garlic & Onion
1 can (about 14 ounces) beef broth
4 medium carrots, peeled and cut into 1-inch chunks
2 medium potatoes, peeled and cut into 1-inch chunks
¾ teaspoon dried thyme, crushed
2 tablespoons Dijon mustard (optional)

1. Combine meat and flour in large plastic food storage bag; toss to coat evenly.

2. Brown meat in hot oil in 6-quart saucepan. Season with salt and pepper, if desired.

3. Add all remaining ingredients except mustard. Bring to a boil; reduce heat to medium-low. Cover; simmer 1 hour or until beef is tender.

4. Blend in mustard, if desired. Garnish and serve with warm crusty French bread, if desired.

Makes 6 to 8 servings

Prep Time: 10 minutes
Cook Time: 1 hour

Bistro Burgundy Stew

1 pound boneless beef sirloin, cut into 1½-inch pieces
3 tablespoons all-purpose flour
6 slices bacon, cut into 1-inch pieces (about ¼ pound)
2 cloves garlic, crushed
3 carrots, peeled and cut into 1-inch pieces (about 1½ cups)
¾ cup Burgundy or other dry red wine
½ cup GREY POUPON® Dijon Mustard
½ cup beef broth or lower sodium beef broth
12 small mushrooms
1½ cups green onions, cut into 1½-inch pieces
Tomato rose and parsley for garnish
Breadsticks (optional)

Coat beef with flour, shaking off excess; set aside.

In large skillet, over medium heat, cook bacon just until done; pour off excess fat. Add beef and garlic; cook until browned. Add carrots, wine, mustard and beef broth. Heat to a boil; reduce heat. Cover; simmer for 30 minutes or until carrots are tender, stirring occasionally. Stir in mushrooms and green onions; cook 10 minutes more, stirring occasionally. Garnish with tomato rose and parsley. Serve with breadsticks, if desired. *Makes 4 servings*

Spicy Chicken Tortilla Casserole

1 tablespoon vegetable oil
1 cup (1 small) chopped green bell pepper
1 cup (1 small) chopped onion
2 cloves garlic, finely chopped
1 pound (about 4) boneless, skinless chicken breast halves, cut into bite-size pieces
2½ cups (24-ounce jar) ORTEGA® Thick & Chunky Salsa, hot, medium or mild
½ cup (2¼-ounce can) sliced ripe olives
6 corn tortillas, cut into halves
2 cups (8 ounces) shredded Monterey Jack or Cheddar cheese
Sour cream (optional)

HEAT oil in large skillet over medium-high heat. Add bell pepper, onion and garlic; cook for 2 to 3 minutes or until vegetables are tender.

ADD chicken; cook, stirring frequently, for 3 to 5 minutes or until chicken is no longer pink in center. Stir in salsa and olives; remove from heat.

PLACE 6 tortilla halves onto bottom of 8-inch square baking pan. Top with half of chicken mixture and 1 cup cheese; repeat layers. Bake, covered, in preheated 350°F oven for 15 to 20 minutes or until bubbly. Serve with sour cream.

Makes 8 servings

Southwestern-Style Beef Stew

¼ cup all-purpose flour
1 teaspoon seasoned salt
¼ teaspoon ground black pepper
2 pounds beef stew meat, cut into bite-size pieces
2 tablespoons vegetable oil
1 large onion, cut into wedges
2 large cloves garlic, finely chopped
1¾ cups (14.5-ounce can) CONTADINA® Stewed Tomatoes, undrained
1¾ cups (16-ounce jar) ORTEGA® Garden Style Salsa, mild
1 cup beef broth
1 tablespoon ground oregano
1 teaspoon ground cumin
½ teaspoon salt
3 large carrots, peeled, cut into 1-inch slices
1¾ cups (15-ounce can) garbanzo beans, drained
1 cup (8-ounce can) baby corn, drained, halved

COMBINE flour, seasoned salt and pepper in medium bowl or large resealable plastic food storage bag. Add meat; toss well to coat.

HEAT oil in large saucepan over medium-high heat. Add meat, onion and garlic; cook for 5 to 6 minutes or until meat is browned on outside and onion is tender. Stir in tomatoes with juice, salsa, beef broth,

oregano, cumin and salt. Bring to a boil; cover. Reduce heat to low; cook, stirring occasionally, for 45 minutes or until meat is tender.

STIR in carrots, beans and baby corn. Increase heat to medium-low. Cook, stirring occasionally, for 30 to 40 minutes or until carrots are tender.

Makes 8 servings

Monterey Black Bean Tortilla Supper

1 pound ground beef, browned and drained
1½ cups bottled salsa
1 (15-ounce) can black beans, drained
4 (8-inch) flour tortillas
2 cups (8 ounces) shredded Wisconsin Monterey Jack cheese*

For authentic Mexican flavor, substitute 2 cups shredded Wisconsin Queso Blanco.

Heat oven to 400°F. Combine ground beef, salsa and beans. In lightly greased 2-quart round casserole, layer 1 tortilla, ⅔ cup meat mixture and ½ cup cheese. Repeat layers 3 times. Bake 30 minutes or until heated through.

Makes 5 to 6 servings

*FAVORITE RECIPE FROM **WISCONSIN MILK MARKETING BOARD***

Southwestern-Style Beef Stew

New Orleans Rice and Sausage

½ pound smoked sausage,* cut into slices
1 can (14½ ounces) stewed tomatoes, Cajun- or Italian-style
¾ cup water
1¾ cups uncooked instant rice
    Dash hot pepper sauce or to taste
1 bag (16 ounces) BIRDS EYE® frozen Farm Fresh Mixtures Broccoli, Corn and Red Peppers

For a spicy dish, use andouille sausage. Any type of kielbasa or turkey kielbasa can also be used.

• Heat sausage in large skillet 2 to 3 minutes.

• Add tomatoes, water, rice and hot pepper sauce; mix well.

• Add vegetables; mix well. Cover and cook over medium heat 5 to 7 minutes or until rice is tender and vegetables are heated through.

Makes 6 servings

Prep Time: 5 minutes
Cook Time: 10 minutes

Oat Bran 'n Broccoli Casserole

1 package (10 ounces) frozen chopped broccoli
⅓ cup sliced green onions
¾ cup water
½ cup part skim ricotta cheese
¼ teaspoon garlic powder
    Dash black pepper
2 cups water
½ teaspoon salt (optional)
¾ cup QUAKER® Oat Bran hot cereal, uncooked
⅔ cup QUAKER® or AUNT JEMIMA® Enriched Hominy Quick Grits*
½ cup plain low-fat yogurt

To use QUAKER® or AUNT JEMIMA® Enriched Hominy Grits, increase water to 2½ cups and simmer time to 15 to 20 minutes. Proceed as directed.

Cook broccoli with green onions in ¾ cup water according to package directions. *Do not drain.* Stir in ricotta, garlic powder and pepper. Cook over medium heat, stirring occasionally, until heated through; set aside.

Bring 2 cups water and salt, if desired, to a boil. Using a wire whisk, gradually add combined oat bran and grits, stirring constantly. Return to a boil; reduce heat and simmer 2 to 4 minutes, stirring frequently, or until oat bran mixture is slightly thickened. Add to broccoli mixture; mix well. Add yogurt; cook until heated through. Serve immediately.

Makes 6 servings

Country Rice & Beans with Chicken & Sausage

8 ounces boneless skinless chicken breasts, cut into strips
8 ounces smoked sausage, sliced
¼ cup coarsely chopped onion
1 tablespoon butter or margarine
3 cups water
1 (8-ounce) package FARMHOUSE® Red Beans & Rice
¼ cup sliced green pepper
¼ cup sliced celery

In large saucepan, sauté chicken, sausage and onion in butter 5 to 7 minutes or until chicken is no longer pink. Add water, beans & rice, contents of seasoning packet, bell pepper and celery. Bring to a boil; cover. Reduce heat and simmer 20 to 25 minutes or until liquid is absorbed.

Makes 6 servings

New Orleans Rice and Sausage

Lasagna Bolognese

1 pound uncooked lasagna noodles

BOLOGNESE SAUCE
**1 tablespoon olive oil
8 ounces mushrooms, sliced
2 teaspoons minced garlic, divided
1¾ pounds ground white meat turkey or lean beef
½ teaspoon salt
½ teaspoon black pepper
6 cups marinara sauce (in jar or refrigerator section)
½ cup slivered fresh basil leaves**

CHEESE LAYERS
**2 cups part-skim ricotta cheese
1 cup (4 ounces) shredded ALPINE LACE® Fat Free Pasteurized Process Skim Milk Cheese Product—For Parmesan Lovers, divided
¾ cup (3 ounces) shredded ALPINE LACE® Reduced Fat Low Moisture Mozzarella Cheese
¾ cup (3 ounces) shredded ALPINE LACE® Fat Free Pasteurized Process Skim Milk Cheese Product—For Mozzarella Lovers**

1. Preheat the oven to 350°F. Spray a 13×9×3-inch baking dish with nonstick cooking spray.

2. To prepare the noodles: Cook the lasagna noodles until al dente, according to package directions. Drain, rinse and drain again. Lay out on wire racks and keep warm.

3. Meanwhile, make the Bolognese Sauce: In a large nonstick skillet, heat the oil over medium-high heat. Add the mushrooms and 1 teaspoon of the garlic; sauté for 7 minutes or until tender. Using a slotted spoon, transfer to a large saucepan.

4. To the same skillet, add the turkey, the remaining teaspoon of garlic, and the salt and pepper. Sauté for 7 minutes or until turkey is no longer pink. Transfer the turkey mixture to the saucepan with the mushrooms and stir in the marinara sauce and basil. Simmer, uncovered, over medium-high heat for 10 minutes or until the flavors are well blended.

5. To assemble the lasagna: Spoon one fourth of the Bolognese Sauce in the baking dish. Layer one third of the lasagna noodles over the sauce, with the edges overlapping. With a spatula, spread one third of the ricotta, then spoon one fourth of the sauce and sprinkle with ¼ cup of the Parmesan. Repeat 2 times. In a small bowl, toss both of the mozzarella cheeses and sprinkle on top of the lasagna. Top with the remaining ¼ cup of Parmesan.

6. Cover with foil and bake for 30 minutes. Uncover and bake 15 minutes longer or until bubbly and hot throughout.

Makes 12 main-dish servings

Quick and Easy Sausage Stew

**1 package (12 ounces) HEBREW NATIONAL® Lean Smoked Turkey Sausage or Beef Polish Sausage, cut into 1-inch slices
1 large onion, chopped
2 cloves garlic, minced
1 red bell pepper, seeded, cut into 1-inch pieces
1 green bell pepper, seeded, cut into 1-inch pieces
1 medium zucchini, cut into ½-inch slices
8 ounces fresh mushrooms, thickly sliced
2 cans (14½ ounces each) stewed tomatoes, undrained
1 teaspoon dried basil leaves
¼ teaspoon crushed red pepper
¼ teaspoon salt**

Cook sausage, onion and garlic in large, deep nonstick skillet over medium-high heat 3 minutes. Add bell peppers, zucchini and mushrooms; cook 5 minutes, stirring occasionally.

Add stewed tomatoes with liquid, basil, crushed pepper and salt. Bring to a boil. Reduce heat. Cover; simmer 25 minutes, stirring occasionally.

Makes 6 servings

Louisiana Jambalaya

- **1½ pounds chicken tenders**
- **½ teaspoon salt**
- **½ teaspoon ground black pepper**
- **1 tablespoon vegetable oil**
- **¾ pound smoked turkey sausage, cut into ¼-inch slices**
- **2 medium onions, chopped**
- **1 large green bell pepper, chopped**
- **1 cup chopped celery**
- **1 clove garlic, minced**
- **2 cups uncooked long grain white rice (not converted)**
- **¼ to ½ teaspoon ground red pepper**
- **2½ cups chicken broth**
- **1 cup sliced green onions**
- **1 medium tomato, chopped**

Season chicken with salt and black pepper. Heat oil in large saucepan or Dutch oven over high heat until hot. Add chicken, stirring until brown on all sides. Add sausage; cook 2 to 3 minutes. Remove chicken and sausage from saucepan; set aside. Add chopped onions, bell pepper, celery and garlic to same saucepan; cook and stir over medium-high heat until crisp-tender. Stir in rice, red pepper, broth and reserved chicken and sausage; bring to a boil. Reduce heat to low; cover and simmer 30 minutes. Stir in green onions and tomato. Serve immediately.

Makes 8 servings

FAVORITE RECIPE FROM **USA RICE FEDERATION**

One-Dish Chicken Bake

- **1 package (6 ounces) STOVE TOP® Stuffing Mix for Chicken**
- **4 boneless skinless chicken breast halves (about 1¼ pounds)**
- **1 can (10¾ ounces) condensed cream of mushroom soup**
- **⅓ cup sour cream or milk**

1. STIR stuffing crumbs, seasoning packet, 1½ cups *hot* water and ¼ cup margarine, cut up, just until moistened; set aside.

2. PLACE chicken in 12×8-inch baking dish. Mix soup and sour cream; pour over chicken. Top with stuffing.

3. BAKE at 375°F for 35 minutes or until chicken is cooked through.   *Makes 4 servings*

Prep Time: 10 minutes
Bake Time: 35 minutes

Quick and Easy Sausage Stew (page 220)

Chicken Ragoût

- 1 package (4.9 ounces) RICE-A-RONI® Chicken & Broccoli Flavor
- 3 tablespoons all-purpose flour
- ¾ teaspoon salt (optional)
- ½ teaspoon black pepper
- 1 pound skinless, boneless chicken breasts or thighs, cut into 1-inch pieces
- 2 tablespoons margarine or butter
- 2 cups sliced mushrooms
- 1 cup thinly sliced carrots
- 1 cup coarsely chopped onion
- 2 cloves garlic, minced
- ½ cup reduced-sodium or regular chicken broth
- ¼ cup dry white wine or additional chicken broth
- 1 teaspoon dried thyme leaves

1. Prepare Rice-A-Roni® Mix as package directs.

2. While Rice-A-Roni® is simmering, combine flour, salt, if desired, and pepper. Coat chicken with flour mixture.

3. In second large skillet, melt margarine over medium heat. Add mushrooms, carrots, onion and garlic; cook 5 minutes, stirring occasionally. Add chicken; continue cooking 4 minutes, stirring occasionally. Add chicken broth, wine and thyme. Reduce heat to low.

4. Simmer 5 to 7 minutes or until chicken is cooked through and carrots are tender.

5. Serve rice topped with chicken mixture.

Makes 4 servings

Chicken & Wild Rice

- 6 cups cooked wild rice (1½ cups uncooked)
- 1 can (10¾ ounces) cream of chicken soup
- 1 can (10¾ ounces) cream of celery soup
- 1 can (about 14 ounces) chicken broth
- 1 can (4 ounces) mushrooms, drained
- 3 cups diced cooked chicken
- ¼ cup chopped green bell pepper
- ¼ cup chopped red bell pepper
- ¼ teaspoon garlic powder
- ½ cup slivered almonds

Preheat oven to 350°F. Grease 13×9-inch casserole.

Mix rice, soups, broth, mushrooms, chicken, bell peppers and garlic powder in large bowl. Spread into prepared dish. Sprinkle with almonds. Bake, covered, 45 minutes. Uncover and continue baking 15 minutes or until heated through.

Makes 10 to 12 servings

FAVORITE RECIPE FROM **MINNESOTA CULTIVATED WILD RICE COUNCIL**

Orange Glazed Chicken and Squash Bake

- 4 broiler-fryer chicken legs
- ½ teaspoon salt
- ¼ teaspoon black pepper
- 2 small acorn squash, quartered lengthwise
- ½ cup orange marmalade
- 1 tablespoon lemon juice
- 1 teaspoon grated lemon peel
- ¼ teaspoon ground nutmeg
- ¼ teaspoon ground cinnamon

Place chicken in single layer on wire rack in large shallow baking pan. Sprinkle salt and pepper over chicken. Place squash in medium baking dish. Add water to cover bottom of dish; cover with foil.

Bake chicken and squash in 375°F oven 25 minutes. Mix marmalade, lemon juice and peel, nutmeg and cinnamon in small bowl. Brush marmalade mixture over chicken. Bake 20 minutes longer. Remove cover from squash. Brush remaining marmalade mixture over chicken and squash. Bake 10 minutes more or until chicken and squash are fork-tender. *Makes 4 servings*

FAVORITE RECIPE FROM **DELMARVA POULTRY INDUSTRY, INC.**

Chicken Ragoût

Southwest Turkey Tenderloin Stew

1 package (about 1½ pounds) turkey tenderloins, cut into ¾-inch pieces
1 tablespoon chili powder
1 teaspoon ground cumin
¾ teaspoon salt
1 red bell pepper, cut into ¾-inch pieces
1 green bell pepper, cut into ¾-inch pieces
¾ cup chopped red or yellow onion
3 cloves garlic, minced
1 can (15½ ounces) chili beans in spicy sauce, undrained
1 can (14½ ounces) chili-style stewed tomatoes, undrained
¾ cup prepared salsa or picante sauce
Fresh cilantro (optional)

Slow Cooker Directions:
PLACE turkey in slow cooker. Sprinkle chili powder, cumin and salt over turkey; toss to coat. Add red bell pepper, green bell pepper, onion, garlic, beans, tomatoes and salsa. Mix well. Cover and cook on LOW 5 hours or until turkey is no longer pink in center and vegetables are crisp-tender. Ladle into bowls. Garnish with cilantro, if desired.

Makes 6 servings

Homespun Turkey 'n Vegetables

1 package (9 ounces) frozen cut green beans, thawed and drained
1 can (14 ounces) sliced carrots, drained
1 can (2.8 ounces) FRENCH'S® French Fried Onions, divided
1 can (16 ounces) whole potatoes, drained
1 can (10¾ ounces) condensed cream of celery soup
¼ cup milk
1 tablespoon FRENCH'S® CLASSIC YELLOW® Mustard
¼ teaspoon garlic powder
1 pound uncooked turkey breast slices

Preheat oven to 375°F. In 12×8-inch baking dish, combine green beans, carrots and *½ can* French Fried Onions. Slice potatoes into halves; arrange as many halves as will fit, cut side down, around edges of baking dish. Combine any remaining potatoes with vegetables in dish. In medium bowl, combine soup, milk, mustard and garlic powder; pour *half* the soup mixture over vegetables. Overlap turkey slices on vegetables. Pour remaining soup mixture over turkey and potatoes. Bake, covered, at 375°F for 40 minutes or until turkey is done. Top turkey with remaining onions; bake, uncovered, 3 minutes or until onions are golden brown.

Makes 4 servings

Country Chicken Stew

2 tablespoons butter or margarine
1 pound boneless skinless chicken breasts, cut into 1-inch cubes
½ pound small red potatoes, cut into ½-inch cubes
2 tablespoons cooking sherry
2 jars (12 ounces each) golden chicken gravy
1 bag (16 ounces) BIRDS EYE® frozen Farm Fresh Mixtures Broccoli, Green Beans, Pearl Onions and Red Peppers
½ cup water

• Melt butter in large saucepan over high heat. Add chicken and potatoes; cook about 8 minutes or until browned, stirring frequently.

• Add sherry; cook until evaporated. Add gravy, vegetables and water.

• Bring to a boil; reduce heat to medium-low. Cover and cook 5 minutes.

Makes 4 to 6 servings

Prep Time: 5 minutes
Cook Time: 20 minutes

Southwest Turkey Tenderloin Stew

Mustard Chicken & Vegetables

- **2 cups (8 ounces) fusilli or rotini, cooked in unsalted water and drained**
- **¼ cup FRENCH'S® Dijon or CLASSIC YELLOW® Mustard**
- **¼ cup vegetable oil**
- **1 tablespoon red wine vinegar**
- **½ teaspoon dried oregano, crumbled**
- **¼ teaspoon black pepper**
- **¼ teaspoon salt**
- **2 pounds chicken pieces, fat trimmed**
- **1 can (10¾ ounces) condensed cream of chicken soup**
- **½ cup milk**
- **1 cup *each* zucchini and yellow squash, cut into 1-inch chunks**
- **1 can (2.8 ounces) FRENCH'S® French Fried Onions, divided**
- **1 medium tomato, cut into wedges**

Preheat oven to 375°F. In large bowl, combine mustard, oil, vinegar and seasonings; mix well. Toss chicken in mustard sauce until coated. Reserve remaining mustard sauce. Arrange chicken in 13×9-inch baking dish. Bake, uncovered, at 375°F for 30 minutes. Stir soup, milk, hot pasta, zucchini, squash and *½ can* French Fried Onions into remaining mustard sauce. Spoon pasta mixture into baking dish, placing it under and around chicken. Bake, uncovered, 15 to 20 minutes or until chicken is done. Top pasta mixture with tomato wedges and top chicken with remaining onions; bake, uncovered, 3 minutes or until onions are golden brown.

Makes 4 to 6 servings

French Veal Casserole

- **1 pound veal steaks**
- **2 tablespoons vegetable oil**
- **1 cup uncooked rice**
- **1 tablespoon chopped onion**
- **2¼ cups water**
- **2 teaspoons salt**
- **2 tablespoons chopped pimientos**
- **½ cup BLUE DIAMOND® Slivered Almonds, toasted**

Cut veal into ½-inch cubes. Brown lightly in oil. Remove meat from pan. Combine rice and onion in same pan and cook, stirring, until rice is golden brown. Add water and salt and bring to a boil. Stir in veal. Turn into casserole dish; cover. Bake at 300°F 50 to 60 minutes or until rice and veal are tender. Just before serving, add pimientos and almonds; fluff rice with fork.

Makes 6 servings

Zesty Cheddar Casserole

- **2 packages (1½ ounces each) 4-cheese pasta sauce mix**
- **2 cups milk**
- **1 cup finely chopped celery**
- **½ cup chopped onion**
- **3 to 4 tablespoons FRANK'S® Original REDHOT® Cayenne Pepper Sauce**
- **1 bag (16 ounces) frozen vegetable combination, such as broccoli, corn and red bell pepper**
- **3 cups diced cooked chicken**
- **6 slices crisply cooked bacon, crumbled**
- **1½ cups (6 ounces) shredded Cheddar cheese, divided**
- **1 package (7½ ounces) refrigerated buttermilk biscuits**

1. Preheat oven to 375°F. Prepare sauce mix according to package directions using milk, *1 cup water* and omitting butter in 3-quart saucepan. Add celery, onion and RedHot® sauce. Cook and stir 1 minute.

2. Stir in vegetables, chicken, bacon and *1 cup* cheese. Spoon into greased 3-quart casserole; cover. Bake 30 minutes; stir. Cut biscuits in half crosswise; arrange around edge of casserole. Sprinkle remaining *½ cup* cheese over biscuits.

3. Bake, uncovered, 15 minutes or until biscuits are golden brown. *Makes 8 servings*

Chicken Stew with Dumplings

2 tablespoons vegetable
  oil
2 cups sliced carrots
1 cup chopped onion
1 large green bell pepper,
  sliced
½ cup sliced celery
2 cans (about 14 ounces
  each) fat-free reduced-
  sodium chicken broth
¼ cup plus 2 tablespoons
  all-purpose flour
2 pounds boneless
  skinless chicken
  breasts, cut into
  1-inch pieces
3 medium potatoes,
  unpeeled and cut into
  1-inch pieces
6 ounces mushrooms,
  halved
¾ cup frozen peas
1 teaspoon dried basil
¾ teaspoon dried
  rosemary
¼ teaspoon dried tarragon
¾ to 1 teaspoon salt
¼ teaspoon black pepper

HERB DUMPLINGS
2 cups biscuit mix
½ teaspoon dried basil
½ teaspoon dried
  rosemary
¼ teaspoon dried tarragon
⅔ cup 2% milk

1. Heat oil in 4-quart Dutch oven over medium heat until hot. Add carrots, onion, bell pepper and celery; cook and stir 5 minutes or until onion is tender. Stir in chicken broth, reserving ½ cup; bring to a boil. Mix reserved ½ cup broth and flour; stir into boiling mixture. Boil, stirring constantly, 1 minute or until thickened. Stir chicken, potatoes, mushrooms, peas and herbs into mixture. Reduce heat to low; simmer, covered, 18 to 20 minutes or until vegetables are almost tender and chicken is no longer pink in center. Add salt and black pepper.

2. For Herb Dumplings, combine biscuit mix and herbs in small bowl; stir in milk to form soft dough. Spoon dumpling mixture on top of stew in 8 large spoonfuls. Cook, uncovered, 10 minutes. Cover and cook 10 minutes or until biscuits are tender and toothpick inserted in center comes out clean. Serve in shallow bowls.

Makes 8 (1¼-cup) servings

Chicken Mexicana Casserole

2½ pounds boneless
  chicken breasts,
  skinned and cut into
  1-inch cubes
2 packages (1.0 ounce
  each) LAWRY'S® Taco
  Spices & Seasonings
2 cans (14½ ounces each)
  whole tomatoes,
  undrained and cut up
3 cups (12 ounces)
  shredded sharp
  cheddar cheese,
  divided
1 can (7 ounces) diced
  green chiles,
  undrained
1 can (12 ounces) whole
  kernel corn, drained
1 package (8¼ ounces)
  corn muffin mix
2 eggs
¼ cup dairy sour cream

In large bowl, toss chicken cubes with Taco Spices & Seasonings and tomatoes; blend well. Add 1 cup cheese. Spread mixture evenly into 13×9×2-inch baking dish. Spoon chiles over chicken mixture; sprinkle with remaining cheese. Set aside. In medium bowl, combine remaining ingredients; blend well. Drop by rounded spoonfuls on top of casserole, spacing evenly. Bake in 350°F oven 50 to 60 minutes or until top is lightly browned and sauce is bubbly. Remove from oven and let stand about 20 minutes before serving.

Makes 10 to 12 servings

Zesty Seafood Lasagna

- **2 packages (1.8 ounces each) white sauce mix**
- **4½ cups milk**
- **1 teaspoon dried basil leaves**
- **½ teaspoon dried thyme leaves**
- **½ teaspoon garlic powder**
- **¾ cup grated Parmesan cheese, divided**
- **3 tablespoons FRANK'S® Original REDHOT® Cayenne Pepper Sauce**
- **9 oven-ready lasagna pasta sheets**
- **2 packages (10 ounces each) frozen chopped spinach, thawed and squeezed**
- **½ pound cooked shrimp**
- **½ pound raw bay scallops or flaked imitation crabmeat**
- **2 cups (8 ounces) shredded mozzarella cheese, divided**

1. Preheat oven to 400°F. Prepare white sauce according to package directions using milk and adding basil, thyme and garlic powder in large saucepan. Stir in *½ cup* Parmesan cheese and RedHot® sauce.

2. Spread *1 cup* sauce on bottom of greased 13×9×2-inch casserole. Layer 3 pasta sheets crosswise over sauce. (Do not let edges touch.) Layer *half* of the spinach and seafood over pasta. Spoon *1 cup* sauce over seafood; sprinkle with *¾ cup* mozzarella cheese.

Repeat layers a second time. Top with final layer of pasta sheets, remaining sauce and cheeses.

3. Cover pan with greased foil. Bake 40 minutes. Remove foil; bake 10 minutes or until top is browned and pasta is fully cooked. Let stand 15 minutes before serving.

Makes 8 servings

Prep Time: 30 minutes
Cook Time: 50 minutes

Salmon Linguini Supper

- **8 ounces linguini, cooked in unsalted water and drained**
- **1 package (10 ounces) frozen peas**
- **1 can (10¾ ounces) condensed cream of celery soup**
- **1 cup milk**
- **¼ cup (1 ounce) grated Parmesan cheese**
- **⅛ teaspoon dried tarragon, crumbled (optional)**
- **1 can (15½ ounces) salmon, drained and flaked**
- **1 egg, slightly beaten**
- **¼ teaspoon salt**
- **¼ teaspoon black pepper**
- **1 can (2.8 ounces) FRENCH'S® French Fried Onions, divided**

Preheat oven to 375°F. Return hot pasta to saucepan; stir in peas, soup, milk, cheese and tarragon; spoon into 12×8-inch baking dish. In medium bowl, using fork, combine salmon, egg, salt, pepper and *½ can*

French Fried Onions. Shape salmon mixture into 4 oval patties. Place patties on pasta mixture. Bake, covered, at 375°F for 40 minutes or until patties are done. Top patties with remaining onions; bake, uncovered, 3 minutes or until onions are golden brown.

Makes 4 servings

String Pie

- **1 pound ground beef**
- **½ cup chopped onion**
- **¼ cup chopped green bell pepper**
- **1 jar (15½ ounces) spaghetti sauce**
- **8 ounces spaghetti, cooked and drained**
- **⅓ cup grated Parmesan cheese**
- **2 eggs, beaten**
- **2 teaspoons butter**
- **1 cup cottage cheese**
- **½ cup (2 ounces) shredded mozzarella cheese**

Preheat oven to 350°F. Cook beef, onion and bell pepper in large skillet over medium-high heat until meat is browned. Drain fat. Stir in spaghetti sauce. Combine spaghetti, Parmesan cheese, eggs and butter in large bowl; mix well. Place on bottom of 13×9-inch baking pan. Spread cottage cheese over top; cover with sauce mixture. Sprinkle with mozzarella cheese. Bake until mixture is thoroughly heated and cheese is melted, about 20 minutes.

Makes 6 to 8 servings

FAVORITE RECIPE FROM **NORTH DAKOTA BEEF COMMISSION**

Zesty Seafood Lasagna

Savory Bean Stew

1 tablespoon olive or
vegetable oil
1 cup frozen vegetable
seasoning blend
(onions, celery, red
and green bell
peppers)
1 can (15½ ounces) chick-
peas, rinsed and
drained
1 can (15 ounces) pinto
beans, rinsed and
drained
1 can (15 ounces) black
beans, rinsed and
drained
1 can (14½ ounces) diced
tomatoes with roasted
garlic, undrained
¾ teaspoon dried thyme
leaves
¾ teaspoon dried sage
leaves
½ to ¾ teaspoon dried
oregano leaves
¾ cup vegetable broth or
chicken broth, divided
1 tablespoon all-purpose
flour

POLENTA
¾ cup yellow cornmeal
¾ teaspoon salt

1. Heat oil in large saucepan
over medium-heat until hot.
Add vegetable seasoning blend;
cook and stir 5 minutes. Stir in
beans, tomatoes and herbs.
Mix ½ cup vegetable broth and
flour. Stir into bean mixture;
bring to a boil. Boil, stirring
constantly, 1 minute. Reduce
heat to low; simmer, covered,
10 minutes. Add remaining
¼ cup broth to stew; season
to taste with salt and pepper.

2. While stew is simmering,
prepare Polenta. Bring 3 cups
water to a boil. Reduce heat
to medium; gradually stir in
cornmeal and salt. Cook 5 to 8
minutes or until cornmeal
thickens and holds its shape,
but is still soft. Season to taste
with pepper. Spread Polenta
over plate and top with stew.

Makes 6 (1-cup) servings

Prep & Cook Time: 30 minutes

Vegetable Sunburst

3 medium carrots, thinly
sliced (about 3 cups)
3 small zucchini, thinly
sliced (about 3 cups)
1 cup (4 ounces) shredded
Cheddar cheese
1 can (2.8 ounces)
FRENCH'S® French
Fried Onions
1 can (10¾ ounces)
condensed cream of
celery soup
¼ cup milk
½ teaspoon seasoned salt
¼ teaspoon garlic powder
¼ teaspoon dried oregano
leaves, crumbled

Preheat oven to 350°F. In
medium saucepan, cook carrots
in boiling water to cover just
until tender-crisp. Place hot
carrots under cold running
water until cool enough to
handle; drain. In 1½-quart
casserole, arrange *half* the
carrots around edge of dish;
place *half* the zucchini in
center. Sprinkle *½ cup* cheese
and *½ can* French Fried Onions
over vegetables. In small bowl,

combine soup, milk and
seasonings. Pour *half* the soup
mixture over onions. Arrange
remaining zucchini around edge
of casserole and remaining
carrots in center. Pour
remaining soup mixture over
vegetables. Bake, covered, at
350°F for 30 minutes or until
vegetables are tender. Top with
remaining cheese and onions;
bake, uncovered, 5 minutes or
until onions are golden brown.

Makes 4 to 6 servings

MICROWAVE DIRECTIONS:
PLACE CARROTS AND ½ CUP WATER
IN MEDIUM MICROWAVE-SAFE BOWL;
MICROWAVE AT HIGH 5 TO
7 MINUTES OR UNTIL CARROTS ARE
TENDER-CRISP. STIR CARROTS
HALFWAY THROUGH COOKING TIME.
DRAIN. PREPARE SOUP MIXTURE AS
DIRECTED. IN 1½-QUART
MICROWAVE-SAFE CASSEROLE, LAYER
VEGETABLES, CHEESE, ONIONS AND
SOUP MIXTURE AS DIRECTED.
MICROWAVE, COVERED, 8 TO
10 MINUTES OR UNTIL VEGETABLES
ARE TENDER. ROTATE DISH HALFWAY
THROUGH COOKING TIME. TOP WITH
REMAINING CHEESE AND ONIONS;
COOK, UNCOVERED, 1 MINUTE OR
UNTIL CHEESE MELTS. LET STAND
5 MINUTES.

Savory Bean Stew

Stacked Burrito Pie

- ½ cup GUILTLESS GOURMET® Mild Black Bean Dip
- 2 teaspoons water
- 5 low-fat flour tortillas (6 inches each)
- ½ cup nonfat sour cream or plain yogurt
- ½ cup GUILTLESS GOURMET® Roasted Red Pepper Salsa
- 1¼ cups (5 ounces) shredded low-fat Monterey Jack cheese
- 4 cups shredded iceberg or romaine lettuce
- ½ cup GUILTLESS GOURMET® Salsa (mild, medium or hot)
- Lime slices and chili pepper (optional)

Preheat oven to 350°F. Combine bean dip and 2 teaspoons water in small bowl; mix well. Line 7½-inch springform pan with 1 tortilla. Spread 2 tablespoons bean dip mixture over tortilla, then spread with 2 tablespoons sour cream and 2 tablespoons red pepper salsa. Sprinkle with ¼ cup cheese. Repeat layers 3 more times. Place remaining tortilla on top and sprinkle with remaining ¼ cup cheese.

Bake 40 minutes or until heated through. (Place sheet of foil under springform pan to catch any juices that may seep through the bottom.) Cool slightly before unmolding. To serve, cut into 4 quarters. Place 1 cup lettuce on 4 serving plates. Top each serving with 1 quarter burrito pie and 2 tablespoons salsa. Garnish with lime slices and pepper, if desired. *Makes 4 servings*

Hot Three-Bean Casserole

- 2 tablespoons olive oil
- 1 cup coarsely chopped onion
- 1 cup chopped celery
- 2 cloves garlic, minced
- 1 can (15 ounces) chick-peas, drained and rinsed
- 1 can (15 ounces) kidney beans, drained and rinsed
- 1 cup coarsely chopped tomato
- 1 can (8 ounces) tomato sauce
- 1 cup water
- 1 to 2 jalapeño peppers, minced*
- 1 tablespoon chili powder
- 2 teaspoons sugar
- 1½ teaspoons ground cumin
- 1 teaspoon salt
- 1 teaspoon dried oregano
- ¼ teaspoon ground black pepper
- 2½ cups (10 ounces) frozen cut green beans

Jalapeño peppers can sting and irritate the skin; wear rubber gloves when handling peppers and do not touch your eyes. Wash hands after handling jalapeño peppers.

1. Heat olive oil in large skillet over medium heat until hot. Add onion, celery and garlic. Cook and stir 5 minutes or until onion is translucent.

2. Add remaining ingredients except green beans. Bring to a boil; reduce heat to low. Simmer, uncovered, 20 minutes. Add green beans. Simmer, uncovered, 10 minutes or until green beans are just tender. Garnish with fresh oregano.
Makes 12 (½-cup) servings

Mexican-Style Chicken

- 1 package (6 ounces) STOVE TOP® Stuffing Mix for Chicken
- 4 boneless skinless chicken breast halves (about 1¼ pounds)
- 1 cup salsa
- 1 cup (4 ounces) KRAFT® Natural Shredded Cheddar Cheese

1. STIR stuffing crumbs, seasoning packet, 1½ cups *hot* water and ¼ cup margarine, cut up, just until moistened.

2. SPOON stuffing in 12×8-inch baking dish. Top with chicken. Pour salsa over chicken; sprinkle with cheese.

3. BAKE at 375°F for 40 minutes or until chicken is cooked through.
Makes 4 servings

Prep Time: 10 minutes
Bake Time: 40 minutes

Nacho Macaroni

8 ounces uncooked elbow macaroni
1 jar (11.5 ounces) GUILTLESS GOURMET® Nacho Dip (mild or spicy)
½ cup skim milk
   Nonstick cooking spray
¼ cup (about 20) crushed GUILTLESS GOURMET® Baked Tortilla Chips (yellow or white corn)

Prepare macaroni according to package directions; drain and keep warm.

Preheat oven to 300°F. Combine nacho dip and milk in 4-cup glass measure; microwave at HIGH 2 minutes. Pour over cooked macaroni; stir to coat well. Coat 2-quart casserole dish with cooking spray. Add macaroni mixture; top with crushed chips.

Bake 20 to 30 minutes or until bubbly and lightly browned on top. Serve hot.

Makes 6 servings

STOVE TOP DIRECTIONS:
COMBINE NACHO DIP AND MILK IN 2-QUART SAUCEPAN; COOK OVER MEDIUM HEAT, STIRRING UNTIL COMPLETELY MIXED. ADD COOKED MACARONI; STIR TO COAT WELL. CONTINUE AS DIRECTED.

Harvest Casserole

2 cups USA lentils, rinsed and cooked
2 cups fresh or frozen broccoli, chopped
1 ½ cups cooked rice
1 ¼ cups (6 ounces) shredded Cheddar cheese
1 tablespoon soy sauce
½ teaspoon salt (optional)
¼ teaspoon dried thyme
¼ teaspoon dried marjoram
¼ teaspoon dried rosemary
4 eggs
1 cup milk

Preheat oven to 350°F.

Mix lentils, broccoli, rice, cheese, soy sauce, salt, thyme, marjoram and rosemary in large bowl. Place mixture in greased 9-inch casserole dish.

Stir together eggs and milk in medium bowl. Pour egg mixture over lentil mixture. Bake 45 minutes or until lightly browned. Top with additional shredded Cheddar cheese, if desired.   *Makes 8 servings*

FAVORITE RECIPE FROM **USA DRY PEA & LENTIL COUNCIL**

Stacked Burrito Pie (page 232)

Barbecue

FEATURING:

Grilled Meat & Chicken

Kabobs

Marinades & Rubs

Barbecue Chicken (page 251)

Southwest Pesto Burgers

CILANTRO PESTO
1 large clove garlic
4 ounces fresh cilantro, stems removed
1 ½ teaspoons bottled minced jalapeño pepper *or*
1 tablespoon bottled sliced jalapeño pepper
¼ teaspoon salt
¼ cup vegetable oil

BURGERS
1 ¼ pounds ground beef
½ teaspoon salt
4 slices Pepper Jack cheese
2 tablespoons light or regular mayonnaise
4 kaiser rolls, split
1 ripe avocado, peeled and sliced
Salsa

1. For pesto, with motor running, drop garlic through feed tube of food processor; process until minced. Add cilantro, jalapeño pepper and ¼ teaspoon salt; process until cilantro is chopped.

2. With motor running, slowly pour oil through feed tube; process until thick paste forms.

3. Prepare barbecue grill for direct cooking.

4. Combine beef, ¼ cup pesto and ½ teaspoon salt in large bowl; mix well. Form into 4 patties. Place patties on grid over medium-hot coals. Grill, uncovered, 4 to 5 minutes per side or until meat is no longer pink in center. Add cheese to patties during last minute of grilling. While patties are cooking, combine mayonnaise and remaining 1 tablespoon pesto in small bowl; mix well. Top patties with mayonnaise mixture. Serve on rolls with avocado and salsa.

Makes 4 servings

Frank's™ Southwest Steak

¾ cup Italian dressing
½ cup minced fresh parsley
⅓ cup FRANK'S® Original REDHOT® Cayenne Pepper Sauce
3 tablespoons lime juice
1 tablespoon FRENCH'S® Worcestershire Sauce
2 pounds boneless sirloin or top round steak (1 ½ inches thick)

1. Place dressing, parsley, RedHot® sauce, juice and Worcestershire in blender or food processor. Cover; process until smooth. Reserve ⅔ cup sauce. Pour remaining sauce over steak in deep dish. Cover; refrigerate 30 minutes.

2. Grill or broil steak 8 minutes per side for medium-rare or to desired doneness. Let stand 5 minutes. Slice steak and serve with reserved sauce.
Makes 6 to 8 servings

Prep Time: 10 minutes
Marinate Time: 30 minutes
Cook Time: 20 minutes

Ranch-Style Fajitas

2 pounds flank or skirt steak
½ cup vegetable oil
⅓ cup lime juice
2 packages (1 ounce each) HIDDEN VALLEY RANCH® Milk Recipe Original Ranch® Salad Dressing Mix
1 teaspoon ground cumin
½ teaspoon black pepper
6 flour tortillas
Lettuce
Guacamole, prepared HIDDEN VALLEY RANCH® Salad Dressing and picante sauce for toppings

Place steak in large baking dish. In small bowl, whisk together oil, lime juice, salad dressing mix, cumin and pepper. Pour mixture over steak. Cover and refrigerate several hours or overnight.

Remove steak; place marinade in small saucepan. Bring to a boil. Grill steak over medium-hot coals 8 to 10 minutes or to desired doneness, turning once and basting with heated marinade during last 5 minutes of grilling. Remove steak and slice diagonally across grain into thin slices. Heat tortillas following package directions. Divide steak strips among tortillas; roll up to enclose. Serve with lettuce and desired toppings. *Makes 6 servings*

Frank's™ Southwest Steak

Zesty Peppered Steaks

4 ounces light cream cheese

½ cup A.1.® Original or A.1.® Bold & Spicy Steak Sauce, divided

1 tablespoon prepared horseradish

4 (4-ounce) beef rib eye steaks, about ¾ inch thick

2 teaspoons coarsely ground black pepper

In small saucepan, over medium heat, stir cream cheese, ¼ cup steak sauce and horseradish until heated through; keep warm.

Brush both sides of steaks with 2 tablespoons steak sauce, dividing evenly. Sprinkle ¼ teaspoon pepper on each side of each steak, pressing into meat and sauce. Grill steaks over medium-high heat or broil 4 inches from heat source 4 minutes on each side or to desired doneness, basting occasionally with remaining 2 tablespoons steak sauce. Serve with warm sauce. Garnish as desired.

Makes 4 servings

Grilled Beef with Two Sauces

1 (1-pound) boneless beef sirloin steak

ROASTED GARLIC SAUCE
¾ cup mayonnaise*
¼ cup Roasted Garlic Purée (recipe follows)
¼ cup GREY POUPON® Dijon Mustard
2 tablespoons chopped parsley
1 tablespoon lemon juice

SUNDRIED TOMATO SAUCE
¾ cup chopped roasted red peppers
½ cup sundried tomatoes, chopped
3 tablespoons GREY POUPON® Dijon Mustard
2 tablespoons chopped parsley
2 to 3 tablespoons olive oil
¼ teaspoon crushed red pepper flakes

*Low-fat mayonnaise may be substituted for regular mayonnaise.

**If sundried tomatoes are very dry, soften in warm water for 15 minutes. Drain before using.

Grill beef over medium heat to desired doneness and chill.

For Roasted Garlic Sauce, in medium bowl, blend all ingredients. Chill at least 1 hour to blend flavors.

For Sundried Tomato Sauce, in medium bowl, combine roasted red peppers, sundried tomatoes, mustard and parsley. Slowly add oil as needed to bind. Add red pepper flakes. Chill at least 1 hour to blend flavors. Bring to room temperature before serving.

To serve, slice beef and arrange on 4 serving plates. Spoon about 2 tablespoons of each sauce onto each plate. Serve with sliced tomatoes and cooled steamed asparagus; garnish as desired. *Makes 4 servings*

ROASTED GARLIC PURÉE:
Remove excess papery outside of 1 head garlic and separate into cloves. Place in 8×8×2-inch baking pan. Add 2 to 3 tablespoons olive oil and 1 cup chicken broth. Bake at 350°F for 25 to 30 minutes or until garlic is soft. Cool and squeeze garlic pulp from skins; discard liquid in pan.

Zesty Peppered Steak

Savory Grilled Tournedos

⅓ cup A.1.® Steak Sauce
¼ cup ketchup
¼ cup orange marmalade
2 tablespoons lemon juice
2 tablespoons minced onion
1 clove garlic, crushed
8 slices bacon (about 5 ounces)
8 (4-ounce) beef tenderloin steaks (tournedos), about 1 inch thick
Mushroom halves, radishes and parsley sprigs for garnish

In small bowl, blend steak sauce, ketchup, marmalade, lemon juice, onion and garlic; set aside.

Wrap a bacon slice around edge of each steak; secure with string or wooden toothpick. Grill steaks over medium-high heat for 10 minutes or to desired doneness, turning occasionally and brushing often with ½ cup prepared sauce. Remove string or toothpicks; serve steaks with remaining sauce. Garnish with mushroom halves, radishes and parsley, if desired.   *Makes 8 servings*

Grilled Dinner Franks with Salsa Cruda

1 package (16 ounces) HEBREW NATIONAL® Quarter Pound Dinner Beef Franks
1 large tomato, seeded and chopped
3 tablespoons chopped cilantro
2 tablespoons finely chopped seeded green bell pepper
2 tablespoons finely chopped red onion
1 jalapeño pepper, seeded and finely chopped
¼ teaspoon salt

Prepare barbecue grill for direct cooking. Grill franks 10 minutes or until heated through and lightly browned. Combine tomato, cilantro, bell pepper, onion, jalapeño pepper and salt in small bowl. Refrigerate until ready to use. Serve franks topped with salsa.

Makes 4 servings

Country Kielbasa Kabobs

½ cup GREY POUPON® COUNTRY DIJON® Mustard
½ cup apricot preserves
⅓ cup minced green onions
1 pound kielbasa, cut into 1-inch pieces
1 large apple, cored and cut into wedges
½ cup frozen pearl onions, thawed
6 small red skin potatoes, parboiled and cut into halves
3 cups shredded red and green cabbage, steamed

Soak 6 (10-inch) wooden skewers in water for 30 minutes. In small bowl, blend mustard, preserves and green onions; set aside ¼ cup mixture.

Alternately thread kielbasa, apple, pearl onions and potatoes on skewers. Grill or broil kabobs for 12 to 15 minutes or until done, turning and brushing with remaining mustard mixture. Heat reserved mustard mixture and toss with steamed cabbage. Serve hot with kabobs. Garnish as desired.

Makes 6 servings

Buffalo Turkey Kabobs

⅔ cup **HELLMANN'S®** or **BEST FOODS®** Real or Light Mayonnaise, divided
1 teaspoon hot pepper sauce
1½ pounds boneless turkey breast, cut into 1-inch cubes
2 red bell peppers or 1 red and 1 yellow bell pepper, cut into 1-inch squares
2 medium onions, cut into wedges
¼ cup (1 ounce) crumbled blue cheese
2 tablespoons milk
1 medium rib celery, minced
1 medium carrot, minced

1. In medium bowl, combine ⅓ cup mayonnaise and hot pepper sauce. Stir in turkey. Let stand at room temperature 20 minutes.

2. On 6 skewers, alternately thread turkey, peppers and onions. Grill or broil 5 inches from heat, brushing with remaining mayonnaise mixture and turning frequently, 12 to 15 minutes.

3. Meanwhile, in small bowl, blend remaining ⅓ cup mayonnaise with blue cheese and milk. Stir in celery and carrot. Serve with kabobs.

Makes 6 servings

Curried Pork Kabobs

1 pound boneless pork loin, cut into ½-inch cubes
1 cup low-fat plain yogurt
2 tablespoons orange juice
1 tablespoon ground coriander
½ teaspoon turmeric
½ teaspoon ground cumin
½ teaspoon salt
¼ teaspoon ground ginger

For marinade, combine all ingredients except pork cubes in medium bowl; blend well. Add pork; stir to coat with marinade. Cover and refrigerate 4 hours or overnight. Prepare grill. Remove pork; discard marinade. Lightly pat pork dry with paper towels. Thread pork evenly onto skewers.* Grill over medium-hot coals about 10 minutes or until pork is nicely browned and barely pink in center, turning frequently. Serve immediately.

Makes 4 servings

Soak bamboo skewers in water 30 minutes to prevent burning.

FAVORITE RECIPE FROM **NATIONAL PORK PRODUCERS COUNCIL**

Buffalo Turkey Kabobs

Micro-Grilled Pork Ribs

- **1 tablespoon firmly packed brown sugar**
- **2 teaspoons ground cumin**
- **1 teaspoon salt**
- **½ teaspoon black pepper Dash ground red pepper (optional)**
- **3 pounds pork back ribs**
- **⅓ cup water**
- **½ cup K.C. MASTERPIECE® Barbecue Sauce Grilled Sweet Potatoes (recipe follows)**

Combine brown sugar, cumin, salt and peppers in small bowl. Rub onto ribs. Arrange ribs in single layer in 13×9-inch microwave-safe baking dish. Pour water over ribs; cover loosely with plastic wrap. Microwave at MEDIUM-HIGH (70% power) 15 minutes, rearranging ribs and rotating dish halfway through cooking time.

Arrange medium-hot **KINGSFORD®** Briquets on one side of grill. Place ribs on grid area opposite briquets. Grill ribs, on a covered grill, 15 to 20 minutes, turning every 5 minutes and basting with barbecue sauce last 10 minutes. (Ribs should be browned and cooked through.) Serve with Grilled Sweet Potatoes.

Makes 4 servings

GRILLED SWEET POTATOES OR BAKING POTATOES:
Slice potatoes into ¼-inch-thick rounds, allowing about ⅓ pound potatoes per serving. Brush both sides of slices lightly with vegetable oil. Place on grid around edges of medium-hot **KINGSFORD®** Briquets. Cook potatoes, on a covered grill, 10 to 12 minutes until golden brown and tender, turning once.

Jamaican Pork Chops with Tropical Fruit Salsa

- **⅔ cup prepared Italian salad dressing**
- **⅓ cup FRANK'S® Original REDHOT® Cayenne Pepper Sauce**
- **⅓ cup lime juice**
- **2 tablespoons brown sugar**
- **2 teaspoons dried thyme leaves**
- **1 teaspoon ground allspice**
- **½ teaspoon ground nutmeg**
- **½ teaspoon ground cinnamon**
- **6 loin pork chops, cut 1 inch thick (about 2½ pounds)**
- **Tropical Fruit Salsa (recipe follows)**

Place salad dressing, RedHot® sauce, lime juice, sugar and seasonings in blender or food processor. Cover and process until smooth. Reserve ½ cup dressing mixture for Tropical Fruit Salsa. Place pork chops in large resealable plastic food storage bag. Pour remaining dressing mixture over chops. Seal bag and marinate in refrigerator 1 hour.

Place chops on grid, reserving dressing mixture. Grill over medium coals 30 minutes or until pork is juicy and barely pink in center, turning and basting frequently with dressing mixture. *Do not baste during last 5 minutes of cooking.* Serve chops with Tropical Fruit Salsa. Garnish as desired.

Makes 6 servings

TROPICAL FRUIT SALSA
- **1 cup finely chopped fresh pineapple**
- **1 ripe mango, peeled, seeded and finely chopped**
- **2 tablespoons finely chopped red onion**
- **1 tablespoon minced fresh cilantro leaves**

Combine pineapple, mango, onion, cilantro and reserved ½ cup dressing mixture in small bowl. Refrigerate until chilled.

Makes about 2½ cups

Prep Time: 20 minutes
Marinate Time: 1 hour
Cook Time: 30 minutes

*Micro-Grilled Pork Ribs and
Grilled Sweet Potatoes*

Grilled Pork Tenderloin Medallions

PEPPER & HERB RUB
- **1 tablespoon dried basil leaves**
- **1 tablespoon garlic salt**
- **1 tablespoon dried thyme leaves**
- **1 ½ teaspoons cracked black pepper**
- **1 ½ teaspoons dried rosemary**
- **1 teaspoon paprika**

PORK
- **12 pork tenderloin medallions (about 1 pound)**

1. For rub, combine basil, salt, thyme, pepper, rosemary and paprika in small bowl.

2. Prepare barbecue grill for direct cooking.

3. Sprinkle rub evenly over both sides of pork, pressing lightly. Spray pork with olive-oil flavored nonstick cooking spray.

4. Place pork on grid over medium-hot coals. Grill, uncovered, 4 to 5 minutes per side or until pork is no longer pink in center.

Makes 4 servings

SERVING SUGGESTION: SERVE MEDALLIONS WITH BOILED RED POTATOES AND STEAMED BROCCOLI.

Hickory Smoked Ham with Maple-Mustard Sauce

- **Hickory chunks or chips for smoking**
- **1 fully cooked boneless ham (about 5 pounds)**
- **¾ cup maple syrup**
- **¾ cup spicy brown mustard or Dijon mustard**

Soak about 4 wood chunks or several handfuls of wood chips in water; drain. If using a canned ham, scrape off any gelatin. If using another type of fully cooked ham, such as a bone-in shank, trim most of the fat, leaving a ⅛-inch layer. (The thinner the fat layer, the better the glaze will adhere to the ham.)

Arrange low **KINGSFORD®** Briquets on each side of a rectangular metal or foil drip pan. Pour hot tap water into pan to fill half full. Add soaked wood (all the chunks or part of the chips) to the fire.

Oil hot grid to help prevent sticking. Place ham on grid directly above drip pan. Grill ham, on a covered grill, 20 to 30 minutes per pound or until a meat thermometer inserted into the thickest part registers 140°F. If your grill has a thermometer, maintain a cooking temperature of about 200°F. For best flavor, cook slowly over low coals, adding a few briquets to both sides

of the fire every hour, or as necessary, to maintain a constant temperature. Add more soaked hickory chips every 20 to 30 minutes.

Meanwhile, prepare Maple-Mustard Sauce by mixing maple syrup and mustard in small bowl; set aside most of the syrup mixture to serve as a sauce. Brush ham with remaining mixture several times during the last 45 minutes of cooking. Let ham stand 10 minutes before slicing. Slice and serve with Maple-Mustard Sauce.

Makes 12 to 15 servings

Note: Most of the hams available today are fully cooked and need only be heated to a temperature of 140°F. If you buy a partially cooked ham, often labeled "cook before eating," it needs to be cooked to 160°F.

Tip: Keep the briquet temperature low and replenish the hickory chips every 20 to 30 minutes.

Grilled Pork Tenderloin Medallions

Cheesy Lamburger

1 pound lean ground
American lamb
¼ cup (1 ounce) shredded
Cheddar cheese
2 tablespoons sweet
pickle relish
2 tablespoons finely
chopped onion
1 tablespoon finely
chopped green bell
pepper
1 teaspoon Dijon mustard
4 multi grain hamburger
buns, toasted
4 lettuce leaves
4 slices tomato

Prepare grill. Combine cheese, relish, onion, pepper and mustard in small bowl. Shape lamb into 8 thin patties about 4 inches in diameter. Spoon cheese mixture onto centers of 4 patties. Top each with another patty, pressing edges to seal filling inside. Place burgers on grid. Grill 4 inches over medium coals 5 minutes on each side or to desired doneness. Serve on buns with lettuce and tomato.

Makes 4 servings

Prep Time: 15 minutes
Cook Time: 10 to 15 minutes

Variation: Substitute dill pickle relish and Monterey Jack or Swiss cheese for the sweet relish and Cheddar.

FAVORITE RECIPE FROM **AMERICAN LAMB COUNCIL**

Southwestern Lamb Grill

1 rack of American lamb,
8 ribs
3 tablespoons stone-
ground mustard
1 tablespoon
Worcestershire sauce
½ teaspoon crushed red
pepper
2 cloves garlic, minced

Trim all visible fat from rack. Stir together remaining ingredients in small bowl. Spread on outside of lamb. (If desired, for maximum flavor, cover and marinate in refrigerator up to 2 days.)

Prepare grill. Place lamb on grid. Grill 6 to 8 inches over hot coals until thermometer registers 145°F for rare or 150°F for medium-rare, turning frequently.   *Makes 2 servings*

CONVENTIONAL DIRECTIONS:
PREPARE LAMB AS DIRECTED. PLACE LAMB ON RACK OVER BROILER PAN. ROAST IN PREHEATED 325°F OVEN UNTIL MEAT THERMOMETER REGISTERS 145°F FOR RARE OR 150°F FOR MEDIUM-RARE.

SERVING SUGGESTION: SLICE RED OR GREEN BELL PEPPERS, ZUCCHINI, CHILI PEPPERS AND CORN TO DESIRED SIZE; BRUSH WITH MIXTURE OF OIL AND CHOPPED FRESH CILANTRO. GRILL 6 TO 8 INCHES OVER HOT COALS UNTIL TENDER.

FAVORITE RECIPE FROM **AMERICAN LAMB COUNCIL**

Western Lamb Riblets

5 pounds lamb riblets,
cut into serving-size
pieces
¾ cup bottled chili sauce
½ cup honey
½ cup beer
¼ cup Worcestershire
sauce
¼ cup finely chopped
onion
1 clove garlic, minced
½ teaspoon crushed red
pepper flakes

Trim excess fat from riblets. In saucepan, combine chili sauce, honey, beer, Worcestershire sauce, onion, garlic and pepper flakes. Bring mixture to a boil. Reduce heat; simmer, covered, 10 minutes. Remove from heat; cool.

Place riblets in plastic bag. Pour cooled marinade over riblets in bag. Close bag securely and refrigerate about 2 hours, turning bag occasionally to distribute marinade evenly.

Drain riblets; reserve marinade. Arrange medium-hot **KINGSFORD**® Briquets around drip pan. Place riblets on grid over drip pan. Cover grill; cook 45 minutes, turning riblets and brushing with marinade twice. Bring remaining marinade to a boil; serve with riblets.

Makes 6 servings

Lamb Sirloin with Honey Mustard Sauce

1 pound American lamb
    sirloin steaks, cut
    ¾ inch thick
Honey Mustard Sauce
    (recipe follows)
¼ teaspoon salt
¼ teaspoon black pepper

Prepare Honey Mustard Sauce; cover and refrigerate until serving time. Sprinkle lamb steaks with salt and black pepper. Grill or broil 4 inches from heat source for 3 to 5 minutes. Turn and continue cooking 3 to 5 minutes or until desired doneness. Serve with sauce. *Makes 4 servings*

Prep Time: 15 minutes
Cook Time: 10 minutes

HONEY MUSTARD SAUCE
1 slice firm-textured
    whole wheat bread
    (1 ounce), torn into
    small pieces
¼ cup plain low-fat yogurt
2 tablespoons brown
    stone-ground mustard
1 tablespoon honey
1 teaspoon snipped fresh
    parsley
1 teaspoon prepared
    horseradish
1 to 2 tablespoons water

Combine torn bread and yogurt in medium bowl. Stir until mixture is fairly smooth. Stir in mustard, honey, parsley and

horseradish; mix well. Stir in 1 to 2 tablespoons water as necessary to reach desired consistency.

Makes about ⅔ cup

FAVORITE RECIPE FROM **AMERICAN LAMB COUNCIL**

Barbecued Leg of Lamb with Cucumber Yogurt Dip

1 (5- to 6-pound) leg of
    lamb, bone removed
    and butterflied
1 onion, thinly sliced
½ cup dry white wine
½ cup FILIPPO BERIO®
    Olive Oil
¼ cup lemon juice
2 cloves garlic, thinly
    sliced
1 tablespoon dried
    oregano leaves
1 bay leaf
    Salt and freshly ground
    black pepper
    Cucumber Yogurt Dip
    (recipe follows)
    Pita bread wedges
2 lemons, cut into wedges

Place lamb in large shallow glass dish. In medium bowl, combine onion, wine, olive oil, lemon juice, garlic, oregano and bay leaf. Pour marinade over lamb; turn to coat both sides. Cover; marinate in refrigerator 3 to 4 hours or overnight, turning occasionally. Remove lamb, reserving marinade.

Brush barbecue grid with olive oil. Grill lamb, on covered grill, over hot coals 20 minutes, basting occasionally with reserved marinade. Turn with tongs. Grill an additional 20 minutes or until desired doneness is reached. Transfer lamb to warm serving platter. Carve into thin slices; season to taste with salt and pepper. Serve with Cucumber Yogurt Dip, pita bread and lemon wedges.

Makes 6 to 8 servings

CUCUMBER YOGURT DIP
2 (8-ounce) containers
    plain yogurt, without
    gelatin
1 large cucumber, peeled
2 tablespoons FILIPPO
    BERIO® Olive Oil
1 tablespoon white
    vinegar
2 cloves garlic, minced
    Salt and white pepper

Line large plastic colander or sieve with large piece of double thickness cheesecloth or large coffee filter. Place colander over deep bowl. Spoon yogurt into colander; cover with waxed paper. Refrigerate until liquid no longer drains from yogurt, about 24 hours. Remove yogurt; place in medium bowl. Discard liquid. Cut cucumber into quarters; remove seeds. Finely chop cucumber; drain on paper towels. Stir cucumber, olive oil, vinegar and garlic into yogurt. Season to taste with salt and pepper. Cover; refrigerate at least 1 hour before serving.

Makes about 2 cups

Grilled Chicken with Orange-Cilantro Salsa

1 cup (11-ounce can) mandarin oranges, drained, ¼ cup juice reserved
1 cup coarsely chopped fresh cilantro
½ cup sliced red onion
¼ cup olive oil
¼ cup red wine vinegar
1 tablespoon ORTEGA® Diced Jalapeños
1 teaspoon salt
1 pound (3 to 4) boneless skinless chicken breast halves

COMBINE oranges with reserved juice, cilantro, onion, oil, vinegar, jalapeños and salt in medium bowl; cover. Chill for at least 2 hours.

GRILL chicken over hot coals in barbecue, turning frequently, for 15 to 20 minutes or until chicken is no longer pink in center. Or, broil chicken in preheated broiler 4 to 5 inches from heat source, turning frequently, for 6 to 8 minutes or until chicken is no longer pink in center. Top each breast with salsa.   *Makes 4 servings*

Jamaican Grilled Chicken

1 whole chicken (4 pounds), cut into pieces *or* 6 whole chicken legs
1 cup coarsely chopped fresh cilantro leaves and stems
½ cup FRANK'S® Original REDHOT® Cayenne Pepper Sauce
⅓ cup vegetable oil
6 cloves garlic, coarsely chopped
¼ cup fresh lime juice (juice of 2 limes)
1 teaspoon grated lime peel
1 teaspoon ground turmeric
1 teaspoon ground allspice

1. Loosen and pull back skin from chicken pieces. Do not remove skin. Place chicken pieces in large resealable plastic food storage bags or large glass bowl.

2. Place remaining ingredients in blender or food processor. Cover; process until smooth. Reserve ⅓ *cup* marinade. Pour remaining marinade over chicken pieces, turning to coat evenly. Seal bags or cover bowl; refrigerate 1 hour.

3. Prepare grill. Reposition skin on chicken pieces. Place chicken on oiled grid. Grill, over medium to medium-low coals, 45 minutes or until chicken is no longer pink near bone and juices run clear, turning and basting often with reserved marinade.
Makes 6 servings

Prep Time: 15 minutes
Marinate Time: 1 hour
Cook Time: 45 minutes

Mango Pineapple Chutney

2 cups diced fresh pineapple
2 kiwi, peeled and diced
1 navel orange, peeled and diced
2 green onions, thinly sliced
½ cup mango chutney, large pieces chopped
2 tablespoons FRANK'S® Original REDHOT® Cayenne Pepper Sauce
2 tablespoons chopped fresh mint or cilantro
1 tablespoon red wine vinegar
½ teaspoon salt

Combine all ingredients in large bowl; toss to coat evenly. Cover; refrigerate 30 minutes.
Makes 3 cups chutney

Prep Time: 20 minutes
Chill Time: 30 minutes

Grilled Chicken with Orange-Cilantro Salsa

Rosemary's Chicken

4 large boneless skinless
    chicken breast halves
    (about 1½ pounds)
¼ cup FRENCH'S® CLASSIC
    YELLOW® Mustard
¼ cup frozen orange juice
    concentrate, undiluted
2 tablespoons cider
    vinegar
2 teaspoons dried
    rosemary leaves,
    crushed
4 strips thick sliced bacon

Place chicken in large
resealable plastic food storage
bag or glass bowl. To prepare
marinade, combine mustard,
orange juice concentrate,
vinegar and rosemary in small
bowl. Pour over chicken. Seal
bag or cover bowl and marinate
in refrigerator 30 minutes.
Wrap 1 strip bacon around
each piece of chicken; secure
with toothpicks.*

Place chicken on grid, reserving
marinade. Grill over medium
coals 25 minutes or until
chicken is no longer pink in
center, turning and basting
often with marinade. *Do not
baste during last 10 minutes
of cooking.* Remove toothpicks
before serving. Garnish as
desired.   *Makes 4 servings*

*Before using, soak toothpicks in
water 20 minutes to prevent
burning.*

Prep Time: 15 minutes
Marinate Time: 30 minutes
Cook Time: 25 minutes

Chicken Ribbons Satay

½ cup creamy peanut
    butter
½ cup water
¼ cup soy sauce
4 cloves garlic, pressed
3 tablespoons lemon juice
2 tablespoons firmly
    packed brown sugar
¾ teaspoon ground ginger
½ teaspoon crushed red
    pepper flakes
4 boneless skinless
    chicken breast halves
Sliced green onion tops
    for garnish

Combine peanut butter, water,
soy sauce, garlic, lemon juice,
brown sugar, ginger and red
pepper flakes in a small
saucepan. Cook over medium
heat 1 minute or until smooth;
cool. Remove garlic from sauce;
discard. Reserve half of sauce
for dipping. Cut chicken
lengthwise into 1-inch-wide
strips. Thread onto 8 metal
or bamboo skewers. (Soak
bamboo skewers in water at
least 20 minutes before using
to prevent them from burning.)

Oil hot grid to help prevent
sticking. Grill chicken, on a
covered grill, over medium-hot
KINGSFORD® Briquets, 6 to
8 minutes or until chicken is no
longer pink in center, turning
once. Baste with sauce once
or twice during cooking. Serve
with reserved sauce garnished
with sliced green onion.
          Makes 4 servings

Lemon Pepper Chicken

⅓ cup lemon juice
¼ cup olive oil
¼ cup finely chopped
    onion
3 cloves garlic, minced
1 tablespoon cracked
    black pepper
1 tablespoon brown sugar
2 teaspoons grated lemon
    peel
¾ teaspoon salt
4 chicken quarters (about
    2½ pounds)

COMBINE lemon juice, oil,
onion, garlic, pepper, sugar,
lemon peel and salt in small
bowl; reserve 2 tablespoons
marinade. Combine remaining
marinade and chicken in large
resealable plastic food storage
bag. Seal bag; knead to coat.
Refrigerate 4 hours or overnight.

REMOVE chicken from
marinade; discard marinade.
Arrange chicken on
microwavable plate; cover
with waxed paper. Microwave
at HIGH 5 minutes. Turn and
rearrange chicken. Cover and
microwave at HIGH 5 minutes.

TRANSFER chicken to grill.
Grill, covered, over medium-
hot coals 15 to 20 minutes or
until chicken is no longer pink
in center and juices run clear,
turning several times and
basting often with reserved
marinade.   *Makes 4 servings*

*SERVING SUGGESTION: SERVE WITH
A MIXED GREEN SALAD AND FRESH
LEMON SLICES.*

Grilled Chicken and Apple with Fresh Rosemary

- ½ cup apple juice
- ¼ cup white wine vinegar
- ¼ cup vegetable oil or light olive oil
- 1 tablespoon chopped fresh rosemary *or* 1 teaspoon dried rosemary leaves, crushed
- ¼ teaspoon salt
- ¼ teaspoon ground black pepper
- 3 boneless skinless chicken breasts, halved
- 2 Washington Golden Delicious apples, cored and sliced into ½-inch-thick rings

1. Combine juice, vinegar, oil, rosemary, salt and pepper in shallow baking dish or bowl. Add chicken and apples; marinate in refrigerator at least 30 minutes.

2. Heat grill. Remove chicken and apples from marinade; arrange on hot grill. Discard marinade. Cook chicken 20 minutes or until cooked through, turning to grill both sides. Cook and turn apples about 6 minutes or until crisp-tender. Serve.

Makes 6 servings

FAVORITE RECIPE FROM **WASHINGTON APPLE COMMISSION**

Barbecue Chicken

- 1 cup prepared barbecue sauce
- ½ cup fresh lemon juice
- ½ cup honey
- 3 tablespoons paprika
- 2 tablespoons olive oil
- 2 teaspoons curry powder
- 1 teaspoon ground cumin
- 1 teaspoon freshly ground black pepper
- ½ teaspoon salt
- 2 packages GALIL® Cut-Up Whole Chicken (about 3½ pounds)

Combine barbecue sauce, lemon juice, honey, paprika, oil, curry, cumin, pepper and salt in medium bowl; mix well. Reserve ¾ cup sauce. Prepare barbecue grill for direct cooking. Grill chicken over medium coals 10 minutes each side. Brush chicken lightly with sauce. Grill about 20 minutes or until chicken is no longer pink in centers or near bone. Serve with reserved sauce.

Makes 8 servings

Grilled Chicken and Apple with Fresh Rosemary

Rotelle with Grilled Chicken Dijon

¾ cup **GREY POUPON®**
  Dijon Mustard, divided
1 tablespoon lemon juice
1 tablespoon olive oil
1 clove garlic, minced
½ teaspoon Italian
  seasoning
1 pound boneless skinless
  chicken breasts
¼ cup margarine or butter
1 cup **COLLEGE INN®**
  Chicken Broth or
  Lower Sodium Chicken
  Broth
1 cup chopped cooked
  broccoli
⅓ cup coarsely chopped
  roasted red peppers
1 pound tri-color rotelle
  or spiral-shaped pasta,
  cooked
¼ cup grated Parmesan
  cheese

In medium bowl, combine ¼ cup mustard, lemon juice, oil, garlic and Italian seasoning. Add chicken, stirring to coat well. Refrigerate for 1 hour.

Grill or broil chicken over medium heat for 6 minutes on each side or until done. Cool slightly; slice into ½-inch strips and set aside.

In large skillet, over medium heat, melt margarine or butter; blend in remaining mustard and chicken broth. Stir in broccoli and peppers; heat through.

In large serving bowl, combine hot cooked pasta, broccoli mixture, chicken and Parmesan cheese, tossing to coat well. Garnish as desired. Serve immediately.

Makes 5 servings

Lime Salsa Chicken

4 broiler-fryer chicken
  breast halves, boned
  and skinned
¼ cup lime juice
2 tablespoons sherry
2 tablespoons light olive
  oil
½ teaspoon dried oregano
  leaves
½ teaspoon garlic salt
  Salsa (recipe follows)
  Avocado slices
  Tortilla chips

For marinade, combine lime juice, sherry, oil, oregano and garlic salt in large glass bowl or resealable plastic food storage bag. Remove 3 tablespoons marinade; set aside for Salsa. Add chicken to remaining marinade; turn to coat. Cover and marinate in refrigerator 1 hour.

Meanwhile, prepare grill and Salsa. Remove chicken, reserving marinade in small saucepan. Bring marinade to a boil; cook 1 minute. Place chicken on grid. Brush marinade over chicken. Grill 8 inches over medium coals about 16 to 20 minutes or until chicken is no longer pink in center, turning and basting frequently with marinade. *Do not baste during last 5 minutes of grilling.* Arrange chicken on platter. Serve with Salsa. Garnish with avocado slices and tortilla chips.

Makes 4 servings

SALSA: Stir together 1 peeled, seeded and chopped tomato, 1 sliced green onion, ¼ cup sliced ripe olives, 3 tablespoons reserved marinade, 1 tablespoon seeded and chopped jalapeño pepper, 1 tablespoon chopped fresh cilantro, 1 tablespoon chopped fresh mint, 1 tablespoon slivered almonds, ¼ teaspoon salt and ¼ teaspoon black pepper; refrigerate.

Makes 1 cup

*FAVORITE RECIPE FROM **DELMARVA POULTRY INDUSTRY, INC.***

Rotelle with Grilled Chicken Dijon

Chicken Shish-Kabobs

¼ cup **CRISCO® Oil**
¼ cup **wine vinegar**
¼ cup **lemon juice**
1 teaspoon **dried oregano leaves**
1 clove **garlic, minced**
¼ teaspoon **black pepper**
1½ pounds **boneless skinless chicken breasts, cut into 1- to 1½-inch cubes**
12 **bamboo or metal skewers (10 to 12 inches long)**
2 medium **tomatoes, cut into wedges**
2 medium **onions, cut into wedges**
1 medium **green bell pepper, cut into 1-inch squares**
1 medium **red bell pepper, cut into 1-inch squares**
4 cups **hot cooked brown rice (cooked without salt or fat)**
Salt (optional)

1. Combine Crisco® Oil, vinegar, lemon juice, oregano, garlic and black pepper in shallow baking dish or glass bowl. Stir well. Add chicken. Stir to coat. Cover. Marinate in refrigerator 3 hours, turning chicken several times.

2. Soak bamboo skewers in water.

3. Prepare grill or heat broiler.

4. Thread chicken, tomatoes, onions and bell peppers alternately on skewers.

5. Place skewers on grill or broiler pan. Grill or broil 5 minutes. Turn. Grill or broil 5 to 7 minutes or until chicken is no longer pink in center. Serve over hot rice. Season with salt and garnish, if desired. *Makes 6 servings*

Grilled Game Hens— Texas Style

1 can (8 ounces) **tomato sauce**
¼ cup **vegetable oil**
1½ teaspoons **chili powder**
1 teaspoon **paprika**
¼ teaspoon **garlic powder**
¼ teaspoon **ground red pepper**
4 **Cornish game hens (1 to 1½ pounds each), cut into halves**

In small bowl, combine all ingredients except game hens. Brush hens generously with tomato mixture. Grill hens, on covered grill, over medium-hot **KINGSFORD®** with Mesquite Charcoal Briquets 45 to 50 minutes or until fork-tender, brushing frequently with tomato mixture. *Makes 4 servings*

Turkey Ham Quesadillas

¼ cup **picante sauce or salsa**
4 (7-inch) **regular or whole wheat flour tortillas**
½ cup **shredded reduced-sodium reduced-fat Monterey Jack cheese**
¼ cup **finely chopped turkey ham or lean ham**
¼ cup **canned green chilies, drained *or* 1 to 2 tablespoons chopped fresh jalapeño peppers to taste**
Nonstick cooking spray
Additional picante sauce or salsa for dipping (optional)
Fat-free or low-fat sour cream (optional)

1. Spread 1 tablespoon picante sauce on each tortilla.

2. Sprinkle cheese, turkey ham and chilies equally over half of each tortilla. Fold over uncovered half to make "sandwich"; spray tops and bottoms of tortilla "sandwiches" with cooking spray.

3. Grill, uncovered, over medium coals 1½ minutes per side or until cheese is melted and tortillas are golden brown, turning once. Quarter each quesadilla and serve with additional picante sauce and fat-free sour cream, if desired. *Makes 8 appetizer servings*

Turkey Burritos

1 tablespoon ground
   cumin
1 tablespoon chili powder
1 ½ teaspoons salt
1 ½ to 2 pounds turkey
   tenderloin, cut into
   ½-inch cubes
   Avocado-Corn Salsa
   (recipe follows,
   optional)
   Lime wedges
   Flour tortillas
   Sour cream (optional)
   Tomato slices for
   garnish

Combine cumin, chili powder
and salt in cup. Place turkey
cubes in a shallow glass dish
or large heavy plastic bag; pour
dry rub over turkey and coat
turkey thoroughly. Let turkey
stand while preparing Avocado-
Corn Salsa. Thread turkey onto
metal or bamboo skewers.
(Soak bamboo skewers in water
at least 20 minutes before using
to prevent them from burning.)

Oil hot grid to help prevent
sticking. Grill turkey, on a
covered grill, over medium
KINGSFORD® Briquets, about
6 minutes or until turkey is no
longer pink in center, turning
once. Remove skewers from
grill; squeeze lime wedges over
skewers. Warm flour tortillas in
microwave oven, or brush each
tortilla very lightly with water
and grill 10 to 15 seconds per
side. Top with Avocado-Corn
Salsa and sour cream, if desired.
Garnish with tomato slices.

Makes 6 servings

AVOCADO-CORN SALSA

2 small to medium-size
   ripe avocados, finely
   chopped
1 cup cooked fresh corn
   or thawed frozen corn
2 medium tomatoes,
   seeded and finely
   chopped
2 to 3 tablespoons
   chopped fresh cilantro
2 to 3 tablespoons lime
   juice
½ to 1 teaspoon minced
   hot green chili pepper
½ teaspoon salt

Gently stir together all
ingredients in medium bowl;
adjust flavors to taste. Cover
and refrigerate until ready to
serve.   *Makes about 1½ cups*

Tip: *This recipe is great for casual
get-togethers. Just prepare the
fixings and let the guests make
their own burritos.*

Dad's Favorite Turkey Kabobs

3 ears corn, cut into
   1-inch pieces
2 medium zucchini, cut
   into ¾-inch pieces
2 red bell peppers, cut
   into 1-inch cubes
2 turkey tenderloins
   (about 1 pound), cut
   into 1-inch cubes
⅓ cup reduced-calorie
   Italian salad dressing
   Additional reduced-
   calorie Italian salad
   dressing

In medium saucepan over high
heat, blanch corn in boiling
water about 1 to 2 minutes.
Remove corn from saucepan
and plunge into cold water.

In large glass bowl, place corn,
zucchini, peppers, turkey and
⅓ cup dressing; cover and
refrigerate 1 to 2 hours.

Drain turkey and vegetables,
discarding marinade.
Alternately thread turkey cubes
and vegetables on 8 skewers,
leaving ½-inch space between
turkey and vegetables.

On outdoor charcoal grill,
cook kabobs 18 to 20 minutes,
brushing with additional
dressing. Turn skewers after
first 10 minutes.

Makes 4 servings

*FAVORITE RECIPE FROM **NATIONAL
TURKEY FEDERATION***

Tuna Steaks with Shrimp Creole Sauce

- 4 tablespoons olive oil, divided
- 1 medium red onion, chopped
- 1 red or yellow bell pepper, seeded and chopped
- 2 ribs celery, sliced
- 2 cloves garlic, minced
- 1 can (14½ ounces) stewed tomatoes
- ¼ cup FRANK'S® Original REDHOT® Cayenne Pepper Sauce
- ¼ cup tomato paste
- ½ teaspoon dried thyme leaves
- 1 bay leaf
- ½ pound medium-size raw shrimp, shelled and deveined
- 4 tuna, swordfish or codfish steaks, cut 1 inch thick (about 1½ pounds)
  Hot cooked rice (optional)

Heat *2 tablespoons* oil in medium skillet over medium-high heat. Add onion, pepper, celery and garlic; cook and stir 1 minute. Stir in tomatoes, RedHot® sauce, tomato paste, thyme and bay leaf. Bring to a boil. Reduce heat to medium-low. Cook 5 minutes, stirring often. Add shrimp; cook 3 minutes or until shrimp turn pink. Remove and discard bay leaf. Set aside shrimp sauce.

Brush both sides of fish steaks with remaining *2 tablespoons* oil. Place steaks on grid. Grill over medium-high coals 10 minutes or until fish flakes easily with a fork,* turning once. Transfer to serving platter. Spoon shrimp sauce over fish. Serve with rice, if desired. Garnish as desired.

Makes 4 servings

*Tuna becomes dry and tough if overcooked. Cook tuna until it is opaque, but still feels somewhat soft in center. Watch carefully while grilling.

Prep Time: 15 minutes
Cook Time: 20 minutes

Grilled Swordfish with Tomato Relish

- 1½ pounds tomatoes, peeled and chopped
- 1½ cups chopped onions
- 1 medium red bell pepper, chopped
- 1 cup sugar
- 1 cup HEINZ® Apple Cider Vinegar
- ½ cup golden raisins
- ⅓ cup HEINZ® 57 Sauce
- 2 teaspoons minced fresh ginger
- 1 clove garlic, crushed
- ½ teaspoon ground coriander
- ¼ teaspoon crushed red pepper
- 2 tablespoons vegetable oil
- 1 tablespoon lemon juice
- ¼ teaspoon lemon pepper seasoning
- ⅛ teaspoon garlic powder
- 6 swordfish steaks, cut ¾ inch thick

For Tomato Relish, combine tomatoes, onions, bell pepper, sugar, vinegar, raisins, Heinz® 57 Sauce, ginger, garlic, coriander and crushed red pepper in large saucepan. Cook, stirring occasionally, over medium-low heat 1 hour or until thick. Transfer to nonaluminum container. Cover; refrigerate. (Mixture may be stored in refrigerator for up to 3 weeks.) Let relish stand at room temperature 1 hour before serving.

For swordfish, combine oil, lemon juice, lemon pepper seasoning and garlic powder in small bowl. Brush mixture over swordfish. Spray grid with nonstick cooking spray. Place swordfish on grid. Grill over medium-hot coals 5 minutes on each side or until fish flakes easily when tested with fork. Serve swordfish topped with Tomato Relish.

Makes 6 servings

Note: Tomato Relish may also be served with chicken, pork, ham or other mild-flavored fish.

Tuna Steak with Shrimp Creole Sauce

Teriyaki Trout

4 whole trout (about
    2 pounds)
¾ cup LAWRY'S® Teriyaki
    Marinade with
    Pineapple Juice,
    divided
½ cup sliced green onions
2 medium lemons, sliced
    Chopped fresh parsley
    (optional)

Pierce skin of trout several times with fork. Brush the inside and outside of each trout with Teriyaki Marinade with Pineapple Juice; stuff with green onions and lemon slices. Place in shallow glass dish. Pour all but ¼ cup Teriyaki Marinade with Pineapple Juice over trout; cover dish. Marinate in refrigerator at least 30 minutes. Heat grill for medium-hot coals. Remove trout from marinade. Place trout in oiled hinged wire grill basket; brush with reserved ¼ cup Teriyaki Marinade with Pineapple Juice. Grill, 4 to 5 inches from heat source, 10 minutes or until trout flakes easily with fork, turning and brushing occasionally with reserved marinade. Sprinkle with parsley, if desired.

Makes 4 servings

Presentation: *For a delicious side dish, cook sliced bell pepper, onion and zucchini brushed with vegetable oil on grill with trout.*

Pineapple Salsa Topped Halibut

PINEAPPLE SALSA
¾ cup diced fresh
    pineapple *or* 1 can
    (8 ounces)
    unsweetened
    pineapple tidbits,
    drained
2 tablespoons finely
    chopped red bell
    pepper
2 tablespoons chopped
    fresh cilantro
2 teaspoons vegetable oil
1 teaspoon bottled
    minced ginger or fresh
    ginger
1 teaspoon bottled
    minced jalapeño
    pepper or fresh
    jalapeño pepper

HALIBUT
4 halibut or swordfish
    steaks (6 ounces
    each), cut ¾ inch
    thick
1 tablespoon garlic-
    flavored olive oil
¼ teaspoon salt

1. For salsa, combine pineapple, bell pepper, cilantro, vegetable oil, ginger and jalapeño pepper in small bowl; mix well.

2. Prepare barbecue grill for direct cooking. Brush halibut with garlic-flavored oil; sprinkle with salt.

3. Grill halibut, on uncovered grill, over medium-hot coals 8 minutes or until halibut flakes easily when tested with fork, turning once.

4. Top halibut with salsa; serve immediately.

Makes 4 servings

Baja Fruited Salmon

1 large navel orange,
    peeled and diced
1 small grapefruit, peeled
    and diced
1 medium tomato, seeded
    and diced
¼ cup diced red onion
1 small jalapeño, seeded
    and finely chopped
2 tablespoons snipped
    fresh cilantro
2 tablespoons red wine
    vinegar
1 tablespoon vegetable oil
½ teaspoon LAWRY'S®
    Seasoned Salt
¼ teaspoon LAWRY'S®
    Garlic Powder with
    Parsley
4 (5-ounce) salmon steaks
    Lemon juice

In medium bowl, combine all ingredients except salmon and lemon juice; refrigerate. Brush salmon steaks with lemon juice. Grill or broil, 5 inches from heat source, 5 to 7 minutes on each side or until fish flakes easily with fork. Spoon chilled fruit salsa over salmon.   *Makes 4 servings*

Presentation: *Serve with pan-fried potatoes. Garnish with lemon slices and parsley.*

Hot Shrimp with Cool Salsa

¼ cup prepared salsa
4 tablespoons fresh lime juice, divided
1 teaspoon honey
1 clove garlic, minced
2 to 4 drops hot pepper sauce
1 pound large shrimp, peeled and deveined, with tails intact
1 cup finely diced honeydew melon
½ cup finely diced unpeeled cucumber
2 tablespoons minced parsley
1 green onion, finely chopped
1½ teaspoons sugar
1 teaspoon olive oil
¼ teaspoon salt

1. To make marinade, combine prepared salsa, 2 tablespoons lime juice, honey, garlic and hot pepper sauce in small bowl. Thread shrimp onto skewers. Brush shrimp with marinade; set aside.

2. To make salsa, combine remaining 2 tablespoons lime juice, melon, cucumber, parsley, onion, sugar, oil and salt in medium bowl; mix well.

3. Grill shrimp over medium coals 4 to 5 minutes or until shrimp are opaque, turning once. Serve with salsa.

Makes 4 servings

Lemon Tarragon Fish

½ cup CRISCO® Oil
1 teaspoon grated lemon peel (optional)
½ cup lemon juice
2 teaspoons dried parsley flakes
2 teaspoons dried tarragon leaves
¼ teaspoon salt
⅛ teaspoon black pepper
4 cod, halibut or haddock steaks (about 1 pound)
2⅔ cups hot cooked rice (cooked without salt or fat)

1. Combine Crisco® Oil, lemon peel (if used), lemon juice, parsley, tarragon, salt and pepper in shallow baking dish. Stir to mix well.

2. Place fish in lemon juice mixture. Turn to coat. Refrigerate 30 minutes, turning after 15 minutes.

3. Prepare grill or heat broiler.

4. Remove fish from marinade; discard marinade. Grill or broil 3 to 5 minutes per side or until fish flakes easily with fork. Serve with hot rice.

Makes 4 servings

Pineapple Salsa Topped Halibut (page 258)

Grilled Stuffed Eggplant

4 baby eggplants*
2 tablespoons olive oil
4 ounces small
    mushrooms, quartered
½ cup finely chopped
    green and/or red bell
    peppers
2 cloves garlic, minced
1 cup chunky-style salsa
1 can (2.8 ounces)
    FRENCH'S® French
    Fried Onions, divided
2 tablespoons crumbled
    goat cheese
1 tablespoon grated
    Parmesan cheese

You may substitute 2 medium eggplants (1½ pounds) for the baby eggplant. Cut eggplants in half lengthwise; proceed as directed.

Cut lengthwise slice ½ inch from top of each eggplant; discard. Using a spoon or melon baller, scoop out pulp leaving ¼-inch shell. Set aside eggplant shells. Finely chop pulp.

Heat oil in large skillet over high heat. Add eggplant pulp and mushrooms; cook about 5 minutes or until liquid is evaporated, stirring often. Add peppers and garlic; cook and stir until peppers are tender. Stir in salsa. Bring to a boil. Reduce heat to medium. Cook and stir 2 minutes. Stir in 1 cup French Fried Onions. Spoon filling into shells, mounding slightly. Sprinkle remaining French Fried Onions and cheeses on top.

Place eggplants on oiled grid. Grill over medium coals 15 minutes or until eggplant shells are tender. Serve warm.
Makes 4 side-dish servings

Skewered Grilled Potatoes

2 pounds red potatoes,
    quartered
⅓ cup cold water
½ cup MIRACLE WHIP®
    Salad Dressing
¼ cup dry white wine or
    chicken broth
2 teaspoons dried
    rosemary leaves,
    crushed
1 teaspoon garlic powder

• Place potatoes and water in 2-quart microwave-safe casserole; cover.

• Microwave at HIGH 12 to 15 minutes or until tender, stirring after 8 minutes. Drain.

• Mix remaining ingredients until well blended. Stir in potatoes. Refrigerate 1 hour. Drain, reserving marinade.

• Arrange potatoes on skewers. Place on grill over hot coals (coals will be glowing). Grill, covered, 6 to 8 minutes or until potatoes are tender and golden brown, brushing occasionally with reserved marinade and turning after 4 minutes.
Makes 8 side-dish servings

Prep Time: 20 minutes plus refrigerating
Grill Time: 8 minutes
Microwave Cook Time:
15 minutes

Grilled Baby Artichokes with RedHot® Pepper Dip

18 baby artichokes* (about
    1½ pounds)
½ teaspoon salt
¼ cup FRANK'S® Original
    REDHOT® Cayenne
    Pepper Sauce
¼ cup butter or margarine,
    melted
    Roasted Pepper Dip
    (page 18)

You may substitute 2 packages (9 ounces each) frozen artichoke halves, thawed and drained. Do not microwave. Brush with REDHOT® butter mixture and grill as directed.

1. Wash and trim tough outer leaves from artichokes. Cut ½ inch off top of artichokes, then cut in half lengthwise. Place artichoke halves, *1 cup water* and salt in 3-quart microwavable bowl. Cover; microwave at HIGH 8 minutes or until just tender. Thread artichoke halves onto metal skewers.

2. Prepare grill. Combine RedHot® sauce and butter in small bowl. Brush mixture over artichokes. Place artichokes on grid. Grill, over hot coals, 5 minutes or until tender, turning and basting often with sauce mixture. Serve artichokes with Roasted Pepper Dip.
Makes 6 servings

Grilled Stuffed Eggplant

Jamaican Grilled Sweet Potatoes

2 large (about 1½ pounds) sweet potatoes or yams
3 tablespoons packed brown sugar
2 tablespoons softened margarine, divided
1 teaspoon ground ginger
2 teaspoons dark rum
1 tablespoon chopped fresh cilantro

1. Pierce potatoes in several places with fork. Place on paper towel in microwave. Microwave at HIGH 5 to 6 minutes or until crisp-tender when tested with fork, rotating ¼ turn halfway through cooking. Let stand 10 minutes. Diagonally slice about ½ inch off ends of potatoes. Continue cutting potatoes diagonally into ¾-inch-thick slices.

2. Combine brown sugar, 1 tablespoon margarine and ginger in small bowl; mix well. Stir in rum, then cilantro; set aside.

3. Melt remaining 1 tablespoon margarine. With half of melted margarine, lightly brush one side of each potato slice. Grill slices, margarine side down, on covered grill over medium coals 4 to 6 minutes or until grillmarked. Brush tops with remaining melted margarine; turn over and grill 3 to 5 minutes or until grillmarked. To serve, spoon rum mixture equally over potato slices.

Makes 6 servings

Savory Herb-Stuffed Onions

1 zucchini, cut lengthwise into ¼-inch-thick slices
Nonstick cooking spray
3 shiitake mushrooms
4 large sweet onions
1 plum tomato, seeded and chopped
2 tablespoons fresh bread crumbs
1 tablespoon fresh basil *or* 1 teaspoon dried basil leaves
1 teaspoon olive oil
¼ teaspoon salt
⅛ teaspoon black pepper
4 teaspoons balsamic vinegar

1. Spray zucchini on both sides with cooking spray. Grill on uncovered grill over medium coals 4 minutes or until grillmarked and tender, turning once. Cool; cut into bite-size pieces.

2. Thread mushrooms onto metal skewers. Grill on covered grill over medium coals 20 to 30 minutes or until grillmarked and tender. Coarsely chop; set aside.

3. Remove stem and root ends of onions, leaving peels intact. Spray onions with cooking spray; grill, root end up, on covered grill over medium coals for 5 minutes or until lightly charred. Remove and let stand until cool enough to handle. Peel and scoop about 1 inch of pulp from stem ends; chop for filling and set whole onions aside.

4. Combine chopped onion, mushrooms, zucchini, tomato, bread crumbs, basil, oil, salt and pepper; mix until well blended. Spoon equal amounts of stuffing mixture into centers of onions.

5. Place each onion on sheet of foil; sprinkle each with 1 tablespoon water. Fold long sides of foil together; fold over short sides. Grill onion packets on covered grill over medium coals 45 to 60 minutes or until tender. Spoon 1 teaspoon vinegar over each onion before serving.

Makes 4 appetizer servings

Sweet & Sour Relish

1 medium onion, chopped
1 rib celery, chopped
½ cup prepared chili sauce
2 tablespoons dark brown sugar
2 tablespoons cider vinegar
Dash dried tarragon leaves

Combine ingredients in medium saucepan. Bring to a boil over medium-high heat. Reduce heat to low; simmer 5 minutes, stirring occasionally. Serve hot or cold. Refrigerate leftovers and reheat if necessary.

Makes 1 cup

SERVING SUGGESTION: SERVE WITH GRILLED BOB EVANS FARMS® BRATWURST, SMOKED SAUSAGE OR KIELBASA.

Jamaican Grilled Sweet Potatoes

Portobello Mushrooms Sesame

- **4 large portobello mushrooms**
- **2 tablespoons sweet cooking rice wine**
- **2 tablespoons reduced-sodium soy sauce**
- **2 cloves garlic, minced**
- **1 teaspoon dark sesame oil**

1. Remove and discard stems from mushrooms; set caps aside. Combine remaining ingredients in small bowl.

2. Brush both sides of mushrooms with soy sauce mixture. Grill mushrooms, top side up, on covered grill over medium coals 3 to 4 minutes. Brush tops with soy sauce mixture and turn over; grill 2 minutes more or until mushrooms are lightly browned. Turn again and grill, basting frequently, 4 to 5 minutes or until tender when pressed with back of spatula. Remove mushrooms and cut diagonally into ½-inch-thick slices.

Makes 4 servings

Thai Marinade

- **½ cup A.1.® Steak Sauce**
- **⅓ cup peanut butter**
- **2 tablespoons soy sauce**

In small nonmetallic bowl, combine steak sauce, peanut butter and soy sauce. Use to marinate beef, poultry or pork for about 1 hour in the refrigerator. *Makes 1 cup*

Wyoming Wild Barbecue Sauce

- **1 cup chili sauce**
- **1 cup ketchup**
- **¼ cup steak sauce**
- **3 tablespoons dry mustard**
- **2 tablespoons horseradish**
- **2 tablespoons TABASCO® pepper sauce**
- **1 tablespoon Worcestershire sauce**
- **1 tablespoon minced garlic**
- **1 tablespoon dark molasses**
- **1 tablespoon red wine vinegar**

Combine ingredients in medium bowl. Whisk until sauce is well blended. Store in 1-quart covered jar in refrigerator up to 7 days. Use as a baste while grilling beef, chicken, pork or game. *Makes 3 cups*

Easy Honey Mustard Barbecue Sauce

- **1 bottle (10.5 ounces) PLOCHMAN'S® Mild Yellow Mustard (about 1 cup)**
- **½ cup barbecue sauce**
- **¼ cup honey**
- **2 tablespoons finely minced onion**

Mix all ingredients. Use as a condiment or brush on chicken, pork chops or seafood.

Makes 2 cups

Prep Time: 5 minutes

Honey Barbecue Sauce

- **1 can (10¾ ounces) condensed tomato soup**
- **½ cup honey**
- **2 tablespoons Worcestershire sauce**
- **2 to 3 tablespoons vegetable oil**
- **1 tablespoon lemon juice**
- **1 teaspoon prepared mustard**
- **Dash ground red pepper or bottled hot pepper sauce (optional)**

Combine ingredients in medium saucepan. Bring to a boil over medium heat. Reduce heat to low and simmer, uncovered, 5 minutes. Use as a baste while grilling beef, ribs or poultry.

Makes about 2 cups

FAVORITE RECIPE FROM **NATIONAL HONEY BOARD**

K.C. Masterpiece® Spread

- **¼ cup K.C. MASTERPIECE® Barbecue Sauce**
- **¼ cup reduced-calorie or regular mayonnaise**

Combine barbecue sauce and mayonnaise in small bowl until smooth. Serve with grilled beef, turkey, chicken or pork.

Makes 1 cup

Honey Strawberry Salsa

1½ cups diced red bell pepper
 1 cup sliced fresh strawberries
 1 cup diced green bell pepper
 1 cup diced fresh tomato
 ¼ cup chopped Anaheim pepper
 2 tablespoons finely chopped fresh cilantro
 ⅓ cup honey
 ¼ cup lemon juice
 1 tablespoon tequila (optional)
 ½ teaspoon crushed dried red chili pepper
 ½ teaspoon salt
 ¼ teaspoon black pepper

Combine ingredients in glass container; mix well. Cover tightly and refrigerate overnight to allow flavors to blend. Serve on grilled fish or chicken.

Makes 3 to 4 cups

*FAVORITE RECIPE FROM **NATIONAL HONEY BOARD***

Rib Ticklin' Barbecue Sauce

½ cup KARO® Light or Dark Corn Syrup
 ½ cup ketchup
 ½ cup finely chopped onion
 ¼ cup cider vinegar
 ¼ cup prepared mustard
 ¼ cup Worcestershire sauce

1. In 1½-quart saucepan, combine corn syrup, ketchup, onion, vinegar, mustard and Worcestershire sauce. Stirring frequently, bring to a boil over medium-high heat. Reduce heat; boil gently 15 minutes or until thickened.

2. Brush on chicken, ribs or beef during last 15 to 20 minutes of grilling, turning frequently. Heat remaining sauce to serve with meat.   *Makes about 2 cups*

Prep Time: 25 minutes

Portobello Mushrooms Sesame (page 264)

Pasta

FEATURING:

Ravioli & Stuffed Pasta

Hearty Baked Pastas

Homemade Sauces

Red Pepper & White Bean Pasta Sauce (page 282)

Broccoli and Beef Pasta

1 pound lean ground beef
2 cloves garlic, minced
1 can (about 14 ounces) beef broth
1 medium onion, thinly sliced
1 cup uncooked rotini pasta
½ teaspoon dried basil leaves
½ teaspoon dried oregano leaves
½ teaspoon dried thyme leaves
1 can (14½ ounces) Italian-style tomatoes, undrained
2 cups broccoli florets *or* 1 package (10 ounces) frozen broccoli, thawed
3 ounces shredded Cheddar cheese or grated Parmesan cheese

1. Combine meat and garlic in large nonstick skillet; cook over high heat 6 to 8 minutes or until meat is no longer pink, breaking meat apart with wooden spoon. Pour off drippings. Place meat mixture in large bowl; set aside.

2. Add broth, onion, pasta, basil, oregano and thyme to skillet. Bring to a boil. Reduce heat to medium-high and boil 10 minutes; add tomatoes and their juice. Increase heat to high and bring to a boil; stir in broccoli. Cook, uncovered, 6 to 8 minutes, stirring occasionally, until broccoli is crisp-tender and pasta is tender. Return meat to skillet and stir 3 to 4 minutes or until heated through.

3. With slotted spoon, transfer pasta to serving platter. Sprinkle with cheese. Cover with lid or tent with foil several minutes until cheese melts. Meanwhile, bring juice left in skillet to a boil over high heat. Boil until thick and reduced to 3 to 4 tablespoons. Spoon over meat.

Makes 4 servings

Prep & Cook Time: 30 minutes

Pasta Paprikash

12 ounces beef round steak, cut into 1-inch cubes
4 tablespoons all-purpose flour, divided
2 cans (about 14 ounces each) beef broth, divided
2 green bell peppers, sliced
1 onion, sliced
2 cloves garlic, minced
2 tablespoons sweet Hungarian paprika
¼ teaspoon black pepper
⅛ teaspoon ground red pepper
1 can (6 ounces) reduced-sodium tomato paste
1 cup reduced-fat sour cream
8 ounces fettuccine, cooked and kept warm

1. Spray large skillet with nonstick cooking spray. Heat over medium heat until hot. Coat beef with 2 tablespoons flour; cook 5 to 8 minutes or until browned. Add 1 cup beef broth and bring to a boil. Reduce heat and simmer, covered, 15 to 20 minutes or until beef is tender. Remove beef from skillet.

2. Add bell peppers, onion and garlic to skillet; cook and stir about 5 minutes or until tender. Stir in remaining 2 tablespoons flour, paprika, black pepper and red pepper; cook, stirring constantly, 1 minute. Stir in tomato paste and ½ cup broth. Add beef and remaining broth and bring to a boil. Reduce heat and simmer, uncovered, 5 to 7 minutes or until sauce is thickened.

3. Stir in sour cream; cook over low heat 1 to 2 minutes, stirring frequently. Season to taste with salt, if desired. Serve over fettuccine.

Makes 4 servings

Broccoli and Beef Pasta

Pasta Bourguignonne

1 pound beef round steak,
visible fat trimmed
and cut into 1½-inch
cubes
3 to 4 tablespoons all-
purpose flour
1 tablespoon olive or
vegetable oil
1 teaspoon dried oregano
leaves
1 teaspoon dried
marjoram leaves
1 teaspoon dried thyme
leaves
2 bay leaves
1 can (about 14 ounces)
beef broth
2 onions, quartered
3 cups sliced mushrooms
2 cups sliced carrots
8 ounces fettuccine,
cooked and kept warm

1. Coat beef with flour. Heat
oil in large saucepan over
medium heat until hot. Add
beef; cook about 8 minutes or
until browned. Add oregano,
marjoram, thyme and bay
leaves; cook 1 minute.

2. Add beef broth to saucepan;
bring to a boil. Reduce heat
and simmer, covered, about
20 minutes or until beef is
tender. Add vegetables; simmer,
covered, 10 to 15 minutes or
until vegetables are tender.
Remove bay leaves. Season
to taste with salt and pepper,
if desired. Serve over pasta.

Makes 4 servings

Country-Style Lasagna

9 lasagna noodles
(2 inches wide)
2 cans (14½ ounces each)
DEL MONTE®
FreshCut™ Diced
Tomatoes with Garlic
& Onion
Milk
2 tablespoons butter or
margarine
3 tablespoons all-purpose
flour
1 teaspoon dried basil,
crushed
1 cup diced cooked ham
2 cups (8 ounces)
shredded mozzarella
cheese

1. Cook noodles according to
package directions; rinse, drain
and separate noodles.

2. Meanwhile, drain tomatoes,
reserving liquid; pour liquid
into measuring cup. Add milk
to measure 2 cups.

3. Melt butter in large saucepan;
stir in flour and basil. Cook
over medium heat 3 minutes,
stirring constantly. Stir in
reserved liquid; cook until
thickened, stirring constantly.
Season to taste with salt and
pepper, if desired. Stir in
tomatoes.

4. Spread thin layer of sauce
on bottom of 11×7-inch or
2-quart baking dish. Top with
3 noodles and ⅓ *each* of sauce,
ham and cheese; repeat layers
twice, ending with cheese.

5. Bake, uncovered, at 375°F,
25 minutes. Serve with grated
Parmesan cheese and garnish,
if desired. *Makes 6 servings*

Prep Time: 15 minutes
Cook Time: 25 minutes

Ravioli with Tomatoes and Zucchini

2 packages (9 ounces
each) fresh or frozen
cheese ravioli or
tortellini
¾ pound hot Italian
sausage, crumbled
2 cans (14½ ounces each)
DEL MONTE®
FreshCut™ Diced
Tomatoes, undrained
1 medium zucchini, thinly
sliced and quartered
1 teaspoon dried basil,
crushed
½ cup ricotta cheese *or*
2 tablespoons grated
Parmesan cheese

1. Cook pasta according to
package directions; drain.

2. Brown sausage in large skillet
or saucepan over medium-high
heat until no longer pink; drain,
reserving sausage in skillet.

3. Add tomatoes, zucchini and
basil to skillet. Cook about
8 minutes or until zucchini is
just tender-crisp, stirring
occasionally. Season with
pepper, if desired.

4. Spoon sauce over hot pasta.
Top with ricotta cheese.
Garnish, if desired.

Makes 4 servings

Pasta Bourguignonne

Linguine with Pumpkin Pork Sauce

- 1¼ pounds boneless pork loin chops, sliced in ¼-inch strips
- 2 tablespoons all-purpose flour
- ½ cup thinly sliced green onions
- 2 to 3 tablespoons vegetable oil
- 2½ cups (1 large) green apple, peeled, cored and thinly sliced
- 3 tablespoons maple syrup
- 1 cup chicken broth
- 1 cup LIBBY'S® Solid Pack Pumpkin
- ½ cup CARNATION® Lowfat or Lite Evaporated Skimmed Milk
- ½ teaspoon dried tarragon
- ½ teaspoon salt
- ¼ teaspoon ground black pepper
- ¼ cup Dijon mustard
- ¾ pound dry linguine, cooked, drained and kept warm

DUST pork with flour in plastic bag. Sauté pork with onions in oil in large skillet until pork is no longer pink. Remove from pan; keep warm. Add apple and maple syrup to pan and cook 1 to 2 minutes or until apple is tender. Remove; keep warm.

ADD broth and pumpkin to same pan; mix well. Slowly add evaporated milk. Mix in tarragon, salt and pepper. Remove from heat; gradually add mustard. Return pork and apple to pan; mix well. Serve over linguine.

Makes 4 to 6 servings

Spicy Ham & Cheese Pasta

- ½ (16-ounce) package corkscrew pasta
- 2 tablespoons olive oil
- 1 large red bell pepper, cut into julienne strips
- 1 small red onion, diced
- 1 large clove garlic, crushed
- 8 ounces cooked ham, cut into ½-inch cubes
- 1 cup ricotta cheese
- 3 tablespoons chopped parsley
- 1 teaspoon TABASCO® pepper sauce
- ¾ teaspoon salt

Prepare pasta as label directs; drain. Meanwhile, in 10-inch skillet over medium heat, in hot olive oil, cook bell pepper, onion and garlic until tender-crisp, about 5 minutes. Add ham cubes; cook 3 minutes longer, stirring occasionally.

In large bowl, toss cooked pasta with ham mixture, ricotta cheese, parsley, TABASCO® sauce and salt; mix well.

Makes 4 servings

Pasta with Sausage and Mustard Sauce

- 1 cup BLUE DIAMOND® Blanched Slivered Almonds
- 5 tablespoons olive oil, divided
- 2 red or green bell peppers, diced
- 1 pound Italian sausage, casing removed
- 3 cloves garlic, chopped finely
- 2 tablespoons chopped fresh basil *or*
  - 1 teaspoon dried basil
- ¾ cup dry white wine
- ¾ cup heavy cream
- 1½ tablespoons Dijon mustard
- ¼ teaspoon black pepper
- 1 pound fresh pasta *or* 8 ounces dried pasta, cooked

Sauté almonds in 1 tablespoon oil until golden; reserve. Add remaining 4 tablespoons oil to pan. Sauté bell peppers and sausage until bell peppers are just tender and sausage is browned and crumbly, about 3 minutes. Stir in garlic, basil, wine and cream. Cook over high heat until liquid thickens and coats the back of a spoon, about 3 minutes. Stir in mustard and black pepper. Add almonds. Toss with hot cooked pasta. *Makes 4 to 6 servings*

Spam™ Confetti Pasta

Nonstick cooking spray
2 cups frozen whole
   kernel corn, thawed
1 (12-ounce) can SPAM®
   Luncheon Meat, cut
   into 2-inch strips
1 red bell pepper, chopped
1 green bell pepper,
   chopped
¾ cup chopped red onion
1½ cups whipping cream
2 tablespoons chili
   powder
¼ teaspoon black pepper
12 ounces angel hair pasta,
   cooked and drained
2 tomatoes, peeled and
   chopped
¼ cup minced fresh
   cilantro

In large skillet coated with cooking spray, sauté corn, Spam®, bell peppers and onion over medium heat 5 minutes or until tender. Transfer mixture to bowl; keep warm. To same skillet, add cream, chili powder and black pepper. Bring to a boil; boil 5 minutes or until cream has thickened slightly, stirring occasionally. Pour over pasta and toss well. Spoon Spam™ mixture over pasta. To serve, sprinkle with tomatoes and cilantro.

Makes 6 servings

Country-Style Cracked Black Pepper Fettuccine

1 (12-ounce) package
   PASTA LABELLA®
   Cracked Black Pepper
   Fettuccine
3 tablespoons butter
2 tablespoons olive oil
½ tablespoon sliced fresh
   garlic
1 cup julienned ham
¾ cup broccoli florets
¾ cup diced tomatoes
¼ cup grated Romano
   cheese
Salt and black pepper

Cook pasta according to package directions. Meanwhile, heat butter and olive oil in large skillet or sauté pan. Sauté garlic, ham, broccoli and tomatoes for 5 minutes. Immediately add hot pasta and toss well with ham and vegetables. Sprinkle with cheese. Season with salt and pepper to taste.

Makes 4 servings

Spam™ Confetti Pasta

Spaghetti Bake

- 1 pound BOB EVANS FARMS® Dinner Link Sausage (regular or Italian)
- 1 (8-ounce) can tomato sauce
- 1 (6-ounce) can tomato paste
- 1 (4-ounce) can sliced mushrooms, drained
- ½ teaspoon salt
- ½ teaspoon dried basil leaves
- ½ teaspoon dried oregano leaves
- 6 ounces spaghetti, cooked according to package directions and drained
- ⅓ cup shredded mozzarella cheese
- 2 tablespoons grated Parmesan cheese
  Fresh basil leaves and tomato slices (optional)

Preheat oven to 375°F. Cut sausage links into bite-size pieces. Cook in medium skillet over medium heat until browned, stirring occasionally. Drain off any drippings; set aside. Combine tomato sauce, tomato paste, mushrooms, salt, dried basil and oregano in large bowl. Add spaghetti and reserved sausage; mix well. Spoon into lightly greased 1½-quart casserole dish; sprinkle with cheeses. Bake 20 to 30 minutes or until heated through. Garnish with fresh basil and tomato slices, if desired. Serve hot. Refrigerate leftovers. *Makes 4 servings*

Tortellini Bake Parmesano

- 1 package (12 ounces) fresh or frozen cheese tortellini or ravioli
- ½ pound lean ground beef
- ½ medium onion, finely chopped
- 2 cloves garlic, minced
- ½ teaspoon dried oregano, crushed
- 1 can (26 ounces) DEL MONTE® Chunky Spaghetti Sauce with Garlic & Herb
- 2 small zucchini, sliced
- ⅓ cup (about 1½ ounces) grated Parmesan cheese

1. Cook pasta according to package directions; rinse and drain.

2. Meanwhile, brown beef with onion, garlic and oregano in large skillet over medium-high heat; drain. Season with salt and pepper, if desired.

3. Add spaghetti sauce and zucchini. Cook 15 minutes or until thickened, stirring occasionally.

4. Arrange half of pasta in oiled 2-quart microwavable dish; top with half *each* of sauce and cheese. Repeat layers ending with cheese; cover.

5. Microwave at HIGH 8 to 10 minutes or until heated through, rotating dish halfway through cooking time.

Makes 4 servings

Cheeseburger Macaroni

- 1 cup uncooked mostaccioli or elbow macaroni
- 1 pound ground beef
- 1 medium onion, chopped
- 1 can (14½ ounces) DEL MONTE® *FreshCut*™ Diced Tomatoes with Basil, Garlic & Oregano
- ¼ cup DEL MONTE® Tomato Ketchup
- 1 cup (4 ounces) shredded Cheddar cheese

1. Cook pasta according to package directions; drain.

2. Brown meat with onion in large skillet; drain. Season with salt and pepper, if desired. Stir in tomatoes, ketchup and pasta; heat through.

3. Top with cheese. Garnish, if desired. *Makes 4 servings*

Prep Time: 8 minutes
Cook Time: 15 minutes

Spaghetti Bake

Angel Hair Carbonara

⅔ cup milk
2 tablespoons margarine
    or butter
1 package (4.8 ounces)
    PASTA RONI® Angel
    Hair Pasta with Herbs
2 cups chopped cooked
    pork or ham
1 package (10 ounces)
    frozen peas
¼ cup sliced green onions

Microwave Directions:

1. In round 3-quart microwavable glass casserole, combine 1½ cups water, milk and margarine. Microwave, uncovered, at HIGH 4 to 5 minutes or until boiling.

2. Gradually add pasta while stirring. Separate pasta with fork, if needed.

3. Stir in contents of seasoning packet.

4. Microwave, uncovered, at HIGH 4 minutes, stirring gently after 2 minutes. Separate pasta with fork, if needed. Stir in pork, frozen peas and onions. Continue to microwave 2 to 3 minutes. Sauce will be thin, but will thicken upon standing.

5. Let stand 3 minutes or until desired consistency. Stir before serving.   *Makes 4 servings*

Tomato Pesto Lasagna

8 ounces lasagna noodles
    (2 inches wide)
1 pound crumbled
    sausage or ground
    beef
1 can (14½ ounces) DEL
    MONTE® *FreshCut*™
    Diced Tomatoes with
    Garlic & Onion,
    undrained
1 can (6 ounces) DEL
    MONTE® Tomato Paste
8 ounces ricotta cheese
1 package (4 ounces)
    pesto sauce*
2 cups (8 ounces)
    shredded mozzarella
    cheese

*Pesto sauce is available frozen or refrigerated at supermarkets.

1. Cook noodles according to package directions; rinse, drain and separate noodles.

2. Meanwhile, brown meat in large skillet; drain. Stir in tomatoes, tomato paste and ¾ cup water.

3. Layer ⅓ meat sauce, then half *each* of noodles, ricotta cheese, pesto and mozzarella cheese in 2-quart casserole or 9-inch square baking dish; repeat layers. Top with remaining sauce. Sprinkle with grated Parmesan cheese, if desired.

4. Bake at 350°F, 30 minutes or until heated through.
          Makes 6 servings

Prep Time: 20 minutes
Cook Time: 30 minutes

Homemade Italian Spaghetti

1 tablespoon olive oil
1 medium onion, chopped
1 medium carrot, chopped
1 rib celery, chopped
1 clove garlic, minced
¾ pound lean ground beef
1 can (28 ounces) Italian
    plum tomatoes,
    undrained
1 can (6 ounces) tomato
    paste
1 cup HOLLAND HOUSE®
    Red Cooking Wine
    with Italian
    Seasonings
¼ cup chopped fresh
    parsley
½ pound spaghetti,
    cooked, drained

Heat oil in large saucepan over medium-high heat. Add onion, carrot, celery and garlic; cook until tender, about 5 minutes. Add ground beef; cook until brown. Add remaining ingredients except spaghetti. Bring to a boil; reduce heat. Simmer 1 hour, stirring occasionally. Serve over cooked spaghetti.   *Makes 6 cups*

Chicken Parmesan Noodle Bake

- 1 package (12 ounces) extra-wide noodles
- 4 boneless chicken breast halves, skinned
- ¼ teaspoon dried rosemary, crushed
- 2 cans (14½ ounces each) DEL MONTE® *FreshCut*™ Diced Tomatoes with Basil, Garlic & Oregano
- ½ cup (2 ounces) shredded mozzarella cheese
- ¼ cup (1 ounce) grated Parmesan cheese

1. Preheat oven to 450°F.

2. Cook noodles according to package directions; drain.

3. Meanwhile, sprinkle chicken with rosemary; season with salt and pepper, if desired. Arrange chicken in 13×9-inch baking dish. Bake, uncovered, 20 minutes or until chicken is no longer pink in center. Drain; remove chicken from dish.

4. Drain tomatoes, reserving liquid. In large bowl, toss reserved liquid with noodles; place in baking dish. Top with chicken and tomatoes; sprinkle with cheeses.

5. Bake 10 minutes or until heated through. Sprinkle with additional Parmesan cheese and garnish, if desired.

Makes 4 servings

Prep & Cook Time: 35 minutes

Santa Fe Pasta

- 8 ounces dried pasta, cooked, drained and kept warm
- 1 tablespoon vegetable oil
- ½ cup (about 6) sliced green onions
- 1 clove garlic, finely chopped
- 8 ounces (about 2) boneless skinless chicken breast halves, cut into 2-inch strips
- 1 cup (1 large) green bell pepper strips
- 1 cup (1 large) red bell pepper strips
- ½ teaspoon salt
- ½ teaspoon chili powder
- ½ teaspoon ground black pepper
- Dash cayenne pepper
- 1½ cups (12 fluid-ounce can) CARNATION® Evaporated Lowfat Milk
- 1 tablespoon cornstarch
- ¼ cup fresh cilantro leaves

HEAT oil in large skillet over medium-high heat. Add green onions and garlic; cook for 1 to 2 minutes. Add chicken, bell peppers, salt, chili powder, black pepper and cayenne pepper; cook for 4 to 5 minutes or until chicken is no longer pink in center.

COMBINE small amount of evaporated milk and cornstarch in small bowl. Add to skillet; gradually stir in remaining evaporated milk and cilantro.

COOK over medium-high heat, stirring occasionally, for 2 to 3 minutes or until mixture is slightly thickened. Serve over pasta.   *Makes 6 servings*

Chicken and Pasta in Cream Sauce

- 5 ounces thin spaghetti, cooked, drained and kept warm
- 6 tablespoons unsalted butter
- 1 tablespoon CHEF PAUL PRUDHOMME'S Poultry Magic®
- ½ pound diced boneless skinless chicken breasts
- ¼ cup finely chopped green onions with tops
- 2 cups heavy cream or half-and-half

Melt butter in large skillet over medium heat. Add Poultry Magic® and chicken; cook 1 minute. Add onions; cook and stir 1 to 2 minutes. Gradually add cream, stirring until well blended. Bring to a boil. Reduce heat to low; simmer, uncovered, 2 to 3 minutes or until sauce starts to thicken, stirring frequently. Add pasta; toss and stir until pasta is heated through, about 2 minutes. Serve immediately.

Makes 2 main-dish servings

Tuscan Pasta

1 pound boneless skinless chicken breasts, cut into 1-inch pieces
1 can (15½ ounces) red kidney beans, rinsed and drained
1 can (15 ounces) tomato sauce
2 cans (14½ ounces each) Italian-style stewed tomatoes
1 jar (4½ ounces) sliced mushrooms, drained
1 medium green bell pepper, chopped
½ cup onion, chopped
½ cup celery, chopped
4 cloves garlic, minced
1 cup water
1 teaspoon dried Italian seasoning
6 ounces thin spaghetti, broken into halves

Slow Cooker Directions:
PLACE all ingredients except spaghetti in slow cooker. Cover and cook on LOW 4 hours or until vegetables are tender.

TURN to HIGH. Stir in spaghetti; cover. Stir again after 10 minutes. Cover and cook 45 minutes or until pasta is tender. Garnish with basil and bell pepper strips, if desired.   *Makes 8 servings*

Mediterranean Pasta

6 to 8 ounces vermicelli
2 half boneless chicken breasts, skinned and cut into 1½×½-inch strips
4 slices bacon, diced
1 can (14½ ounces) DEL MONTE® *FreshCut*™ Diced Tomatoes with Garlic & Onion
1 can (15 ounces) DEL MONTE® Tomato Sauce
½ teaspoon dried rosemary, crushed
1 package (9 ounces) frozen artichoke hearts, thawed
½ cup pitted ripe olives, sliced lengthwise

1. Cook pasta according to package directions; drain.

2. Season chicken with salt and pepper, if desired. In large skillet, cook bacon over medium-high heat until almost crisp. Add chicken; cook until browned on both sides. Drain.

3. Stir in tomatoes, tomato sauce and rosemary. Cook 15 minutes, stirring occasionally. Add artichokes and olives; heat through.

4. Spoon sauce over hot pasta just before serving. Sprinkle with crumbled feta cheese and chopped parsley, if desired.
Makes 4 to 6 servings

Chicken Pesto Mozzarella

6 to 8 ounces linguine or corkscrew pasta
4 half boneless chicken breasts, skinned
1 tablespoon olive oil
1 can (14½ ounces) DEL MONTE® *FreshCut*™ Diced Tomatoes with Basil, Garlic & Oregano, undrained
½ medium onion, chopped
⅓ cup sliced ripe olives
4 teaspoons pesto sauce*
¼ cup (1 ounce) shredded mozzarella cheese

*Pesto sauce is available frozen or refrigerated at supermarkets.

1. Cook pasta according to package directions; drain.

2. Meanwhile, season chicken with salt and pepper, if desired. In large skillet, brown chicken in hot oil over medium-high heat. Add tomatoes, onion and olives; bring to a boil. Cover and cook 8 minutes over medium heat.

3. Remove cover; cook about 8 minutes or until chicken is no longer pink in center.

4. Spread 1 teaspoon pesto over each chicken breast; top with cheese. Cover and cook until cheese is melted. Serve over pasta. Garnish, if desired.
Makes 4 servings

Prep Time: 10 minutes
Cook Time: 25 minutes

Tuscan Pasta

California Walnut Noodles

DRESSING
- ½ cup plain nonfat yogurt
- ½ cup orange juice
- 3 tablespoons balsamic vinegar or wine vinegar
- 2 tablespoons brown sugar
- 2 teaspoons sesame oil
- 1½ teaspoons grated fresh ginger *or* ½ teaspoon ground ginger
- ½ teaspoon crushed red pepper (optional)
- 2 cloves garlic, minced
- Salt to taste (optional)

NOODLES
- 12 ounces uncooked spaghetti or linguine
- 2 cups diced cooked skinless chicken breasts
- 1 red or green bell pepper, halved, seeded and thinly sliced
- 1 cucumber, halved, seeded and thinly sliced
- ½ cup chopped green onions
- 2 teaspoons minced jalapeño pepper or other hot chili pepper
- 2 tablespoons chopped cilantro (optional)
- ⅔ cup Savory California Walnut Sprinkles (recipe follows)

For dressing, whisk together yogurt, orange juice, vinegar, sugar, oil, ginger, crushed red pepper, garlic and salt in large bowl. Set aside.

Cook pasta according to package directions. Drain and rinse well; drain again. Toss pasta and ¾ cup dressing in large bowl. Combine chicken, bell pepper, cucumber, green onions, jalapeño pepper and cilantro with remaining dressing. Arrange pasta on large platter or in shallow bowl. Spoon chicken mixture down center. Just before serving, top each serving with ¼ of the walnut sprinkles.

Makes 4 servings

SAVORY CALIFORNIA WALNUT SPRINKLES
- 4 ounces (1 cup) chopped California walnuts
- ½ cup fresh white bread crumbs
- 1 tablespoon paprika
- ¼ teaspoon cayenne pepper
- ¼ teaspoon salt (optional)

Preheat oven to 325°F. In food processor, process walnuts until finely ground; transfer to small bowl. Add bread crumbs; stir to combine. Spread mixture in even layer on ungreased baking sheet. Bake 15 minutes, stirring frequently, until mixture is golden brown and crisp. Stir in paprika, cayenne pepper and salt. Cool to room temperature.

Makes 1¼ cups

*FAVORITE RECIPE FROM **WALNUT MARKETING BOARD***

Turkey Stuffed Pasta Italiano

- 1 pound ground California turkey
- 1 cup minced onion
- 1 cup grated peeled eggplant
- 2 cloves garlic, minced
- Salt and black pepper
- 1 can (28 ounces) tomatoes, undrained
- 1 can (8 ounces) tomato sauce
- 1 cup red wine or water
- 1 teaspoon garlic salt
- 1 teaspoon dried oregano leaves
- 1 teaspoon dried basil leaves
- ½ teaspoon dried tarragon leaves
- ½ teaspoon crushed red pepper
- 1 package (12 ounces) uncooked jumbo pasta shells
- ½ cup grated Parmesan cheese
- ¾ cup (3 ounces) shredded mozzarella cheese

In large nonstick skillet, brown turkey, onion, eggplant and garlic until turkey is no longer pink; drain. Season with salt and pepper; reserve. In small saucepan, simmer tomatoes with juice, tomato sauce, wine and seasonings for 15 minutes. Cook pasta shells until done, but still firm; drain. In large bowl, combine turkey mixture and Parmesan cheese with half the tomato sauce mixture. Stuff shells; place in 13×9-inch pan.

Spoon remaining sauce mixture over shells; top with mozzarella cheese. Bake at 350°F for 30 minutes.

Makes 8 to 10 servings

Note: *Shells can be stuffed ahead of time and refrigerated. Add sauce and mozzarella cheese just before baking. Increase cooking time by 8 to 10 minutes.*

FAVORITE RECIPE FROM **CALIFORNIA POULTRY INDUSTRY FEDERATION**

Penne with Eggplant and Turkey Sausage

1 pound Italian turkey sausage, cut into 1-inch rings
1 medium eggplant, cut into ½-inch cubes
3 cups prepared chunky vegetable spaghetti sauce
12 ounces penne pasta, cooked according to package directions
4 ounces Asiago cheese, grated

1. In large nonstick skillet, over medium heat, sauté turkey sausage and eggplant 12 to 15 minutes or until sausage is no longer pink and eggplant is soft and lightly browned. Add spaghetti sauce to turkey mixture and simmer 3 minutes or until heated throughout.

2. To serve, spoon sauce over penne and top with cheese.

Makes 8 servings

FAVORITE RECIPE FROM **NATIONAL TURKEY FEDERATION**

Peppy Pesto Toss

8 ounces uncooked ziti or mostaccioli
1 package (16 ounces) frozen bell pepper and onion strips, thawed
½ pound deli turkey breast or smoked turkey breast, cut ½ inch thick
1 cup half-and-half
½ cup pesto sauce
¼ cup grated Parmesan or Asiago cheese

1. Cook pasta according to package directions.

2. Add pepper and onion mixture to pasta water during last 2 minutes of cooking. Meanwhile, cut turkey into ½-inch cubes.

3. Drain pasta and vegetables in colander.

4. Combine half-and-half, pesto and turkey in saucepan used to prepare pasta. Cook 2 minutes or until heated through. Return pasta and vegetables to saucepan; toss well.

5. Sprinkle with cheese. Serve immediately.

Makes 4 servings

Peppy Pesto Toss

Penne with Arrabiatta Sauce

- ½ pound uncooked penne or other tube-shaped pasta
- 2 tablespoons olive oil or oil from sun-dried tomatoes
- 8 cloves garlic
- 1 can (28 ounces) crushed tomatoes in purée
- ¼ cup chopped sun-dried tomatoes packed in oil
- 3 tablespoons FRANK'S® Original REDHOT® Cayenne Pepper Sauce
- 8 kalamata olives, pitted and chopped*
- 6 fresh basil leaves *or* 1½ teaspoons dried basil leaves
- 1 tablespoon capers

To pit olives, place olives on cutting board. Press each with side of knife until split. Remove pits.

1. Cook pasta according to package directions; drain.

2. Heat oil in large nonstick skillet over medium heat. Add garlic; cook until golden, stirring frequently. Add remaining ingredients. Bring to a boil. Simmer, partially covered, 10 minutes. Stir occasionally.

3. Toss pasta with *half* of the sauce mixture. Spoon into serving bowl. Pour remaining sauce mixture over pasta. Garnish with fresh basil or parsley, if desired.

*Makes 4 servings
(3 cups sauce)*

Red Pepper & White Bean Pasta Sauce

- 12 ounces uncooked penne or ziti pasta
- 1 teaspoon olive oil
- 3 cloves garlic, chopped
- 1 jar (11.5 ounces) GUILTLESS GOURMET® Roasted Red Pepper Salsa
- ¾ cup canned cannellini beans (white kidney beans), rinsed well
- ½ cup low-sodium chicken or vegetable broth, defatted
- ⅓ cup chopped fresh cilantro
- ¼ cup crumbled feta cheese
  Fresh thyme sprigs (optional)

Cook pasta according to package directions. Drain and keep warm.

Meanwhile, heat oil in medium nonstick skillet over medium-high heat until hot. Add garlic; cook and stir 30 seconds or until softened. *Do not brown.* Add salsa, beans, broth and cilantro; bring just to a boil, stirring occasionally. (If mixture appears too thick, add water, 1 tablespoon at a time, to desired consistency.) To serve, place pasta in large serving bowl. Add salsa mixture; toss to coat well. Sprinkle with feta cheese. Garnish with thyme, if desired. *Makes 4 servings*

Sweet Peppered Pasta

- 3 tablespoons MAZOLA® Corn Oil
- ½ cup finely chopped onion
- ½ cup minced red bell pepper
- ½ cup minced yellow bell pepper
- 3 large cloves garlic, minced
- ⅓ cup water
- 2 tablespoons chopped fresh basil
- 1 chicken-flavor bouillon cube
- ¼ teaspoon crushed red pepper
- 7 ounces MUELLER'S® Pasta Ruffles (about 2⅔ cups), cooked and drained
  Salad greens (optional)

1. In large skillet, heat corn oil over medium-high heat. Add onion, red and yellow bell peppers and garlic; cook and stir 4 minutes.

2. Stir in water, basil, bouillon cube and crushed red pepper. Bring to a boil, stirring occasionally. Reduce heat to low; simmer 4 minutes.

3. Spoon over pasta in large bowl; toss to coat well. Serve on assorted salad greens, if desired. *Makes 6 servings*

Penne with Arrabiatta Sauce

Lemon Pepper Pasta with Piccata-Style Vegetables

1 (12-ounce) package PASTA LABELLA® Lemon Pepper Pasta
1 tablespoon extra-virgin olive oil
2 tablespoons butter
1 cup julienned red onions
1 cup julienned carrots
2 teaspoons minced garlic
1 cup white wine
1½ tablespoon capers
1 cup julienned snow peas
Salt and black pepper to taste
2 tablespoons chopped parsley
⅓ cup grated Parmesan cheese

Cook pasta according to package directions. In large skillet, heat olive oil and butter. Add onions, carrots and garlic and sauté for 4 minutes. Add in wine and capers and simmer for 2 minutes. Mix in hot pasta and snow peas; toss and blend well. Season with salt and pepper and sprinkle with parsley. Top with Parmesan cheese and serve.

Makes 3 servings

Chili Pepper Pasta with Jalapeño Butter Sauce

1 (12-ounce) package PASTA LABELLA® Chili Pepper Pasta
4½ tablespoons butter
¼ cup diced jalapeño peppers
½ teaspoon minced garlic
1½ cups diced tomatillo tomatoes
2 tablespoons chopped fresh cilantro
½ cup white wine
3 tablespoons fresh lime juice
Salt and black pepper to taste
¼ cup grated Romano cheese

Cook pasta according to package directions. Over medium heat, melt butter in large sauté pan. Add jalapeños, garlic and tomatillos to pan and sauté for 3 to 4 minutes. Add cilantro, wine, lime juice, salt and pepper. Simmer sauce for 2 to 3 minutes and toss in hot pasta. Mix well and portion in bowls. Top with Romano cheese and serve.

Makes 4 servings

Fettuccine with Olive Pesto

10 ounces dried fettuccine
1½ cups whole pitted California ripe olives
3 tablespoons drained capers
4 teaspoons lemon juice
1 tablespoon olive oil
2 teaspoons Dijon mustard
2 to 3 cloves garlic, peeled
¼ cup finely chopped fresh basil
¼ cup grated Parmesan cheese
Basil sprigs

Cook fettuccine according to package directions. While pasta cooks, combine olives, capers, lemon juice, oil, mustard and garlic in food processor or blender. Process until coarsely puréed. Stir in chopped basil and cheese; set aside. Drain pasta well and transfer to a large warm serving bowl. Spoon pesto over pasta and mix gently. Garnish with basil sprigs. *Makes 4 servings*

Prep Time: 15 minutes
Cook Time: 15 minutes

*FAVORITE RECIPE FROM **CALIFORNIA OLIVE INDUSTRY***

Pasta with Sunflower Kernels

- ½ cup sunflower oil
- 3 sprigs parsley, chopped
- 3 cloves garlic, minced
- 1 teaspoon grated lemon peel
- ½ teaspoon salt
- ½ teaspoon black pepper
- 8 ounces tomato, spinach or plain spaghetti, cooked, drained
- ⅔ cup grated Parmesan cheese
- ½ cup roasted sunflower kernels

Heat sunflower oil in small skillet over medium-high heat. Add parsley, garlic and lemon peel; cook and stir 1 minute. Add salt and pepper. Pour over hot pasta. Add Parmesan cheese and sunflower kernels; toss lightly.   *Makes 4 servings*

FAVORITE RECIPE FROM **NATIONAL SUNFLOWER ASSOCIATION**

Pineapple-Raisin Fettuccine

- 8 ounces crushed pineapple in natural juice
- ⅓ cup raisins
- 2 tablespoons white vinegar
- 4 teaspoons brown sugar
- 1 tablespoon low-sodium soy sauce
- 2 teaspoons cornstarch, dissolved in ¼ cup water
- 4 ounces fettuccine
- 4 teaspoons olive oil

In small saucepan, combine pineapple, raisins, vinegar, brown sugar, soy sauce and cornstarch mixture. Cook until clear and mixture thickens, about 3 to 4 minutes, stirring occasionally. Set aside.

In large pan, prepare fettuccine according to package directions. Drain, toss with olive oil, then with pineapple-raisin sauce. Warm sauce briefly, if necessary.

Makes 4 servings

Note: *This sauce is especially good as an accompaniment to chicken, pork or ham.*

FAVORITE RECIPE FROM **THE SUGAR ASSOCIATION**

Sonoma Fettuccine Alfredo

- ½ pound dried fettuccine pasta
- 1 jar (8 ounces) SONOMA Marinated Dried Tomatoes, undrained
- 1½ cups whipping cream, divided
- 1 cup (3 ounces) grated fresh Parmesan cheese, divided
- Salt and black pepper to taste
- 3 tablespoons chopped chives
- ½ teaspoon nutmeg

Cook pasta in large pot of boiling salted water 5 to 8 minutes or until just tender; drain well. Meanwhile, drain tomato marinade oil into large skillet; snip tomatoes in half and reserve. Add ½ cup cream to skillet. Cook over high heat, stirring constantly, about 3 minutes or until slightly thickened. Reduce heat to medium; add cooked pasta and mix gently. Add ½ cup cheese, ½ cup cream and reserved tomatoes; mix in gently. Repeat with remaining ½ cup cheese and ½ cup cream; mix again. Season with salt and pepper. Transfer to warmed individual pasta bowls or large platter. Sprinkle with chives and nutmeg. Serve immediately.

Makes 4 servings

Pasta Primavera

2 tablespoons butter or
margarine
1 medium onion, finely
chopped
1 clove garlic, minced
¾ pound asparagus, cut
diagonally into
1½-inch pieces
½ pound fresh
mushrooms, sliced
1 medium zucchini, sliced
1 carrot, sliced
1 cup half-and-half or
light cream
½ cup chicken broth
1 tablespoon all-purpose
flour
2 teaspoons dried basil
leaves, crushed
1 pound uncooked
fettuccine
¾ cup (3 ounces)
SARGENTO® Fancy
Shredded Parmesan
& Romano Cheese

In large skillet over medium
heat, melt butter. Add onion
and garlic; cook and stir until
onion is tender. Add asparagus,
mushrooms, zucchini and
carrot; cook, stirring
constantly, 2 minutes. *Increase
heat to high.* Combine half-and-
half, broth, flour and basil in
small bowl; add to skillet. Bring
mixture to a boil. Boil, stirring
occasionally, until thickened.

Meanwhile, cook fettuccine
according to package
directions; drain. In serving
bowl, place hot fettuccine,
sauce and Parmesan &
Romano Cheese; toss gently.

Makes 8 servings

Manicotti Florentine

1 package (10 ounces)
frozen chopped
spinach
½ cup chopped onion
1 clove garlic, minced
½ cup uncooked QUAKER®
Oat Bran hot cereal
½ cup low-fat cottage
cheese
2 teaspoons dried basil
leaves, crumbled,
divided
½ teaspoon dried oregano
leaves, crumbled
8 manicotti noodles,
uncooked
2 cans (8 ounces each)
low-sodium tomato
sauce, divided
¼ cup (1 ounce) shredded
part-skim mozzarella
cheese

Heat oven to 375°F. Cook
spinach according to package
directions with onion and
garlic. Cool slightly; drain. Stir
in oat bran, cottage cheese,
1 teaspoon basil and oregano;
set aside. Cook manicotti in
boiling water 4 minutes; drain.

Spread 1½ cans tomato sauce
on bottom of 11×7-inch baking
dish. Stuff each manicotti with
about 3 tablespoons spinach
mixture; arrange in baking
dish. Pour remaining ½ can
sauce over manicotti. Sprinkle
with remaining 1 teaspoon
basil. Top with mozzarella
cheese. Cover; bake 25 to
30 minutes or until bubbly.

Makes 4 servings

Rigatoni with Creamy Tomato Sauce

8 ounces dry pasta
(rigatoni or penne),
cooked, drained and
kept warm
1 tablespoon olive oil
½ cup diced onion
2 tablespoons dry
vermouth or white
wine
1¾ cups (14.5-ounce can)
CONTADINA® Pasta
Ready™ Chunky
Tomatoes, Primavera
½ cup heavy cream
1 cup California ripe
olives, halved
½ cup grated Parmesan
cheese
¼ cup sliced green onions

In large skillet, heat oil; add
onion and sauté 4 to 5 minutes.
Add vermouth; cook 1 minute.
Stir in tomatoes and juice,
cream, pasta, olives and
Parmesan cheese; toss well.
Sprinkle with green onions.

Makes 4 servings

Pasta Primavera

Hot Sesame Noodles

1 package (16 ounces) uncooked linguini
1 teaspoon dark sesame oil
3 tablespoons olive oil
3 tablespoons sesame seeds
2 cloves garlic, minced
⅔ cup chunky peanut butter
1 cup chicken broth
⅓ cup reduced-sodium soy sauce
3 to 4 tablespoons FRANK'S® Original REDHOT® Cayenne Pepper Sauce
1½ teaspoons sugar
1 large green onion, sliced

1. Cook linguini according to package directions. Rinse under cold water; drain well. Toss linguini with sesame oil in large bowl.

2. Heat olive oil in large nonstick skillet over medium heat. Add sesame seeds and garlic; cook and stir constantly 1 minute or until seeds are golden. Add peanut butter; stir until well blended. Stir in broth, soy sauce, RedHot® sauce and sugar. Bring just to a boil.

3. Pour sauce over linguini; toss to coat evenly. Sprinkle with green onion. Serve immediately.

Makes 4 servings (2 cups sauce)

Note: *Sesame noodles may be served cold, if desired. Chill linguini and sauce separately. Toss just before serving.*

Penne with Artichokes

1 package (10 ounces) frozen artichoke hearts
1¼ cups water
2 tablespoons lemon juice
5 cloves garlic
2 tablespoons olive oil, divided
2 ounces oil-packed sun-dried tomatoes, drained
2 small dried hot red chilies, crushed
2 tablespoons chopped fresh parsley
¼ teaspoon salt
¼ teaspoon black pepper
¾ cup fresh bread crumbs
1 tablespoon chopped garlic
12 ounces uncooked penne, cooked, drained and kept warm
1 tablespoon grated Romano cheese

Cook artichoke hearts in water and lemon juice in medium saucepan over medium heat until tender. Cool artichoke hearts; cut into quarters. Reserve artichoke cooking liquid.

Cook and stir 5 whole cloves garlic in 1½ tablespoons oil in large skillet over medium-high heat until golden. Reduce heat to low. Add artichoke hearts and tomatoes; simmer 1 minute. Stir in reserved artichoke cooking liquid, chilies, parsley, salt and pepper. Simmer 5 minutes. Remove and discard whole cloves garlic.

Meanwhile, cook and stir bread crumbs and 1 tablespoon chopped garlic in remaining ½ tablespoon oil. Pour artichoke sauce over penne in large bowl; toss gently to coat. Sprinkle with bread crumb mixture and cheese. *Makes 4 to 6 servings*

FAVORITE RECIPE FROM **NATIONAL PASTA ASSOCIATION**

Pasta with Roasted Red Pepper Sauce

12 ounces uncooked linguine or spaghetti
1 can (28 ounces) low-sodium peeled, chopped tomatoes
1 jar (11.5 ounces) GUILTLESS GOURMET® Roasted Red Pepper Salsa
⅓ cup (about 20) crushed GUILTLESS GOURMET® Baked Tortilla Chips (yellow or white corn)
¼ cup chopped fresh cilantro

Cook pasta according to package directions. Drain and keep warm.

Combine tomatoes and salsa in small saucepan or microwave-safe dish; cook over medium heat or microwave at HIGH until thoroughly heated. Place pasta on serving platter; pour sauce over pasta. Sprinkle with crushed chips and cilantro. Serve hot. *Makes 4 servings*

Penne with Artichokes

Three Cheese Vegetable Lasagna

1 teaspoon olive oil
1 large onion, chopped
3 cloves garlic, minced
1 can (28 ounces) no-salt-added tomato purée
1 can (14½ ounces) no-salt-added tomatoes, undrained and chopped
2 cups (6 ounces) sliced fresh mushrooms
1 medium zucchini, finely chopped
1 large green bell pepper, chopped
2 teaspoons dried basil leaves, crushed
1 teaspoon *each* salt and sugar (optional)
½ teaspoon *each* red pepper flakes and dried oregano leaves, crushed
2 cups (15 ounces) SARGENTO® Light Ricotta Cheese
1 package (10 ounces) frozen chopped spinach, thawed and squeezed dry
2 egg whites
2 tablespoons (½ ounce) SARGENTO® Fancy Supreme Shredded Parmesan Cheese
8 ounces lasagna noodles, cooked according to package directions, without oil or salt
¾ cup (3 ounces) *each* SARGENTO® Light Fancy Shredded Mozzarella and Mild Cheddar Cheese, divided

Preheat oven to 375°F. Spray large skillet with nonstick vegetable spray. Heat oil in large skillet over medium heat; add onion and garlic. Cook until tender, stirring occasionally. Add tomato purée, tomatoes and liquid, mushrooms, zucchini, bell pepper, basil, salt, sugar, pepper flakes and oregano. Bring to a boil; reduce heat to low. Cover and simmer 10 minutes or until vegetables are crisp-tender.

Combine ricotta cheese, spinach, egg whites and Parmesan cheese in medium bowl; mix well. Spread 1 cup sauce on bottom of 13×9-inch baking dish. Layer 3 lasagna noodles over sauce. Top with half the ricotta cheese mixture and 2 cups remaining sauce. Repeat layering with 3 more lasagna noodles, remaining ricotta mixture and 2 cups sauce. Combine mozzarella and Cheddar cheeses. Sprinkle ¾ cup cheese mixture over sauce. Top with remaining lasagna noodles and sauce. Cover with foil; bake 30 minutes. Uncover; bake 15 minutes more. Sprinkle with remaining ¾ cup cheese mixture. Let stand 10 minutes before serving.

Makes 10 servings

Penne Primavera with Sundried Tomato Sauce

4 cups assorted cut-up vegetables (zucchini, eggplant, peppers, mushrooms)
½ cup GREY POUPON® Dijon Mustard, divided
1 tablespoon olive oil
1 (7-ounce) jar sundried tomato strips in oil, drained
1 clove garlic, minced
2 cups light cream or half-and-half
1 tablespoon chopped fresh basil leaves
1 pound penne pasta, cooked
Grated Parmesan cheese (optional)

In large bowl, combine vegetables, 2 tablespoons mustard and oil. Place vegetables on broiler pan; broil for 8 to 10 minutes or until golden and tender, stirring occasionally.

In medium saucepan, over medium heat, sauté sundried tomato strips and garlic for 2 minutes. Reduce heat to low and stir in light cream or half-and-half, remaining mustard and basil; heat through.*

In large serving bowl, combine hot cooked pasta, vegetables and cream sauce, tossing to coat well. Serve immediately with Parmesan cheese.

Makes 6 servings

*If sauce thickens upon standing before tossing with pasta, thin with additional light cream or half-and-half.

Ravioli with Roasted Red Pepper Alfredo Sauce

- 1 package (10 ounces) DI GIORNO® Alfredo Sauce
- 1 jar (7 ounces) roasted red peppers, drained, sliced
- ½ cup toasted chopped walnuts
- 1 package (9 ounces) DI GIORNO® Four Cheese Ravioli, cooked, drained

HEAT sauce, peppers and walnuts in saucepan on medium heat.

TOSS with hot ravioli. Sprinkle with additional toasted chopped walnuts and chopped fresh parsley, if desired.

Makes 4 servings

Prep Time: 10 minutes
Cook Time: 10 minutes

Vegetable Macaroni & Cheese

- 1 box (14 ounces) macaroni and cheese
- 1 bag (16 ounces) BIRDS EYE® frozen Farm Fresh Mixtures Broccoli, Cauliflower and Carrots*

Or, substitute any other BIRDS EYE® frozen Farm Fresh Mixtures variety.

• Cook macaroni and cheese according to package directions. Add vegetables during last 5 minutes of cooking time. Continue preparing recipe according to package directions.

Makes about 4 servings

Cook Time: 15 to 20 minutes

Penne Primavera with Sundried Tomato Sauce (page 290)

Garden Primavera Pasta

- 6 ounces bow-tie pasta
- 1 jar (6 ounces) marinated artichoke hearts, undrained
- 2 cloves garlic, minced
- ½ teaspoon dried rosemary, crushed
- 1 medium green bell pepper, cut into thin strips
- 1 large carrot, cut into 3-inch-julienne strips
- 1 medium zucchini, cut into 3-inch-julienne strips
- 1 can (14½ ounces) DEL MONTE® *FreshCut*™ Diced Tomatoes with Garlic & Onion, undrained
- 12 small pitted ripe olives (optional)

1. Cook pasta according to package directions; drain.

2. Drain artichokes, reserving marinade. Combine pasta with 3 tablespoons artichoke marinade; toss to coat. Set aside. Cut artichoke hearts in half.

3. Cook garlic with rosemary in 1 tablespoon artichoke marinade in large skillet over medium-high heat until garlic is tender. Add all remaining ingredients except pasta and artichokes. Cook 4 to 5 minutes or until vegetables are tender-crisp and sauce is thickened.

4. Stir in artichoke hearts; spoon over pasta. Serve with grated Parmesan cheese, if desired.   *Makes 4 servings*

Tortellini with Three-Cheese Tuna Sauce

- 1 pound uncooked cheese-filled spinach or egg tortellini
- 2 green onions, thinly sliced
- 1 clove garlic, minced
- 1 tablespoon butter or margarine
- 1 cup low-fat ricotta cheese
- ½ cup low-fat milk
- 1 can (9 ounces) STARKIST® Tuna, drained and broken into chunks
- ½ cup (2 ounces) shredded low-fat mozzarella cheese
- ¼ cup grated Parmesan or Romano cheese
- 2 tablespoons chopped fresh basil *or* 2 teaspoons dried basil leaves, crushed
- 1 teaspoon grated lemon peel
  Fresh tomato wedges, red peppers and basil leaves for garnish (optional)

In large saucepan, cook tortellini in boiling salted water according to package directions. When tortellini are almost done, in separate large saucepan, cook and stir onions and garlic in butter 2 minutes. Whisk in ricotta cheese and milk. Add tuna, cheeses, basil and lemon peel.

Cook over medium-low heat until mixture is heated through and cheeses are melted.

Drain pasta; add to sauce. Toss well to coat; garnish if desired. Serve immediately.
            Makes 4 to 5 servings

Prep Time: 25 minutes

Linguine with White Clam Sauce

- 8 ounces linguine or spaghetti
- 2 tablespoons butter
- 1 tablespoon all-purpose flour
- 1 (10-ounce) can clam juice
- 1 tablespoon dried parsley leaves
- 1 teaspoon dried thyme leaves
- 2 (6½-ounce) cans minced clams

Prepare pasta according to package directions; drain.

Melt butter in small saucepan; add flour and mix. Add clam juice and stir until smooth. Add parsley and thyme; cook over low heat for 5 minutes. Add clams to mixture and cook 5 minutes more. Serve over pasta.   *Makes 4 servings*

FAVORITE RECIPE FROM **NATIONAL PASTA ASSOCIATION**

Garden Primavera Pasta

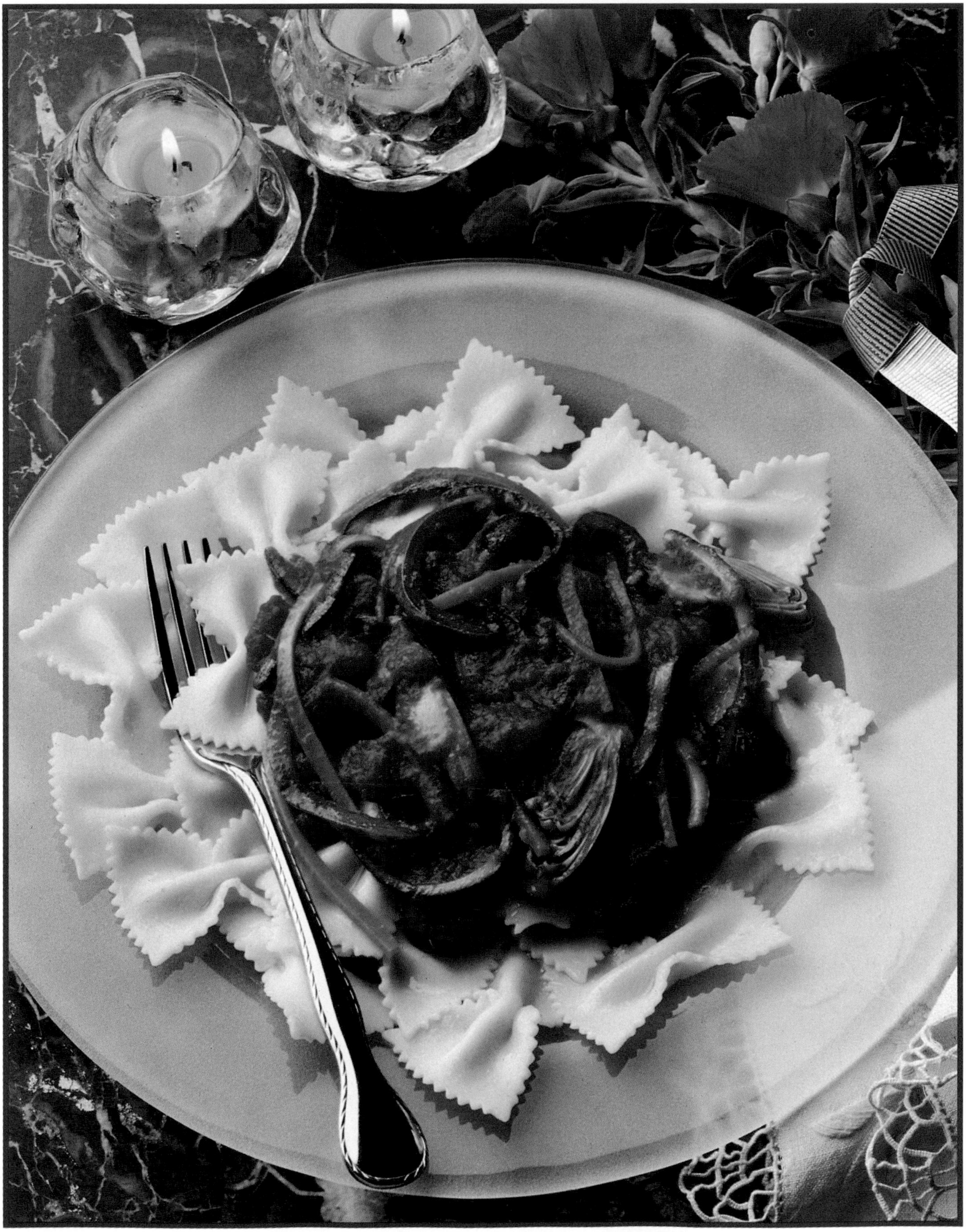

Seafood Lasagna with Spaghetti Squash and Broccoli

1 tablespoon olive oil
1 cup minced shallots
16 small mushrooms, cut in half
1 tablespoon minced garlic (2 to 4 cloves)
1 teaspoon dried thyme leaves
3 tablespoons all-purpose flour
2 cups dry white wine or chicken broth
1 cup bottled clam juice
¼ teaspoon freshly ground nutmeg
  Ground black pepper to taste
1½ pounds cooked seafood mixture of firm-textured fish (such as salmon) and scallops, cut into bite-size pieces, divided
6 lasagna noodles, cooked and drained
4 ounces (1½ to 2 cups) stuffing mix
1 (10-ounce) package frozen chopped broccoli, thawed
1 pound JARLSBERG LITE™ Cheese, shredded
3 cups cooked spaghetti squash

Heat oil in large skillet over medium-high heat. Sauté shallots, mushrooms, garlic and thyme in oil 4 minutes or until shallots begin to brown. Add flour; cook, stirring constantly, 2 to 3 minutes. Add wine, clam juice, nutmeg and pepper. Boil 3 minutes to thicken and reduce liquid. Add fish pieces and simmer 3 minutes. Add scallops; remove skillet from heat and set aside.

Arrange 3 lasagna noodles on bottom of 3½-quart rectangular baking dish. Evenly sprinkle with stuffing mix. Reserve 1 cup sauce mixture; spoon remaining sauce mixture over stuffing mix. Cover evenly with broccoli, ⅔ of cheese and 2 cups spaghetti squash. Cover with remaining lasagna noodles, cheese, reserved sauce mixture and remaining spaghetti squash. Press down firmly.* Cover tightly with tented foil and bake at 350°F, 45 to 50 minutes or until heated through.

Makes 10 to 12 servings

Recipe can be made ahead up to this point and refrigerated. Bring to room temperature before baking.

Tip: To cook spaghetti squash, pierce in several places and place on baking sheet in 350°F oven for 1 hour or until tender when pierced with knife. When squash is cool, cut in half, scoop out seeds and remove strands with two forks. Squash may be prepared ahead and refrigerated until needed.

Crab Basil Fettuccine

3 tablespoons margarine or butter
3 tablespoons olive oil
2 tomatoes, peeled, seeded and chopped
1 clove garlic, minced
⅓ cup whipping cream
½ cup HOLLAND HOUSE® White Cooking Wine
½ cup chopped fresh basil
½ cup cooked fresh or frozen crabmeat
¼ cup freshly grated Parmesan cheese, divided
¼ cup chopped fresh parsley, divided
1 pound fettuccine, cooked and drained

Melt margarine and oil in medium saucepan over medium heat. Add tomatoes and garlic; simmer until tomatoes are softened. Add whipping cream and cooking wine; simmer 10 minutes. Stir in basil and crabmeat; simmer 3 minutes. Add ½ of cheese and ½ of parsley. Serve over cooked fettuccine. Sprinkle with remaining cheese and parsley. *Makes 6 servings*

Pasta Verde de Mar

- 1 pound cod fillets
- 1 can (about 14 ounces) chicken broth
- 8 ounces fresh spinach linguine or fettuccine
- 3 tablespoons olive oil, divided
- 2 cloves garlic, crushed
- 6 green onions, diagonally sliced into ½-inch pieces
- 1 yellow bell pepper, cut into ¼-inch strips
- ½ cup chopped fresh basil *or* 1 tablespoon dried basil, crushed
- ¼ teaspoon red pepper flakes
- 8 cherry tomatoes, cut into quarters
- ¼ cup chopped parsley
- 1 (8-ounce) jar sun-dried tomatoes (optional)

Place cod fillets in 10-inch skillet with chicken broth. (If desired, add 1 slice lemon, 1 bay leaf and a few peppercorns to liquid.) Bring liquid to a boil; cover and immediately reduce heat to low. Simmer for 8 to 10 minutes or until fish is opaque. As fish simmers, cook pasta according to package directions. Drain; toss with 1 tablespoon olive oil and keep warm.

Remove fish from skillet; keep warm. Pour off cooking liquid, reserving ½ cup. Preheat dry skillet over high heat; add remaining 2 tablespoons olive oil. Add garlic, green onions, bell pepper, basil and red pepper flakes and stir-fry 3 to 5 minutes or until vegetables are tender-crisp. Remove pan from heat; add cherry tomatoes, parsley and sun-dried tomatoes, if desired, and mix well.

Use fork to break cod into 2-inch pieces; add fish and reserved cooking liquid to vegetables. Add pasta to skillet and toss gently with two forks to combine. Serve immediately.

Makes 4 servings

*FAVORITE RECIPE FROM **NATIONAL FISHERIES INSTITUTE***

Salmon Tortellini

- 1 package (7 ounces) cheese-filled tortellini, cooked and drained
- 1 container (8 ounces) PHILADELPHIA BRAND® Soft Cream Cheese with Smoked Salmon
- ½ cup finely chopped cucumber
- 1 teaspoon dried dill weed *or* 2 teaspoons fresh dill

• Lightly toss hot tortellini with remaining ingredients. Serve immediately.

Makes 6 to 8 servings

Prep Time: 25 minutes

Milano Shrimp Fettuccine

- 4 ounces egg or spinach fettuccine
- ½ pound medium shrimp, peeled and deveined
- 1 clove garlic, minced
- 1 tablespoon olive oil
- 1 can (14½ ounces) DEL MONTE® *FreshCut*™ Diced Tomatoes with Basil, Garlic & Oregano, undrained
- ½ cup whipping cream
- ¼ cup sliced green onions

1. Cook pasta according to package directions; drain.

2. Cook shrimp and garlic in hot oil in large skillet over medium-high heat until shrimp are pink and opaque.

3. Stir in tomatoes; simmer 5 minutes. Blend in cream and green onions; heat through. *Do not boil.* Serve over hot pasta.

Makes 3 to 4 servings

Prep & Cook Time: 20 minutes

Shrimp & Asparagus Fettuccine

12 ounces uncooked
    fettuccine
1 box (10 ounces) BIRDS
    EYE® frozen Asparagus
    Cuts*
1 tablespoon vegetable oil
1 package (16 ounces)
    frozen, uncooked
    cocktail-size shrimp
1 jar (12 ounces) prepared
    alfredo sauce
1 jar (4 ounces) sliced
    pimiento, drained

*Or, substitute 1½ cups BIRDS
EYE® frozen Green Peas or
BIRDS EYE® frozen Broccoli
Cuts.*

• Cook pasta according to
package directions, adding
asparagus to water 8 minutes
before pasta is done. Drain;
keep warm.

• Meanwhile, heat oil in large
skillet over medium-high heat.
Add shrimp; cover and cook
3 minutes or until shrimp turn
pink. Drain excess liquid,
leaving shrimp and about
2 tablespoons liquid in skillet.
Reduce heat to low. Stir in
alfredo sauce and pimiento.
Cover; cook 5 minutes. *Do not
boil.*

• Toss fettuccine and asparagus
with shrimp mixture.

Makes about 4 servings

Prep Time: 5 minutes
Cook Time: 20 minutes

Shrimp with Pasta

1 package fresh angel hair
    pasta
2 tablespoons extra-virgin
    olive oil
2 tablespoons chopped
    onion
1 teaspoon chopped garlic
12 medium shrimp, peeled
    and deveined
½ cup dry white wine
1 cup fish stock or bottled
    clam juice
2 teaspoons chopped
    Italian parsley
1 teaspoon chopped fresh
    basil leaves
½ teaspoon salt
2 tablespoons lemon juice
1 teaspoon Worcestershire
    sauce
¼ teaspoon TABASCO®
    pepper sauce

Boil large pot of water and cook
pasta according to package
instructions. Meanwhile, heat
olive oil in sauté pan until very
hot. Sauté onion and garlic
until lightly browned. Add
shrimp and sauté until pink;
remove and keep warm.

Add white wine and fish stock
to pan. Bring to a boil; add
parsley, basil, salt, lemon juice,
Worcestershire and TABASCO®
sauce. Return shrimp to pan
and simmer for about
30 seconds on each side.
Remove shrimp and arrange
over pasta; pour sauce over
shrimp.   *Makes 2 servings*

Winter Pesto Pasta with Shrimp

12 ounces uncooked
    fettuccine
1 cup chopped fresh kale,
    washed and stems
    removed
½ cup fresh basil leaves
¼ cup grated Parmesan
    cheese
2 cloves garlic, halved
⅛ teaspoon salt
1 cup plain nonfat yogurt
1 teaspoon vegetable oil
1 pound medium shrimp,
    peeled and deveined
1 medium red bell pepper,
    cut into bite-sized
    pieces

Cook pasta according to
package directions. While pasta
is cooking, purée kale, basil,
Parmesan cheese, garlic and
salt in food processor or
blender until smooth. Stir in
yogurt.

Heat oil in large skillet over
medium-low heat. Sauté shrimp
and bell pepper 4 minutes or
until shrimp are opaque.

When pasta is done, drain and
transfer to serving bowl. Add
kale mixture; toss well. Add
shrimp and bell pepper; toss
gently. Serve immediately.

Makes 4 servings

FAVORITE RECIPE FROM **NATIONAL PASTA
ASSOCIATION**

Shrimp & Asparagus Fettuccine

Bow Ties Alle Portofino

1 pound uncooked bow tie, radiatore or other medium pasta

1 pound small frozen shrimp, thawed *or* 1 pound medium fresh shrimp, peeled and deveined

12 sun-dried tomatoes, rehydrated, drained and cut into thin strips

8 fresh plum tomatoes, chopped

2 bunches arugula, washed and torn into bite-sized pieces

6 sprigs fresh Italian parsley, coarsely chopped

½ small bunch fresh basil, leaves picked and coarsely chopped

¼ cup olive or vegetable oil

Juice of 1 lemon

Salt and freshly ground black pepper to taste

Cook pasta according to package directions. While pasta is cooking, steam shrimp until opaque. Place shrimp in large mixing bowl. Add sun-dried tomatoes, fresh tomatoes, arugula, parsley and basil; toss gently.

When pasta is done, drain well; immediately add to shrimp mixture. Add oil, lemon juice, salt and pepper; toss well. Serve immediately.

Makes 6 servings

FAVORITE RECIPE FROM **NATIONAL PASTA ASSOCIATION**

Pasta Carbonara

½ cup sliced California ripe olives

½ cup sliced mushrooms

½ cup crumbled cooked bacon

¼ cup minced green onions with tops

½ teaspoon coarsely ground black pepper

3 tablespoons margarine

1 cup whipping cream

¾ cup grated Parmesan cheese

3 large eggs, lightly beaten

7 ounces linguine, cooked, drained and kept warm

Microwave Directions:
Combine olives, mushrooms, bacon, onions and pepper in small bowl; set aside.

Melt margarine in 2-quart microwave-safe casserole at HIGH 1 minute. Stir in olive mixture. Microwave at HIGH 1 minute. Add whipping cream, cheese and eggs; mix well. Microwave at HIGH 3 to 5 minutes, stirring every minute or until sauce is thickened. Pour over linguine; toss well.

Makes 6 servings

FAVORITE RECIPE FROM **CALIFORNIA OLIVE INDUSTRY**

Squid Mediterranean

2 pounds cleaned whole squid (body and tentacles only)

1 tablespoon olive oil

¾ cup finely chopped onion

1 clove garlic, minced

2 (16-ounce) cans Italian-style tomatoes, drained and chopped

3 tablespoons sliced black olives

1 tablespoon capers

½ teaspoon dried oregano

¼ teaspoon dried marjoram

⅛ teaspoon crushed red pepper

Cut body of squid into ½-inch slices; set aside. Heat olive oil in large skillet; add onion and garlic. Cook until onion is tender. Add squid and remaining ingredients. Bring to a boil. Cover; reduce heat and simmer 30 minutes or until squid is tender. *Makes 4 servings*

Prep Time: 45 minutes

FAVORITE RECIPE FROM **NATIONAL FISHERIES INSTITUTE**

Bow Ties Alle Portofino

Golden Apple-Salmon Pasta

8 ounces salmon, thawed if necessary, cut into ¾-inch chunks*
2 tablespoons butter or margarine, divided
1 cup sliced mushrooms
¾ cup diagonally sliced asparagus**
¼ cup chopped onion
¼ teaspoon dried oregano
⅛ teaspoon *each* salt and black pepper
⅓ cup half-and-half
1 Golden Delicious apple, cored and diced
4 ounces fettuccine noodles or spaghetti, cooked and drained
Grated Parmesan cheese

Eight ounces tiny pink shrimp can be substituted for salmon.

**One-half cup thawed frozen peas can be substituted for asparagus. Add peas with apple.*

Sauté salmon in 1 tablespoon butter 5 minutes or until barely cooked; remove from skillet. Sauté mushrooms, asparagus and onion in remaining 1 tablespoon butter 2 minutes. Add seasonings and half-and-half; cook and stir on high heat 1 minute. Add apple and salmon; cook and stir 30 seconds or until vegetables are tender and salmon flakes easily when tested with fork. Serve over hot fettuccine. Sprinkle with Parmesan cheese.

Makes 2 or 3 servings

FAVORITE RECIPE FROM WASHINGTON APPLE COMMISSION

Spinach Pesto

1 bunch fresh spinach, washed, dried and chopped
1 cup fresh parsley
⅔ cup grated Parmesan cheese
½ cup walnut pieces
6 cloves CHRISTOPHER RANCH Fresh Garlic, crushed
4 flat anchovy fillets
1 tablespoon dried tarragon leaves
1 teaspoon dried basil leaves
1 teaspoon salt
½ teaspoon black pepper
¼ teaspoon anise or fennel seed
1 cup olive oil
Pasta twists, spaghetti or shells, cooked, drained and kept warm
Mixed salad (optional)

Place spinach, parsley, cheese, walnuts, garlic, anchovies, tarragon, basil, salt, pepper and anise in food processor. Process until smooth. With motor running, add oil in thin stream. Adjust seasonings, if desired. Pour desired amount of sauce over pasta; toss gently to coat. Serve with salad, if desired. Garnish as desired.

Makes 2 cups sauce

Note: Keep any remaining sauce covered in refrigerator for up to 1 week.

Zesty Artichoke Pesto Sauce

¾ cup (6-ounce jar) marinated artichoke hearts, chopped, marinade reserved
1 cup (1 small) sliced onion
1¾ cups (14.5-ounce can) CONTADINA® Dalla Casa Buitoni Recipe Ready Diced Tomatoes, undrained
⅔ cup (6-ounce can) CONTADINA® Dalla Casa Buitoni Italian Paste with Tomato Pesto
1 cup water
½ teaspoon salt
Hot cooked pasta

Heat reserved artichoke marinade in large saucepan over medium-high heat until warm. Add onion; cook for 3 to 4 minutes or until tender. Add artichoke hearts, tomatoes and juice, tomato paste, water and salt. Bring to a boil; reduce heat to low. Cook, stirring occasionally, for 10 to 15 minutes. Serve over pasta.

Makes 6 to 8 servings

SAVORY CAPER AND OLIVE SAUCE: Eliminate artichoke hearts. Heat 2 tablespoons olive oil in large saucepan over medium-high heat. Add onion; cook for 3 to 4 minutes or until tender. Add tomatoes and juice, tomato paste, water, salt, ¾ cup sliced and quartered zucchini, ½ cup (2¼-ounce can) drained sliced ripe olives and 2 tablespoons CROSSE & BLACKWELL® Capers. Proceed as directed.

Spinach Pesto

An Uncommon Pasta Sauce

**2 tablespoons olive oil
1 medium onion, chopped
3 cups boiling water
1 package (3 ounces) *or*
    2 cups SONOMA
    Dried Tomato Halves,
    cut into quarters
1 large clove garlic,
    quartered
2 tablespoons chopped
    parsley
1 tablespoon chopped
    fresh basil *or*
    1 teaspoon dried basil
    leaves, crushed
2 teaspoons chopped
    fresh oregano *or*
    ¾ teaspoon dried
    oregano leaves,
    crushed
2 teaspoons lemon juice
1 teaspoon salt
¼ teaspoon black pepper
    Pasta, cooked, drained
    and kept warm
    Grated Parmesan
    cheese (optional)**

Heat oil in large skillet over medium heat. Add onion; sauté 5 minutes. Combine water and tomato halves in medium bowl; set aside 2 to 3 minutes. Drain well.

Place ⅔ of rehydrated tomato halves and garlic in blender or food processor; process until smooth. Add to onion in skillet. Stir in remaining ⅓ rehydrated tomato halves. Bring to a boil; reduce heat. Simmer, uncovered, 10 minutes.

Stir in parsley, basil, oregano, lemon juice, salt and pepper; simmer 1 minute. Remove from heat. Serve over pasta. Sprinkle with cheese, if desired.

Makes 2½ to 3 cups sauce

Warm Tomato-Pepper Sauce

**2½ quarts chopped red bell
    peppers
5 cups thinly sliced green
    onions
3 tablespoons minced
    garlic
⅓ cup olive oil
8 quarts California
    tomatoes, seeded and
    diced
1⅔ cups grated Parmesan
    cheese
1 cup chopped parsley
2½ teaspoons black pepper
¾ teaspoon cayenne
    pepper
3 pounds penne pasta,
    cooked**

1. Sauté bell peppers, onions and garlic in oil in large skillet over medium-high heat until vegetables are tender-crisp.

2. Stir in tomatoes; cook over high heat until sauce thickens, 10 to 15 minutes.

3. Stir in remaining ingredients except pasta. Serve sauce over hot pasta.   *Makes 24 servings*

*FAVORITE RECIPE FROM **CALIFORNIA TOMATO COMMISSION***

Basic Tomato Sauce

**1 teaspoon vegetable oil
1 medium onion, chopped
2 cloves garlic, chopped
2 (28-ounce) cans whole
    tomatoes
1 (6-ounce) can tomato
    paste
2 teaspoons dried Italian
    seasoning
2 bay leaves
    Salt and black pepper to
    taste**

In medium heavy-bottom saucepan, stir together oil, onion and garlic. Cook over low heat, stirring often, until onion is very soft and aromatic, about 6 to 8 minutes. In food processor or blender, purée tomatoes. Add tomatoes, tomato paste, Italian seasoning and bay leaves to onions and bring to a simmer over medium-high heat. Reduce heat to very low and let sauce simmer slowly for 30 minutes, stirring bottom often to prevent burning. If you are adding meatballs, do so at this time, and simmer them in the sauce for 20 minutes, stirring often. If you are not adding meatballs, simmer the sauce for another 20 minutes (50 minutes total). Season to taste with salt and pepper. Remove bay leaves before serving.

Makes 4 servings

*FAVORITE RECIPE FROM **NATIONAL PASTA ASSOCIATION***

Traditional Spaghetti Sauce

- 12 ounces dried CONTADINA® Dalla Casa Buitoni Spaghetti, cooked, drained and kept warm
- 1 pound mild Italian sausage
- ½ cup chopped onion
- 1¾ cups (14.5-ounce can) CONTADINA® Dalla Casa Buitoni Pasta Ready Chunky Tomatoes with Olive Oil, Garlic & Spices, undrained
- 1 cup water or chicken broth
- ⅔ cup (6-ounce can) CONTADINA® Dalla Casa Buitoni Italian Paste with Tomato Pesto
- 1 tablespoon chopped fresh parsley

Crumble sausage into large skillet. Cook over medium-high heat, stirring to break up sausage, for 4 to 5 minutes or until no longer pink. Add onion; cook for 2 to 3 minutes. Drain. Stir in tomatoes and juice, water, tomato paste and parsley. Bring to a boil. Reduce heat to low; cook for 10 to 15 minutes or until flavors are blended. Serve sauce over pasta.   *Makes 4 to 6 servings*

Sherry Cheese Sauce

- 2 tablespoons margarine or butter
- 2 tablespoons all-purpose flour
- ⅛ teaspoon white pepper
- 1 cup milk
- 2 tablespoons HOLLAND HOUSE® Sherry Cooking Wine
- 4 ounces (1 cup) shredded Cheddar cheese
- 1 teaspoon dry mustard
- 1 teaspoon Worcestershire sauce

Melt margarine in small saucepan; blend in flour and pepper. Cook over medium heat until smooth and bubbly, about 1 minute. Gradually add milk and cooking wine. Cook until mixture boils and thickens, stirring constantly. Boil 1 minute. Stir in cheese, mustard and Worcestershire sauce. Cook over low heat until cheese is melted.

Makes 1⅓ cups

An Uncommon Pasta Sauce (page 302)

International Fare

FEATURING:

Asian Stir-Fries

Mexican Meals

European Classics

Thai Beef and Noodle Toss (page 310)

305

Sweet and Spicy Chicken Stir-Fry

1½ cups uncooked long-grain white rice
1 can (8 ounces) DEL MONTE® Pineapple Chunks In Its Own Juice, undrained
4 boneless chicken breast halves, skinned and cut bite-size
2 tablespoons vegetable oil
1 large green bell pepper, cut into strips
¾ cup sweet and sour sauce
⅛ to ½ teaspoon red pepper flakes

1. Cook rice according to package directions.

2. Drain pineapple, reserving ⅓ cup juice.

3. Stir-fry chicken in hot oil in large skillet over medium-high heat until no longer pink in center. Add bell pepper and reserved pineapple juice; stir-fry 2 minutes or until tender-crisp.

4. Add sweet and sour sauce, red pepper flakes and pineapple; stir-fry 3 minutes or until heated through.

5. Spoon rice onto serving plate; top with chicken mixture. Garnish, if desired.

Makes 4 servings

Prep Time: 5 minutes
Cook Time: 20 minutes

Orange Ginger Chicken & Rice

1 package (6.9 ounces) RICE-A-RONI® With ⅓ Less Salt Chicken Flavor
1 tablespoon margarine or butter
1 cup orange juice
¾ pound boneless skinless chicken breasts, cut into thin strips
2 cloves garlic, minced
¼ teaspoon ground ginger
Dash red pepper flakes (optional)
1½ cups carrots, cut into short thin strips *or* 3 cups broccoli flowerets

1. In large skillet, sauté Rice-A-Roni® Mix and margarine over medium heat, stirring frequently until vermicelli is golden brown.

2. Stir in 1½ cups water, orange juice, chicken, garlic, ginger, red pepper flakes, if desired, and contents of seasoning packet; bring to a boil over high heat.

3. Cover; reduce heat. Simmer 10 minutes.

4. Stir in carrots.

5. Cover; continue to simmer 5 to 10 minutes or until liquid is absorbed and rice is tender.

Makes 4 servings

Stir-Fry Tomato Beef

1 cup uncooked long-grain white rice
1 pound flank steak
1 tablespoon cornstarch
1 tablespoon soy sauce
2 cloves garlic, minced
1 teaspoon minced fresh ginger *or* ¼ teaspoon ground ginger
1 tablespoon vegetable oil
1 can (14½ ounces) DEL MONTE® Original Recipe Stewed Tomatoes

1. Cook rice according to package directions.

2. Meanwhile, cut meat in half lengthwise, and then cut crosswise into thin slices.

3. Combine cornstarch, soy sauce, garlic and ginger in medium bowl. Add meat; toss to coat.

4. Heat oil in large skillet over high heat. Add meat; cook, stirring constantly, until browned. Add tomatoes; cook until thickened, about 5 minutes, stirring frequently.

5. Serve meat mixture over hot cooked rice. Garnish, if desired.

Makes 4 to 6 servings

Prep Time: 10 minutes
Cook Time: 20 minutes

Sweet and Spicy Chicken Stir-Fry

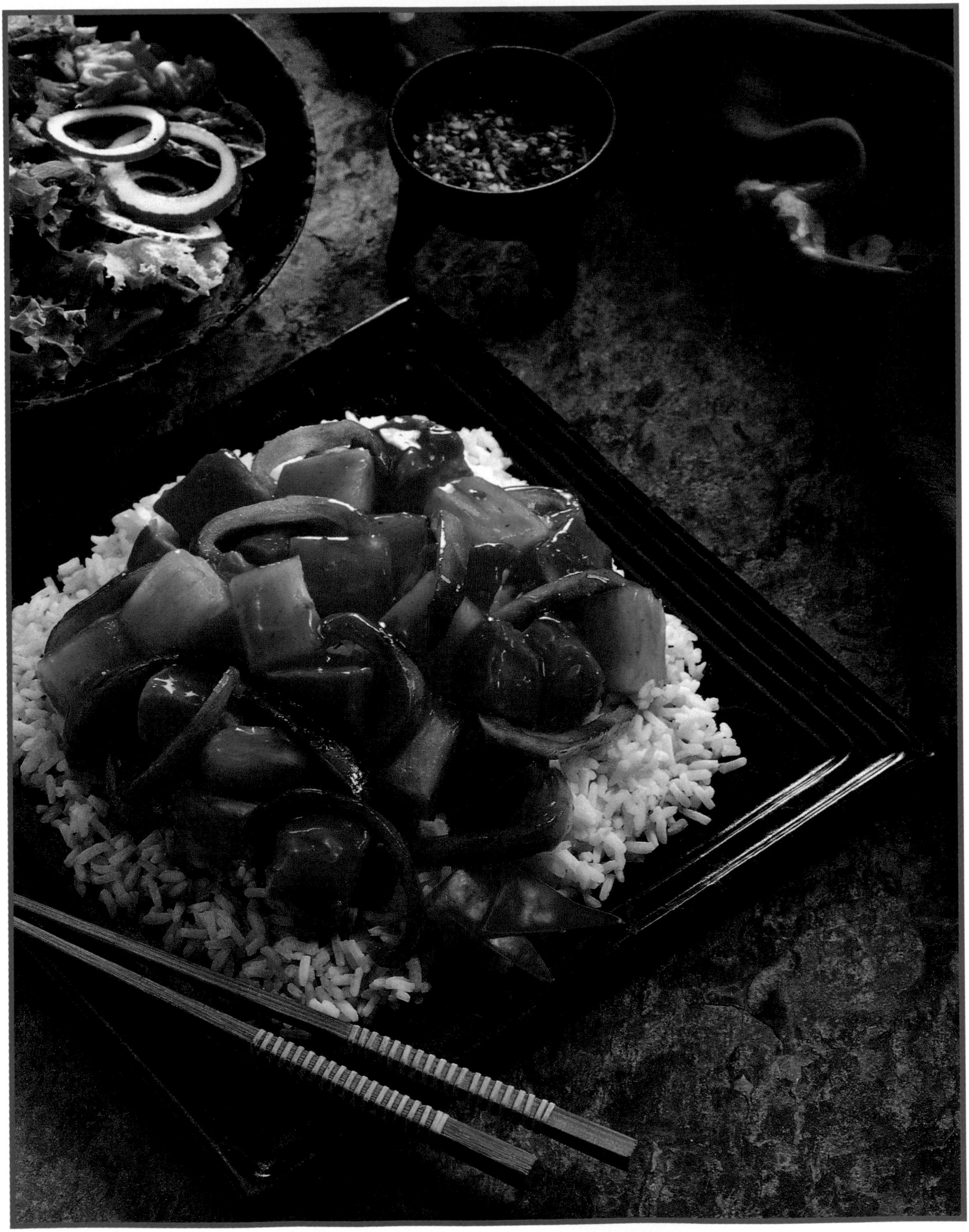

Savory Pork & Apple Stir-Fry

- 1 package (7.2 ounces) RICE-A-RONI® Rice Pilaf
- 1⅓ cups apple juice or apple cider, divided
- 1 pound boneless pork loin, pork tenderloin or boneless skinless chicken breast halves
- 1 teaspoon paprika
- 1 teaspoon dried thyme
- ½ teaspoon ground sage or poultry seasoning
- ½ teaspoon salt (optional)
- 2 tablespoons margarine or butter
- 2 apples, cored and sliced
- 1 teaspoon cornstarch
- ⅓ cup coarsely chopped walnuts

1. Prepare Rice-A-Roni® Mix as package directs, substituting 1 cup water and 1 cup apple juice for water in directions.

2. While Rice-A-Roni® is simmering, cut pork into 1½×¼-inch strips. Combine seasonings; toss with pork.

3. In second large skillet, melt margarine over medium heat. Stir-fry pork 3 to 4 minutes or just until pork is no longer pink.

4. Add apples; stir-fry 2 to 3 minutes or until apples are almost tender. Add combined remaining ⅓ cup apple juice and cornstarch. Stir-fry 1 to 2 minutes or until thickened to form glaze.

5. Stir in nuts. Serve rice topped with pork mixture.

Makes 4 servings

Chinese Flatbreads

- 1 pound frozen white bread dough, thawed Sesame oil
- 1½ to 2 teaspoons LAWRY'S® Garlic Salt with Parsley
- 2 green onions, thinly sliced
- 2 teaspoons sesame seeds

On well-floured work surface, roll dough into rectangle, about 15×6 inches. Brush lightly with sesame oil. Sprinkle with Garlic Salt with Parsley and green onions. Starting from long edge, roll dough up jelly-roll fashion. With serrated knife, cut dough into 1-inch slices and flatten each slice slightly by pressing with heel of hand. Arrange slices on baking sheet sprayed with nonstick cooking spray. Brush tops lightly with sesame oil and sprinkle with sesame seeds. Cover and let rise in warm place 30 minutes. Bake in 350°F oven 15 minutes or until golden.

Makes 4 servings

Hint: *Breads can be baked ahead and frozen. Reheat 5 minutes in 350°F oven.*

Crystal Shrimp with Sweet & Sour Sauce

- ½ cup KIKKOMAN® Sweet & Sour Sauce
- 1 tablespoon water
- 2 teaspoons cornstarch
- ½ pound medium-size raw shrimp, peeled and deveined
- 1 egg white, beaten
- 2 tablespoons vegetable oil, divided
- 1 clove garlic, minced
- 2 carrots, cut diagonally into thin slices
- 1 medium-size green bell pepper, chunked
- 1 medium onion, chunked
- 1 tablespoon sesame seed, toasted

Blend sweet & sour sauce and water; set aside. Measure cornstarch into large plastic food storage bag. Coat shrimp with egg white; drain off excess egg. Add shrimp to cornstarch in bag; shake bag to coat shrimp. Heat 1 tablespoon oil in hot wok or large skillet over medium-high heat. Add garlic; stir-fry 10 seconds, or until fragrant. Add shrimp and stir-fry 2 minutes, or until pink; remove. Heat remaining 1 tablespoon oil in same pan over high heat. Add carrots, bell pepper and onion; stir-fry 4 minutes. Add shrimp and sweet & sour sauce mixture. Cook and stir until shrimp and vegetables are coated with sauce. Remove from heat; stir in sesame seed. Serve immediately.

Makes 4 servings

Persian Chicken Breasts

1 medium lemon
2 teaspoons olive oil
1 teaspoon ground cinnamon
½ teaspoon salt
¼ teaspoon black pepper
¼ teaspoon turmeric
4 boneless skinless chicken breast halves
4 flour tortillas or soft lavash

1. Peel lemon rind into long strips with paring knife; reserve for garnish, if desired. Juice lemon and combine with oil, cinnamon, salt, pepper and turmeric in large heavy-duty resealable plastic food storage bag. Gently massage ingredients in bag to mix thoroughly; add chicken. Seal bag and turn to coat thoroughly. Refrigerate 4 hours or overnight.

2. Remove chicken from marinade and gently shake to remove excess. Grill chicken 5 to 7 minutes per side or until chicken is no longer pink in center, brushing occasionally with marinade. Discard remaining marinade. Serve chicken with lightly grilled tortillas or lavash and red and yellow grilled peppers, if desired.   *Makes 4 servings*

Chinese Vegetable Salad

1 bag (16 ounces) BIRDS EYE® frozen Farm Fresh Mixtures Broccoli, Carrots and Water Chestnuts
½ pound cooked shrimp*
½ cup sweet and sour sauce or dressing
1 can (3 ounces) chow mein noodles

Or, substitute ½ pound chicken for shrimp. Cut into thin strips and brown in 2 teaspoons hot oil.

• Cook vegetables according to package directions.

• Combine vegetables and cooked shrimp; toss with sweet and sour sauce.

• Serve over chow mein noodles or toss with noodles. Serve warm or chilled.
          Makes 4 to 5 servings

Prep Time: 2 minutes
Cook Time: 10 to 12 minutes

Persian Chicken Breast

Sweet & Sour Mustard Pork

- **1 pound boneless pork, cut into strips**
- **¼ cup GREY POUPON® Dijon Mustard, divided**
- **3 teaspoons soy sauce, divided**
- **1 (3-ounce) package chicken-flavored ramen noodles**
- **1 (8-ounce) can pineapple chunks, drained, reserving juice**
- **½ cup water**
- **2 tablespoons firmly packed light brown sugar**
- **½ teaspoon grated fresh ginger**
- **1 tablespoon cornstarch**
- **2 cups broccoli flowerettes**
- **½ cup chopped red or green cabbage**
- **½ cup chopped red bell pepper**
- **½ cup coarsely chopped onion**
- **2 tablespoons vegetable oil**

In medium bowl, combine pork strips, 2 tablespoons mustard and 1 teaspoon soy sauce. Refrigerate 1 hour.

In small bowl, combine remaining mustard and soy sauce, chicken flavor packet from noodles, reserved pineapple juice, water, brown sugar, ginger and cornstarch; set aside. Cook ramen noodles according to package directions; drain and set aside.

In large skillet, over medium-high heat, stir-fry vegetables in oil until tender-crisp; remove from skillet. Add pork mixture; stir-fry 3 to 4 minutes or until done. Return vegetables to skillet with pineapple chunks and cornstarch mixture; heat until mixture thickens and begins to boil. Add cooked noodles, tossing to coat well. Garnish as desired. Serve immediately.

Makes 4 servings

Thai Beef and Noodle Toss

- **1 pound beef round tip steaks, cut ⅛ to ¼ inch thick**
- **1 to 2 jalapeño peppers,* minced**
- **2 cloves garlic, minced**
- **2 tablespoons dark sesame oil, divided**
- **1 (3-ounce) package beef-flavored instant ramen noodles**
- **1 cup diagonally sliced carrots**
- **½ cup chopped green onions**
- **½ cup A.1.® Thick & Hearty Steak Sauce**
- **¼ cup water**
- **¼ cup PLANTERS® Unsalted Peanuts, chopped**
- **2 tablespoons chopped fresh cilantro or parsley**

Remove interior ribs and seeds if a milder flavor is desired.

Cut steaks crosswise into 1-inch-wide strips; cut each strip in half. In large bowl, toss steaks, jalapeños and garlic with 1 tablespoon oil; set aside.

Break noodles into 3 or 4 pieces; set aside seasoning packet. Cook noodles according to package directions; drain and rinse. Meanwhile, heat large skillet or wok over medium-high heat; stir-fry reserved steak mixture in batches 30 to 60 seconds or until steak is desired doneness. Remove steak mixture from skillet; keep warm.

In same skillet, in remaining 1 tablespoon oil, stir-fry carrots and green onions until tender. Add cooked noodles, steak sauce, water, peanuts and cilantro; sprinkle with reserved seasoning packet. Heat mixture until hot, stirring occasionally. Return warm steak mixture to skillet; mix lightly. Serve immediately.

Makes 4 servings

Sweet & Sour Mustard Pork

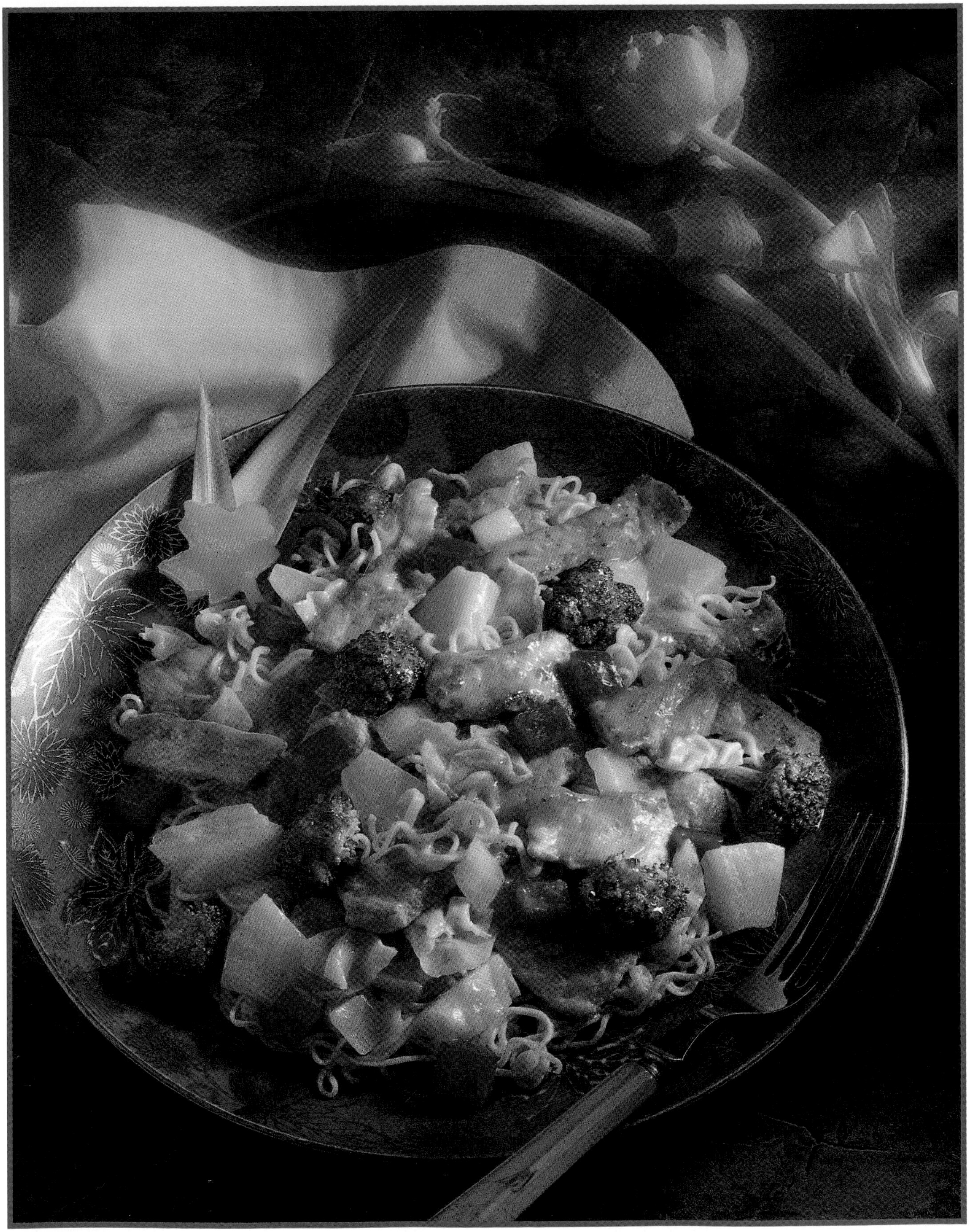

Spaghetti with Beef and Black Pepper Sauce

8 ounces uncooked spaghetti
5 ounces beef fillet, shredded
½ cup plus 2 tablespoons LEE KUM KEE® Black Pepper Sauce, divided
1 tablespoon vegetable oil
1 ounce onion, shredded
1 ounce green bell pepper, shredded
1 ounce red bell pepper, shredded

1. Cook spaghetti in boiling water 10 minutes. Rinse with cold water and drain.

2. Marinate beef with 2 tablespoons pepper sauce 5 minutes.

3. Heat oil in wok. Sauté onion until fragrant. Add beef and stir-fry until cooked. Add spaghetti, bell peppers and ½ cup pepper sauce. Stir well and serve.

Makes 4 to 6 servings

Southwestern Chilies Rellenos

2 tablespoons olive oil
½ teaspoon white pepper
½ teaspoon salt
½ teaspoon ground red pepper
¼ teaspoon ground cloves
4 cans (4 ounces each) whole green chilies, drained and seeded
1½ cups (6 ounces) shredded Wisconsin Cheddar cheese
1½ cups (6 ounces) shredded Wisconsin Monterey Jack cheese
1 package (16 ounces) egg roll wrappers
1 egg yolk *plus* 1 teaspoon water
Vegetable oil

Combine olive oil and seasonings in small bowl. Add chilies; toss to coat. Let stand 1 hour. Combine cheeses in separate small bowl.

For each chili relleno, place 1 chili in center of 1 egg roll wrapper; top with ¼ cup cheese mixture. Brush edges of wrapper with egg yolk mixture. Fold edges lengthwise over filling, overlapping edges; press together. Seal ends, enclosing filling.

Heat vegetable oil in heavy saucepan over medium-high heat until oil reaches 375°F. Fry chilies rellenos, a few at a time, in hot oil 2 to 3 minutes or until golden brown. Drain on paper towels. *Makes 6 servings*

FAVORITE RECIPE FROM **WISCONSIN MILK MARKETING BOARD**

Border Scramble

1 pound BOB EVANS FARMS® Original Recipe Roll Sausage
1½ cups chopped cooked potatoes
1½ cups chopped onions
1½ cups chopped tomatoes
¾ cup chopped green bell pepper
¼ to ½ cup picante sauce
½ to 1 tablespoon hot pepper sauce
½ teaspoon garlic powder
½ teaspoon salt
4 (9-inch) flour tortillas
2 cups prepared meatless chili
½ cup (2 ounces) shredded Cheddar cheese

Crumble sausage into large skillet. Cook over medium heat until browned, stirring occasionally. Drain off any drippings. Add all remaining ingredients except tortillas, chili and cheese; simmer 20 minutes or until vegetables are crisp-tender. To warm tortillas, microwave 1 minute at HIGH between paper towels. Place 1 cup sausage mixture in center of each tortilla; fold tortilla over filling to close. Heat chili in small saucepan until hot, stirring occasionally. Top each folded tortilla with ½ cup chili and 2 tablespoons cheese. Serve hot. Refrigerate leftovers. *Makes 4 servings*

Microwave Black Bean & Cream Cheese Enchiladas

- 1 cup frozen corn
- ⅔ cup chopped green bell pepper
- ½ cup chopped onion
- 1 package (8 ounces) low-fat cream cheese
- 1 cup GUILTLESS GOURMET® Salsa (mild, medium or hot), divided
- 10 corn tortillas (6 inches each)
- 10 tablespoons GUILTLESS GOURMET® Black Bean Dip (mild or spicy)
- 1 cup GUILTLESS GOURMET® Nacho Dip (mild or spicy)
- Lime wedges and fresh sage leaves (optional)

Microwave Directions:
Place corn, pepper and onion in 2-cup glass measure. Cover with vented plastic wrap; microwave at HIGH 3 minutes or until heated through. Stir; let stand, covered, until ready to use. Cut cream cheese into 10 equal portions; roll each portion into long tube. Pour half the salsa in 13×9-inch glass baking dish.

To soften tortillas, stack 5 tortillas and wrap in damp paper towel; microwave at HIGH 35 seconds.

To assemble enchiladas, spread 1 tablespoon bean dip in center of each tortilla. Place 1 cheese tube on top of dip in center. Drizzle 1 heaping tablespoonful corn mixture over cheese. Roll up tortilla and place seam side down in dish. Repeat with remaining softened tortillas. Soften remaining 5 tortillas and assemble as directed. Pour remaining ½ cup salsa over top. Pour nacho dip over salsa. Cover with vented plastic wrap; microwave at HIGH 10 minutes. Let stand 3 minutes before serving. Garnish with lime and sage, if desired.

Makes 10 servings

Baked Chilies Rellenos

- 4 small to medium poblano chili peppers
- 1 cup cooked brown rice
- ½ cup cooked corn (fresh, canned or frozen)
- ¼ cup GUILTLESS GOURMET® Spicy Nacho Dip
- 1 tablespoon chopped fresh cilantro
- ¼ cup low-fat sour cream
- ¼ cup GUILTLESS GOURMET® Salsa (mild, medium or hot)

To prepare peppers, preheat broiler. Place peppers on baking sheet; broil about 10 minutes, turning as skins blister. (Avoid charring peppers; blister peppers evenly.) Remove peppers from oven; *turn off broiler.* Immerse peppers in bowl of ice water; allow to cool. Remove peppers from ice water and gently scrape away blistered skin, being careful not to tear the flesh.* Make lengthwise slit in each pepper and carefully scrape out seeds and membranes.

Preheat oven to 350°F. Combine rice, corn, nacho dip and cilantro in small bowl. Stuff peppers evenly with rice mixture; press peppers to close, squeezing with fingertips. Arrange peppers in small baking dish.

Bake 20 to 30 minutes or until heated through. To serve, dollop each pepper with 1 tablespoon sour cream and 1 tablespoon salsa.   *Makes 4 peppers*

*Chili peppers can sting and irritate the skin; wear plastic gloves when handling peppers and do not touch eyes. Wash hands after handling.

Chicken Enchiladas

1¾ cups fat free sour cream
½ cup chopped green onions
⅓ cup minced fresh cilantro
1 tablespoon minced fresh jalapeño chili pepper
1 teaspoon ground cumin
1 tablespoon vegetable oil
12 ounces boneless, skinless chicken breasts, cut into 3×1-inch strips
1 teaspoon minced garlic
8 flour tortillas (8-inch)
1 cup (4 ounces) shredded ALPINE LACE® Reduced Fat Cheddar Cheese
1 cup bottled chunky salsa (medium or hot)
1 small ripe tomato, chopped
Sprigs of cilantro (optional)

1. Preheat the oven to 350°F. Spray a 13×9×3-inch baking dish with nonstick cooking spray.

2. In a small bowl, mix together the sour cream, green onions, cilantro, jalapeño pepper and cumin.

3. Spray a large nonstick skillet with the cooking spray, pour in the oil and heat over medium-high heat. Add the chicken and garlic and sauté for 4 minutes or until the juices run clear when the chicken is pierced with a fork.

4. Divide the chicken strips among the 8 tortillas, placing them down the center of the tortillas. Top with the sour cream mixture, then roll them up and place them, seam side down, in the baking dish.

5. Sprinkle with the cheese, cover with foil and bake for 30 minutes or until bubbly. Spoon the salsa in a strip down the center and sprinkle the salsa with the tomato. Garnish with the sprigs of cilantro, if you wish. Serve hot!

Makes 8 servings

Mexicali Pizzas

2 (9-inch) flour tortillas
2 cups (8 ounces) shredded Monterey Jack cheese
1 can (15 ounces) VEG-ALL® Mixed Vegetables, drained
1 cup chopped tomato
½ cup finely chopped green onions
½ cup finely chopped green bell pepper
3 tablespoons chopped mild green chilies
¼ cup sliced pitted ripe olives

1. Place tortillas on lightly greased baking sheet. Sprinkle one tortilla with ½ cup cheese; top with half of Veg-All®, tomato, green onions, pepper and chilies.

2. Sprinkle with ½ cup cheese; top with 2 tablespoons olives.

3. Repeat procedure with second tortilla.

4. Bake at 425°F about 10 to 12 minutes or until cheese is melted and tortillas are crisp.

Makes 2 (9-inch) pizzas

Chicken Rellenos

8 small poblano or green bell peppers (about 2 ounces each)
1 can (8½ ounces) whole kernel corn, drained
2 cans (4 ounces each) chunk white chicken, drained
1 can (4 ounces) sliced mushrooms, drained
1 cup (4 ounces) shredded Monterey Jack cheese
2 tablespoons chopped pimientos
1 or 2 canned jalapeño peppers, finely chopped
1 clove garlic, minced
1 tablespoon vegetable oil

Remove tops from poblano peppers; scoop out and discard seeds. Mix corn, chicken, mushrooms, cheese, pimientos, jalapeño peppers and garlic; spoon mixture into poblano peppers. Heat oil in large skillet over medium-high heat; cook peppers, browning all sides. Reduce heat to low. Cover; cook, turning occasionally, until peppers are tender, 5 to 10 minutes.   *Makes 4 servings*

FAVORITE RECIPE FROM **CANNED FOOD INFORMATION COUNCIL**

Chicken Enchiladas

Smothered Mexican Pork Chops

1 tablespoon vegetable oil
4 boneless thin-cut pork chops (about ¾ pound)
1 can (14½ ounces) chunky tomatoes, salsa- or Cajun-style
1 can (16 ounces) black beans
2 cups BIRDS EYE® frozen Farm Fresh Mixtures Broccoli, Corn and Red Peppers*

Or, substitute 2 cups BIRDS EYE® frozen Corn.

• Heat oil in large skillet over high heat. Add pork; cook until browned, about 4 minutes per side.

• Add tomatoes; reduce heat to medium. Cover and cook 5 minutes. Uncover and push pork to side of skillet.

• Add beans and vegetables. Place pork on top of vegetables. Increase heat to medium-high; cover and cook 5 minutes or until heated through.

Makes about 4 servings

Prep Time: 5 minutes
Cook Time: 20 minutes

Shredded Pork Tacos

3 cups shredded or finely chopped cooked roast pork
1 cup chopped onion
1 clove garlic, minced
1 to 3 tablespoons diced jalapeño pepper
12 small flour tortillas, warmed
3 cups shredded lettuce
2 cups diced tomatoes
¾ cup (3 ounces) shredded Cheddar cheese
Salsa (optional)

In medium nonstick skillet, cook and stir onion and garlic over medium heat 5 minutes or until soft and translucent. Add cooked pork; toss lightly. Heat thoroughly; stir in jalapeño pepper. On each tortilla, spoon ¼ cup pork mixture, a portion of lettuce, tomatoes and 1 tablespoon cheese; top with salsa, if desired.

Makes 6 servings

Prep Time: 15 minutes

*FAVORITE RECIPE FROM **NATIONAL PORK PRODUCERS COUNCIL***

Mexicali Cornbread con Queso

1 (8½-ounce) package yellow cornbread mix
2 cups (8 ounces) shredded Wisconsin Cheddar or Monterey Jack cheese, divided
1 pound ground beef
1 (15-ounce) can pinto beans, drained
1 package taco seasoning mix
Chopped tomatoes
Sliced avocado
Sour cream

Heat oven to 350°F. Prepare cornbread mix according to package directions, adding 1 cup shredded Wisconsin cheese to batter. Pour batter in equal amounts into two separate greased 9-inch round baking pans. Bake 8 to 12 minutes; cool.

Brown ground beef; drain. Add beans, seasoning mix and water according to seasoning mix package directions. Continue cooking until slightly thickened.

Place one cornbread round on serving platter; top with half of meat mixture and ½ cup cheese. Place the other cornbread round on top and cover with remaining meat mixture and cheese. Cut into wedges to serve. Top with chopped tomatoes, avocado slices and sour cream.

Makes 8 servings

*FAVORITE RECIPE FROM **WISCONSIN MILK MARKETING BOARD***

Smothered Mexican Pork Chop

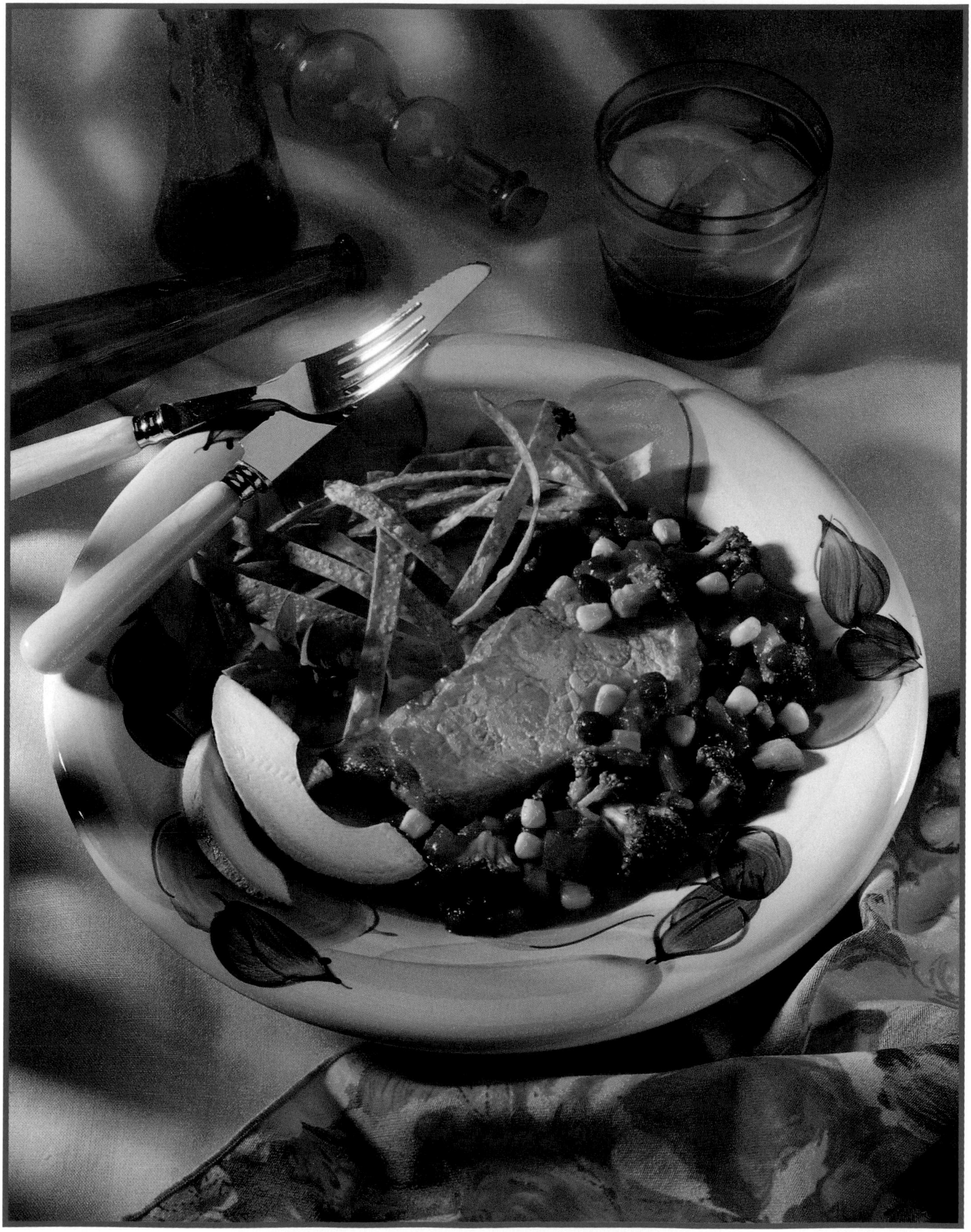

Mexican Lasagna

4 boneless skinless
    chicken breast halves
2 tablespoons vegetable
    oil
2 teaspoons chili powder
1 teaspoon ground cumin
1 can (14½ ounces) diced
    tomatoes with garlic,
    drained
1 can (8 ounces) tomato
    sauce
1 teaspoon hot pepper
    sauce (optional)
1 cup part-skim ricotta
    cheese
1 can (4 ounces) diced
    green chilies
¼ cup chopped fresh
    cilantro, divided
12 (6-inch) corn tortillas
1 cup (4 ounces) shredded
    Cheddar cheese

PREHEAT oven to 375°F.

CUT chicken into ½-inch pieces. Heat oil in large skillet over medium heat until hot. Add chicken, chili powder and cumin. Cook about 4 minutes or until browned, stirring occasionally. Stir in tomatoes, tomato sauce and hot pepper sauce, if desired; bring to a boil. Reduce heat; simmer 2 minutes.

COMBINE ricotta cheese, chilies and 2 tablespoons cilantro in small bowl; mix until well blended.

SPOON half of chicken mixture into bottom of 12×8-inch baking dish. Top with 6 tortillas, ricotta cheese mixture, remaining tortillas, remaining

chicken mixture, Cheddar cheese and remaining cilantro. Bake 25 minutes or until heated through.

Makes 6 to 8 servings

Taco Bake

TACO MEAT FILLING
1 pound ground beef
½ cup chopped onion
1 package taco seasoning

TACO CRUST
1¾ to 2 cups all-purpose
    flour, divided
1 package RED STAR®
    Active Dry Yeast or
    QUICK-RISE™ Yeast
1 tablespoon sugar
2 teaspoons finely
    chopped onion
¾ teaspoon salt
⅔ cup warm water
2 tablespoons oil
½ cup crushed corn chips

TOPPINGS
1 cup shredded Cheddar
    cheese
1 cup shredded lettuce
1½ cups chopped tomatoes

Brown ground beef with onion; drain. Add taco seasoning. Prepare taco filling according to seasoning packet directions.

Preheat oven to 375°F. In medium bowl, combine 1 cup flour, yeast, sugar, onion and salt; mix well. Add warm water (120° to 130°F) and oil to flour mixture. Mix by hand until almost smooth. Stir in corn chips and enough remaining flour to make a stiff batter. Spread in well-greased 10-inch pie pan, forming a rim around

edge. Cover; let rise in warm place about 20 minutes (10 minutes for Quick-Rise™ Yeast). Spread meat filling over dough. Bake at 375°F 30 to 35 minutes or until edge is crisp and light golden brown. Sprinkle cheese, lettuce and tomatoes on top. Serve immediately.

Makes 4 to 6 servings

Arroz Mexicana

1 medium onion, chopped
2 cloves garlic, crushed
½ teaspoon dried oregano
    leaves
1 tablespoon vegetable oil
¾ cup uncooked long-grain
    white rice
1 can (14½ ounces) DEL
    MONTE® FreshCut™
    Diced Tomatoes
1 medium green bell
    pepper, chopped

1. Cook onion, garlic and oregano in hot oil in large skillet until onion is tender.

2. Stir in rice; cook until golden, stirring frequently.

3. Drain tomatoes, reserving liquid; pour liquid into measuring cup. Add water to measure 1½ cups. Stir into rice; bring to a boil.

4. Reduce heat to medium; cover. Simmer 15 minutes or until rice is tender. Stir in tomatoes and bell pepper; cook 5 minutes.

Makes 4 to 6 servings

Prep Time: 5 minutes
Cook Time: 27 minutes

Mexican Lasagna

Empanadas

¼ **cup raisins**
1 **tablespoon apple cider vinegar**
1 **pound ground beef or turkey**
1 **cup (1 small) chopped onion**
2 **cloves garlic, finely chopped**
1¾ **cups (16-ounce jar) ORTEGA® Thick & Chunky Salsa, hot, medium or mild, divided**
¼ **cup slivered almonds**
2 **tablespoons brown sugar**
½ **teaspoon ground cinnamon**
¼ **teaspoon salt**
1 **loaf (1 pound) frozen bread dough, thawed**
½ **cup (2 ounces) shredded Monterey Jack cheese**
1 **egg, lightly beaten**

COMBINE raisins and vinegar in small bowl; soak 15 to 20 minutes or until raisins are plump.

COMBINE beef, onion and garlic in large skillet; cook over medium-high heat 4 to 5 minutes or until no longer pink; drain. Add ½ cup salsa, almonds, raisin mixture, sugar, cinnamon and salt. Bring to a boil. Cook 3 to 4 minutes or until flavors are blended.

DIVIDE dough into 6 pieces; roll into balls. On well-floured board, roll each ball into a 6-inch circle. Place ½ cup beef filling on bottom half of circle; sprinkle with cheese. Fold top half of dough over filling; crimp edges with tines of fork. Pierce top with fork. Place on greased cookie sheet; brush with egg.

BAKE in preheated 375°F oven 20 to 25 minutes or until golden. Serve with remaining 1½ cups salsa.

Makes 6 servings

Tip: ORTEGA® Salsas make great accompaniments for these authentic beef-filled pies. Prepare smaller empanadas and serve as appetizers to a Mexican meal.

Oven-Roasted Turkey Breast Fajitas

2 **teaspoons vegetable oil**
1 **medium onion, sliced**
1 **cup green or red bell pepper strips (or combination)**
4 **kosher flour tortillas (6 or 7 inches), warmed**
12 **ounces HEBREW NATIONAL® Sliced Oven Roasted Turkey Breast**
8 **thin slices ripe avocado**
¾ **cup prepared salsa**

Heat oil in small nonstick skillet over medium heat. Add onion and pepper strips; cook until tender. Fill each tortilla with 3 ounces turkey breast, ½ cup onion mixture, 2 slices avocado and 3 tablespoons salsa. Roll up tortilla; serve immediately.

Makes 4 servings

Tacos Picadillos

¾ **pound ground pork**
1 **medium onion, chopped**
½ **teaspoon ground cinnamon**
½ **teaspoon ground cumin**
1½ **cups DEL MONTE® Traditional Salsa**
⅓ **cup DEL MONTE® Seedless Raisins**
⅓ **cup toasted chopped almonds**
6 **flour tortillas**

1. Brown meat with onion and spices in large skillet over medium-high heat. Season to taste with salt and pepper, if desired.

2. Stir in salsa and raisins. Cover and cook 10 minutes. Remove cover; cook 5 minutes or until thickened, stirring occasionally.

3. Stir in almonds just before serving. Fill tortillas with meat mixture; roll to enclose. Serve with lettuce, cilantro and sour cream, if desired.

Makes 6 servings

Prep Time: 5 minutes
Cook Time: 25 minutes

Helpful Hint: If ground pork is not available, boneless pork may be purchased. Cut pork into 1-inch cubes before grinding in food processor.

Spicy Chicken Tostada

- 4 (7-inch) flour tortillas
  Nonstick cooking spray
- 1 tablespoon all-purpose flour
- 2 teaspoons chili powder
- ¼ teaspoon garlic powder
- ¼ teaspoon salt
- 12 chicken tenders (about 14 ounces)
- 1 tablespoon olive oil
- 2 cups shredded iceberg lettuce
- ½ cup (2 ounces) shredded Monterey Jack cheese
- 1 large tomato, diced
- 1 cup diced avocado
- ½ cup salsa

PREHEAT oven to 450°F. Spray both sides of tortillas with cooking spray. Arrange tortillas on large baking sheet. Bake 4 to 5 minutes or until crisp and light brown. Cool.

COMBINE flour, chili powder, garlic powder and salt on sheet of waxed paper. Lightly coat chicken tenders with flour mixture.

HEAT oil in large nonstick skillet over medium heat until hot. Add chicken; cook, turning once about 6 minutes or until browned and no longer pink in center.

PLACE tortillas on 4 plates. Top each with lettuce, 3 chicken tenders, cheese, tomato, avocado and salsa.

Makes 4 servings

Vegetable & Cheese Fajitas

- ¾ cup sliced onion
- 1 cup *each* sliced yellow and red bell peppers
- 1 cup zucchini strips
- 1 clove garlic, minced
- ¾ teaspoon minced jalapeño pepper
- ¾ teaspoon chili powder
  Salt (optional)
- 2 flour tortillas
- ¼ cup (1 ounce) JARLSBERG LITE™ Cheese

Coat medium skillet with nonstick cooking spray. Cook onion, bell peppers, zucchini, garlic and jalapeño, adding a little water if necessary, until soft. Add chili powder and salt to taste, if desired. Evenly divide vegetable mixture between tortillas. Sprinkle 2 tablespoons cheese on each tortilla and roll up.

Makes 2 servings

Spicy Chicken Tostada

Arroz con Pollo

4 slices bacon
1½ pounds (about 6) boneless skinless chicken breasts
1 cup chopped onion
1 cup chopped green bell pepper
2 large cloves garlic, finely chopped
2 cups uncooked long-grain white rice
2½ cups (24-ounce jar) ORTEGA® Garden Style Salsa, mild
1¾ cups chicken broth
1 cup (8-ounce can) CONTADINA® Tomato Sauce
1 teaspoon salt
½ teaspoon ground cumin
Chopped fresh parsley

COOK bacon in large saucepan over medium-high heat until crispy; remove from saucepan. Crumble bacon; set aside. Add chicken to saucepan; cook, turning frequently, 5 to 7 minutes or until golden on both sides. Remove from saucepan; keep warm. Discard all but 2 tablespoons drippings from saucepan.

ADD onion, bell pepper and garlic; cook 3 to 4 minutes or until crisp-tender. Add rice; cook 2 to 3 minutes. Stir in salsa, chicken broth, tomato sauce, salt and cumin. Bring to a boil. Place chicken over rice mixture; reduce heat to low. Cover; cook 20 to 25 minutes or until most of moisture is absorbed and chicken is no longer pink in center. Sprinkle with bacon and parsley.

Makes 4 to 6 servings

Chicken Fajitas

¼ cup orange juice
2 tablespoons lime juice
2 tablespoons lemon juice
1 clove garlic, minced
4 boneless skinless chicken breast halves
1 teaspoon chili powder
½ teaspoon salt
1 tablespoon vegetable oil
1 *each* red, green and yellow bell pepper, cut into strips
1 medium onion, sliced
10 flour tortillas, warmed
1 cup sour cream
1 cup salsa
1 can (2¼ ounces) sliced black olives, drained

Combine juices and garlic in large bowl. Season chicken with chili powder and salt. Place chicken in juice mixture, turning to coat. Cover; marinate in refrigerator 30 minutes. Remove chicken. Place marinade in small saucepan. Bring to a boil over medium-high heat; keep warm. Place chicken on broiler rack or grill about 6 inches from heat. Broil or grill, turning and basting with marinade, 10 minutes or until no longer pink in center. Heat oil in large skillet over medium-high heat until hot. Add peppers and onion; cook and stir about 5 minutes or until onion is tender. Slice chicken into strips; add to pepper-onion mixture. Divide chicken-pepper mixture evenly in centers of tortillas. Roll up tortillas; top each with dollop of sour cream, salsa and olives. *Makes 5 servings*

*FAVORITE RECIPE FROM **NATIONAL BROILER COUNCIL***

Turkey Tortilla Flats

4 (9-inch) flour tortillas
1 pound California-grown ground turkey
¼ pound mushrooms, very thinly sliced
⅓ cup tomato sauce
4 green onions, chopped
1 egg white
2 cloves fresh garlic, minced
½ teaspoon ground allspice
½ teaspoon dried oregano leaves
¼ teaspoon freshly ground black pepper
12 soft sun-dried tomato halves, cut into strips and soaked in water
¾ cup shredded Monterey Jack cheese
3 tablespoons shelled pistachio nuts

Place tortillas in single layer on 2 baking sheets. In large bowl, combine turkey, mushrooms, tomato sauce, green onions, egg white, garlic, allspice, oregano, pepper and tomato strips. Spoon mixture over tortillas, allowing ½-inch border around edge. Sprinkle with shredded cheese and nuts. Bake at 425°F 10 to 12 minutes or until tortillas are golden brown around edges and meat is cooked through.

Makes 4 servings

*FAVORITE RECIPE FROM **CALIFORNIA POULTRY INDUSTRY FEDERATION***

Arroz con Pollo

Beef & Bean Burritos

Nonstick cooking spray
½ pound beef round steak, cut into ½-inch pieces
3 cloves garlic, minced
1 can (about 15 ounces) pinto beans, rinsed and drained
1 can (4 ounces) diced mild green chilies, drained
¼ cup finely chopped cilantro
6 (6-inch) flour tortillas
½ cup (2 ounces) shredded reduced-fat Cheddar cheese

1. Spray nonstick skillet with cooking spray; heat over medium heat until hot. Add steak and garlic; cook and stir 5 minutes or until steak is cooked to desired doneness. Stir beans, chilies and cilantro into skillet; cook and stir 5 minutes or until heated through.

2. Spoon steak mixture evenly down center of each tortilla; sprinkle with cheese. Fold bottom end of tortilla over filling; roll to enclose. Garnish, if desired.   *Makes 6 servings*

Brazilian Corn and Shrimp Moqueca Casserole

2 tablespoons olive oil
½ cup chopped onion
¼ cup chopped green bell pepper
¼ cup tomato sauce
2 tablespoons chopped parsley
½ teaspoon TABASCO® pepper sauce
1 pound medium cooked shrimp
Salt to taste
2 tablespoons all-purpose flour
1 cup milk
1 can (16 ounces) cream-style corn
Grated Parmesan cheese

In large oven-proof skillet over medium-high heat, heat oil. Add onion, bell pepper, tomato sauce, parsley and TABASCO® sauce; cook, stirring occasionally, 5 minutes. Add shrimp and salt. Cover and reduce heat to low; simmer 2 to 3 minutes. Preheat oven to 375°F. Sprinkle flour over shrimp mixture; stir. Add milk gradually, stirring after each addition. Cook over medium heat until mixture thickens. Remove from heat. Pour corn over mixture; do not stir. Sprinkle with Parmesan cheese. Bake 30 minutes or until browned.   *Makes 4 servings*

West Indies Curried Drumsticks

12 broiler-fryer chicken drumsticks
¾ teaspoon salt, divided
½ teaspoon paprika
1 tablespoon cornstarch
1 tablespoon sugar
1 cup orange juice
2 cloves garlic, crushed
1½ teaspoons curry powder
1 teaspoon grated orange peel
½ teaspoon ground ginger
½ cup chopped cashews

Place chicken in large baking dish; sprinkle with ½ teaspoon salt and paprika. Bake in 375°F oven 30 minutes. Mix cornstarch and sugar in small saucepan. Stir in orange juice, garlic, curry powder, orange peel, ginger and remaining ¼ teaspoon salt. Cook and stir over medium heat until mixture boils and thickens. Pour sauce over chicken; bake, basting once with pan juices, about 25 minutes more or until chicken is fork-tender. Sprinkle cashews over chicken.

Makes 6 servings

*FAVORITE RECIPE FROM **DELMARVA POULTRY INDUSTRY, INC.***

Beef & Bean Burrito

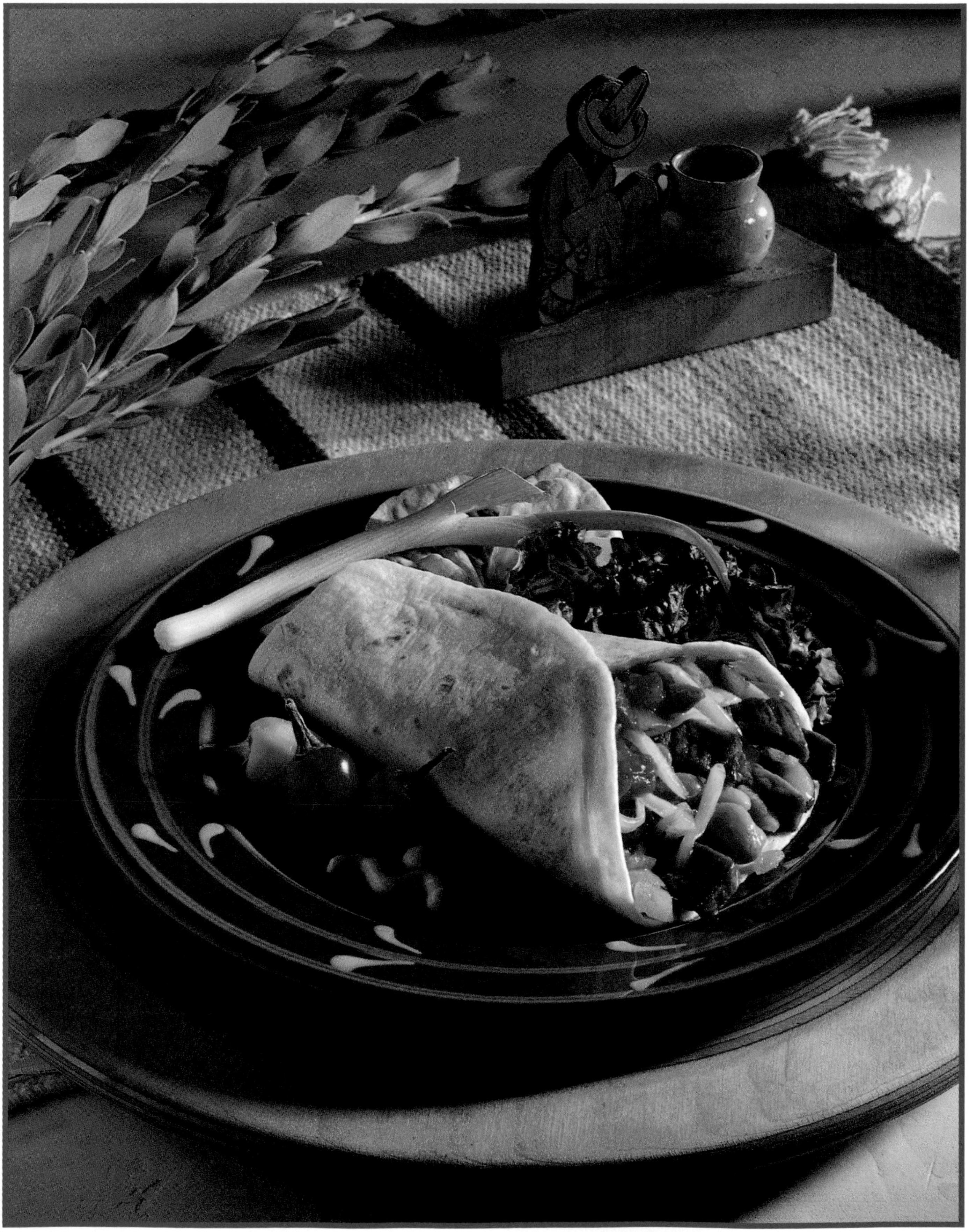

Turkish Chicken with Spiced Date Sauce

- 4 boneless skinless chicken breasts *or*
  1 pound turkey breast slices
  Vegetable cooking spray
- 1 cup low-sodium chicken broth
- 1 box (8 ounces) DOLE® Chopped Dates or Pitted Dates, chopped
- ½ cup chopped onion
- 2 tablespoons apricot or peach fruit spread
- ½ teaspoon ground cinnamon
  Hot cooked rice (optional)

• **PLACE** chicken in large skillet sprayed with vegetable cooking spray. Cook over medium heat about 5 minutes on each side (2 minutes on each side for turkey) or until chicken is no longer pink in center. Remove chicken from skillet; cover and keep warm.

• **ADD** chicken broth, dates and onion to skillet; bring to a boil, stirring occasionally. Reduce heat to low; cook 8 minutes or until liquid is reduced by half.

• **STIR** apricot spread and cinnamon into sauce until blended; spoon over chicken. Garnish with parsley, if desired. Serve with hot rice, if desired.

Makes 4 servings

Prep Time: 10 minutes
Cook Time: 20 minutes

Falafel

- ¾ cup sliced green onions
- ½ cup sliced celery
- 2 cloves garlic, minced
- 1 can (15 ounces) garbanzo beans, drained
- 1 can (15 ounces) pinto beans, rinsed and drained
- 1 egg
- 2 tablespoons flour
- 2 teaspoons lemon juice
- ½ teaspoon salt
- ½ teaspoon ground cumin
- ¼ teaspoon black pepper
- 2 cans (15 ounces each) whole tomatoes, drained and coarsely chopped
- ½ cup chopped cucumber
- 2 teaspoons sliced pitted ripe olives
- 1 cup plain nonfat yogurt
- ½ teaspoon dried mint leaves
- 4 pita breads, cut into halves

Heat small skillet; spray with nonstick cooking spray. Cook and stir onions, celery and garlic until tender; remove from heat. Process beans in food processor until smooth. Combine bean mixture, egg, flour, juice, salt, cumin and pepper in large bowl; stir in cooked vegetables. Form mixture into eight patties. Heat large skillet; spray with cooking spray. Cook patties over medium-low heat until lightly browned, about 5 minutes per side.

Combine tomatoes, cucumber and olives in small bowl. Combine yogurt and mint in separate small bowl. Serve falafel with pita breads; serve with tomato and yogurt mixtures. *Makes 8 servings*

*FAVORITE RECIPE FROM **CANNED FOOD INFORMATION COUNCIL***

Indian Vegetable Curry

- 2 to 3 teaspoons curry powder
- 1 can (16 ounces) sliced potatoes, drained
- 1 bag (16 ounces) BIRDS EYE® frozen Farm Fresh Mixtures Broccoli, Cauliflower and Carrots
- 1 can (15 ounces) chick-peas, drained
- 1 can (14½ ounces) stewed tomatoes
- 1 can (about 14 ounces) vegetable or chicken broth
- 2 tablespoons cornstarch

• Stir curry powder in large skillet over high heat until fragrant, about 30 seconds.

• Stir in potatoes, vegetables, chick-peas and tomatoes; bring to a boil. Reduce heat to medium-high; cover and cook 8 minutes.

• Blend vegetable broth with cornstarch; stir into vegetables. Cook until thickened.

Makes about 6 servings

Prep Time: 5 minutes
Cook Time: 15 minutes

Caribbean Jerk-Style Pork

¾ cup DOLE® Pineapple Juice or Pineapple Orange Juice, divided
1 tablespoon prepared yellow mustard
1 teaspoon dried thyme leaves
¼ teaspoon crushed red pepper
12 ounces pork loin chops or chicken breasts, cut into strips
Vegetable cooking spray
½ cup DOLE® Golden or Seedless Raisins
½ cup sliced DOLE® Green Onions
2 medium firm DOLE® Bananas, cut diagonally into ¼-inch slices
Hot cooked rice or noodles (optional)

• **STIR** ½ cup juice, mustard, thyme and red pepper in small bowl; set aside.

• **PLACE** pork in large nonstick skillet sprayed with vegetable cooking spray. Cook 3 to 5 minutes or until pork is no longer pink; remove from skillet.

• **ADD** remaining ¼ cup juice to skillet; stir in raisins and green onions. Cook and stir 1 minute.

• **RETURN** pork to skillet with reserved mustard mixture; cover and cook 2 minutes or until heated through. Stir in bananas. Serve over hot rice, if desired.   *Makes 4 servings*

Coq au Vin

2 slices bacon, cut into ½-inch pieces
1 chicken (3½ pounds), cut up
1 onion, coarsely chopped
1 cup mushrooms, cut into halves
1 red bell pepper, coarsely chopped
¾ cup red wine or dry white wine
1 cup chicken broth, divided
2 cloves garlic, minced
1 teaspoon dried thyme
¼ teaspoon black pepper
¼ cup all-purpose flour
Chopped parsley (optional)
Hot cooked noodles

COOK bacon in large skillet over medium heat until crisp. Remove and set aside. Add chicken to skillet; cook 10 minutes or until golden brown, turning occasionally.

ADD onion, mushrooms, bell pepper, wine, ¾ cup chicken broth, garlic, thyme and black pepper; bring to a boil. Reduce heat to low. Cover and simmer 25 minutes.

COMBINE remaining ¼ cup broth and flour; stir until smooth. Stir into skillet. Simmer, uncovered, 5 minutes or until thickened. Season to taste with salt and black pepper. Top with reserved bacon and parsley, if desired. Serve with noodles.

Makes 4 servings

Coq au Vin

Greek-Style Grilled Feta

- ¼ cup thinly sliced sweet onion
- 1 package (8 ounces) feta cheese, sliced horizontally
- ¼ cup thinly sliced green bell pepper
- ¼ cup thinly sliced red bell pepper
- ½ teaspoon dried oregano leaves
- ¼ teaspoon garlic pepper or ground black pepper
- 24 (½-inch) slices French bread

1. Spray 14-inch-long sheet of foil with nonstick cooking spray. Place onion slices in center of foil and top with feta slices. Sprinkle with bell pepper slices, oregano and garlic pepper.

2. Seal foil by bringing the 2 long sides together above the food; fold down in a series of locked folds. Fold the short ends up and over again. Press folds firmly to seal foil packet. Place foil packet on grid upside down and grill on covered grill over hot coals 15 minutes. Turn packet over; grill on covered grill 15 minutes more.

3. Open packet carefully and serve immediately with slices of French bread.

Makes 8 servings

Greek Lamb Braised with Vegetables

- ¼ cup FILIPPO BERIO® Olive Oil
- 2½ pounds lean boneless lamb, cut into 1½-inch cubes
- 1 cup chicken broth
- ½ cup dry white wine
- 2 medium carrots, diagonally cut into 1-inch pieces
- 2 ribs celery, diagonally cut into 1-inch pieces
- ½ medium bulb fennel, cut into ¼-inch-thick slices lengthwise through stem
- 1 (14-ounce) can artichoke hearts, drained and cut into quarters lengthwise
- 3 green onions, cut into 1½-inch pieces
  Salt and black pepper
- 8 ounces uncooked orzo pasta
  Chopped fresh parsley

In Dutch oven, heat olive oil over medium-high heat until hot. Add lamb; cook and stir 5 minutes or until lightly browned. Add chicken broth and wine; cover. Bring mixture to a boil. Reduce heat to low; simmer 1½ hours. Add carrots, celery, fennel, artichokes and green onions. Simmer 15 to 20 minutes or until lamb and vegetables are tender. Season to taste with salt and pepper. Meanwhile, cook orzo until *al dente*. Drain. Serve lamb mixture over orzo. Top with parsley.

Makes 6 servings

Paella a la Española

- 2 tablespoons margarine or butter
- 1¼ to 1½ pounds chicken thighs, skinned
- 1 package (7.2 ounces) RICE-A-RONI® Rice Pilaf
- 1 can (14½ or 16 ounces) tomatoes or stewed tomatoes, undrained
- ½ teaspoon turmeric (optional)
- ⅛ teaspoon hot pepper sauce or black pepper
- 8 ounces cooked deveined peeled medium shrimp
- 1 cup frozen peas
  Lemon wedges

1. In large skillet, melt margarine over medium heat. Add chicken; cook 2 minutes on each side or until browned. Remove from skillet; set aside, reserving drippings. Keep warm.

2. In same skillet, sauté rice pilaf mix in reserved drippings over medium heat until pasta is lightly browned. Stir in 1½ cups water, tomatoes, turmeric, if desired, pepper sauce and contents of seasoning packet. Bring to a boil over high heat; stir in chicken.

3. Cover; reduce heat. Simmer 20 minutes. Stir in shrimp and peas.

4. Cover; continue to simmer 5 to 10 minutes or until liquid is absorbed and rice is tender. Serve with lemon wedges.

Makes 4 servings

Greek-Style Grilled Feta

Chicken Tikka
(TANDOORI-STYLE GRILLED CHICKEN)

- 2 chickens (3 pounds each), cut up
- 1 pint nonfat yogurt
- ½ cup FRANK'S® Original REDHOT® Cayenne Pepper Sauce
- 1 tablespoon grated peeled fresh ginger
- 3 cloves garlic, minced
- 1 tablespoon paprika
- 1 tablespoon cumin seeds, crushed *or* 1½ teaspoons ground cumin
- 2 teaspoons salt
- 1 teaspoon ground coriander

Remove skin and visible fat from chicken pieces. Rinse with cold water and pat dry. Randomly poke chicken all over with tip of sharp knife. Place chicken in resealable plastic food storage bags or large glass bowl. Combine yogurt, RedHot® sauce, ginger, garlic, paprika, cumin, salt and coriander in small bowl; mix well. Pour over chicken pieces, turning pieces to coat evenly. Seal bags or cover bowl and marinate in refrigerator 1 hour or overnight.

Place chicken on oiled grid, reserving marinade. Grill over medium coals 45 minutes or until chicken is no longer pink near bone and juices run clear, turning and basting often with marinade. *Do not baste during last 10 minutes of cooking.* Discard any remaining marinade. Serve warm.

Makes 6 to 8 servings

Moroccan Brisket with Olives

- 2 first cut (about 2½ pounds each) *or* 1 whole HEBREW NATIONAL® Fresh Brisket (5 to 6 pounds), well trimmed
- ½ teaspoon salt
- ½ teaspoon freshly ground black pepper
- 2 tablespoons olive oil
- 2 large onions, chopped
- 1 carrot, peeled and thinly sliced
- 1 rib celery, chopped
- 3 cloves garlic, minced
- 1 can (16 ounces) stewed tomatoes, undrained
- 1 tablespoon lemon juice
- 2 teaspoons grated fresh ginger
- ¼ teaspoon crushed saffron *or* ½ teaspoon turmeric
- 1 cup kalamata olives, pitted and cut into halves
- 2 tablespoons packed light brown sugar

Heat oven to 325°F. Sprinkle brisket with salt and pepper. Heat oil in large skillet over medium-high heat. Add onions, carrot, celery and garlic; cook 8 minutes, stirring occasionally. Add tomatoes with liquid, lemon juice, ginger and saffron; bring to a boil. Spoon half of tomato mixture evenly into large roasting pan; top with brisket. Spoon remaining tomato mixture evenly over brisket. Cover; bake 3 to 3¼ hours or until brisket is fork-tender.

Transfer brisket to cutting board; tent with aluminum foil. Let stand 10 minutes. Skim fat from sauce; discard fat. Transfer sauce to medium saucepan; add olives and brown sugar. Cook over medium heat until thickened, stirring constantly. Slice brisket across the grain into ¼-inch-thick slices; transfer to serving platter. Spoon sauce over brisket.

Makes 12 servings

Chicken Tikka

Hot Sausages with Caponata

- 1 package (12 ounces) HEBREW NATIONAL® Beef Hot Sausage
- ¼ cup plus 2 tablespoons olive oil, divided
- 1 medium eggplant, peeled and cut into ½-inch pieces
- 1 large onion, chopped
- 3 cloves garlic, minced
- 1 can (14½ ounces) stewed tomatoes, undrained
- 2 tablespoons drained capers
- 2 tablespoons balsamic or red wine vinegar
- ¼ teaspoon red pepper flakes
- ¼ teaspoon salt
- ¼ cup chopped fresh basil

Cook sausage in large deep nonstick skillet over medium heat about 5 minutes or until browned. Transfer sausage to plate; set aside. Heat ¼ cup oil in same skillet; add eggplant. Cook over medium heat 5 minutes or until just tender. Transfer to bowl; set aside.

Heat remaining 2 tablespoons oil in same skillet over medium-high heat. Add onion and garlic; cook 5 minutes or until onion is tender. Add tomatoes and juice; reduce heat to medium and simmer 5 minutes. Stir in capers, reserved eggplant, vinegar, red pepper and salt. Cover; simmer 10 minutes, stirring occasionally.

Add reserved sausage to skillet. Simmer, uncovered, 10 minutes or until sauce thickens and sausage is heated through. Sprinkle with basil.

Makes 4 servings

Paella

- ¼ cup FILIPPO BERIO® Olive Oil
- 1 pound boneless skinless chicken breasts, cut into 1-inch strips
- ½ pound Italian sausage, cut into 1-inch slices
- 1 onion, chopped
- 3 cloves garlic, minced
- 2 cans (about 14 ounces each) chicken broth
- 2 cups uncooked long-grain white rice
- 1 (8-ounce) bottle clam juice
- 1 (2-ounce) jar chopped pimientos, drained
- 2 bay leaves
- 1 teaspoon salt
- ¼ teaspoon saffron threads, crumbled (optional)
- 1 pound raw shrimp, peeled and deveined
- 1 (16-ounce) can whole tomatoes, drained
- 1 (10-ounce) package frozen peas, thawed
- 12 littleneck clams, scrubbed
- ¼ cup water
  Fresh herb sprig (optional)

Preheat oven to 350°F. In large skillet, heat olive oil over medium heat until hot. Add chicken; cook and stir 8 to 10 minutes or until brown on all sides. Remove with slotted spoon; set aside. Add sausage to skillet; cook and stir 8 to 10 minutes or until brown. Remove with slotted spoon; set aside. Add onion and garlic to skillet; cook and stir 5 to 7 minutes or until onion is tender. Transfer chicken, sausage, onion and garlic to large casserole.

Add chicken broth, rice, clam juice, pimientos, bay leaves, salt and saffron, if desired, to chicken mixture. Cover; bake 30 minutes. Add shrimp, tomatoes and peas; stir well. Cover; bake an additional 15 minutes or until rice is tender, liquid is absorbed and shrimp are opaque. Remove bay leaves.

Meanwhile, combine clams and water in stockpot or large saucepan. Cover; cook over medium heat 5 to 10 minutes or until clams open; remove clams immediately as they open. Discard any clams with unopened shells. Place clams on top of paella. Garnish with herb sprig, if desired.

Makes 4 to 6 servings

Paella

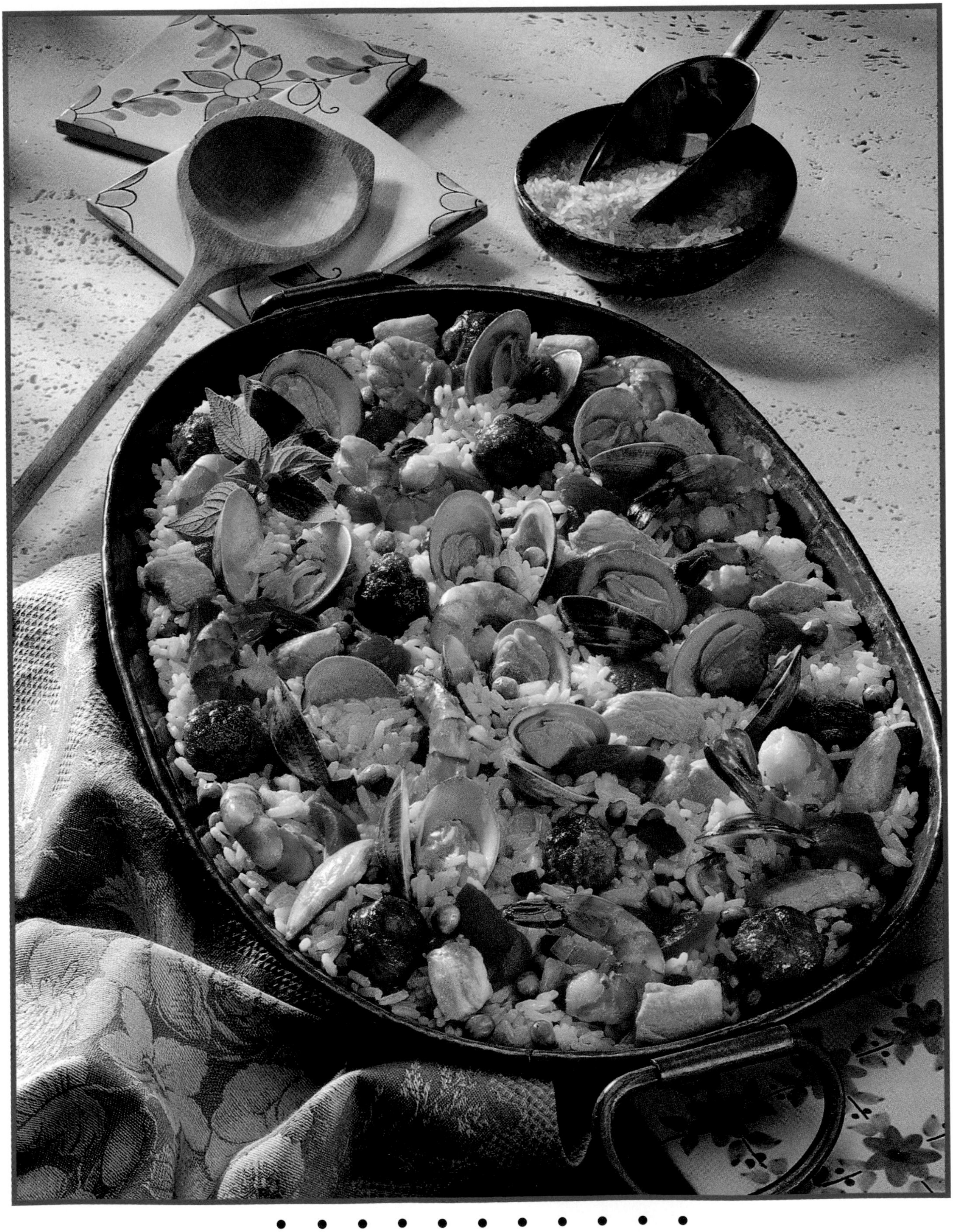

Milanese Chicken & Rice Skillet

- 1 pound boneless skinless chicken breasts, thinly sliced
- 2 tablespoons olive or vegetable oil
- 1 cup sliced green onions
- ¼ cup *each* chopped green and red bell pepper
- 2 to 3 cloves garlic, minced
- 1 teaspoon dried oregano leaves
- 1 can (14½-ounce) diced tomatoes, undrained
- 1 can (about 14 ounces) chicken broth
- ¼ teaspoon black pepper
- 1 cup FARMHOUSE® Natural Long Grain White Rice
- ½ cup small pitted ripe olives
- ⅓ cup frozen peas, thawed
- ¼ cup grated Parmesan cheese
- 2 tablespoons chopped fresh basil *or* 2 teaspoons dried basil leaves
- 2 tablespoons chopped fresh parsley *or* 2 teaspoons dried parsley flakes

In large skillet, sauté chicken in oil until no longer pink in center. Add green onions, bell peppers, garlic and oregano; stir to coat. Add tomatoes, chicken broth and black pepper; bring to a boil. Stir in rice. Cover; reduce heat and cook 20 minutes or until most of the liquid is absorbed. Stir in olives, peas, cheese, basil and parsley.
Makes 4 servings (8 cups)

Chicken Milano

- 2 cloves garlic, minced
- 2 boneless skinless chicken breasts, halved (about 1¼ pounds)
- ½ teaspoon dried basil leaves
- ⅛ teaspoon red pepper flakes (optional)
- Salt and black pepper
- 1 tablespoon olive oil
- 1 can (14½ ounces) DEL MONTE® *FreshCut*™ Diced Tomatoes with Basil, Garlic & Oregano, undrained
- 1 can (14½ ounces) DEL MONTE® *FreshCut*™ Cut Green Italian Beans or Blue Lake Cut Green Beans, drained
- ¼ cup whipping cream

1. Rub garlic over chicken. Sprinkle with basil and red pepper, if desired. Season with salt and black pepper.

2. Brown chicken in oil in skillet over medium-high heat. Stir in tomatoes.

3. Cover; simmer 5 minutes. Uncover; reduce heat to medium and cook 8 to 10 minutes or until liquid is slightly thickened and chicken is tender.

4. Stir in green beans and cream; heat through. *Do not boil.* *Makes 4 servings*

Prep & Cook Time: 25 minutes

Vesuvio Roasted Chicken and Potatoes

- 1 GALIL® Chicken (about 3¾ pounds)
- ⅓ cup olive oil
- 2 tablespoons fresh lemon juice
- 4 cloves garlic, minced
- 3 large baking potatoes, peeled and cut into quarters lengthwise
- Salt
- Freshly ground black pepper

Preheat oven to 375°F. Place chicken, breast side down, on rack in oiled large shallow roasting pan. Combine oil, lemon juice and garlic in small bowl; brush over chicken. Set aside remaining oil mixture. Bake chicken 30 minutes.

Turn chicken breast side up. Add potatoes to roasting pan. Brush chicken and potatoes with remaining oil mixture; sprinkle with salt and pepper to taste. Bake about 50 minutes or until internal temperature of chicken reaches 180°F on meat thermometer inserted into thickest part of thigh and potatoes are browned and tender. Baste with pan juices every 20 minutes of baking time. Transfer chicken to cutting board; tent with aluminum foil. Let stand 5 to 10 minutes before serving.
Makes 4 to 6 servings

Mediterranean Stew

1 medium butternut or acorn squash, peeled and cut into 1-inch cubes
2 cups unpeeled 1-inch eggplant cubes
2 cups sliced zucchini
1 can (15½ ounces) chick-peas (garbanzo beans), rinsed and drained
1 package (10 ounces) frozen cut okra
1 can (8 ounces) tomato sauce
1 cup chopped onion
1 medium tomato, chopped
1 medium carrot, thinly sliced
½ cup reduced-sodium vegetable broth
⅓ cup raisins
1 clove garlic, minced
½ teaspoon ground cumin
½ teaspoon ground turmeric
¼ to ½ teaspoon ground red pepper
¼ teaspoon ground cinnamon
¼ teaspoon paprika
6 to 8 cups hot cooked couscous or rice
Fresh parsley (optional)

Slow Cooker Directions: COMBINE all ingredients except couscous and parsley in slow cooker; mix well. Cover and cook on LOW 8 to 10 hours or until vegetables are crisp-tender. Serve over couscous. Garnish with parsley, if desired.
Makes 6 servings

Main Dish Moroccan Rice

½ cup chopped onion
1 tablespoon olive oil
2 cups uncooked brown rice
4 cups chicken broth
3 cups mushroom slices
1 cup sliced carrots
1½ teaspoons grated orange peel
¼ to ½ teaspoon ground cinnamon
⅛ teaspoon white pepper
2 cups red or green California seedless grapes
1 tablespoon chopped parsley

Cook and stir onion in oil in large skillet until tender; stir in rice and cook 2 minutes. Add chicken broth, mushrooms, carrots, orange peel, cinnamon and pepper. Cover; simmer 40 minutes. Stir in grapes and parsley; cover and simmer 5 minutes or until rice is tender. *Makes 4 servings*

*FAVORITE RECIPE FROM **CALIFORNIA TABLE GRAPE COMMISSION***

Mediterranean Stew

Side Dishes

FEATURING:

Vegetable Gratins

Potato Dishes

Rice & Beans

Ratatouille Stuffed Zucchini (page 338)

337

Sautéed Pickle Spears

- **3 tablespoons all-purpose flour**
- **½ cup seasoned dry bread crumbs**
- **4 HEBREW NATIONAL® Kosher Pickles, drained and quartered lengthwise** *or* **12 Kosher Pickle Spears, well drained**
- **2 eggs, beaten**
- **¼ cup vegetable oil, olive oil or garlic-flavored olive oil**
- **Ketchup or HEBREW NATIONAL® Deli Mustard**

Place flour on small plate. Place bread crumbs on another small plate. Coat each pickle spear with flour. Dip into egg; roll in bread crumbs.* Set aside.

Heat oil in large nonstick skillet over medium heat. Line large plate with paper towels. Add 4 pickle spears at a time to hot oil. Cook 1 to 2 minutes each side or until golden brown. Remove to prepared plate. Repeat with remaining pickle spears. Serve warm or at room temperature with ketchup or mustard for dipping.

Makes 12 servings

*Breaded pickles may be covered and refrigerated up to 2 hours before cooking.

Ratatouille Stuffed Zucchini

- **2 medium zucchini**
- **½ cup chopped onion**
- **1 clove garlic, minced**
- **1 tablespoon margarine, divided**
- **½ cup chopped green bell pepper**
- **½ cup chopped peeled eggplant**
- **½ cup chopped tomato**
- **¼ cup EGG BEATERS® Healthy Egg Substitute**
- **1 teaspoon dried basil leaves**
- **19 low-salt round buttery crackers, divided**
- **1 tablespoon grated Parmesan cheese**

Halve each zucchini lengthwise; scoop out center portions, leaving ¼-inch shell. Chop 1 cup scooped out zucchini filling; reserve.

In large nonstick skillet, over medium heat, sauté onion and garlic in 2 teaspoons margarine until tender. Stir in bell pepper, eggplant, tomato and reserved chopped zucchini; cook until tender-crisp, about 5 minutes. Remove from heat; stir in Egg Beaters® and basil.

Coarsely break 15 crackers; stir into vegetable mixture. Spoon vegetable mixture into zucchini shells. Place zucchini shells in 12×8×2-inch baking dish.

Melt remaining 1 teaspoon margarine. Crush remaining crackers; in small bowl, toss with melted margarine until well coated. Stir in cheese; sprinkle over vegetable mixture. Bake at 375°F for 20 to 25 minutes or until hot.

Makes 4 servings

Prep Time: 25 minutes
Cook Time: 35 minutes

Welsh Rarebit

- **½ cup HELLMANN'S® or BEST FOODS® Real or Light Mayonnaise or Low Fat Mayonnaise Dressing**
- **3 tablespoons flour**
- **½ teaspoon dry mustard**
- **½ teaspoon Worcestershire sauce**
- **¾ cup beer**
- **2 cups (8 ounces) shredded Cheddar cheese**
- **8 slices white or whole wheat bread, toasted, halved diagonally**
- **3 large tomatoes, cut into 16 slices**

1. In 2-quart saucepan, combine mayonnaise, flour, dry mustard and Worcestershire sauce. Stirring constantly, cook over low heat 1 minute.

2. Gradually stir in beer until thick and smooth *(do not boil)*. Stir in cheese until melted.

3. Arrange 4 toast halves and 4 tomato slices alternately on each of 4 serving plates; spoon on cheese sauce. Serve immediately.

Makes 4 servings

Top to bottom: Bagel Dogs with Zesty BBQ Sauce (page 391) and Sautéed Pickle Spears

Oven-Fried Tex-Mex Onion Rings

½ cup plain dry bread crumbs
⅓ cup yellow cornmeal
1½ teaspoons chili powder
⅛ to ¼ teaspoon ground red pepper
⅛ teaspoon salt
1 tablespoon plus 1½ teaspoons margarine, melted
2 medium onions (about 10 ounces), sliced ⅜ inch thick
2 egg whites

1. Preheat oven to 450°F. Spray large nonstick baking sheet with nonstick cooking spray; set aside.

2. Combine bread crumbs, cornmeal, chili powder, pepper and salt in medium shallow dish; mix well. Stir in margarine and 1 teaspoon water.

3. Separate onion slices into rings. Place egg whites in large bowl; beat lightly. Add onions; toss lightly to coat evenly. Transfer to bread crumb mixture; toss to coat evenly. Place in single layer on prepared baking sheet.

4. Bake 12 to 15 minutes or until onions are tender and coating is crisp.

Makes 6 servings

Vegetable Sauté

2 tablespoons FILIPPO BERIO® Olive Oil
2 yellow squash, trimmed and cut into 1-inch chunks
1 medium onion, sliced
4 baby eggplants, trimmed and cut into halves lengthwise
1 medium yellow bell pepper, cut into ¼-inch strips
8 baby carrots, peeled and trimmed
8 cherry tomatoes, cut into halves
1 tablespoon chopped garlic
1 tablespoon chopped fresh thyme*
½ cup coarsely chopped fresh basil*
　Salt and freshly ground black pepper
　Fresh thyme sprig (optional)

Omit herbs if fresh herbs are unavailable. Do not substitute dried herb leaves.

In large heavy skillet, heat olive oil over medium-high heat until hot. Add squash, onion, eggplants, bell pepper and carrots. Cook, stirring constantly, 5 minutes. Add tomatoes, garlic and thyme. Cook, stirring constantly, 3 minutes or until vegetables are tender-crisp. Stir in basil. Season to taste with salt and black pepper. Garnish with thyme sprig, if desired.

Makes 6 servings

Mexican Cheese Fritters

1 cup reduced-fat biscuit mix
1 cup cornmeal
1½ cups low-fat buttermilk
1 cup (4 ounces) shredded JARLSBERG LITE™ Cheese
1 can (4 ounces) diced green chilies
2 cups frozen corn, thawed
½ to 1 teaspoon ground cumin
¼ to ½ teaspoon ground red pepper
　Prepared enchilada sauce, fresh or jarred green or red salsa and additional JARLSBERG LITE™ Cheese

Combine all ingredients except enchilada sauce, salsa and additional cheese; let stand ½ hour. On hot nonstick griddle, brushed with oil, drop batter by tablespoonfuls to make 2-inch fritters. Turn fritters when edges look dry. Serve with enchilada sauce, salsa and additional cheese.

Makes 8 to 10 servings

Oven-Fried Tex-Mex Onion Rings

Escalloped Corn

2 tablespoons butter or
   margarine
½ cup chopped onion
3 tablespoons all-purpose
   flour
1 cup milk
4 cups frozen corn,
   thawed, divided
½ teaspoon salt
½ teaspoon dried thyme
   leaves
¼ teaspoon black pepper
⅛ teaspoon ground
   nutmeg
   Fresh thyme (optional)

Slow Cooker Directions:
HEAT butter in small saucepan over medium heat. Add onion; cook and stir 5 minutes or until tender. Add flour. Cook over medium heat 1 minute, stirring constantly. Stir in milk and heat to a boil. Boil 1 minute or until thickened, stirring constantly.

PROCESS half the corn in food processor or blender until coarsely chopped. Combine milk mixture, processed and whole corn, salt, dried thyme, pepper and nutmeg in slow cooker. Cover and cook on LOW 3½ to 4 hours or until mixture is bubbly around edge. Garnish with fresh thyme, if desired.   *Makes 6 servings*

Variation: If desired, add ½ cup (2 ounces) shredded Cheddar cheese and 2 tablespoons grated Parmesan cheese before serving; stir until melted. Garnish with additional shredded Cheddar cheese, if desired.

Spicy Corn Pudding

¼ cup all-purpose flour
½ teaspoon baking powder
4 egg whites
2 whole eggs
2 packages (9 ounces
   each) frozen corn,
   thawed and well
   drained
1¼ cups half-and-half
1 cup milk
4 tablespoons FRANK'S®
   Original REDHOT®
   Cayenne Pepper Sauce
1 cup (4 ounces) shredded
   Cheddar cheese

1. Preheat oven to 325°F. Combine flour and baking powder in small bowl. Beat egg whites and eggs in large bowl until foamy. Gradually whisk in flour mixture until smooth. Stir in corn, half-and-half, milk and RedHot® sauce.

2. Pour mixture into greased 12×8-inch baking dish. Set dish in larger shallow roasting pan. Fill roasting pan halfway with water. Bake, uncovered, 1 hour or until knife inserted near center comes out clean. Sprinkle with cheese during last 5 minutes of baking.

3. Transfer pudding from roasting pan to wire rack; let stand 15 minutes before serving.
   Makes 8 side-dish servings

Prep Time: 15 minutes
Cook Time: 1 hour

Iowa Corn Pudding

½ cup egg substitute *or*
   2 large eggs
2 large egg whites
3 tablespoons all-purpose
   flour
1 tablespoon sugar
½ teaspoon freshly ground
   black pepper
1 can (16½ ounces)
   cream-style corn
2 cups fresh corn kernels
   or frozen corn, thawed
   and drained
1 cup (4 ounces) shredded
   ALPINE LACE®
   American Flavor
   Pasteurized Process
   Cheese Product
½ cup finely chopped red
   bell pepper
⅓ cup 2% low-fat milk
1 tablespoon unsalted
   butter substitute
¼ teaspoon paprika
   Sprigs of fresh parsley

1. Preheat the oven to 350°F. Spray an 8-inch round baking dish with nonstick cooking spray. (A deep-dish pie plate works well.) Place in the oven to heat.

2. Meanwhile, in a large bowl, using an electric mixer set on high, beat the egg substitute (or the whole eggs) and egg whites with the flour, sugar and black pepper until smooth. Stir in the creamed corn, corn kernels, cheese, bell pepper and milk. Pour into the hot baking dish.

3. Dot with the butter and sprinkle with the paprika. Bake, uncovered, for 55 minutes or until set. Let stand for 15 minutes before serving. Garnish with the parsley.

Makes 6 servings

Orange-Spice Glazed Carrots

1 package (32 ounces) baby carrots
½ cup packed brown sugar
½ cup orange juice
3 tablespoons butter or margarine
¾ teaspoon ground cinnamon
¼ teaspoon ground nutmeg
2 tablespoons cornstarch
¼ cup water

Slow Cooker Directions: COMBINE all ingredients except cornstarch and water in slow cooker. Cover and cook on LOW 3½ to 4 hours or until carrots are crisp-tender. Spoon carrots into serving bowl. Remove juices to small saucepan. Heat to a boil. Mix cornstarch and water in small bowl until blended. Stir into saucepan. Boil 1 minute or until thickened; stir constantly. Pour over carrots.

Makes 6 servings

Hot & Spicy Glazed Carrots

2 tablespoons vegetable oil
2 dried red chili peppers
1 pound carrots, peeled and cut diagonally into ⅛-inch slices
¼ cup KIKKOMAN® Teriyaki Baste & Glaze

Heat oil in hot wok or large skillet over high heat. Add peppers and stir-fry until darkened; remove and discard. Add carrots; reduce heat to medium. Stir-fry 4 minutes or until tender-crisp. Stir in teriyaki baste & glaze and cook until carrots are glazed. Serve immediately.

Makes 4 servings

Iowa Corn Pudding (page 342)

Apricot-Glazed Beets

- 1 large bunch fresh beets *or* 1 pound loose beets
- 1 cup apricot nectar
- 1 tablespoon cornstarch
- 2 tablespoons cider vinegar or red wine vinegar
- 8 dried apricot halves, cut into strips
- ¼ teaspoon salt
  Additional apricot halves (optional)

Cut tops off beets, leaving at least 1 inch of stems (do not trim root ends). Scrub beets under running water with soft vegetable brush, being careful not to break skins. Place beets in medium saucepan; cover with water. Cover. Bring to a boil over high heat; reduce heat to medium. Simmer beets about 20 minutes or until just barely firm when pierced with fork and skins rub off easily. (Larger beets will take longer to cook.) Transfer to plate; cool. Rinse pan.

Combine apricot nectar and cornstarch in same saucepan; stir in vinegar. Add apricot strips and salt. Cook over medium heat until mixture thickens.

Cut roots and stems from beets on plate.* Peel, halve and cut beets into ¼-inch-thick slices. Add beet slices to apricot mixture; toss gently to coat.

Transfer to warm serving dish. Garnish as desired. Serve immediately with additional apricot halves, if desired.

Makes 4 side-dish servings

*Do not cut beets on cutting board; the juice will stain the board.

Baked Spiced Squash

- 2 boxes (12 ounces each) BIRDS EYE® frozen Cooked Winter Squash, thawed
- 2 egg whites, lightly beaten
- ¼ cup brown sugar
- 2 teaspoons butter or margarine, melted
- 1 teaspoon cinnamon
- ½ cup herbed croutons, coarsely crushed

• Preheat oven to 400°F. Combine squash, egg whites, sugar, butter and cinnamon; mix well.

• Pour into 1-quart baking dish sprayed with nonstick cooking spray.

• Bake 20 to 25 minutes or until center is set.

• Remove from oven; sprinkle crushed croutons on top. Bake 5 to 7 minutes longer or until croutons are browned.

Makes 6 to 8 servings

Prep Time: 5 minutes
Cook Time: 25 to 35 minutes

Spaghetti Squash with Black Beans & Zucchini

- 1 spaghetti squash (about 3 pounds), cut into halves
- 1 can (16 ounces) zucchini with Italian-style tomato juice
- 1 can (15 ounces) black beans, rinsed and drained
- 2 large cloves garlic, minced

Place squash, cut sides down, in baking dish; add ½ inch water. Bake at 350°F until just tender when pierced with fork, about 30 minutes. Place squash on serving plate; fluff squash strands with fork.

During last 10 minutes of baking, heat zucchini, beans and garlic in medium saucepan. Spoon into squash; toss.

Makes 8 servings

*FAVORITE RECIPE FROM **CANNED FOOD INFORMATION COUNCIL***

Baked Spiced Squash

Green 'n' White Vegetables au Gratin

VEGETABLES
  ¼ **teaspoon salt**
  2 pounds fresh broccoli, separated into florets and trimmed
  1 medium-size head cauliflower, separated into florets and trimmed (about 2 pounds)

AU GRATIN SAUCE
  1½ **cups 2% low-fat milk**
  2 tablespoons all-purpose flour
  1 teaspoon Worcestershire sauce
  ¼ **teaspoon crushed red pepper flakes**
  ⅛ **teaspoon ground nutmeg**
  2 cups (8 ounces) shredded ALPINE LACE® Reduced Fat Cheddar Cheese

1. To prepare the Vegetables: Half-fill a large saucepan with water, add the salt and bring to a boil over high heat.

2. Add the broccoli and cook, uncovered, for 10 minutes or until tender. Using a slotted spoon, transfer the broccoli to a colander to drain. Arrange the broccoli around the edge of a large round platter and keep warm.

3. To the same boiling water, add the cauliflower florets and cook, uncovered, for 8 minutes or until tender. Drain and arrange the cauliflower in the center of the platter.

4. While the vegetables cook, make the Au Gratin Sauce: In a medium-size saucepan, combine the milk, flour, Worcestershire, red pepper flakes and nutmeg. Bring to a boil, stirring constantly, over medium-high heat.

5. Reduce the heat to medium and stir until thickened. Then add the cheese and stir until melted. Drizzle the sauce over the vegetables and serve immediately.

Makes 6 servings

Green Beans and Tomatoes Provençal

  1 pound fresh green beans, trimmed
  ¼ **cup FILIPPO BERIO® Olive Oil**
  1 clove garlic, crushed Salt and black pepper
  3 shallots, sliced
  3 tomatoes, cored and cut crosswise in half
  ¼ **cup dry bread crumbs**
  2 tablespoons chopped fresh Italian parsley
  1 tablespoon chopped fresh thyme *or* 1 teaspoon dried thyme leaves Additional fresh Italian parsley (optional)

Preheat oven to 400°F. Steam green beans 6 minutes; place in 13×9-inch dish. In small bowl, combine olive oil and garlic; drizzle 1 tablespoon olive oil mixture over beans. Season to taste with salt and pepper.

In large nonstick skillet, heat remaining olive oil mixture over medium heat until hot. Add shallots; cook and stir 2 minutes. Add tomatoes; cook 1 minute, turning halfway through cooking time.

Place tomatoes, cut side up, and shallots on top of beans. In small bowl, combine bread crumbs, 2 tablespoons parsley and thyme. Sprinkle over top of tomatoes and beans. Drizzle with oil remaining in skillet. Bake 15 to 20 minutes or until golden brown. Garnish with additional parsley, if desired.

Makes 6 servings

Grilled Country Dijon Vegetables

  ⅓ **cup GREY POUPON® COUNTRY DIJON® Mustard**
  ⅓ **cup olive oil**
  ¼ **cup balsamic vinegar**
  ¼ **cup chopped parsley**
  2 tablespoons chopped chives
  1 tablespoon minced garlic
  4 baby eggplants
  2 Spanish onions
  2 medium zucchini
  2 medium yellow squash
  2 roasted red peppers, cut into strips

In bowl, whisk mustard, oil, vinegar, parsley, chives and garlic until blended; set aside.

Cut each eggplant and onion crosswise into 4 slices; cut zucchini and yellow squash into 8 slices each.

Grill vegetables, basting with ¾ cup mustard mixture. Grill onions about 6 to 8 minutes and remaining vegetables 2 to 3 minutes. To serve, arrange vegetables on serving platter; top with pepper strips and drizzle with remaining mustard mixture.

Makes 6 to 8 servings

Stuffed Tomatoes

**4 large firm tomatoes
1 cup EGG BEATERS®
    Healthy Egg Substitute
½ teaspoon dried dill
    weed, crumbled
4 teaspoons bread crumbs**

Microwave Directions:
Cut tops off tomatoes; scoop out and reserve pulp. Chop ⅓ cup pulp; set aside. Discard any remaining pulp.

In lightly greased 1½-quart microwavable bowl, beat together Egg Beaters® and dill; cover. Microwave at HIGH 2 to 3 minutes or until set but slightly moist, stirring lightly after 1½ minutes. Stir in chopped tomato pulp.

Arrange tomatoes in 9-inch microwavable pie plate; spoon 1 teaspoon bread crumbs into each tomato. Divide egg mixture evenly among tomatoes; cover. Microwave at HIGH 2 to 3 minutes or until heated through, rotating dish after 1 minute. Serve immediately.

Makes 4 servings

Creamed Spinach

**3 cups water
2 bags (10 ounces each)
    fresh spinach, washed,
    stems removed and
    chopped
2 teaspoons margarine
2 tablespoons all-purpose
    flour
1 cup skim milk
2 tablespoons grated
    Parmesan cheese
⅛ teaspoon ground white
    pepper
Ground nutmeg**

1. Bring water to a boil; add spinach. Reduce heat and simmer, covered, about 5 minutes or until spinach is wilted. Drain well. Set aside.

2. Melt margarine in small saucepan; stir in flour and cook over medium-low heat 1 minute, stirring constantly. Using wire whisk, stir in milk; bring to a boil. Cook, whisking constantly, 1 to 2 minutes or until mixture thickens. Stir in cheese and pepper.

3. Stir spinach into sauce; heat thoroughly. Spoon into serving bowl; sprinkle lightly with nutmeg. Garnish as desired.

Makes 4 servings

Blazing Veggie Medley

**1 (12-ounce) package
    rotini or corkscrew
    pasta
2 tablespoons olive oil
2 small yellow squash
    (6 ounces each),
    sliced
2 small zucchini
    (6 ounces each),
    sliced
1 small eggplant
    (1 pound), cut into
    ½-inch pieces
1 medium onion, sliced
1 medium green bell
    pepper, seeded and
    sliced
1 (8-ounce) package fresh
    mushrooms, sliced
1 (26-ounce) jar
    NEWMAN'S OWN®
    Diavolo Sauce
Grated Parmesan
    cheese (optional)**

Prepare pasta according to package directions. Drain; keep warm. Meanwhile, heat olive oil in 12-inch skillet over medium-high heat. Add vegetables; cook until lightly browned and tender, about 15 minutes, stirring often.

Stir in Newman's Own® Diavolo Sauce; heat to boiling. Reduce heat to low; cover and simmer 10 minutes to blend flavors. Spoon sauce over pasta on warm large platter; toss to serve. Serve with grated Parmesan cheese, if desired.

Makes 4 servings

Cheesy Mushroom au Gratin

- 3 tablespoons Wisconsin butter, divided
- ¼ cup all-purpose flour
- 3 cups hot, not scalded, milk
- ½ cup (2 ounces) shredded Wisconsin Colby cheese
- ½ cup (2 ounces) shredded Wisconsin Muenster cheese
- ¾ teaspoon salt
- ¾ teaspoon hot pepper sauce
- ¼ teaspoon ground nutmeg
- 8 ounces sliced fresh mushrooms
- 6 ounces sliced shiitake mushrooms
- ½ cup sliced green onions
- 1 ½ teaspoons dried fines herbes, crumbled *or* ½ teaspoon *each:* dried parsley flakes, dried chervil leaves, dried tarragon leaves, freeze-dried chives
- 12 slices bread, toasted
- ¼ cup plus 2 tablespoons grated Wisconsin Asiago cheese
  Cooked asparagus tips for garnish
  Additional shredded Wisconsin cheese for garnish

1. In large skillet, melt 2 tablespoons butter; whisk in flour. Cook on low heat 3 to 4 minutes. Slowly whisk in hot milk, stirring well. Bring sauce to a boil; reduce heat and simmer 5 to 6 minutes, stirring occasionally.

2. Stir in Colby and Muenster until melted. Season cheese sauce with salt, hot pepper sauce and nutmeg; set aside.

3. In separate large skillet, melt remaining 1 tablespoon butter; add mushrooms, green onions and fines herbes. Cook on medium-high heat until mushrooms are golden brown, 10 to 12 minutes. Stir mushroom mixture into cheese sauce.

4. Lightly butter six individual shallow ramekins or single-serving casserole dishes. Place 2 slices toasted bread in each dish; top with ½ cup mushroom sauce and sprinkle with 1 tablespoon Asiago. Bake in preheated 400°F oven 8 to 10 minutes or until browned and bubbly.

5. To serve, top with asparagus and additional shredded cheese. *Makes 6 servings*

FAVORITE RECIPE FROM **WISCONSIN MILK MARKETING BOARD**

Tangy Asparagus Linguini

- 2 tablespoons light margarine
- ¼ cup finely chopped onion
- 3 cloves garlic, minced
- 8 ounces fresh asparagus, peeled and sliced diagonally into ½-inch pieces
- 2 tablespoons dry white wine
- 2 tablespoons fresh lemon juice
  Freshly ground black pepper
- 5 ounces linguini, cooked and drained
- ¼ cup (1 ounce) SARGENTO® Grated Parmesan Cheese
- ¾ cup (3 ounces) SARGENTO® Preferred Light® Fancy Shredded Mozzarella Cheese

Melt margarine over medium heat in large skillet. Cook and stir onion and garlic until onion is soft. Add asparagus; cook and stir an additional 2 minutes. Add wine and lemon juice; cook an additional minute. Season with pepper to taste. Remove from heat. In large bowl, toss hot pasta, Parmesan cheese and asparagus mixture. Remove to serving platter; sprinkle with mozzarella cheese. Garnish, if desired. Serve immediately.

Makes 4 servings

Crumb-Topped Snowball

- **1 large head cauliflower (about 1¼ pounds)**
- **¼ cup butter or margarine**
- **1 cup fresh bread crumbs (about 2 slices)**
- **2 green onions, thinly sliced**
- **2 eggs, hard cooked and finely chopped**
- **2 tablespoons lemon juice**

Remove and discard leaves and stem from cauliflower. Cut around core with paring knife, being careful not to separate florets from head; remove and discard core. Rinse.

Pour 1 inch of water into large saucepan. Place cauliflower in water, stem side down; cover. Bring to a boil over high heat; reduce heat to low. Simmer 10 to 12 minutes or until crisp-tender; drain. Place cauliflower in 8-inch square baking dish. Preheat oven to 375°F. Melt butter over medium heat in small skillet. Stir in bread crumbs and onions; cook until crumbs are lightly browned. Stir in eggs and lemon juice. Press crumb mixture evenly over top of cauliflower. Place any extra crumb mixture in baking dish. Bake 10 minutes or until crumb mixture is crispy and lightly browned. Garnish, if desired. Serve immediately.

Makes 6 side-dish servings

Fresh Vegetable Basil Medley

- **3 small zucchini**
- **3 small yellow squash**
- **2 medium carrots**
- **4 teaspoons vegetable oil**
- **2 teaspoons dried basil leaves**
- **Fresh basil leaves (optional)**

Cut vegetables into julienned strips. Heat oil in large skillet over medium-high heat. Add carrots; cook 1 minute. Add zucchini, squash and dried basil; cook and stir until vegetables are crisp-tender. Garnish with fresh basil, if desired. Serve hot. Refrigerate leftovers.

Makes 4 to 6 side-dish servings

FAVORITE RECIPE FROM **BOB EVANS FARMS**®

Fresh Vegetable Basil Medley

Harvest Vegetable Scallop

**4 carrots, thinly sliced
1 package (10 ounces) frozen chopped broccoli, thawed and drained
1 can (2.8 ounces) FRENCH'S® French Fried Onions, divided
5 small red potatoes, sliced ⅛ inch thick
1 jar (8 ounces) pasteurized processed cheese spread
¼ cup milk
Ground black pepper
Seasoned salt**

Preheat oven to 375°F. In 12×8-inch baking dish, combine carrots, broccoli and *½ can* French Fried Onions. Tuck potato slices into vegetable mixture at an angle. Dot vegetables evenly with cheese spread. Pour milk over vegetables; sprinkle with seasonings as desired. Bake, covered, at 375°F for 30 minutes or until vegetables are tender. Top with remaining onions; bake, uncovered, 3 minutes or until onions are golden brown.

Makes 6 servings

MICROWAVE DIRECTIONS: IN 12×8-INCH MICROWAVABLE DISH, PREPARE VEGETABLES AS ABOVE. TOP WITH CHEESE SPREAD, MILK AND SEASONINGS AS ABOVE. COOK, COVERED, AT HIGH 12 TO 14 MINUTES OR UNTIL VEGETABLES ARE TENDER, ROTATING DISH HALFWAY THROUGH COOKING TIME. TOP WITH REMAINING ONIONS; COOK, UNCOVERED, 1 MINUTE. LET STAND 5 MINUTES.

Polenta with Italian-Style Vegetables

**1 cup chopped onion, divided
1 clove garlic, minced
2 cups water
2 cups chicken broth
1½ cups yellow cornmeal
2 cups cut-up cauliflower (1-inch pieces)
1 can (16 ounces) no-salt-added whole tomatoes, drained and coarsely chopped
1 can (16 ounces) no-salt-added sliced carrots, drained
1 can (8 ounces) whole green beans, drained
½ teaspoon dried basil leaves
2 teaspoons balsamic or red wine vinegar**

Spray large saucepan with cooking spray and heat until hot. Add ½ cup onion and garlic; cook and stir until tender. Add water and chicken broth; heat to a boil. Gradually stir cornmeal into boiling broth mixture. Reduce heat and simmer, stirring frequently, until thickened, about 10 minutes. Pour mixture into greased 8×4-inch loaf pan. Refrigerate until firm, several hours or overnight.

Remove polenta from pan; cut into 16 slices. Spray large skillet with cooking spray; cook polenta slices over medium-low heat until browned on both sides.

Spray another large skillet with cooking spray and heat until hot. Add cauliflower and remaining ½ cup onion; sauté until cauliflower is crisp-tender, about 10 minutes. Stir in remaining ingredients; cook over medium heat until hot. Arrange polenta slices on serving platter; top with vegetable mixture.

Makes 8 servings

FAVORITE RECIPE FROM CANNED FOOD INFORMATION COUNCIL

Guiltless Zucchini

**Nonstick cooking spray
4 medium zucchini, sliced
⅓ cup chopped onion
4 cloves garlic, minced
¼ teaspoon dried oregano leaves
½ cup GUILTLESS GOURMET® Medium Salsa
¼ cup (1 ounce) shredded low-fat mozzarella cheese**

Coat large nonstick skillet with cooking spray; heat over medium heat until hot. Add zucchini; cook and stir 5 minutes. Add onion, garlic and oregano; cook 5 minutes more or until zucchini and onion are lightly browned. Stir in salsa. Bring just to a boil. Reduce heat to low; simmer 5 minutes more or until zucchini is crisp-tender. Sprinkle cheese on top; cover and cook 1 to 2 minutes or until cheese melts. Serve hot.

Makes 4 servings

Guiltless Zucchini

Eggplant Chutney

2 large eggplants
(2½ pounds),
unpeeled and cut into
½-inch cubes
1 small onion, finely
chopped
3 tablespoons minced
garlic
3 tablespoons minced
fresh ginger
3 tablespoons packed
light brown sugar
1 teaspoon dried
rosemary
1 teaspoon dried anise or
fennel seeds
½ teaspoon dried thyme
leaves
2 tablespoons balsamic
vinegar
1 tablespoon dark sesame
oil
¼ cup dark raisins
½ cup reduced-sodium
chicken broth
2 tablespoons coarsely
chopped walnuts

1. Preheat oven to 450°F.
Arrange eggplant on 15×10-
inch jelly-roll pan lined with
foil. Add onion, garlic, ginger,
brown sugar, rosemary, anise
and thyme; toss to combine.
Drizzle with vinegar and oil;
stir to coat. Bake 1½ hours or
until eggplant is browned and
shriveled, stirring every 30
minutes.

2. Stir raisins into eggplant
mixture and drizzle with
chicken broth; bake 10 minutes
or until broth is absorbed.
Remove from oven; stir in
walnuts. Cool.

3. Serve on crackers or lavash
as an appetizer, or serve warm
or at room temperature as a
condiment with roasted meats
and poultry, if desired. Garnish
with kale and orange slices,
if desired. Store chutney in
airtight container up to 10 days
in refrigerator or 3 months in
freezer.

Makes about 2¾ cups

Barley Mounds in Avocado Pears

2¼ cups water, divided
½ cup medium pearled
barley
1 package (8 to
10 ounces) frozen
mixed vegetables
2 tablespoons margarine
1 clove garlic, minced
2 tablespoons all-purpose
flour
¼ teaspoon salt
¼ teaspoon dry mustard
¼ teaspoon black pepper
½ cup milk
½ cup sliced fresh
mushrooms
¾ cup (3 ounces)
crumbled or grated
Gruyère cheese,
divided
2 tablespoons chopped
parsley
3 avocado pears, Winter
Nellis pears or other
firm green winter
pears

1. In medium saucepan, bring
1½ cups water to a boil. Stir in
barley. Reduce heat; cover and
simmer 45 minutes, stirring
occasionally. Drain.

2. In another medium saucepan,
bring ¼ cup water to a boil.
Add vegetables. Bring to a boil
again, then remove from heat
and drain. Set aside.

3. In 1-quart saucepan, melt
margarine. Add garlic; cook
1 minute. Stir in flour, salt,
dry mustard and pepper; blend
well. Whisk in remaining
½ cup water and milk to
smooth consistency; cook
over medium heat until sauce
thickens. Remove from heat;
add mushrooms, ½ cup cheese,
parsley, barley and vegetables.
Mix well.

4. Peel pears, if desired. Cut
into halves; remove seeds,
keeping shells intact. Arrange
pear halves in 10-inch baking
dish or pan. Mound equal
portions barley-vegetable
mixture into pear halves.
Sprinkle with remaining ¼ cup
cheese. Bake in preheated
350°F oven 20 minutes or
until cheese melts and barley-
vegetable mixture is heated
through.   *Makes 6 servings*

*FAVORITE RECIPE FROM **NORTH DAKOTA
BARLEY COUNCIL***

Spiced Cranberry-Orange Mold

- 1 bag (12 ounces) fresh cranberries*
- ½ cup sugar*
- 1½ cups boiling water
- 1 package (8-serving size) *or* 2 packages (4-serving size) JELL-O® Brand Cranberry, Orange or Lemon Flavor Gelatin
- ¼ teaspoon salt (optional)
- 1 cup cold water*
- 1 tablespoon lemon juice
- ¼ teaspoon ground cinnamon
- ⅛ teaspoon ground cloves
- 1 orange, sectioned and diced
- ½ cup chopped nuts

Or use 1 can (16 ounces) whole berry cranberry sauce; omit sugar and reduce cold water to ½ cup.

Finely chop cranberries in food processor; mix with sugar. Set aside.

Stir boiling water into gelatin and salt in large bowl 2 minutes or until gelatin is completely dissolved. Stir in cold water, lemon juice, cinnamon and cloves. Refrigerate about 1½ hours or until thickened (spoon drawn through gelatin leaves a definite impression).

Stir in cranberries, orange and nuts. Spoon into 5-cup mold that has been lightly sprayed with no-stick cooking spray. Refrigerate about 4 hours or until firm. Unmold. Garnish as desired. *Makes 10 servings*

Acorn Squash Filled with Savory Spinach

- 4 small acorn squash
- 2 tablespoons FILIPPO BERIO® Olive Oil
- 1 (10-ounce) package frozen chopped spinach, thawed and drained
- 8 ounces ricotta cheese
- 1 tablespoon grated Parmesan cheese
- ¼ teaspoon black pepper
- ⅛ teaspoon salt
- ⅛ teaspoon ground nutmeg

Preheat oven to 325°F. Cut squash crosswise in half. Scoop out seeds and fibers; discard. Brush insides and outsides of squash halves with olive oil. Place in large shallow roasting pan. Bake, uncovered, 35 to 40 minutes or until tender when pierced with fork.

In medium bowl, combine spinach, ricotta cheese, Parmesan cheese, pepper, salt and nutmeg. Spoon equal amounts of spinach mixture into squash halves. Bake, uncovered, an additional 10 to 15 minutes or until heated through.

Makes 8 servings

Acorn Squash Filled with Savory Spinach

Herbed Potato Chips

Olive oil-flavored
  nonstick cooking
  spray
2 medium-sized red
  potatoes (about
  ½ pound), unpeeled
1 tablespoon olive oil
2 tablespoons minced
  fresh dill, thyme or
  rosemary *or*
  2 teaspoons dried dill
  weed, thyme or
  rosemary
¼ teaspoon garlic salt
⅛ teaspoon black pepper
1¼ cups nonfat sour cream

1. Preheat oven to 450°F. Spray large nonstick baking sheets with nonstick cooking spray; set aside.

2. Cut potatoes crosswise into very thin slices, about ¹⁄₁₆ inch thick. Pat dry with paper towels. Arrange potato slices in single layer on prepared baking sheets; coat potatoes with nonstick cooking spray.

3. Bake 10 minutes; turn slices over. Brush with oil. Combine dill, garlic salt and pepper in small bowl; sprinkle evenly onto potato slices. Continue baking 5 to 10 minutes or until potatoes are golden brown. Cool on baking sheets.

4. Serve with sour cream.

Makes about 60 chips

Sautéed Garlic Potatoes

2 pounds boiling potatoes,
  peeled and cut into
  1-inch pieces
3 tablespoons FILIPPO
  BERIO® Olive Oil
6 cloves garlic, skins on
1 tablespoon lemon juice
1 tablespoon chopped
  fresh chives
1 tablespoon chopped
  fresh parsley
  Salt and freshly ground
  black pepper

Place potatoes in large colander; rinse under cold running water. Drain well; pat dry. In large nonstick skillet, heat olive oil over medium heat until hot. Add potatoes in single layer. Cook, stirring and turning frequently, 10 minutes or until golden brown. Add garlic. Cover; reduce heat to low and cook very gently, shaking pan and stirring mixture occasionally, 15 to 20 minutes or until potatoes are tender when pierced with fork. Remove garlic; discard skins. In small bowl, crush garlic; stir in lemon juice. Add garlic mixture to potatoes; mix well. Cook 1 to 2 minutes or until heated through. Transfer to serving dish; sprinkle with chives and parsley. Season to taste with salt and pepper.

Makes 4 servings

Rosemary Hash Potatoes

2 tablespoons olive oil
1 clove garlic, minced
2 teaspoons snipped fresh
  rosemary leaves
1½ pounds red skin
  potatoes, unpeeled
  and cut into ½-inch
  cubes
½ teaspoon salt
½ teaspoon black pepper
  Fresh rosemary sprig
  and tomato wedges
  (optional)

Heat oil in large skillet over medium heat until hot. Add garlic and snipped rosemary; cook and stir 2 minutes. Add potatoes, salt and pepper. Cook 5 minutes, stirring occasionally. Reduce heat to medium-low; cook, uncovered, about 20 minutes or until potatoes are golden brown and crisp, turning occasionally. Garnish with rosemary sprig and tomato, if desired. Serve hot. Refrigerate leftovers.

Makes 4 to 6 side-dish servings

*FAVORITE RECIPE FROM **BOB EVANS FARMS**®*

Herbed Potato Chips

Double-Baked Potatoes

- 3 large Idaho potatoes
- 4 tablespoons skim milk, warmed
- 1 cup (4 ounces) shredded reduced-fat Cheddar cheese
- ¾ cup corn
- ½ teaspoon chili powder
- 1 tablespoon finely chopped fresh oregano *or* ½ teaspoon dried oregano leaves
- 1 cup chopped onion
- ½ to 1 cup chopped poblano chili peppers
- 3 cloves garlic, minced
- ½ teaspoon salt
- ¼ teaspoon black pepper
- 3 tablespoons chopped cilantro

1. Preheat oven to 400°F. Scrub potatoes under running water with soft vegetable brush; rinse. Pierce each potato with fork. Wrap each potato in aluminum foil. Bake about 1 hour or until fork-tender. Remove potatoes; cool slightly. *Reduce oven temperature to 350°F.*

2. Cut potatoes in half lengthwise; scoop out inside being careful not to tear shells. Set shells aside. Beat potatoes in large bowl with electric mixer until coarsely mashed. Add milk; beat until smooth. Stir in cheese, corn, chili powder and oregano. Set aside.

3. Spray medium skillet with nonstick cooking spray. Add onion, poblano peppers and garlic; cook and stir 5 to 8 minutes or until tender. Stir in salt and black pepper.

4. Spoon potato mixture into reserved potato shells. Sprinkle with onion mixture. Place stuffed potatoes in small baking pan. Bake 20 to 30 minutes or until heated through. Sprinkle with cilantro.

Makes 6 servings

Southwestern Twice-Baked Spuds

- 2 baking potatoes with skins (about 6 ounces each)
- ½ cup GUILTLESS GOURMET® Nacho Dip (mild or spicy)
- ¼ cup finely chopped green onions
- ¼ teaspoon coarsely ground black pepper
- 2 tablespoons GUILTLESS GOURMET® Salsa (mild, medium or hot)
- 2 tablespoons chopped fresh cilantro
- Nasturtium flowers (optional)

Preheat oven to 400°F. Scrub potatoes with vegetable brush; pierce in several places with fork. Bake potatoes 45 to 50 minutes or until fork-tender. Remove from oven; cool potatoes until safe enough to handle.

Reduce oven temperature to 300°F. Slice potatoes in half lengthwise. Form 4 shells by scooping out most of potato pulp, being careful not to pierce skin. Place pulp in large bowl; mash with potato masher or whip with electric mixer. Add nacho dip, onions and pepper. Blend until smooth. Add salsa and cilantro; mix until blended. Fill potato shells with equal amount of potato mixture, heaping to form mounds. Wrap skins in foil, leaving tops open. Place on baking sheet.

Bake 25 minutes or until heated through. Serve hot. Garnish with edible flowers, if desired.

Makes 4 servings

Double-Baked Potato

Cheese and Pepper Stuffed Potato Skins

6 large russet potatoes
(about ¾ pound each),
scrubbed
4 tablespoons FRANK'S®
Original REDHOT®
Cayenne Pepper
Sauce, divided
2 tablespoons butter,
melted
1 large red bell pepper,
seeded and finely
chopped
1 cup chopped green
onions
1 cup (4 ounces) shredded
Cheddar cheese

1. Preheat oven to 450°F. Wrap potatoes in foil; bake about 1 hour 15 minutes or until fork tender. Let stand until cool enough to handle. Cut each potato in half lengthwise; scoop out insides, leaving a ¼-inch-thick shell. Cut shells in half crosswise. Place shells on large baking sheet.

2. Preheat broiler. Combine 1 tablespoon RedHot® sauce and butter in small bowl; brush on inside of each potato shell. Broil shells, 6 inches from heat, 8 minutes or until golden brown and crispy.

3. Combine remaining 3 tablespoons RedHot® sauce with remaining ingredients in large bowl. Spoon about 1 tablespoon mixture into each potato shell. Broil 2 minutes or until cheese melts. Cut each piece in half to serve.

Makes 12 servings

Toluca Taters

1 package (1.48 ounces)
LAWRY'S® Spices &
Seasonings for Chili
1 pound ground turkey
1 can (15¼ ounces)
kidney beans,
undrained
1 can (14½ ounces) whole
peeled tomatoes,
undrained and cut up
½ cup water
8 medium russet potatoes,
washed and pierced
with fork
1 cup (4 ounces) shredded
cheddar cheese
½ cup thinly sliced green
onions

Microwave Directions:
In large glass bowl, prepare Spices & Seasonings for Chili with ground turkey, kidney beans, tomatoes and water according to package microwave directions; keep warm. Microwave potatoes at HIGH 25 minutes, turning over after 12 minutes. Cut potatoes lengthwise and stir inside with fork to fluff. Top each potato half with ½ to ¾ cup prepared chili, 2 tablespoons cheese and 1 tablespoon green onions.

Makes 8 servings

Presentation: *Top with sour cream, if desired. Serve with a mixed green salad and fresh fruit.*

Hint: *This recipe is a great way to use leftover chili.*

Cheesy Potato Pancakes

1½ quarts prepared instant
mashed potatoes,
cooked dry and cooled
1½ cups (6 ounces)
shredded Wisconsin
Colby or Muenster
cheese
4 eggs, lightly beaten
1½ cups all-purpose flour,
divided
¾ cup chopped fresh
parsley
⅓ cup chopped fresh
chives
1½ teaspoons dried thyme,
rosemary or sage
leaves
2 eggs, lightly beaten

1. In large bowl, combine potatoes, cheese, 4 beaten eggs, ¾ cup flour and herbs; mix well. Cover and refrigerate at least 4 hours before molding and preparing.

2. To prepare, form 18 (3-inch) patties. Dip in 2 beaten eggs and dredge in remaining ¾ cup flour. Cook each patty in nonstick skillet 3 minutes per side or until crisp, golden brown and heated through.

3. Serve warm with eggs or omelets, or serve with sour cream and sliced pan-fried apples or applesauce, if desired.

Makes 4 to 6 servings

Variation: *Substitute Wisconsin Cheddar or Smoked Cheddar for Colby or Muenster.*

FAVORITE RECIPE FROM **WISCONSIN MILK MARKETING BOARD**

Cheese and Pepper Stuffed Potato Skins

Potato-Swiss Galette

- 2 tablespoons butter substitute
- 1 pound yellow onions, sliced ¼ inch thick (2 cups)
- 1 teaspoon minced garlic Nonstick cooking spray
- 2 pounds unpeeled small red-skinned potatoes, sliced ¼ inch thick (4 cups)
- ½ teaspoon salt
- ¼ teaspoon freshly ground black pepper
- 1 cup (4 ounces) shredded ALPINE LACE® Reduced Fat Swiss Cheese
- ¼ cup minced fresh parsley
- ½ teaspoon snipped fresh rosemary leaves *or* ¼ teaspoon dried rosemary

1. In large nonstick skillet, melt butter over medium-high heat. Add onions and garlic; sauté for 5 minutes or until softened. Spray both sides of potatoes with cooking spray; sprinkle with salt and pepper. Add potatoes to skillet with onion mixture. Sauté for 5 minutes or until golden brown on both sides. Cover; cook, stirring occasionally, for 10 minutes or until potatoes are tender.

2. In small bowl, toss the cheese with parsley and rosemary. Sprinkle over potatoes and toss gently just until cheese has melted. *Makes 6 servings*

Tomato Scalloped Potatoes

- 1 can (14½ ounces) DEL MONTE® *FreshCut*™ Diced Tomatoes, undrained
- 1 pound red potatoes, thinly sliced
- 1 medium onion, chopped
- ½ cup whipping cream
- 1 cup (4 ounces) shredded Swiss cheese
- 3 tablespoons grated Parmesan cheese

1. Preheat oven to 350°F.

2. Drain tomatoes, reserving liquid; pour liquid into measuring cup. Add water to measure 1 cup.

3. Add reserved liquid, potatoes and onion to large skillet; cover. Cook 10 minutes or until tender.

4. Place potato mixture in 1-quart baking dish; top with tomatoes and cream. Sprinkle with cheeses.

5. Bake 20 minutes or until hot and bubbly. Sprinkle with chopped parsley, if desired.
Makes 6 servings

Prep Time: 8 minutes
Cook Time: 30 minutes

Roasted Garlic Mashed Potatoes

- 1 large bulb garlic Olive oil
- ¼ cup chopped green onions
- ¼ cup margarine or butter
- 2½ pounds potatoes, peeled, cubed and cooked
- 1½ cups milk
- ½ cup GREY POUPON® Dijon Mustard
- ½ cup shredded Cheddar cheese (2 ounces)
- ¼ cup chopped parsley Salt and black pepper to taste

To roast garlic, peel off loose paperlike skin from bulb. Coat garlic bulb lightly with olive oil; wrap in foil. Place in small baking pan. Bake at 400°F for 40 to 45 minutes; cool. Separate cloves. Squeeze cloves to extract pulp; discard skins.

In large saucepan, over medium heat, sauté garlic pulp and green onions in margarine until tender. Add cooked potatoes, milk, mustard and cheese. Mash potato mixture until smooth and well blended. Stir in parsley; season with salt and pepper. Serve immediately.
Makes 8 servings

Country-Style Mashed Potatoes

4 pounds Yukon gold or Idaho potatoes, unpeeled and cut into 1-inch pieces
6 large cloves garlic, peeled
½ cup nonfat sour cream
½ cup skim milk, warmed
2 tablespoons margarine
2 tablespoons finely chopped fresh rosemary *or* **1 teaspoon dried rosemary**
2 tablespoons finely chopped fresh thyme *or* **½ teaspoon dried thyme leaves**
2 tablespoons finely chopped parsley

1. Place potatoes and garlic in medium saucepan; cover with water. Bring to a boil. Reduce heat and simmer, covered, about 15 minutes or until potatoes are fork-tender. Drain well.

2. Place potatoes and garlic in large bowl. Beat with electric mixer just until mashed. Beat in sour cream, milk and margarine until almost smooth. Mix in rosemary, thyme and parsley.

Makes 8 (¾-cup) servings

Zippy Scalloped Potatoes

Nonstick cooking spray
3 large baking potatoes (about 2½ pounds)
1 jar (11.5 ounces) GUILTLESS GOURMET® Nacho Dip (mild or spicy)
¾ cup skim milk
Fresh cilantro leaves and red pepper strips (optional)

Preheat oven to 350°F. Coat microwavable 2-quart rectangular dish or round casserole with cooking spray.

Scrub potatoes with vegetable brush; thinly slice potatoes. (Slice in food processor, if desired.) Layer in prepared dish. Cover with vented plastic wrap or lid; microwave at HIGH 10 minutes or until potatoes are fork-tender.

Combine nacho dip and milk in 4-cup glass measure; microwave at HIGH 2 minutes. Pour over potatoes; gently stir to coat potato slices. Cover and bake 30 minutes. Uncover; bake 10 minutes more or until heated through. Let stand 5 minutes before serving. Garnish with cilantro and pepper, if desired.

Makes 8 servings

Country-Style Mashed Potatoes

Spicy Spanish Rice

- 1 teaspoon canola oil
- 1 cup uncooked white rice
- 1 medium onion, chopped
- 2 cups chicken stock or canned low-sodium chicken broth, defatted
- 1 cup GUILTLESS GOURMET® Salsa (mild, medium or hot)
  Green chili pepper strips (optional)

Heat large skillet over medium-high heat until hot. Add oil; swirl to coat skillet. Add rice; cook and stir until lightly browned. Remove rice to small bowl. Add onion to same skillet; cook and stir until onion is translucent. Add chicken stock and salsa to skillet; return rice to skillet. Bring to a boil. Reduce heat to low; cover and simmer until liquid is absorbed and rice is tender. Serve hot. Garnish with pepper strips, if desired.   *Makes 4 servings*

Jalapeño Green Rice

- 1 poblano chili, peeled and seeded*
- ½ medium onion
- ½ cup parsley, loosely packed
- 2 cloves garlic
- 2 cups chicken stock, divided
- 1 tablespoon vegetable oil
- 1 cup uncooked rice
- 1 tablespoon TABASCO® jalapeño sauce
- ½ teaspoon salt

*To peel chili: Roast chili over a gas burner, under a broiler or on a griddle, turning until skin is blistered and charred on all sides. Place in a plastic bag; close and let steam 15 minutes. Under running water, remove skin from pepper. Slit pepper to open; wash out seeds and remove veins.

Combine poblano chili, onion, parsley and garlic with ½ cup chicken stock in blender; blend until smooth. Set aside. In 3-quart skillet, heat oil over medium-high heat. Add rice and cook over medium heat until golden, stirring constantly. Add remaining chicken stock, chili mixture, TABASCO® sauce and salt. Bring to a boil; stir once or twice. Reduce heat; cover and simmer 20 minutes or until rice is tender and liquid is absorbed.

Makes 6 servings

"Wild" Black Beans

- 2 cups cooked wild rice
- 1 can (15 ounces) black beans, undrained
- 1 cup canned or thawed frozen corn, drained
- ½ cup chopped red bell pepper
- 1 small jalapeño pepper, seeded and chopped
- 1 tablespoon red wine vinegar
- 1 cup (4 ounces) shredded Monterey Jack cheese
- ¼ cup chopped fresh cilantro

Preheat oven to 350°F. In 1½-quart baking dish, combine wild rice, beans, corn, bell pepper, jalapeño and vinegar. Cover; bake 20 minutes. Top with cheese; bake, uncovered, 10 minutes. Garnish with cilantro.

Makes 6 to 8 servings

*FAVORITE RECIPE FROM **MINNESOTA CULTIVATED WILD RICE COUNCIL***

Rice Pilaf with Dried Cherries and Almonds

½ cup slivered almonds
2 tablespoons margarine
2 cups uncooked converted rice
½ cup chopped onion
1 can (about 14 ounces) vegetable broth
1½ cups water
½ cup dried cherries

1. Cook and stir almonds in large nonstick skillet over medium heat until lightly browned. Remove from skillet; cool.

2. Melt margarine in same skillet over low heat. Add rice and onion; cook and stir until rice is lightly browned. Add broth and water. Bring to a boil over high heat; reduce heat to low. Simmer, covered, 15 minutes.

3. Stir in almonds and cherries. Simmer 5 minutes or until liquid is absorbed and rice is tender. Garnish as desired.

Makes 12 servings

Green Rice

2 Anaheim chilies
1 jalapeño pepper
1 tablespoon margarine or olive oil
¼ cup sliced green onions
¼ cup snipped cilantro
1 recipe Arroz Blanco (recipe follows)
¼ teaspoon dried oregano leaves

Chop chilies and jalapeño pepper in food processor until minced, but not liquefied. Melt margarine in large skillet over low heat. Add chilies mixture; cook 1 minute over medium heat. Stir in onions and cilantro; cook 15 to 30 seconds. Add Arroz Blanco and oregano; heat.

Makes 6 servings

ARROZ BLANCO
1 tablespoon margarine
½ cup chopped onion
2 cloves garlic, minced
1 cup uncooked rice*
2 cups chicken broth

*Recipe based on regular-milled long-grain white rice.

Melt margarine in 2- to 3-quart saucepan over medium heat. Add onion and garlic; cook until onion is tender. Add rice and chicken broth. Bring to a boil; stir. Reduce heat; cover and simmer 15 minutes or until rice is tender and liquid is absorbed. Fluff with fork.

Makes 6 servings

FAVORITE RECIPE FROM **USA RICE FEDERATION**

White Rice Turkish Style

1 tablespoon FILIPPO BERIO® Olive Oil
1 small onion, sliced
½ green bell pepper, seeded and cut into thin strips
2 cups chicken broth, beef broth or water
1 (2-ounce) jar sliced pimientos, drained
1 cup uncooked long-grain rice
1 (8½-ounce) can small peas, drained
Salt

In 3-quart saucepan, heat olive oil over medium heat until hot. Add onion and bell pepper; cook and stir 5 to 7 minutes or until tender. Add chicken broth and pimientos. Reduce heat to low; simmer 5 minutes. Stir in rice. Cover; simmer 15 minutes or until rice is tender and liquid is absorbed. Remove from heat; let stand, covered, 5 to 10 minutes. Stir in peas. Season to taste with salt.

Makes 4 to 6 servings

Cheese Strata

BASIC STRATA
- 3 tablespoons butter or margarine
- 6 slices bread, crusts removed
- 3 cups (12 ounces) shredded cheddar cheese, divided
- 6 eggs
- 2 cups milk
- 1 tablespoon LAWRY'S® Minced Onion with Green Onion Flakes
- 1 teaspoon LAWRY'S® Seasoned Salt
- ¼ teaspoon LAWRY'S® Garlic Powder with Parsley

Lightly grease 13×9×2-inch baking dish with butter; arrange bread slices on bottom of dish. Sprinkle with half of cheddar cheese. In medium bowl, beat together eggs, milk, Minced Onion with Green Onion Flakes, Seasoned Salt and Garlic Powder with Parsley. Pour mixture over bread and cheese. Sprinkle with remaining cheddar cheese. Bake, uncovered, in 350°F oven 35 minutes or until light golden brown. Let stand 5 minutes before serving.

Makes 6 servings

HERB STRATA: Add 2 tablespoons LAWRY'S® Pinch of Herbs to Basic Strata egg and milk mixture.

ITALIAN-HERB STRATA: To Herb Strata variation, add ¼ cup sliced black olives to each cheese layer and top with diced tomatoes. Serve with LAWRY'S® Original-Style Spaghetti Sauce Spices & Seasonings prepared as directed on package.

Gourmet Grits

- ½ pound BOB EVANS FARMS® Italian Roll Sausage
- 3 cups water
- 1 cup uncooked white grits
- ½ (10-ounce) package frozen chopped spinach, thawed and squeezed dry
- ¼ cup grated Parmesan cheese
- ¼ cup chopped sun-dried tomatoes
- ¼ cup olive oil
- 1 clove garlic, chopped

Crumble sausage into medium skillet. Cook over medium heat until browned, stirring occasionally. Drain off any drippings; set aside. Bring water to a rapid boil in large saucepan. While stirring, add grits in steady stream until mixture thickens into smooth paste. Reduce heat to low; simmer 5 to 7 minutes, stirring frequently to prevent sticking. Stir in sausage, spinach, cheese and tomatoes. Pour into greased 9×5-inch loaf pan. Refrigerate until cool and firm.

Unmold. Slice into ½-inch-thick slices. Heat oil in large skillet over medium-high heat until hot. Add garlic; cook and stir 30 seconds or until soft. Add grit slices, 4 to 5 at a time, and cook until golden brown on both sides. Repeat until all slices are cooked. Serve hot. Garnish with mozzarella cheese slices, if desired. Refrigerate leftovers.

Makes 4 to 6 side-dish servings

Spaghetti Pancakes

- ½ pound spaghetti, cooked and cooled
- 2 eggs, beaten
- ⅓ to ½ cup freshly grated Parmesan cheese
- Salt and freshly ground black pepper to taste
- 3 tablespoons butter, divided

In mixing bowl, combine spaghetti, eggs, cheese, salt and pepper. Heat 2 tablespoons butter in 10-inch skillet until it starts to foam. Add spaghetti mixture and press down with spatula to form a compact cake.

Sauté over medium heat about 10 minutes or until bottom is nicely browned. Dot top with remaining 1 tablespoon butter. Cover pan with serving dish and invert pancake onto dish. Slide pancake back into pan, browned side up. Cook until underside is brown. Slide out onto serving dish. Cut into wedges and serve hot.

Makes 4 servings

FAVORITE RECIPE FROM **NORTH DAKOTA WHEAT COMMISSION**

Gourmet Grits

Green Chili Rice

1 cup uncooked white rice
1 can (about 14 ounces) fat-free reduced-sodium chicken broth plus water to measure 2 cups
1 can (4 ounces) chopped mild green chilies
½ medium yellow onion, peeled and diced
1 teaspoon dried oregano leaves
½ teaspoon salt (optional)
½ teaspoon cumin seeds
3 green onions, thinly sliced
⅓ to ½ cup fresh cilantro leaves

Combine rice, chicken broth mixture, chilies, yellow onion, oregano, salt, if desired, and cumin in large saucepan. Bring to a boil, uncovered, over high heat. Reduce heat to low; cover and simmer 18 minutes or until liquid is absorbed and rice is tender. Stir in green onions and cilantro. Garnish as desired.   *Makes 6 servings*

Chili Bean Ragoût

1 cup chopped onion
1 cup sliced celery
1 cup cubed green bell pepper
2 cloves garlic, minced
3 to 4 teaspoons chili powder
1 teaspoon dried oregano leaves
1 teaspoon dried basil leaves
½ teaspoon dried thyme leaves
1 can (17 ounces) lima beans, drained
1 can (16 ounces) no-salt-added whole tomatoes, undrained and coarsely chopped
1 can (16 ounces) ½-less-salt whole kernel corn, drained
1 can (15½ ounces) kidney beans, drained
1 can (15 ounces) black-eyed peas, drained
Hot cooked rice or cornbread

Spray bottom of large saucepan with nonstick cooking spray; heat over high heat. Cook and stir onion, celery, bell pepper and garlic until tender. Stir in chili powder, oregano, basil and thyme; cook 1 minute. Stir in lima beans, tomatoes, corn, kidney beans and black-eyed peas; heat to boiling. Reduce heat and simmer, uncovered, 10 minutes. Serve over rice or cornbread.   *Makes 8 servings*

FAVORITE RECIPE FROM **CANNED FOOD INFORMATION COUNCIL**

Red Rice

3 slices bacon, cut into bite-size pieces
1 large onion, chopped
½ teaspoon LAWRY'S® Garlic Powder with Parsley
1 cup chicken broth
3 medium tomatoes, chopped
1 cup uncooked long-grain rice
1 can (15¼ ounces) kidney beans, drained
1 teaspoon LAWRY'S® Seasoned Salt
Chopped parsley for garnish (optional)

In large deep skillet, cook bacon until light brown. Drain, reserving 1 tablespoon fat. Add onion, bacon, reserved fat and Garlic Powder with Parsley to skillet. Cook and stir until onion is translucent. Add chicken broth; bring to a boil. Stir in tomatoes, rice, beans and Seasoned Salt. Reduce heat; cover and simmer 20 to 25 minutes or until liquid is absorbed. Let stand 2 minutes before serving. Garnish with parsley, if desired.
Makes 6 servings

Green Chili Rice

Shrimp Stuffing

- 1 package (6 ounces) KELLOGG'S® CROUTETTES® Stuffing Mix
- ½ cup chopped celery
- ½ cup sliced green onions
- ¼ cup chopped green bell pepper
- 1 can (10¾ ounces) condensed cream of mushroom soup
- ¾ cup water
- ¼ teaspoon salt
- ½ teaspoon Cajun seasoning
- 1 teaspoon dry mustard
- 1 teaspoon lemon juice
- 1 pound raw shrimp, cleaned and cut into quarters
- 2 tablespoons margarine, melted
- ½ cup (2 ounces) shredded part-skim mozzarella cheese

Microwave Directions:
1. In 4-quart microwavable mixing bowl, combine all ingredients except cheese. Cover with plastic wrap, leaving a corner open as a vent. Microwave at HIGH 9 minutes, stirring after 3 and 6 minutes, or until stuffing is hot and shrimp are cooked. (When stirring stuffing, carefully remove plastic from bowl to allow steam to escape.)

2. Stir cheese into hot stuffing before serving.

Makes 8 servings

RANGE-TOP DIRECTIONS: IN 12-INCH SKILLET, COOK SHRIMP IN MARGARINE OVER MEDIUM HEAT JUST UNTIL SHRIMP START TO CHANGE COLOR. STIR IN REMAINING INGREDIENTS EXCEPT CHEESE, TOSSING GENTLY TO MOISTEN. COVER AND CONTINUE COOKING 5 MINUTES LONGER OVER LOW HEAT. REMOVE FROM HEAT AND STIR IN CHEESE.

Pork Fried Rice

- 2½ cups uncooked long-grain white rice
- 4 pork chops, diced
- 2 tablespoons vegetable oil
- 1 medium onion, finely chopped
- 1 can (14½ ounces) DEL MONTE® Peas and Carrots, drained
- 3 green onions, sliced
- 3 to 4 tablespoons soy sauce

1. Cook rice according to package directions.

2. Cook meat in hot oil in large skillet or wok until no longer pink in center, stirring occasionally. Add chopped onion; cook until tender.

3. Stir in rice, peas and carrots, green onions and soy sauce; heat through, stirring frequently. Season with pepper, if desired.

Makes 4 servings

Prep & Cook Time: 30 minutes

Mixed Vegetable Saucepan Stuffing

- ½ cup *each* chopped onion, celery, carrot and mushrooms
- 2 tablespoons margarine or butter
- 1 (13¾-fluid ounce) can COLLEGE INN® Lower Sodium Chicken Broth
- ⅓ cup GREY POUPON® COUNTRY DIJON® Mustard
- ½ teaspoon poultry seasoning
- ¼ teaspoon dried rosemary leaves
- 5 cups dried bread stuffing cubes
- ⅓ cup PLANTERS® Walnuts, chopped
- 2 tablespoons chopped parsley

In large saucepan, over medium-high heat, sauté onion, celery, carrot and mushrooms in margarine until tender. Stir in chicken broth, mustard, poultry seasoning and rosemary. Heat mixture to a boil; reduce heat. Cover and simmer for 5 minutes. Add bread cubes, walnuts and parsley, stirring to coat well. Cover; let stand for 5 minutes. Fluff with fork before serving.

Makes 5 servings

Tabbouleh with Scallops in Citrus Dressing

SALAD
6 ounces (about 1 cup) cracked bulgur wheat
3 tablespoons lemon juice
3 tablespoons FILIPPO BERIO® Olive Oil, divided
4 to 6 green onions, thinly sliced
2 tablespoons chopped fresh Italian parsley
½ teaspoon salt
Freshly ground black pepper
1 pound sea scallops

DRESSING
Juice of 1 lemon
Juice of 1 lime
1 tablespoon chopped fresh dill*
1 tablespoon FILIPPO BERIO® Olive Oil
1 shallot, finely chopped
1 small clove garlic, minced
¼ teaspoon salt
Freshly ground black pepper
Sprigs of fresh dill and lemon and lime slices (optional)

Omit dill if fresh is unavailable. Do not substitute dried dill weed.

For Salad, in medium bowl, cover bulgur with warm water; soak 30 minutes. Drain well; press out any excess water. Add 3 tablespoons lemon juice, 2 tablespoons olive oil, green onions, parsley and ½ teaspoon salt; mix well. Cover and refrigerate at least 30 minutes. Season to taste with pepper.

Meanwhile, in large skillet, heat remaining 1 tablespoon olive oil over medium-high heat until hot. Add scallops; cook and stir 2 to 3 minutes or until opaque and lightly browned. Transfer scallops to shallow glass dish.

For Dressing, in small bowl, whisk together lemon juice, lime juice, dill, 1 tablespoon olive oil, shallot, garlic and ¼ teaspoon salt. Season to taste with pepper. Pour mixture over scallops; marinate 15 minutes. Drain scallops, reserving dressing.

To serve, place a portion of bulgur mixture on one side of 4 serving plates; arrange scallops on other side. Drizzle dressing over bulgur mixture. Garnish with sprigs of dill and slices of lemon and lime, if desired. *Makes 4 servings*

Risi Bisi

1½ cups uncooked converted long-grain white rice
¾ cup chopped onion
2 cloves garlic, minced
2 cans (about 14 ounces each) reduced-sodium chicken broth
⅓ cup water
¾ teaspoon Italian seasoning
½ teaspoon dried basil leaves
½ cup frozen peas, thawed
¼ cup grated Parmesan cheese
¼ cup toasted pine nuts (optional)

Slow Cooker Directions:
COMBINE rice, onion and garlic in slow cooker. Heat broth and water in small saucepan to a boil. Stir boiling liquid, Italian seasoning and basil into rice mixture. Cover and cook on LOW 2 to 3 hours or until liquid is absorbed. Add peas. Cover and cook 1 hour. Stir in cheese. Spoon rice into serving bowl. Sprinkle with pine nuts, if desired.
Makes 6 servings

Orzo with Spinach and Red Pepper

4 ounces uncooked orzo
1 teaspoon olive oil
1 medium red bell pepper, diced
3 cloves garlic, minced
1 package (10 ounces) frozen chopped spinach, thawed and squeezed dry
¼ cup grated Parmesan cheese
½ teaspoon minced fresh oregano or basil (optional)
¼ teaspoon lemon pepper

1. Prepare orzo according to package directions; drain well and set aside.

2. Spray large nonstick skillet with nonstick cooking spray. Heat skillet over medium-high heat until hot; add oil, tilting skillet to coat bottom. Add bell pepper and garlic; cook and stir 2 to 3 minutes or until bell pepper is crisp-tender. Add orzo and spinach; stir until evenly mixed and heated through. Remove from heat and stir in cheese, oregano, if desired, and lemon pepper. Garnish as desired.

Makes 6 servings

Almond Brown Rice Stuffing

⅓ cup slivered almonds
2 teaspoons margarine
2 medium tart apples, cored and diced
½ cup chopped onion
½ cup chopped celery
½ teaspoon poultry seasoning
¼ teaspoon dried thyme leaves
¼ teaspoon ground white pepper
3 cups cooked brown rice (cooked in chicken broth)

Cook almonds in margarine in large skillet over medium-high heat until browned. Add apples, onion, celery, poultry seasoning, thyme and pepper; cook until vegetables are tender-crisp. Stir in rice; cook until thoroughly heated. Serve or use as stuffing for poultry or pork roast. Stuffing may be baked in covered baking dish at 375°F for 15 to 20 minutes.

Makes 6 servings

MICROWAVE DIRECTIONS: COMBINE ALMONDS AND MARGARINE IN 2- TO 3-QUART MICROWAVABLE BAKING DISH. COOK AT HIGH 2 TO 3 MINUTES OR UNTIL BROWNED. ADD APPLES, ONION, CELERY, POULTRY SEASONING, THYME AND PEPPER. COVER WITH WAXED PAPER AND COOK AT HIGH 2 MINUTES. STIR IN RICE; COOK AT HIGH 2 TO 3 MINUTES, STIRRING AFTER 1½ MINUTES, OR UNTIL THOROUGHLY HEATED. SERVE AS ABOVE.

Variations: For Mushroom Stuffing, add 2 cups (about 8 ounces) sliced mushrooms; cook with apples, onion, celery and seasonings. For Raisin Stuffing, add ½ cup raisins; cook with apples, onion, celery and seasonings.

FAVORITE RECIPE FROM USA RICE FEDERATION

Broccoli Rice au Gratin

1 cup GUILTLESS GOURMET® Nacho Dip (mild or spicy)
⅓ cup skim milk
1 cup cooked rice
2 cups chopped broccoli (1 package frozen, thawed)
Nonstick cooking spray

Preheat oven to 250°F. Combine nacho dip and milk in small saucepan; mix thoroughly. Heat over medium heat until warmed but not boiling, stirring occasionally. Stir rice into cheese mixture; set aside.

Steam broccoli until crisp-tender. Add to cheese mixture, stirring gently. Coat 8-inch square baking dish with cooking spray. Spread broccoli and rice mixture into prepared dish. Bake 15 minutes or until heated through. Serve hot.

Makes 4 servings

CAULIFLOWER RICE AU GRATIN: Substitute cauliflower for broccoli. Sprinkle with chopped fresh parsley, if desired.

Orzo with Spinach and Red Pepper

Apple Stuffing

1 cup finely chopped
    onion
½ cup finely chopped
    celery
½ cup finely chopped
    unpeeled apple
1½ cups MOTT'S® Natural
    Apple Sauce
1 (8-ounce) package
    stuffing mix (original
    or cornbread)
1 cup low-fat reduced-
    sodium chicken broth
1½ teaspoons dried thyme
    leaves
1 teaspoon ground sage
½ teaspoon salt
½ teaspoon black pepper

1. Spray medium nonstick
skillet with nonstick cooking
spray. Heat over medium heat
until hot. Add onion and celery;
cook and stir about 5 minutes
or until transparent. Add apple;
cook and stir about 3 minutes
or until golden. Transfer to
large bowl. Stir in apple sauce,
stuffing mix, chicken broth,
thyme, sage, salt and black
pepper.

2. Loosely stuff chicken or
turkey just before roasting or
place stuffing in greased 8-inch
square pan. Cover pan; bake in
preheated 350°F oven 20 to 25
minutes or until hot. Refrigerate
leftovers.   *Makes 8 servings*

*Note: Cooked stuffing can also be
used to fill centers of cooked acorn
squash.*

Fruited Rice Pilaf

2½ cups water
1 cup uncooked rice
2 tablespoons butter or
    margarine
1 medium tomato,
    chopped
⅓ cup minced dried apples
¼ cup minced dried
    apricots
¼ cup sliced green onions
¾ teaspoon LAWRY'S®
    Seasoned Salt
¼ teaspoon LAWRY'S®
    Garlic Powder with
    Parsley
3 tablespoons sliced
    almonds

In 2-quart saucepan, bring
water to a boil; add rice and
butter. Return to a boil. Reduce
heat; cover and simmer 15
minutes. Add remaining
ingredients except almonds;
cook 5 to 10 minutes longer
or until rice is tender. Stir in
almonds. Garnish with apple
slices and celery leaves, if
desired.   *Makes 4 servings*

*Presentation: Serve with baked
pork chops, roasted meats or
poultry.*

*Hint: For variety and added flavor,
add ¼ teaspoon curry powder to
cooked rice.*

Lemon Rice

1 cup uncooked rice*
1 teaspoon margarine
    (optional)
1 clove garlic, minced
1 teaspoon grated lemon
    peel
⅛ to ¼ teaspoon black
    pepper
2 cups chicken broth
2 tablespoons snipped
    parsley

**Recipe based on regular-milled
long-grain white rice.*

Combine rice, margarine, if
desired, garlic, lemon peel,
pepper and chicken broth in
2- to 3-quart saucepan. Bring
to a boil; stir once or twice.
Reduce heat; cover and simmer
15 minutes or until rice is
tender and liquid is absorbed.
Stir in parsley.

Makes 6 servings

FAVORITE RECIPE FROM **USA RICE
FEDERATION**

Apple-Rice Medley

- 1 package (6 ounces) long-grain and wild rice mix
- 1 cup (4 ounces) shredded mild Cheddar cheese, divided
- 1 cup chopped Washington Golden Delicious apple
- 1 cup sliced mushrooms
- ½ cup thinly sliced celery

Prepare rice mix according to package directions. Preheat oven to 350°F. Add ½ cup cheese, apple, mushrooms and celery to rice; toss to combine. Spoon mixture into 1-quart casserole. Bake 15 minutes. Top with remaining ½ cup cheese; bake until cheese melts, about 10 minutes.

Makes 4 servings

MICROWAVE DIRECTIONS: COMBINE COOKED RICE, ½ CUP CHEESE, APPLE, MUSHROOMS AND CELERY AS DIRECTED; SPOON MIXTURE INTO 1-QUART MICROWAVABLE DISH. MICROWAVE AT HIGH 3 TO 4 MINUTES OR UNTIL HEATED THROUGH. TOP MIXTURE WITH REMAINING ½ CUP CHEESE; MICROWAVE AT HIGH 1 MINUTE OR UNTIL CHEESE MELTS.

FAVORITE RECIPE FROM WASHINGTON APPLE COMMISSION

Mexican Rice

- 2 tablespoons butter or margarine
- ½ cup chopped onion
- 2 cloves garlic, finely chopped
- 1¾ cups (16-ounce jar) ORTEGA® Thick & Chunky Salsa, hot, medium or mild or Garden Style Salsa, medium or mild
- 1¼ cups water
- ¾ cup (1 large) shredded carrot
- ½ cup frozen peas, thawed
- 1 cup uncooked long-grain white rice

MELT butter in large saucepan over medium heat. Add onion and garlic; cook 2 to 3 minutes or until onion is tender. Stir in salsa, water, carrot and peas. Bring to a boil; stir in rice. Reduce heat to low; cook, covered, 25 to 30 minutes or until liquid is absorbed and rice is tender. *Makes 8 servings*

Tip: Serve this traditional side dish to complete any Mexican meal.

Mexican Rice

Sandwiches & Pizzas

FEATURING:

Picnic Favorites

Hamburgers

Meat & Veggie Pizzas

Albondigas Meatball Sandwich (page 397)

Tuna Monte Cristo Sandwiches

4 thin slices (2 ounces) Cheddar cheese
4 slices sourdough or challah (egg) bread
½ pound deli tuna salad
1 egg, beaten
¼ cup milk
2 tablespoons butter or margarine

1. Place 1 slice cheese on each bread slice. Spread tuna salad evenly over two slices of cheese-topped bread. Close sandwiches with remaining bread slices.

2. Combine egg and milk in shallow bowl. Dip sandwiches in egg mixture, turning to coat well.

3. Melt butter in large nonstick skillet over medium heat. Add sandwiches; cook 4 to 5 minutes per side or until bread is golden brown and cheese is melted.
Makes 2 servings

Prep & Cook Time: 20 minutes

SERVING SUGGESTION: SERVE WITH TORTILLA CHIPS AND A CHILLED FRESH FRUIT SALAD.

Hot Crab and Cheese on Muffins

4 English muffins, split
1 tablespoon butter or margarine
3 green onions, chopped
⅓ cup chopped red bell pepper
½ pound fresh crabmeat, drained and flaked*
1 to 2 teaspoons hot pepper sauce
1 cup (4 ounces) shredded Cheddar cheese
1 cup (4 ounces) shredded Monterey Jack cheese

Two cans (6 ounces each) fancy crabmeat, drained, can be substituted for fresh crabmeat.

1. Preheat broiler. Place muffin halves on lightly greased baking sheet. Broil 4 inches from heat 2 minutes or until muffins are lightly toasted. Place on large microwavable plate.

2. Melt butter in medium skillet over medium heat. Add green onions and bell pepper; cook and stir 3 to 4 minutes or until tender. Remove from heat; stir in crabmeat, pepper sauce and cheeses. Spoon about ⅓ cup crab mixture onto each muffin half.

3. Microwave at HIGH 2 to 3 minutes, rotating platter once, or until crab mixture is heated through. *Makes 8 servings*

Prep & Cook Time: 12 minutes

Chicken & Spinach Muffuletta

6 boneless skinless chicken breast halves
Salt and black pepper
1 tablespoon olive oil
¼ cup prepared pesto
¼ cup chopped pitted black olives
¼ cup chopped pitted green olives
1 round loaf (16 ounces) Hawaiian or French bread
2 cups fresh spinach leaves, washed
4 ounces sliced mozzarella cheese

SEASON chicken with salt and pepper. Heat oil in large skillet over medium heat until hot. Add chicken; cook 4 minutes on each side or until no longer pink in center. Cut cooked chicken into strips before assembling sandwich.

COMBINE pesto and olives in small bowl. Cut bread horizontally in half. Spread bottom half of bread with pesto mixture. Top with spinach, chicken, cheese and top half of bread. Cut into wedges.
Makes 6 servings

Tuna Monte Cristo Sandwich

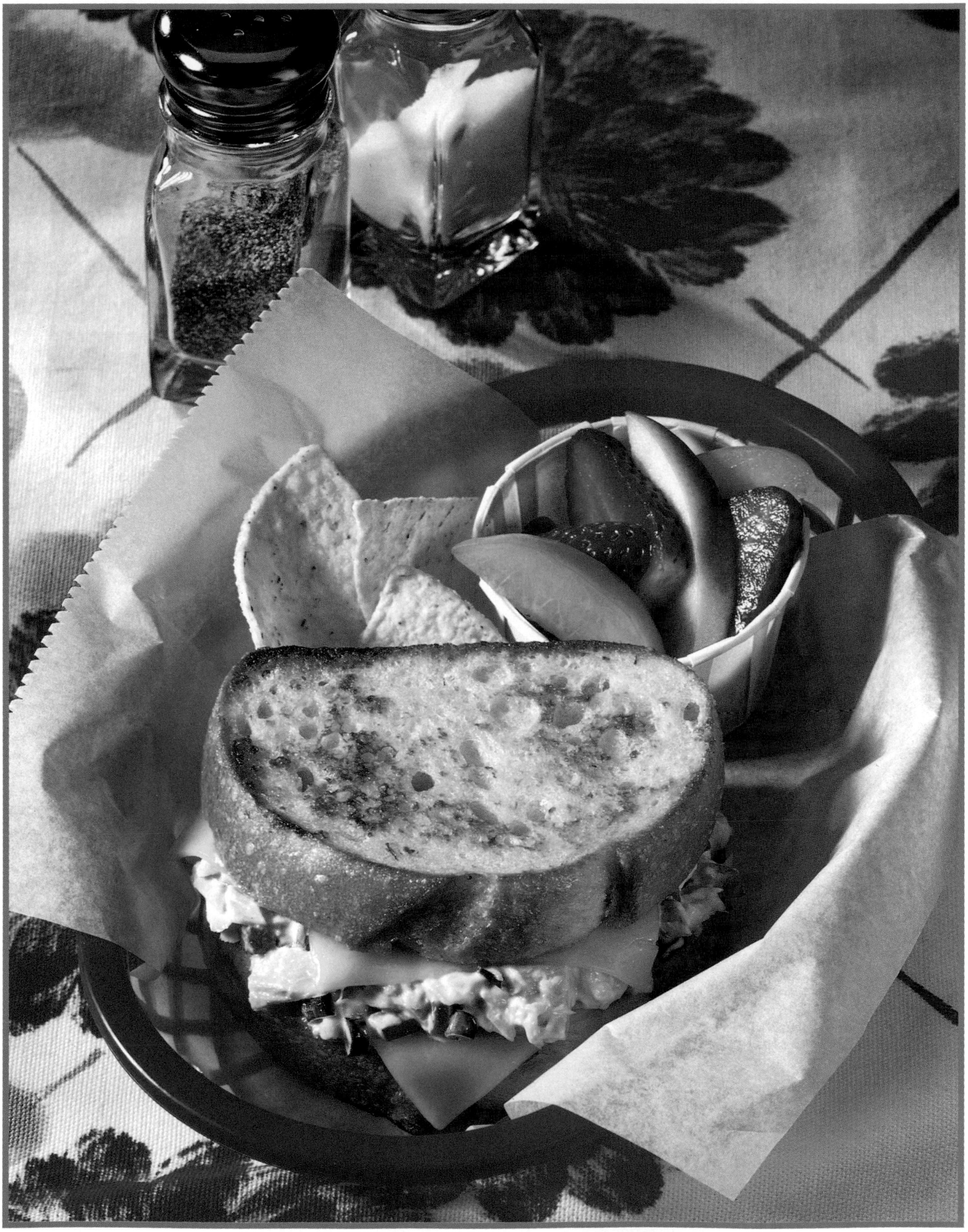

Veggie Club Sandwiches

¼ **cup reduced-fat mayonnaise**
1 **clove garlic, minced**
⅛ **teaspoon dried marjoram leaves**
⅛ **teaspoon dried tarragon leaves**
8 **slices Savory Summertime Oat Bread (page 438) or whole-grain bread**
8 **washed leaf lettuce leaves**
1 **large tomato, thinly sliced**
1 **small cucumber, thinly sliced**
4 **slices reduced-fat Cheddar cheese**
1 **medium red onion, thinly sliced and separated into rings**
½ **cup alfalfa sprouts**

1. To prepare mayonnaise spread, combine mayonnaise, garlic, marjoram and tarragon in small bowl. Refrigerate until ready to use.

2. To assemble sandwiches, spread each of 4 bread slices with 1 tablespoon mayonnaise spread. Divide lettuce, tomato, cucumber, cheese, onion and sprouts among bread slices. Top with remaining bread. Cut sandwiches into halves and serve immediately.

Makes 4 sandwiches

Grilled Cheese 'n' Tomato Sandwiches

8 **slices whole wheat bread, divided**
6 **ounces part-skim mozzarella cheese, cut into 4 slices**
1 **large tomato, cut into 8 thin slices**
⅓ **cup yellow cornmeal**
2 **tablespoons grated Parmesan cheese**
1 **teaspoon dried basil leaves**
½ **cup EGG BEATERS® Healthy Egg Substitute**
¼ **cup skim milk**
2 **tablespoons margarine, divided**
1 **cup low-salt tomato sauce, heated**

On each of 4 bread slices, place 1 cheese slice and 2 tomato slices; top with remaining bread slices. Combine cornmeal, Parmesan cheese and basil on waxed paper. In shallow bowl, combine Egg Beaters® and milk. Melt 1 tablespoon margarine in large nonstick griddle or skillet. Dip sandwiches in egg mixture; coat with cornmeal mixture. Transfer 2 sandwiches to griddle. Cook sandwiches 3 minutes on each side or until golden. Repeat using remaining margarine and sandwiches. Cut sandwiches in half; serve warm with tomato sauce for dipping.

Makes 4 servings

Prep Time: 20 minutes
Cook Time: 14 minutes

The Meatless Dagwood

¾ **pound deli egg salad**
¼ **cup coarsely chopped pitted kalamata or black olives**
6 **slices marble rye or pumpernickel bread**
4 **thin slices (2 ounces) brick or provolone cheese**
2 **dill pickles, thinly sliced**
2 **romaine or red leaf lettuce leaves**

1. Combine egg salad and olives in small bowl.

2. Layer sandwich ingredients as follows: 1 slice bread, 1 slice cheese, ¼ egg-olive mixture, 1 pickle slice, 1 slice bread, 1 lettuce leaf, 1 slice cheese, ¼ egg-olive mixture and 1 slice bread.

3. Repeat to make a second sandwich. Serve immediately.

Makes 2 servings

Prep Time: 10 minutes

Veggie Club Sandwich

Southern Barbecue Sandwich

- **1 pound boneless sirloin or flank steak***
- **¾ cup FRENCH'S® Worcestershire Sauce, divided**
- **½ cup ketchup**
- **½ cup light molasses**
- **¼ cup FRENCH'S® Classic Yellow® Mustard**
- **2 tablespoons FRANK'S® Original REDHOT® Cayenne Pepper Sauce**
- **½ teaspoon hickory salt**
- **4 sandwich buns, split**

*You may substitute 1 pound pork tenderloin for the steak. Cook pork until meat is juicy and barely pink in center or substitute leftover sliced steak for the grilled steak. Stir into sauce and heat through.

Place steak in large resealable plastic food storage bag. Pour ½ cup Worcestershire over steak. Seal bag and marinate meat in refrigerator 20 minutes.

To prepare barbecue sauce, combine ketchup, molasses, remaining ¼ cup Worcestershire, mustard, RedHot® sauce and hickory salt in medium saucepan. Bring to a boil over high heat. Reduce heat to low. Cook 5 minutes or until slightly thickened, stirring occasionally. Set aside.

Place steak on grid, discarding marinade. Grill over hot coals 15 minutes, turning once. Remove steak from grid; let stand 5 minutes. Cut steak diagonally into thin slices. Stir meat into barbecue sauce. Cook until heated through, stirring often. Serve steak and sauce in sandwich buns. Garnish as desired. *Makes 4 servings*

Prep Time: 15 minutes
Marinate Time: 20 minutes
Cook Time: 25 minutes

Broiled Chicken, Avocado and Papaya Sandwich

- **½ cup teriyaki sauce**
- **¼ cup honey**
- **2 teaspoons olive oil**
- **1 pound boneless skinless chicken breasts**
- **1 loaf (16 ounces) sourdough bread**
- **1 large avocado, peeled and sliced**
- **1 medium papaya, peeled and sliced**
- **1 medium tomato, sliced**
- **⅓ cup ranch salad dressing**
- **½ cup cashews, chopped**

1. Combine teriyaki sauce, honey and oil in medium bowl; whisk to combine. Reserve ¼ cup marinade. Add chicken to remaining marinade, turning to coat well. Cover with plastic wrap; refrigerate at least 1 hour, turning chicken occasionally.

2. Remove chicken from marinade; discard marinade. Place chicken on broiler pan coated with nonstick cooking spray. Broil 4 to 5 inches from heat source 10 to 12 minutes on each side or until chicken is no longer pink in center, brushing occasionally with reserved ¼ cup marinade. Set aside; cool. Cut chicken into ½-inch-thick slices.

3. Cut sourdough bread in half lengthwise. Hollow out inside of bread halves, leaving ¼-inch shell. Discard extra bread.

4. To complete recipe, layer chicken on bottom of bread shell. Top with avocado, papaya and tomato. Drizzle ranch dressing over top and sprinkle with cashews. Cover with bread shell top. Press down firmly and cut into slices. For picnics, wrap in plastic wrap and keep cold. *Makes 6 servings*

SERVING SUGGESTION: SERVE WITH FRESH FRUIT SUCH AS CANTALOUPE AND RASPBERRIES. SPARKLING FRUIT SELTZER IS A REFRESHING BEVERAGE.

Southern Barbecue Sandwich

Beefy Calzones

- 1 pound ground beef
- ¼ cup finely chopped onion
- ¼ cup finely chopped green bell pepper
- 2 cloves garlic, minced
- 1 (15-ounce) can tomato sauce
- ½ cup A.1.® Thick & Hearty Steak Sauce
- 1 teaspoon Italian seasoning
- 2 (11-ounce) packages refrigerated pizza crust dough
- 2 cups shredded mozzarella cheese (8 ounces)

In large skillet, over medium-high heat, cook beef, onion, pepper and garlic until beef is no longer pink, stirring to break up meat; drain. Keep warm.

In small skillet, over medium-high heat, heat tomato sauce, steak sauce and Italian seasoning to a boil. Reduce heat to low; simmer 5 minutes or until slightly thickened. Stir 1 cup tomato sauce mixture into beef mixture; set aside. Keep remaining tomato sauce mixture warm.

Unroll pizza dough from 1 package; divide into 4 equal pieces. Roll each piece into 6-inch square; spoon ⅓ cup reserved beef mixture onto center of each square. Top with ¼ cup cheese. Fold dough over to form triangle. Press edges together, sealing well with tines of fork. Place on lightly greased baking sheets. Repeat with remaining dough, filling and cheese to make a total of 8 calzones. Bake at 400°F 20 minutes or until golden brown. Serve with warm sauce. Garnish as desired.

Makes 8 servings

Open-Faced Reuben with Mustard-Caraway Hollandaise

- ¼ cup butter or margarine
- 1 teaspoon caraway seeds
- 1 package (1¼ ounces) hollandaise sauce mix
- 2 tablespoons Dijon mustard or German-style mustard
- Dash ground red pepper
- 4 slices pumpernickel or rye bread
- 8 ounces sliced pastrami
- 1⅓ to 2 cups sauerkraut, drained
- 1 green bell pepper, thinly sliced in rings
- 3 ounces thinly sliced or shredded Swiss cheese
- Dash paprika or ground red pepper

1. Place butter and caraway in 1- to 2-quart saucepan. Cook over medium heat until butter is melted. Mix in hollandaise mix with wire whisk. While whisking, slowly add water according to package directions. Add mustard and ground red pepper; whisk until bubbly. Simmer and stir 1 minute or until thickened; set aside.

2. Preheat broiler. Place bread on baking sheet. Broil 4 inches from heat 1½ to 2 minutes per side or until crisp; set aside. Place pastrami on plate; cover with plastic wrap. Microwave at HIGH 1 minute or until heated through; set aside. Place sauerkraut in small bowl. Cover with plastic wrap and microwave at HIGH 1 minute or until heated through; set aside.

3. Spread 2 to 3 teaspoons sauce on each slice of toast. Place pastrami on toast; top with sauerkraut. Drizzle each serving with about 1 tablespoon sauce. Lay 2 pepper rings on sauerkraut; top with cheese. Sprinkle with paprika. Broil 2 to 3 minutes or until cheese bubbles. Serve with remaining sauce to spoon over individual servings. *Makes 4 servings*

Prep & Cook Time: 20 minutes

SERVING SUGGESTION: SERVE WITH PICKLES, CELERY AND CARROT STICKS.

Mediterranean Chicken Salad Sandwiches

- **4 boneless skinless chicken breast halves**
- **1 teaspoon dried basil leaves**
- **¼ teaspoon salt**
- **¼ teaspoon black pepper**
- **1 cup chopped cucumber**
- **½ cup mayonnaise**
- **¼ cup chopped roasted red pepper**
- **¼ cup pitted black olive slices**
- **¼ cup yogurt**
- **¼ teaspoon garlic powder**
- **6 Kaiser rolls, split**
  Additional mayonnaise
  Lettuce leaves

PLACE chicken, ½ cup water, basil, salt and black pepper in medium saucepan; bring to a boil. Reduce heat; simmer, covered, 10 to 12 minutes or until chicken is no longer pink in center. Remove chicken from saucepan; cool. Cut into ½-inch pieces.

COMBINE chicken, cucumber, ½ cup mayonnaise, red pepper, olives, yogurt and garlic powder in medium bowl; toss to coat well.

SPREAD rolls with additional mayonnaise. Top with lettuce and chicken salad mixture.

Makes 6 servings

Southwestern Sloppy Joes

- **1 pound lean ground round**
- **1 cup chopped onion**
- **¼ cup chopped celery**
- **¼ cup water**
- **1 can (10 ounces) diced tomatoes and green chilies, undrained**
- **1 can (8 ounces) no-salt-added tomato sauce**
- **4 teaspoons brown sugar**
- **½ teaspoon ground cumin**
- **¼ teaspoon salt**
- **9 whole wheat hamburger buns**

1. Heat large nonstick skillet over high heat. Add beef, onion, celery and water. Reduce heat to medium. Cook and stir 5 minutes or until meat is no longer pink. Drain fat.

2. Stir in tomatoes and green chilies, tomato sauce, brown sugar, cumin and salt; bring to a boil over high heat. Reduce heat; simmer 20 minutes or until mixture thickens. Serve on buns. Garnish as desired.

Makes 9 (⅓-cup) servings

Southwestern Sloppy Joe

Grilled Feta Burgers

- ½ **pound lean ground sirloin**
- ½ **pound ground turkey breast**
- 2 **teaspoons grated lemon peel**
- 1 **teaspoon olive oil**
- 1 **teaspoon dried oregano**
- ¼ **teaspoon salt**
- ⅛ **teaspoon black pepper**
- 1 **ounce feta cheese Cucumber Raita (recipe follows)**
- 4 **slices tomato**
- 4 **whole wheat hamburger buns**

1. Combine sirloin, turkey, lemon peel, oil, oregano, salt and pepper; mix well and shape into 8 patties. Make small depression in each of 4 patties and place ¼ of the cheese in each depression. Cover each with remaining 4 patties, sealing edges to form burgers.

2. Grill burgers 10 to 12 minutes or until thoroughly cooked, turning once. Serve with Cucumber Raita and tomato slice on whole wheat bun.

Makes 4 burgers

CUCUMBER RAITA
- 1 **cup plain nonfat yogurt**
- ½ **cup finely chopped cucumber**
- 1 **tablespoon minced fresh mint**
- 1 **clove garlic, minced**
- ¼ **teaspoon salt**

Combine all ingredients in small bowl. Cover and refrigerate until ready to use.

Makes about 1½ cups

Barbecued Cheese Burgers

BARBECUE SPREAD
- ¼ **cup reduced-calorie mayonnaise**
- ¼ **cup bottled barbecue sauce**
- ¼ **cup red or green pepper hamburger relish**

BURGERS
- 1½ **pounds ground lean turkey or ground beef round**
- ⅓ **cup bottled barbecue sauce**
- ⅓ **cup minced red onion**
- 1 **teaspoon hot red pepper sauce**
- ½ **teaspoon garlic salt**
- 6 **sesame seed hamburger buns, split**
- 6 **slices (1 ounce each) ALPINE LACE® Fat Free Pasteurized Process Skim Milk Cheese Product—For Cheddar Lovers**

1. To make the Barbecue Spread: In a small bowl, stir all of the spread ingredients together until well blended. Cover and refrigerate.

2. To make the Burgers: In a medium-size bowl, mix the turkey, barbecue sauce, onion, hot pepper sauce and garlic salt. Form into 6 patties (5 inches each), about 1¼ inches thick. Cover with plastic wrap and refrigerate for at least 30 minutes or overnight.

3. To cook the Burgers: Preheat the grill (or broiler). Grill over medium-hot coals (or broil) 4 inches from the heat for 4 minutes on each side for medium or until cooked the way you like them. Place the buns alongside the burgers for the last 5 minutes to heat, if you wish. Top each burger with a slice of cheese.

4. To serve, spread the insides of the buns with the Barbecue Spread and stuff each bun with a burger. *Makes 6 burgers*

Spamburger® Hamburgers

- 1 **(12-ounce) can SPAM® Luncheon Meat**
- 3 **tablespoons mayonnaise**
- 6 **hamburger buns, split**
- 6 **lettuce leaves**
- 2 **tomatoes, sliced**
- 6 **(1-ounce) slices American cheese**

Slice Spam® into 6 slices (3×¼-inch). In large skillet, sauté Spam® until lightly browned. Spread mayonnaise on buns. Layer Spam® and remaining ingredients on bun bottoms. Cover with bun tops.

Makes 6 servings

Grilled Feta Burger

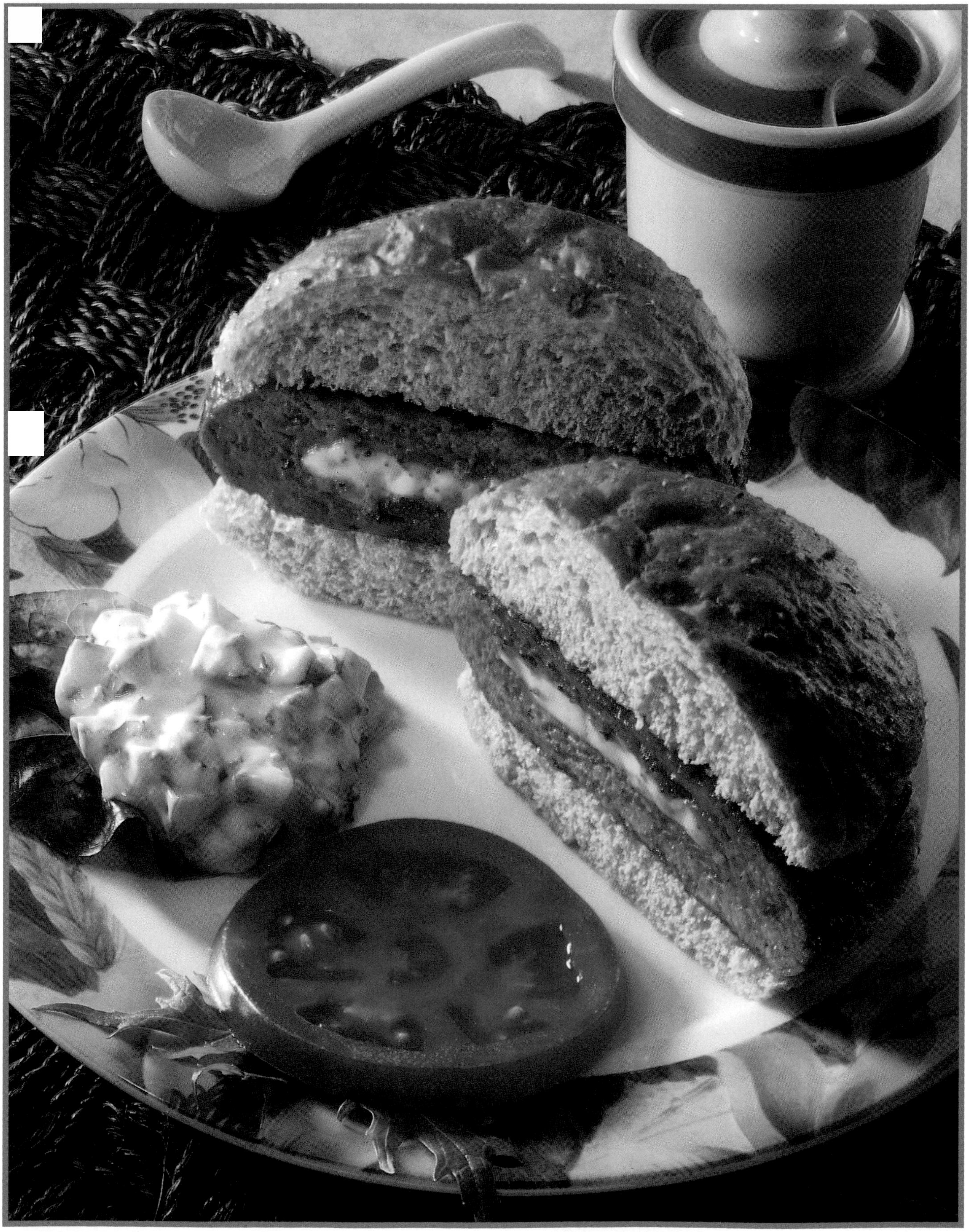

Fresh Rockfish Burgers

8 ounces skinless rockfish or scrod fillet
1 egg white
¼ cup dry bread crumbs
1 green onion, finely chopped
1 tablespoon finely chopped parsley
2 teaspoons fresh lime juice
1½ teaspoons capers
1 teaspoon Dijon mustard
¼ teaspoon salt
⅛ teaspoon black pepper
Nonstick cooking spray
4 grilled whole wheat English muffins
4 leaf lettuce leaves
4 slices tomato
Additional Dijon mustard (optional)

1. Finely chop rockfish and place in medium bowl. Add egg white, bread crumbs, onion, parsley, lime juice, capers, mustard, salt and pepper; gently combine with fork. Shape into 4 patties.

2. Spray heavy grillproof cast iron skillet or griddle with nonstick cooking spray; place on grid over hot coals to heat. Spray tops of burgers with additional cooking spray. Place burgers in hot skillet; grill on covered grill over hot coals 4 to 5 minutes or until burgers are browned on both sides, turning once. Serve on English muffins with lettuce, tomato slice and additional Dijon mustard, if desired.

Makes 4 servings

Broiled Turkey Burgers

1 pound ground turkey
¼ cup finely chopped green onions
¼ cup finely chopped parsley
2 tablespoons dry red wine
1 teaspoon Italian seasoning
¼ teaspoon salt
¼ teaspoon black pepper
4 whole wheat hamburger buns

1. Preheat broiler.

2. Combine turkey, onions, parsley, wine, Italian seasoning, salt and pepper in large bowl; mix well. Shape turkey mixture into 4 (¾-inch-thick) burgers.

3. Spray rack of broiler pan with nonstick cooking spray; place burgers on rack. Broil burgers, 4 inches from heat source, 5 to 6 minutes per side or until burgers are no longer pink in centers. Serve on whole wheat buns with lettuce, grilled pineapple slice and bell pepper strips, if desired.

Makes 4 servings

Dijon Bacon Cheeseburgers

1 cup shredded Cheddar cheese (4 ounces)
5 tablespoons GREY POUPON® Dijon Mustard,* divided
2 teaspoons dried minced onion
1 teaspoon prepared horseradish*
1 pound lean ground beef
4 onion sandwich rolls, split and toasted
1 cup shredded lettuce
4 slices tomato
4 slices bacon, cooked and cut into halves

*5 tablespoons GREY POUPON Horseradish Mustard may be substituted for Dijon mustard; omit horseradish.

In small bowl, combine cheese, 3 tablespoons mustard, onion and horseradish; set aside.

In medium bowl, combine ground beef and remaining mustard; shape mixture into 4 patties. Grill or broil burgers over medium heat 5 minutes on each side or until desired doneness; top with cheese mixture and cook until cheese melts, about 2 minutes. Top each roll bottom with ¼ cup shredded lettuce, 1 tomato slice, burger, 2 bacon pieces and roll top. Serve immediately.

Makes 4 burgers

Fresh Rockfish Burger

Vegetarian Burgers

- ½ cup A.1.® Steak Sauce, divided
- ¼ cup plain yogurt
- ⅔ cup PLANTERS® Slivered Almonds
- ⅔ cup PLANTERS® Salted Peanuts
- ⅔ cup PLANTERS® Sunflower Kernels
- ½ cup chopped green bell pepper
- ¼ cup chopped onion
- 1 clove garlic, minced
- 1 tablespoon REGINA® Red Wine Vinegar
- 4 (5-inch) pita breads, cut into halves
- 4 lettuce leaves
- 4 tomato slices

In small bowl, combine ¼ cup steak sauce and yogurt; set aside. In food processor or blender, process almonds, peanuts, sunflower kernels, bell pepper, onion and garlic until coarsely chopped. With motor running, slowly add remaining steak sauce and vinegar until blended; shape mixture into 4 patties. Grill burgers over medium heat 1½ minutes on each side or until heated through, turning once. Split open top edge of each pita bread. Layer lettuce, burger, tomato slice and 2 tablespoons prepared sauce in each pita bread half. Serve immediately.

Makes 4 servings

Swiss Burgers

- 1 package (about 1¼ pounds) PERDUE® Fresh Ground Turkey, Ground Turkey Breast Meat or Ground Chicken
- ½ cup thinly sliced scallions
- 1 teaspoon Worcestershire sauce
- 4 ounces fresh white mushrooms, thinly sliced
- 2 teaspoons olive oil
- ½ teaspoon salt
  Ground black pepper to taste
- 4 to 5 slices Swiss cheese Dijon mustard
- 4 to 5 Kaiser rolls
- 6 to 8 tablespoons sour cream

Prepare outdoor grill or preheat broiler. In large bowl, combine ground turkey, scallions and Worcestershire sauce. Shape mixture into 4 or 5 patties.

To grill: When coals are medium-hot, place burgers on hottest area of cooking surface of grill; cook 1 to 2 minutes on each side to brown. Move burgers to edge of grill; cook 4 to 6 minutes longer on each side or until thoroughly cooked, juices run clear and burgers spring back to the touch.

To broil: Place burgers on rack in broiling pan 4 inches from heat source. Broil 4 to 6 minutes on each side or until burgers are thoroughly cooked and spring back to the touch.

While burgers are cooking, toss mushrooms with oil and sprinkle lightly with salt and pepper. Place mushrooms on sheet of heavy-duty aluminum foil. Grill or broil along with burgers during last 1 to 2 minutes of cooking time.

When burgers are cooked through, place 1 slice Swiss cheese on each; cook 1 minute longer or just enough to melt cheese. To serve, spread mustard on bottom halves of rolls; cover with a burger and an equal portion of mushrooms. Top each with a generous dollop of sour cream and remaining roll half.

Makes 4 to 5 servings

Inside-Out Brie Burgers

1 pound ground beef
5 tablespoons A.1.®
 Original or A.1.® Bold
 & Spicy Steak Sauce,
 divided
3 ounces Brie, cut into
 4 slices
¼ cup dairy sour cream
2 tablespoons chopped
 green onion
1 medium-size red bell
 pepper, cut into
 ¼-inch rings
4 (2½-inch) slices Italian
 or French bread, cut
 into halves
4 radicchio or lettuce
 leaves

In medium bowl, combine beef and 3 tablespoons steak sauce; shape into 8 thin patties. Place 1 slice Brie in center of each of 4 patties. Top with remaining patties. Seal edges to form 4 patties; set aside.

In small bowl, combine sour cream, remaining 2 tablespoons steak sauce and green onion; set aside.

Grill burgers over medium heat or broil 6 inches from heat source 7 minutes on each side or until beef is no longer pink. Place pepper rings on grill or under broiler; cook with burgers until tender, about 4 to 5 minutes. Top each of 4 bread slice halves with radicchio leaf, pepper ring, burger, 2 tablespoons reserved sauce and another bread slice half. Serve immediately. Garnish as desired. *Makes 4 servings*

Ranch Burgers

1 ¼ pounds lean ground beef
¾ cup prepared HIDDEN
 VALLEY RANCH®
 Original Ranch® Salad
 Dressing
¾ cup dry bread crumbs
¼ cup minced onions
1 teaspoon salt
¼ teaspoon black pepper
 Sesame seed buns
 Lettuce, tomato slices
 and red onion slices
 (optional)
 Additional Original
 Ranch® Salad Dressing

In large bowl, combine beef, ¾ cup salad dressing, bread crumbs, onions, salt and pepper. Shape into 6 patties. Grill over medium-hot coals 4 to 5 minutes for medium doneness. Place on sesame seed buns with lettuce, tomato and red onion slices, if desired. Serve with a generous amount of additional salad dressing.

Makes 6 servings

Inside-Out Brie Burger

Hot Dogs with Dijon Kraut

- 1 (14-ounce) can sauerkraut
- ¼ cup GREY POUPON® Dijon Mustard
- ¼ cup prepared barbecue sauce
- ⅓ cup chopped onion
- 1 tablespoon sweet pickle relish
- 1 teaspoon caraway seeds
- 6 hot dogs, grilled
- 6 oblong sandwich buns or hot dog rolls, toasted
- 1½ cups shredded Cheddar cheese (6 ounces)

In medium saucepan, over medium heat, heat sauerkraut, mustard, barbecue sauce, onion, pickle relish and caraway seeds to a boil; reduce heat. Cover; simmer 2 minutes. Keep warm.

Place hot dogs in buns; top each with ¼ cup cheese. Broil 1 minute or until cheese melts. Top with sauerkraut mixture and serve immediately.

Makes 6 servings

Grilled Garden Spam™ Salad Sandwiches

- 1 (12-ounce) can SPAM® Luncheon Meat, finely cubed
- 1 cup (4 ounces) shredded Swiss cheese, divided
- ½ cup thinly sliced celery
- ½ cup chopped green bell pepper
- ⅓ cup mayonnaise or salad dressing
- ½ teaspoon dried thyme leaves
- ¼ cup butter or margarine, softened
- 12 slices caraway rye bread
- 1 tomato, thinly sliced
- 1 small onion, thinly sliced and separated into rings

In medium bowl, combine Spam®, ½ cup cheese, celery, bell pepper, mayonnaise and thyme; mix well. Spread butter on one side of each bread slice. Spread ½ cup Spam™ mixture on unbuttered side of each of 6 bread slices. Top each with tomato slices, onion rings and about 1 tablespoon of the remaining ½ cup cheese. Top with remaining bread slices, buttered side up. In large skillet or griddle over medium heat, cook sandwiches until cheese melts and sides are golden brown. *Makes 6 servings*

California Ham and Cheese Pitas

- 2 cups chopped honey-baked ham
- 1 cup shredded Cheddar cheese (4 ounces)
- ½ cup chopped red or green bell pepper
- ⅓ cup GREY POUPON® COUNTRY DIJON® Mustard
- ⅓ cup low-fat plain yogurt
- 1 tablespoon chopped cilantro
- 5 (6-inch) whole wheat pita breads, split open
- 1¼ cups alfalfa sprouts
- 2 small tomatoes, sliced
- 1 ripe medium avocado, peeled, pitted and sliced

In small bowl, combine ham, cheese, bell pepper, mustard, yogurt and cilantro. Chill until serving time.

To serve, line each pita with ¼ cup sprouts, tomato and avocado slices; spoon ham filling into pitas. Serve immediately.

Makes 5 servings

Indian Sandwiches

1 ¼ cups soft cheese
(farmer, ricotta, pot,
goat or cottage)
1 small tomato, seeded
and diced
½ cup thinly sliced
cucumber
½ cup diced green bell
pepper
½ cup plain low-fat yogurt
⅓ cup thinly sliced carrot
⅓ cup mixed fresh herbs
(such as parsley, basil,
dill or mint)
1 tablespoon candied
ginger
½ teaspoon TABASCO®
pepper sauce
Salt to taste
4 pita bread pockets or
wheat tortillas, sliced
into halves

In medium bowl, combine
cheese, tomato, cucumber, bell
pepper, yogurt, carrot, herbs,
ginger, TABASCO® sauce and
salt. Serve in pita bread
pockets or rolled in wheat
tortillas. *Makes 8 servings*

Ham and Swiss Sandwiches with Citrus Mayonnaise

¼ cup GREY POUPON®
Dijon Mustard
¼ cup mayonnaise*
1 tablespoon lime juice
1 tablespoon honey
½ teaspoon grated lime
peel
¼ teaspoon ground black
pepper
8 (½-inch-thick) slices
black bread
1 cup shredded lettuce
8 slices tomato
4 ounces sliced Swiss
cheese
12 ounces sliced honey-
baked ham

*Low-fat mayonnaise may be
substituted for the regular
mayonnaise.*

In small bowl, blend mustard,
mayonnaise, lime juice, honey,
lime peel and pepper. Spread
about 1 tablespoon mustard
mixture on each bread slice.
On each of 4 bread slices, layer
¼ cup lettuce, 2 tomato slices,
1 ounce cheese and 3 ounces
ham. Top with remaining bread
slices. Serve with remaining
mustard mixture.
Makes 4 sandwiches

Bagel Dogs with Zesty BBQ Sauce

1 ½ cups ketchup
⅓ cup finely chopped
onion
¼ cup packed light brown
sugar
1 tablespoon cider vinegar
1 tablespoon Worcestershire
sauce*
1 teaspoon hot pepper
sauce
Dash liquid smoke
(optional)
8 HEBREW NATIONAL®
Bagel Dogs

*Use a kosher-certified
Worcestershire sauce that does
not contain any fish product.*

Combine ketchup, onion, sugar,
vinegar, Worcestershire, hot
sauce and liquid smoke, if
desired, in small saucepan.
Bring to a boil over medium-
high heat. Reduce heat; simmer
5 minutes, stirring occasionally.

Heat bagel dogs according to
package directions. Serve bagel
dogs with sauce.
Makes 8 servings

Bistro Turkey Sandwiches

- ¼ cup reduced-calorie mayonnaise
- 2 tablespoons finely chopped fresh basil
- 2 tablespoons chopped drained sun-dried tomatoes in oil
- 2 tablespoons finely chopped pitted kalamata olives
- ⅛ teaspoon red pepper flakes
- 1 loaf focaccia bread, quartered and split *or* 8 slices sourdough bread
- 1 jar (7 ounces) roasted red bell peppers, drained and rinsed
- 4 romaine or red leaf lettuce leaves
- 2 packages (4 ounces each) HEBREW NATIONAL® Sliced Oven Roasted or Smoked Turkey Breast

Combine mayonnaise, basil, sun-dried tomatoes, olives and red pepper flakes in small bowl; mix well. Spread evenly over cut sides of bread. Remove excess liquid from roasted red bell peppers with paper towels. Layer roasted peppers, lettuce and turkey breast between bread slices.

Makes 4 servings

Smoked Turkey and Provolone Croissants

- ⅓ cup GREY POUPON® COUNTRY DIJON® Mustard
- 2 tablespoons mayonnaise*
- 1 tablespoon chopped fresh basil leaves
- 4 croissants, split horizontally
- 1 cup fresh spinach leaves
- 6 ounces deli sliced smoked turkey breast
- 1 small red onion, thinly sliced
- 4 ounces deli sliced provolone cheese
- 1 medium tomato, thinly sliced

Low-fat mayonnaise may be substituted for the regular mayonnaise.

In small bowl, blend mustard, mayonnaise and basil. Spread mustard mixture on cut sides of each croissant. Layer spinach leaves, turkey, onion, cheese and tomato on croissant bottoms; replace croissant tops. Serve immediately.

Makes 4 sandwiches

Creole Hero Sandwich

- ½ cup reduced-fat mayonnaise
- 3 tablespoons chopped chives or green onions
- 2 tablespoons FRANK'S® Original REDHOT® Cayenne Pepper Sauce
- 1 tablespoon small capers
- 1 large loaf French bread (about 20 inches long)
- 3 pounds thinly sliced luncheon meats and cheeses, such as Canadian bacon, roast beef, salami and provolone or Muenster cheese
- 4 plum tomatoes, thinly sliced
- 1 red onion, thinly sliced
- 2 cups shredded romaine or iceburg lettuce

1. Combine mayonnaise, chives, RedHot® sauce, and capers in small bowl. Split bread in half lengthwise. Remove about ¾-inch depth of bread on both sides. Spread mayonnaise mixture inside both halves of bread.

2. Layer luncheon meats, cheeses, tomatoes, onion and lettuce over bottom half of bread. Cover with top half, pressing closed.

3. Cut crosswise into ½-inch-thick slices, securing slices with sandwich picks.

Makes about 12 servings

Bistro Turkey Sandwich

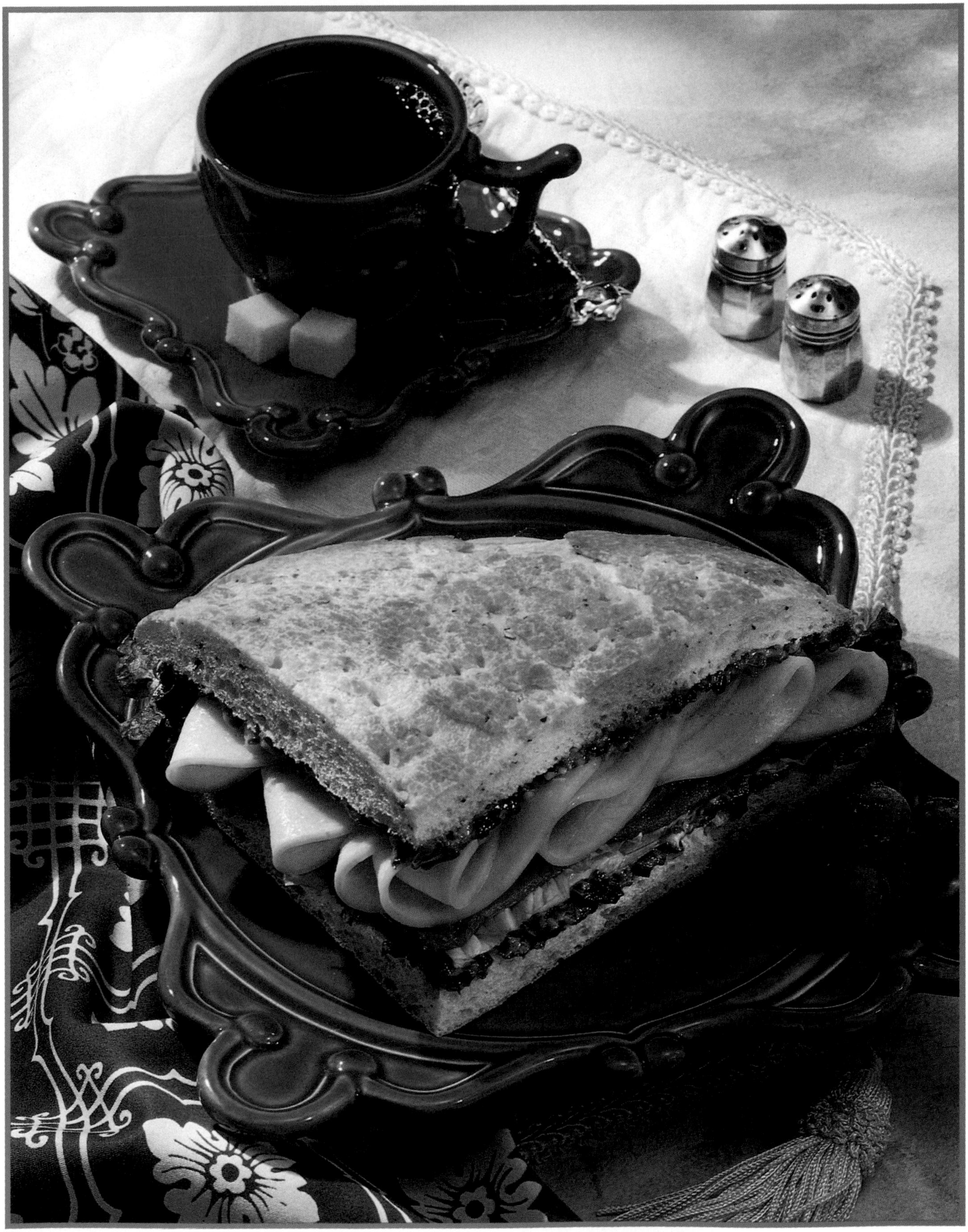

Tabbouli Lamb Sandwich

1 can (14½ ounces) DEL MONTE® *FreshCut*™ Diced Tomatoes with Garlic & Onion, undrained
½ cup uncooked bulgur wheat
1½ cups diced cooked lamb or beef
¾ cup diced cucumber
3 tablespoons minced fresh mint or parsley
1 tablespoon lemon juice
1 tablespoon olive oil
3 pita breads, cut into halves

1. Drain tomatoes, reserving liquid; pour liquid into measuring cup. Add water, if needed, to measure ¾ cup.

2. Bring reserved liquid to a boil in small saucepan; add bulgur. Reduce heat to low; cover. Simmer 20 minutes or until bulgur is tender. Cool.

3. Combine tomatoes, meat, cucumber, mint, lemon juice and oil in medium bowl. Stir in cooled bulgur. Season with salt and pepper, if desired.

4. Spoon about ½ cup tabbouli into each pita bread half.

Makes 6 sandwiches
(½ pita each)

Prep & Cook Time: 25 minutes

Open-Faced Zucchini and Roasted Red Pepper Melts

½ cup HELLMANN'S® or BEST FOODS® Real or Light Mayonnaise or Low Fat Mayonnaise Dressing
1 clove garlic, minced
1 tablespoon chopped fresh basil *or*
   1 teaspoon dried basil leaves
1½ teaspoons chopped fresh oregano *or*
   ½ teaspoon dried oregano leaves
½ teaspoon freshly ground black pepper
1 loaf (14 inches) Italian bread, sliced lengthwise, then cut crosswise in half
1 large zucchini, sliced diagonally into 8 slices
1 jar (7¼ ounces) roasted red peppers, drained and cut into quarters *or* 2 medium red bell peppers, roasted, peeled and cut into quarters
½ cup (2 ounces) shredded mozzarella cheese

1. In small bowl, blend mayonnaise, garlic, basil, oregano and black pepper. Brush cut sides of bread with half the mayonnaise mixture. Broil 5 inches from heat 2 minutes or until golden brown. Remove; set aside.

2. Brush zucchini slices with remaining mayonnaise mixture. Broil 2 minutes, turning once.

3. Top each half of bread alternately with zucchini and red pepper. Sprinkle with cheese.

4. Broil 1 to 2 minutes or until golden brown and cheese melts.
Makes 4 sandwiches

Grilled Salami Sandwich

½ cup drained HEBREW NATIONAL® Sauerkraut
½ teaspoon caraway seeds
4 slices rye bread
2 tablespoons prepared oil and vinegar based coleslaw dressing, divided
4 ounces HEBREW NATIONAL® Beef Salami or Lean Beef Salami Chub, thinly sliced
1 tablespoon parve margarine, divided

Combine sauerkraut and caraway seeds in small bowl. Heat medium nonstick skillet over medium heat. For each sandwich, spread 1 bread slice with 1 tablespoon coleslaw dressing. Cover with salami, sauerkraut mixture and second bread slice. Spread outside of sandwich with margarine. Cook in skillet 6 minutes or until lightly browned on each side. Repeat with remaining ingredients.

Makes 2 servings

Grilled Club Sandwiches

1 long thin loaf
    (18 inches) French
    bread
½ cup mayonnaise
¼ cup FRENCH'S® Deli
    Brown Mustard
2 tablespoons finely
    chopped red onion
2 tablespoons horseradish
½ pound sliced smoked
    boiled ham
½ pound sliced honey-
    baked deli turkey
1 large ripe tomato, sliced
8 ounces Brie cheese,
    thinly sliced
1 bunch watercress,
    washed and drained

Cut bread in half lengthwise.
Combine mayonnaise, mustard,
onion and horseradish in small
bowl; mix well. Spread mixture
on both halves of bread. Layer
ham, turkey, tomato, cheese
and watercress on bottom half
of bread. Cover with top half;
press down firmly. Cut loaf
crosswise into 1½-inch pieces.
Thread two mini sandwiches
through crusts onto metal
skewer. Repeat with remaining
sandwiches.

Place sandwiches on well-oiled
grid. Grill over medium-low
coals about 5 minutes or until
cheese is melted and bread is
toasted, turning once. Serve
warm.   *Makes 6 servings*

Prep Time: 15 minutes
Cook Time: 5 minutes

Salami Western

4 eggs
1 ¼ cups (5 ounces)
    HEBREW NATIONAL®
    Beef Salami or Lean
    Beef Salami Chub,
    diced
1 teaspoon parve
    margarine
¼ cup chopped onion
¼ cup chopped seeded
    green bell pepper
4 soft rolls, split

Beat eggs in medium bowl;
stir in salami. Melt margarine
in large nonstick skillet over
medium heat. Add onion and
pepper; cook and stir 5 minutes
or until tender. Add egg mixture;
cook, stirring frequently, 5 to
7 minutes or until eggs are set.
Spoon onto rolls. Serve
immediately.

Makes 4 servings

Grilled Salami Sandwich (page 394)

Eggplant & Pepper Cheese Sandwiches

- 1 (8-ounce) eggplant, cut into 18 slices
  Salt and black pepper to taste
- ⅓ cup GREY POUPON® COUNTRY DIJON® Mustard
- ¼ cup olive oil
- 2 tablespoons REGINA® Red Wine Vinegar
- ¾ teaspoon dried oregano leaves
- 1 clove garlic, crushed
- 6 (4-inch) pieces French bread, cut into halves
- 1 (7-ounce) jar roasted red peppers, cut into strips
- 1½ cups shredded mozzarella cheese (6 ounces)

Place eggplant slices on greased baking sheet, overlapping slightly. Sprinkle lightly with salt and pepper. Bake at 400°F for 10 to 12 minutes or until tender.

Blend mustard, oil, vinegar, oregano and garlic. Brush eggplant slices with ¼ cup mustard mixture; broil eggplant 1 minute.

Brush cut sides of French bread with remaining mustard mixture. Layer 3 slices eggplant, a few red pepper strips and ¼ cup cheese on each bread bottom. Place on broiler pan with roll tops, cut-sides up; broil until cheese melts. Close sandwiches with bread tops and serve immediately.

Makes 6 sandwiches

Walnut Chicken Salad Sandwich

- ⅔ cup nonfat plain yogurt
- ½ cup finely chopped celery
- ½ cup finely chopped fresh spinach *or* 3 tablespoons drained thawed frozen chopped spinach
- ¼ cup chopped green onions
- 1 tablespoon lemon juice
- 1 tablespoon chopped fresh dill or tarragon *or* ½ teaspoon dried dill weed or tarragon leaves
- 1 teaspoon ground mustard
- 3 cups diced cooked chicken breasts
- 1 apple, cored and diced
- ½ cup (2 ounces) chopped California walnuts
  Salt and black pepper (optional)
- 4 pita breads, cut into halves
- 4 iceberg lettuce leaves or other crisp lettuce leaves

In large bowl, combine yogurt, celery, spinach, onions, lemon juice, dill and mustard. Stir in chicken, apple and walnuts. Season with salt and pepper, if desired. Spoon ½ cup salad into each pita bread half; tuck in lettuce leaf.

Makes 4 sandwiches

FAVORITE RECIPE FROM **WALNUT MARKETING BOARD**

Spiral Sandwich Rounds

- 1 container (5 ounces) garlic and herb cheese spread, at room temperature
- 3 tablespoons finely chopped pimientos, well drained
- 2 tablespoons FRANK'S® Original REDHOT® Cayenne Pepper Sauce
- 6 (8-inch) flour tortillas
- ½ cup watercress or fresh cilantro, washed and finely chopped
- 8 ounces thinly sliced smoked turkey
- 4 ounces thinly sliced Muenster cheese
- ½ small red onion, very thinly sliced

1. Beat cheese spread, pimientos and RedHot® sauce in medium bowl until smooth. Spread rounded tablespoon mixture onto each tortilla leaving ½-inch border. Sprinkle with watercress.

2. Layer turkey, cheese and onion evenly over tortillas. Roll up tortillas jelly-roll style. Wrap each roll with plastic wrap. Refrigerate 30 minutes.

3. Cut rolls diagonally into 1-inch pieces. Skewer with frillpicks to serve.

Makes 6 servings

Note: *You may substitute ⅔ cup pimiento cheese spread for herb cheese and pimientos. Mix in RedHot® sauce and proceed as above.*

Onion & Pepper Cheesesteaks

- 2 medium onions, thinly sliced
- 1 cup red, yellow and/or green bell pepper strips
- 2 tablespoons margarine or butter
- ½ cup GREY POUPON® Dijon Mustard, divided
- 1 tablespoon honey
- 4 (6- to 8-inch) steak rolls
- 8 frozen sandwich steaks, cooked
- 1 cup shredded Cheddar cheese (4 ounces)

In large skillet, over medium-high heat, sauté onions and bell pepper in margarine until tender. Stir in 6 tablespoons mustard and honey; reduce heat and cook 2 minutes. Keep warm.

Cut rolls in half lengthwise, not cutting completely through rolls; brush cut sides of rolls with remaining mustard. Broil rolls, cut-sides up, until golden. Top each roll with cooked steaks, onion mixture and cheese. Broil 1 minute more or until cheese melts. Close sandwiches and serve immediately.

Makes 4 servings

Albondigas Meatball Sandwiches

- 1¾ cups (16-ounce jar) ORTEGA® Thick & Chunky Salsa, mild
- 1 cup (8-ounce can) CONTADINA® Tomato Sauce
- 1 tablespoon ORTEGA® Diced Jalapeños
- ½ teaspoon sugar
- ¼ teaspoon ground cinnamon
- ⅛ teaspoon ground cloves
- 1 pound ground beef
- 1 egg
- ⅓ cup plain dried bread crumbs
- ⅓ cup finely chopped onion
- ¼ cup finely chopped fresh parsley
- 6 (6-inch) sourdough rolls, split

COMBINE salsa, tomato sauce, jalapeños, sugar, cinnamon and cloves in medium bowl.

COMBINE beef, egg, bread crumbs, onion and parsley in large bowl; mix well. Form into 24 (1-inch) meatballs.

COOK meatballs in large skillet over medium-high heat 6 to 8 minutes or until brown. Add salsa mixture; bring to a boil. Cover; reduce heat to low. Cook, stirring occasionally, 20 to 25 minutes or until meatballs are no longer pink in centers. Place 4 meatballs in each roll; top with salsa mixture. *Makes 6 servings*

Sizzling Chicken Sandwiches

- 4 boneless skinless chicken breast halves (about 1 pound)
- 1 package (1.27 ounces) LAWRY'S® Spices & Seasonings for Fajitas
- 1 cup chunky salsa
- ¼ cup water
  Lettuce
- 4 large sandwich buns
- 4 slices Monterey Jack cheese
  Red onion slices
  Avocado slices
  Additional chunky salsa

In large resealable plastic bag, place chicken. In small bowl, combine Spices & Seasonings for Fajitas, 1 cup salsa and water; pour over chicken. Marinate in refrigerator 2 hours. Heat grill for medium coals or heat broiler. Remove chicken, reserving marinade. Grill or broil, 4 to 5 inches from heat source, 5 to 7 minutes on each side or until chicken is no longer pink in center, basting frequently with marinade. Place on lettuce-lined sandwich buns. Top with cheese, onion, avocado and additional salsa.

Makes 4 servings

Note: *Do not baste chicken with marinade during last 5 minutes of cooking.*

Artichoke Heart, Olive and Goat Cheese Pizza

New York-Style Pizza
    Crust (page 406)
2 teaspoons olive oil
2 teaspoons minced fresh
    rosemary *or*
    1 teaspoon dried
    rosemary
3 cloves garlic, minced
½ cup (2 ounces) shredded
    reduced-fat Monterey
    Jack cheese, divided
1 jar (14 ounces) water-
    packed artichoke
    hearts, drained and
    cut into quarters
3 oil-packed sun-dried
    tomatoes, drained and
    cut into slices
2½ ounces soft ripe goat
    cheese, such as
    Montrachet, sliced or
    crumbled
10 kalamata olives, pitted
    and cut into halves
    (about ¼ cup)

1. Prepare New York-Style Pizza Crust. Preheat oven to 500°F. Brush surface of prepared crust with olive oil. Sprinkle with rosemary and garlic and brush again to coat with oil. Bake about 4 minutes or until crust begins to turn golden.

2. Sprinkle with ¼ cup Monterey Jack cheese, leaving 1-inch border. Top with artichokes, tomatoes, goat cheese and olives. Sprinkle with remaining ¼ cup Monterey Jack cheese. Return to oven and bake 3 to 4 minutes more or until crust is deep golden and Monterey Jack cheese is melted. Cut into 8 wedges.

Makes 4 servings

Vegetable Pizza with Oat Bran Crust

1 cup uncooked QUAKER®
    Oat Bran hot cereal
1 cup all-purpose flour
1 teaspoon baking powder
¾ cup skim milk
3 tablespoons vegetable
    oil
1 tablespoon uncooked
    QUAKER® Oat Bran
    hot cereal
1 can (8 ounces) low-
    sodium tomato sauce
1 cup sliced mushrooms
    (about 3 ounces)
1 medium green, red or
    yellow bell pepper, or
    combination, cut into
    rings
½ cup chopped onion
1¼ cups (5 ounces)
    shredded part-skim
    mozzarella cheese
½ teaspoon dried oregano
    leaves or Italian
    seasoning

Combine 1 cup oat bran, flour and baking powder. Add milk and oil; mix well. Let stand 10 minutes.

Heat oven to 425°F. Lightly spray 12-inch round pizza pan with vegetable oil cooking spray or oil lightly. Sprinkle with 1 tablespoon oat bran. With lightly oiled fingers, pat dough out evenly; shape edge to form rim. Bake 18 to 20 minutes. Spread sauce evenly over partially baked crust. Top with vegetables; sprinkle with cheese and oregano. Bake an additional 12 to 15 minutes or until golden brown. Cut into 8 wedges.   *Makes 4 servings*

*Artichoke Heart, Olive and
Goat Cheese Pizza*

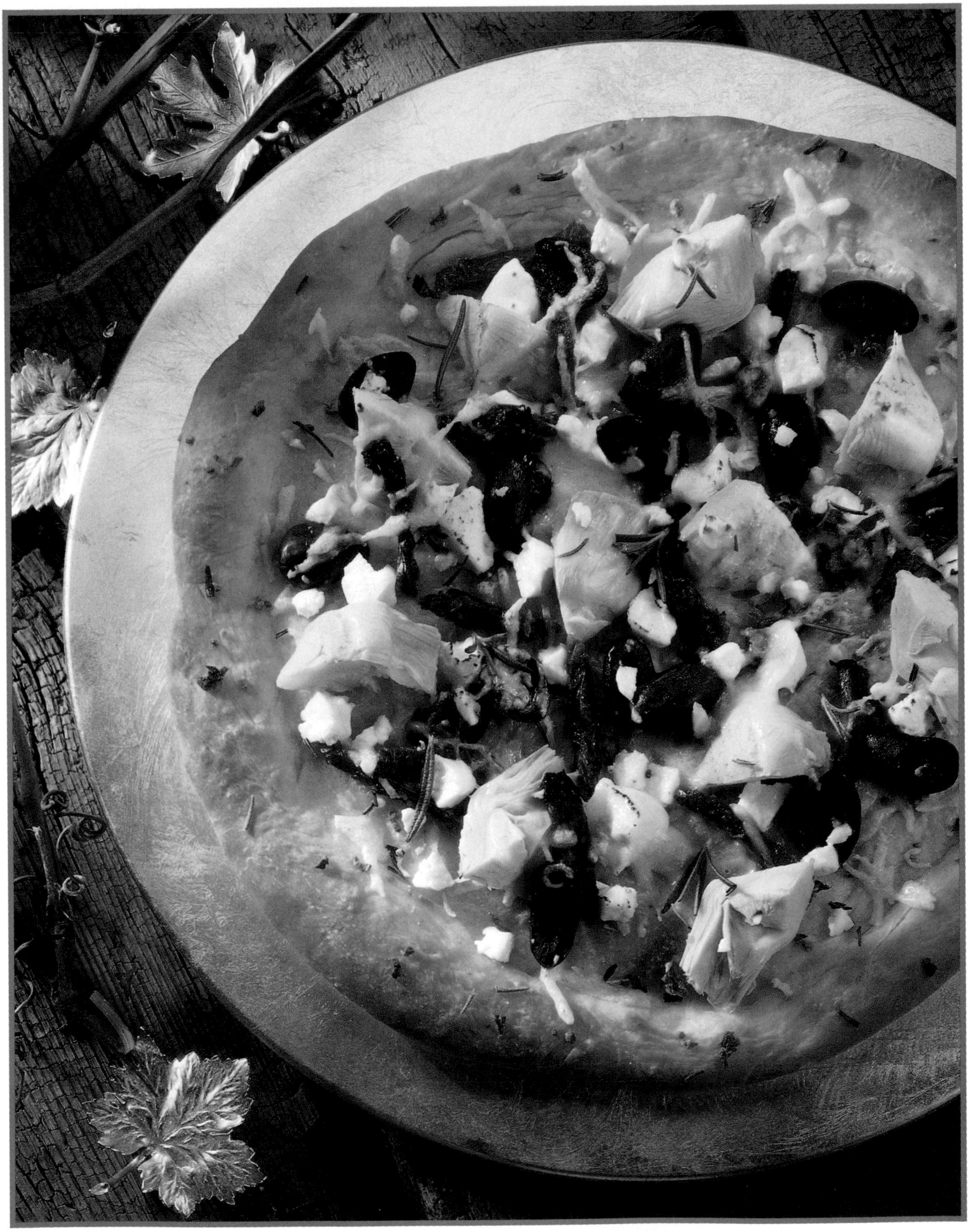

Quick and Hearty Pizza

CRUST
- ½ cup warm water
- 1 package quick-rising active dry yeast
- 2 teaspoons vegetable oil
- ¼ teaspoon salt
- ½ cup whole wheat flour
- 1 cup all-purpose flour

TOPPING
- 1 cup sliced mushrooms
- 1 clove garlic, thinly sliced
- 1 can (8 ounces) no-salt-added tomato sauce
- ½ teaspoon chopped fresh basil
- ⅛ teaspoon black pepper
- 1 green bell pepper, seeded and sliced into rings
- ½ cup Italian-style smoked turkey sausage, sliced
- ½ cup (2 ounces) shredded part-skim mozzarella cheese

1. Preheat oven to 450°F. Pour water and yeast into medium bowl. Stir until completely dissolved. Using wire whisk, stir in oil, salt and whole wheat flour until blended. Using wooden spoon, stir in all-purpose flour until soft dough forms. Turn dough out onto lightly floured surface. Knead dough 5 minutes.

2. Spray medium bowl with olive oil-flavored nonstick cooking spray. Place dough in bowl; cover with plastic wrap. Let dough rest 15 to 20 minutes.

Spray 12-inch pizza pan with nonstick cooking spray. Roll out dough to about ½-inch thickness. Press dough into prepared pizza pan. Set aside.

3. Spray large skillet with nonstick cooking spray. Add mushrooms, garlic and 2 tablespoons water. Cook and stir over high heat 5 minutes or until water evaporates and mushrooms are lightly browned. Reduce heat to low. Add tomato sauce, basil and black pepper; mix well. Spread sauce on pizza crust. Top sauce with bell pepper rings, sausage and cheese. Bake 12 to 14 minutes or until cheese is golden.

Makes 4 servings

Herbed Chicken with Boursin Pizza

- Cornmeal Crust (page 404) or New York-Style Pizza Crust (page 406)
- ¼ cup dry white wine
- 1 tablespoon lemon juice
- 2 tablespoons olive oil, divided
- 1 clove garlic, minced
- ½ teaspoon dried oregano
- ½ teaspoon dried basil
- ½ teaspoon black pepper
- 1 pound boneless skinless chicken breast
- Nonstick cooking spray
- ¾ cup crumbled light Boursin cheese
- ½ cup chopped fresh basil
- 2 tablespoons chopped fresh chives

1. Prepare Cornmeal Crust.

2. Combine white wine, lemon juice, 1 tablespoon olive oil, garlic, oregano, dried basil and pepper in medium bowl. Transfer wine mixture to large resealable plastic food storage bag. Add chicken to bag; seal bag and knead to coat chicken with marinade. Place in refrigerator and marinate at least 2 hours or overnight.

3. Remove chicken from marinade; discard remaining marinade. Spray large skillet with cooking spray; heat over medium heat until hot. Add chicken; cook and stir 12 to 15 minutes or until chicken is golden brown and no longer pink in center. Remove chicken to cutting board. When chicken is cool enough to handle, cut into ½-inch pieces.

4. Preheat oven to 450°F.

5. Press dough into prepared pan. Brush dough with remaining 1 tablespoon olive oil. Top dough with chicken, Boursin cheese, fresh basil and chives. Bake 18 to 20 minutes or until crust is golden brown and cheese is melted.

Makes 8 servings

BBQ Beef Pizza

- **½ pound lean ground beef**
- **1 medium green bell pepper**
- **⅔ cup prepared barbecue sauce**
- **1 (14-inch) prepared pizza crust**
- **3 to 4 onion slices, rings separated**
- **½ (2¼-ounce) can sliced black olives, drained**
- **1 cup (4 ounces) shredded cheese (Colby and Monterey Jack mix)**

1. Preheat oven to 400°F. Place meat in large skillet; cook over high heat 6 to 8 minutes or until meat is no longer pink, breaking meat apart with wooden spoon. Pour off drippings; remove from heat.

2. While meat is cooking, seed bell pepper and slice into ¼-inch-thick rings. Add barbecue sauce to cooked meat in skillet. Place pizza crust on baking pan. Spread meat mixture over pizza crust to within ½ inch of edge. Arrange onion slices and pepper rings over meat. Sprinkle with olives and cheese. Bake 8 minutes or until cheese is melted. Cut into 8 wedges.

Makes 3 to 4 servings

***Prep & Cook Time:** 20 minutes*

Spam™ French Bread Pizza

- **1 onion, chopped**
- **1 green bell pepper, chopped**
- **1 cup sliced fresh mushrooms**
- **1 tablespoon vegetable oil**
- **1 (16-ounce) loaf French bread**
- **1 (12-ounce) can SPAM® Luncheon Meat, cubed**
- **1 cup chunky-style spaghetti sauce**
- **2 cups (8 ounces) shredded mozzarella cheese**

Heat oven to 425°F. In large skillet, sauté vegetables in oil 3 to 4 minutes or until tender. Cut bread in half lengthwise. Remove soft center, leaving two bread shells. Spoon vegetables and Spam® into bread shells. Spoon spaghetti sauce over Spam®. Sprinkle with cheese. Place shells on baking sheet. Bake 10 to 15 minutes or until cheese is melted and bubbly.

Makes 8 servings

Herbed Chicken with Boursin Pizza (page 400)

Thai Chicken Pizza

2 boneless skinless chicken breast halves (½ pound)
2 teaspoons Thai seasoning
Nonstick cooking spray
2 tablespoons pineapple juice
1 tablespoon peanut butter
1 tablespoon oyster sauce
1 teaspoon Thai chili paste*
2 (10-inch) flour tortillas
½ cup shredded carrot
½ cup sliced green onions
½ cup red bell pepper slices
¼ cup chopped cilantro
½ cup (2 ounces) shredded mozzarella cheese

*Thai chili paste is available at some larger supermarkets and at Asian markets.

1. Preheat oven to 400°F. Cut chicken breasts crosswise into thin slices, each about 1½×½ inch. Sprinkle with Thai seasoning. Let stand 5 minutes. Spray large nonstick skillet with cooking spray; heat over medium heat until hot. Add chicken; cook and stir 3 minutes or until chicken is lightly browned and no longer pink in center.

2. Combine pineapple juice, peanut butter, oyster sauce and chili paste in small bowl until smooth.

3. Place tortillas on baking sheets. Spread peanut butter mixture over tortillas. Divide chicken, carrot, green onions, bell pepper and cilantro evenly between each tortilla. Sprinkle with cheese. Bake 5 minutes or until tortillas are crisp and cheese is melted. Cut into wedges. *Makes 4 servings*

Sausage Pizza Piena

1 tablespoon olive oil
1 onion, chopped
1 red bell pepper, diced
1 green bell pepper, diced
1 pound turkey sausage, casing removed
1 teaspoon dried marjoram leaves
1 pound thawed frozen bread dough, at room temperature
2 cups (8 ounces) shredded mozzarella cheese
2 eggs, lightly beaten
3 tablespoons FRANK'S® Original REDHOT® Cayenne Pepper Sauce
1 tablespoon milk
Grated Parmesan cheese
Sesame seeds

1. Heat oil in large nonstick skillet. Add onion and bell peppers; cook 5 minutes or until tender. Add sausage and marjoram. Cook and stir 5 minutes or until meat is no longer pink. Drain well; cool.

2. Preheat oven to 375°F. Cut dough in half. Roll half of dough into 14×10-inch rectangle on lightly floured board. (Let dough rest 5 minutes if dough springs back when rolling.) Pat onto bottom and 1 inch up sides of greased 13×9×2-inch baking pan. Roll out remaining half of dough to 13×9-inch rectangle; keep covered.

3. Stir mozzarella cheese, eggs and RedHot® sauce into sausage mixture; toss to coat evenly. Spoon evenly over bottom dough. Cover sausage mixture with top half of dough. Pinch top and bottom edges of dough to seal. Brush top lightly with milk. Sprinkle with Parmesan cheese and sesame seeds.

4. Bake 25 minutes or until golden and bread sounds hollow when tapped. Let stand 10 minutes. Cut into squares to serve. *Makes 6 to 8 servings*

Prep Time: 30 minutes
Bake Time: 25 minutes

Personal Pizzas

1 pound BOB EVANS
FARMS® Italian Roll
Sausage
1 (8-ounce) can tomato
sauce or pizza sauce
½ teaspoon garlic powder
½ teaspoon dried oregano
leaves
¼ teaspoon dried basil
leaves
8 English muffins *or*
1 pound loaf Italian
bread, cut into 1-inch
slices
3 cups (12 ounces)
shredded Cheddar or
mozzarella cheese or
a combination, divided
1 (4-ounce) can mushroom
stems and pieces,
drained
6 to 8 pimiento-stuffed
green olives, sliced

Preheat oven to 425°F. Crumble
sausage into medium skillet.
Cook over medium heat until
lightly browned, stirring
occasionally. Drain on paper
towels; set aside. Combine
tomato sauce and seasonings
in small bowl; spread evenly on
muffins. Layer ⅔ of cheese on
top of sauce. Layer sausage,
mushrooms and olives evenly
over cheese. Sprinkle with
remaining cheese. Bake 15 to
20 minutes or until bubbly.
Serve hot. Refrigerate leftovers.

Makes 8 servings

Pesto Dijon Pizza

½ cup chopped parsley*
⅓ cup GREY POUPON®
Dijon Mustard
¼ cup PLANTERS®
Walnuts, chopped*
1 tablespoon olive oil*
2 tablespoons grated
Parmesan cheese,*
divided
1½ teaspoons dried basil
leaves,* divided
2 (8-ounce) packages
small prepared pizza
crusts
4 ounces thinly sliced deli
baked ham
3 plum tomatoes, sliced
1 cup shredded
mozzarella cheese
(4 ounces)

**One (7-ounce) container
prepared pesto sauce may be
substituted for parsley, walnuts,
olive oil, 1 tablespoon Parmesan
cheese and 1 teaspoon basil. Stir
the mustard into prepared pesto
sauce.*

In small bowl, combine
parsley, mustard, walnuts, oil,
1 tablespoon Parmesan cheese
and 1 teaspoon basil. Divide
mixture and spread evenly onto
each pizza crust. Top each
crust with 2 ounces ham,
tomato slices and mozzarella
cheese. Sprinkle with remaining
Parmesan cheese and basil.
Place on baking sheet. Bake at
450°F for 8 to 10 minutes or
until cheese melts. Cut into
wedges; serve warm.

*Makes 4 main-dish or
8 appetizer servings*

Vegetable Pizza

2 to 3 cups BIRDS EYE®
frozen Farm Fresh
Mixtures Broccoli, Red
Peppers, Onions and
Mushrooms
1 Italian bread shell or
pizza crust, about
12 inches
1 to 1½ cups shredded
mozzarella cheese
Dried oregano, basil or
Italian seasoning

• Preheat oven according to
directions on pizza crust
package.

• Rinse vegetables in colander
under warm water. Drain well;
pat with paper towel to remove
excess moisture.

• Spread crust with half the
cheese and all the vegetables.
Sprinkle with herbs; top with
remaining cheese.

• Follow baking directions on
pizza crust package; bake until
hot and bubbly.

Makes 3 to 4 servings

Prep Time: 5 minutes
Cook Time: 15 minutes

Corn and Tomato Pizza

Cornmeal Crust (recipe
follows)
1½ cups frozen corn,
thawed
1½ cups chopped seeded
plum tomatoes
¼ cup chopped fresh basil
3 cloves garlic, minced
1 teaspoon dried oregano
leaves
½ teaspoon coarse ground
black pepper
2 tablespoons Dijon
mustard (optional)
1 cup (4 ounces) shredded
reduced-fat part-skim
mozzarella cheese
2 tablespoons grated
Parmesan cheese

1. Prepare Cornmeal Crust.
Preheat oven to 450°F.

2. Combine corn, tomatoes,
basil, garlic, oregano and pepper
in medium bowl.

3. Spread mustard over
prepared crust, if desired.
Sprinkle crust with mozzarella
cheese; top with corn mixture
and Parmesan cheese. Bake
18 to 20 minutes or until crust
is golden brown and cheese is
melted. Cut into 8 wedges.

Makes 4 servings

CORNMEAL CRUST

1 cup warm water (110°
to 115°F)
2 tablespoons sugar or
honey
1 package (¼ ounce)
active dry yeast or
quick-rising yeast
2 to 2½ cups all-purpose
flour, divided
1 cup plus 1 tablespoon
cornmeal, divided
¼ teaspoon salt (optional)

1. Combine water and sugar
in small bowl; stir to dissolve
sugar. Sprinkle yeast on top;
stir to combine. Let stand
5 to 10 minutes or until foamy.

2. Combine 2 cups flour, 1 cup
cornmeal and salt, if desired, in
large bowl. Stir in yeast mixture.
Mix until mixture forms soft
dough. Remove dough to lightly
floured surface. Knead 5 to 10
minutes, adding remaining
½ cup flour, if necessary, until
dough is smooth and elastic.

3. Place dough in large bowl
coated with nonstick cooking
spray. Turn dough in bowl so
top is coated with cooking
spray; cover with towel. Let
dough rise in warm place about
1½ hours or until doubled in
bulk. Punch down dough and
pat into disk. Gently stretch
dough into 14- to 15-inch circle.

4. Spray 14-inch pizza pan with
nonstick cooking spray; sprinkle
with remaining 1 tablespoon
cornmeal. Press dough into
pan. Follow topping and baking
directions for individual recipes.

Makes 1 thick 14-inch crust

Pesto Pita Pizzas

1 envelope (½ ounce)
pesto sauce mix
½ cup water
¼ cup tomato sauce,
preferably no salt
added
4 (6-inch) rounds pita
bread or ready-made
pizza crusts
½ cup (2 ounces) grated
reduced-fat Monterey
Jack cheese
½ cup (2 ounces) chopped
California walnuts
1 teaspoon dried mixed
Italian herbs or Italian
seasoning

Combine pesto sauce mix and
water; blend well. *Omit the oil
called for in package directions.*
Microwave at HIGH 3 minutes,
stirring once, or boil on
stovetop 3 minutes.

Preheat oven to 450°F. Stir
tomato sauce into pesto mix
and spread each pita with
about 2 tablespoons sauce.
Sprinkle each with 2 tablespoons
cheese and 2 tablespoons
walnuts. Sprinkle each pizza
lightly with Italian herbs. Place
on baking sheet and bake 8 to
10 minutes or until sauce is
bubbling and cheese is melted.

Makes 4 pizzas

*FAVORITE RECIPE FROM WALNUT
MARKETING BOARD*

Corn and Tomato Pizza

Zucchini, Black Bean and Sun-Dried Tomato Pizza

½ cup sun-dried tomatoes
1 large seeded peeled tomato, chopped
1 (12-inch) prepared pizza crust
1 cup drained canned black beans
¾ cup grated carrots
1 tablespoon olive oil
1½ cups sliced zucchini
1 small onion, cut into thin slices
¼ teaspoon red pepper flakes
⅔ cup part-skim mozzarella cheese

1. Preheat oven to 425°F. Place sun-dried tomatoes in small bowl; cover with boiling water. Let stand 15 minutes; drain. Coarsely chop.

2. Place tomato and sun-dried tomatoes in food processor. Process using on/off pulsing action until tomatoes are finely chopped.

3. Place crust on baking sheet. Spread with tomato mixture. Top with beans and carrots.

4. Heat oil in medium skillet over medium heat until hot. Add zucchini, onion and pepper. Cook and stir 5 minutes or just until zucchini and onion are soft. Arrange on pizza. Sprinkle with cheese.

5. Bake 12 to 15 minutes or until cheese is melted and pizza is hot. Cut into 8 slices.

Makes 4 servings

Barbecue Chicken Pizza

New York-Style Pizza Crust (recipe follows)
6 ounces boneless skinless chicken breast
2 teaspoons olive oil
¼ to ⅓ cup prepared barbecue sauce
½ medium red onion, thinly sliced
½ green bell pepper, diced
½ cup (2 ounces) shredded reduced-fat Monterey Jack cheese
¼ cup fresh cilantro leaves

1. Prepare New York-Style Pizza Crust. Preheat oven to 500°F.

2. Slice chicken into ¼-inch-thick strips. Bring 4 cups water to a boil in large saucepan over high heat. Stir in chicken; cover and remove from heat. Let stand 3 to 4 minutes or until chicken is no longer pink in center. Drain; set aside.

3. Brush oil evenly over prepared crust. Spread barbecue sauce over crust leaving 1-inch border. Arrange onions over sauce. Top with chicken, bell pepper and cheese. Bake 10 minutes or until crust is dark golden brown. Sprinkle with cilantro and cut into 8 wedges.

Makes 4 servings

NEW YORK-STYLE PIZZA CRUST

⅔ cup warm water (110° to 115°F)
1 teaspoon sugar
½ of 1(¼-ounce) package quick-rising yeast
1¾ cups all-purpose or bread flour
½ teaspoon salt
1 tablespoon cornmeal

1. Combine water and sugar in small bowl; stir to dissolve sugar. Sprinkle yeast on top; stir to combine. Let stand 5 minutes until foamy.

2. Combine flour and salt in large bowl. Stir in yeast mixture. Mix until mixture forms soft dough. Remove dough to lightly floured surface. Knead dough 5 minutes or until smooth and elastic, adding additional flour as needed. Place in bowl coated with nonstick cooking spray. Turn dough in bowl so top is coated with cooking spray; cover with towel. Let rise in warm place 30 minutes or until doubled in bulk.

3. Punch dough down; place on lightly floured surface and knead 2 minutes or until smooth. Pat dough into 7-inch disk. Let rest 2 to 3 minutes. Pat and gently stretch dough from edges until dough seems to not stretch anymore. Let rest 2 to 3 minutes. Continue patting and stretching until dough is 12 to 14 inches in diameter. Spray 12- to 14-inch pizza pan with cooking spray; sprinkle with cornmeal. Press dough into pan. Preheat oven to 500°F. Follow topping and baking directions for individual recipes, baking pizza on bottom rack of oven.

Makes 1 thin 14-inch crust

Fresh Tomato Pizza

New York-Style Pizza Crust (page 406)
1 to 1¼ pounds ripe tomatoes, cored
1 tablespoon olive oil
3 to 4 cloves garlic, minced
½ cup (2 ounces) shredded Monterey Jack cheese or part-skim mozzarella cheese
2 tablespoons grated Parmesan cheese
Cracked black pepper
10 to 12 fresh basil leaves

1. Prepare New York-Style Pizza Crust. Preheat oven to 500°F.

2. Slice tomatoes and place between double layers of paper towels. Press gently to remove juice.

3. Combine oil and garlic in small bowl. Brush oil mixture over entire surface of prepared crust. Pierce surface with fork 12 to 14 times. Sprinkle with Monterey Jack cheese leaving 1-inch border. Bake 3 to 4 minutes or until crust is light golden and cheese is melted.

4. Arrange tomato slices over cheese. Sprinkle with Parmesan cheese and pepper. Bake 4 to 6 minutes or until crust is dark golden. Cut into 8 wedges. Top with whole or slivered basil leaves. *Makes 4 servings*

Southwestern Pizza

1 prebaked pizza crust
1 cup GUILTLESS GOURMET® Barbecue Black Bean Dip
½ onion, sliced
½ bell pepper, sliced
½ cup frozen corn
½ cup GUILTLESS GOURMET® Spicy Nacho Dip

Preheat oven to 400°F. Spread prepared pizza crust with bean dip. Arrange onion, bell pepper and corn on bean dip. Microwave nacho dip in small microwavable bowl at HIGH 2 to 3 minutes or heat in small saucepan over medium heat until warm. Drizzle nacho dip over pizza.

Bake 10 minutes or until heated through. To serve, cut into 8 slices.

Makes 1 pizza (8 slices)

Zucchini, Black Bean and Sun-Dried Tomato Pizza (page 406)

Breakfast & Brunch

FEATURING:

Omelets & Quiche

Pancakes & French Toast

Dishes for Entertaining

Western Omelet (page 412)

Huevos Rancheros Ortega® Style

- 2 tablespoons vegetable oil
- 1 cup (1 small) sliced onion
- 1 cup (1 small) sliced green or red bell pepper
- 2 cloves garlic, finely chopped
- 1¾ cups (16-ounce jar) ORTEGA® Garden Style Salsa, medium or mild
- ½ cup (4-ounce can) ORTEGA® Diced Green Chiles
- ¼ teaspoon ground oregano
- 1 package (10) ORTEGA® Tostada Shells, warmed
- 10 fried or poached eggs
- 1 cup (4 ounces) shredded Cheddar or Monterey Jack cheese
  Sliced green onions (optional)

HEAT oil in large skillet over medium-high heat. Add onion, bell pepper and garlic; cook for 3 to 4 minutes or until vegetables are tender and onion is slightly golden. Add salsa, chiles and oregano. Bring to a boil. Remove from heat.

TOP each tostada shell with ⅓ cup sauce, 1 egg, cheese and green onions.

Makes 10 servings

Tip: This traditional Mexican morning meal is usually served with refried beans on the side.

Sausage Vegetable Frittata

- 5 eggs
- ¼ cup milk
- 2 tablespoons grated Parmesan cheese
- ½ teaspoon dried oregano leaves
- ½ teaspoon black pepper
- 1 (10-ounce) package BOB EVANS FARMS® Skinless Link Sausage
- 2 tablespoons butter or margarine
- 1 small zucchini, sliced (about 1 cup)
- ½ cup shredded carrots
- ⅓ cup sliced green onions with tops
- ¾ cup (6 ounces) shredded Swiss cheese
  Carrot curls (optional)

Whisk eggs in medium bowl; stir in milk, Parmesan cheese, oregano and pepper. Set aside. Cook sausage in large skillet over medium heat until browned, turning occasionally. Drain off any drippings. Remove sausage from skillet and cut into ½-inch lengths. Melt butter in same skillet. Add zucchini, shredded carrots and onions; cook and stir over medium heat until tender. Top with sausage, then Swiss cheese. Pour egg mixture over vegetable mixture. Stir gently to combine. Cook, without stirring, over low heat 8 to 10 minutes or until center is almost set. Remove from heat. Let stand 5 minutes before cutting into wedges; serve hot. Garnish with carrot curls, if desired. Refrigerate leftovers.

Makes 4 to 6 servings

Mexican Frittata

- 2 whole eggs
- 4 egg whites
- 2 tablespoons skim milk
- ¼ teaspoon coarsely ground black pepper
  Nonstick cooking spray
- ¼ cup chopped red bell pepper
- ¼ cup chopped green onions
- ¼ cup sliced fresh mushrooms
- ¼ cup GUILTLESS GOURMET® Mild Nacho Dip
- ¼ cup GUILTLESS GOURMET® Roasted Red Pepper Salsa
  Orange slices and fresh oregano sprigs (optional)

Combine eggs, egg whites, milk and black pepper in small bowl; beat well. Coat medium nonstick skillet with cooking spray; heat skillet over medium-high heat until hot. Add bell pepper, onions and mushrooms; cook and stir until tender. Remove vegetables from skillet; set aside.

Add egg mixture to same skillet; cook over low heat until egg mixture is set, gently lifting edge with spatula to allow uncooked egg to flow under cooked portion. *Do not stir.* Drop spoonfuls of nacho dip on top. Top with vegetables. Cover; let stand 3 to 5 minutes. Cut in half; serve with salsa. Garnish with orange slices and oregano, if desired.

Makes 2 servings

Huevos Rancheros Ortega® Style

Roasted Red Pepper Omelet

Nonstick cooking spray
¼ cup chopped green onions
¼ cup sliced fresh mushrooms
½ cup GUILTLESS GOURMET® Roasted Red Pepper Salsa
8 egg whites, at room temperature
4 egg yolks
⅓ cup skim milk
1 tablespoon reduced calorie mayonnaise
¼ teaspoon coarsely ground black pepper
¼ cup GUILTLESS GOURMET® Nacho Dip (mild or spicy)

Preheat oven to 350°F. Coat large nonstick skillet with cooking spray; heat over medium-high heat until hot. Add onions and mushrooms; cook and stir until tender. Stir in salsa; remove from heat and set aside.

Beat egg whites in large bowl with electric mixer on high speed until stiff peaks form; set aside. Combine egg yolks, milk, mayonnaise and pepper in another large bowl; blend well. Fold egg whites into egg yolk mixture. Coat 8-inch *ovenproof* omelet pan or heavy skillet with cooking spray; heat over medium heat until hot. Pour egg mixture into skillet; gently smooth surface. Reduce heat to medium-low; cook 5 minutes or until puffy and light brown on bottom, gently lifting omelet at edge to judge color. *Do not stir.*

Place in oven; bake 10 minutes or until knife inserted in center comes out clean. Spoon reserved vegetable mixture over half the omelet; drop small spoonfuls nacho dip onto vegetable mixture. Loosen omelet with spatula; fold omelet in half. Gently slide onto warm serving platter. Serve hot.   *Makes 4 servings*

Double Onion Quiche

3 cups thinly sliced yellow onions
3 tablespoons butter or margarine
1 cup thinly sliced green onions
3 eggs
1 cup heavy cream
½ cup grated Parmesan cheese
¼ teaspoon hot pepper sauce
1 package (1 ounce) HIDDEN VALLEY RANCH® Milk Recipe Original Ranch® salad dressing mix
1 (9-inch) deep-dish pastry shell, baked, cooled
Fresh oregano sprig for garnish

Preheat oven to 350°F. In medium skillet, cook and stir yellow onions in butter about 10 minutes. Add green onions; cook 5 minutes. Remove from heat; cool.

In large bowl, whisk eggs until frothy. Whisk in cream, cheese, pepper sauce and salad dressing mix. Stir in cooled onion mixture. Pour egg and onion mixture into cooled pastry shell. Bake until top is browned and knife inserted in center comes out clean, 35 to 40 minutes. Cool on wire rack 10 minutes before slicing. Garnish with oregano.
        Makes 8 servings

Western Omelet

½ cup finely chopped red or green bell pepper
⅓ cup cubed cooked potato
2 slices turkey bacon, diced
¼ teaspoon dried oregano leaves
2 teaspoons margarine, divided
1 cup EGG BEATERS® Healthy Egg Substitute
Fresh oregano sprig for garnish

In 8-inch nonstick skillet, over medium heat, sauté bell pepper, potato, turkey bacon and dried oregano in 1 teaspoon margarine until tender. Remove from skillet; keep warm.

In same skillet, over medium heat, melt remaining 1 teaspoon margarine. Pour Egg Beaters® into skillet. Cook, lifting edges to allow uncooked portion to flow underneath. When almost set, spoon vegetable mixture over half of omelet. Fold other half over vegetable mixture; slide onto serving plate. Garnish with fresh oregano.
        Makes 2 servings

Easy Morning Strata

- 1 pound BOB EVANS FARMS® Original Recipe Roll Sausage
- 8 eggs
- 10 slices bread, cut into cubes (about 10 cups)
- 3 cups milk
- 2 cups (8 ounces) shredded Cheddar cheese
- 2 cups (8 ounces) sliced fresh mushrooms
- 1 (10-ounce) package frozen cut asparagus, thawed and drained
- 2 tablespoons butter or margarine, melted
- 2 tablespoons all-purpose flour
- 1 tablespoon dry mustard
- 2 teaspoons dried basil leaves
- 1 teaspoon salt

Crumble sausage into large skillet. Cook over medium heat until browned, stirring occasionally. Drain off any drippings. Whisk eggs in large bowl. Add sausage and remaining ingredients; mix well. Spoon into greased 13×9-inch baking dish. Cover; refrigerate 8 hours or overnight. Preheat oven to 350°F. Bake 60 to 70 minutes or until knife inserted near center comes out clean. Let stand 5 minutes before cutting into squares; serve hot. Refrigerate leftovers.

Makes 10 to 12 servings

SERVING SUGGESTION: SERVE WITH SLICES OF FRESH PLUMS.

Quiche Lorraine Florentine

- 1 (10-ounce) package frozen chopped spinach, thawed and well drained
- 1 cup shredded Swiss cheese (4 ounces)
- 4 slices bacon, cooked and crumbled
- 2 tablespoons chopped green onions
- 1 (9-inch) unbaked pastry shell
- 3 eggs, slightly beaten
- 1 cup light cream or half-and-half
- ¼ cup GREY POUPON® Dijon Mustard

Combine spinach, cheese, bacon and green onions. Spoon mixture evenly into pastry shell.

In small bowl, blend eggs, cream and mustard. Pour evenly over spinach mixture. Bake at 375°F for 35 to 40 minutes or until knife inserted in center comes out clean. Let stand 10 minutes before serving. To serve, cut into wedges.   *Makes 8 servings*

Easy Morning Strata

Apple and Brie Omelet

- **2 large Golden Delicious apples**
- **2 tablespoons butter or margarine, divided**
- **½ teaspoon ground nutmeg**
- **4 ounces Brie cheese**
- **2 green onions**
- **8 large eggs, lightly beaten**

1. Place large serving platter in oven and preheat to 200°F. Peel, core and slice apples; place in microwavable container. Top with 1 tablespoon butter and nutmeg. Cover and microwave at HIGH 3 minutes; set aside. While apples cook, trim rind from Brie cheese; thinly slice. Thinly slice green onions. Set cheese and onions aside.

2. Heat large nonstick skillet (or large skillet sprayed with nonstick cooking spray) over medium heat until hot. Add 1½ teaspoons butter; spread over pan surface. Pour in half of eggs. Let cook, without stirring, 1 to 2 minutes, or until set on bottom. With rubber spatula, lift sides of omelet and slightly tilt pan to allow uncooked portion of egg to flow underneath. Cover pan and cook 2 to 3 minutes or until eggs are set but still moist on top. Remove platter from oven; slide omelet into center. Spread apples evenly over entire omelet, reserving a few slices to garnish top, if desired.

Evenly space cheese slices over apples. Sprinkle with onions, reserving a few slices for garnish. Return platter to oven.

3. Repeat directions in step 2 to cook remaining eggs. When cooked, slide spatula around edges to be certain omelet is loose. Carefully flip second omelet over and place on top of cheese, apple and onion mixture. Place reserved apple and onion slices on top in decorative pattern. Cut into wedges to serve.

Makes 4 servings

Prep & Cook Time: 20 minutes

Ham and Cheese Frittata

- **1 tablespoon vegetable oil**
- **1 cup chopped red onion**
- **½ cup chopped green bell pepper**
- **1 teaspoon minced garlic**
- **1 cup (6 ounces) slivered ALPINE LACE® Boneless Cooked Ham**
- **1 cup egg substitute *or* 4 large eggs**
- **3 large egg whites**
- **1 cup (4 ounces) shredded ALPINE LACE® Reduced Fat Cheddar Cheese, divided**
- **¼ cup whole fresh tarragon leaves *or* 2 teaspoons dried tarragon**
- **½ teaspoon salt**
- **¼ teaspoon cracked black pepper**
- **2 large plum tomatoes, thinly sliced**

1. Preheat the broiler. In a large broilerproof skillet, heat the oil over medium-high heat. Add the onion, bell pepper and garlic and sauté for 5 minutes or until soft. Stir in the ham and cook 3 minutes more.

2. In a medium size bowl, whisk the egg substitute (or the 4 whole eggs) with the egg whites until foamy; fold in ½ cup of the cheese, the tarragon, salt and black pepper. Pour over the vegetable-ham mixture.

3. Reduce the heat and cook, uncovered, for 6 minutes or just until the egg mixture is set around the edges. Arrange the tomato slices on top of the frittata, in a circle around the edge and in a cluster in the center. Sprinkle with the remaining ½ cup of cheese.

4. Slide the skillet under the broiler 1 minute or until the frittata is set in the center. Serve immediately right from the skillet.   *Makes 4 servings*

Apple and Brie Omelet

Breakfast Burritos

- 6 ounces breakfast sausage
- 1¾ cups (1-pound can) ORTEGA® Refried Beans
- 1 tablespoon butter or margarine
- 8 eggs, lightly beaten
- 8 soft taco-size (8-inch) flour tortillas, warmed
- ½ cup (2 ounces) shredded Cheddar cheese
- ¼ cup chopped fresh tomato
- ¼ cup chopped green bell pepper
  ORTEGA® Thick & Chunky Salsa, mild or Garden Style Salsa, mild or Thick & Smooth Taco Sauce, medium

COOK sausage, stirring to break into pieces, in large skillet over medium-high heat for 4 to 5 minutes or until no longer pink in center; drain. Stir in refried beans; heat for 3 to 4 minutes. Reduce heat to low; cook, stirring frequently, for 5 minutes. Remove from skillet; keep warm.

MELT butter in medium skillet over medium heat. Add eggs; cook, stirring constantly, for 3 to 4 minutes or until eggs are of desired consistency.

PLACE ⅓ cup sausage mixture down center of each tortilla. Top with 2 tablespoons eggs, 1 tablespoon cheese, 1 teaspoon tomato and 1 teaspoon bell pepper; fold into burritos. Serve immediately with salsa or taco sauce. *Makes 8 servings*

Chile Tortilla Brunch Casserole

- 2 cans (7 ounces each) ORTEGA® Whole Green Chiles, split in half
- 6 corn tortillas, cut into strips
- 4 cups (16 ounces) shredded Monterey Jack cheese
- 1 cup (1 medium) chopped tomato
- 4 tablespoons (about 3) chopped green onions, divided
- 8 eggs
- ½ cup milk
- ½ teaspoon salt
- ½ teaspoon ground black pepper
- ½ teaspoon ground cumin
  ORTEGA® Thick & Chunky Salsa, hot, medium or mild

LAYER 1 can chile halves, 3 tortillas and 2 cups cheese in greased 9-inch square baking pan. Top with tomato and *2 tablespoons* green onions. Layer remaining 1 can chile halves, 3 tortillas and 2 cups cheese over tomato. Beat eggs, milk, salt, pepper and cumin in medium bowl; pour over chile mixture.

BAKE, uncovered, in preheated 350°F. oven for 40 to 45 minutes or until center is set. Cool in pan on wire rack for 10 minutes; sprinkle with *remaining 2 tablespoons* green onions. Serve with salsa. *Makes 8 servings*

Cheesy Salsa Omelet

- 1 cup egg substitute
- 1 tablespoon skim milk
  Nonstick cooking spray
- ¼ cup sliced fresh mushrooms
- ¼ cup chopped green onions
- ¼ cup GUILTLESS GOURMET® Nacho Dip (mild or spicy)
- ¼ cup GUILTLESS GOURMET® Salsa (mild, medium or hot)

Combine egg substitute and milk in small bowl; beat well. Coat medium nonstick skillet with cooking spray; heat over medium-high heat until hot. Add mushrooms and onions; cook and stir 2 to 3 minutes or until vegetables are softened. Remove vegetables from skillet; set aside.

Add egg mixture to same skillet; cook over low heat until egg mixture sets, gently lifting edge with spatula to allow uncooked egg to flow under cooked portion. *Do not stir.* Top with reserved vegetable mixture. Drop spoonfuls of nacho dip over vegetable mixture. Cover tightly; let stand 3 to 5 minutes. Fold omelet in half. Gently slide onto warm serving platter. Cut in half; serve each half with 2 tablespoons salsa. *Makes 2 servings*

Zucchini Mushroom Frittata

- 1 ½ cups EGG BEATERS® Healthy Egg Substitute
- ½ cup (2 ounces) shredded reduced-fat Swiss cheese
- ¼ cup skim milk
- ½ teaspoon garlic powder
- ¼ teaspoon seasoned pepper
- 1 medium zucchini, shredded (1 cup)
- 1 medium tomato, chopped
- 1 (4-ounce) can sliced mushrooms, drained
  Tomato slices and fresh basil leaves for garnish

In medium bowl, combine Egg Beaters®, cheese, milk, garlic powder and seasoned pepper; set aside.

Spray 10-inch ovenproof nonstick skillet lightly with nonstick cooking spray. Over medium-high heat, sauté zucchini, tomato and mushrooms in skillet until tender. Pour egg mixture into skillet, stirring well. Cover; cook over low heat for 15 minutes or until cooked on bottom and almost set on top. Remove lid and place skillet under broiler for 2 to 3 minutes or until desired doneness. Slide onto serving platter; cut into wedges to serve. Garnish with tomato slices and basil.

Makes 6 servings

Prep Time: 20 minutes
Cook Time: 20 minutes

Easy Brunch Quiche

- 1 package (8 ounces) refrigerated crescent dinner rolls
- 1 ½ cups (6 ounces) shredded Monterey Jack cheese, divided
- ½ cup (4-ounce can) ORTEGA® Diced Green Chiles
- ½ cup chopped onion
- 4 eggs, lightly beaten
- 1 cup milk
- ¼ cup chopped fresh cilantro
- 2 tablespoons Dijon mustard
  ORTEGA® Thick & Chunky Salsa, mild or Garden Style Salsa, mild

UNROLL crescent roll dough; press onto bottom of greased 13×9-inch baking pan. Bake in preheated 375°F. oven for 5 to 8 minutes or until lightly golden; remove from oven. Sprinkle with ¾ cup cheese. Top with chiles, onion and remaining ¾ cup cheese.

COMBINE eggs, milk, cilantro and mustard in medium bowl. Pour evenly over cheese mixture.

BAKE, uncovered, in preheated 375°F. oven for 25 to 30 minutes or until knife inserted near center comes out clean. Cool in pan on wire rack for 5 minutes. Cut into pieces; serve topped with salsa.

Makes 12 servings

Farmstand Frittata

- ½ cup chopped onion
- 1 medium red bell pepper, cut into thin strips
- 1 cup broccoli florets, blanched, drained
- 1 cup cooked quartered unpeeled red-skinned potatoes
- 6 egg whites
- 1 cup cholesterol-free egg substitute
- 1 tablespoon chopped fresh parsley
- ½ teaspoon salt
- ¼ teaspoon ground black pepper
- ½ cup (2 ounces) shredded reduced-fat Cheddar cheese

1. Spray large nonstick ovenproof skillet with nonstick cooking spray; heat over medium heat until hot. Add onion and bell pepper; cook and stir 3 minutes or until crisp-tender.

2. Add broccoli and potatoes; cook and stir 1 to 2 minutes or until heated through.

3. Whisk together egg whites, egg substitute, parsley, salt and black pepper in medium bowl.

4. Spread vegetables in even layer in skillet. Pour egg white mixture over vegetables; cover and cook over medium heat 10 to 12 minutes or until egg mixture is set.

5. Preheat broiler. Top frittata with cheese. Broil 4 inches from heat 1 minute or until cheese is bubbly. Cut into wedges.

Makes 5 servings

Silver Dollar Pancakes with Mixed Berry Topping

1 ¼ cups all-purpose flour
2 tablespoons sugar
2 teaspoons baking soda
1 ½ cups buttermilk
½ cup EGG BEATERS®
   Healthy Egg Substitute
3 tablespoons margarine,
   melted, divided
   Mixed Berry Topping
   (recipe follows)

In large bowl, combine flour, sugar and baking soda. Stir in buttermilk, Egg Beaters® and 2 tablespoons margarine just until blended.

Brush large nonstick griddle or skillet with some of remaining margarine; heat over medium-high heat. Using 1 heaping tablespoon batter for each pancake, spoon batter onto griddle. Cook until bubbly; turn and cook until lightly browned. Repeat with remaining batter using remaining margarine as needed. Serve hot with Mixed Berry Topping.

Makes 28 (2-inch) pancakes

MIXED BERRY TOPPING: In medium saucepan, over medium-low heat, combine 1 (12-ounce) package frozen mixed berries,* thawed, ¼ cup honey and ½ teaspoon grated gingerroot (*or* ⅛ teaspoon ground ginger). Cook and stir just until hot and well blended. Serve over pancakes.

*Three cups mixed fresh berries may be substituted.

Harvest Apple Oatmeal

1 cup apple juice
1 cup water
1 medium apple, cored
   and chopped
1 cup uncooked old-
   fashioned rolled oats
¼ cup raisins
⅛ teaspoon ground
   cinnamon
⅛ teaspoon salt

Microwave Directions:
Combine apple juice, water and apple in 2-quart microwavable bowl. Microwave at HIGH 3 minutes, stirring halfway through cooking time. Add oats, raisins, cinnamon and salt; stir until well blended. Microwave at MEDIUM (50%) 4 to 5 minutes or until thick; stir before serving. Garnish with apple slices, if desired.

Makes 2 servings

CONVENTIONAL DIRECTIONS: BRING APPLE JUICE, WATER AND APPLE TO A BOIL IN MEDIUM SAUCEPAN OVER MEDIUM-HIGH HEAT. STIR IN OATS, RAISINS, CINNAMON AND SALT UNTIL WELL BLENDED. COOK, UNCOVERED, OVER MEDIUM HEAT 5 TO 6 MINUTES OR UNTIL THICK, STIRRING OCCASIONALLY.

Black Bean Pancakes & Salsa

1 cup GUILTLESS
   GOURMET® Black
   Bean Dip (mild or
   spicy)
2 egg whites
½ cup unbleached
   all-purpose flour
½ cup skim milk
1 tablespoon canola oil
   Nonstick cooking spray
½ cup fat-free sour cream
½ cup GUILTLESS
   GOURMET® Salsa
   (mild, medium or hot)
   Yellow tomatoes and
   fresh mint leaves
   (optional)

For pancake batter, place bean dip, egg whites, flour, milk and oil in blender or food processor; blend until smooth. Refrigerate 2 hours or overnight.

Preheat oven to 350°F. Coat large nonstick skillet with cooking spray; heat over medium heat until hot. For each pancake, spoon 2 tablespoons batter into skillet; cook until bubbles form and break on pancake surface. Turn pancakes over; cook until lightly browned on other side. Place on baking sheet; keep warm in oven. Repeat to make 16 small pancakes. (If batter becomes too thick, thin with more milk.) Serve hot with sour cream and salsa. Garnish with tomatoes and mint, if desired.

Makes 4 servings

Silver Dollar Pancakes with Mixed Berry Topping

Sunrise French Toast

2 cups cholesterol-free
　egg substitute
½ cup evaporated
　skimmed milk
1 teaspoon grated orange
　peel
1 teaspoon vanilla
¼ teaspoon ground
　cinnamon
1 jar (10 ounces) no-
　sugar-added orange
　marmalade
1 loaf (1 pound) Italian
　bread, cut into
　½-inch-thick slices
　(about 20 slices)
　Powdered sugar
　Maple-flavored syrup
　(optional)

1. Preheat oven to 400°F. Combine egg substitute, milk, peel, vanilla and cinnamon in medium bowl. Set aside.

2. Spread 1 tablespoon marmalade over 1 bread slice to within ½ inch of edge. Top with another bread slice. Repeat with remaining marmalade and bread.

3. Spray griddle or large skillet with nonstick cooking spray; heat over medium heat until hot. Dip sandwiches in egg substitute mixture. *Do not soak.* Cook sandwiches in batches 2 to 3 minutes on each side or until golden brown.

4. Transfer sandwiches to 15×10-inch jelly-roll pan. Bake 10 to 12 minutes or until sides are sealed. Dust with powdered sugar and serve with syrup.

Makes 5 servings

Cheesy Corn Batter Cakes

1¼ cups all-purpose flour
2 tablespoons sugar
1 teaspoon baking powder
½ teaspoon salt
1½ cups 2% low fat milk
¼ cup egg substitute *or*
　1 large egg
2 tablespoons unsalted
　butter substitute,
　melted
1 cup (4 ounces) shredded
　ALPINE LACE®
　American Flavor
　Pasteurized Process
　Cheese Product
1 cup fresh or frozen and
　thawed corn kernels

1. Spray a large nonstick griddle or skillet with nonstick cooking spray and heat over medium heat.

2. In a medium-size bowl, mix the flour, sugar, baking powder and salt.

3. In a small bowl, whisk together the milk, egg substitute (or the whole egg) and butter.

4. Using your hands, make a hole in the center of the flour mixture and pour in the milk mixture. Using a wooden spoon, stir just until combined. Fold in the cheese and corn.

5. Spoon the batter by ¼ cupfuls onto the griddle. Cook for about 3 minutes or just until the cakes are covered with bubbles. Flip over and cook 2 minutes more or until golden brown. Serve for brunch with maple syrup or honey.

Makes 12 (4-inch) batter cakes

PB & J French Toast

¼ cup blueberry preserves,
　or any flavor
6 slices whole wheat
　bread
¼ cup creamy peanut
　butter
½ cup EGG BEATERS®
　Healthy Egg Substitute
¼ cup skim milk
2 tablespoons margarine
1 large banana, sliced
1 tablespoon honey
1 tablespoon orange juice
1 tablespoon PLANTERS®
　Dry Roasted Unsalted
　Peanuts, chopped
　Low-fat vanilla yogurt
　(optional)

Spread preserves evenly over 3 bread slices. Spread peanut butter evenly over remaining bread slices. Press preserves and peanut butter slices together to form 3 sandwiches; cut each diagonally in half. In shallow bowl, combine Egg Beaters® and milk. In large nonstick griddle or skillet, over medium-high heat, melt margarine. Dip each sandwich in egg mixture to coat; transfer to griddle. Cook sandwiches 2 minutes on each side or until golden. Keep warm.

In small bowl, combine banana slices, honey, orange juice and peanuts. Arrange sandwiches on platter; top with banana mixture. Serve warm with a dollop of yogurt, if desired.

Makes 6 servings

Sunrise French Toast

Country Skillet Hash

2 tablespoons butter or margarine
4 pork chops (¾ inch thick), diced
¼ teaspoon black pepper
¼ teaspoon cayenne pepper (optional)
1 medium onion, chopped
2 cloves garlic, minced
1 can (14½ ounces) DEL MONTE® FreshCut™ Whole New Potatoes, drained and diced
1 can (14½ ounces) DEL MONTE® FreshCut™ Diced Tomatoes, undrained
1 medium green bell pepper, chopped
½ teaspoon dried thyme, crushed

1. Melt butter in large skillet over medium heat. Add meat; cook, stirring occasionally, until no longer pink in center. Season with black pepper and cayenne pepper, if desired.

2. Add onion and garlic; cook until tender. Stir in potatoes, tomatoes, bell pepper and thyme. Cook 5 minutes, stirring frequently. Season with salt, if desired. *Makes 4 servings*

Prep Time: 10 minutes
Cook Time: 15 minutes

Tip: The hash may be topped with a poached or fried egg.

Make-Ahead Breakfast Casserole

2½ cups seasoned croutons
1 pound BOB EVANS FARMS® Original Recipe Roll Sausage
4 eggs
2¼ cups milk
1 (10½-ounce) can condensed cream of mushroom soup
1 (10-ounce) package frozen chopped spinach, thawed and squeezed dry
1 (4-ounce) can mushrooms, drained and chopped
1 cup (4 ounces) shredded sharp Cheddar cheese
1 cup (4 ounces) shredded Monterey Jack cheese
¼ teaspoon dry mustard
Fresh herb sprigs and carrot strips (optional)
Picante sauce or salsa (optional)

Spread croutons on bottom of greased 13×9-inch baking dish. Crumble sausage into medium skillet. Cook over medium heat until browned, stirring occasionally. Drain off any drippings. Spread over croutons. Whisk eggs and milk in large bowl until blended. Stir in soup, spinach, mushrooms, cheeses and mustard. Pour egg mixture over sausage and croutons. Refrigerate overnight.

Preheat oven to 325°F. Bake egg mixture 50 to 55 minutes or until set and lightly browned on top. Garnish with herb sprigs and carrot, if desired. Serve hot with picante sauce, if desired. Refrigerate leftovers. *Makes 10 to 12 servings*

Walnut Chicken Pinwheels

2 boneless skinless chicken breasts, halved
12 to 14 spinach leaves
1 package (4 ounces) ALOUETTE® Garlic et Herbs Classique Cheese
5 ounces roasted red peppers, sliced, or 5 ounces pimiento slices
¾ cup finely chopped California walnuts

Pound chicken to about ¼-inch thickness with flat side of meat mallet or chef's knife. Cover each chicken piece with spinach leaves. Spread each with Alouette®. Top with pepper slices and walnuts. Carefully roll up each breast and secure with wooden toothpicks. Bake at 400°F 20 to 25 minutes or until cooked through. Chill. Remove toothpicks before serving, then slice into ½-inch rounds. Serve cold.
Makes about 35 appetizers or 8 main-dish servings

Country Skillet Hash

Asparagus-Swiss Soufflé

- ¼ **cup unsalted butter substitute**
- ½ **cup chopped yellow onion**
- ¼ **cup all-purpose flour**
- ½ **teaspoon salt**
- ¼ **teaspoon cayenne pepper**
- 1 **cup 2% low fat milk**
- 1 **cup (4 ounces) shredded ALPINE LACE® Reduced Fat Swiss Cheese**
- 1 **cup egg substitute** *or* **4 large eggs**
- 1 **cup coarsely chopped fresh asparagus pieces, cooked, or frozen asparagus pieces, thawed and drained**
- 3 **large egg whites**

1. Preheat the oven to 325°F. Spray a 1½-quart soufflé dish with nonstick cooking spray.

2. In a large saucepan, melt the butter over medium heat, add the onion and sauté for 5 minutes or until soft. Stir in the flour, salt and pepper and cook for 2 minutes or until bubbly. Add the milk and cook, stirring constantly, for 5 minutes or until the sauce thickens. Add the cheese and stir until melted.

3. In a small bowl, whisk the egg substitute (or the whole eggs). Whisk in a little of the hot cheese sauce, then return this egg mixture to the saucepan and whisk until well blended. Remove from the heat and fold in the drained asparagus.

4. In a medium-size bowl, using an electric mixer set on high, beat the egg whites until stiff peaks form. Fold the hot cheese sauce into the whites, then spoon into the soufflé dish.

5. Place the soufflé on a baking sheet and bake for 50 minutes or until golden brown and puffy. *Makes 8 servings*

Chicken Cordon Bleu Bake

- 8 **slices day-old white or whole-wheat bread, crusts removed**
- 8 **thin slices (1 ounce each) ALPINE LACE® Reduced Fat Swiss Cheese**
- 2 **tablespoons unsalted butter substitute**
- ¼ **cup all-purpose flour**
- 1⅔ **cups 2% low fat milk**
- ½ **teaspoon freshly ground black pepper**
- ¼ **teaspoon salt**
- 12 **thin slices (½ ounce each) skinless roasted chicken or turkey**
- 12 **thin slices (½ ounce each) ALPINE LACE® Boneless Cooked Ham**
- 1 **cup thin strips yellow onion**

1. Preheat the oven to 350°F. Butter a 13×9×3-inch ovenproof dish. Cut bread into 32 triangles, 4 triangles each slice. Line the bottom of the dish with 16 triangles, overlapping as you go along. Cut the cheese into 3½×¼-inch strips.

2. In a medium-size saucepan, melt the butter over medium heat. Stir in the flour and cook until bubbly. Whisk in the milk, pepper and salt. Cook, whisking constantly, for 5 minutes or until slightly thickened.

3. Spread ¼ of the sauce in the baking dish. Layer ⅓ of the chicken, ⅓ of the cheese, ⅓ of the ham, ⅓ of the onion and ¼ of the sauce. Repeat 2 times. Top with the remaining 16 triangles of bread, placing them around the edge and down the center.

4. Bake for 40 minutes or until puffy and golden brown. Let stand for 10 minutes before serving. *Makes 8 servings*

Asparagus-Swiss Soufflé

Spam™ Hash Brown Bake

- 1 (32-ounce) package frozen hash brown potatoes, thawed slightly
- ½ cup butter or margarine, melted
- 1 teaspoon salt
- 1 teaspoon black pepper
- ½ teaspoon garlic powder
- 2 cups (8 ounces) shredded Cheddar cheese
- 1 (12-ounce) can SPAM® Luncheon Meat, cubed
- 1 (10¾-ounce) can cream of chicken soup
- 1½ cups sour cream
- ½ cup milk
- ½ cup chopped onion
- 1 (4.25-ounce) jar CHI-CHI'S® Diced Green Chilies, drained
- 2 cups crushed potato chips

Heat oven to 350°F. In large bowl, combine potatoes, melted butter, salt, pepper and garlic powder. In separate large bowl, combine cheese, Spam®, soup, sour cream, milk, onion and green chilies. Add Spam™ mixture to potato mixture; mix well. Pour into 2-quart baking dish. Sprinkle with potato chips. Bake 45 to 60 minutes or until thoroughly heated.

Makes 8 servings

Spam™ Cakes

- 1½ cups pancake mix
- 1 cup milk
- 1 egg
- 1 tablespoon vegetable oil
- 1 (7-ounce) can SPAM® Luncheon Meat, finely chopped
- Syrup or honey

In large bowl, combine pancake mix, milk, egg and oil. Stir in Spam®. Using ⅓ cup for each pancake, pour batter onto greased griddle; cook until browned on bottom. Turn and cook until browned. Serve with syrup or honey.

Makes 6 servings
(12 pancakes)

Cinnamon-Raisin Rolls

- 1 package (16 ounces) hot roll mix, plus ingredients to prepare mix
- ⅓ cup raisins
- 4 tablespoons margarine, softened, divided
- ¼ cup granulated sugar
- 2 teaspoons ground cinnamon
- ½ teaspoon ground nutmeg
- 1½ cups powdered sugar
- 1 to 2 tablespoons skim milk, divided
- ½ teaspoon vanilla

1. Preheat oven to 375°F. Spray 13×9-inch baking pan with nonstick cooking spray.

2. Prepare hot roll mix according to package directions; mix in raisins. Knead dough on lightly floured surface until smooth and elastic, about 5 minutes. Cover dough with plastic wrap; let stand 5 minutes.

3. Roll out dough on floured surface to 16×10-inch rectangle. Spread dough with 2 tablespoons margarine. Combine granulated sugar, cinnamon and nutmeg in small bowl; sprinkle evenly over dough. Roll up dough starting at long end. Pinch edge of dough to seal.

4. Gently stretch sealed dough until about 18 inches long. Cut dough into 1-inch pieces; place, cut side up, in prepared pan. Cover pan loosely with towel. Let stand 20 to 30 minutes or until doubled in size.

5. Bake 20 to 25 minutes or until golden. Cool in pan on wire rack 2 to 3 minutes. Remove from pan; cool on wire rack.

6. Combine powdered sugar, remaining 2 tablespoons margarine, 1 tablespoon milk and vanilla in medium bowl. Add additional 1 tablespoon milk to make thin glaze, if desired. Spread glaze over warm rolls.

Makes 1½ dozen rolls

Quicky Sticky Buns

¼ cup KARO® Light or Dark Corn Syrup
¼ cup coarsely chopped pecans
3 tablespoons packed brown sugar, divided
2 tablespoons softened MAZOLA® Margarine, divided
1 can (8 ounces) refrigerated crescent dinner rolls
1 teaspoon ground cinnamon

1. Preheat oven to 350°F.

2. In small bowl, combine corn syrup, pecans, 2 tablespoons brown sugar and 1 tablespoon margarine. Spoon about 2 teaspoons mixture into each of 9 (2½-inch) muffin pan cups.

3. Unroll entire crescent roll dough; pinch seams together to form one rectangle.

4. Combine remaining 1 tablespoon brown sugar and cinnamon. Spread dough with remaining 1 tablespoon margarine; sprinkle with cinnamon mixture. Roll up from short end. Cut into 9 slices. Place one slice in each prepared muffin pan cup.

5. Bake 25 minutes or until golden brown. Immediately invert pan onto cookie sheet or tray; cool 10 minutes.

Makes 9 buns

Prep Time: 15 minutes
Bake Time: 25 minutes, plus cooling

Triple Berry Breakfast Parfait

2 cups vanilla sugar-free nonfat yogurt
¼ teaspoon ground cinnamon
1 cup sliced strawberries
½ cup blueberries
½ cup raspberries
1 cup low-fat granola without raisins

1. Combine yogurt and cinnamon in small bowl. Combine strawberries, blueberries and raspberries in medium bowl.

2. For each parfait, layer ¼ cup fruit mixture, 2 tablespoons granola and ¼ cup yogurt mixture in parfait glass. Repeat layers. Garnish with mint leaves, if desired.

Makes 4 servings

Triple Berry Breakfast Parfait

Breads & Muffins

FEATURING:

Quick Breads

Scones & Biscuits

Coffee Cakes

Cranberry Poppy Seed Loaf (page 433)

429

Pumpkin Harvest Bread

1½ cups all-purpose flour
½ cup ALBERS® Yellow
    Corn Meal
2 teaspoons ground
    cinnamon
1½ teaspoons baking
    powder
1 teaspoon baking soda
½ teaspoon ground
    nutmeg
¼ teaspoon salt
1 cup LIBBY'S® Solid Pack
    Pumpkin
2 eggs
½ cup granulated sugar
½ cup packed brown sugar
¼ cup vegetable oil
¼ cup applesauce
½ cup raisins

COMBINE flour, cornmeal, cinnamon, baking powder, baking soda, nutmeg and salt in medium bowl. Beat pumpkin, eggs, granulated sugar, brown sugar, oil and applesauce in large mixer bowl. Beat in flour mixture just until blended. Stir in raisins. Spoon into greased, floured 9×5-inch loaf pan.

BAKE in preheated 350°F. oven for 50 to 55 minutes or until wooden pick inserted in center comes out clean. Cool in pan on wire rack for 5 to 10 minutes. Remove to wire rack to cool completely.

Makes 18 servings

Orange Fruit Bread

2 cups all-purpose flour
¼ cup sugar
1½ teaspoons baking
    powder
½ teaspoon baking soda
½ teaspoon salt
¼ cup Prune Purée
    (page 434) or prepared
    prune butter
¾ cup orange juice
½ cup orange marmalade
    Grated peel of 1 orange
1 package (6 ounces)
    mixed dried fruit bits
¼ cup chopped toasted
    pecans

Preheat oven to 350°F. Coat 8½×4½×2¾-inch loaf pan with vegetable cooking spray. In mixer bowl, combine flour, sugar, baking powder, baking soda and salt. Add prune purée; beat at low speed until blended. Add juice, marmalade and orange peel. Beat at low speed just until blended. Stir in fruit bits and pecans. Spoon batter into prepared pan. Bake in center of oven about 1 hour until pick inserted into center comes out clean. Cool in pan 5 minutes; remove from pan to wire rack. Cool completely. For best flavor, wrap securely and store overnight before slicing. Serve with orange marmalade, if desired.

Makes 1 loaf (12 slices)

FAVORITE RECIPE FROM **CALIFORNIA PRUNE BOARD**

Maple-Walnut Bread

1 cup packed brown sugar
¼ cup Prune Purée
    (page 434) or
    prepared prune butter
2 egg whites
1½ teaspoons maple
    flavoring
¾ cup low-fat buttermilk
2 cups all-purpose flour
2 teaspoons baking
    powder
½ teaspoon baking soda
½ teaspoon salt
⅓ cup finely chopped
    toasted walnuts

Preheat oven to 350°F. Coat 8½×4½×2¾-inch loaf pan with vegetable cooking spray. In mixer bowl, beat sugar, prune purée, egg whites and maple flavoring until well blended. Mix in buttermilk until blended. In medium bowl, combine flour, baking powder, baking soda and salt; stir into sugar mixture. Stir in walnuts. Spoon batter into prepared pan. Bake in center of oven 50 minutes or until pick inserted into center comes out clean. Cool in pan 5 minutes; remove from pan to wire rack. Cool completely before slicing.

Makes 1 loaf (12 slices)

FAVORITE RECIPE FROM **CALIFORNIA PRUNE BOARD**

Pumpkin Harvest Bread

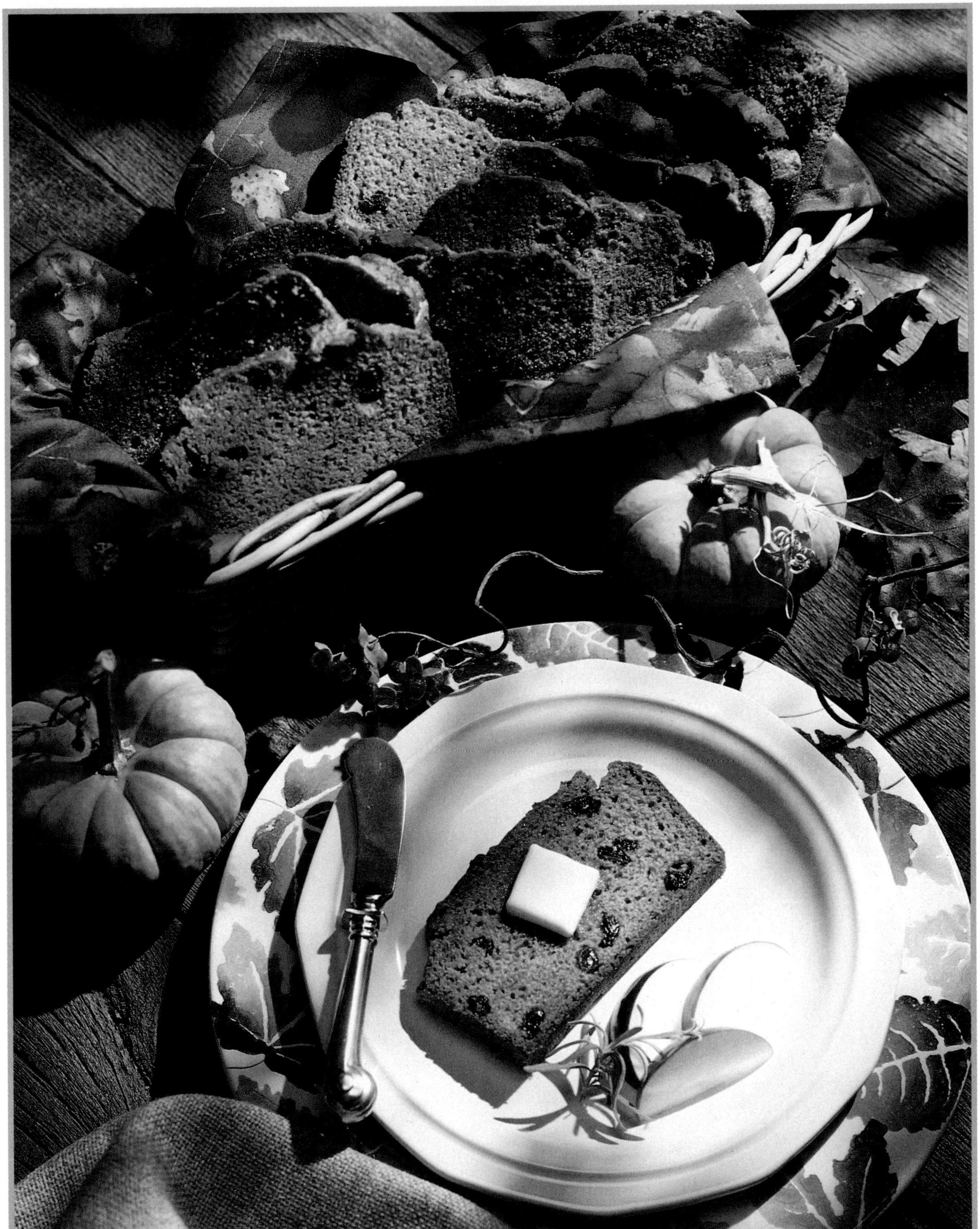

Cherry Banana Bread

1 jar (10 ounces)
    maraschino cherries
1¾ cups all-purpose flour
1½ teaspoons baking
    powder
½ teaspoon baking soda
½ teaspoon salt
⅔ cup firmly packed brown
    sugar
⅓ cup butter or margarine,
    softened
2 eggs
1 cup mashed ripe
    bananas
½ cup chopped macadamia
    nuts
1 tablespoon raw brown
    sugar (optional)

Drain maraschino cherries, reserving 2 tablespoons juice. Cut cherries into quarters; set aside.

Combine flour, baking powder, baking soda and salt; set aside.

In medium bowl, combine ⅔ cup brown sugar, butter, eggs and reserved cherry juice; mix with electric mixer on medium speed until ingredients are thoroughly combined. Add flour mixture and bananas alternately, beginning and ending with flour mixture. Stir in cherries and nuts. Lightly spray 9×5×3-inch loaf pan with nonstick cooking spray. Spread batter evenly in pan. Sprinkle batter with raw brown sugar.

Bake in preheated 350°F oven about 1 hour, or until golden brown and wooden pick inserted in center comes out clean.

Remove from pan and cool on wire rack. Store in tightly covered container or foil.
Makes 1 loaf (about 16 slices)

FAVORITE RECIPE FROM **CHERRY MARKETING INSTITUTE, INC.**

Golden Apple Buttermilk Bread

1½ cups unsifted
    all-purpose flour
1 cup whole wheat flour
½ cup natural bran cereal
1 teaspoon baking soda
½ teaspoon baking powder
¼ teaspoon ground ginger
1⅓ cups buttermilk
¾ cup sugar
¼ cup vegetable oil
1 large egg
1 teaspoon grated orange
    peel
1 cup chopped Golden
    Delicious apples

1. Heat oven to 350°F. Grease 9×5-inch loaf pan. In medium bowl, combine flours, bran, baking soda, baking powder and ginger. In large bowl, beat together buttermilk, sugar, oil, egg and orange peel.

2. Add flour mixture to buttermilk mixture, stirring just until combined. Fold in apples. Spread batter into prepared pan and bake 45 to 50 minutes or until wooden toothpick inserted in center comes out clean. Cool bread in pan 10 minutes. Remove from pan and cool on wire rack.
Makes 1 loaf (8 servings)

FAVORITE RECIPE FROM **WASHINGTON APPLE COMMISSION**

Chocolate-Chocolate Chip Bread

⅔ cup sugar
⅓ cup Prune Purée
    (page 434) or
    prepared prune butter
2 egg whites
¼ cup semisweet
    miniature chocolate
    chips, melted
½ cup nonfat milk
1 teaspoon vanilla
1⅓ cups all-purpose flour
½ teaspoon baking powder
½ teaspoon salt
¼ teaspoon baking soda
⅓ cup semisweet
    miniature chocolate
    chips

Preheat oven to 350°F. Coat 8½×4½×2¾-inch loaf pan with vegetable cooking spray. In mixer bowl, beat sugar, prune purée, egg whites and melted chocolate chips until well blended. Mix in milk and vanilla. In medium bowl, combine flour, baking powder, salt and baking soda; stir into sugar mixture just until blended. Stir in chocolate chips. Spoon batter into prepared pan. Bake in center of oven 40 to 45 minutes or until springy to the touch and pick inserted into center comes out clean. Cool in pan 5 minutes; remove from pan to wire rack. Cool completely before slicing.
Makes 1 loaf (12 slices)

FAVORITE RECIPE FROM **CALIFORNIA PRUNE BOARD**

Low-Fat Pumpkin Bread

1 cup Prune Purée
 (page 434) or
 prepared prune butter
1 cup packed brown sugar
1 cup granulated sugar
1 cup egg substitute
1 cup canned solid pack
 pumpkin
2⅔ cups all-purpose flour
2 teaspoons baking
 powder
1 teaspoon baking soda
1 teaspoon ground
 cinnamon
½ teaspoon salt
½ teaspoon ground cloves
¼ teaspoon ground ginger
¼ teaspoon ground nutmeg

Preheat oven to 350°F. Coat two 8½×4½×2¾-inch loaf pans with vegetable cooking spray. In mixer bowl, beat prune purée with sugars until well blended. Beat in egg substitute and pumpkin just until blended. In medium bowl, combine flour, baking powder, baking soda, cinnamon, salt, cloves, ginger and nutmeg; stir into prune purée mixture until well blended. Spoon batter into prepared pans, dividing equally. Bake in center of oven 1 hour or until pick inserted into centers comes out clean. Cool in pans 10 minutes; remove from pans to wire racks to cool completely. Serve with fat-free cream cheese, if desired.

*Makes 2 loaves
(16 slices per loaf)*

FAVORITE RECIPE FROM **CALIFORNIA PRUNE BOARD**

Lemon Cranberry Loaves

1¼ cups finely chopped
 fresh cranberries
½ cup finely chopped
 walnuts
¼ cup granulated sugar
1 package DUNCAN
 HINES® Moist Deluxe
 Lemon Supreme Cake
 Mix
1 package (3 ounces)
 cream cheese,
 softened
¾ cup milk
4 eggs
 Confectioners sugar

1. Preheat oven to 350°F. Grease and flour two 8½×4½-inch loaf pans.

2. Stir together cranberries, walnuts and granulated sugar in large bowl; set aside.

3. Combine cake mix, cream cheese and milk in large bowl. Beat at medium speed with electric mixer for 2 minutes. Add eggs, 1 at a time, beating for an additional 2 minutes. Fold in cranberry mixture. Pour into pans. Bake at 350°F for 45 to 50 minutes or until toothpick inserted in centers comes out clean. Cool in pans 15 minutes. Loosen loaves from pans. Invert onto cooling rack. Turn right side up. Cool completely. Dust with confectioners sugar.

Makes 24 slices

Tip: To quickly chop cranberries or walnuts, use food processor fitted with steel blade and pulse until evenly chopped.

Cranberry Poppy Seed Loaf

2½ cups all-purpose flour
¾ cup granulated sugar
2 tablespoons poppy
 seeds
1 tablespoon baking
 powder
1 cup skim milk
⅓ cup margarine, melted
¼ cup EGG BEATERS®
 Healthy Egg Substitute
2 teaspoons grated lemon
 peel
1 teaspoon vanilla extract
1 cup fresh or frozen
 cranberries, chopped
 Powdered Sugar Glaze
 (optional, recipe
 follows)

In large bowl, combine flour, sugar, poppy seeds and baking powder; set aside.

In small bowl, combine milk, margarine, Egg Beaters®, lemon peel and vanilla. Stir milk mixture into flour mixture just until moistened. Stir in cranberries. Spread batter into greased 8½×4½×2¼-inch loaf pan. Bake at 350°F for 60 to 70 minutes or until toothpick inserted in center comes out clean. Cool in pan on wire rack. Drizzle with Powdered Sugar Glaze, if desired.

Makes 12 servings

POWDERED SUGAR GLAZE: In small bowl, combine 1 cup powdered sugar and 5 to 6 teaspoons water until smooth.

Apple-Cinnamon Bread

⅓ cup packed brown sugar
⅓ cup granulated sugar
3 egg whites
¼ cup Prune Purée (recipe follows) or prepared prune butter
⅔ cup buttermilk
1¾ cups all-purpose flour
1 teaspoon ground cinnamon
¾ teaspoon baking powder
¾ teaspoon baking soda
½ teaspoon salt
¼ teaspoon ground nutmeg
¼ teaspoon ground cloves
¾ cup peeled and finely chopped apple (spooned, not packed, into cup)

Preheat oven to 375°F. Coat 8½×4½×2¾-inch loaf pan with vegetable cooking spray. In mixer bowl, beat sugars, egg whites and prune purée until well blended. Mix in buttermilk until blended. In medium bowl, combine flour, cinnamon, baking powder, baking soda, salt, nutmeg and cloves; stir into sugar mixture just until blended. Stir in apple. Spoon batter into prepared pan. Bake in center of oven 45 to 50 minutes or until pick inserted into center comes out clean. Cool in pan 5 minutes; remove from pan to wire rack. Cool completely before slicing.

Makes 1 loaf (12 slices)

PRUNE PURÉE: Combine 1⅓ cups (8 ounces) pitted prunes and 6 tablespoons hot water in food processor or blender. Pulse on and off until prunes are finely chopped and smooth. Store leftovers in covered container in refrigerator for up to two months. *Makes 1 cup*

*FAVORITE RECIPE FROM **CALIFORNIA PRUNE BOARD***

Orchard Fruit Bread

3 cups all-purpose flour or oat flour blend
⅔ cup sugar
1 teaspoon baking soda
2 eggs, beaten
1 carton (8 ounces) lemon low-fat yogurt
⅓ cup vegetable oil
1 teaspoon grated lemon peel
1 can (15 ounces) DEL MONTE® LITE® Fruit Cocktail, drained
½ cup chopped walnuts or pecans

1. Preheat oven to 350°F. Combine flour, sugar and baking soda; mix well.

2. Blend eggs with yogurt, oil and lemon peel. Add dry ingredients along with fruit cocktail and nuts; stir just enough to blend. Spoon into greased 9×5-inch loaf pan.

3. Bake 60 to 70 minutes or until wooden pick inserted into center comes out clean. Let stand in pan 10 minutes. Turn out onto wire rack; cool completely. *Makes 1 loaf*

Boston Brown Bread

3 (16-ounce) emptied and cleaned vegetable cans
½ cup rye flour
½ cup yellow cornmeal
½ cup whole wheat flour
3 tablespoons sugar
1 teaspoon baking soda
¾ teaspoon salt
½ cup chopped walnuts
½ cup raisins
1 cup buttermilk*
⅓ cup molasses

Soured fresh milk may be substituted. To sour, place 1 tablespoon lemon juice plus enough milk to equal 1 cup in 2-cup measure. Stir; let stand 5 minutes before using.

Slow Cooker Directions:
SPRAY vegetable cans and 1 side of three 6-inch squares of aluminum foil with nonstick cooking spray; set aside. Combine rye flour, cornmeal, whole wheat flour, sugar, baking soda and salt in large bowl. Stir in walnuts and raisins. Whisk buttermilk and molasses in medium bowl until blended. Add buttermilk mixture to dry ingredients; stir until well mixed. Spoon mixture evenly into prepared cans. Place 1 piece of foil, greased side down, on top of each can. Secure foil with rubber bands or cotton string.

PLACE filled cans in slow cooker. Pour boiling water into slow cooker to come halfway up sides of cans. (Make sure foil tops do not touch boiling water.) Cover and cook on LOW 4 hours or until skewer inserted in centers comes out clean. To remove bread, lay cans on side; roll and tap gently on all sides until bread releases. Cool completely on wire racks.   *Makes 3 loaves*

Orange Marmalade Bread

3 cups all-purpose flour
4 teaspoons baking powder
1 teaspoon salt
½ cup chopped walnuts
2 eggs, lightly beaten
¾ cup SMUCKER'S® Simply Fruit Orange Marmalade
¾ cup milk
¼ cup honey
2 tablespoons vegetable oil

Preheat oven to 350°F. Grease 9×5×3-inch loaf pan. Into large bowl, sift together flour, baking powder and salt. Stir in nuts. In small bowl, combine eggs, marmalade, milk, honey and oil; blend well. Add to flour mixture; stir only until flour is well moistened (batter will be lumpy). Turn batter into prepared pan. Bake 65 to 70 minutes or until lightly browned and wooden toothpick inserted in center comes out clean. Cool in pan on wire rack 10 minutes. Remove from pan; cool completely on rack.
     Makes 1 loaf

Mexicale Corn Bread

Nonstick cooking spray
1 cup whole wheat flour
1 cup cornmeal
2 tablespoons sugar
1 tablespoon baking powder
2 teaspoons chili powder
1 cup frozen corn
1 egg
¾ cup skim milk
¾ cup GUILTLESS GOURMET® Spicy Nacho Dip
Fresh currants (optional)

Preheat oven to 325°F. Coat 8×8-inch glass baking dish with cooking spray. Combine flour, cornmeal, sugar, baking powder and chili powder in large bowl. Stir in corn until corn is coated with flour mixture. Combine egg, milk and nacho dip in small bowl until well blended. Stir egg mixture into corn mixture just until moistened. *Do not overmix.* Pour into prepared dish. Bake 25 minutes or until golden brown. Let stand 10 minutes. To serve, cut into 12 squares. Garnish with currants, if desired.   *Makes 12 servings*

Boston Brown Bread (page 434)

Spicy Cheese Bread

2 packages (¼ ounce each) active dry yeast
1 teaspoon granulated sugar
½ cup warm water (110°F)
8¾ cups all-purpose flour, divided
3 cups shredded Jarlsberg or Swiss cheese
2 tablespoons fresh chopped rosemary *or* 2 teaspoons dried rosemary
1 tablespoon salt
1 tablespoon TABASCO® pepper sauce
2 cups milk
4 large eggs, lightly beaten

Combine yeast, sugar and warm water. Let stand 5 minutes until foamy. Meanwhile, in large bowl, combine 8 cups flour, cheese, rosemary, salt and TABASCO® sauce. In small saucepan, heat milk until warm (120° to 130°F).

Stir milk into flour mixture. Set aside 1 tablespoon beaten egg. Add remaining eggs to flour mixture with foamy yeast mixture; stir until soft dough forms.

On lightly floured surface, knead dough 5 minutes or until smooth and elastic, kneading in remaining ¾ cup flour. Shape dough into a ball; place in large greased bowl. Cover with towel and let rise in warm place until doubled, about 1½ hours.

Grease two large cookie sheets. Punch down dough and divide in half. Cut each half in three strips and braid. Place braids on greased cookie sheets. Cover and let rise in warm place until almost doubled, 30 minutes to 1 hour. Preheat oven to 375°F. Brush braids with reserved egg. Bake about 45 minutes or until braids sound hollow when tapped. Remove to wire racks to cool.

Makes 2 braids

Taco Bread

1 pound (16 ounces) frozen bread dough, thawed
1½ cups (6 ounces) grated cheddar cheese
1 package (1 ounce) LAWRY'S® Taco Spices & Seasonings
3 tablespoons IMPERIAL® Margarine, melted

On baking sheet, stretch dough into 14×8-inch rectangle. Sprinkle with cheese and Taco Spices & Seasonings; drizzle with margarine. Roll up, jelly-roll fashion, and place seam side down on baking sheet. Bake in 350°F oven 20 to 25 minutes or until golden brown. Cool.

Makes 6 servings

Presentation: *Serve bread slices as a spicy complement to hearty soups.*

Last Minute Tomato Swirl Bread

2 loaves (16 ounces each) frozen bread dough, thawed according to package directions
2 large cloves garlic, pressed
1 jar (8 ounces) SONOMA Marinated Tomatoes, drained and blotted with paper towels
3 tablespoons grated Parmesan cheese
2 tablespoons dried basil leaves
Cornmeal
1 egg, beaten

Preheat oven to 400°F. On lightly floured surface, roll and pat one loaf of dough into 12×7-inch rectangle. Gently sprinkle half of garlic over dough. Distribute half of tomatoes evenly over dough, leaving ½-inch border. Sprinkle with half of cheese and basil. Starting from one long edge, tightly roll up dough jelly-roll style. Carefully pinch seam to seal. Quickly repeat procedure with second loaf. Sprinkle baking sheets with cornmeal. Place loaves on baking sheets, seam sides down. Brush with egg. *Do not let rise. Bake immediately* 25 to 30 minutes or until loaves are browned and sound hollow when tapped. Remove to racks to cool before slicing. If desired, loaves can be frozen up to 1 month.

Makes 2 loaves (24 slices)

Last Minute Tomato Swirl Bread

Bran and Honey Rye Breadsticks

- 1 package (¼ ounce) active dry yeast
- 1 teaspoon sugar
- 1½ cups warm water (110°F)
- 3¾ cups all-purpose flour, divided
- 1 tablespoon honey
- 1 tablespoon vegetable oil
- ½ teaspoon salt
- 1 cup rye flour
- ½ cup whole bran cereal
  Skim milk

1. Dissolve yeast and sugar in warm water in large bowl. Let stand 10 minutes. Add 1 cup all-purpose flour, honey, oil and salt. Beat with electric mixer at medium speed 3 minutes. Stir in rye flour, bran cereal and additional 2 cups all-purpose flour or enough to make moderately stiff dough.

2. Knead dough on lightly floured surface 10 minutes or until smooth and elastic, adding remaining ¾ cup all-purpose flour as necessary to prevent sticking. Place in greased bowl; turn over to grease surface. Cover with damp cloth; let rise in warm place 40 to 45 minutes or until doubled in bulk.

3. Spray 2 baking sheets with nonstick cooking spray. Punch dough down. Divide into 24 equal pieces on lightly floured surface. Roll each piece into an 8-inch rope. Place on prepared baking sheets. Cover with damp cloth; let rise in warm place 30 to 35 minutes or until doubled in bulk.

4. Preheat oven to 375°F. Brush breadsticks with milk. Bake 18 to 20 minutes or until breadsticks are golden brown. Remove from baking sheets. Cool on wire racks.

Makes 24 breadsticks

Savory Summertime Oat Bread

- ½ cup finely chopped onion
- 2 cups whole wheat flour
- 4¼ to 4½ cups all-purpose flour, divided
- 2 cups uncooked rolled oats
- ¼ cup sugar
- 2 packages (¼ ounce each) quick-rising active dry yeast
- 1½ teaspoons salt
- 1½ cups water
- 1¼ cups skim milk
- ¼ cup margarine
- 1 cup finely shredded carrots
- 3 tablespoons dried parsley leaves
- 1 tablespoon margarine, melted

1. Spray small nonstick skillet with nonstick cooking spray; heat over medium heat until hot. Cook and stir onion 3 minutes or until tender. Set aside.

2. Stir together whole wheat flour, 1 cup all-purpose flour, oats, sugar, yeast and salt in large mixer bowl. Heat water, milk and ¼ cup margarine in medium saucepan over low heat until mixture reaches 120° to 130°F. Add to flour mixture. Blend at low speed just until dry ingredients are moistened; beat 3 minutes at medium speed. Stir in carrots, onion, parsley and remaining 3¼ to 3½ cups all-purpose flour until dough is no longer sticky.

3. Knead dough on lightly floured surface 5 to 8 minutes or until smooth and elastic. Place in large bowl lightly sprayed with cooking spray. Cover and let rise in warm place about 30 minutes or until doubled in bulk.

4. Spray two 8×4-inch loaf pans with cooking spray. Punch dough down. Cover and let rest 10 minutes. Shape into 2 loaves; place in pans. Brush with melted margarine. Cover; let rise in warm place 30 minutes or until doubled in bulk. Meanwhile, preheat oven to 350°F.

5. Bake 40 to 45 minutes or until bread sounds hollow when tapped. Remove from pans; cool on wire racks.

Makes 2 loaves (24 slices)

Honey of a Whole Wheat Bread (for bread machines)

1-POUND LOAF
1½ teaspoons RED STAR® Active Dry Yeast
1⅓ cups bread flour
⅔ cup whole wheat flour
1½ teaspoons salt
2 teaspoons butter, cut into small pieces
2 tablespoons honey (80°F)
¼ cup milk (80°F)
¼ cup water (80°F)
1 large egg, at room temperature

1½-POUND LOAF
2¼ teaspoons RED STAR® Active Dry Yeast
2 cups bread flour
1 cup whole wheat flour
2 teaspoons salt
1 tablespoon butter, cut into small pieces
¼ cup honey (80°F)
½ cup milk (80°F)
¼ cup water (80°F)
1 large egg, at room temperature

Place ingredients in pan in order specified by bread machine owner's manual. Set bread machine on basic/ standard bread-making setting; select medium or normal baking cycle. Cool bread to room temperature before slicing.   *Makes 1 loaf*

Cajun Bubble Bread

¼ cup (½ stick) unsalted butter
2 green onions, finely chopped
2 cloves garlic, minced
2 teaspoons Cajun seasoning spice blend*
4 tablespoons FRANK'S® Original REDHOT® Cayenne Pepper Sauce
¼ cup chopped almonds, divided
2 pounds thawed frozen bread dough
¾ cup (3 ounces) shredded Monterey Jack-Cheddar cheese blend, divided
2 tablespoons grated Parmesan cheese, divided

*If Cajun seasoning is unavailable, substitute ¾ teaspoon each Italian seasoning and chili powder, and ½ teaspoon celery seeds.

1. Melt butter in small saucepan. Add onions, garlic and Cajun spice; cook over medium-low heat 3 minutes or just until tender. Remove from heat; stir in RedHot® sauce.

2. Grease 10-inch tube pan or 12-cup Bundt pan.** Sprinkle bottom of tube pan with *1 tablespoon* almonds. Cut bread dough into 24 (1-inch) pieces; shape into balls. Dip dough balls, one at a time, into butter mixture. Place in a single layer in bottom of tube pan. Sprinkle with *¼ cup* Monterey Jack-Cheddar cheese, *1 tablespoon* almonds and *2 teaspoons* Parmesan cheese.

3. Repeat layers twice with remaining ingredients. Cover with plastic wrap; let rise in warm place 1½ hours or until doubled in size.

4. Preheat oven to 375°F. Bake 35 minutes or until golden brown. (Loosely cover with foil during last 15 minutes if bread browns too quickly.) Loosen bread from sides of pan. Invert immediately onto serving plate; serve warm.

Makes 8 servings

**You may substitute 2 (8×4-inch) loaf pans.

Prep Time: 30 minutes
Rise Time: 1½ hours
Cook Time: 35 minutes

RedHot® Parmesan Biscuits

- 4 cups all-purpose flour
- ½ cup grated Parmesan cheese
- 2 tablespoons baking powder
- 2 teaspoons sugar
- 1 teaspoon baking soda
- 6 tablespoons cold butter, cut into pieces
- 6 tablespoons cold solid vegetable shortening
- 1 cup plus 2 tablespoons buttermilk, divided
- ½ cup FRANK'S® Original REDHOT® Cayenne Pepper Sauce
- Sesame seeds (optional)

1. Preheat oven to 450°F. Place flour, cheese, baking powder, sugar and baking soda in blender or food processor.* Cover; process 30 seconds. Add butter and shortening; process, pulsing on and off, until fine crumbs form. Transfer to large bowl.

2. Add *1 cup* buttermilk and RedHot® sauce. Stir together just until mixture starts to form a ball. (Dough will be dry. Do not overmix.)

3. Turn out dough onto lightly floured board. With palms of hands, gently knead 8 times. Using floured rolling pin or hands, roll dough to ¾-inch thickness. Using 2½-inch round biscuit cutter, cut out 16 biscuits, re-rolling dough as necessary.

4. Place biscuits 2 inches apart on large foil-lined baking sheet. Brush tops with remaining *2 tablespoons* buttermilk; sprinkle with sesame seeds, if desired. Bake 12 to 15 minutes or until golden.

Makes 16 biscuits

Or, place dry ingredients in large bowl. Cut in butter and shortening until fine crumbs form using pastry blender or 2 knives. Add buttermilk and RedHot® sauce; mix just until moistened. Continue with step 3.

Country Biscuits

- 2 cups all-purpose flour
- 1 tablespoon baking powder
- 1 teaspoon salt
- ⅓ CRISCO® Stick or ⅓ cup CRISCO® all-vegetable shortening
- ¾ cup milk

1. Preheat oven to 425°F. **Combine** flour, baking powder and salt in medium bowl. **Cut** in Crisco® using pastry blender (or two knives) to form coarse crumbs. **Add** milk. **Mix** with fork until dry mixture is moistened. **Form** dough into a ball.

2. Transfer dough to lightly floured surface. **Knead** gently 8 to 10 times. **Roll** out dough to ½-inch thickness. **Cut** with floured 2-inch round cutter. **Place** on ungreased baking sheet.

3. Bake at 425°F. 12 to 14 minutes or until golden.

Makes 12 to 16 biscuits

Chive Whole Wheat Drop Biscuits

- 1¼ cups whole wheat flour
- ¾ cup all-purpose flour
- 3 tablespoons toasted wheat germ, divided
- 1 tablespoon baking powder
- 1 tablespoon chopped fresh chives *or* 1 teaspoon dried chives
- 2 teaspoons sugar
- 3 tablespoons margarine
- 1 cup skim milk
- ½ cup shredded low-fat process American cheese

1. Preheat oven to 450°F. Spray baking sheet with nonstick cooking spray. Combine flours, 2 tablespoons wheat germ, baking powder, chives and sugar in medium bowl. Cut in margarine with pastry blender or two knives until mixture resembles coarse meal. Add milk and American cheese; stir until just combined.

2. Drop dough by rounded teaspoonfuls onto prepared baking sheet about 1 inch apart. Sprinkle with remaining 1 tablespoon wheat germ. Bake 10 to 12 minutes or until golden brown. Remove immediately from baking sheet. Serve warm.

Makes 12 servings

RedHot® Parmesan Biscuits

Herb Biscuits

¼ cup hot water (130°F)
1½ teaspoons (½ package) fast-rising active dry yeast
2½ cups all-purpose flour
3 tablespoons sugar
1½ teaspoons baking powder
½ teaspoon baking soda
½ teaspoon salt
5 tablespoons cold margarine, cut into pieces
2 teaspoons finely chopped fresh parsley *or* ½ teaspoon dried parsley flakes
2 teaspoons finely chopped fresh basil *or* ½ teaspoon dried basil leaves
2 teaspoons finely chopped fresh chives *or* ½ teaspoon dried chives
¾ cup buttermilk

1. Preheat oven to 425°F. Spray cookie sheet with nonstick cooking spray.

2. Combine hot water and yeast in small cup; let stand 2 to 3 minutes. Combine flour, sugar, baking powder, baking soda and salt in medium bowl; cut in margarine using pastry blender or 2 knives until mixture resembles coarse crumbs. Mix in parsley, basil and chives. Stir in buttermilk and yeast mixture to make soft dough. Turn out dough onto lightly floured surface. Knead 15 to 20 times.

3. Roll to ½-inch thickness. Cut hearts or other shapes with 2½-inch cookie cutter. Place biscuits on prepared cookie sheet. Bake 12 to 15 minutes or until browned. Cool on wire racks. Serve immediately.

Makes 18 biscuits

Sonoma Dried Tomato and Vegetable Biscuits

¼ cup SONOMA Dried Tomato Halves
2½ cups unbleached all-purpose flour
1 tablespoon sugar
2 teaspoons baking powder
2 teaspoons salt
½ teaspoon baking soda
¼ teaspoon black pepper
½ teaspoon active dry yeast
2 tablespoons warm water (110° to 115°F)
1 cup cold vegetable shortening, cut into ½-inch cubes
½ cup vegetables, cut into ¼-inch cubes (carrot, yellow squash, green bell pepper and zucchini)
2 teaspoons *each* fresh minced parsley, basil and dill *or* 1 scant teaspoon *each* dried parsley, basil and dill
1 large clove garlic, minced
¾ cup buttermilk

Preheat oven to 375°F. In small bowl, cover tomatoes with boiling water; set aside 10 minutes. In large bowl, mix flour, sugar, baking powder, salt, baking soda and pepper. In another small bowl, dissolve yeast in warm water; set aside. Cut shortening into flour mixture until crumbs resemble coarse meal. Blend yeast mixture into flour mixture to form dough. *Thoroughly* drain and mince tomatoes; combine with vegetables, herbs and garlic. Add half the vegetable mixture and half the buttermilk to the dough; mix well and repeat with remaining vegetable mixture and buttermilk. Turn out dough onto floured surface and knead several times, adding more flour only if necessary. Pat or roll out dough to ¾-inch thickness; cut out dough with 3-inch biscuit cutter. Place biscuits, 2 inches apart, on greased or parchment-lined baking sheet. Bake 20 to 24 minutes or until lightly browned and cooked through.

Makes 8 biscuits

Herb Biscuits

Pear Scones

2½ cups all-purpose flour
1 cup plus 1 tablespoon
    granulated sugar,
    divided
½ cup whole wheat flour
1 tablespoon baking
    powder
½ teaspoon baking soda
½ teaspoon ground ginger
2 tablespoons cold
    margarine
2 tablespoons cold butter
1 pear, cored and
    shredded
½ cup buttermilk

Preheat oven to 400°F. Spray baking sheets with nonstick cooking spray; set aside. In food processor, combine all-purpose flour, 1 cup sugar, whole wheat flour, baking powder, baking soda and ginger; process until blended. Add margarine and butter; process until mixture resembles coarse crumbs. Transfer to large bowl. Stir in pear and buttermilk until soft dough forms.

Turn out dough onto lightly floured surface. Knead 8 to 10 times. Roll out dough into ½-inch thickness; cut into rounds with lightly floured 2½-inch biscuit cutter. Sprinkle remaining 1 tablespoon sugar over tops of scones. Bake 10 to 15 minutes or until golden brown and wooden pick inserted in center comes out clean. Remove from baking sheets. Cool on wire racks 10 minutes.

Makes about 30 scones

FAVORITE RECIPE FROM **THE SUGAR ASSOCIATION, INC.**

Cranberry Scones

2½ cups all-purpose flour
½ cup packed brown sugar
1 tablespoon baking
    powder
1 teaspoon baking soda
¾ teaspoon salt
½ teaspoon ground
    cinnamon
¼ cup Prune Purée
    (page 434) or
    prepared prune butter
2 tablespoons cold
    margarine or butter
1 container (8 ounces)
    nonfat vanilla yogurt
¾ cup dried cranberries
1 egg white, lightly beaten
1 tablespoon granulated
    sugar

Preheat oven to 400°F. Coat baking sheet with vegetable cooking spray. In large bowl, combine flour, brown sugar, baking powder, baking soda, salt and cinnamon. Cut in prune purée and margarine with pastry blender until mixture resembles coarse crumbs. Mix in yogurt just until blended. Stir in cranberries. On floured surface, roll or pat dough to ¾-inch thickness. Cut out with 2½- to 3-inch biscuit cutter, re-rolling scraps as needed, but handling as little as possible. Arrange on prepared baking sheet, spacing 2 inches apart. Brush with egg white and sprinkle with granulated sugar. Bake in center of oven about 15 minutes or until golden brown and springy to the touch. *Makes 12 scones*

FAVORITE RECIPE FROM **CALIFORNIA PRUNE BOARD**

Apple Cheddar Scones

1½ cups unsifted
    all-purpose flour
½ cup toasted wheat germ
3 tablespoons sugar
2 teaspoons baking
    powder
½ teaspoon salt
2 tablespoons butter
1 small Rome apple, cored
    and chopped
¼ cup shredded Cheddar
    cheese
1 large egg white
½ cup low-fat (1%) milk

1. Heat oven to 400°F. Grease 8-inch round cake pan. In medium bowl, combine flour, wheat germ, sugar, baking powder and salt. With two knives or pastry blender, cut in butter until the size of coarse crumbs. Toss apple and cheese in flour mixture.

2. Beat together egg white and milk until well combined. Add to flour mixture, mixing with fork until dough forms. Turn out dough onto lightly floured surface and knead 6 times.

3. Spread dough evenly in prepared cake pan and score deeply with knife into 6 wedges. Bake 25 to 30 minutes or until top springs back when gently pressed. Let stand 5 minutes; remove from pan. Cool before serving.

Makes 6 scones

FAVORITE RECIPE FROM **WASHINGTON APPLE COMMISSION**

Cranberry Scones

Dill Sour Cream Scones

- 2 cups all-purpose flour
- 2 teaspoons baking powder
- ½ teaspoon baking soda
- ½ teaspoon salt
- 4 tablespoons butter or margarine
- 2 eggs
- ½ cup sour cream
- 1 tablespoon chopped fresh dill *or* 1 teaspoon dried dill weed

Preheat oven to 425°F.

Combine flour, baking powder, baking soda and salt in large bowl. Cut in butter with pastry blender or 2 knives until mixture resembles coarse crumbs. Beat eggs with fork in small bowl. Add sour cream and dill; beat until well combined. Stir into flour mixture until mixture forms soft dough that pulls away from side of bowl.

Turn out dough onto well-floured surface. Knead dough 10 times. Roll out dough into 9×6-inch rectangle with lightly floured rolling pin. Cut dough into 6 (3-inch) squares. Cut each square diagonally in half, making 12 triangles. Place triangles, 2 inches apart, onto *ungreased* baking sheets.

Bake 10 to 12 minutes or until golden brown and wooden pick inserted in center comes out clean. Cool on wire rack 10 minutes. Serve warm or cool completely.

Makes 12 scones

Fruited Oat Scones

- 1½ cups all-purpose flour
- 1¼ cups QUAKER® Oats (quick or old fashioned, uncooked)
- ¼ cup sugar
- 1 tablespoon baking powder
- ¼ teaspoon salt (optional)
- ⅓ cup (5⅓ tablespoons) margarine
- 1 (6-ounce) package diced dried mixed fruit (1⅓ cups)
- ½ cup milk
- 1 egg, slightly beaten
- 1 teaspoon sugar
- ⅛ teaspoon ground cinnamon

Preheat oven to 375°F. Combine flour, oats, ¼ cup sugar, baking powder and salt; mix well. Cut in margarine until mixture resembles coarse crumbs; stir in fruit. Add milk and egg, mixing just until moistened. Shape dough to form a ball. Turn out onto floured surface; knead gently 6 times. On lightly greased cookie sheet, pat out dough to form 8-inch circle. With sharp knife, score round into 12 wedges; sprinkle with combined 1 teaspoon sugar and cinnamon. Bake about 30 minutes or until golden brown. Break apart; serve warm. *Makes 1 dozen scones*

Buttermilk Oatmeal Scones

- 2 cups all-purpose flour, sifted
- 1 cup uncooked rolled oats
- ⅓ cup granulated sugar
- 1 tablespoon baking powder
- ½ teaspoon baking soda
- ⅛ teaspoon salt
- 6 tablespoons cold unsalted margarine, cut into small pieces
- 1 cup buttermilk

Preheat oven to 375°F. Grease baking sheets; set aside.

Combine flour, oats, sugar, baking powder, baking soda and salt in large bowl. Cut in margarine with pastry blender or process in food processor until mixture resembles coarse crumbs. Add buttermilk; stir with fork until soft dough forms. Turn out dough onto lightly floured surface; knead 10 to 12 times. Roll out dough to ½-inch-thick rectangle with lightly floured rolling pin. Cut dough into circles with lightly floured 1½-inch biscuit cutter. Place on prepared baking sheets. Brush tops with aditional buttermilk and sprinkle with additional sugar. Bake 18 to 20 minutes or until golden brown and wooden pick inserted in center comes out clean. Remove from baking sheets. Cool on wire racks 10 minutes. Serve warm or cool completely.

Makes about 30 scones

FAVORITE RECIPE FROM **THE SUGAR ASSOCIATION, INC.**

White Chocolate Chunk Muffins

2½ cups all-purpose flour
1 cup packed brown sugar
⅓ cup unsweetened cocoa
   powder
2 teaspoons baking soda
½ teaspoon salt
1⅓ cups buttermilk
6 tablespoons butter or
   margarine, melted
2 eggs, beaten
1½ teaspoons vanilla
1½ cups chopped white
   chocolate

Preheat oven to 400°F. Grease 12 (3½-inch) large muffin cups; set aside.

Combine flour, sugar, cocoa, baking soda and salt in large bowl. Combine buttermilk, butter, eggs and vanilla in small bowl until blended. Stir into flour mixture just until moistened. Fold in white chocolate. Spoon into prepared muffin cups, filling half full.

Bake 25 to 30 minutes or until wooden pick inserted in center comes out clean. Cool in pan on wire rack 5 minutes. Remove from pan. Cool on wire rack 10 minutes. Serve warm or cool completely.

Makes 12 jumbo muffins

Oreo® Muffins

1¾ cups all-purpose flour
½ cup sugar
1 tablespoon DAVIS®
   Baking Powder
½ teaspoon salt
¾ cup milk
⅓ cup sour cream
1 egg
¼ cup margarine, melted
20 OREO® Chocolate
   Sandwich Cookies,
   coarsely chopped

In medium bowl, combine flour, sugar, baking powder and salt; set aside.

In small bowl, combine milk, sour cream and egg; stir into flour mixture with margarine until just blended. Gently stir in cookies. Spoon batter into 12 greased 2½-inch muffin cups.

Bake at 400°F for 20 to 25 minutes or until toothpick inserted in center comes out clean. Remove from pan; cool on wire rack. Serve warm or cold.　　*Makes 1 dozen muffins*

White Chocolate Chunk Muffins

Broccoli & Cheddar Muffins

**3 cups buttermilk baking
    and pancake mix**
2 eggs, lightly beaten
⅔ cup milk
1 teaspoon dried basil
**1 cup shredded Cheddar
    cheese**
**1 box (10 ounces) BIRDS
    EYE® frozen Chopped
    Broccoli, thawed and
    drained**

• Preheat oven to 350°F.
Combine baking mix, eggs,
milk and basil. Mix until
moistened. *(Do not overmix.)*

• Add cheese and broccoli; stir
just to combine. Add salt and
pepper to taste.

• Spray 12 muffin cups with
nonstick cooking spray. Pour
batter into muffin cups. Bake
25 to 30 minutes or until
golden brown.

• Cool 5 minutes in pan. Loosen
sides of muffins with knife;
remove from pan and serve
warm.

Makes 1 dozen large muffins

Prep Time: 5 to 10 minutes
Bake Time: 25 to 30 minutes

Fresh Ginger and Lemon Muffins

1 cup sugar, divided
**¼ cup coarsely chopped
    peeled fresh ginger**
**1 tablespoon grated
    lemon peel**
2 eggs
1 cup low-fat buttermilk
**⅓ cup Prune Purée
    (page 434) or
    prepared prune butter**
**2 cups plus 2 tablespoons
    all-purpose flour**
¾ teaspoon baking soda
½ teaspoon salt

Preheat oven to 375°F. Coat
twelve 2¾-inch (⅓-cup
capacity) muffin cups with
vegetable cooking spray. In
bowl of food processor fitted
with metal blade, process
½ cup sugar, ginger and lemon
peel about 30 seconds or until
mixture is finely chopped. In
large mixer bowl, using mixer
set on high, beat eggs and
remaining ½ cup sugar 3 to
5 minutes or until mixture
increases in volume and
becomes thick and pale in
color. Beat in buttermilk, prune
purée and ginger mixture. In
medium bowl, combine flour,
baking soda and salt. Fold flour
mixture into egg mixture; mix
just until blended. Spoon batter
into prepared muffin cups,
dividing equally. Bake in center
of oven about 18 minutes or
until muffins are lightly browned
and springy to the touch.
Remove muffins to wire rack to
cool slightly. Serve warm.

Makes 12 muffins

*FAVORITE RECIPE FROM **CALIFORNIA
PRUNE BOARD***

Anjou Pear Cheese Muffins

2 cups all-purpose flour
**¾ cup (3 ounces) shredded
    Swiss cheese**
¼ cup packed brown sugar
**3 teaspoons baking
    powder**
½ teaspoon salt
⅔ cup milk
1 egg, slightly beaten
**2 tablespoons vegetable
    oil**
**1 USA Anjou pear, finely
    chopped**
½ cup chopped nuts

Preheat oven to 400°F. Grease
12 (2½-inch) muffin cups; set
aside.

Combine flour, cheese, sugar,
baking powder and salt in large
bowl. Combine milk, egg and
oil in small bowl. Stir into flour
mixture with pear and nuts just
until moistened. Spoon evenly
into prepared muffin cups.

Bake 20 to 25 minutes or until
wooden pick inserted near
center comes out clean. Cool
on wire rack 10 minutes. Serve
warm or cool completely.

Makes 12 muffins

Note: *Muffins may be frozen in
aluminum foil or plastic food
storage bags. Reheat, unthawed,
at 350°F 20 to 25 minutes or until
thoroughly heated.*

*FAVORITE RECIPE FROM **OREGON
WASHINGTON CALIFORNIA PEAR
BUREAU***

Broccoli & Cheddar Muffins

Orange and Blueberry Cornmeal Muffins

1½ cups frozen apple juice concentrate, thawed
½ cup Prune Purée (page 434) or prepared prune butter
½ cup buttermilk
3 eggs
2½ cups all-purpose flour
½ cup cornmeal
1½ teaspoons baking soda
½ teaspoon salt
2 teaspoons grated orange peel
2 cups fresh or frozen blueberries, divided

Preheat oven to 375°F. Coat eighteen 2¾-inch (⅓-cup capacity) muffin cups with vegetable cooking spray. In large bowl, beat juice concentrate, prune purée, buttermilk and eggs until well blended. In medium bowl, combine flour, cornmeal, baking soda and salt. Add flour mixture and orange peel to concentrate mixture; mix just until blended. Stir in 1½ cups blueberries. Spoon batter into prepared muffin cups, dividing equally. Top batter with remaining blueberries. Bake in center of oven about 20 minutes or until springy to the touch and pick inserted into centers comes out clean. Remove muffins to wire racks to cool slightly. Serve warm. *Makes 18 muffins*

*FAVORITE RECIPE FROM **CALIFORNIA PRUNE BOARD***

Norwegian Almond Muffins

2 cups all-purpose flour, divided
1 package RED STAR® Active Dry Yeast or QUICK•RISE™ Yeast
¼ cup sugar
1 teaspoon salt
1 teaspoon ground cardamom
½ cup water
¼ cup milk
¼ cup butter or margarine
¼ cup almond paste
1 egg
½ teaspoon almond extract
⅛ cup cherry preserves
1 tablespoon sugar
¼ cup chopped almonds

Preheat oven to 350°F.

Combine 1 cup flour, yeast, ¼ cup sugar, salt and cardamom in small bowl; mix well. Heat water, milk, butter and almond paste until very warm (120° to 130°F; butter does not need to melt). Add to flour mixture. Add egg and almond extract. Beat with electric mixer at low speed until moistened. Beat 3 minutes at medium speed. By hand, gradually stir in remaining 1 cup flour to make soft batter.

Spoon batter into well-greased muffin cups. Cover; let rise in warm place 1 to 1½ hours (30 to 45 minutes for QUICK•RISE™ Yeast).

Before baking, make an indentation in top of each muffin; spoon about ½ teaspoon cherry preserves into each muffin. Combine 1 tablespoon sugar and almonds; sprinkle over muffins. Bake 20 to 25 minutes or until golden brown. Cool in pans 3 minutes; remove from pans. *Makes 12 muffins*

Cranberry Oat Bran Muffins

2 cups all-purpose flour
1 cup oat bran
½ cup packed brown sugar
2 teaspoons baking powder
½ teaspoon baking soda
½ teaspoon salt (optional)
½ cup MIRACLE WHIP® Light Reduced Calorie Salad Dressing
3 egg whites, slightly beaten
½ cup skim milk
⅓ cup orange juice
1 teaspoon grated orange peel
1 cup coarsely chopped cranberries

Preheat oven to 375°F. Line 12 medium muffin cups with paper baking cups or spray with nonstick cooking spray. Mix together dry ingredients. Add combined dressing, egg whites, milk, juice and peel; mix just until moistened. Fold in cranberries. Fill prepared muffin cups almost full. Bake 15 to 17 minutes or until golden brown.

Makes 12 muffins

Orange and Blueberry Cornmeal Muffins

Apple Streusel Mini Muffins

¼ cup chopped pecans
2 tablespoons brown sugar
1 tablespoon all-purpose flour
2 teaspoons butter or margarine, melted
1 package (7 ounces) apple cinnamon muffin mix plus ingredients to prepare mix
½ cup shredded peeled apple

1. Preheat oven to 425°F. Coat 18 mini muffin cups with nonstick cooking spray.

2. Combine pecans, brown sugar and flour in small bowl. Drizzle with butter; toss until mixture is moistened.

3. Prepare muffin mix according to package directions. Stir in apple. Fill each muffin cup ⅔ full. Sprinkle approximately 1 teaspoon pecan mixture on top of each muffin. Bake 12 to 15 minutes or until golden brown. Cool slightly. Serve warm.   *Makes 18 mini muffins*

Prep & Cook Time: 30 minutes

Regular-Size Muffins: Grease 6 (2½-inch) muffin cups. Prepare topping and batter as directed. Fill muffin cups ⅔ full of batter. Sprinkle approximately 1 tablespoon pecan mixture on top of each muffin. Bake 18 to 20 minutes or until golden brown.

Makes 6 regular-size muffins

Carrot Pineapple Muffins

4 cups grated carrots (spooned, not packed, into cup)
1 cup granulated sugar
1 cup packed brown sugar
1 can (8 ounces) crushed pineapple in unsweetened pineapple juice, undrained
1 cup Prune Purée (page 434) or prepared prune butter
4 egg whites
2 teaspoons vanilla
2 cups all-purpose flour
2 teaspoons baking soda
2 teaspoons ground cinnamon
½ teaspoon salt
¾ cup raisins (optional)

Preheat oven to 375°F. Coat eighteen 2¾-inch (⅓-cup capacity) muffin cups with vegetable cooking spray. In large bowl, beat carrots, sugars, pineapple and juice, prune purée, egg whites and vanilla until well blended. In medium bowl, combine flour, baking soda, cinnamon and salt. Add flour mixture to carrot mixture; mix just until blended. Stir in raisins, if desired. Spoon batter into prepared muffin cups, dividing equally. Bake in center of oven about 20 to 25 minutes or until springy to the touch and pick inserted into centers comes out clean. Cool in pans 15 minutes. Remove to wire racks. Serve warm.   *Makes 18 muffins*

*FAVORITE RECIPE FROM **CALIFORNIA PRUNE BOARD***

Peachy Oat Bran Muffins

1½ cups oat bran
½ cup all-purpose flour
⅓ cup firmly packed brown sugar
2 teaspoons baking powder
1 teaspoon ground cinnamon
½ teaspoon salt
¾ cup low-fat milk
1 egg, beaten
¼ cup vegetable oil
1 can (15 ounces) DEL MONTE® LITE® Yellow Cling Sliced Peaches, drained and chopped
⅓ cup chopped walnuts

1. Preheat oven to 425°F. Combine oat bran, flour, brown sugar, baking powder, cinnamon and salt; mix well.

2. Combine milk, egg and oil. Add to dry ingredients; stir just enough to blend. Fold in fruit and nuts.

3. Fill greased muffin cups with batter. Sprinkle with granulated sugar, if desired.

4. Bake 20 to 25 minutes or until golden brown.
Makes 12 medium muffins

Prep Time: 10 minutes
Cook Time: 25 minutes

Tip: Muffins can be frozen and reheated in microwave or toaster oven.

Apple Streusel Mini Muffins

Blueberry Yogurt Muffins

- **2 cups QUAKER® Oat Bran hot cereal, uncooked**
- **¼ cup firmly packed brown sugar**
- **2 teaspoons baking powder**
- **1 carton (8 ounces) plain low-fat yogurt**
- **2 egg whites, slightly beaten**
- **¼ cup skim milk**
- **¼ cup honey**
- **2 tablespoons vegetable oil**
- **1 teaspoon grated lemon peel**
- **½ cup fresh or frozen blueberries**

Heat oven to 425°F. Line 12 medium muffin cups with paper baking cups.

Combine oat bran, brown sugar and baking powder. Add combined yogurt, egg whites, skim milk, honey, oil and lemon peel, mixing just until moistened. Fold in blueberries. Fill muffin cups almost full.

Bake 18 to 20 minutes or until golden brown.

Makes 12 muffins

Tips: *To freeze muffins, wrap securely in foil or place in freezer bag. Seal, label and freeze. To reheat frozen muffins, unwrap muffins. Microwave at HIGH about 30 seconds per muffin.*

Nutmeg Strawberry Muffins

- **2 cups stemmed and halved (quartered, if large) California strawberries (about 1 pint)**
- **2 cups plus 1 tablespoon sugar, divided**
- **½ cup plus 1 tablespoon cornmeal, divided**
- **3¼ teaspoons nutmeg, divided**
- **3 cups all-purpose flour**
- **1 teaspoon salt**
- **1 teaspoon baking soda**
- **1¼ cups vegetable oil**
- **4 eggs, beaten**
- **1 cup chopped walnuts**

Preheat oven to 375°F. Toss strawberries with 1 tablespoon sugar in medium bowl; set aside. Combine 1 tablespoon sugar, 1 tablespoon cornmeal and ¼ teaspoon nutmeg for topping; set aside. Combine flour, remaining sugar, ½ cup cornmeal, 3 teaspoons nutmeg, salt and baking soda in large bowl. Add oil and eggs to strawberry mixture; mix gently. Add strawberry mixture and walnuts to flour mixture; mix just until dry ingredients are moistened. Measure ⅓ cup batter into 24 paper-lined or greased 2¾-inch muffin cups. Sprinkle reserved topping mixture evenly over muffins.

Bake in center of oven about 25 minutes or until springy to the touch and wooden toothpick inserted into centers comes out clean. Cooled muffins can be wrapped and frozen for up to 2 months.

Makes 24 muffins

NUTMEG STRAWBERRY BREAD: Prepare batter as directed. Pour into two greased 8×4-inch loaf pans; sprinkle loaves with topping mixture. Bake in preheated 375°F oven about 1 hour 10 minutes or until toothpick inserted into centers comes out clean. Cool on rack.

Makes 2 loaves

FAVORITE RECIPE FROM **CALIFORNIA STRAWBERRY COMMISSION**

Blueberry Yogurt Muffins

Three-Berry Kuchen

- 1¾ cups all-purpose flour, divided
- 2 teaspoons baking powder
- ½ teaspoon baking soda
- ½ teaspoon salt
- ⅔ cup MOTT'S® Apple Sauce
- 4 egg whites
- ¼ cup nonfat plain yogurt
- 2 tablespoons granulated sugar
- 1 teaspoon grated lemon peel
- 2 cups assorted fresh or thawed frozen blueberries, raspberries or blackberries
- ¼ cup firmly packed light brown sugar
- 2 tablespoons margarine

1. Preheat oven to 350°F. Spray 10-inch round cake pan with nonstick cooking spray.

2. In small bowl, combine 1½ cups flour, baking powder, baking soda and salt.

3. In large bowl, whisk together apple sauce, egg whites, yogurt, granulated sugar and lemon peel.

4. Add flour mixture to apple sauce mixture; stir until well blended. Spread batter into prepared pan.

5. Sprinkle berries over batter. Combine remaining ¼ cup flour and brown sugar in small bowl. Cut in margarine with pastry blender or fork until mixture resembles coarse crumbs. Sprinkle over berries.

6. Bake 50 to 55 minutes or until lightly browned. Cool on wire rack 20 minutes. Serve warm or cool completely. Cut into 9 slices.

Makes 9 servings

Cherry Cheese Danish Ring

- 1 sheet (½ of 17¼-ounce package) frozen puff pastry
- 3 tablespoons unsalted butter substitute, melted and divided
- 1 cup (4 ounces) shredded ALPINE LACE® Reduced Sodium Muenster Cheese
- ⅓ cup plus 2 tablespoons sifted confectioners' sugar, divided
- 1 large egg yolk
- 1 teaspoon grated lemon peel
- ¼ teaspoon almond extract
- 1 cup dried cherries or cranberries, coarsely chopped
- 1 cup sliced almonds (optional)

1. Preheat the oven to 375°F. Spray a baking sheet with nonstick cooking spray.

2. On a lightly floured board, pat out the dough to a 14×18-inch rectangle and brush with 2 tablespoons of the butter.

3. In the bowl of a food processor, place the cheese, the ⅓ cup of confectioners' sugar, the egg yolk, lemon peel and almond extract. Process for 15 seconds or just until blended. *(Avoid overprocessing.)* Spread over the dough, leaving a ½-inch border. Sprinkle evenly with the cherries.

4. Starting at one of the wide ends, roll up dough jelly-roll-style. Place dough on the baking sheet, seam side down, forming a 12-inch circle and pinching the ends together.

5. Using scissors, cut at 1-inch intervals from the outside of the ring toward (but not through) the center. Twist each section half a turn, allowing the filling to show. Brush the top with the remaining tablespoon of butter. Sprinkle with the almonds, if you wish.

6. Bake for 20 minutes or just until light brown. Using a large spatula, carefully slide the ring onto the rack to cool for 15 minutes, then sprinkle with the remaining 2 tablespoons of confectioners' sugar.

Makes 1 (16-inch) danish

Three-Berry Kuchen

Orange Streusel Coffeecake

Cocoa Streusel (recipe follows)
¾ cup (1½ sticks) butter or margarine, softened
1 cup sugar
3 eggs
1 teaspoon vanilla extract
½ cup dairy sour cream
3 cups all-purpose flour
2 teaspoons baking powder
1 teaspoon baking soda
1 cup orange juice
2 teaspoons freshly grated orange peel
½ cup orange marmalade or apple jelly

Prepare Cocoa Streusel. Heat oven to 350°F. Generously grease 12-cup fluted tube pan. In large bowl, beat butter and sugar until well blended. Add eggs and vanilla; beat well. Add sour cream; beat until blended. Stir together flour, baking powder and baking soda; add alternately with orange juice to butter mixture, beating until well blended. Stir in orange peel. Spread marmalade in bottom of prepared pan; sprinkle half of streusel over marmalade. Pour half of batter into pan, spreading evenly. Sprinkle remaining streusel over batter; spread remaining batter evenly over streusel. Bake about 1 hour or until toothpick inserted in center of cake comes out clean. Loosen cake from side of pan with metal spatula; immediately invert onto serving plate.

Makes 12 servings

COCOA STREUSEL: Stir together ⅔ cup packed light brown sugar, ½ cup chopped walnuts, ¼ cup **HERSHEY'S** Cocoa and ½ cup **MOUNDS®** Sweetened Coconut Flakes, if desired.

Lemon Crème Tea Ring

1 pound frozen bread dough, thawed
3 tablespoons unsalted butter substitute, melted, divided
1 cup shredded ALPINE LACE® Reduced Sodium Muenster Cheese
½ cup plus ¾ cup sifted confectioners' sugar
2 tablespoons 2% low fat milk
1 large egg yolk
1 teaspoon grated lemon peel
1½ teaspoons vanilla extract, divided
½ cup seedless golden raisins
2 tablespoons fresh lemon juice

1. Spray a 15×10-inch baking sheet with nonstick cooking spray.

2. To make the tea ring: On a lightly floured board, pat out the dough into a 16×12-inch rectangle and brush with 2 tablespoons of the butter substitute.

3. In a food processor or blender, process the cheese, ½ cup of the sugar, the milk, egg yolk, lemon peel and 1 teaspoon vanilla for 15 seconds or just until blended. *(Avoid overprocessing.)* Spread the cheese mixture over the dough, leaving a ½-inch border, then sprinkle evenly with the raisins.

4. Starting at one of the narrow ends, roll up the dough jelly-roll style. Place on the baking sheet, seam side down, then form into a circle, pinching the ends together. Using scissors, cut at ½-inch intervals from the outside of the ring toward, but not through, the center. Slightly twist each section a half turn, allowing the filling to show. Cover and let rise for 1 hour or until doubled in size.

5. Preheat the oven to 375°F. Uncover the ring and brush the top with the remaining tablespoon of butter substitute. Bake for 20 minutes or just until golden brown. Using a large spatula, carefully slide the tea ring onto a wire rack to cool for 15 minutes.

6. While the tea ring is cooling, make the icing: In a small bowl, beat the remaining ¾ cup sugar, lemon juice and the remaining ½ teaspoon vanilla until smooth. Using a small spoon, drizzle the icing over the top of the warm tea ring. *Makes 14 servings*

Pecan Sticky Buns

DOUGH*
4½ to 5½ cups all-purpose flour, divided
½ cup granulated sugar
1½ teaspoons salt
2 packages (¼ ounce each) active dry yeast
¾ cup warm milk (105° to 115°F)
½ cup warm water (105° to 115°F)
¼ cup (½ stick) MAZOLA® Margarine or butter, softened
2 eggs

GLAZE
½ cup KARO® Light or Dark Corn Syrup
½ cup packed light brown sugar
¼ cup (½ stick) MAZOLA® Margarine or butter
1 cup pecans, coarsely chopped

FILLING
½ cup firmly packed light brown sugar
1 teaspoon ground cinnamon
2 tablespoons MAZOLA® Margarine or butter, melted

To use frozen bread dough, thaw two 1-pound loaves frozen bread dough in refrigerator overnight. Press loaves together and roll to a 20×12-inch rectangle; complete as recipe directs.

1. For Dough: In large bowl, combine 2 cups flour, granulated sugar, salt and yeast. Stir in milk, water and softened margarine until blended. Stir in eggs and enough additional flour (about 2 cups) to make a soft dough. Knead on floured surface until smooth and elastic, about 8 minutes. Cover dough and let rest on floured surface 10 minutes.

2. For Glaze: In small saucepan over low heat, stir corn syrup, brown sugar and margarine until smooth. Pour into 13×9×2-inch baking pan. Sprinkle with pecans; set aside.

3. For Filling: Combine brown sugar and cinnamon. Roll dough into 20×12-inch rectangle. Brush dough with 2 tablespoons melted margarine; sprinkle with brown sugar mixture. Starting from a long side, roll up jelly-roll fashion. Pinch seam to seal. Cut into 15 slices. Place cut side up in prepared pan. Cover tightly. Refrigerate 2 to 24 hours.

4. Preheat oven to 375°F. Uncover pan and let stand at room temperature 10 minutes. Bake 28 to 30 minutes or until tops are browned. Invert onto serving tray. Serve warm or cool completely.

Makes 15 rolls

Orange Streusel Coffeecake (page 458)

Cookies & Brownies

FEATURING:

Bar Cookies

Biscotti & Shaped Cookies

Homemade Candy

Chocolate Espresso Brownies (page 482)

461

Chocolate Crackletops

- 2 cups all-purpose flour
- 2 teaspoons baking powder
- 2 cups granulated sugar
- ½ cup (1 stick) butter or margarine
- 4 squares (1 ounce each) unsweetened baking chocolate, chopped
- 4 large eggs, lightly beaten
- 2 teaspoons vanilla extract
- 1¾ cups "M&M's"® Chocolate Mini Baking Bits
  Additional granulated sugar

Combine flour and baking powder; set aside. In 2-quart saucepan over medium heat combine 2 cups sugar, butter and chocolate, stirring until butter and chocolate are melted; remove from heat. Gradually stir in eggs and vanilla. Stir in flour mixture until well blended. Chill mixture 1 hour. Stir in "M&M's"® Chocolate Mini Baking Bits; chill mixture an additional 1 hour.

Preheat oven to 350°F. Line cookie sheets with foil. With sugar-dusted hands, roll dough into 1-inch balls; roll balls in additional granulated sugar. Place about 2 inches apart onto prepared cookie sheets. Bake 10 to 12 minutes. *Do not overbake.* Cool completely on wire racks. Store in tightly covered container.

Makes about 5 dozen cookies

Brownie Turtle Cookies

- 2 squares (1 ounce each) unsweetened baking chocolate
- ⅓ cup solid vegetable shortening
- 1 cup granulated sugar
- ½ teaspoon vanilla extract
- 2 large eggs
- 1¼ cups all-purpose flour
- ½ teaspoon baking powder
- ½ teaspoon salt
- 1 cup "M&M's"® Milk Chocolate Mini Baking Bits, divided
- 1 cup pecan halves
- ⅓ cup caramel ice cream topping
- ⅓ cup shredded coconut
- ⅓ cup chopped pecans

Preheat oven to 350°F. Lightly grease cookie sheets; set aside. Heat chocolate and shortening in 2-quart saucepan over low heat, stirring constantly until melted; remove from heat. Mix in sugar, vanilla and eggs. Blend in flour, baking powder and salt. Stir in ⅔ *cup "M&M's"® Milk Chocolate Mini Baking Bits.* For each cookie, arrange 3 pecan halves, with ends almost touching at center, on prepared cookie sheets. Drop dough by rounded teaspoonfuls onto center of each group of pecans. Bake 8 to 10 minutes. *Do not overbake.* Cool on wire racks. In small bowl combine ice cream topping, coconut and chopped nuts; top each cookie with about 1½ teaspoons mixture. Press remaining ⅓ *cup "M&M's"® Milk Chocolate Mini Baking Bits* into topping.

Makes about 2½ dozen cookies

Double Chocolate Walnut Drops

- ¾ cup (1½ sticks) butter or margarine, softened
- ¾ cup granulated sugar
- ¾ cup firmly packed light brown sugar
- 1 large egg
- 1 teaspoon vanilla extract
- 2¼ cups all-purpose flour
- ⅓ cup unsweetened cocoa powder
- 1 teaspoon baking soda
- ½ teaspoon salt
- 1¾ cups "M&M's"® Chocolate Mini Baking Bits
- 1 cup coarsely chopped English or black walnuts

Preheat oven to 350°F. Lightly grease cookie sheets; set aside. In large bowl cream butter and sugars until light and fluffy; beat in egg and vanilla. In medium bowl combine flour, cocoa powder, baking soda and salt; add to creamed mixture. Stir in "M&M's"® Chocolate Mini Baking Bits and nuts. Drop by heaping tablespoonfuls about 2 inches apart onto prepared cookie sheets. Bake 12 to 14 minutes for chewy cookies or 14 to 16 minutes for crispy cookies. Cool completely on wire racks. Store in tightly covered container.

Makes about 4 dozen cookies

Variation: *Shape dough into 2-inch-thick roll. Cover with plastic wrap; refrigerate. When ready to bake, slice dough into ¼-inch-thick slices and bake as directed.*

Chocolate Crackletops

Chocolate Surprise Cookies

2¾ cups all-purpose flour
¾ cup unsweetened cocoa powder
½ teaspoon baking powder
½ teaspoon baking soda
1 cup margarine or butter, softened
1½ cups packed light brown sugar
½ cup plus 1 tablespoon granulated sugar, divided
2 eggs
1 teaspoon vanilla
1 cup chopped pecans, divided
1 package (9 ounces) caramels coated in milk chocolate
3 squares (1 ounce each) white chocolate, coarsely chopped

PREHEAT oven to 375°F. Place flour, cocoa, baking powder and baking soda in medium bowl; stir to combine. Set aside.

BEAT margarine, brown sugar and ½ cup granulated sugar with electric mixer at medium speed until light and fluffy; beat in eggs and vanilla. Gradually add flour mixture and ½ cup pecans. Beat at low speed, scraping down side of bowl occasionally. Refrigerate dough, covered, 15 minutes or until firm enough to roll into balls.

PLACE remaining ½ cup pecans and 1 tablespoon sugar in shallow dish. Roll tablespoonful of dough around 1 caramel candy, covering completely; press one side into nut mixture.

Place, nut side up, on ungreased cookie sheet. Repeat with additional dough and candies, placing 3 inches apart.

BAKE 10 to 12 minutes or until set and slightly cracked. Let stand on cookie sheet 2 minutes. Transfer cookies to wire rack; cool completely.

PLACE white chocolate pieces in small resealable plastic freezer bag; seal bag. Microwave at MEDIUM (50% power) 2 minutes. Turn bag over; microwave at MEDIUM 2 to 3 minutes or until melted. Knead bag until chocolate is smooth. Cut off tiny corner of bag; drizzle white chocolate onto cookies. Let stand until white chocolate is set, about 30 minutes.

Makes about 3½ dozen cookies

Chocolate Sugar Cookies

3 squares BAKER'S® Unsweetened Chocolate
1 cup (2 sticks) margarine or butter
1 cup sugar
1 egg
1 teaspoon vanilla
2 cups flour
1 teaspoon baking soda
¼ teaspoon salt
Additional sugar

Microwave chocolate and margarine in large microwavable bowl on HIGH 2 minutes or until margarine is melted. Stir until chocolate is completely melted.

Stir 1 cup sugar into melted chocolate mixture until well blended. Stir in egg and vanilla until completely blended. Mix in flour, baking soda and salt. Refrigerate 30 minutes.

Heat oven to 375°F. Shape dough into 1-inch balls; roll in additional sugar. Place, 2 inches apart, on *ungreased* cookie sheets. (If flatter, crisper cookies are desired, flatten balls with bottom of drinking glass.)

Bake 8 to 10 minutes or until set. Remove from cookie sheets to cool on wire racks.
Makes about 3½ dozen cookies

Prep Time: 15 minutes
Chill Time: 30 minutes
Bake Time: 8 to 10 minutes

JAM-FILLED CHOCOLATE SUGAR COOKIES: Prepare Chocolate Sugar Cookie dough as directed. Roll in finely chopped nuts in place of sugar. Make indentation in each ball; fill center with your favorite jam. Bake as directed.

CHOCOLATE-CARAMEL SUGAR COOKIES: Prepare Chocolate Sugar Cookie dough as directed. Roll in finely chopped nuts in place of sugar. Make indentation in each ball; bake as directed. Microwave 1 package (14 ounces) caramels with 2 tablespoons milk in microwavable bowl on HIGH 3 minutes or until melted, stirring after 2 minutes. Fill centers of cookies with caramel mixture. Drizzle with melted BAKER'S® Semi-Sweet Chocolate.

Chewy Brownie Cookies

1½ cups firmly packed light brown sugar
⅔ CRISCO® Stick or ⅔ cup CRISCO® all-vegetable shortening
1 tablespoon water
1 teaspoon vanilla
2 eggs
1½ cups all-purpose flour
⅓ cup unsweetened baking cocoa
¼ teaspoon baking soda
½ teaspoon salt
2 cups semisweet chocolate chips (12-ounce package)

1. **Heat** oven to 375°F. **Place** sheets of foil on countertop for cooling cookies.

2. **Combine** brown sugar, shortening, water and vanilla in large bowl. **Beat** at medium speed of electric mixer until well blended. **Beat** eggs into creamed mixture.

3. **Combine** flour, cocoa, baking soda and salt. Mix into creamed mixture at low speed just until blended. **Stir** in chocolate chips.

4. **Drop** rounded measuring tablespoonfuls of dough 2 inches apart onto *ungreased* baking sheet.

5. **Bake** one baking sheet at a time at 375°F for 7 to 9 minutes, or until cookies are set. DO NOT OVERBAKE. **Cool** 2 minutes on baking sheet. **Remove** cookies to foil to cool completely.
Makes about 3 dozen cookies

Double Chocolate Oat Cookies

1 package (12 ounces) semisweet chocolate pieces, divided
½ cup margarine or butter, softened
½ cup sugar
1 egg
¼ teaspoon vanilla
¾ cup all-purpose flour
¾ cup QUAKER® Oats (quick or old fashioned, uncooked)
1 teaspoon baking powder
¼ teaspoon baking soda
¼ teaspoon salt (optional)

Preheat oven to 375°F. Melt 1 cup chocolate pieces in small saucepan; set aside. Beat margarine and sugar until fluffy; add melted chocolate, egg and vanilla. Add combined flour, oats, baking powder, baking soda and salt; mix well. Stir in remaining chocolate pieces. Drop by rounded tablespoonfuls onto *ungreased* cookie sheet. Bake 8 to 10 minutes. Cool 1 minute on cookie sheet; remove to wire rack.
Makes about 3 dozen cookies

Chocolate Surprise Cookies (page 464)

Cherry Chocolate Chip Walnut Cookies

1 cup sugar
¼ cup Prune Purée (page 434) or prepared prune butter *or* 1 jar (2½ ounces) first-stage baby food prunes
¼ cup water
2 tablespoons nonfat milk
1 teaspoon vanilla
½ teaspoon instant espresso coffee powder *or* 1 teaspoon instant coffee granules
1 cup all-purpose flour
½ cup unsweetened cocoa powder
¾ teaspoon baking soda
½ teaspoon salt
½ cup dried sour cherries
¼ cup chopped walnuts
¼ cup semisweet chocolate chips

Preheat oven to 350°F. Coat baking sheets with vegetable cooking spray. In large bowl, whisk together sugar, prune purée, water, milk, vanilla and espresso powder until mixture is well blended, about 1 minute. Combine flour, cocoa, baking soda and salt; mix into prune purée mixture until well blended. Stir in cherries, walnuts and chocolate chips. Spoon 12 equal mounds of dough onto prepared baking sheets, spacing at least 2 inches apart. Bake in center of oven 18 to 20 minutes or until set and tops of cookies feel dry to the touch. Cool on baking sheets 2 minutes; remove to wire rack to cool completely.

Makes 12 large cookies

Tip: In chocolate baked goods using prune purée, the addition of coffee powder enhances the chocolate flavor.

FAVORITE RECIPE FROM **CALIFORNIA PRUNE BOARD**

Original Nestlé® Toll House® Chocolate Chip Cookies

2¼ cups all-purpose flour
1 teaspoon baking soda
1 teaspoon salt
1 cup (2 sticks) butter, softened
¾ cup granulated sugar
¾ cup packed brown sugar
1 teaspoon vanilla extract
2 eggs
2 cups (12-ounce package) NESTLÉ® TOLL HOUSE® Semi-Sweet Chocolate Morsels
1 cup chopped nuts

Combine flour, baking soda and salt in small bowl. Beat butter, granulated sugar, brown sugar and vanilla in large mixer bowl. Add eggs, one at a time, beating well after each addition; gradually beat in flour mixture. Stir in morsels and nuts. Drop by rounded tablespoonfuls onto *ungreased* baking sheets. Bake in preheated 375°F. oven for 9 to 11 minutes or until golden brown. Cool on baking sheets for 2 minutes; remove to wire racks to cool completely.

Makes about 5 dozen cookies

Pan Cookie Variation: Prepare dough as directed. Spread into greased 15½×10½-inch jelly-roll pan. Bake in preheated 375°F. oven for 20 to 25 minutes or until golden brown. Cool in pan on wire rack. *Makes 4 dozen bars*

Slice and Bake Cookie Variation: Prepare dough as directed. Divide in half; wrap in wax paper. Chill for 1 hour or until firm. Shape each half into 15-inch log; wrap in wax paper. Chill for 30 minutes. Cut into ½-inch-thick slices; place on ungreased baking sheets. Bake in preheated 375°F. oven for 8 to 10 minutes or until golden brown. Cool on baking sheets for 2 minutes; remove to wire racks to cool completely.

Makes about 5 dozen cookies

Cherry Chocolate Chip Walnut Cookies

Spicy Lemon Crescents

- 1 cup (2 sticks) butter or margarine, softened
- 1 ½ cups powdered sugar, divided
- ½ teaspoon lemon extract
- ½ teaspoon grated lemon zest
- 2 cups cake flour
- ½ cup finely chopped almonds, walnuts or pecans
- 1 teaspoon ground cinnamon
- ½ teaspoon ground cardamom
- ½ teaspoon ground nutmeg
- 1 ¾ cups "M&M's"® Chocolate Mini Baking Bits

Preheat oven to 375°F. Lightly grease cookie sheets; set aside. In large bowl cream butter and *½ cup sugar;* add lemon extract and zest until well blended. In medium bowl combine flour, nuts, cinnamon, cardamom and nutmeg; add to creamed mixture until well blended. Stir in "M&M's"® Chocolate Mini Baking Bits. Using 1 tablespoon of dough at a time, form into crescent shapes; place about 2 inches apart onto prepared cookie sheets. Bake 12 to 14 minutes or until edges are golden. Cool 2 minutes on cookie sheets. Gently roll warm crescents in remaining *1 cup sugar.* Cool completely on wire racks. Store in tightly covered container.

Makes about 2 dozen cookies

Apple Sauce Gingerbread Cookies

- 4 cups all-purpose flour
- 2 teaspoons ground ginger
- 2 teaspoons ground cinnamon
- 1 teaspoon baking soda
- ½ teaspoon salt
- ¼ teaspoon ground nutmeg
- ½ cup margarine, softened
- 1 cup sugar
- ⅓ cup light (gold label) molasses
- 1 cup MOTT'S® Natural Apple Sauce
  Decorator Icing (recipe follows)

Sift together flour, ginger, cinnamon, baking soda, salt and nutmeg; set aside. In bowl, with electric mixer at high speed, beat margarine, sugar and molasses until creamy. Alternately blend in dry ingredients and apple sauce. Cover and chill dough for several hours or overnight.

Preheat oven to 375°F. On floured surface, roll out dough to ⅛-inch thickness with lightly floured rolling pin. Cut with floured gingerbread man cutter or other shapes. Place on greased baking sheet. Bake 12 minutes or until done. Remove from sheet; cool on wire rack. Frost with Decorator Icing as desired. After icing dries, store in airtight container.

Makes 2½ dozen (5½-inch) cookies

DECORATOR ICING: Mix 2 cups confectioners' sugar and 1 tablespoon water. Add more water, 1 teaspoon at a time, until icing holds its shape and can be piped through a decorating tube.

Snow Covered Almond Crescents

- 1 cup (2 sticks) margarine or butter, softened
- ¾ cup powdered sugar
- ½ teaspoon almond extract *or* 2 teaspoons vanilla
- 1 ¾ cups all-purpose flour
- ¼ teaspoon salt (optional)
- 1 cup QUAKER® Oats (quick or old fashioned, uncooked)
- ½ cup finely chopped almonds
  Powdered sugar

Preheat oven to 325°F. Beat margarine, sugar and almond extract until well blended. Add flour and salt; mix until well blended. Stir in oats and almonds. Using level measuring tablespoonfuls, shape dough into crescents. Bake on *ungreased* cookie sheet 14 to 17 minutes or until bottoms are light golden brown. Remove to wire rack. Sift additional powdered sugar generously over warm cookies. Cool completely. Store tightly covered.

Makes about 3 dozen cookies

Bird's Nest Cookies

1⅓ cups (3½ ounces) flaked coconut
1 cup (2 sticks) butter or margarine, softened
½ cup granulated sugar
1 large egg
½ teaspoon vanilla extract
2 cups all-purpose flour
¾ teaspoon salt
1¾ cups "M&M's"® Semi-Sweet Chocolate Mini Baking Bits, divided

Preheat oven to 300°F. Spread coconut on *ungreased* cookie sheet. Toast in oven, stirring until coconut just begins to turn light golden, about 25 minutes. Remove coconut from cookie sheet; set aside. *Increase oven temperature to 350°F.* In large bowl cream butter and sugar until light and fluffy; beat in egg and vanilla. In medium bowl combine flour and salt; blend into creamed mixture. Stir in *1 cup "M&M's"® Semi-Sweet Chocolate Mini Baking Bits.* Form dough into 1¼-inch balls. Roll heavily in toasted coconut. Place 2 inches apart on lightly greased cookie sheets. Make indentation in center of each cookie with thumb. Bake 12 to 14 minutes or until coconut is golden brown. Remove cookies to wire racks; immediately fill indentations with remaining *"M&M's"® Semi-Sweet Chocolate Mini Baking Bits,* using scant teaspoonful for each cookie. Cool completely.

Makes about 3 dozen cookies

Chocolate Macadamia Chewies

¾ cup (1½ sticks) butter or margarine, softened
⅔ cup firmly packed light brown sugar
1 large egg
1 teaspoon vanilla extract
1¾ cups all-purpose flour
¾ teaspoon baking soda
¼ teaspoon salt
¾ cup (3½ ounces) coarsely chopped macadamia nuts
½ cup shredded coconut
1¾ cups "M&M's"® Chocolate Mini Baking Bits

Preheat oven to 350°F. In large bowl cream butter and sugar until light and fluffy; beat in egg and vanilla. In medium bowl combine flour, baking soda and salt; blend into creamed mixture. Blend in nuts and coconut. Stir in "M&M's"® Chocolate Mini Baking Bits. Drop by heaping teaspoonfuls about 2 inches apart onto *ungreased* cookie sheets; flatten slightly with back of spoon. Bake 8 to 10 minutes or until set. *Do not overbake.* Cool 1 minute on cookie sheets; cool completely on wire racks. Store in tightly covered container.

Makes about 4 dozen cookies

Low Fat Molasses Jumbles

½ cup Prune Purée (page 434) or prepared prune butter
½ cup sugar
½ cup molasses
1 egg
2 cups all-purpose flour
2 teaspoons ground cinnamon
1 teaspoon ground ginger
½ teaspoon baking soda
½ teaspoon salt
Additional sugar

Preheat oven to 350°F. Coat baking sheets with vegetable cooking spray. In large bowl, mix prune purée, sugar and molasses until well blended. Add egg; mix well. Combine remaining ingredients except additional sugar; stir into prune purée mixture just until blended. Roll heaping tablespoonfuls of dough in additional sugar. Place on baking sheets, spacing 2 inches apart. With fork, flatten dough in crisscross fashion until ½ inch thick. Bake in center of oven about 12 to 13 minutes or until set and bottoms are lightly browned. Remove from baking sheets to wire racks to cool completely.

Makes 30 (2½-inch) cookies

Tip: For easy cleanup, measure molasses in a cup that has been lightly sprayed with vegetable cooking spray.

FAVORITE RECIPE FROM **CALIFORNIA PRUNE BOARD**

Chocolate Banana Walnut Drops

½ cup (1 stick) butter or margarine, softened
½ cup solid vegetable shortening
1¼ cups firmly packed light brown sugar
1 large egg
1 medium banana, mashed (about ½ cup)
2¼ cups all-purpose flour
1 teaspoon baking soda
1 teaspoon ground cinnamon
½ teaspoon ground nutmeg
¼ teaspoon salt
2 cups uncooked quick-cooking or old-fashioned oats
1 cup coarsely chopped walnuts
1¾ cups "M&M's"® Chocolate Mini Baking Bits

Preheat oven to 350°F. In large bowl cream butter, shortening and sugar until light and fluffy; beat in egg and banana. In medium bowl combine flour, baking soda, cinnamon, nutmeg and salt; blend into creamed mixture. Blend in oats and nuts. Stir in "M&M's"® Chocolate Mini Baking Bits. Drop by tablespoonfuls about 2 inches apart onto *ungreased* cookie sheets. Bake 8 to 10 minutes or just until set. *Do not overbake.* Cool 1 minute on cookie sheets; cool completely on wire racks. Store in tightly covered container.

Makes about 3 dozen cookies

Biscotti for Dunking

¾ cup sugar
¼ cup Prune Purée (page 434) or prepared prune butter
Grated peel of 1 orange
½ cup egg substitute
½ teaspoon almond extract
2½ cups all-purpose flour
¼ cup toasted whole almonds, cut in half
1 tablespoon anise seeds (optional)
1½ teaspoons baking powder
¼ teaspoon salt

Preheat oven to 325°F. Coat baking sheet with vegetable cooking spray and dust with flour. In mixer bowl, beat sugar, prune purée and orange peel at low speed until well blended. Add egg substitute and almond extract; beat until blended. In medium bowl, combine remaining ingredients; mix into sugar mixture until well blended. Divide mixture in half and form into 2 equal 14-inch logs. Place on prepared baking sheet, spacing at least 2 inches apart. Bake in center of oven about 30 minutes or until golden brown. Remove from baking sheet to wire rack to cool 5 minutes. With serrated knife, cut diagonally into ½-inch slices. Lay slices flat on baking sheet and bake about 15 minutes longer, turning once, until dry. Remove from baking sheet to wire rack to cool completely. Store in airtight container.

Makes 56 cookies

FAVORITE RECIPE FROM CALIFORNIA PRUNE BOARD

Crispy Oat Drops

1 cup (2 sticks) butter or margarine, softened
½ cup granulated sugar
½ cup firmly packed light brown sugar
1 large egg
2 cups all-purpose flour
½ cup uncooked quick-cooking or old-fashioned oats
1 teaspoon cream of tartar
½ teaspoon baking soda
¼ teaspoon salt
1¾ cups "M&M's"® Semi-Sweet Chocolate Mini Baking Bits
1 cup toasted rice cereal
½ cup shredded coconut
½ cup coarsely chopped pecans

Preheat oven to 350°F. In large bowl cream butter and sugars until light and fluffy; beat in egg. In medium bowl combine flour, oats, cream of tartar, baking soda and salt; blend flour mixture into creamed mixture. Stir in "M&M's"® Semi-Sweet Chocolate Mini Baking Bits, cereal, coconut and pecans. Drop by heaping tablespoonfuls about 2 inches apart onto *ungreased* cookie sheets. Bake 10 to 13 minutes or until lightly browned. Cool completely on wire racks. Store in tightly covered container.

Makes about 4 dozen cookies

Chocolate Banana Walnut Drops

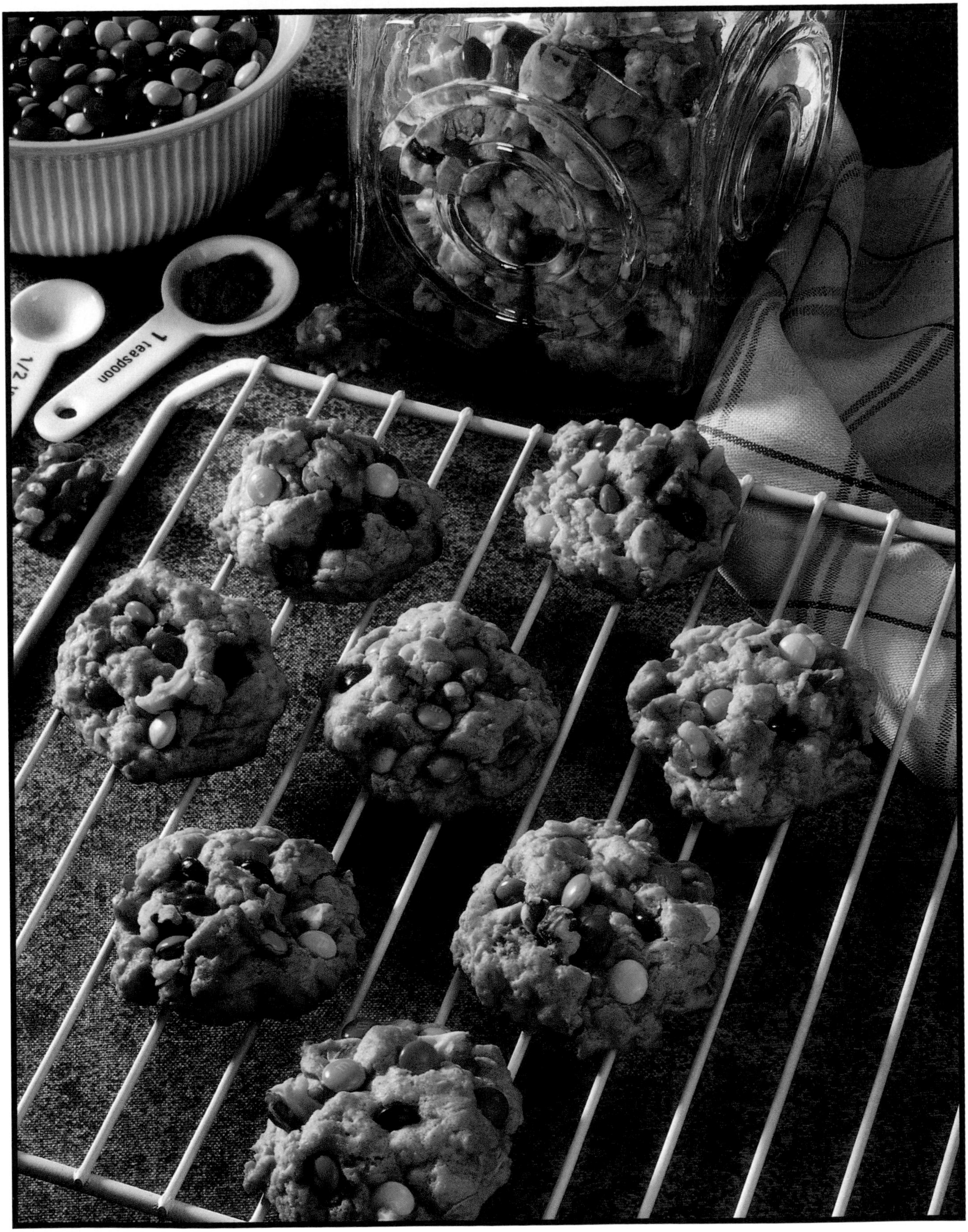
1 teaspoon

Oatmeal Cookies

1 cup all-purpose flour
1 teaspoon baking powder
½ teaspoon baking soda
½ teaspoon salt
¼ cup MOTT'S® Cinnamon Apple Sauce
2 tablespoons margarine
½ cup granulated sugar
½ cup firmly packed light brown sugar
1 egg
1 teaspoon vanilla extract
1⅓ cups uncooked rolled oats
½ cup raisins (optional)

1. Preheat oven to 375°F. Spray cookie sheet with nonstick cooking spray.

2. In small bowl, combine flour, baking powder, baking soda and salt.

3. In large bowl, place apple sauce. Cut in margarine with pastry blender or fork until margarine breaks into pea-sized pieces. Add granulated sugar, brown sugar, egg and vanilla; stir until well blended.

4. Add flour mixture to apple sauce mixture; stir until well blended. Fold in oats and raisins, if desired.

5. Drop rounded teaspoonfuls of dough 2 inches apart onto prepared cookie sheet.

6. Bake 10 to 12 minutes or until lightly browned. Cool 5 minutes on cookie sheet. Remove to wire rack; cool completely.

Makes 3 dozen cookies

Oatmeal Scotchies

1¼ cups all-purpose flour
1 teaspoon baking soda
½ teaspoon salt
½ teaspoon ground cinnamon
1 cup (2 sticks) butter or margarine, softened
¾ cup granulated sugar
¾ cup packed brown sugar
2 eggs
1 teaspoon vanilla extract *or* grated peel of 1 orange
3 cups quick or old-fashioned oats
1⅔ cups (11-ounce package) NESTLÉ® TOLL HOUSE® Butterscotch Flavored Morsels

COMBINE flour, baking soda, salt and cinnamon in small bowl. Beat butter, granulated sugar, brown sugar, eggs and vanilla in large mixer bowl. Gradually beat in flour mixture. Stir in oats and morsels. Drop by rounded tablespoonfuls onto *ungreased* baking sheets.

BAKE in preheated 375°F. oven for 7 to 8 minutes for chewy cookies; 9 to 10 minutes for crisp cookies. Cool on baking sheets for 2 minutes; remove to wire racks to cool completely.
Makes about 4 dozen cookies

Pan Cookie Variation: SPREAD dough into greased 15½×10½-inch jelly-roll pan. Bake in preheated 375°F. oven for 18 to 22 minutes or until very lightly browned. Cool completely on wire rack.
Makes 4 dozen bars

Peanut Butter Cookies

⅓ cup Prune Purée (page 434) or prepared prune butter *or* 1 jar (2½ ounces) first-stage baby food prunes
⅓ cup granulated sugar
⅓ cup packed brown sugar
¼ cup creamy peanut butter
¼ cup honey
2 tablespoons vegetable oil
1 egg white
1 teaspoon vanilla
1½ cups all-purpose flour
½ teaspoon salt
½ teaspoon baking soda

Preheat oven to 375°F. Coat baking sheets with vegetable cooking spray. In mixer bowl, beat prune purée, sugars, peanut butter, honey, oil, egg white and vanilla 1 minute at medium speed until well blended. Combine flour, salt and baking soda; beat into prune purée mixture until well blended. With hands moistened with water to prevent sticking, shape generous tablespoonfuls of dough into balls. Place on prepared baking sheets, spacing 3 inches apart. With fork, flatten dough in crisscross fashion until ½ inch thick. Bake in center of oven 10 to 11 minutes or until light golden brown. Cool on baking sheets 1 minute; remove to wire racks to cool completely.
Makes 24 cookies

FAVORITE RECIPE FROM ***CALIFORNIA PRUNE BOARD***

Gingersnaps

2 ½ cups all-purpose flour
1 ½ teaspoons ground
 ginger
 1 teaspoon baking soda
 1 teaspoon ground
 allspice
 ½ teaspoon salt
1 ½ cups sugar
 2 tablespoons margarine,
 softened
 ½ cup MOTT'S® Apple
 Sauce
 ¼ cup GRANDMA'S®
 Molasses

1. Preheat oven to 375°F. Spray cookie sheet with nonstick cooking spray.

2. In medium bowl, sift together flour, ginger, baking soda, allspice and salt.

3. In large bowl, beat sugar and margarine with electric mixer at medium speed until blended. Whisk in apple sauce and molasses.

4. Add flour mixture to apple sauce mixture; stir until well blended.

5. Drop rounded tablespoonfuls of dough 1 inch apart onto prepared cookie sheet. Flatten each slightly with moistened fingertips.

6. Bake 12 to 15 minutes or until firm. Cool completely on wire rack.

Makes 3 dozen cookies

Jumbles

½ cup (1 stick) butter or
 margarine, softened
 ½ cup granulated sugar
 ¼ cup firmly packed light
 brown sugar
 1 large egg
1 ¼ cups all-purpose flour
 ½ teaspoon baking soda
1 ¾ cups "M&M's"®
 Chocolate Mini Baking
 Bits
 1 cup raisins
 1 cup chopped walnuts

Preheat oven to 350°F. Lightly grease cookie sheets. Cream butter and sugars until light and fluffy; beat in egg. Combine flour and baking soda; blend into creamed mixture. Stir in remaining ingredients. Drop by rounded tablespoonfuls onto cookie sheets. Bake 13 to 15 minutes. Cool 2 to 3 minutes on cookie sheets; cool completely on wire racks.

Makes about 3 dozen cookies

Top to bottom: Oatmeal Cookies (page 472) and Gingersnaps

Happy Cookie Pops

**1½ cups granulated sugar
1 cup butter-flavored solid
    vegetable shortening
2 large eggs
1 teaspoon vanilla extract
2¾ cups all-purpose flour
1 teaspoon baking powder
½ teaspoon baking soda
1¾ cups "M&M's"®
    Chocolate Mini Baking
    Bits, divided
Additional granulated
    sugar
2½ dozen flat wooden ice
    cream sticks
Prepared frostings
Tubes of decorator's
    icing**

In large bowl cream 1½ cups sugar and shortening until light and fluffy; beat in eggs and vanilla. In medium bowl combine flour, baking powder and baking soda; blend into creamed mixture. Stir in *1¼ cups "M&M's"® Chocolate Mini Baking Bits.* Wrap and refrigerate dough 1 hour.

Preheat oven to 375°F. Roll 1½ tablespoons dough into ball and roll in granulated sugar. Insert ice cream stick into each ball. Place about 2 inches apart onto ungreased cookie sheets; gently flatten, using bottom of small plate. On half the cookies, make a smiling face by placing some of the remaining *"M&M's"® Chocolate Mini Baking Bits* on the surface; leave other cookies for decorating after baking.

Bake all cookies 10 to 12 minutes or until golden. Cool 2 minutes on cookie sheets; cool completely on wire racks. Decorate cookies as desired using frostings, decorator's icing and remaining *"M&M's"® Chocolate Mini Baking Bits.* Store in single layer in tightly covered container.

Makes 2½ dozen cookies

Variation: For chocolate cookies, combine ⅓ cup unsweetened cocoa powder with flour, baking powder and baking soda; continue as directed.

Peanut Butter Bears

**1 cup SKIPPY® Creamy
    Peanut Butter
1 cup (2 sticks) MAZOLA®
    Margarine or butter,
    softened
1 cup packed brown sugar
⅔ cup KARO® Light or
    Dark Corn Syrup
2 eggs
4 cups all-purpose flour,
    divided
1 tablespoon baking
    powder
1 teaspoon ground
    cinnamon (optional)
¼ teaspoon salt**

1. In large bowl with mixer at medium speed, beat peanut butter, margarine, brown sugar, corn syrup and eggs until smooth. Reduce speed; beat in 2 cups flour, baking powder, cinnamon and salt. With spoon stir in remaining 2 cups flour. Wrap dough in plastic wrap; refrigerate 2 hours.

2. Preheat oven to 325°F. Divide dough in half; set half aside.

3. On floured surface, roll out half the dough to ⅛-inch thickness. Cut with floured bear cookie cutter. Repeat with remaining dough.

4. Bake bears on *ungreased* cookie sheets 10 minutes or until lightly browned. Remove from cookie sheets; cool completely on wire rack. Decorate as desired.

Makes about 3 dozen bears

Prep Time: 35 minutes plus chilling
Bake Time: 10 minutes plus cooling

Note: Use scraps of dough to make bear faces. Make one small ball of dough for muzzle. Form 3 smaller balls of dough and press gently to create eyes and nose; bake as directed. If desired, use frosting to create paws, ears and bow ties.

Happy Cookie Pops

PB & J Cookie Sandwiches

½ cup butter or margarine, softened
½ cup creamy peanut butter
¼ cup solid vegetable shortening
1 cup firmly packed light brown sugar
1 large egg
1 teaspoon vanilla extract
1⅔ cups all-purpose flour
1 teaspoon baking soda
½ teaspoon baking powder
1 cup "M&M's"® Milk Chocolate Mini Baking Bits
½ cup finely chopped peanuts
½ cup grape or strawberry jam

Preheat oven to 350°F. In large bowl cream butter, peanut butter, shortening and sugar until light and fluffy; beat in egg and vanilla. In medium bowl combine flour, baking soda and baking powder; blend into creamed mixture. Stir in "M&M's"® Milk Chocolate Mini Baking Bits and nuts. Drop by rounded teaspoonfuls onto ungreased cookie sheets. Bake 8 to 10 minutes or until light golden. Let cool 2 minutes on cookie sheets; remove to wire racks to cool completely. Just before serving, spread ½ teaspoon jam on bottom of one cookie; top with second cookie. Store in tightly covered container.

Makes about 2 dozen sandwich cookies

Spicy Fruit and Oatmeal Hermits

½ cup packed light brown sugar
⅓ cup Prune Purée (page 434) or prepared prune butter
⅓ cup granulated sugar
¼ cup water
2 tablespoons nonfat milk
2 teaspoons vanilla
1 cup all-purpose flour
1½ teaspoons pumpkin pie spice
1 teaspoon instant espresso coffee powder *or* 2 teaspoons instant coffee granules
1 teaspoon baking soda
½ teaspoon salt
1½ cups rolled oats
1¼ cups mixed dried fruit bits

Preheat oven to 350°F. Coat baking sheets with vegetable cooking spray. In large bowl, beat brown sugar, prune purée, granulated sugar, water, milk and vanilla about 1 minute until well blended. Combine flour, spice, espresso powder, baking soda and salt; stir into sugar mixture until well blended. Stir in oats and dried fruit. Drop rounded tablespoonfuls of dough onto prepared baking sheets, spacing 2 inches apart. Bake in center of oven about 12 minutes or until cookies are golden brown and soft on top. Remove cookies from baking sheets to wire racks to cool completely.

Makes 20 cookies

Tip: Purchase mixed dried fruits chopped into bits or purchase individual dried fruits and chop them to make your own dried fruit mix. Start with chopped prunes, apricots or peaches and add raisins, currants, cherries or cranberries.

FAVORITE RECIPE FROM **CALIFORNIA PRUNE BOARD**

Colorific Chocolate Chip Cookies

1 cup (2 sticks) butter or margarine, softened
⅔ cup granulated sugar
½ cup firmly packed light brown sugar
1 large egg
1 teaspoon vanilla extract
2 cups all-purpose flour
¾ teaspoon baking soda
¾ teaspoon salt
1¾ cups "M&M's"® Semi-Sweet Chocolate Mini Baking Bits
¾ cup chopped nuts (optional)

Preheat oven to 375°F. In large bowl cream butter and sugars until light and fluffy; beat in egg and vanilla. In medium bowl combine flour, baking soda and salt; blend into creamed mixture. Stir in "M&M's"® Semi-Sweet Chocolate Mini Baking Bits and nuts, if desired. Drop by heaping tablespoonfuls about 2 inches apart onto *ungreased* cookie sheets. Bake 9 to 12 minutes or until lightly browned. Cool 1 minute on cookie sheets; cool completely on wire racks.

Makes about 3 dozen cookies

Hint: For chewy cookies bake 9 to 10 minutes; for crispy cookies bake 11 to 12 minutes.

Pan Cookie Variation: Prepare dough as directed; spread into lightly greased 15×10×1-inch jelly-roll pan. Bake at 375°F for 18 to 22 minutes. Cool completely before cutting into 35 (2-inch) squares. For a more festive look, reserve ½ cup baking bits to sprinkle on top of dough before baking.

Chewy Oatmeal Trail Mix Cookies

¾ **BUTTER FLAVOR* CRISCO® Stick or ¾ cup BUTTER FLAVOR CRISCO® all-vegetable shortening**
1¼ **cups firmly packed light brown sugar**
⅓ **cup milk**
1 **egg**
1½ **teaspoons vanilla**
2½ **cups uncooked quick oats**
1 **cup all-purpose flour**
½ **teaspoon baking soda**
½ **teaspoon salt**
¼ **teaspoon cinnamon**
1 **cup semisweet or milk chocolate chips**
¾ **cup raisins**
¾ **cup coarsely chopped walnuts, pecans or peanuts**
½ **cup sunflower seeds**

*Butter Flavor CRISCO® is artificially flavored.

1. Heat oven to 375°F. **Grease** baking sheets with shortening. **Place** sheets of foil on countertop for cooling cookies.

2. Combine shortening, brown sugar, milk, egg and vanilla in large bowl. **Beat** at medium speed of electric mixer until well blended.

3. Combine oats, flour, baking soda, salt and cinnamon. **Mix** into shortening mixture at low speed just until blended. **Stir** in chocolate chips, raisins, nuts and sunflower seeds.

4. Drop rounded tablespoonfuls of dough 2 inches apart onto prepared baking sheets.

5. Bake one baking sheet at a time at 375°F for 10 to 12 minutes, or until lightly browned. *Do not overbake.* **Cool** 2 minutes on baking sheets. **Remove** cookies to foil to cool completely.

Makes about 3 dozen cookies

Note: You may substitute 3 cups of prepared trail mix (available in grocery or health food stores) for the chips, raisins, nuts and sunflower seeds.

Valentine Stained Glass Hearts

½ **cup butter or margarine, softened**
¾ **cup granulated sugar**
2 **eggs**
1 **teaspoon vanilla extract**
2⅓ **cups all-purpose flour**
1 **teaspoon baking powder**
Red hard candies, crushed (about ⅓ cup)
Frosting (optional)

Cream butter and sugar in mixing bowl. Beat in eggs and vanilla. Sift flour and baking powder together. Gradually stir in flour mixture until dough is very stiff. Cover and chill. *Dough needs to chill 3 hours to overnight.*

Preheat oven to 375°F. Roll out dough to ⅛-inch thickness on lightly floured surface. To prevent cookies from becoming tough and brittle, do not incorporate too much flour. Cut out cookies using large heart-shaped cookie cutter or use sharp knife and cut heart design. Transfer cookies to foil-lined baking sheet. Using small heart-shaped cookie cutter, cut out and remove heart design from center of each cookie. Fill cutout sections with crushed candy. Bake 7 to 9 minutes or until cookies are lightly browned and candy has melted. *Do not overcook.*

Remove from oven; immediately slide foil off baking sheet. Cool completely; carefully loosen cookies from foil. Pipe decorative borders with frosting around edges, if desired.

Makes about 2½ dozen medium cookies

*Favorite recipe from **The Sugar Association, Inc.***

Marbled Biscotti

½ cup (1 stick) butter or
   margarine, softened
1 cup granulated sugar
2 large eggs
1 teaspoon vanilla extract
2½ cups all-purpose flour
1 teaspoon baking powder
1 teaspoon baking soda
1¾ cups "M&M's"®
   Chocolate Mini Baking
   Bits, divided
1 cup slivered almonds,
   toasted*
¼ cup unsweetened cocoa
   powder
2 tablespoons instant
   coffee granules

*To toast almonds, spread in
single layer on baking sheet.
Bake at 350°F for 7 to 10
minutes until light golden,
stirring occasionally. Remove
almonds from pan and cool
completely before using.*

Preheat oven to 350°F. Lightly
grease cookie sheets; set aside.
In large bowl cream butter and
sugar until light and fluffy; beat
in eggs and vanilla. In medium
bowl combine flour, baking
powder and baking soda; blend
into creamed mixture. *Dough
will be stiff.* Stir in *1¼ cups
"M&M's"® Chocolate Mini
Baking Bits* and nuts. Divide
dough in half. Add cocoa
powder and coffee granules to
half of the dough, mixing to
blend. On well-floured surface,
gently knead doughs together
just enough to marble. Divide
dough in half and gently roll
each half into 12×2-inch log;

place on prepared cookie
sheets at least 4 inches apart.
Press remaining *½ cup
"M&M's"® Chocolate Mini
Baking Bits* onto outside of
both logs. Bake 25 minutes.
Dough will spread. Cool logs
15 to 20 minutes. Slice each
log into 12 slices; arrange on
cookie sheet cut side down.
Bake an additional 10 minutes.
(For softer biscotti, omit second
baking.) Cool completely. Store
in tightly covered container.

Makes 24 pieces

Ultimate Sugar Cookies

1¼ cups granulated sugar
1 BUTTER FLAVOR*
   CRISCO® Stick or
   1 cup BUTTER FLAVOR
CRISCO® all-vegetable
   shortening
2 eggs
¼ cup light corn syrup or
   regular pancake syrup
1 tablespoon vanilla
3 cups plus 4 tablespoons
   all-purpose flour,
   divided
¾ teaspoon baking powder
½ teaspoon baking soda
½ teaspoon salt
   Granulated sugar or
   colored sugar crystals

*Butter Flavor CRISCO® is
artificially flavored.*

1. Place sugar and shortening
in large bowl. Beat at medium
speed of electric mixer until
well blended. Add eggs, syrup
and vanilla; beat until well
blended and fluffy.

2. Combine 3 cups flour,
baking powder, baking soda
and salt. Add gradually to
shortening mixture, beating at
low speed until well blended.

3. Divide dough into 4 equal
pieces. Wrap with plastic wrap.
Refrigerate 1 hour or until firm.

4. Heat oven to 375°F. Place
sheets of foil on countertop for
cooling cookies.

5. Spread about 1 tablespoon
flour on large sheet of waxed
paper. Place disk of dough on
floured paper; flatten slightly
with hands. Turn dough over;
cover with another large sheet
of waxed paper. Roll dough to
¼-inch thickness. Remove top
sheet of waxed paper. Cut into
desired shapes with floured
cookie cutters. Place 2 inches
apart on *ungreased* baking
sheets. Repeat with remaining
dough and flour.

6. Sprinkle with granulated
sugar.

7. Bake one baking sheet at a
time at 375°F for 5 to 9 minutes
or until edges of cookies
are lightly browned. *Do not
overbake.* Cool 2 minutes on
baking sheet. Remove cookies
to foil to cool completely.

Makes about 3½ dozen cookies

Soft Apple Cider Cookies

- **1 cup firmly packed light brown sugar**
- **½ cup margarine, softened**
- **½ cup apple cider**
- **½ cup EGG BEATERS® Healthy Egg Substitute**
- **2¼ cups all-purpose flour**
- **1½ teaspoons ground cinnamon**
- **1 teaspoon baking soda**
- **¼ teaspoon salt**
- **2 medium apples, peeled and diced (about 1½ cups)**
- **¾ cup almonds, chopped Cider Glaze (recipe follows)**

In large bowl, with electric mixer at medium speed, beat sugar and margarine until creamy. Add cider and Egg Beaters®; beat until smooth. With electric mixer at low speed, gradually blend in flour, cinnamon, baking soda and salt. Stir in apples and almonds.

Drop dough by tablespoonfuls, 2 inches apart, onto greased baking sheets. Bake at 375°F for 10 to 12 minutes or until golden brown. Remove from sheets; cool on wire racks. Drizzle with Cider Glaze.

Makes 4 dozen cookies

Prep Time: 30 minutes
Cook Time: 12 minutes

CIDER GLAZE: In small bowl, combine 1 cup powdered sugar and 2 tablespoons apple cider until smooth.

Doubly Chocolate Mint Cookies

- **1 HERSHEY'₅S Cookies 'n' Mint Milk Chocolate Bar (7 ounces)**
- **½ cup (1 stick) butter or margarine, softened**
- **¾ cup sugar**
- **1 egg**
- **1 teaspoon vanilla extract**
- **1 cup all-purpose flour**
- **⅓ cup HERSHEY'₅S Cocoa**
- **½ teaspoon baking soda**
- **⅛ teaspoon salt**
- **1 cup coarsely chopped nuts (optional)**

Heat oven to 350°F. Cut chocolate bar into small pieces. In large bowl, beat butter, sugar, egg and vanilla until light and fluffy. Combine flour, cocoa, baking soda and salt; add butter mixture, beating until well blended. Stir in chocolate and nuts, if desired. Drop rounded teaspoonfuls onto *ungreased* cookie sheet. Bake 10 to 12 minutes or until set. Cool slightly; remove to wire rack. Cool completely.

Makes about 2½ dozen cookies

Soft Apple Cider Cookies

Triple Chocolate Brownies

3 squares (1 ounce each) unsweetened chocolate, coarsely chopped
2 squares (1 ounce each) semisweet chocolate, coarsely chopped
½ cup margarine or butter
1 cup all-purpose flour
½ teaspoon salt
¼ teaspoon baking powder
1½ cups sugar
3 large eggs
1 teaspoon vanilla
¼ cup sour cream
½ cup milk chocolate chips
Powdered sugar (optional)

PREHEAT oven to 350°F. Lightly grease 13×9-inch baking pan.

PLACE unsweetened chocolate, semisweet chocolate and margarine in medium microwavable bowl. Microwave at HIGH 2 minutes or until margarine is melted; stir until chocolate is completely melted. Cool to room temperature.

PLACE flour, salt and baking powder in small bowl; stir to combine.

BEAT sugar, eggs and vanilla in large bowl with electric mixer at medium speed until slightly thickened. Beat in chocolate mixture until well combined. Add flour mixture; beat at low speed until blended. Add sour cream; beat at low speed until combined. Stir in milk chocolate chips. Spread mixture evenly into prepared pan.

BAKE 20 to 25 minutes or until wooden pick inserted into center comes out almost clean. *Do not overbake.* Cool brownies completely in pan on wire rack. Cut into 2-inch squares. Place powdered sugar in fine-mesh strainer; sprinkle over brownies, if desired.

STORE tightly covered at room temperature or freeze up to 3 months.

Makes 2 dozen brownies

Fabulous Blonde Brownies

1¾ cups all-purpose flour
1 teaspoon baking powder
¼ teaspoon salt
1 cup (6 ounces) white chocolate chips
1 cup (4 ounces) blanched whole almonds, coarsely chopped
1 cup English toffee bits
⅔ cup margarine or butter, softened
1½ cups packed light brown sugar
2 eggs
2 teaspoons vanilla

PREHEAT oven to 350°F. Lightly grease 13×9-inch baking pan.

COMBINE flour, baking powder and salt in small bowl; mix well.

COMBINE white chocolate, almonds and toffee in medium bowl; mix well.

BEAT margarine and brown sugar in large bowl with electric mixer at medium speed until light and fluffy. Beat in eggs and vanilla. Add flour mixture; beat at low speed until well blended. Stir in ¾ cup of white chocolate mixture. Spread evenly into prepared pan.

BAKE 20 minutes. Immediately after removing brownies from oven, sprinkle remaining white chocolate mixture evenly over brownies. Press down lightly. Return pan to oven; bake 15 to 20 minutes or until wooden pick inserted into center comes out clean. Cool brownies completely in pan on wire rack. Cut into 2×1½-inch bars.

STORE tightly covered at room temperature or freeze up to 3 months.

Makes 3 dozen brownies

Triple Chocolate Brownies

Peanut Butter Marbled Brownies

4 ounces cream cheese, softened
½ cup peanut butter
2 tablespoons sugar
1 egg
1 package (20 to 22 ounces) brownie mix plus ingredients to prepare mix
¾ cup lightly salted cocktail peanuts

PREHEAT oven to 350°F. Lightly grease 13×9-inch baking pan; set aside.

BEAT cream cheese, peanut butter, sugar and egg in medium bowl with electric mixer at medium speed until blended; set aside.

PREPARE brownie mix according to package directions.

SPREAD brownie mixture evenly in prepared pan. Spoon peanut butter mixture in dollops over brownie mixture. Swirl peanut butter mixture into brownie mixture with tip of knife. Sprinkle peanuts on top; lightly press peanuts down.

BAKE 30 to 35 minutes or until wooden pick inserted into center comes out almost clean. *Do not overbake.* Cool brownies completely in pan on wire rack. Cut into 2-inch squares.

STORE tightly covered at room temperature or freeze up to 3 months.

Makes 2 dozen brownies

One Bowl® Brownies

4 squares BAKER'S® Unsweetened Chocolate
¾ cup (1½ sticks) margarine or butter
2 cups sugar
3 eggs
1 teaspoon vanilla
1 cup flour
1 cup chopped nuts (optional)

HEAT oven to 350°F (325°F for glass baking dish). Line 13×9-inch baking pan with foil extending over edges to form handles. Grease foil.

MICROWAVE chocolate and margarine in large microwavable bowl on HIGH 2 minutes or until margarine is melted. Stir until chocolate is completely melted.

STIR sugar into chocolate until well blended. Mix in eggs and vanilla. Stir in flour and nuts until well blended. Spread in prepared pan.

BAKE 30 to 35 minutes or until toothpick inserted into center comes out with fudgy crumbs. **Do not overbake.** Cool in pan. Lift out of pan onto cutting board. Cut into squares.

Makes 24 fudgy brownies

TOP OF STOVE PREPARATION:
MELT CHOCOLATE AND MARGARINE IN HEAVY 3-QUART SAUCEPAN ON VERY LOW HEAT, STIRRING CONSTANTLY. REMOVE FROM HEAT. CONTINUE AS DIRECTED.

Chocolate Espresso Brownies

4 squares (1 ounce each) unsweetened chocolate
1 cup sugar
¼ cup Prune Purée (page 434) or prepared prune butter
3 egg whites
1 to 2 tablespoons instant espresso coffee powder
1 teaspoon baking powder
1 teaspoon salt
1 teaspoon vanilla
½ cup all-purpose flour
Powdered sugar (optional)

Preheat oven to 350°F. Coat 8-inch square baking pan with vegetable cooking spray. In small heavy saucepan, melt chocolate over very low heat, stirring until melted and smooth. Remove from heat; cool. In mixer bowl, beat chocolate and remaining ingredients except flour and powdered sugar at medium speed until well blended; mix in flour. Spread batter evenly in prepared pan. Bake in center of oven about 30 minutes or until pick inserted into center comes out clean. Cool completely in pan on wire rack. Dust with powdered sugar. Cut into 1⅓-inch squares.

Makes 36 brownies

*FAVORITE RECIPE FROM **CALIFORNIA PRUNE BOARD***

Peanut Butter Marbled Brownies

Ultimate Rocky Road Cups

¾ cup (1½ sticks) butter or margarine
4 squares (1 ounce each) unsweetened baking chocolate
1½ cups granulated sugar
3 large eggs
1 cup all-purpose flour
1¾ cups "M&M's"® Chocolate Mini Baking Bits
¾ cup coarsely chopped peanuts
1 cup mini marshmallows

Preheat oven to 350°F. Generously grease 24 (2½-inch) muffin cups or line with foil liners. Place butter and chocolate in large microwave-safe bowl. Microwave at HIGH 1 minute; stir. Microwave at HIGH an additional 30 seconds; stir until chocolate is completely melted. Add sugar and eggs, one at a time, beating well after each addition. Blend in flour. In separate bowl combine "M&M's"® Chocolate Mini Baking Bits and nuts; stir 1 cup baking bits mixture into brownie batter. Divide batter evenly among prepared muffin cups. Bake 20 minutes. Combine remaining baking bits mixture with marshmallows; divide evenly among muffin cups, topping hot brownies. Return to oven; bake 5 minutes longer. Cool completely before removing from muffin cups. Store in tightly covered container. *Makes 24 cups*

MINI ULTIMATE ROCKY ROAD CUPS: Prepare recipe as directed, dividing batter among 60 generously greased 2-inch mini muffin cups. Bake 15 minutes. Sprinkle with topping mixture; bake 5 minutes longer. Cool completely before removing from cups.

Makes about 60 mini cups

ULTIMATE ROCKY ROAD SQUARES: Prepare recipe as directed, spreading batter into generously greased 13×9×2-inch baking pan. Bake 30 minutes. Sprinkle with topping mixture; bake 5 minutes longer. Cool.

Makes 24 squares

Fudgy Double Chocolate Brownies

1⅓ cups unsweetened cocoa powder
1 cup all-purpose flour
1 teaspoon baking powder
½ teaspoon baking soda
½ teaspoon salt
⅓ cup Prune Purée (page 434) or prepared prune butter *or* 1 jar (2½ ounces) first-stage baby food prunes
¼ cup nonfat milk
1 tablespoon vegetable oil
1 tablespoon instant espresso coffee powder
1 tablespoon vanilla
6 egg whites
2 cups sugar
⅔ cup semisweet chocolate chips

Preheat oven to 325°F. Coat 15½×10½×1-inch baking pan with vegetable cooking spray. In medium bowl, combine cocoa, flour, baking powder, baking soda and salt; set aside. In small bowl, whisk together prune purée, milk, oil, espresso powder and vanilla until well blended, about 1 minute. In mixer bowl, beat egg whites and sugar on medium speed 30 seconds; increase speed to high and beat 2½ minutes more until mixture is thick, but not stiff. Add prune purée mixture; beat until well blended, about 15 seconds. Fold in flour mixture. Fold in chocolate chips. Spread batter evenly in prepared pan. Bake in center of oven 25 to 30 minutes or until springy to the touch and pick inserted into center comes out almost clean. Cool completely in pan on wire rack. Cut into bars with knife dipped into hot water.

Makes 20 brownies

FAVORITE RECIPE FROM **CALIFORNIA PRUNE BOARD**

Caramel-Layered Brownies

4 squares BAKER'S®
   Unsweetened
   Chocolate
¾ cup (1½ sticks)
   margarine or butter
2 cups sugar
3 eggs
1 teaspoon vanilla
1 cup flour
1 cup BAKER'S®
   Semi-Sweet Real
   Chocolate Chips
1½ cups chopped nuts
1 package (14 ounces)
   caramels
⅓ cup evaporated milk

HEAT oven to 350°F.

MICROWAVE chocolate and margarine in large microwavable bowl on HIGH 2 minutes or until margarine is melted. **Stir until chocolate is completely melted.**

STIR sugar into melted chocolate mixture. Mix in eggs and vanilla until well blended. Stir in flour. Remove 1 cup of batter; set aside. Spread remaining batter in greased 13×9-inch pan. Sprinkle with chips and 1 cup nuts.

MICROWAVE caramels and milk in same bowl on HIGH 4 minutes, stirring after 2 minutes. Stir until caramels are completely melted and smooth. Spoon over chips and nuts, spreading to edges of pan. Gently spread reserved batter over caramel mixture. Sprinkle with remaining ½ cup nuts.

BAKE 40 minutes or until toothpick inserted into center comes out with fudgy crumbs. **Do not overbake.** Cool in pan. Cut into squares.

Makes 24 fudgy brownies

Prep Time: 20 minutes
Bake Time: 40 minutes

Double-Decker Confetti Brownies

¾ cup (1½ sticks) butter
   or margarine, softened
1 cup granulated sugar
1 cup firmly packed light
   brown sugar
3 large eggs
1 teaspoon vanilla extract
2½ cups all-purpose flour,
   divided
2½ teaspoons baking
   powder
½ teaspoon salt
⅓ cup unsweetened cocoa
   powder
1 tablespoon butter or
   margarine, melted
1 cup "M&M's"® Semi-
   Sweet Chocolate Mini
   Baking Bits, divided

Preheat oven to 350°F. Lightly grease 13×9×2-inch baking pan; set aside. In large bowl cream butter and sugars until light and fluffy; beat in eggs and vanilla. In medium bowl combine *2¼ cups flour,* baking powder and salt; blend into creamed mixture. Divide batter in half. Blend together cocoa powder and melted butter; stir into half of dough. Spread cocoa dough evenly into prepared baking pan. Stir remaining *¼ cup flour* and

½ *cup "M&M's"® Semi-Sweet Chocolate Mini Baking Bits* into remaining dough; spread evenly over cocoa dough in pan. Sprinkle with remaining ½ *cup "M&M's"® Semi-Sweet Chocolate Mini Baking Bits.* Bake 25 to 30 minutes or until edges start to pull away from sides of pan. Cool completely. Cut into bars. Store in tightly covered container.

Makes 24 brownies

Peanut Butter Chips and Jelly Bars

1½ cups all-purpose flour
½ cup sugar
¾ teaspoon baking powder
½ cup (1 stick) cold butter
   or margarine
1 egg, beaten
¾ cup grape jelly
1⅔ cups (10-ounce
   package) REESE'S®
   Peanut Butter Chips,
   divided

Heat oven to 375°F. Grease 9-inch square baking pan. Stir together flour, sugar and baking powder. With pastry blender, cut in butter until mixture resembles coarse crumbs. Add egg; blend well. Reserve half of mixture; press remaining mixture onto bottom of prepared pan. Spread jelly over crust. Sprinkle 1 cup peanut butter chips over jelly. Stir together reserved crumb mixture with remaining ⅔ cup chips; sprinkle over top. Bake 25 to 30 minutes or until lightly browned. Cool completely in pan on wire rack. Cut into bars.

Makes about 16 bars

Marvelous Cookie Bars

½ cup (1 stick) butter or margarine, softened
1 cup firmly packed light brown sugar
2 large eggs
1⅓ cups all-purpose flour
1 cup uncooked quick-cooking or old-fashioned oats
⅓ cup unsweetened cocoa powder
1 teaspoon baking powder
½ teaspoon salt
¼ teaspoon baking soda
½ cup chopped walnuts, divided
1 cup "M&M's"® Semi-Sweet Chocolate Mini Baking Bits, divided
½ cup cherry preserves
¼ cup shredded coconut

Preheat oven to 350°F. Lightly grease 9×9×2-inch baking pan; set aside. In large bowl cream butter and sugar until light and fluffy; beat in eggs. In medium bowl combine flour, oats, cocoa powder, baking powder, salt and baking soda; blend into creamed mixture. Stir in ¼ cup nuts and ¾ cup "M&M's"® Semi-Sweet Chocolate Mini Baking Bits. Reserve 1 cup dough; spread remaining dough into prepared pan. Combine preserves, coconut and remaining ¼ cup nuts; spread evenly over dough to within ½ inch of edge. Drop reserved dough by rounded teaspoonfuls over preserves mixture; sprinkle with remaining ¼ cup "M&M's"® Semi-Sweet Chocolate Mini Baking Bits.

Bake 25 to 30 minutes or until slightly firm near edges. Cool completely. Cut into bars. Store in tightly covered container.

Makes 16 bars

Lemon Crème Bars

CRUST
2 cups sifted all-purpose flour
¾ cup sifted confectioners' sugar
1 teaspoon grated lemon rind
½ cup unsalted butter, at room temperature
2 tablespoons cold water

LEMON FILLING
½ cup egg substitute *or* 2 large eggs
1¾ cups granulated sugar
¾ cup (3 ounces) shredded ALPINE LACE® Reduced Sodium Muenster Cheese
1½ cups sifted all-purpose flour
1 tablespoon baking powder
⅔ cup fresh lemon juice
1 teaspoon grated lemon rind
¼ cup slivered almonds (optional)
3 tablespoons sifted confectioners' sugar
Additional grated lemon rind (optional)

1. To make the Crust: Preheat the oven to 350°F and butter a 13×9×2-inch baking pan. In a medium-size bowl, mix the flour, confectioners' sugar and lemon rind, then work in the butter with your fingers until coarse crumbs form. Add the water and continue mixing until a dough forms. Press evenly onto the bottom of the baking pan and bake for 10 minutes.

2. While the crust is baking, make the Lemon Filling: In a medium-size bowl, whisk the egg substitute (or the whole eggs) until light yellow. Whisk in the granulated sugar, cheese, flour, baking powder, lemon juice and lemon rind until well blended. Pour the egg mixture over the hot crust and sprinkle with the almonds, if you wish. Return to the oven and bake 25 minutes longer or until the filling is set.

3. Cool the cookies in the pan on a wire rack for 10 minutes, then cut into 36 (2×1½-inch) bars. Cool on wire racks. Dust with the confectioners' sugar. Garnish with additional lemon rind, if you wish. Refrigerate in an airtight container.

Makes 3 dozen bars

Rainbow Blondies

1 cup (2 sticks) butter or margarine, softened
1 ½ cups firmly packed light brown sugar
1 large egg
1 teaspoon vanilla extract
2 cups all-purpose flour
½ teaspoon baking soda
1¾ cups "M&M's"® Semi-Sweet or Milk Chocolate Mini Baking Bits
1 cup chopped walnuts or pecans

Preheat oven to 350°F. Lightly grease 13×9×2-inch baking pan; set aside. In large bowl cream butter and sugar until light and fluffy; beat in egg and vanilla. In medium bowl combine flour and baking soda; add to creamed mixture just until combined. *Dough will be stiff.* Stir in "M&M's"® Chocolate Mini Baking Bits and nuts. Spread dough into prepared baking pan. Bake 30 to 35 minutes or until toothpick inserted in center comes out with moist crumbs. *Do not overbake.* Cool completely. Cut into bars. Store in tightly covered container.

Makes 24 bars

Peanut Butter Crispy Treats

4 cups toasted rice cereal
1¾ cups "M&M's"® Milk Chocolate Mini Baking Bits
4 cups mini marshmallows
½ cup creamy peanut butter
¼ cup butter or margarine
⅛ teaspoon salt

Combine cereal and "M&M's"® Milk Chocolate Mini Baking Bits in lightly greased baking pan; set aside. Melt marshmallows, peanut butter, butter and salt in heavy saucepan over low heat, stirring occasionally until mixture is smooth. Pour melted mixture over cereal mixture, tossing lightly until thoroughly coated. Gently shape into 1½-inch balls with buttered fingers. Place on waxed paper; cool at room temperature until set. Store in tightly covered container.

Makes about 3 dozen

Variation: *After cereal mixture is thoroughly coated, press lightly into greased 13×9×2-inch pan. Cool completely; cut into bars. Makes 24 bars.*

Lemon Crème Bars (page 486)

Spiced Chocolate Pecan Squares

COOKIE BASE
- 1 cup all-purpose flour
- ½ cup packed light brown sugar
- ½ teaspoon baking soda
- ¼ cup (½ stick) butter or margarine, softened

TOPPING
- 1 package (8 ounces) semisweet chocolate baking squares
- 2 large eggs
- ¼ cup packed light brown sugar
- ¼ cup light corn syrup
- 2 tablespoons FRENCH'S® Worcestershire Sauce
- 1 tablespoon vanilla extract
- 1½ cups chopped pecans or walnuts, divided

Preheat oven to 375°F. To prepare cookie base, place flour, ½ cup sugar and baking soda in food processor or bowl of electric mixer. Process or mix 10 seconds. Add butter. Process or beat 30 seconds or until mixture resembles fine crumbs. Press evenly into bottom of greased 9-inch baking pan. Bake 15 minutes.

Meanwhile, to prepare topping, place chocolate in microwave-safe bowl. Microwave, uncovered, at HIGH 2 minutes or until chocolate is melted, stirring until chocolate is smooth; set aside.

Place eggs, ¼ cup sugar, corn syrup, Worcestershire and vanilla in food processor or bowl of electric mixer. Process or beat until well blended. Add melted chocolate. Process or beat until smooth. Stir in *1 cup nuts.* Pour chocolate mixture over cookie base. Sprinkle with remaining *½ cup nuts.* Bake 40 minutes or until toothpick inserted into center comes out with slightly fudgy crumbs. (Cookie will be slightly puffed along edges.) Cool completely on wire rack. To serve, cut into squares. *Makes 16 servings*

Prep Time: 20 minutes
Cook Time: 55 minutes

Pumpkin Jingle Bars

- ¾ cup MIRACLE WHIP® Salad Dressing
- 1 two-layer spice cake mix
- 1 (16-ounce) can pumpkin
- 3 eggs
  Sifted confectioners' sugar
  Vanilla frosting
  Red and green gum drops, sliced

Mix first 4 ingredients in large bowl at medium speed of electric mixer until well blended. Pour into greased 15½×10½×1-inch jelly-roll pan. Bake at 350°F, 18 to 20 minutes or until edges pull away from sides of pan. Cool. Sprinkle with sugar. Cut into bars. Decorate with frosting and gum drops.
Makes about 3 dozen bars

Prep Time: 5 minutes
Cook Time: 20 minutes

Pear Mince Oatmeal Bars

- ¾ cup butter or margarine, softened
- ¾ cup packed brown sugar
- 1½ cups all-purpose flour
- 1¼ cups uncooked quick-cooking oats
- ½ cup chopped walnuts
- ½ teaspoon salt
- ½ teaspoon baking soda
- 2 USA Anjou pears, cored and chopped
- 1 cup prepared mincemeat
- 1 teaspoon lemon juice
- ½ teaspoon grated lemon peel

Preheat oven to 375°F. Cream butter and sugar. Stir in flour, oats, nuts, salt and baking soda until crumbly. Press ⅔ of flour mixture into ungreased 13×9-inch baking pan.

Combine pears, mincemeat, lemon juice and peel; spread over crumb crust. Top with remaining crumb mixture; pat lightly. Bake 25 to 30 minutes or until crust is golden. Cut into bars.

Makes 30 to 35 bars

*FAVORITE RECIPE FROM **OREGON WASHINGTON CALIFORNIA PEAR BUREAU***

Spiced Chocolate Pecan Squares

Colorful Caramel Bites

1 cup plus 6 tablespoons all-purpose flour, divided

1 cup uncooked quick-cooking or old-fashioned oats

¾ cup firmly packed light brown sugar

½ teaspoon baking soda

¼ teaspoon salt

¾ cup (1½ sticks) butter or margarine, melted

1¾ cups "M&M's"® Semi-Sweet Chocolate Mini Baking Bits, divided

1½ cups chopped pecans, divided

1 jar (12 ounces) caramel ice cream topping

Preheat oven to 350°F. Combine *1 cup flour,* oats, sugar, baking soda and salt; blend in melted butter to form crumbly mixture. Press half the crumb mixture onto bottom of 9×9×2-inch baking pan; bake 10 minutes. Sprinkle with *1 cup "M&M's"® Semi-Sweet Chocolate Mini Baking Bits* and *1 cup nuts.* Blend remaining *6 tablespoons flour* with caramel topping; pour over top. Combine remaining crumb mixture, remaining *¾ cup "M&M's"® Semi-Sweet Chocolate Mini Baking Bits* and remaining *½ cup nuts;* sprinkle over caramel layer. Bake 20 to 25 minutes or until golden brown. Cool completely. Cut into squares.

Makes 36 bars

Chocolate Oat Shortbread

1 cup (2 sticks) butter, softened

1 cup powdered sugar

2 teaspoons vanilla extract

1½ cups all-purpose flour

1 cup uncooked quick-cooking or old-fashioned oats

¼ cup unsweetened cocoa powder

1 teaspoon ground cinnamon

1¾ cups "M&M's"® Chocolate Mini Baking Bits, divided

Preheat oven to 325°F. Lightly grease 13×9×2-inch pan. Cream butter and sugar until light and fluffy; add vanilla. Combine flour, oats, cocoa powder and cinnamon; blend into creamed mixture. Stir in *1 cup "M&M's"® Chocolate Mini Baking Bits;* press dough into prepared pan. Sprinkle remaining *¾ cup "M&M's"® Chocolate Mini Baking Bits* over dough; press in lightly. Bake 20 to 25 minutes or until set. Cool completely; cut into triangles. *Makes 36 to 48 bars*

Rich Cocoa Fudge

3 cups sugar

⅔ cup HERSHEY'®S Cocoa or HERSHEY'®S European Style Cocoa

⅛ teaspoon salt

1½ cups milk

¼ cup (½ stick) butter or margarine

1 teaspoon vanilla extract

Line 8- or 9-inch square pan with foil, extending foil over edges of pan. Butter foil. In heavy 4-quart saucepan, stir together sugar, cocoa and salt; stir in milk. Cook over medium heat, stirring constantly, until mixture comes to a full rolling boil. Boil, without stirring, until mixture reaches 234°F on candy thermometer or until small amount of mixture dropped into very cold water forms a soft ball that flattens when removed from water. (Bulb of thermometer should not rest on bottom of saucepan.) Remove from heat. Add butter and vanilla. (Do not stir.) Cool at room temperature to 110°F (lukewarm). Beat with wooden spoon until fudge thickens and just begins to lose some of its gloss. Quickly spread into prepared pan; cool completely. Use foil to lift fudge out of pan; peel off foil. Cut into squares. Store in tightly covered container at room temperature.

Makes about 3 dozen pieces

Note: *For best results, do not double this recipe.*

NUTTY RICH COCOA FUDGE: Beat cooked fudge as directed. Immediately stir in 1 cup chopped almonds, pecans or walnuts; quickly spread into prepared pan.

Top to bottom: Colorful Caramel Bites and Chocolate Oat Shortbread

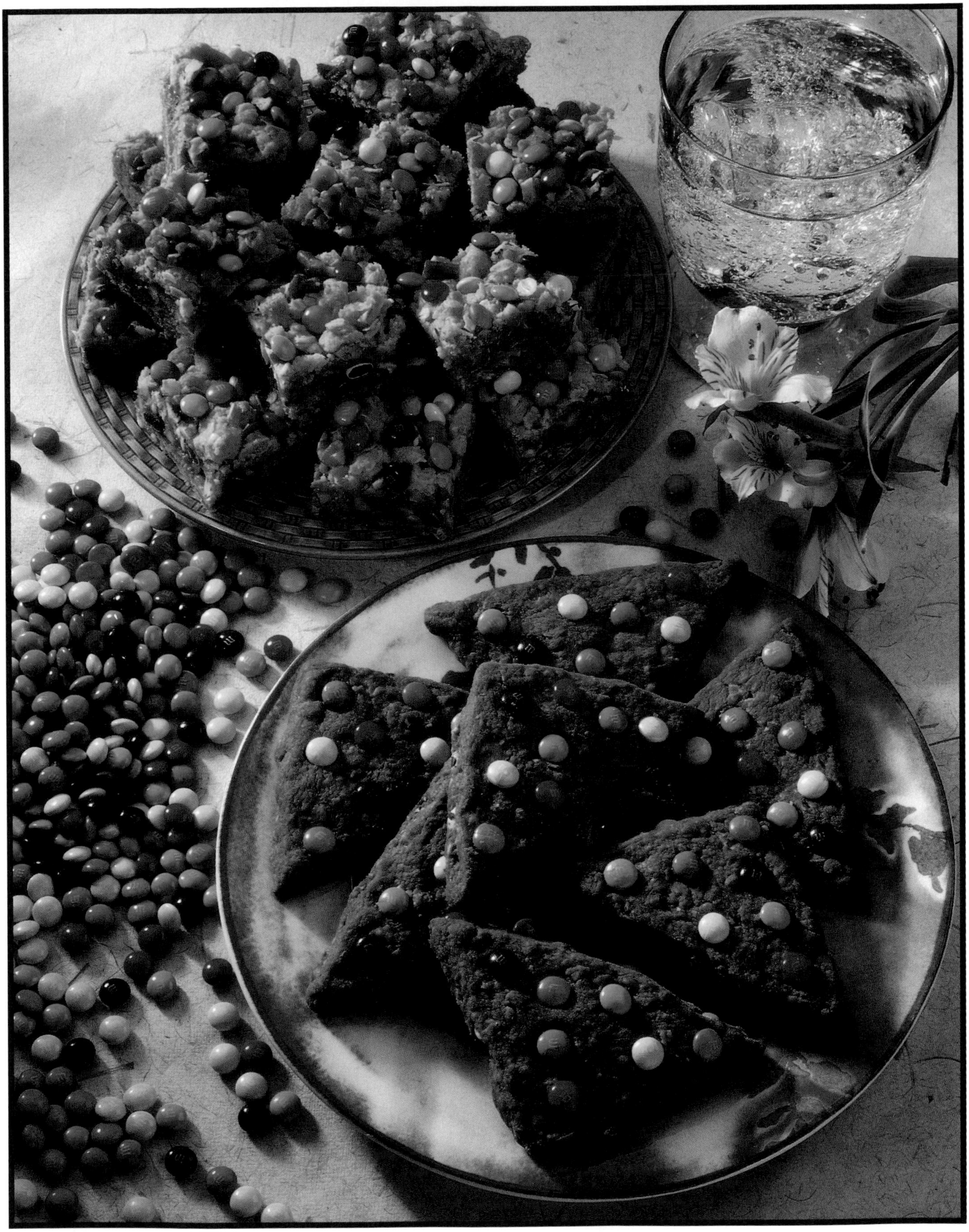

Fast 'n' Fabulous Dark Chocolate Fudge

- ½ cup KARO® Light or Dark Corn Syrup
- ⅓ cup evaporated milk
- 3 cups (18 ounces) semisweet chocolate chips
- ¾ cup confectioners sugar, sifted
- 2 teaspoons vanilla
- 1 cup coarsely chopped nuts (optional)

Microwave Directions:

1. Line 8-inch square baking pan with plastic wrap.

2. In 3-quart microwavable bowl, combine corn syrup and evaporated milk; stir until well blended. Microwave at HIGH 3 minutes. Stir in chocolate chips until melted.

3. Stir in confectioners sugar, vanilla and nuts. With wooden spoon, beat until thick and glossy.

4. Spread in prepared pan. Refrigerate 2 hours or until firm. *Makes 25 squares*

Prep Time: 10 minutes plus chilling

MARVELOUS MARBLE FUDGE: Omit nuts. Prepare as directed in steps 1 through 3; spread in prepared pan. Drop ⅓ cup SKIPPY® Creamy Peanut Butter over fudge in small dollops. Swirl fudge to marbleize. Continue as directed.

DOUBLE PEANUT BUTTER CHOCOLATE FUDGE: Prepare as directed in steps 1 and 2. In step 3, stir in ⅓ cup SKIPPY® SUPER CHUNK® Peanut Butter. Spread in prepared pan. Drop additional ⅓ cup peanut butter over fudge in small dollops. With small spatula, swirl fudge to marbleize. Continue as directed.

Chocolate-Coated Almond Brittle

- 1¾ cups sugar
- ⅓ cup KARO® Light Corn Syrup
- ¼ cup water
- 1 cup (2 sticks) MAZOLA® Margarine or butter
- 1½ cups finely chopped, toasted blanched almonds
- Chocolate Glaze (recipe follows)
- 3 cups coarsely chopped, toasted blanched almonds, divided

1. In heavy 2-quart saucepan, combine sugar, corn syrup and water. Stirring constantly, bring to a boil over medium heat. Cover; cook 1 minute. Remove cover. Add margarine. Stirring constantly, cook until temperature on candy thermometer reaches 290°F or small amount of mixture dropped into very cold water separates into threads that are hard but not brittle. Remove from heat.

2. Quickly stir in 1½ cups finely chopped almonds just until blended. Immediately pour into ungreased 15½×10½×1-inch baking pan, spreading quickly. Cool a few minutes until film forms on top.

3. Using wide metal spatula, mark surface into 1½-inch squares, beginning from outside, working toward center. Without breaking through film surface, press along marked lines. When spatula can be pressed to bottom of pan in all lines, candy is shaped. Cool.

4. Remove from pan and break into squares. Dip each square into Chocolate Glaze; coat with remaining chopped almonds. Place on waxed paper-lined tray. Refrigerate 20 to 25 minutes or until chocolate sets. Store in single layer in tightly covered container.
Makes about 2 pounds

CHOCOLATE GLAZE: In 1-quart saucepan combine 3 squares (1 ounce each) semisweet chocolate, 3 squares (1 ounce each) unsweetened chocolate, ⅓ cup MAZOLA® Margarine or butter and 1½ tablespoons KARO® Light or Dark Corn Syrup. Stir over very low heat just until smooth. Remove from heat; beat with wooden spoon until cool but still pourable.
Makes about 1 cup

Prep Time: 60 minutes plus cooling

Classic Peanut Brittle

MAZOLA NO STICK®
Corn Oil Cooking
Spray
1 cup KARO® Light or
Dark Corn Syrup
1 cup sugar
¼ cup water
2 tablespoons MAZOLA®
Margarine or butter
1½ cups peanuts
1 teaspoon baking soda

1. Spray large cookie sheet and metal spatula with cooking spray; set aside.

2. In heavy 3-quart saucepan, combine corn syrup, sugar, water and margarine. Stirring constantly, cook over medium heat until sugar dissolves and mixture comes to a boil.

3. Without stirring, cook until temperature reaches 280°F on candy thermometer or small amount of mixture dropped into very cold water separates into threads that are hard but not brittle.

4. Gradually stir in peanuts. Stirring frequently, continue cooking until temperature reaches 300°F or small amount of mixture dropped into very cold water separates into threads that are hard and brittle. Remove from heat; stir in baking soda.

5. Immediately pour mixture onto cookie sheet. With metal spatula, spread mixture evenly to edges. Cool. Break into pieces.

Makes about 1½ pounds

Almond Butter Crunch

1 cup BLUE DIAMOND®
Blanched Slivered
Almonds
½ cup butter
½ cup sugar
1 tablespoon light corn
syrup

Line bottom and sides of 8- or 9-inch cake pan with aluminum foil (*not* plastic wrap or wax paper). Butter foil heavily; set aside. Combine almonds, butter, sugar and corn syrup in 10-inch skillet. Bring to a boil over medium heat, stirring constantly. Boil, stirring constantly, until mixture turns golden brown, about 5 to 6 minutes. Working quickly, spread candy in prepared pan. Cool about 15 minutes or until firm. Remove candy from pan by lifting edges of foil. Peel off foil. Cool thoroughly. Break into pieces.

Makes about ¾ pound

Fast 'n' Fabulous Dark Chocolate Fudge (page 492)

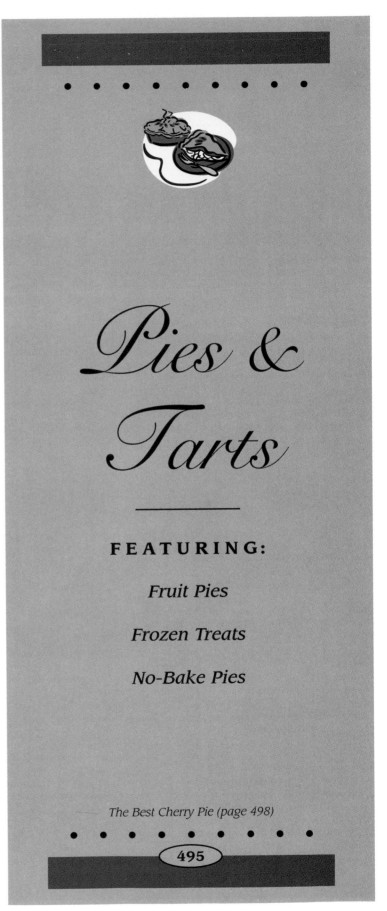

Pies & Tarts

FEATURING:

Fruit Pies

Frozen Treats

No-Bake Pies

The Best Cherry Pie (page 498)

495

Nectarine Pecan Tart

PECAN CRUST
1 cup wafer crumbs
½ cup pecan pieces
2 tablespoons sugar
3 tablespoons unsalted butter, melted

CREAM CHEESE FILLING
1 package (8 ounces) plus 1 package (3 ounces) cream cheese, softened
3 tablespoons sugar
2 tablespoons orange juice
½ teaspoon vanilla

FRUIT TOPPING
2 ripe nectarines
4 tablespoons apricot jelly

1. For crust, preheat oven to 350°F. Process wafer crumbs, pecans and 2 tablespoons sugar in food processor until coarse crumbs form. Transfer to small bowl; stir in butter. Pat evenly on bottom and 1 inch up side of 8-inch springform pan.

2. Bake 15 minutes or until lightly browned. Cool completely on wire rack.

3. For filling, beat cream cheese, 3 tablespoons sugar, juice and vanilla in medium bowl with electric mixer at low speed until blended. Increase speed to high; beat 2 minutes or until fluffy. Pour into crust, spreading evenly to side. Cover; refrigerate 3 hours or until set.

4. For topping, halve and slice nectarines. Arrange over cream cheese mixture.

5. Remove side of springform pan from tart; place on serving platter. Melt jelly in small saucepan, whisking constantly, over low heat. Cool 1 minute. Drizzle jelly over nectarines. Refrigerate, uncovered, 20 minutes or until set.

Makes 6 servings

Note: *For best results, serve tart same day as assembled.*

Rice Pudding Pear Tart

½ (15-ounce) package refrigerated pie crust
2 cups dry red wine
1 teaspoon ground cinnamon
2 large pears, peeled, cut into halves and cored
2 cups cooked rice
2 cups half-and-half
½ cup plus 1 tablespoon sugar, divided
2 tablespoons butter or margarine
¼ teaspoon salt
2 eggs, beaten
1 teaspoon vanilla extract

Preheat oven to 450°F. Prepare pie crust according to package directions. Place in 10-inch tart pan. Bake 8 to 10 minutes or until lightly browned; set aside. *Reduce oven temperature to 350°F.*

Place wine and cinnamon in 10-inch skillet; bring to a boil. Add pears; reduce heat, cover and poach 10 minutes. Carefully turn pears in liquid; poach 5 to 10 minutes or until tender. Remove from wine; set aside.

Combine rice, half-and-half, ½ cup sugar, butter and salt in 3-quart saucepan. Cook over medium heat 12 to 15 minutes or until slightly thickened. Gradually stir ¼ of hot rice pudding mixture into eggs; return mixture to saucepan, stirring constantly. Continue to cook 1 to 2 minutes. Stir in vanilla. Pour rice pudding mixture into prepared crust. Place pears, cut sides down, on cutting surface. Cut thin lengthwise slices into each pear one third of the way down from stem end. Fan pears over pudding mixture.

Bake 30 minutes or until pudding is set. Remove from oven; sprinkle with remaining 1 tablespoon sugar. Place tart in oven about 4 to 5 inches from heat; broil 1 to 2 minutes or until top is browned. Cool before serving. Garnish as desired. Tart can be made ahead, if desired.

Makes 1 (10-inch) tart

FAVORITE RECIPE FROM **USA RICE FEDERATION**

Nectarine Pecan Tart

The Best Cherry Pie

Reduced-Fat Pie Pastry (recipe follows)
2 bags (12 ounces each) frozen no-sugar-added cherries, thawed and well drained
¾ cup plus 2 teaspoons sugar, divided
1 tablespoon plus 1½ teaspoons cornstarch
1 tablespoon plus 1½ teaspoons quick-cooking tapioca
1 teaspoon skim milk

1. Preheat oven to 425°F.

2. Roll ⅔ of pie pastry on lightly floured surface into 9½-inch circle. Gently press pastry into 8-inch pie pan.

3. Combine cherries, ¾ cup sugar, cornstarch and tapioca in large bowl. Spoon cherry mixture into pastry. Roll remaining pastry into circle large enough to fit top of pie; trim off any excess pastry. Cover pie with crust. Press edges of top and bottom crust together; trim and flute. Cut steam vents in top of pie; brush with milk and sprinkle with remaining 2 teaspoons sugar.

4. Bake 10 minutes. *Reduce heat to 375°F;* bake 45 to 50 minutes or until pie is bubbly and crust is golden. (Cover edge of crust with aluminum foil, if necessary, to prevent burning.) Cool on wire rack; serve warm.

Makes 8 servings

REDUCED-FAT PIE PASTRY
2 cups all-purpose flour
2 tablespoons sugar
½ teaspoon baking powder
¼ teaspoon salt
7 tablespoons cold shortening
6 to 8 tablespoons ice water, divided

1. Combine flour, sugar, baking powder and salt in medium bowl. Cut in shortening with pastry blender or 2 knives until mixture resembles coarse crumbs. Mix in water, 1 tablespoon at a time, until stiff dough is formed.

2. Cover dough with plastic wrap; refrigerate 30 minutes.

Makes 1 (8-inch) double crust

Pumpkin Pecan Pie

3 eggs, divided
1 cup solid pack pumpkin
1 cup sugar, divided
½ teaspoon ground cinnamon
¼ teaspoon ground ginger
⅛ teaspoon ground cloves
Easy-As-Pie Crust (page 499) *or* 1 (9-inch) frozen deep-dish pie crust*
⅔ cup KARO® Light or Dark Corn Syrup
2 tablespoons MAZOLA® Margarine or butter, melted
1 teaspoon vanilla
1 cup coarsely chopped pecans or walnuts

*Do not thaw frozen pie crust. Preheat oven and cookie sheet. Pour filling into crust. Bake on cookie sheet.

1. Preheat oven to 350°F.

2. In small bowl, combine 1 egg, pumpkin, ⅓ cup sugar, cinnamon, ginger and cloves. Spread evenly in bottom of pie crust.

3. In medium bowl, beat remaining 2 eggs slightly. Stir in corn syrup, remaining ⅔ cup sugar, margarine and vanilla until blended. Stir in pecans; carefully spoon over pumpkin mixture.

4. Bake 50 to 60 minutes or until filling is set around edge. Cool completely on wire rack.

Makes 8 servings

Prep Time: 15 minutes
Bake Time: 50 minutes, plus cooling

Classic Pecan Pie

3 eggs
1 cup sugar
1 cup KARO® Light or Dark Corn Syrup
2 tablespoons MAZOLA® Margarine or butter, melted
1 teaspoon vanilla
1½ cups pecans
Easy-As-Pie Crust (page 499) *or* 1 (9-inch) frozen deep-dish pie crust*

*To use prepared frozen pie crust: Do not thaw. Preheat oven and cookie sheet. Pour filling into frozen crust. Bake on cookie sheet. (Insulated cookie sheet not recommended.)

1. Preheat oven to 350°F.

2. In medium bowl with fork, beat eggs slightly. Add sugar, corn syrup, margarine and vanilla; stir until well blended. Stir in pecans. Pour into pie crust.

3. Bake 50 to 55 minutes or until knife inserted halfway between center and edge comes out clean. Cool on wire rack.   *Makes 8 servings*

ALMOND AMARETTO PIE: Substitute 1 cup sliced almonds for pecans. Add 2 tablespoons almond-flavored liqueur and ½ teaspoon almond extract to filling.

BUTTERSCOTCH PECAN PIE: Omit margarine; add ¼ cup heavy or whipping cream to filling.

CHOCOLATE CHIP WALNUT PIE: Substitute 1 cup walnuts, coarsely chopped, for pecans. Sprinkle ½ cup semisweet chocolate chips over bottom of pie crust. Carefully pour filling into pie crust.

CHOCOLATE COCONUT PECAN PIE: Reduce pecans to ½ cup; coarsely chop. Add ⅔ cup flaked coconut and ⅓ cup semisweet chocolate chips to filling.

CRANBERRY PECAN PIE: Reduce sugar to ⅔ cup; use 1 cup pecans, coarsely chopped. Add 1 cup coarsely chopped cranberries and 1 tablespoon grated orange peel with pecans.

KENTUCKY BOURBON PECAN PIE: Add 2 tablespoons bourbon to filling.

Easy-As-Pie Crust

1 ¼ cups unsifted flour
⅛ teaspoon salt
½ cup MAZOLA® Margarine
2 to 3 tablespoons cold water

1. In medium bowl, combine flour and salt. With pastry blender or 2 knives, cut in margarine until mixture resembles fine crumbs.

2. Sprinkle water over mixture while tossing to blend well. Press dough firmly into ball.

3. On lightly floured surface, roll into 12-inch circle. Fit loosely into 9-inch pie plate. Trim and flute edge. Fill and bake according to recipe.
          Makes 1 (9-inch) crust

Baked Pie Shell: *Preheat oven to 450°F. Pierce pie crust thoroughly with fork. Bake 12 to 15 minutes or until light golden brown.*

Pumpkin Pecan Pie (page 498)

Pineapple Fruit Tart

¼ **cup ground almonds (about 2 tablespoons whole almonds)**
¼ **cup butter or margarine, softened**
¼ **cup sugar**
2 **tablespoons milk**
½ **teaspoon almond extract**
¾ **cup all-purpose flour**
2 **packages (3 ounces each) cream cheese, softened**
2 **tablespoons sour cream**
¼ **cup apricot preserves, divided**
1 **teaspoon vanilla extract**
1 **can (15¼ ounces) DEL MONTE® Pineapple Spears In Its Own Juice, drained**
2 **kiwifruits, peeled, sliced and halved**
1 **cup sliced strawberries**

1. Combine almonds, butter, sugar, milk and almond extract; mix well. Blend in flour. Chill dough 1 hour.

2. Press dough evenly onto bottom and up side of tart pan with removable bottom.

3. Bake at 350°F 15 to 18 minutes or until golden brown. Cool.

4. Combine cream cheese, sour cream, 1 tablespoon apricot preserves and vanilla. Spread onto crust. Arrange pineapple, kiwi and strawberries over cream cheese mixture.

5. Heat remaining 3 tablespoons apricot preserves in small saucepan over low heat. Spoon over fruit. *Makes 8 servings*

Cherry-Cheese Tart Jubilee

1 **container (15 ounces) Wisconsin Ricotta cheese**
⅓ **cup sour cream**
⅓ **cup sugar**
3 **tablespoons almond-flavored liqueur**
2 **tablespoons all-purpose flour**
1 **teaspoon grated orange peel**
¼ **teaspoon salt**
2 **eggs, separated**
1 **prebaked and cooled 9½-inch Tart Shell (recipe follows)**
3 **cups Northwest frozen pitted dark sweet cherries, partially thawed**
2 **tablespoons red currant jelly, melted**
2 **to 3 tablespoons toasted sliced almonds**

Preheat oven to 350°F.

Press cheese through sieve into large bowl. Mix in sour cream, sugar, liqueur, flour, orange peel and salt. Beat in egg yolks. In another bowl, beat egg whites to form soft peaks; fold into cheese mixture. Pour into prepared Tart Shell. Bake 50 to 60 minutes or until lightly browned, puffy and set. Cool on rack.

Just before serving, arrange partially thawed cherries on tart. Brush cherries with jelly. Garnish with almonds. Serve immediately.

Makes 8 servings

TART SHELL: Preheat oven to 425°F. In large bowl, mix 1 cup flour, 1 tablespoon sugar and ¼ teaspoon salt. Add 6 tablespoons cold butter, cut into chunks. Cut in with pastry blender until mixture resembles coarse meal. Beat 1 egg yolk with 2 tablespoons ice water. Add to flour mixture. Mix with fork and gather into ball. Roll out dough on lightly floured surface into 11-inch circle. Fit into 9½-inch tart pan with removable bottom. Fold pastry overhang back toward inside and press firmly against side of pan, allowing pastry to extend slightly above top. Refrigerate 10 minutes. Prick tart shell all over with fork; line with foil. Fill with pie weights, dried beans or rice. Bake 14 minutes. Remove foil and weights; bake 10 to 15 minutes or longer until lightly browned and cooked through. Cool on wire rack.

Makes 1 (9½-inch) tart shell

FAVORITE RECIPE FROM **WISCONSIN MILK MARKETING BOARD**

Pineapple Fruit Tart

Hazelnut Plum Tart

- **1 cup hazelnuts**
- **¼ cup firmly packed light brown sugar**
- **1 cup all-purpose flour**
- **⅓ cup FILIPPO BERIO® Olive Oil**
- **1 egg, separated**
- **Pinch salt**
- **3 tablespoons granulated sugar**
- **2 teaspoons cornstarch**
- **½ teaspoon grated lime peel**
- **Pinch ground nutmeg**
- **Pinch ground cloves**
- **1¼ pounds plums (about 5 large), cut into halves and pitted**
- **3 tablespoons currant jelly**
- **Sweetened whipped cream (optional)**

Preheat oven to 375°F. Grease 9-inch tart pan with removable bottom with olive oil.

Place hazelnuts in food processor; process until coarsely chopped. Remove ¼ cup for garnish; set aside. Add brown sugar; process until nuts are finely ground. Add flour, ⅓ cup olive oil, egg yolk and salt; process until combined. (Mixture will be crumbly.)

Spoon mixture into prepared pan. Press firmly in even layer onto bottom and up side. Brush inside of crust with egg white. Place in freezer 10 minutes.

In large bowl, combine granulated sugar, cornstarch, lime peel, nutmeg and cloves.

Cut each plum half into 4 wedges. Add to sugar mixture; toss until combined. Arrange plums in overlapping circles in crust; spoon any remaining sugar mixture over plums. Place tart on baking sheet.

Bake 45 to 50 minutes or until fruit is tender and juices are thickened. Cool 30 minutes on wire rack. Place currant jelly in small saucepan; heat over low heat, stirring frequently, until melted. Brush over plums; sprinkle with reserved hazelnuts. Serve tart warm or at room temperature with whipped cream, if desired.

Makes 6 servings

Cranberry Apple Nut Pie

- **Rich Pie Pastry (recipe follows)**
- **1 cup sugar**
- **3 tablespoons all-purpose flour**
- **¼ teaspoon salt**
- **4 cups sliced peeled tart apples (4 large apples)**
- **2 cups fresh cranberries**
- **½ cup golden raisins**
- **½ cup coarsely chopped pecans**
- **1 tablespoon grated lemon peel**
- **2 tablespoons butter or margarine**
- **1 egg, beaten**

Preheat oven to 425°F. Divide pie pastry in half. Roll one half on lightly floured surface to form 13-inch circle. Fit into 9-inch pie plate; trim edges. Reroll scraps and cut into

decorative shapes, such as holly leaves and berries, for garnish; set aside.

Combine sugar, flour and salt in large bowl. Stir in apples, cranberries, raisins, pecans and lemon peel; toss well. Spoon fruit mixture into unbaked pie crust. Dot with butter. Roll remaining half of pie pastry on lightly floured surface to form 11-inch circle. Place over filling. Trim and seal edges; flute. Cut 3 slits in center of top crust. Moisten pastry cutouts and decorate as desired. Lightly brush top crust with egg.

Bake 35 to 40 minutes or until apples are tender when pierced with a fork and pastry is golden brown. Cool in pan on wire rack. Serve warm or cool completely.

Makes 1 (9-inch) pie

RICH PIE PASTRY
- **2 cups all-purpose flour**
- **¼ teaspoon salt**
- **6 tablespoons butter**
- **6 tablespoons lard**
- **6 to 8 tablespoons cold water**

Combine flour and salt in medium bowl. Cut in butter and lard with pastry blender or 2 knives until mixture resembles coarse crumbs. Sprinkle water, 1 tablespoon at a time, over flour mixture, mixing until flour is moistened. Shape dough into ball. Roll, fill and bake as recipe directs.

Makes pastry for 1 (9-inch) double pie crust

Note: *For single crust, cut recipe in half.*

Orange Pumpkin Tart

1 ½ cups all-purpose flour
1 cup uncooked QUAKER® Oats (quick or old fashioned), divided
1 cup plus 2 tablespoons granulated sugar, divided
¾ cup (1 ½ sticks) margarine
2 tablespoons water
1 can (16 ounces) pumpkin (1 ¾ cups)
1 egg white
1 teaspoon pumpkin pie spice
½ cup powdered sugar
2 teaspoons orange juice
½ teaspoon grated orange peel

Preheat oven to 400°F. Combine flour, ¾ cup oats and ½ cup granulated sugar; cut in margarine until crumbly. Reserve ¾ cup oat mixture. Mix remaining oat mixture with water until dough is moistened. Divide into 2 parts; press each onto cookie sheet to form a 12×5-inch tart. Combine pumpkin, egg white, ½ cup granulated sugar and pumpkin pie spice. Spread over tarts. Top with combined remaining ¼ cup oats, remaining 2 tablespoons granulated sugar and reserved oat mixture. Bake 25 minutes or until golden. Cool. Drizzle with combined remaining ingredients. Refrigerate leftovers.

Makes 12 servings

Elegant and Easy Pear Tart

1 can (29 ounces) USA Bartlett pears, undrained
2 packages (3 ⅛ to 3 ½ ounces each) vanilla pudding mix
Milk
¼ cup almond-flavored liqueur*
1 (8-inch) pastry shell, baked and cooled
Apricot Glaze (recipe follows)

½ teaspoon almond extract can be substituted.

Drain pears; reserve 1 cup liquid. Prepare pudding according to package directions substituting reserved pear liquid for part of milk; stir in liqueur. Pour into pastry shell; chill until set. Slice pears and arrange over pudding. Brush with warm Apricot Glaze; refrigerate until cold. *Makes 1 (8-inch) tart*

APRICOT GLAZE: Heat ½ cup apricot or peach preserves and 1 tablespoon almond-flavored liqueur or pear liquid. Press through sieve; discard pulp.

Makes about ⅓ cup

*FAVORITE RECIPE FROM **PACIFIC COAST CANNED PEAR SERVICE***

Hazelnut Plum Tart (page 502)

Amaretto Coconut Cream Pie

¼ cup flaked coconut
1 container (8 ounces) thawed nondairy whipped topping, divided
1 container (8 ounces) coconut cream-flavored or vanilla-flavored yogurt
¼ cup amaretto liqueur
1 package (4-serving size) instant coconut pudding and pie filling mix
1 prepared (9-inch) graham cracker pie crust
Fresh strawberries and mint leaves (optional)

PREHEAT oven to 350°F. To toast coconut, place coconut on baking sheet. Bake 4 to 5 minutes or until golden brown, stirring frequently. Cool completely.

PLACE 2 cups whipped topping, yogurt and amaretto in large bowl. Add pudding mix. Beat with wire whisk or electric mixer on low speed 1 to 2 minutes or until thickened.

POUR pudding mixture into crust; spread remaining whipped topping over filling. Sprinkle with toasted coconut. Garnish with fresh strawberries and mint leaves, if desired. Refrigerate. *Makes 8 servings*

Chocolate Mudslide Frozen Pie

1 cup (6 ounces) NESTLÉ® TOLL HOUSE® Semi-Sweet Chocolate Morsels
1 teaspoon TASTER'S CHOICE® Original Freeze Dried Coffee
1 teaspoon hot water
¾ cup sour cream
½ cup granulated sugar
1 teaspoon vanilla extract
1 prepared (9-inch) chocolate crumb crust
1½ cups heavy whipping cream
1 cup powdered sugar
¼ cup NESTLÉ® TOLL HOUSE® Baking Cocoa
2 tablespoons NESTLÉ® TOLL HOUSE® Semi-Sweet Chocolate Mini Morsels

MELT 1 cup morsels in small heavy-duty saucepan over *lowest possible heat.* When morsels begin to melt, remove from heat; stir. Return to heat for a few seconds at a time, stirring until smooth. Remove from heat; cool 10 minutes.

COMBINE coffee and water in medium bowl. Add sour cream, granulated sugar and vanilla; stir until sugar is dissolved. Stir in melted chocolate until smooth. Spread into crust; chill.

BEAT cream, powdered sugar and cocoa in small bowl until stiff peaks form. Spread or pipe over chocolate layer. Sprinkle with mini morsels. Freeze at least 6 hours or until firm.
Makes 8 servings

Peanut Butter Cream Pie

¾ cup powdered sugar
⅓ cup creamy peanut butter
1 baked (9-inch) pie crust
1 cup milk
1 cup sour cream
1 package (4-serving size) instant French vanilla pudding and pie filling mix
5 peanut butter candy cups, divided
2 cups thawed nondairy whipped topping

COMBINE powdered sugar and peanut butter with fork in medium bowl until blended. Spread evenly in bottom of pie crust.

PLACE milk and sour cream in large bowl. Add pudding mix. Beat with wire whisk or electric mixer 1 to 2 minutes or until thickened.

POUR half of filling over peanut butter mixture. Coarsely chop 4 candy cups; sprinkle over filling. Top with remaining filling.

SPREAD whipped topping over filling. Cut remaining candy cup into 8 pieces; place on top of pie. Refrigerate.

Makes 8 servings

Amaretto Coconut Cream Pie

Fudgy Bittersweet Brownie Pie

12 squares (1 ounce each) bittersweet chocolate*
½ cup margarine or butter
2 eggs
½ cup sugar
1 cup all-purpose flour
½ teaspoon salt
1½ cups prepared hot fudge sauce, divided
1½ cups prepared caramel topping, divided
¾ cup chopped pecans, divided

*If unavailable, substitute 4 squares unsweetened chocolate plus 8 squares semisweet chocolate.

PREHEAT oven to 350°F. Grease 10-inch tart pan with removable bottom or 9-inch square baking pan; set aside.

MELT chocolate and margarine in small heavy saucepan over low heat, stirring constantly; set aside.

BEAT eggs in medium bowl with electric mixer at medium speed 30 seconds. Gradually beat in sugar; beat 1 minute. Beat in chocolate mixture, scraping down side of bowl once. Beat in flour and salt at low speed until just combined, scraping down side of bowl once. Spread mixture evenly in prepared pan.

BAKE 25 minutes or until center is just set. Cool pie completely in pan on wire rack. To serve, cut pie into 12 wedges, or 12 squares if using square pan.

PLACE fudge sauce in small microwavable bowl. Microwave at HIGH until hot, stirring once. Spoon 2 tablespoons each fudge sauce and caramel topping over each serving. Top each serving with chopped pecans. *Makes 12 servings*

Mud Pie

1¼ cups chocolate graham cracker crumbs
3 tablespoons sugar
¼ cup Prune Purée (page 434) or prepared prune butter
1 quart fat-free coffee ice cream or frozen yogurt
1 cup prepared fat-free fudge sauce
½ cup low-fat nondairy whipped topping

Preheat oven to 375°F. Coat 9-inch pie plate with vegetable cooking spray. In large bowl, mix crumbs and sugar. Cut in prune purée until mixture resembles coarse crumbs. Press onto bottom and side of prepared pie plate. Bake in center of oven 15 minutes. Cool completely. Soften ice cream slightly. Spoon evenly into pie shell. Freeze until firm. Cover ice cream with fudge sauce. Cut into wedges and serve immediately or cover and return to freezer up to 1 week before serving. Top each serving with 1 tablespoon whipped topping. *Makes 8 servings*

*Favorite recipe from **California Prune Board***

Raspberry Chocolate Mousse Pie

40 chocolate wafer cookies
½ cup butter, melted
7 tablespoons sugar
5 egg yolks
6 squares (1 ounce each) semisweet chocolate, melted, cooled slightly
3 tablespoons raspberry-flavored liqueur (optional)
3½ cups thawed nondairy whipped topping

PLACE cookies in food processor or blender; process with on/off pulses until finely crushed. Combine cookie crumbs and butter in medium bowl; mix well. Press onto bottom and 1 inch up side of 9-inch springform pan.

COMBINE ½ cup water and sugar in medium sucepan. Bring to a boil over medium-high heat. Boil 1 minute.

PLACE egg yolks in large bowl. Gradually whisk in hot sugar mixture. Return mixture to medium saucepan; whisk over low heat 1 to 2 minutes or until mixture is thick and creamy. Remove from heat; pour mixture back into large bowl.

WHISK in melted chocolate and liqueur, if desired. Beat mixture until cool. Fold in whipped topping. Pour mixture into prepared crust. Freeze until firm. Allow pie to stand at room temperature 20 minutes before serving. Remove side of pan. *Makes 16 servings*

Double Chocolate Mousse Pie

1 ¼ cups chocolate graham
    cracker crumbs
3 tablespoons sugar
¼ cup Prune Purée (page
    434) or prepared
    prune butter
3 cups nonfat milk
2 packages (3.4 ounces
    each) instant
    chocolate pudding mix
1 ½ cups low-fat nondairy
    whipped topping,
    divided
    Chocolate curls
    (optional)

Preheat oven to 375°F. Coat 9-inch pie plate with vegetable cooking spray. In large bowl, combine crumbs and sugar. Cut in prune purée with pastry blender until mixture resembles coarse crumbs. Press evenly onto bottom and side of prepared pie plate. Bake in center of oven 15 minutes. Cool completely on wire rack.

Meanwhile, in large bowl, combine milk and pudding mixes; whisk 2 minutes. Fold in 1 cup whipped topping. Spoon into prepared crust. Chill at least 2 hours. Pipe remaining whipped topping along edge. Garnish with chocolate curls, if desired. Cut into wedges.

Makes 8 servings

*FAVORITE RECIPE FROM **CALIFORNIA PRUNE BOARD***

Mocha Ice Cream Pie

2 cups coffee or vanilla
    ice cream, softened
1 prepared (9-inch)
    chocolate pie crust
1 jar (12 ounces) hot
    caramel ice cream
    topping, divided
2 cups chocolate ice
    cream, softened
2 cups thawed nondairy
    whipped topping
1 English toffee bar
    (1.4 ounces), chopped

SPREAD coffee ice cream in bottom of pie crust. Freeze 10 minutes or until semi-firm.

SPREAD half of caramel topping over coffee ice cream. Spread chocolate ice cream over caramel. Freeze 10 minutes or until semi-firm.

SPREAD remaining caramel topping over chocolate ice cream. Spoon whipped topping into pastry bag fitted with star decorating tip. Pipe rosettes on top of pie. Sprinkle toffee over topping.

FREEZE pie until firm, 6 hours or overnight. Allow pie to stand at room temperature 15 minutes before serving.

Makes 8 servings

Double Chocolate Mousse Pie

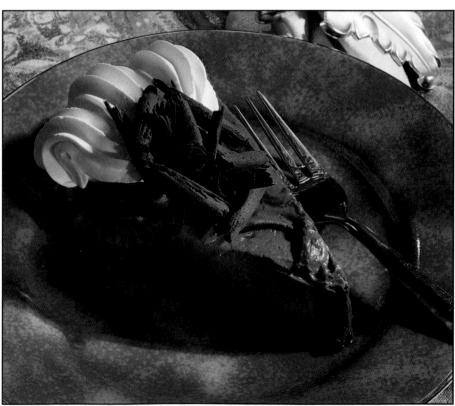

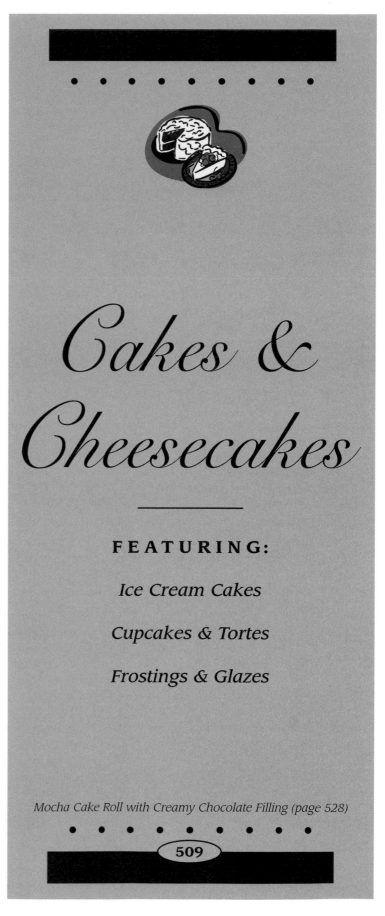

Cakes & Cheesecakes

FEATURING:

Ice Cream Cakes

Cupcakes & Tortes

Frostings & Glazes

Mocha Cake Roll with Creamy Chocolate Filling (page 528)

Chocolate-Raspberry Layer Cake

1 cup water
½ cup Prune Purée (page 434) or prepared prune butter
3 egg whites
1½ teaspoons vanilla
1 cup plus 2 tablespoons all-purpose flour
1 cup plus 2 tablespoons granulated sugar
¾ cup unsweetened cocoa powder
1½ teaspoons baking powder
¼ teaspoon baking soda
¼ teaspoon salt
⅔ cup no-sugar-added raspberry spread
¼ cup raspberry- or orange-flavored liqueur
1½ cups crushed fresh raspberries
Additional fresh raspberries for garnish
Powdered sugar
1½ cups low-fat nondairy whipped topping

Preheat oven to 350°F. Coat two 8-inch round layer cake pans with vegetable cooking spray. In mixer bowl, beat water, prune purée, egg whites and vanilla at medium speed until well blended. In medium bowl, combine flour, granulated sugar, cocoa, baking powder, baking soda and salt; mix into prune purée mixture until well blended. Spread batter equally in prepared pans. Bake in center of oven about 20 minutes or until toothpick inserted into centers comes out clean. Cool in pans 10 minutes; remove from pans to wire racks to cool completely. Refrigerate 1 hour.

Using serrated knife, carefully split each layer horizontally. Place one layer on cake plate. In small bowl, mix raspberry spread with liqueur; spread about ⅓ of mixture over cake layer. Spread with ½ cup crushed raspberries. Repeat layers two more times. Place remaining cake layer on top, cut side down, and press gently. Cover and refrigerate several hours or overnight. Garnish with whole raspberries and dust with powdered sugar. Cut into wedges. Dollop each wedge with 2 tablespoons whipped topping.

Makes 12 servings

FAVORITE RECIPE FROM CALIFORNIA PRUNE BOARD

Hershey's® Special Chocolate Cake

1¼ cups all-purpose flour
⅓ cup HERSHEY'S® Cocoa
1 teaspoon baking soda
6 tablespoons extra light corn oil spread
1 cup sugar
1 cup skim milk
1 tablespoon white vinegar
½ teaspoon vanilla extract
Special Cocoa Frosting or Almond Frosting (recipes follow)

Heat oven to 350°F. Spray two 8-inch round baking pans with vegetable cooking spray. In small bowl, stir together flour, cocoa and baking soda. In medium saucepan over low heat, melt corn oil spread; stir in sugar. Remove from heat. Add milk, vinegar and vanilla to mixture in saucepan; stir. Add flour mixture; stir with whisk until well blended. Pour batter into prepared pans.

Bake 20 minutes or until wooden pick inserted into centers comes out clean. Cool 10 minutes; remove from pans to wire racks. Cool completely. To assemble, place one cake layer on serving plate; spread half of frosting over top. Set second cake layer on top; spread remaining frosting over top. Refrigerate 2 to 3 hours or until chilled before serving. Garnish as desired. Cover; refrigerate leftover cake.

Makes 12 servings

SPECIAL COCOA FROSTING: In small bowl, stir together 1 envelope (1.3 ounces) dry whipped topping mix, ½ cup cold skim milk, 1 tablespoon HERSHEY'S® Cocoa and ½ teaspoon vanilla extract. Beat on high speed of electric mixer until soft peaks form.

ALMOND FROSTING: Omit ½ teaspoon vanilla extract. Add ¼ teaspoon almond extract.

Chocolate-Raspberry Layer Cake

Spicy Butterscotch Snack Cake

1 cup (2 sticks) butter or margarine, softened
1 cup granulated sugar
2 eggs
½ teaspoon vanilla extract
½ cup applesauce
2½ cups all-purpose flour
1½ to 2 teaspoons ground cinnamon
1 teaspoon baking soda
½ teaspoon salt
1⅔ cups (10-ounce package) HERSHEY'S Butterscotch Chips
1 cup chopped pecans (optional)
Powdered sugar or frozen non-dairy whipped topping, thawed (optional)

Heat oven to 350°F. Lightly grease 13×9-inch baking pan. In large bowl, beat butter and granulated sugar until light and fluffy. Add eggs and vanilla; beat well. Mix in applesauce. Stir together flour, cinnamon, baking soda and salt; gradually add to butter mixture, beating until well blended. Stir in butterscotch chips and pecans, if desired. Spread into prepared pan. Bake 35 minutes or until wooden pick inserted into center comes out clean. Cool completely in pan. Dust with powdered sugar or serve with whipped topping, if desired.

Makes 12 servings

Pecan Spice Cake

MAZOLA NO STICK® Corn Oil Cooking Spray
1 package (18¼ ounces) spice cake mix plus ingredients as label directs
½ cup finely chopped pecans
Coconut-Pecan Filling (recipe follows)
Luscious Chocolate Frosting (recipe follows)

1. Preheat oven to 350°F. Spray 2 (9-inch) round cake pans with cooking spray. Prepare cake mix as label directs; stir in pecans. Pour batter into pans.

2. Bake as directed. Cool on wire racks 10 minutes. Remove from pans; cool completely. When cool, split layers horizontally in half.

3. Place one cake layer on serving plate. Spread with one-third of Coconut-Pecan Filling. Top with second cake layer; spread with about ⅔ cup Luscious Chocolate Frosting. Top with third cake layer; spread with one-third of filling. Top with fourth cake layer. Frost side of cake with remaining frosting. Spread top of cake with remaining filling.

4. Refrigerate 2 hours or until set.

Makes 12 to 16 servings

Prep Time: 1 hour
Bake Time: 30 minutes, plus cooling

COCONUT-PECAN FILLING

¾ cup sugar
½ cup KARO® Light Corn Syrup
½ cup evaporated milk
½ cup (1 stick) MAZOLA® Margarine or butter
3 egg yolks, slightly beaten
1 teaspoon vanilla
1⅓ cups flaked coconut
1 cup finely chopped pecans

1. In medium saucepan combine sugar, corn syrup, evaporated milk, margarine, egg yolks and vanilla. Stirring frequently, cook over medium heat until thickened, 10 to 12 minutes. Remove from heat. Stir in coconut and pecans.

2. Cool until thick enough to spread, stirring occasionally.

Makes about 2¼ cups

Prep Time: 15 minutes, plus cooling

LUSCIOUS CHOCOLATE FROSTING

1 package (3 ounces) cream cheese
¼ cup KARO® Light Corn Syrup
2 tablespoons MAZOLA® Margarine or butter
2 cups confectioners' sugar
⅓ cup unsweetened cocoa
½ teaspoon vanilla

1. In small bowl beat cream cheese, corn syrup and margarine until creamy. Beat in confectioners' sugar, cocoa and vanilla until frosting is of spreading consistency.

Makes 1⅓ cups

Prep Time: 10 minutes

Mott's®
Peppermint Cake

CAKE

2¼ cups cake flour
2 teaspoons baking powder
1 teaspoon salt
½ teaspoon baking soda
1½ cups sugar
2 tablespoons margarine
½ cup MOTT'S® Natural Apple Sauce
½ cup skim milk
4 egg whites
1 teaspoon vanilla extract

PEPPERMINT FROSTING

1½ cups sugar
¼ cup water
2 egg whites
¼ teaspoon cream of tartar
½ teaspoon peppermint extract
½ ounce crushed starlight candies

1. Preheat oven to 375°F. Spray 9-inch round cake pan with nonstick cooking spray.

2. **To prepare Cake,** in medium bowl, combine flour, baking powder, salt and baking soda. In large bowl, beat 1½ cups sugar and margarine with electric mixer at medium speed until blended. Whisk in apple sauce, milk, 4 egg whites and vanilla extract.

3. Add flour mixture to apple sauce mixture; stir until well blended. Pour into prepared cake pan.

4. Bake 35 to 40 minutes or until toothpick inserted into center comes out clean. Cool completely on wire rack. Split cake horizontally in half to make 2 layers.

5. **To prepare Peppermint Frosting,** in top of double boiler, whisk together 1½ cups sugar, water, 2 egg whites and cream of tartar. Cook, whisking occasionally, over simmering water 4 minutes or until mixture is hot and sugar is dissolved. Remove from heat; stir in peppermint extract. Beat with electric mixer at high speed 3 minutes or until mixture forms stiff peaks.

6. Place 1 cake layer on serving plate. Spread with layer of Peppermint Frosting. Top with second cake layer. Frost top and side with remaining frosting. Sprinkle top and side of cake with crushed candies. Cut into 12 slices. Refrigerate leftovers.   *Makes 12 servings*

Pecan Spice Cake (page 512)

Chocolate Mayonnaise Cake

2 cups all-purpose flour
²/₃ cup unsweetened cocoa
1¼ teaspoons baking soda
¼ teaspoon baking powder
3 eggs
1²/₃ cups sugar
1 teaspoon vanilla
1 cup HELLMANN'S® or BEST FOODS® Real or Light Mayonnaise
1¹/₃ cups water

1. Preheat oven to 350°F. Grease and flour bottoms of two 9×1½-inch round cake pans.

2. In medium bowl, combine flour, cocoa, baking soda and baking powder; set aside.

3. In large bowl, with mixer at high speed, beat eggs, sugar and vanilla, scraping bowl occasionally, 3 minutes or until smooth and creamy. Reduce speed to low; beat in mayonnaise until blended. Add flour mixture in 4 additions alternately with water, beginning and ending with flour mixture. Pour into prepared pans.

4. Bake 30 to 35 minutes or until cake springs back when touched lightly in center. Cool in pans on wire racks 10 minutes. Remove from pans; cool completely on racks. Fill and frost as desired.

Makes 1 (9-inch) layer cake

Black Forest Chocolate Fudge Cake

2 cups cake flour
1 cup unsweetened cocoa powder
1 teaspoon baking powder
½ teaspoon salt
1½ cups packed brown sugar
2 eggs
1 egg white
1 cup Prune Purée (page 434) or prepared prune butter
¾ cup nonfat milk
4 teaspoons vanilla
1 cup boiling water
2 tablespoons instant espresso coffee powder
2 teaspoons baking soda
2 cups frozen pitted unsweetened dark sweet cherries, coarsely chopped, thawed and well drained
½ cup chopped toasted walnuts
Mocha Glaze (recipe follows)
Chocolate Drizzle (optional, recipe follows)
Fresh cherries or frozen cherries, thawed
Mint sprigs for garnish

Preheat oven to 350°F. Coat 12- to 16-cup Bundt or other tube pan with vegetable cooking spray. In large bowl, combine flour, cocoa, baking powder and salt; mix in brown sugar.

In medium bowl, whisk eggs, egg white, prune purée, milk and vanilla. In 2-cup measure, combine boiling water, espresso powder and baking soda. Stir prune purée and water mixtures into flour mixture; mix just until blended. Pour half the batter into prepared pan; sprinkle cherries and walnuts evenly over batter. Top with remaining batter. Bake in center of oven about 45 minutes or until toothpick inserted into center comes out clean. Cool in pan on wire rack 15 minutes; remove from pan. Cool completely on wire rack. Prepare Mocha Glaze. Spoon over cake, allowing glaze to run down sides. Prepare Chocolate Drizzle, if desired. Drizzle over glaze. Fill cake center with additional cherries and garnish with mint.

Makes 16 servings

MOCHA GLAZE: Place 1 cup powdered sugar in small bowl. Dissolve ⅛ teaspoon instant espresso coffee powder in 4 teaspoons water. Stir into sugar until smooth, adding 1 teaspoon water, if needed, for desired consistency.

CHOCOLATE DRIZZLE: In top of double boiler or bowl set over simmering water, melt 2 tablespoons semisweet chocolate chips. Stir in 2 teaspoons hot water until blended. Cool until desired consistency.

*FAVORITE RECIPE FROM **CALIFORNIA PRUNE BOARD***

Mocha Marble Pound Cake

- **2 cups all-purpose flour**
- **2 teaspoons baking powder**
- **1 teaspoon baking soda**
- **½ teaspoon salt**
- **1 cup sugar**
- **¼ cup margarine, softened**
- **1 teaspoon vanilla extract**
- **½ cup EGG BEATERS® Healthy Egg Substitute**
- **1 (8-ounce) container low-fat coffee yogurt**
- **¼ cup unsweetened cocoa Mocha Yogurt Glaze (recipe follows)**

In small bowl, combine flour, baking powder, baking soda and salt; set aside.

In large bowl, with electric mixer at medium speed, beat sugar, margarine and vanilla until creamy. Add Egg Beaters®; beat until smooth. With mixer at low speed, add yogurt alternately with flour mixture, beating well after each addition. Remove half of batter to medium bowl. Add cocoa to batter remaining in large bowl; beat until blended. Alternately spoon coffee and chocolate batters into greased 9×5×3-inch loaf pan. With knife, cut through batters to create marbled effect.

Bake at 325°F for 60 to 65 minutes or until toothpick inserted into center comes out clean. Cool in pan on wire rack 10 minutes. Remove from pan; cool completely on wire rack. Frost with Mocha Yogurt Glaze.

Makes 16 servings

Prep Time: 20 minutes
Cook Time: 65 minutes

MOCHA YOGURT GLAZE: In small bowl, combine ½ cup powdered sugar, 1 tablespoon unsweetened cocoa and 1 tablespoon low-fat coffee yogurt until smooth; add more yogurt if necessary to make spreading consistency.

Lemon Semolina Syrup Cake

- **2 cups farina or semolina flour**
- **1 cup sugar**
- **1½ teaspoons baking powder**
- **¼ teaspoon salt**
- **2 cups plain low-fat yogurt**
- **2 tablespoons FILIPPO BERIO® Extra Light Tasting Olive Oil**
- **Finely grated peel of 1 lemon**
- **12 to 15 walnut halves**
- **1 cup light corn syrup**
- **2 tablespoons lemon juice**
- **Fresh strawberries (optional)**

Preheat oven to 350°F. Grease 9-inch springform pan with olive oil.

In large bowl, combine farina, sugar, baking powder and salt. With wooden spoon or spatula, mix in yogurt, 2 tablespoons olive oil and lemon peel until well blended. *Do not use electric mixer.* Pour batter into prepared pan. Score top of batter with tip of sharp knife, making 12 to 15 squares or diamond shapes, about ½ inch deep. (Marks will not remain completely visible before baking, but will show slightly when baked.) Place walnut half in center of each square or diamond shape.

Bake 45 minutes or until golden brown and toothpick inserted into center comes out clean. Meanwhile, in small saucepan, combine corn syrup and lemon juice. Heat over medium heat, stirring frequently, until mixture is hot.

When cake tests done, remove from oven. Make ½-inch-deep cuts through scored portions, cleaning knife after each cut. Immediately pour hot syrup over cake in pan. Let stand 1 to 2 hours or until syrup is absorbed and cake is cool. Remove side of pan; serve garnished with strawberries, if desired. Cover; refrigerate any remaining cake.

Makes 10 to 12 servings

Apple-Gingerbread Mini Cakes

1 large Cortland or
   Jonathan apple, cored
   and cut into quarters
1 package (14½ ounces)
   gingerbread cake and
   cookie mix
1 large egg
   Powdered sugar

Microwave Directions:
1. Lightly grease 10 (6- to 7-ounce) custard cups; set aside. Grate apple in food processor or with hand-held grater. Combine grated apple, cake mixture, 1 cup water and egg in medium bowl; stir until well blended. Spoon about ⅓ cup mixture into each custard cup, filling cups half full.

2. Arrange 5 cups in microwave. Microwave at HIGH 2 minutes. Rotate cups ½ turn. Microwave 1 minute more or until cakes are springy when touched lightly and look a little moist on top. Cool on wire rack. Repeat with remaining cakes.

3. To unmold cakes, run a small knife around edge of custard cups to loosen cakes while still warm. Invert onto cutting board and tap lightly until cakes drop out. Place on plates. Dust with powdered sugar. Serve warm or at room temperature.

Makes 10 (single-serving) cakes

Prep & Cook Time: 20 minutes

SERVING SUGGESTION: SERVE WITH WHIPPED CREAM, VANILLA ICE CREAM OR CRÈME ANGLAISE.

Orange Carrot Cake

1 cup margarine or butter,
   softened
1 cup GRANDMA'S®
   Molasses Unsulphured
4 eggs
½ cup orange juice
1 cup all-purpose flour
1 cup whole wheat flour
2 teaspoons baking soda
1 teaspoon ground
   cinnamon
½ teaspoon salt
2 cups shredded carrots
½ cup chopped walnuts

FROSTING
1 package (3 ounces)
   cream cheese,
   softened
2 tablespoons margarine
   or butter, softened
1½ cups powdered sugar
1 teaspoon grated orange
   peel

Heat oven to 350°F. Grease two 8- or 9-inch round cake pans. In large bowl, combine margarine, molasses, eggs and orange juice; mix well. Stir in flours, baking soda, cinnamon and salt; mix well. Stir in carrots and walnuts. Pour into prepared pans. Bake at 350°F 30 to 35 minutes or until toothpick inserted into centers comes out clean. Cool 15 minutes; remove from pans. Cool completely.

In small bowl, combine all frosting ingredients; beat until smooth. Place one layer of cake on serving plate; spread top with frosting. Top with second layer; spread top with frosting.   *Makes 12 servings*

Gingerbread

½ cup packed brown sugar
⅓ cup Prune Purée (page
   434) or prepared
   prune butter or 1 jar
   (2½ ounces) first-
   stage baby food
   prunes
1 egg
2 tablespoons vegetable
   shortening
2 teaspoons vanilla
1 cup molasses
2⅓ cups all-purpose flour
2 teaspoons baking soda
1½ teaspoons ground
   ginger
1 teaspoon ground
   cinnamon
½ teaspoon ground cloves
½ teaspoon dry mustard
½ teaspoon salt
1 cup boiling water

Preheat oven to 375°F. Coat 9-inch square baking pan with vegetable cooking spray. In mixer bowl, beat brown sugar, prune purée, egg, shortening and vanilla at high speed 1 minute; beat in molasses until well blended. In medium bowl, combine flour, baking soda, spices and salt; mix into sugar mixture in three additions, alternating with water. Pour batter evenly into prepared pan. Bake in center of oven 35 to 40 minutes or until springy to the touch. Cool completely in pan on wire rack.

Makes 16 servings

*FAVORITE RECIPE FROM **CALIFORNIA PRUNE BOARD***

Apple-Gingerbread Mini Cakes

Cassata

2 cups (15 ounces)
   SARGENTO® Part-Skim
   Ricotta Cheese
¼ cup sugar
3 tablespoons orange-
   flavored liqueur
⅓ cup finely chopped
   mixed candied fruit
¼ cup chopped almonds
1¼ cups mini semisweet
   chocolate chips,
   divided
1 prepared pound cake
   (10¾ ounces)
1 teaspoon instant coffee
   dissolved in ¼ cup
   boiling water
6 tablespoons unsalted
   butter or margarine,
   cut into 8 pieces,
   chilled
   Chopped almonds for
   garnish (optional)

In bowl, combine ricotta cheese, sugar and liqueur; beat until light and fluffy, about 3 minutes. Fold in candied fruit, ¼ cup chopped almonds and ¼ cup chocolate chips. Set aside.

Cut pound cake in half horizontally using sharp serrated knife. Cut each half horizontally in half again. Place top layer of pound cake, top side down, on serving platter. Spread one third ricotta mixture evenly over cake. Repeat procedure twice, using two cake layers and remaining ricotta mixture; stack layers. Top with remaining cake layer; press slightly to compact layers. Cover with plastic wrap; chill at least 2 hours.

Meanwhile, combine remaining 1 cup chocolate chips and coffee in top of double boiler over hot, not boiling, water. Stir constantly until chocolate is melted. Add butter pieces, one at a time, stirring constantly, until all butter is added and melted. Remove from heat; chill to spreading consistency, about 2 to 2½ hours. Spread top and sides of cake with frosting. Garnish top with chopped almonds, if desired.   *Makes 12 servings*

Tip: Cake may be made 1 day in advance, covered with plastic wrap and refrigerated. Let stand at room temperature about 30 minutes before slicing.

Flag Cake

2 pints strawberries
1 package (12 ounces)
   pound cake, cut into
   8 slices
1⅓ cups blueberries,
   divided
1 tub (8 ounces) COOL
   WHIP® Whipped
   Topping, thawed

SLICE 1 cup strawberries; set aside. Halve remaining strawberries; set aside.

LINE bottom of 12×8-inch baking dish with cake slices. Top with 1 cup sliced strawberries, 1 cup blueberries and all of whipped topping.

PLACE strawberry halves and remaining ⅓ cup blueberries over whipped topping to create a flag design.

REFRIGERATE until ready to serve.   *Makes 15 servings*

Mom's Favorite White Cake

2¼ cups cake flour
1 tablespoon baking
   powder
½ teaspoon salt
1½ cups sugar
½ cup margarine or butter,
   softened
4 egg whites
2 teaspoons vanilla
1 cup milk
   Strawberry Frosting
   (recipe follows)
   Fruit Filling (recipe
   follows)
   Fresh strawberries
   (optional)

PREHEAT oven to 350°F. Line bottoms of two 9-inch round cake pans with waxed paper; lightly grease paper. Combine flour, baking powder and salt in medium bowl; set aside.

BEAT sugar and margarine in large bowl with electric mixer at medium speed until light and fluffy. Add egg whites, two at a time, beating well after each addition. Add vanilla; beat until blended. With electric mixer at low speed, add flour mixture alternately with milk, beating well after each addition. Pour batter evenly into prepared pans.

BAKE 25 minutes or until toothpick inserted into centers comes out clean. Cool layers in pans on wire rack 10 minutes. Loosen edges and invert layers onto rack to cool completely.

PREPARE Strawberry Frosting and Fruit Filling. To fill and frost cake, place one layer on cake plate; spread top with Fruit Filling. Place second layer over filling. Frost top and sides with Strawberry Frosting. Place strawberries on top of cake, if desired. Refrigerate; allow cake to stand at room temperature 15 minutes before serving.

Makes 12 servings

STRAWBERRY FROSTING

   2 envelopes (1.3 ounces each) whipped topping mix
   ²/₃ cup milk
   1 cup (6 ounces) white chocolate chips, melted
   ¼ cup strawberry jam

BEAT whipped topping mix and milk in medium bowl with electric mixer on low speed until blended. Beat on high speed 4 minutes or until topping thickens and forms peaks. With mixer at low speed, beat melted chocolate into topping. Add jam; beat until blended. Chill 15 minutes or until of spreading consistency.

FRUIT FILLING

   1 cup Strawberry Frosting (recipe above)
   1 can (8 ounces) crushed pineapple, drained
   1 cup sliced strawberries

COMBINE Strawberry Frosting, pineapple and strawberries in medium bowl; mix well.

Best-Ever Short Cake

   2 cups all-purpose flour
   2 tablespoons sugar
   1 tablespoon baking powder
   1 teaspoon salt
   ¾ cup shortening
   1 cup milk
   2 boxes (10 ounces each) BIRDS EYE® frozen Strawberries, thawed
Whipped topping (optional)

• Preheat oven to 450°F. Combine flour, sugar, baking powder and salt.

• Cut shortening into flour mixture until mixture resembles coarse cornmeal.

• Blend in milk; mix well. Spread dough in 9×9-inch baking pan.

• Bake 15 minutes. Serve warm or let cool; top with strawberries before serving. Garnish with whipped topping, if desired.

Makes 6 to 9 servings

Best-Ever Short Cake

Apple Pie Chocolate Brownie Cake

Apple Topping (recipe follows)
1 cup all-purpose flour
⅔ cup sugar
¼ cup HERSHEY'S Cocoa or HERSHEY'S European Style Cocoa
1 teaspoon baking powder
½ teaspoon salt
¾ cup water
⅔ cup shortening
1 egg
1 teaspoon vanilla extract

Prepare Apple Topping. Heat oven to 375°F. Grease and flour 9-inch square baking pan. In medium bowl, stir together flour, sugar, cocoa, baking powder and salt. Add water, shortening, egg and vanilla; beat until smooth and well blended. Spread into prepared pan. *Carefully* spoon prepared topping over chocolate batter to within ½ inch of edges. *Do not stir.* Bake 35 to 40 minutes or until chocolate is set and cakelike. Cool completely in pan on wire rack. Serve with whipped topping, if desired. Garnish as desired.

Makes 8 to 10 servings

APPLE TOPPING
1 can (20 ounces) apple pie filling
½ teaspoon lemon juice
½ teaspoon ground cinnamon

In small bowl, stir together apple pie filling, lemon juice and cinnamon.

Brownie Sundae Cake

1 (19- to 21-ounce) package fudge brownie mix, prepared according to package directions for cake-like brownies
1 cup "M&M's" Semi-Sweet Chocolate Mini Baking Bits
½ cup chopped nuts (optional)
1 quart vanilla ice cream, softened
¼ cup caramel or butterscotch ice cream topping

Line 2 (9-inch) round cake pans with aluminum foil, extending slightly over edges of pans. Lightly spray bottoms with vegetable cooking spray; set aside. Preheat oven as brownie mix package directs. Divide brownie batter evenly between pans; sprinkle ½ cup "M&M's" Semi-Sweet Chocolate Mini Baking Bits and ¼ cup nuts, if desired, over each pan. Bake 23 to 25 minutes or until edges begin to pull away from sides of pan. Cool completely. Remove layers by lifting foil from pans.

To assemble cake, place one brownie layer, topping-side down, in 9-inch springform pan. Carefully spread ice cream over brownie layer; drizzle with ice cream topping. Place second brownie layer on top of ice cream layer, topping-side up; press down, lightly. Wrap in plastic wrap and freeze until firm. Remove from freezer about 15 minutes before serving. Remove side of pan. Cut into wedges. *Makes 12 slices*

Charlotte Russe

2 cups boiling water
1 package (8-serving size) *or* 2 packages (4-serving size each) JELL-O® Brand Black Cherry, Cherry or Orange Flavor Gelatin
1 quart vanilla ice cream, softened (4 cups)
12 ladyfingers, split*
COOL WHIP® Whipped Topping, thawed

Or use thin strips of sponge cake.

Stir boiling water into gelatin in medium bowl 2 minutes until dissolved. Spoon in ice cream, stirring until melted and smooth. Refrigerate until thickened (or when spoon drawn through mixture leaves definite impression).

Meanwhile, trim about 1 inch off one end of each split ladyfinger. Place ladyfingers, cut ends down, around side of 8-inch springform pan. Spoon gelatin mixture into pan. Refrigerate 4 hours or until firm. Remove side of pan. Garnish with whipped topping. Decorate as desired.

Makes 10 servings

Prep Time: 20 minutes
Chill Time: 4 hours

Brownie Sundae Cake

Black Bottom Cheesecake Cups

CHEESECAKE FILLING
1 container (8 ounces) fat-free cream cheese
¼ cup sugar
1 egg

CHOCOLATE BATTER
1½ cups all-purpose flour
¾ cup sugar
⅓ cup unsweetened cocoa powder
1 teaspoon baking soda
½ teaspoon salt
1 cup water
⅓ cup Prune Purée (page 434) or prepared prune butter or 1 jar (2½ ounces) first-stage baby food prunes
1 tablespoon instant espresso coffee powder or 2 tablespoons instant coffee granules
1 tablespoon white vinegar
2 teaspoons vanilla
½ cup semisweet chocolate chips

ALMOND TOPPING
¼ cup finely chopped blanched almonds
2 tablespoons sugar

Preheat oven to 350°F. Line eighteen 2¾-inch (⅓-cup capacity) muffin cups with cupcake liners. Coat liners lightly with vegetable cooking spray. To make filling, in small mixer bowl, beat filling ingredients at medium speed until smooth; set aside.

To make chocolate batter, in large bowl, combine first five batter ingredients. In medium bowl, beat water, prune purée, espresso powder, vinegar and vanilla until blended. Mix into flour mixture. Spoon into muffin cups, dividing equally. Top each with heaping teaspoonful of cream cheese mixture. Sprinkle with chocolate chips.

To make topping, mix almonds and sugar; sprinkle over chocolate chips. Bake in center of oven about 25 minutes or until toothpick inserted into chocolate portion comes out clean. Cool in pans 5 minutes; remove from pans to wire racks to cool completely.

Makes 18 cupcakes

*FAVORITE RECIPE FROM **CALIFORNIA PRUNE BOARD***

Cherry-Topped Icebox Cake

20 whole graham crackers, divided
1 package (6-serving size) JELL-O® Vanilla or Chocolate Flavor Instant Pudding & Pie Filling
2 cups cold milk
1¾ cups thawed COOL WHIP® Whipped Topping
2 cans (21 ounces each) cherry pie filling

Line 13×9-inch pan with ⅓ of the graham crackers, breaking crackers, if necessary.

Prepare pudding mix with cold milk as directed on package. Let stand 5 minutes. Gently stir in whipped topping. Spread ½ of the pudding mixture over crackers. Add second layer of crackers; top with remaining pudding mixture. Add third layer of crackers. Top with cherry pie filling. Refrigerate 3 hours.   *Makes 12 servings*

CHOCOLATE-FROSTED ICEBOX CAKE: Prepare Cherry-Topped Icebox Cake as directed, substituting ¾ cup ready-to-spread chocolate fudge frosting for the cherry pie filling. Carefully spread frosting over top layer of graham crackers.

Apple Praline Bundt Cake

1 can (20 ounces) sliced apples, drained
½ cup granulated sugar
½ cup packed light brown sugar
1 cup vegetable oil
4 eggs
1½ cups all-purpose flour
2 teaspoons ground cinnamon
1½ teaspoons baking powder
1½ teaspoons baking soda
1½ teaspoons dried mint
¼ teaspoon ground nutmeg
¾ cup chopped walnuts, divided
Praline Sauce (page 523)

Preheat oven to 350°F.

Finely chop apples to measure 1½ cups; place apples in large bowl, reserving remaining slices. Add sugars and oil. Add eggs, one at a time. Add combined flour, cinnamon, baking powder, baking soda, mint and nutmeg; mix well. Add ½ cup walnuts.

Spoon batter into greased and floured 12-cup fluted cake pan. Bake 50 minutes or until cake begins to pull away from side of pan. Cool cake in pan on wire rack 10 minutes; remove from pan and cool on wire rack.

Pierce warm cake with long-tined fork; spoon half of Praline Sauce over cake. Arrange remaining apple slices on top of cake; spoon remaining Praline Sauce over apples and sprinkle with remaining ¼ cup walnuts.

Makes 10 to 12 servings

PRALINE SAUCE
6 tablespoons margarine or butter
¾ cup packed light brown sugar
¼ cup brandy or apple juice

Heat margarine in small saucepan until melted; stir in brown sugar and brandy. Heat to boiling; reduce heat and simmer until sauce is thickened to the consistency of honey, 5 to 8 minutes.

Makes about ⅔ cup

*FAVORITE RECIPE FROM **CANNED FOOD INFORMATION COUNCIL***

Quick Chocolate Cupcakes

1 ½ **cups all-purpose flour**
¾ **cup sugar**
¼ **cup HERSHEY'S Cocoa**
1 **teaspoon baking soda**
½ **teaspoon salt**
1 **cup water**
¼ **cup vegetable oil**
1 **tablespoon white vinegar**
1 **teaspoon vanilla extract**

Heat oven to 375°F. Line muffin cups (2½ inches in diameter) with paper baking cups. In medium bowl, stir together flour, sugar, cocoa, baking soda and salt. Add water, oil, vinegar and vanilla; beat with whisk just until batter is smooth and well blended. Fill muffin cups ⅔ full with batter. Bake 16 to 18 minutes or until wooden pick inserted into center comes out clean. Remove from pans to wire racks. Cool completely. Frost as desired.

Makes 18 cupcakes

Black Bottom Cheesecake Cups (page 522)

Lemon Poppy Seed Cake

6 tablespoons margarine, softened
½ cup firmly packed light brown sugar
½ cup plain low-fat yogurt
1 egg
2 egg whites
3 teaspoons fresh lemon juice
1¾ cups all-purpose flour
1 teaspoon baking powder
½ teaspoon baking soda
¼ teaspoon salt
⅓ cup skim milk
2 tablespoons poppy seeds
1 tablespoon grated lemon peel

LEMON GLAZE
1 cup powdered sugar
2 tablespoons plus 1½ teaspoons lemon juice
½ teaspoon poppy seeds

Preheat oven to 350°F. Grease and flour 6-cup Bundt pan. Beat margarine in large bowl with electric mixer until fluffy. Beat in brown sugar, yogurt, whole egg, egg whites and 3 teaspoons lemon juice. Set aside. Combine flour, baking powder, baking soda and salt in medium bowl. Add flour mixture to margarine mixture alternately with milk, beginning and ending with flour mixture. Mix in 2 tablespoons poppy seeds and lemon peel. Pour batter into prepared pan.

Bake about 40 minutes or until cake is golden brown and toothpick inserted into center comes out clean. Cool in pan on wire rack 10 minutes. Remove from pan to wire rack; cool completely.

For Lemon Glaze, mix powdered sugar with 2 tablespoons plus 1½ teaspoons lemon juice until desired consistency. Spoon glaze over cake and sprinkle with ½ teaspoon poppy seeds.

Makes 12 servings

Holiday Fruit Cake

1 (16-ounce) package HONEY MAID® Grahams, finely rolled (about 5 cups crumbs)
½ teaspoon ground cinnamon
½ teaspoon ground allspice
¼ teaspoon ground cloves
¾ cup seedless raisins
1 cup pitted dates, snipped
12 ounces (about 1½ cups) mixed candied fruit
1 cup PLANTERS® Walnut Pieces, chopped
½ cup orange juice
⅓ cup light corn syrup

In large bowl, combine crumbs, cinnamon, allspice, cloves, raisins, dates, candied fruit and walnuts. Stir together orange juice and corn syrup; add to crumb mixture, blending until moistened. Press firmly into foil-lined 8½×4½×2½-inch loaf pan; cover tightly. Store at least 2 days in refrigerator before serving. Cake will keep several weeks in refrigerator.

Makes 1 (8-inch) loaf

Lemon Meringue Torte

MERINGUE
4 egg whites
¼ teaspoon cream of tartar
1 cup sugar

LEMON LAYER
4 egg yolks
½ cup sugar
Grated peel of 1 lemon
¼ cup fresh lemon juice
1 cup whipping cream
Candied lemon peel (optional)

Preheat oven to 275°F. To prepare meringue, beat egg whites and cream of tartar in medium bowl with electric mixer on medium speed until frothy. Gradually beat in 1 cup sugar on high speed until stiff peaks form. Draw 9-inch circle on heavy brown paper. Place on baking sheet; spread meringue inside circle to form 8- to 9-inch round. Bake 1 hour. *Turn off oven;* cool completely in oven. Meanwhile, to prepare lemon layer, beat egg yolks in top of double boiler. Stir in ½ cup sugar, grated peel and juice. Place over hot, not boiling, water; cook 5 to 8 minutes or until thickened, stirring constantly. Remove top of double boiler; cover and set aside to cool.

Place cooled meringue round on serving plate. Spread with lemon layer. Refrigerate until set. Just before serving, beat cream in medium bowl with electric mixer on high speed until stiff peaks form; spread over lemon filling. Garnish with candied peel, if desired. Refrigerate leftovers.

Makes 8 servings

FAVORITE RECIPE FROM **BOB EVANS FARMS**®

Chocolate Cream Torte

1 package DUNCAN
   HINES® Moist Deluxe
   Devil's Food Cake Mix
1 package (8 ounces)
   cream cheese,
   softened
½ cup sugar
1 teaspoon vanilla extract
1 cup finely chopped
   pecans
1 cup whipping cream,
   chilled
   Strawberry halves for
   garnish
   Mint leaves for garnish

1. Preheat oven to 350°F. Grease and flour two 8- or 9-inch round cake pans.

2. Prepare, bake and cool cake following package directions for basic recipe. Chill layers for ease in splitting.

3. Place cream cheese, sugar and vanilla extract in small bowl. Beat at low speed with electric mixer until smooth. Add pecans; stir until blended. Set aside. Beat whipping cream in small bowl until stiff peaks form. Fold whipped cream into cream cheese mixture.

4. To assemble, split each cake layer in half horizontally (see Tip). Place one cake layer on serving plate. Spread top with ¼ of filling. Repeat with remaining layers and filling. Garnish with strawberry halves and mint leaves, if desired. Refrigerate until ready to serve.

Makes 12 to 16 servings

Tip: *To split layers evenly, measure cake with ruler. Divide into 2 equal layers. Mark with toothpicks. Cut through layers with serrated knife, using toothpicks as guide.*

Rum and Spumoni Layered Torte

1 package (18 to 19
   ounces) moist butter
   recipe yellow cake mix
3 eggs
½ cup butter or margarine,
   softened
⅓ cup plus 2 teaspoons
   rum, divided
⅓ cup water
1 quart spumoni ice
   cream, softened
1 cup whipping cream
1 tablespoon powdered
   sugar
   Chopped mixed candied
   fruit
   Red and green sugars
   for decorating
   (optional)

Preheat oven to 375°F. Grease and flour 15½×10½×1-inch jelly-roll pan. Combine cake mix, eggs, butter, ⅓ cup rum and water in large bowl. Beat with electric mixer at low speed until moistened. Beat at high speed 4 minutes. Pour evenly into prepared pan.

Bake 20 to 25 minutes or until toothpick inserted into center comes out clean. Cool in pan 10 minutes. Turn out of pan onto wire rack; cool completely.

Cut cake into three 10×5-inch pieces. Place one cake layer on serving plate. Spread with half the softened ice cream. Cover with second cake layer. Spread with remaining ice cream. Place remaining cake layer on top. Gently push down. Wrap cake in plastic wrap and freeze at least 4 hours.

Just before serving, combine cream, powdered sugar and remaining 2 teaspoons rum in small chilled bowl. Beat at high speed with chilled beaters until stiff peaks form. Remove cake from freezer. Spread thin layer of whipped cream mixture over top of cake. Place star tip in pastry bag; fill with remaining whipped cream mixture. Pipe rosettes around outer top edges of cake. Place candied fruit in narrow strip down center of cake. Sprinkle colored sugars over rosettes, if desired. Serve immediately.

Makes 8 to 10 servings

Chocolate and Raspberry Cream Torte

- **6 tablespoons (40% oil) lower fat margarine**
- **1 cup sugar**
- **1 cup skim milk**
- **1 tablespoon white vinegar**
- **½ teaspoon vanilla extract**
- **1¼ cups all-purpose flour**
- **⅓ cup HERSHEY'S Cocoa or HERSHEY'S European Style Cocoa**
- **1 teaspoon baking soda**
- **¼ cup red raspberry jam Raspberry Cream (recipe follows)**

Heat oven to 350°F. Spray 15½×10½×1-inch jelly-roll pan with vegetable cooking spray. In medium saucepan over low heat, melt margarine; stir in sugar. Remove from heat; stir in milk, vinegar and vanilla. In small bowl, stir together flour, cocoa and baking soda; gradually add to sugar mixture, stirring with whisk until well blended. Pour batter into prepared pan.

Bake 16 to 18 minutes or until wooden pick inserted into center comes out clean. Cool 10 minutes; remove from pan to wire rack. Cool completely. To assemble, cut cake crosswise into four equal pieces. Place one piece on serving plate; spread 1 tablespoon jam over top. Carefully spread a scant ¾ cup Raspberry Cream over jam. Repeat procedure with remaining cake layers, jam and Raspberry Cream, ending with plain layer on top. Spread remaining 1 tablespoon jam over top. Spoon or pipe remaining Raspberry Cream over jam. Refrigerate torte until ready to serve. Garnish as desired. Cover; refrigerate leftover torte.

Makes 15 servings

RASPBERRY CREAM: Thaw and thoroughly drain 1 package (10 ounces) frozen red raspberries. In blender container, place raspberries. Cover; blend until smooth. Strain in sieve; discard seeds. In small bowl, prepare 1 envelope (1.3 ounces) dry whipped topping mix as directed on package, using ½ cup cold skim milk, omitting vanilla and adding 2 to 3 drops red food color, if desired. Fold in puréed raspberries.

Makes about 2¼ cups

Linzer Torte

- **½ cup whole almonds, toasted**
- **1½ cups all-purpose flour**
- **1 teaspoon ground cinnamon**
- **¼ teaspoon salt**
- **¾ cup granulated sugar**
- **½ cup butter or margarine, softened**
- **½ teaspoon grated lemon peel**
- **1 egg**
- **¾ cup raspberry or apricot jam Sifted powdered sugar**

Process almonds in food processor until ground, but not pasty. Preheat oven to 375°F. Combine flour, almonds, cinnamon and salt in medium bowl; set aside. Beat granulated sugar, butter and lemon peel in large bowl with electric mixer at medium speed about 5 minutes or until light and fluffy, scraping down side of bowl once. Beat in egg until well blended. Beat in flour mixture at low speed until well blended.

Spoon ⅔ of dough onto bottom of 10-inch tart pan with removable bottom. Pat dough evenly over bottom and up side of pan. Spread jam over bottom of dough. Roll remaining ⅓ of dough on lightly floured surface into 10×5-inch rectangle. Cut dough into ten ½-inch-wide strips using pizza wheel or sharp knife.

Arrange 4 or 5 strips of dough lengthwise across jam. Arrange another 4 or 5 strips of dough crosswise across top. Trim and press ends of dough strips into edge of crust. Bake 25 to 35 minutes or until crust is golden brown. Cool completely in pan on wire rack. Remove torte from pan. Sprinkle with powdered sugar. Cut into wedges. Store, tightly covered, at room temperature 1 to 2 days.

Makes 12 servings

Chocolate and Raspberry Cream Torte

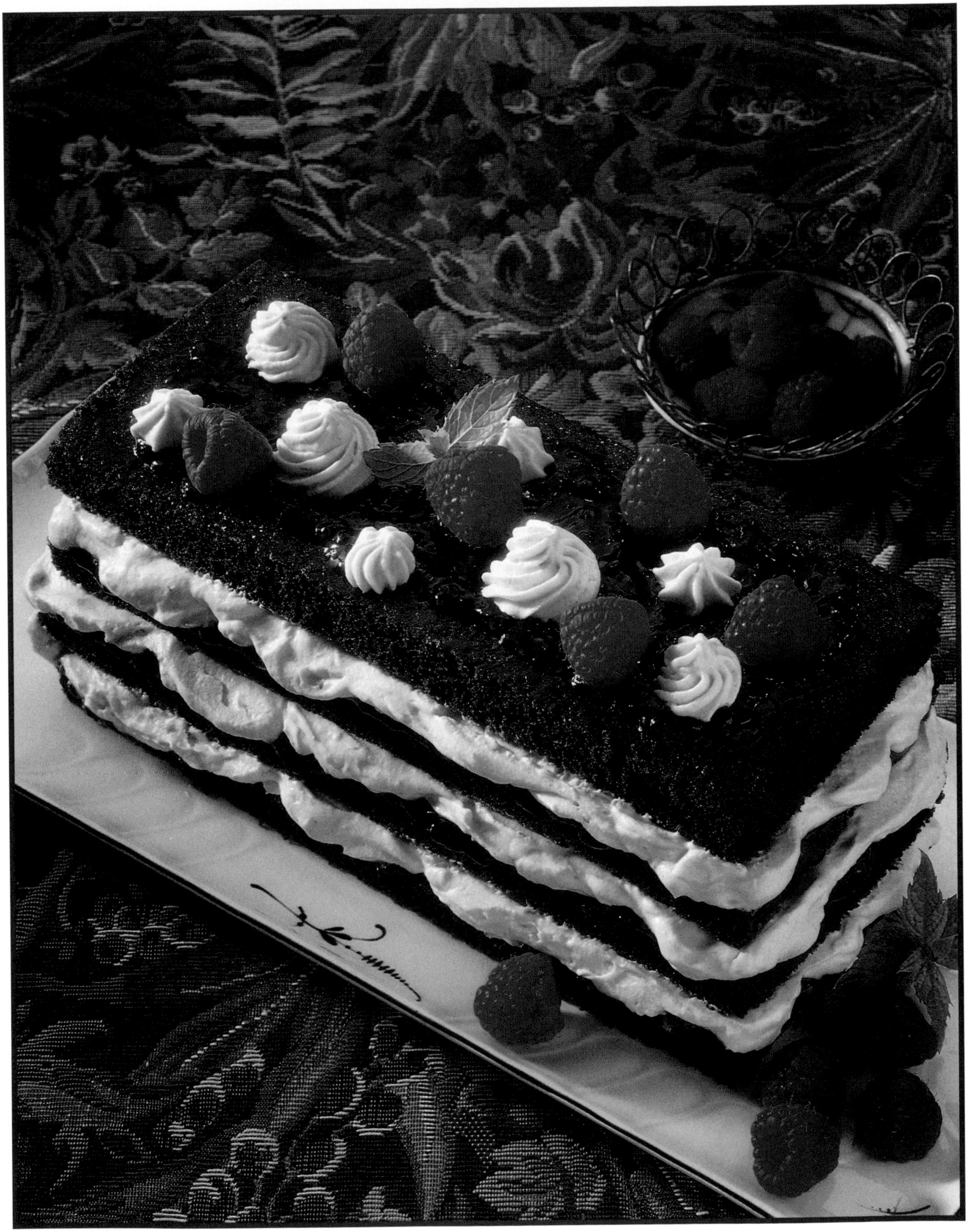

Chocolate-Raspberry Jelly Roll

¾ **cup granulated sugar**
2 **eggs**
3 **egg whites**
¼ **cup Prune Purée (page 434) or prepared prune butter**
1 **tablespoon vanilla**
1 **cup all-purpose flour**
¼ **cup unsweetened cocoa powder**
¼ **teaspoon salt**
 Powdered sugar
½ **cup raspberry preserves**
¾ **cup low-fat nondairy whipped topping**
½ **pint fresh raspberries**
 Mint sprigs for garnish

Preheat oven to 425°F. Coat 13×9-inch baking pan with vegetable cooking spray. Line pan with parchment or waxed paper; coat paper with vegetable cooking spray. In top of double boiler or bowl set over simmering water, combine granulated sugar, eggs and egg whites. Beat at high speed with portable electric mixer until tripled in volume, about 5 minutes. Beat in prune purée and vanilla, mixing until well blended; remove from heat. In medium bowl, combine flour, cocoa and salt. Sift flour mixture over egg mixture; gently fold in just until blended. Spread batter evenly in prepared pan. Bake in center of oven 10 minutes or until springy to the touch.

Meanwhile, lay cloth tea towel on work surface; dust evenly with powdered sugar. When cake is done, immediately loosen edges and invert onto towel. Gently peel off paper. Roll cake up in towel from narrow end. Place seam side down on wire rack; cool completely. Gently unroll cooled cake; spread with preserves. Reroll cake without towel. Place seam side down on serving plate. Dust with powdered sugar. Cut into ¾-inch slices. Top each serving with dollop of whipped topping and some raspberries. Garnish with mint sprig.

Makes 12 servings

FAVORITE RECIPE FROM **CALIFORNIA PRUNE BOARD**

Mocha Cake Roll with Creamy Chocolate Filling

¾ **cup granulated sugar**
2 **eggs**
3 **egg whites**
¼ **cup Prune Purée (page 434) or prepared prune butter**
¼ **cup coffee-flavored liqueur, divided**
2 **tablespoons instant coffee granules**
1 **cup all-purpose flour**
¼ **cup unsweetened cocoa powder, divided**
¼ **teaspoon salt**
 Powdered sugar
1½ **cups low-fat nondairy whipped topping**
 Additional low fat nondairy whipped topping and chocolate covered coffee beans for garnish

Preheat oven to 425°F. Coat 13×9×2-inch baking pan with vegetable cooking spray. Line pan with parchment or waxed paper; coat paper with vegetable cooking spray. In top of double boiler or bowl set over simmering water, combine granulated sugar, eggs and egg whites. Beat at high speed with portable electric mixer until tripled in volume, about 5 minutes. Beat in prune purée, 2 tablespoons liqueur and coffee granules until well blended; remove from heat. In medium bowl, combine flour, 2 tablespoons cocoa and salt. Sift flour mixture over egg mixture; gently fold in just until blended. Spread batter evenly in prepared pan. Bake in center of oven 10 minutes or until springy to the touch.

Meanwhile, lay cloth tea towel on work surface; dust evenly with powdered sugar. When cake is done, immediately loosen edges and invert onto towel. Gently peel off paper. Roll cake up in towel from narrow end. Place seam side down on wire rack; cool completely. Gently unroll cooled cake; brush with remaining 2 tablespoons liqueur. Combine whipped topping with remaining 2 tablespoons cocoa. Spread evenly over moistened cake. Reroll cake without towel. Place seam side down on serving plate. Dust with powdered sugar. Garnish with additional whipped topping and coffee beans. Cut into slices.

Makes 12 servings

FAVORITE RECIPE FROM **CALIFORNIA PRUNE BOARD**

Blueberry Angel Food Cake Rolls

1 package DUNCAN
  HINES® Angel Food
  Cake Mix
  Confectioners sugar
1 can (21 ounces)
  blueberry pie filling
¼ cup confectioners sugar
  Mint leaves for garnish
  (optional)

1. Preheat oven to 350°F. Line two 15½×10½×1-inch jelly-roll pans with aluminum foil.

2. Prepare cake following package directions. Divide into pans. Spread evenly. Cut through batter with knife or spatula to remove large air bubbles. Bake at 350°F for 15 minutes or until set. Invert cakes at once onto clean, lint-free dishtowels dusted with confectioners sugar. Remove foil carefully. Roll up each cake with towel jelly-roll fashion, starting at short end. Cool completely.

3. Unroll cakes. Spread about 1 cup blueberry pie filling to within 1 inch of edges on each cake. Reroll and place seam-side down on serving plate. Dust with ¼ cup confectioners sugar. Garnish with mint leaves, if desired.

Makes 2 cakes (8 servings each)

Philly 3-Step™ Toffee Crunch Cheesecake

2 (8-ounce) packages
  PHILADELPHIA
  BRAND® Cream
  Cheese, softened
½ cup sugar
½ teaspoon vanilla
2 eggs
1 ready-to-use graham
  cracker pie crust
  (6 ounces or 9 inches)
4 (1.4-ounce) bars
  chocolate covered
  English toffee,
  chopped (1 cup)

1. MIX cream cheese, sugar and vanilla at medium speed with electric mixer until well blended. Add eggs; mix until blended.

2. POUR into crust. Sprinkle with toffee.

3. BAKE at 350°F, 40 minutes or until center is almost set. Cool. Refrigerate 3 hours or overnight.   *Makes 8 servings*

Blueberry Angel Food Cake Roll

Raspberry-Swirled Cheesecake

14 chocolate sandwich
   cream cookies
3 tablespoons margarine
   or butter, melted
1 package (8 ounces)
   cream cheese,
   softened
1 cup powdered sugar
1 tablespoon lemon juice
1 teaspoon vanilla
2½ cups thawed nondairy
   whipped topping
¼ cup seedless raspberry
   jam
   Mint leaves, chocolate
   drizzle and fresh
   raspberries (optional)

PLACE cookies in food
processor or blender; process
with on/off pulses until finely
crushed. Add margarine;
process with pulses until
blended. Press crumb mixture
onto bottom of 8-inch
springform pan; refrigerate.

BEAT cream cheese in large
bowl with electric mixer at
medium speed until creamy.
Add sugar; beat well. Add
lemon juice and vanilla; beat
until smooth. Add whipped
topping; stir with mixing spoon
until blended. Pour into
prepared crust.

MAKE 20 to 25 holes in
cheesecake with teaspoon. Stir
jam until smooth.* Place jam in
holes. Gently swirl jam with tip
of knife.

REFRIGERATE cheesecake
2 hours. Garnish with mint
leaves, chocolate drizzle and
fresh raspberries, if desired.

Makes 9 servings

*If raspberry jam remains lumpy,
place in small microwavable
bowl. Microwave at HIGH 30
to 45 seconds; stir.*

Marble Cheesecake

HERSHEY'S Chocolate
   Crumb Crust (recipe
   follows)
3 packages (8 ounces
   each) cream cheese,
   softened
1 cup sugar, divided
½ cup dairy sour cream
2½ teaspoons vanilla
   extract, divided
3 tablespoons all-purpose
   flour
3 eggs
¼ cup HERSHEY'S Cocoa
1 tablespoon vegetable oil

Prepare Hershey's Chocolate
Crumb Crust. Heat oven to
450°F. In large bowl, on
medium speed of electric
mixer, beat cream cheese,
¾ cup sugar, sour cream and
2 teaspoons vanilla until
smooth. Gradually add flour,
beating well. Add eggs, 1 at a
time, beating well after each
addition.

In medium bowl, stir together
cocoa and remaining ¼ cup
sugar. Add oil, remaining ½
teaspoon vanilla and 1½ cups

cream cheese mixture; blend
well. Spoon plain and
chocolate batters alternately
into prepared crust, ending
with spoonfuls of chocolate
batter; gently swirl with knife
for marbled effect. Bake 10
minutes. *Without opening oven
door, reduce temperature to
250°F;* continue baking 30
minutes. *Turn off oven;* without
opening door, leave cheesecake
in oven 30 minutes. Remove
from oven to wire rack. With
knife, immediately loosen
cheesecake from side
of pan; cool completely.
Refrigerate several hours or
overnight; remove side of pan.
Cover; refrigerate leftover
cheesecake.

Makes 10 to 12 servings

HERSHEY'S CHOCOLATE
CRUMB CRUST
1¼ cups vanilla wafer
   crumbs (about
   40 wafers)
⅓ cup powdered sugar
⅓ cup HERSHEY'S Cocoa
¼ cup (½ stick) butter or
   margarine, melted

Heat oven to 350°F. In medium
bowl, stir together crumbs,
powdered sugar and cocoa;
blend in butter. Press mixture
onto bottom and ½ inch up
side of 9-inch springform pan.
Bake 8 minutes; cool crust
completely.

Raspberry-Swirled Cheesecake

Lemon Cheesecake

CRUST
- 35 vanilla wafers
- ¾ cup slivered almonds, toasted
- ⅓ cup sugar
- ¼ cup butter or margarine, melted

FILLING
- 3 packages (8 ounces each) cream cheese, softened
- ¾ cup sugar
- 4 eggs
- ⅓ cup whipping cream
- ¼ cup lemon juice
- 1 tablespoon grated lemon peel
- 1 teaspoon vanilla

TOPPING
- 1 pint strawberries
- 2 tablespoons sugar

1. Preheat oven to 375°F. For crust, combine wafers, almonds and ⅓ cup sugar in food processor; process until fine crumbs are formed. Combine sugar mixture with melted butter in medium bowl. Press mixture evenly onto bottom and 1 inch up side of 9-inch springform pan. Set aside.

2. For filling, beat cream cheese and ¾ cup sugar in large bowl on high speed of electric mixer 2 to 3 minutes or until fluffy. Add eggs, 1 at a time, beating after each addition. Add whipping cream, lemon juice, lemon peel and vanilla; beat just until blended. Pour into prepared crust. Place springform pan on baking sheet. Bake 45 to 55 minutes or until set. Loosen cake from rim of pan with knife or small spatula. Cool completely on wire rack. Cover and refrigerate at least 10 hours or overnight.

3. For topping, hull and slice strawberries. Combine with sugar in medium bowl. Let stand 15 minutes. Serve over cheesecake.

Makes 16 servings

Philly 3-Step™ Piña Colada Cheesecake

- 2 (8-ounce) packages PHILADELPHIA BRAND® Cream Cheese, softened
- ½ cup sugar
- ½ teaspoon vanilla
- 2 eggs
- ⅓ cup piña colada frozen concentrated tropical fruit mixer, thawed
- 1 ready-to-use graham cracker pie crust (6 ounces or 9 inches)

1. MIX cream cheese, sugar and vanilla at medium speed with electric mixer until well blended. Add eggs; mix until blended. Blend in piña colada mixer.

2. POUR into crust.

3. BAKE at 350°F, 40 minutes or until center is almost set. Cool. Refrigerate 3 hours or overnight. Garnish with fresh fruit. Serve with Crimson Raspberry Sauce (recipe follows), if desired.

Makes 8 servings

CRIMSON RASPBERRY SAUCE: Place 2 packages (10 ounces each) frozen raspberries, thawed, in heavy 2-quart saucepan. Bring to a boil. Boil over high heat, stirring frequently, 7 minutes. Strain. Stir in 1 teaspoon fresh lemon juice. *Makes 2½ cups*

Prep Time: 10 minutes
Cook Time: 40 minutes

STRAWBERRY DAIQUIRI CHEESECAKE: Substitute strawberry daiquiri frozen concentrated tropical fruit mixer, thawed, for piña colada mixer.

LIME MARGARITA CHEESECAKE: Substitute margarita frozen concentrated tropical fruit mixer, thawed, for piña colada mixer.

Chocolate Marble Praline Cheesecake

CRUST
- 1 package DUNCAN HINES® Golden Sugar Cookie Mix
- 1 egg
- ¼ cup CRISCO® Oil or CRISCO® PURITAN® Canola Oil
- 1 ½ tablespoons water
- ½ cup finely chopped pecans

FILLING
- 1 ¼ cups packed brown sugar
- 2 tablespoons all-purpose flour
- 3 packages (8 ounces each) cream cheese, softened
- 3 eggs, lightly beaten
- 1 ½ teaspoons vanilla extract
- 1 square (1 ounce) unsweetened chocolate, melted
- 20 to 25 pecan halves (½ cup)
- Caramel flavor topping

1. Preheat oven to 350°F.

2. For crust, combine cookie mix, 1 egg, oil, water and chopped pecans in large bowl. Stir until thoroughly blended. Reserve 1 cup dough; set aside (see Note). Press remaining mixture onto bottom of ungreased 9-inch springform pan. Bake at 350°F for 22 to 24 minutes or until edge is light brown and center is set. Remove from oven.

3. For filling, combine brown sugar and flour in small bowl; set aside. Place cream cheese in large bowl. Beat at low speed with electric mixer, adding brown sugar mixture gradually. Add beaten eggs and vanilla extract, mixing only until incorporated. Remove 1 cup batter to small bowl; add melted chocolate. Pour remaining plain batter onto warm crust. Drop spoonfuls of chocolate batter over plain batter. Run knife through batters to marbleize. Arrange pecan halves around top edge. Bake at 350°F for 45 to 55 minutes or until set. Loosen cake from side of pan with knife or spatula. Cool completely on rack. Refrigerate 2 hours or until ready to serve.

4. To serve, remove side of pan. Glaze top of cheesecake with caramel flavor topping. Cut into slices and serve with additional caramel flavor topping, if desired.

Makes 12 to 16 servings

Note: To bake reserved cookie dough, press ¼ cup dough into 3-inch circle on ungreased baking sheet. Repeat with remaining dough. Bake at 375°F for 8 to 10 minutes or until light golden brown. Cool 1 minute on baking sheet. Remove to cooling rack.

Makes 4 large cookies

Lemon Cheesecake (page 532)

Philly 3-Step™ Chocolate Chip Cookie Dough Cheesecake

- 2 (8-ounce) packages PHILADELPHIA BRAND® Cream Cheese, softened
- ½ cup sugar
- ½ teaspoon vanilla
- 2 eggs
- ¾ cup prepared chocolate chip cookie dough, divided
- 1 ready-to-use graham cracker pie crust (6 ounces or 9 inches)

1. MIX cream cheese, sugar and vanilla at medium speed with electric mixer until well blended. Add eggs; mix until blended. Drop ½ cup of the cookie dough by level teaspoonfuls into batter; fold gently.

2. POUR into crust. Dot with level teaspoonfuls of remaining ¼ cup cookie dough.

3. BAKE at 350°F, 40 minutes or until center is almost set. Cool. Refrigerate 3 hours or overnight.   *Makes 8 servings*

Prep Time: 10 minutes
Cook Time: 40 minutes

COOKIES AND CREAM CHEESECAKE: Omit cookie dough. Substitute chocolate-flavored pie crust for graham cracker pie crust. Stir ½ cup chopped chocolate sandwich cookies into batter. Sprinkle with additional ¼ cup chopped chocolate sandwich cookies before baking.

Marbled Pumpkin Cheesecake Squares

- ¼ cup reduced-fat cream cheese, softened
- 2 tablespoons granulated sugar
- 3 tablespoons egg substitute
- 1 cup packed brown sugar
- ½ cup Prune Purée (page 434) or prepared prune butter
- 2 egg whites
- 1½ teaspoons vanilla
- 1 cup all-purpose flour
- 1 teaspoon baking powder
- ¾ teaspoon ground cinnamon
- ¼ teaspoon ground ginger
- ¼ teaspoon salt
- ⅛ teaspoon ground cloves
- ¾ cup canned pumpkin

Preheat oven to 350°F. Coat 8-inch square baking dish or pan with vegetable cooking spray. In small bowl, beat cream cheese and granulated sugar until blended. Gradually add egg substitute, beating until blended. Set aside. In large bowl, beat brown sugar, prune purée, egg whites and vanilla until well blended. In medium bowl, combine flour, baking powder, cinnamon, ginger, salt and cloves; stir into brown sugar mixture until well blended. Beat in pumpkin. Spread batter evenly in prepared baking dish. Drop heaping tablespoonfuls of cream cheese mixture over batter. Using knife, gently swirl cream cheese mixture into batter. Bake in center of oven

25 to 30 minutes or until toothpick inserted into center comes out clean. Cool in baking dish 15 minutes. Cut into squares. Serve warm with fat-free vanilla ice cream or frozen yogurt, if desired.
Makes 9 servings

Note: This recipe can be made a day ahead. Cool, cover and store at room temperature. Reheat in 350°F oven 10 to 15 minutes before serving.

FAVORITE RECIPE FROM **CALIFORNIA PRUNE BOARD**

Chocolate Raspberry Cheesecake

CRUST
- 1½ cups finely crushed chocolate sandwich cookies
- 2 tablespoons butter or margarine, melted

FILLING
- 4 (8-ounce) packages PHILADELPHIA BRAND® Cream Cheese, softened, divided
- ¾ cup sugar
- 1 teaspoon vanilla
- 3 eggs
- ½ cup sour cream
- 6 squares BAKER'S® Semi-Sweet Chocolate, melted, slightly cooled
- ⅓ cup strained red raspberry preserves

TOPPING
- 6 squares BAKER'S® Semi-Sweet Chocolate
- ¼ cup whipping cream

• Heat oven to 325°F.

CRUST
• Mix crumbs and butter; press onto bottom of 9-inch springform pan.

FILLING
• Beat 3 packages cream cheese, sugar and vanilla at medium speed with electric mixer until well blended. Add eggs, 1 at a time, mixing at low speed after each addition, just until blended. Blend in sour cream; pour over crust.

• Beat remaining package cream cheese and 6 squares melted chocolate at medium speed with electric mixer until well blended. Add preserves; mix well. Drop rounded tablespoonfuls of chocolate mixture over plain cream cheese mixture; do not swirl.

• Bake 1 hour and 15 minutes to 1 hour and 20 minutes or until center is almost set. Run knife or metal spatula around rim of pan to loosen cake; cool before removing rim of pan.

TOPPING
• Melt remaining chocolate and whipping cream over low heat, stirring until smooth. Spread over cooled cheesecake. Refrigerate 4 hours or overnight. Garnish with COOL WHIP® Whipped Topping, raspberries and mint leaves.

Makes 12 servings

Prep Time: 30 minutes
Cook Time: 1 hour 20 minutes

Chocolate Turtle Cheesecake

24 chocolate sandwich cookies, ground (about 2¾ cups)
2 tablespoons butter or margarine, melted
2 packages (8 ounces each) cream cheese, softened
⅓ cup sugar
¼ cup sour cream
2 eggs
1 teaspoon vanilla
½ cup prepared caramel sauce
½ cup prepared fudge sauce
½ cup pecan halves

1. Preheat oven to 350°F. Combine ground cookies and butter in medium bowl; pat evenly onto bottom and 1 inch up side of 9-inch springform pan. Place in freezer while preparing filling.

2. Beat cream cheese in large bowl with electric mixer until fluffy. Beat in sugar, sour cream, eggs and vanilla until smooth. Pour mixture into prepared crust.

3. Bake cheesecake 30 to 35 minutes or until almost set in center. Cool on wire rack. Refrigerate, loosely covered, 8 hours or up to 3 days.

4. Remove side of springform pan from cheesecake; place on serving plate. Drizzle caramel and fudge sauces over cake; cut cake into wedges. Top each serving with 2 to 3 pecan halves.   *Makes 12 servings*

Philly 3-Step™ Cheesecake

2 (8-ounce) packages PHILADELPHIA BRAND® Cream Cheese *or* PHILADELPHIA BRAND® Neufchâtel Cheese, ⅓ Less Fat Than Cream Cheese, softened
½ cup sugar
½ teaspoon vanilla
2 eggs
1 ready-to-use graham cracker crumb crust (6 ounces or 9 inches)

1. MIX cream cheese, sugar and vanilla with electric mixer on medium speed until well blended. Add eggs; mix until blended.

2. POUR into crust.

3. BAKE at 350°F, 40 minutes or until center is almost set. Cool. Refrigerate 3 hours or overnight.   *Makes 8 servings*

Prep Time: 10 minutes
Cook Time: 40 minutes

FRUIT TOPPED CHEESECAKE: Top with 2 cups assorted cut-up fruit *or* 1 (21-ounce) can cherry pie filling.

LEMON CHEESECAKE: Stir 1 tablespoon fresh lemon juice and ½ teaspoon grated lemon peel into batter.

CHOCOLATE CHIP CHEESECAKE: Stir ½ cup miniature semisweet chocolate chips into batter. Sprinkle with additional ¼ cup chips before baking.

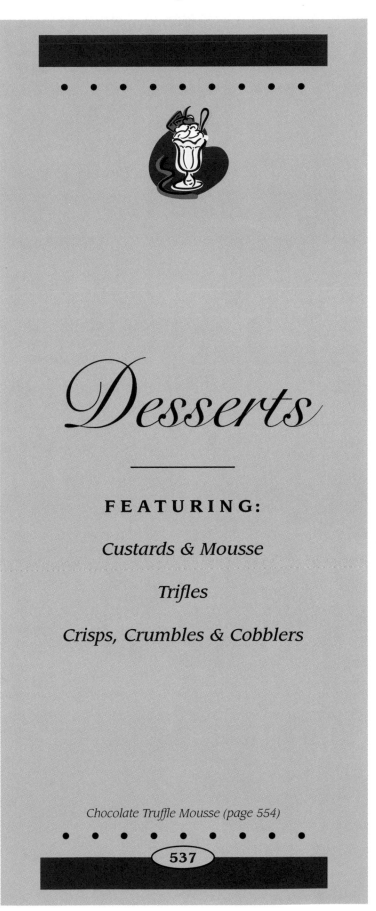

Desserts

FEATURING:

Custards & Mousse

Trifles

Crisps, Crumbles & Cobblers

Chocolate Truffle Mousse (page 554)

Fantasy in Berries

- 1 bag (12 ounces) frozen unsweetened raspberries, thawed
- ¼ cup plus 2 tablespoons sugar, divided
- 1 tablespoon fresh lemon juice
- 2 cups sliced fresh strawberries
- 1 cup fresh raspberries
- 1 cup fresh blueberries
- 1 cup low-fat ricotta cheese
- 1 teaspoon vanilla extract
- ¼ teaspoon almond extract

1. Place thawed frozen raspberries, ¼ cup sugar and lemon juice in blender or food processor; blend until smooth. Pour through strainer to remove seeds. Spoon 3 tablespoons raspberry sauce on each of 8 plates. Tilt each plate, rotating to spread raspberry sauce over bottom of plate.

2. Arrange ¼ cup sliced strawberries, 2 tablespoons fresh raspberries and 2 tablespoons fresh blueberries on top of sauce on each plate.

3. Place cheese, remaining 2 tablespoons sugar and vanilla and almond extracts in clean blender or food processor; blend until smooth and satiny. Spoon cheese mixture into pastry bag and pipe onto berries, using about 2 tablespoons per serving. Garnish with mint sprigs and edible flowers, such as pansies, violets or nasturtiums, if desired.

Makes 8 servings

Apple-Cranberry Crisp

- 1½ cups QUAKER® Oats (quick or old fashioned, uncooked)
- ½ cup firmly packed brown sugar
- ⅓ cup all-purpose flour
- ½ teaspoon ground cinnamon
- ⅓ cup vegetable shortening, melted
- 1 tablespoon water
- 1 can (16 ounces) whole berry cranberry sauce
- 2 tablespoons cornstarch
- 5 cups peeled and thinly sliced apples (about 5 medium)

Preheat oven to 375°F. For topping, combine oats, brown sugar, flour and cinnamon; mix well. Stir in melted shortening and water; mix until crumbly. Set aside.

For filling, combine cranberry sauce and cornstarch in large saucepan; mix well. Heat over medium heat, stirring occasionally, 2 minutes or until sauce bubbles. Add apples, tossing to coat. Spread into 8-inch baking dish. Crumble topping over fruit. Bake 25 to 35 minutes or until apples are tender. Serve warm with whipped cream or ice cream, if desired. *Makes 9 servings*

Fruit Pizza

- 1 (20-ounce) package refrigerated sliceable sugar cookies
- 1 (8-ounce) package PHILADELPHIA BRAND® Cream Cheese, softened
- ⅓ cup sugar
- ½ teaspoon vanilla Assorted fruit
- ½ cup KRAFT® Orange Marmalade, Peach or Apricot Preserves
- 2 tablespoons cold water

- Freeze cookie dough 1 hour.

- Heat oven to 375°F. Slice cookie dough into ⅛-inch slices. Arrange cookie slices, slightly overlapping, on foil-lined 14-inch pizza pan; press lightly to form crust.

- Bake 12 minutes or until golden brown. Cool. Invert onto serving plate; carefully remove foil. Invert onto right side.

- Beat cream cheese, sugar and vanilla in small bowl with electric mixer on medium speed until well blended. Spread over crust.

- Arrange fruit over cream cheese layer. Mix marmalade and water; spoon over fruit. Refrigerate. Cut into wedges.
Makes 10 to 12 servings

Suggested Fruit: *Banana slices, kiwi slices, strawberries, blueberries, raspberries, red or green grape halves, pineapple chunks, maraschino cherry halves, thinly sliced peaches, pears or apples, or mandarin orange segments.*

Fantasy in Berries

Double Dipped Apples

MAZOLA NO STICK®
Corn Oil Cooking
Spray
5 medium apples
5 wooden sticks
1 package (14 ounces)
caramel candies
¼ cup KARO® Light or
Dark Corn Syrup
¾ cup chopped walnuts
1 cup (6 ounces)
semisweet chocolate
chips
1 teaspoon MAZOLA®
Corn Oil

1. Spray small cookie sheet with cooking spray; set aside. Wash and dry apples; insert stick into stem end.

2. In small deep microwavable bowl, microwave caramels and corn syrup at HIGH 3 to 4 minutes or until caramels are melted and smooth, stirring after each minute.

3. Dip apples in hot caramel mixture, turning to coat well. Allow caramel to drip from apples for a few seconds, then scrape excess from bottom of apples. Roll bottom half in walnuts. Place on prepared cookie sheet. Refrigerate at least 15 minutes.

4. In small microwavable bowl, microwave chocolate and corn oil at HIGH 1 to 2 minutes; stir until melted.

5. Drizzle apples with chocolate. Refrigerate 10 minutes or until chocolate is firm. Wrap apples individually; store in refrigerator.

Makes 5 apples

Chocolate Baskets with Berries

4 to 6 ounces semisweet
or bittersweet
chocolate, chopped
1 cup fresh blueberries,
raspberries or sliced
strawberries
2 tablespoons Grand
Marnier, Chambord,
Cointreau or sugar
1 cup frozen raspberry
yogurt or sorbet

1. Invert two 6-ounce custard cups onto baking sheet. Cover each cup with piece of foil, smoothing surface to make sure foil stays in place. Coat foil with nonstick cooking spray.

2. Melt chocolate in small heavy saucepan over low heat. Remove from heat; let stand 10 minutes. Spoon into pastry bag fitted with small writing tip.

3. Slowly drizzle chocolate over each cup. (If chocolate drizzles too fast, let cool. If it becomes too firm, remove from bag and reheat.) Refrigerate 10 minutes. Repeat procedure; refrigerate 1 hour. Carefully remove custard cups and foil from baskets. Store in airtight container in refrigerator until ready to serve.

4. Combine fruit and liqueur in small bowl. Cover and refrigerate until ready to serve.

5. Spoon frozen yogurt into chocolate baskets on serving plates. Spoon fruit mixture evenly over yogurt and around chocolate baskets.

Makes 2 servings

Chocolate Plunge

⅔ cup KARO® Light or
Dark Corn Syrup
½ cup heavy cream
8 squares (1 ounce each)
semisweet chocolate
Assorted fresh fruit

1. In medium saucepan, combine corn syrup and cream. Bring to a boil over medium heat. Remove from heat.

2. Add chocolate; stir until completely melted.

3. Serve warm as a dip for fruit. *Makes 1½ cups*

Prep Time: 10 minutes

MICROWAVE DIRECTIONS: IN MEDIUM MICROWAVABLE BOWL, COMBINE CORN SYRUP AND CREAM. MICROWAVE AT HIGH 1½ MINUTES OR UNTIL BOILING. ADD CHOCOLATE; STIR UNTIL COMPLETELY MELTED. SERVE AS DIRECTED.

Note: Chocolate Plunge can be made a day ahead. Store covered in refrigerator. Reheat before serving.

Tip: Try some of these "dippers": candied pineapple, dried apricots, waffle squares, ladyfingers, cubed pound cake, macaroons, pretzels, croissants, mint cookies or peanut butter cookies.

Brownie Baked Alaskas

2 purchased brownies (2½ inches square)
2 scoops fudge swirl ice cream (or favorite flavor)
⅓ cup semisweet chocolate chips
2 tablespoons light corn syrup or milk
2 egg whites
¼ cup sugar

1. Preheat oven to 500°F. Place brownies on small cookie sheet; top each with scoop of ice cream and place in freezer.

2. Melt chocolate chips in small saucepan over low heat. Stir in corn syrup; set aside and keep warm.

3. Beat egg whites to soft peaks in small bowl. Gradually beat in sugar; continue beating until stiff peaks form. Spread egg white mixture over ice cream and brownies with small spatula (ice cream and brownies should be completely covered with egg white mixture).

4. Bake 2 to 3 minutes or until meringue is golden. Spread chocolate sauce on serving plates; place baked Alaskas over sauce.   *Makes 2 servings*

Cherry-Chocolate Crumble

1½ cups graham cracker crumbs
3 tablespoons sugar
¼ cup Prune Purée (page 434) or prepared prune butter
¼ cup semisweet miniature chocolate chips
2 cans (20 ounces each) cherry pie filling

Preheat oven to 375°F. In medium bowl, mix crumbs and sugar. Cut in prune purée with pastry blender until mixture resembles coarse crumbs. Mix in chocolate chips. Spread pie filling evenly in 8-inch square baking dish or pan; cover evenly with crumb mixture. Bake in center of oven about 20 minutes or until cherries are bubbly and topping is lightly browned. Cool on wire rack 15 minutes. Serve warm, topped with fat-free vanilla frozen yogurt, if desired.

Makes 8 servings

*FAVORITE RECIPE FROM **CALIFORNIA PRUNE BOARD***

Double Dipped Apples (page 540)

Fresh Berry Pizza

**Ginger Cookie Crust
(recipe follows)**
**1 ½ cups fat-free ricotta
cheese**
3 tablespoons sugar
1 tablespoon lemon juice
**2 teaspoons grated lemon
peel**
1 pint fresh raspberries
½ pint fresh blueberries

1. Prepare Ginger Cookie Crust; cool. Gently slide onto flat serving platter or board.

2. Combine cheese, sugar, lemon juice and lemon peel in medium bowl. Stir until smooth. Spread evenly over crust leaving ½- to 1-inch border. Arrange raspberries and blueberries on top. Serve, or cover with plastic wrap and refrigerate up to 6 hours. Cut into 8 wedges. Garnish as desired. *Makes 8 servings*

GINGER COOKIE CRUST
35 vanilla wafers
20 gingersnaps
1 egg white, lightly beaten

1. Preheat oven to 375°F. Combine vanilla wafers and gingersnaps in food processor or blender; process until coarse crumbs form. Transfer to medium bowl. Stir egg white into crumbs until evenly mixed.

2. Spray 12- to 14-inch pizza pan with nonstick cooking spray. Press crumb mixture evenly into pan. Bake on center rack in oven 8 to 10 minutes or until firm and lightly browned. Cool in pan.
*Makes 1 (12- to 14-inch)
crust (8 servings)*

Apple Cobbler

1 ½ cups all-purpose flour
**⅓ cup plus 1 tablespoon
sugar, divided**
**2 teaspoons baking
powder**
1 teaspoon baking soda
**1 teaspoon ground
cinnamon, divided**
½ teaspoon salt
**3 tablespoons Prune
Purée (page 434) or
prepared prune butter**
**1 tablespoon cold butter
or margarine**
¾ cup nonfat milk
**1 can (21 ounces) apple
pie filling**

Preheat oven to 400°F. In large bowl, mix flour, ⅓ cup sugar, baking powder, baking soda, ½ teaspoon cinnamon and salt. Cut in prune purée and butter with pastry blender until mixture resembles coarse crumbs. Mix in milk just until blended. Spread pie filling evenly in 8-inch square baking dish or pan. Spoon batter over pie filling in 6 equal mounds. Combine remaining 1 tablespoon sugar and ½ teaspoon cinnamon; sprinkle over batter. Bake in center of oven about 35 minutes or until top is baked through and springy to the touch. Serve with fat-free vanilla ice cream, if desired.
Makes 6 servings

*FAVORITE RECIPE FROM **CALIFORNIA
PRUNE BOARD***

Fresh Berry
Cobbler Cake

**1 pint fresh berries
(blueberries,
blackberries,
raspberries and/or
strawberries)**
1 cup all-purpose flour
1 ¼ cups sugar, divided
1 teaspoon baking powder
¼ teaspoon salt
**3 tablespoons butter or
margarine**
½ cup milk
1 tablespoon cornstarch
**1 cup cold water
Additional berries
(optional)**

Preheat oven to 375°F. Place 1 pint berries in 9×9-inch baking pan; set aside. Combine flour, ½ cup sugar, baking powder and salt in large bowl. Cut in butter with pastry blender or two knives until coarse crumbs form. Stir in milk. Spoon over berries. Combine remaining ¾ cup sugar and cornstarch in small bowl. Stir in water until sugar mixture dissolves; pour over berry mixture. Bake 35 to 40 minutes or until lightly browned. Serve warm or cool completely. Garnish with additional berries, if desired.
Makes 6 servings

*FAVORITE RECIPE FROM **BOB EVANS
FARMS**®*

Fresh Berry Pizza

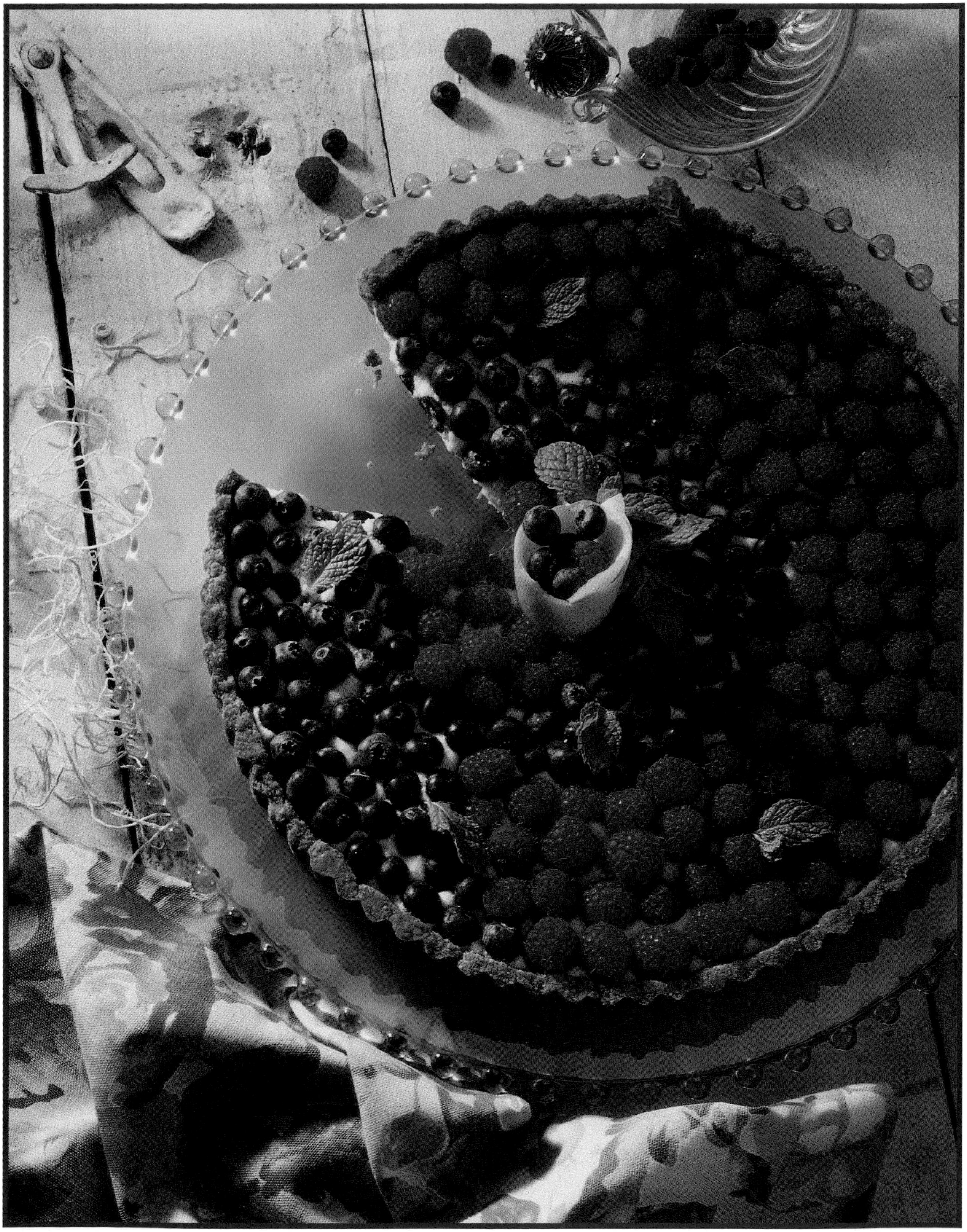

Tempting Apple Trifles

½ cup skim milk
1½ teaspoons cornstarch
4½ teaspoons dark brown sugar
1 egg white
½ teaspoon canola oil
½ teaspoon vanilla
½ teaspoon rum extract, divided
¼ cup unsweetened apple cider, divided
2 tablespoons raisins
½ teaspoon ground cinnamon
1 cup peeled and chopped Golden Delicious apple
1 cup ½-inch angel food cake cubes, divided

To prepare custard, combine milk and cornstarch in small heavy saucepan; stir until cornstarch is completely dissolved. Add brown sugar, egg white and oil; blend well. Slowly bring to a boil over medium-low heat until thickened, stirring constantly with whisk. Remove from heat; stir in vanilla and ¼ teaspoon rum extract. Set aside; cool completely.

Combine 2 tablespoons cider, raisins and cinnamon in medium saucepan; bring to a boil over medium-low heat. Add apple and cook until apple is fork-tender and all liquid has been absorbed, stirring frequently. Remove from heat; set aside to cool.

To assemble, place ¼ cup cake cubes in bottom of 2 small trifle or dessert dishes. Combine remaining 2 tablespoons cider and ¼ teaspoon rum extract in small bowl; mix well. Spoon 1½ teaspoons cider mixture over cake in each dish. Top each with ¼ of custard mixture and ¼ cup cooked apple mixture. Repeat layers. Serve immediately. Garnish with fresh mint, if desired.

Makes 2 servings

Apple Cranberry Buckle

6 medium Granny Smith apples, peeled, cored and thinly sliced
¾ cup dried cranberries or dried cherries
⅓ cup orange juice
⅔ cup packed light brown sugar
1½ cups plus 2 tablespoons all-purpose flour, divided
1¼ teaspoons ground cinnamon
¼ teaspoon ground cloves
¾ cup plus 1 teaspoon granulated sugar, divided
1½ teaspoons baking powder
1 egg
⅓ cup milk
¼ cup margarine or butter, melted
1 cup apple butter
2 tablespoons amaretto liqueur (optional)
Mint leaves (optional)

PREHEAT oven to 375°F. Place apples and cranberries in 11×7-inch baking dish. Drizzle orange juice over fruit.

COMBINE brown sugar, 2 tablespoons flour, cinnamon and cloves in small bowl. Pour over apple mixture; toss to coat.

COMBINE remaining 1½ cups flour, ¾ cup granulated sugar and baking powder in medium bowl. Add egg, milk and margarine; stir with mixing spoon to blend. Drop tablespoonfuls over top of apple mixture.

SPRINKLE remaining 1 teaspoon granulated sugar over topping. Bake 35 minutes or until topping is lightly browned and apples are tender. Cool buckle slightly in pan on wire rack.

COMBINE apple butter and liqueur, if desired, in small microwavable bowl. Microwave at HIGH 1 minute or until warm. Spoon 1 to 2 tablespoonfuls sauce over each serving. Garnish with mint leaves, if desired.   *Makes 8 servings*

Berry Delicious Trifles

1 package (4-serving size) instant vanilla pudding and pie filling mix
2¼ cups milk
1 cup sliced strawberries
1 cup raspberries
1 cup blueberries
1 frozen pound cake (10¾ ounces), thawed
2 tablespoons orange-flavored liqueur or orange juice
¼ cup orange marmalade
Sweetened whipped cream and mint leaves (optional)

BEAT pudding mix and milk in medium bowl with electric mixer at low speed 2 minutes; set aside. Combine strawberries, raspberries and blueberries in medium bowl; set aside.

SLICE cake into 12 slices, each about ½ inch wide. Brush one side of each piece with liqueur; spread marmalade over liqueur.

CUT cake slices in half lengthwise. Place 4 pieces of cake each against side of 6 martini or parfait glasses with marmalade side toward center of glass.

PLACE ¼ cup berries in bottom of each glass; top each with heaping ⅓ cup pudding mix and then ¼ cup berries. Refrigerate 30 minutes. Garnish with sweetened whipped cream and mint leaves, if desired.

Makes 6 servings

Poached Pears with Raspberry Sauce

4 cups cran-raspberry juice cocktail
2 cups Rhine or Riesling wine
¼ cup sugar
2 cinnamon sticks, broken into halves
4 to 5 firm Bosc or Anjou pears, peeled, cored and seeded
1 package (10 ounces) frozen raspberries in syrup, thawed
Fresh berries (optional)

Slow Cooker Directions:
COMBINE juice, wine, sugar and cinnamon stick halves in slow cooker. Submerge pears in mixture. Cover and cook on LOW 3½ to 4 hours or until pears are tender. Remove and discard cinnamon sticks.

PROCESS raspberries in food processor or blender until smooth; strain out seeds. Spoon raspberry sauce onto serving plates; place pear on top of sauce. Garnish with fresh berries, if desired.

Makes 4 to 5 servings

Berry Delicious Trifle

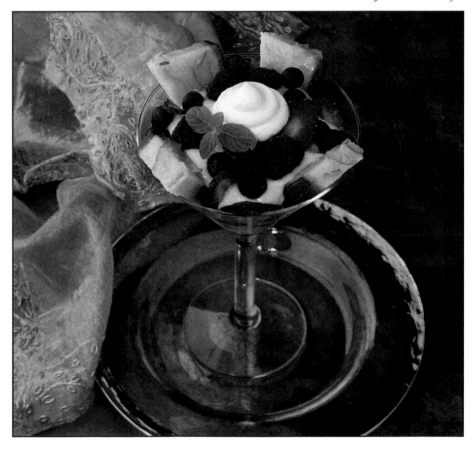

Blue-Ribbon Apricot Dessert

12 ounces dried apricots
2 cups water
1 cup sugar, divided
2 cups all-purpose flour
¼ cup cold margarine
2 cups rolled oats
½ teaspoon baking soda
½ cup Prune Purée (page 434) or prepared prune butter *or* 2 jars (2½ ounces each) first-stage baby food prunes
1 egg
1 teaspoon vanilla

In heavy 2- to 3-quart saucepan, bring apricots and water to a boil over medium-high heat. Reduce heat to low; cover and simmer, stirring occasionally, until apricots are tender, about 40 minutes. Strain apricots in sieve, reserving ¼ cup liquid. Cool. In food processor fitted with metal blade, purée drained apricots, reserved ¼ cup liquid and ¼ cup sugar until smooth; set aside. Preheat oven to 375°F. In large bowl, place flour. Cut in margarine with pastry blender until mixture resembles coarse crumbs. Stir in oats, baking soda and remaining ¾ cup sugar. In small bowl, mix prune purée, egg and vanilla until smooth; mix into oat mixture until mixture is moist and crumbly. Coat 13×9×2-inch baking pan with vegetable cooking spray.

Press 3 cups crumb mixture firmly into bottom of pan. Bake in center of oven 10 minutes or until golden brown. Spread apricot mixture evenly over hot crust. Sprinkle remaining crumb mixture evenly over filling and pat gently. Bake in center of oven 20 to 25 minutes or until golden brown. Cool in pan on wire rack. Cut into bars. Serve warm or at room temperature.

Makes 16 servings

FAVORITE RECIPE FROM **CALIFORNIA PRUNE BOARD**

Summertime Fruit Medley

2 large ripe peaches, peeled and sliced
2 large ripe nectarines, sliced
1 large mango, peeled and cut into 1-inch chunks
1 cup blueberries
2 cups orange juice
¼ cup amaretto *or* ½ teaspoon almond extract
2 tablespoons sugar

1. Combine peaches, nectarines, mango and blueberries in large bowl.

2. Whisk orange juice, amaretto and sugar in small bowl until sugar is dissolved. Pour over fruit mixture; toss. Marinate 1 hour at room temperature, gently stirring occasionally. Garnish with mint, if desired.

Makes 8 servings

Baked Apple Crisp

8 cups thinly sliced unpeeled apples (about 8 medium)
2 tablespoons granulated sugar
4½ teaspoons lemon juice
4 teaspoons ground cinnamon, divided
1½ cups MOTT'S® Natural Apple Sauce
1 cup uncooked rolled oats
½ cup firmly packed light brown sugar
⅓ cup all-purpose flour
⅓ cup evaporated skimmed milk
¼ cup nonfat dry milk powder
1 cup vanilla nonfat yogurt

1. Preheat oven to 350°F. Spray 2-quart casserole with nonstick cooking spray.

2. In large bowl, toss apple slices with granulated sugar, lemon juice and 2 teaspoons cinnamon. Spoon into prepared dish. Spread apple sauce evenly over apple mixture.

3. In medium bowl, combine oats, brown sugar, flour, evaporated milk, dry milk powder and remaining 2 teaspoons cinnamon. Spread over apple sauce.

4. Bake 35 to 40 minutes or until lightly browned and bubbly. Cool slightly; serve warm. Top each serving with dollop of yogurt.

Makes 12 servings

Banana Caramel Shortcake

1 ½ **cups all-purpose flour**
⅓ **cup sugar**
2 **teaspoons baking powder**
½ **teaspoon baking soda**
½ **teaspoon salt**
½ **teaspoon ground nutmeg**
3 **tablespoons Prune Purée (page 434) or prepared prune butter**
1 **tablespoon cold butter or margarine**
1 **container (8 ounces) plain nonfat yogurt**
4 **ripe bananas, sliced**
1 **cup prepared fat-free caramel sauce**
1 **cup low-fat nondairy whipped topping**
Additional low-fat nondairy whipped topping (optional)
8 **teaspoons toasted slivered almonds**

Preheat oven to 400°F. Coat baking sheet with vegetable cooking spray. In large bowl, mix flour, sugar, baking powder, baking soda, salt and nutmeg. Cut in prune purée and butter with pastry blender until mixture resembles coarse crumbs. Mix in yogurt just until blended.

Spoon onto baking sheet in 8 equal mounds. Bake in center of oven about 20 minutes or until lightly browned and springy to the touch. Remove from baking sheet to wire rack to cool. To serve, cut each shortcake horizontally into halves; place bottom half on serving plate. Cover each with ¹⁄₁₆ of banana slices, 1 tablespoon caramel sauce, 2 tablespoons whipped topping, remaining shortcake half, ¹⁄₁₆ of banana slices and 1 tablespoon caramel sauce. Dollop with 2 tablespoons whipped topping, if desired. Sprinkle with 1 teaspoon almonds.

Makes 8 servings

FAVORITE RECIPE FROM **CALIFORNIA PRUNE BOARD**

Spiced Apple & Cranberry Compote

2 ½ **cups cranberry juice cocktail**
1 **package (6 ounces) dried apples**
½ **cup (2 ounces) dried cranberries**
½ **cup Rhine wine or apple juice**
½ **cup honey**
2 **cinnamon sticks, broken into halves**
Frozen yogurt or ice cream (optional)
Additional cinnamon sticks (optional)

Slow Cooker Instructions:
MIX juice, apples, cranberries, wine, honey and cinnamon stick halves in slow cooker. Cover and cook on LOW 4 to 5 hours or until liquid is absorbed and fruit is tender. Remove and discard cinnamon stick halves. Ladle compote into bowls. Serve warm, at room temperature or chilled with scoop of frozen yogurt or ice cream and garnish with additional cinnamon sticks, if desired. *Makes 6 servings*

Swedish Apple Nut Strip

1 ½ **cups all-purpose flour**
3 **tablespoons sugar, divided**
½ **teaspoon salt**
½ **cup margarine**
1 **egg, lightly beaten**
1 **cup MOTT'S® Cinnamon Apple Sauce**
¼ **cup finely chopped walnuts**
1 **teaspoon ground cinnamon**

Preheat oven to 375°F. In bowl, mix flour, 2 tablespoons sugar and salt; cut in margarine until mixture is crumbly. Stir in egg; shape dough into ball. Cover; refrigerate 15 minutes. Divide dough in half. On lightly greased baking sheet, shape each half into 10×2-inch rectangle. Make a 1-inch-wide indentation down center length of each rectangle; fill each with ½ cup apple sauce. Mix remaining 1 tablespoon sugar, walnuts and cinnamon; sprinkle on dough along sides of apple sauce filling. Bake 20 minutes. Cool slightly on wire rack. Cut into 1-inch diagonal slices. Cool completely. Store in airtight container. *Makes 20 bars*

Apple Strudel

- 1 sheet (½ of a 17¼-ounce package) frozen puff pastry
- 1 cup (4 ounces) shredded ALPINE LACE® Reduced Sodium Muenster Cheese
- 2 large Granny Smith apples, peeled, cored and sliced ⅛ inch thick (12 ounces)
- ⅓ cup golden raisins
- 2 tablespoons apple brandy (optional)
- ¼ cup granulated sugar
- ¼ cup packed light brown sugar
- ½ teaspoon ground cinnamon
- 2 tablespoons unsalted butter substitute, melted

1. To shape the pastry: Thaw the pastry for 20 minutes. Preheat the oven to 350°F. On a floured board, roll the pastry into a 15×12-inch rectangle.

2. To make the filling: Sprinkle the cheese on the dough, leaving a 1-inch border. Arrange the apples on top. Sprinkle with the raisins, then the brandy, if you wish. In a small cup, mix both of the sugars with the cinnamon, then sprinkle over the apple filling.

3. Starting from one of the wide ends, roll up jelly-roll style. Place on a baking sheet, seam side down, tucking the ends under. Using a sharp knife, make 7 diagonal slits on the top, then brush with the butter. Bake for 35 minutes or until golden brown.

Makes 18 servings

Cinnamon-Spice Apple Crisp

- 1½ pounds tart baking apples
- 2 tablespoons granulated sugar
- 1 tablespoon lemon juice
- ⅔ cup packed light brown sugar
- ½ cup all-purpose flour
- ⅓ cup quick-cooking oats
- ½ teaspoon ground cinnamon
- ¼ teaspoon ground nutmeg
- ¼ teaspoon ground ginger
- ¼ teaspoon ground mace
- 5 tablespoons cold margarine, cut into pieces

1. Preheat oven to 375°F.

2. Mix apples, granulated sugar and lemon juice in large bowl; arrange in ungreased 1½-quart glass casserole.

3. Combine brown sugar, flour, oats, cinnamon, nutmeg, ginger and mace in medium bowl. Cut in margarine with pastry blender or 2 knives until mixture resembles coarse crumbs. Sprinkle brown sugar mixture over apples.

4. Bake, uncovered, about 30 minutes or until apples are tender and topping is golden. Serve warm with frozen yogurt, if desired. Sprinkle with additional ground cinnamon, if desired. *Makes 6 servings*

Cranberry-Walnut Pear Wedges

- 3 firm ripe pears
- ¼ cup triple sec*
- 2 tablespoons orange juice
- ½ cup prepared cranberry fruit relish
- ¼ cup finely chopped walnuts
- ¼ cup (1 ounce) crumbled blue cheese

*Omit liqueur, if desired. Increase orange juice to ¼ cup. Add 2 tablespoons honey and 2 tablespoons balsamic vinegar to marinade.

1. Cut each pear lengthwise into quarters. Using a melon ball scoop, grapefruit spoon or sharp knife, remove cores.

2. Place pears in resealable plastic food storage bag. Pour triple sec and orange juice over pears; seal bag. Turn bag over several times to coat pears evenly. Refrigerate at least 1 hour, turning bag occasionally.

3. Drain pears; discard marinade. Place pears on serving platter. Spoon cranberry relish evenly into cavities in pears; sprinkle with walnuts and cheese. Garnish, if desired.

Makes 12 servings

Almond-Pear Strudel

5 to 6 cups thinly sliced crisp pears (about 5)
1 tablespoon grated lemon peel
1 tablespoon lemon juice
⅓ cup plus 1 teaspoon sugar, divided
2 teaspoons ground cinnamon
1 teaspoon ground nutmeg
6 sheets (¼ pound) phyllo dough
4 tablespoons melted butter or margarine, divided
½ teaspoon almond extract
¾ cup slivered almonds, toasted, divided

1. Place sliced pears in large microwavable container. Stir in lemon peel and lemon juice. Microwave at HIGH 6 minutes or until tender; cool. Combine ⅓ cup sugar, cinnamon and nutmeg in small bowl; cover. Cover pears and refrigerate overnight.

2. Lay 2 sheets of plastic wrap on work surface to make 20-inch square. Place 1 phyllo sheet in middle of plastic wrap. (Cover remaining dough with damp kitchen towel to prevent drying.) Brush 1 teaspoon melted butter onto phyllo sheet. Place second phyllo sheet over first; brush with 1 teaspoon butter. Repeat layering with remaining sheets of phyllo.

Cover phyllo and remaining butter with plastic wrap. Refrigerate overnight or up to 1 day.

3. To complete recipe, preheat oven to 400°F. Drain reserved pears; toss with reserved sugar mixture and almond extract. Melt reserved butter. Uncover phyllo dough. Spread pear mixture evenly over phyllo leaving 3-inch strip on far long side. Sprinkle pear mixture with ½ cup toasted almonds. Brush strip with 2 teaspoons melted butter.

4. Beginning at long side of phyllo opposite strip, roll up jelly-roll style, forming strudel. Place seam-side down onto buttered baking sheet. Brush top with 1 teaspoon butter. Bake 20 minutes or until golden. Brush with 1 teaspoon butter. Stir remaining ¼ cup almonds and 1 teaspoon sugar with remaining butter; sprinkle on top of strudel. Bake 5 minutes more. Cool 10 minutes; sprinkle with powdered sugar, if desired.

Makes 8 servings

Cranberry-Walnut Pear Wedge
(page 548)

Tiramisu

2 packages (3 ounces each) ladyfingers, thawed if frozen, split in half horizontally
¾ cup brewed espresso*
2 tablespoons coffee liqueur or brandy (optional)
1 package (8 ounces) cream cheese, softened
2 tablespoons sugar
⅓ cup sour cream
½ cup whipping cream
2 tablespoons unsweetened cocoa powder, divided
Chocolate curls and mint leaves (optional)

Use fresh brewed espresso, instant espresso powder prepared according to directions on jar or 2 teaspoons instant coffee powder dissolved in ¾ cup hot water.

PLACE ladyfingers on baking sheet, uncovered, 8 hours or overnight to dry. Or dry ladyfingers by placing on microwavable plate. Microwave at MEDIUM-HIGH (70% power) 1 minute; turn ladyfingers over. Microwave at MEDIUM-HIGH 1 to 1½ minutes or until dry.

COMBINE espresso and liqueur, if desired, in small bowl. Dip half the ladyfingers in espresso mixture; place in bottom of 2-quart serving bowl.

BEAT cream cheese and sugar with electric mixer at medium speed until fluffy; add sour cream, beating until blended. Add whipping cream, beating until smooth. Spread half the cheese mixture over ladyfingers.

PLACE 1 tablespoon cocoa in fine strainer. Lightly tap rim of strainer and dust cocoa over cheese layer.

DIP remaining ladyfingers in espresso mixture. Place over cheese mixture in serving bowl.

SPREAD remaining cheese mixture over ladyfingers. Dust remaining 1 tablespoon cocoa over cheese layer. Refrigerate, covered, 4 hours or overnight. Garnish with chocolate curls and mint leaves, if desired.

Makes 6 servings

Steamed Southern Sweet Potato Custard

1 can (16 ounces) cut sweet potatoes, drained
1 can (12 ounces) evaporated milk, divided
½ cup packed brown sugar
2 eggs, lightly beaten
1 teaspoon ground cinnamon
½ teaspoon ground ginger
¼ teaspoon salt
Whipped cream (optional)
Ground nutmeg (optional)

Slow Cooker Directions:
PROCESS sweet potatoes with about ¼ cup milk in food processor or blender until smooth. Add remaining milk, brown sugar, eggs, cinnamon, ginger and salt; process until well mixed. Pour into ungreased 1-quart soufflé dish. Cover tightly with foil. Crumple large sheet (about 15×12 inches) of foil; place in bottom of slow cooker. Pour 2 cups water over foil. Make foil handles* and place soufflé dish on top of foil strips.

TRANSFER dish to slow cooker using foil handles; lay foil strips over top of dish. Cover and cook on HIGH 2½ to 3 hours or until skewer inserted into center comes out clean. Using foil strips, lift dish from slow cooker and transfer to wire rack. Uncover; let stand 30 minutes. Garnish with whipped cream and nutmeg, if desired.
Makes 4 servings

To make foil handles, tear off three 18×3-inch strips of heavy-duty foil. Crisscross the strips so they resemble the spokes of a wheel. Place the dish or food in the center of the strips. Pull the foil strips up and over and place into the slow cooker. Leave them in while cooking so you can easily lift the item out again when ready.

Tiramisu

Cold Cherry Mousse with Vanilla Sauce

- 1 envelope whipped topping mix
- ½ cup skim milk
- ½ teaspoon vanilla extract
- 2 envelopes unflavored gelatin
- ½ cup sugar
- ½ cup cold water
- 1 package (16 ounces) frozen unsweetened cherries, thawed, undrained and divided
- 1 tablespoon fresh lemon juice
- ½ teaspoon almond extract
  Vanilla Sauce (recipe follows)

Prepare whipped topping according to package directions using milk and vanilla; set aside. Combine gelatin and sugar in small saucepan; stir in water. Let stand 5 minutes to soften. Heat over low heat until gelatin is completely dissolved. Cool to room temperature. Set aside 1 cup cherries without juice for garnish. Place remaining cherries and juice in blender. Add lemon juice, almond extract and gelatin mixture; process until blended. Fold cherry purée into whipped topping. Pour mixture into Bundt pan or ring mold. Refrigerate 4 hours or overnight until jelled.

To serve, unmold mousse onto large serving plate. Spoon remaining 1 cup cherries into center of mousse. Serve with Vanilla Sauce.

Makes 6 servings

VANILLA SAUCE

- 4½ teaspoons cherry brandy *or* 1 teaspoon vanilla extract *plus* ½ teaspoon cherry extract
- ¾ cup melted vanilla ice milk or low-fat ice cream, cooled

Stir brandy into ice milk in small bowl; blend well.

Makes ¾ cup

Strawberry Miracle Mold

- 1½ cups boiling water
- 2 packages (4-serving size) JELL-O® Brand Strawberry Flavor Gelatin
- 1¾ cups cold water
- ½ cup MIRACLE WHIP® Salad Dressing
  Assorted fruit

Stir boiling water into gelatin in medium bowl 2 minutes until dissolved. Stir in cold water. Gradually whisk gelatin into salad dressing in large bowl until well blended.

Pour into 1-quart mold or glass serving bowl that has been lightly sprayed with non-stick cooking spray. Refrigerate 2 hours until firm. Unmold onto serving plate. Serve with fruit.

Makes 4 to 6 servings

Prep Time: 10 minutes plus refrigerating

Crème Caramel

- ½ cup sugar, divided
- 1 tablespoon hot water
- 2 cups skim milk
- ⅛ teaspoon salt
- ½ cup cholesterol-free egg substitute
- ½ teaspoon vanilla
- ⅛ teaspoon maple extract

Heat ¼ cup sugar in heavy saucepan over low heat, stirring constantly until melted and straw colored. Remove from heat; stir in water. Return to heat; stir 5 minutes or until mixture is dark caramel color. Divide melted sugar evenly among 6 custard cups. Set aside.

Preheat oven to 350°F. Combine milk, remaining ¼ cup sugar and salt in medium bowl. Add egg substitute, vanilla and maple extract; mix well. Pour ½ cup mixture into each custard cup. Place cups in heavy baking pan and pour 1 to 2 inches hot water into pan.

Bake 40 to 45 minutes or until knife inserted near edge of each cup comes out clean. Cool on wire rack. Refrigerate 4 hours or overnight. Before serving, run knife around edge of custard cup. Invert custard onto serving plate; remove cup.

Makes 6 servings

Color-Bright Ice Cream Sandwiches

¾ cup butter, softened
¾ cup creamy peanut
    butter
1¼ cups firmly packed light
    brown sugar
1 large egg
1 teaspoon vanilla extract
1½ cups all-purpose flour
1 teaspoon baking soda
¼ teaspoon salt
1¾ cups "M&M's"®
    Chocolate Mini Baking
    Bits, divided
2 quarts vanilla or
    chocolate ice cream,
    slightly softened

Preheat oven to 350°F. In large bowl, cream butter, peanut butter and sugar until light and fluffy; beat in egg and vanilla. In medium bowl, combine flour, baking soda and salt; blend into creamed mixture. Stir in 1⅓ cups "M&M's"® Chocolate Mini Baking Bits. Shape dough into 1¼-inch balls. Place about 2 inches apart on ungreased cookie sheets. Gently flatten to about ½-inch thickness with fingertips. Place 7 or 8 of the remaining "M&M's"® Chocolate Mini Baking Bits on each cookie; press in lightly. Bake 10 to 12 minutes or until edges are light brown. *Do not overbake.* Cool about 1 minute on cookie sheets; cool completely on wire racks. Assemble cookies in pairs with about ⅓ cup ice cream; press cookies together lightly. Wrap each sandwich in plastic wrap; freeze until firm.

Makes about 24 sandwiches

Apricot Foster Sundae

1 can (15¼ ounces) DEL
    MONTE® Unpeeled
    Apricot Halves in
    Heavy Syrup,
    undrained
⅓ cup firmly packed brown
    sugar
2 tablespoons butter or
    margarine
1 pint vanilla ice cream

1. Drain apricot syrup into small saucepan. Bring to a boil. Reduce heat to medium-low; simmer 4 minutes.

2. Stir in brown sugar and butter; cook until thickened, stirring constantly. Add apricots; heat through. Spoon over scoops of vanilla ice cream.

Makes 4 servings

Prep & Cook Time: 7 minutes

Color-Bright Ice Cream Sandwiches

Chocolate Truffle Mousse

1 cup whipping cream, divided
1 egg yolk
2 tablespoons corn syrup
2 tablespoons margarine or butter
4 squares (1 ounce each) semisweet chocolate, coarsely chopped
4 squares (1 ounce each) milk chocolate, coarsely chopped
5 teaspoons powdered sugar
½ teaspoon vanilla
  Sweetened whipped cream, fresh raspberries and mint leaves (optional)

WHISK ½ cup cream, egg yolk, corn syrup and margarine in medium heavy saucepan over medium heat until mixture simmers. Continue whisking while mixture simmers 2 minutes. Remove from heat; add chocolates, stirring until smooth. Cool to room temperature.

BEAT remaining ½ cup cream in medium bowl with electric mixer at high speed until soft peaks form. Add powdered sugar and vanilla; beat until stiff peaks form.

STIR whipped cream into chocolate mixture. Pour into medium serving bowl. Chill 4 hours or overnight. Garnish with sweetened whipped cream, fresh strawberries and mint leaves, if desired.

Makes 6 servings

Bavarian Rice Cloud with Bittersweet Chocolate Sauce

1 envelope unflavored gelatin
1½ cups skim milk
3 tablespoons sugar
2 cups cooked rice
2 cups frozen light whipped topping, thawed
1 tablespoon almond-flavored liqueur
½ teaspoon vanilla extract
  Vegetable cooking spray
  Bittersweet Chocolate Sauce (recipe follows)
2 tablespoons sliced almonds, toasted

Sprinkle gelatin over milk in small saucepan; let stand 1 minute or until gelatin is softened. Cook over low heat, stirring constantly, until gelatin dissolves. Add sugar and stir until dissolved. Add rice; stir until well blended. Cover and chill until the consistency of unbeaten egg whites. Fold in whipped topping, liqueur and vanilla. Spoon into 4-cup mold coated with cooking spray. Cover and chill until firm. Unmold onto serving platter. Spoon Bittersweet Chocolate Sauce over rice dessert. Sprinkle with almonds.

Makes 10 servings

BITTERSWEET CHOCOLATE SAUCE

3 tablespoons cocoa
3 tablespoons sugar
½ cup low-fat buttermilk
1 tablespoon almond-flavored liqueur

Combine cocoa and sugar in small saucepan. Add buttermilk, mixing well. Place over medium heat; cook until sugar dissolves. Stir in liqueur; remove from heat.

FAVORITE RECIPE FROM **USA RICE FEDERATION**

Brownie Berry Parfaits

1 box (10 ounces) BIRDS EYE® frozen Raspberries*
4 large prepared brownies, cut into cubes
1 pint vanilla or chocolate ice cream
4 tablespoons chocolate syrup
2 tablespoons chopped walnuts

Or, substitute BIRDS EYE® frozen Strawberries.

• Thaw raspberries according to package directions.

• Divide half the brownie cubes among four parfait glasses. Top with half the ice cream and raspberries. Repeat layers with remaining brownie cubes, ice cream and raspberries.

• Drizzle chocolate syrup over each dessert; sprinkle with walnuts. *Makes 4 servings*

Brownie Berry Parfaits

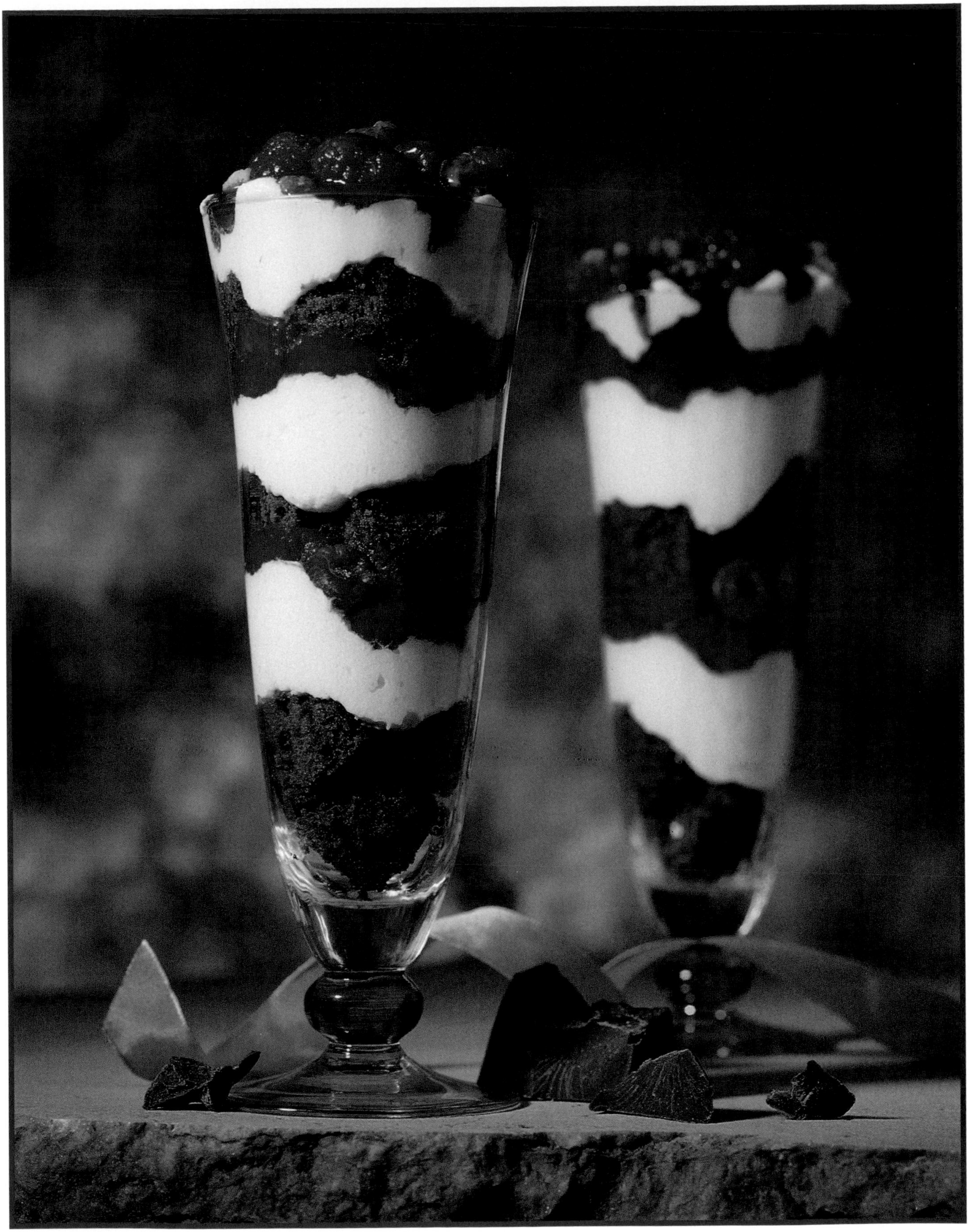

Black Forest Parfaits

- 1 package (8 ounces)
  PHILADELPHIA
  BRAND® Cream
  Cheese, softened
- 2 cups cold milk
- 1 package (4-serving size)
  JELL-O® Chocolate
  Flavor Instant Pudding
  & Pie Filling
- 1 can (21 ounces) cherry
  pie filling
- 1 tablespoon cherry
  liqueur
- ½ cup chocolate wafer
  cookie crumbs

BEAT cream cheese with ½ cup milk at low speed until smooth. Add pudding mix and remaining milk. Beat until smooth, 1 to 2 minutes.

MIX cherry pie filling and liqueur. Reserve a few cherries for garnish, if desired. Spoon ½ of pudding mixture evenly into individual dessert dishes; sprinkle with cookie crumbs. Top with pie filling, then with remaining pudding mixture. Refrigerate until ready to serve. Garnish with reserved cherries and additional cookie crumbs, if desired.

Makes 4 to 6 servings

Rich Chocolate Pudding

- ⅔ cup sugar
- ¼ cup unsweetened cocoa
- 3 tablespoons cornstarch
- 2 cups 2% milk
- 1 egg
- ½ teaspoon vanilla
- 1 tablespoon butter or
  margarine

1. Combine sugar, cocoa and cornstarch in medium saucepan; whisk in milk. Cook over medium-high heat, stirring frequently, until mixture boils; boil 1 minute, stirring constantly.

2. Beat egg in small bowl. Whisk about ½ cup hot milk mixture into egg; whisk egg mixture back into saucepan. Cook over medium heat 2 minutes, stirring constantly.

3. Remove pudding from heat; stir in vanilla and butter. Pour into serving dishes. Serve warm or cover and refrigerate until ready to serve.

Makes 4 servings

RICH MOCHA PUDDING: Add 1 to 1½ teaspoons instant coffee crystals to sugar mixture in step 1.

Funky Devil's Fudge Sauce

- 1 can (14 ounces)
  sweetened condensed
  milk (*not* evaporated
  milk)
- 1 package (12 ounces)
  semisweet chocolate
  chips
- ¼ cup whole milk
- 3 tablespoons FRANK'S®
  Original REDHOT®
  Cayenne Pepper Sauce
- Ice cream or pound
  cake (optional)

Microwave Directions:
Combine condensed milk, chocolate and whole milk in large microwavable bowl. Microwave at HIGH 3 minutes or until chocolate is melted, stirring once. Add RedHot® sauce; stir until smooth. Serve over ice cream or cake. Garnish as desired. Refrigerate any leftover sauce.*

Makes 2½ cups

*Leftover sauce may be reheated in microwave. Microwave and stir 30 seconds at a time. If sauce becomes too thick, just stir in small amount of whole milk.

Prep Time: 5 minutes
Cook Time: 3 minutes

Tip: *This sauce is also great as a fondue dipping sauce. Serve with cubed pound cake, apple wedges, fresh strawberries, orange segments, sliced peeled kiwifruit and cubed fresh pineapple.*

Note: *RedHot® Sauce does add a hot "bite" to this sauce.*

Creamy Cappuccino Frozen Dessert

- **1 package (8 ounces) cream cheese, softened**
- **1 can (14 ounces) sweetened condensed milk**
- **½ cup chocolate-flavored syrup**
- **1 tablespoon instant coffee powder**
- **1 tablespoon hot water**
- **1½ cups frozen whipped topping, thawed**
- **1 prepared chocolate crumb crust (6 ounces)**
- **¼ cup chopped pecans, toasted**
- **Additional chocolate-flavored syrup**

1. For dessert, beat cream cheese in large bowl with electric mixer at medium speed 2 to 3 minutes or until fluffy. Add milk and ½ cup syrup; beat at low speed until well blended.

2. Dissolve coffee powder in hot water in small bowl. Slowly stir into cream cheese mixture. Fold in whipped topping; spoon mixture into crust. Sprinkle with pecans. Cover and freeze overnight.

3. To complete recipe, let dessert stand in refrigerator 10 to 15 minutes before serving. Cut into wedges. For topping, drizzle with additional syrup.

Makes 16 servings

Mocha Parfait

- **1½ tablespoons margarine**
- **⅓ cup unsweetened cocoa powder**
- **1 cup boiling water**
- **½ cup sugar**
- **1 tablespoon instant coffee granules**
- **1 teaspoon vanilla**
- **1 pint coffee-flavored nonfat frozen yogurt**
- **12 whole coffee beans (optional)**

Melt margarine in heavy saucepan over low heat. Add cocoa; cook and stir 3 minutes. Add boiling water, sugar and coffee; cook and stir until thickened. Remove from heat; stir in vanilla. Cool.

Place 2 tablespoons frozen yogurt in bottom of each of 4 parfait glasses. Top each with 1 tablespoon sauce. Top sauce with another 2 tablespoons frozen yogurt; top frozen yogurt with 2 tablespoons sauce. Repeat layering of 2 tablespoons frozen yogurt and 2 tablespoons sauce twice more. Top each parfait with 3 coffee beans, if desired.

Makes 4 servings

Creamy Cappuccino Frozen Dessert

Acknowledgments

The publisher would like to thank the companies and organizations listed below for the use of their recipes and photos in this publication.

Alpine Lace Brands, Inc.

American Italian Pasta Company

American Lamb Council

BC–USA

Best Foods Division,
   CPC International Inc.

Birds Eye ®

Blue Diamond Growers

Bob Evans Farms®

California Apricot Advisory Board

California Beef Council

California Olive Industry

California Poultry Industry
   Federation

California Prune Board

California Strawberry Commission

California Table Grape Commission

California Tomato Commission

California Tree Fruit Agreement

Canned Food Information Council

Chef Paul Prudhomme's Magic
   Seasoning Blends®

Cherry Marketing Institute, Inc.

Christopher Ranch Garlic

Colorado Potato Administrative
   Committee

Dean Foods Vegetable Company

Delmarva Poultry Industry, Inc.

Del Monte Corporation

Dole Food Company, Inc.

Farmhouse Foods Company

Filippo Berio Olive Oil

Florida Department of Agriculture
   & Consumer Services, Bureau of
   Seafood and Aquaculture

Golden Grain/Mission Pasta

Grandma's Molasses, a division
   of Cadbury Beverages Inc.

Guiltless Gourmet, Incorporated

Heinz U.S.A.

Hershey Foods Corporation

Holland House, a division of
   Cadbury Beverages Inc.

Hormel Foods Corporation

The HV Products Company

Jolly Time® Pop Corn

Kahlúa® Liqueur

Kellogg Company

Kikkoman International Inc.

The Kingsford Products Company

Kraft Foods, Inc.

Lawry's® Foods, Inc.

M&M/MARS

McIlhenny Company

Minnesota Cultivated Wild Rice
   Council

MOTT'S® Inc., a division of
   Cadbury Beverages Inc.

Nabisco, Inc.

National Broiler Council

National Fisheries Institute

National Foods, Inc.

National Honey Board

National Pasta Association

National Pork Producers Council

National Sunflower Association

National Turkey Federation

Nestlé USA

Newman's Own, Inc.®

Norseland, Inc.

North Dakota Barley Council

North Dakota Beef Commission

North Dakota Wheat Commission

Oregon Washington California
   Pear Bureau

Oscar Mayer Foods Corporation

Pacific Coast Canned Pear Service

Perdue Farms Incorporated

The Procter & Gamble Company

The Quaker® Kitchens

Ralston Foods, Inc.

Reckitt & Colman Inc.

RED STAR® Yeast & Products,
   a Division of Universal Foods
   Corporation

Sargento® Foods Inc.

The J.M. Smucker Company

Sonoma® Dried Tomato

StarKist® Seafood Company

The Sugar Association, Inc.

Sunkist Growers

USA Dry Pea & Lentil Council

USA Rice Federation

Walnut Marketing Board

Washington Apple Commission

Wisconsin Milk Marketing Board

Index

INDEX

INDEX

METRIC CONVERSION CHART

VOLUME MEASUREMENTS (dry)

⅛ teaspoon = 0.5 mL

¼ teaspoon = 1 mL

½ teaspoon = 2 mL

¾ teaspoon = 4 mL

1 teaspoon = 5 mL

1 tablespoon = 15 mL

2 tablespoons = 30 mL

¼ cup = 60 mL

⅓ cup = 75 mL

½ cup = 125 mL

⅔ cup = 150 mL

¾ cup = 175 mL

1 cup = 250 mL

2 cups = 1 pint = 500 mL

3 cups = 750 mL

4 cups = 1 quart = 1 L

VOLUME MEASUREMENTS (fluid)

1 fluid ounce (2 tablespoons) = 30 mL

4 fluid ounces (½ cup) = 125 mL

8 fluid ounces (1 cup) = 250 mL

12 fluid ounces (1½ cups) = 375 mL

16 fluid ounces (2 cups) = 500 mL

WEIGHTS (mass)

½ ounce = 15 g

1 ounce = 30 g

3 ounces = 90 g

4 ounces = 120 g

8 ounces = 225 g

10 ounces = 285 g

12 ounces = 360 g

16 ounces = 1 pound = 450 g

DIMENSIONS

1/16 inch = 2 mm

⅛ inch = 3 mm

¼ inch = 6 mm

½ inch = 1.5 cm

¾ inch = 2 cm

1 inch = 2.5 cm

OVEN TEMPERATURES

250°F = 120°C

275°F = 140°C

300°F = 150°C

325°F = 160°C

350°F = 180°C

375°F = 190°C

400°F = 200°C

425°F = 220°C

450°F = 230°C

BAKING PAN SIZES

Utensil	Size in Inches/Quarts	Metric Volume	Size in Centimeters
Baking or Cake Pan (square or rectangular)	8×8×2	2 L	20×20×5
	9×9×2	2.5 L	23×23×5
	12×8×2	3 L	30×20×5
	13×9×2	3.5 L	33×23×5
Loaf Pan	8×4×3	1.5 L	20×10×7
	9×5×3	2 L	23×13×7
Round Layer Cake Pan	8×1½	1.2 L	20×4
	9×1½	1.5 L	23×4
Pie Plate	8×1¼	750 mL	20×3
	9×1¼	1 L	23×3
Baking Dish or Casserole	1 quart	1 L	—
	1½ quart	1.5 L	—
	2 quart	2 L	—